Overreached on All Sides

Overreached on All Sides

*The Freedmen's Bureau Administrators
in Texas, 1865–1868*

WILLIAM L. RICHTER

TEXAS A&M UNIVERSITY PRESS
College Station

Dedicated to Inez, and in memory of Bob

Library of Congress Cataloging-in-Publication Data

Richter, William L. (William Lee), 1942–
    Overreached on all sides : the Freedmen's Bureau administrators in
Texas, 1865–1868 / William L. Richter. — 1st ed.
        p   cm.
    Includes bibliographical references and index.
    ISBN 0-89096-473-4
    1. Reconstruction–Texas.   2. Texas–Politics and government–
1865–1950.   3. United States. Bureau of Refugees, Freedmen, and
Abandoned Lands.   4. Freedmen–Texas.   I. Title.
F391.R543   1991
976.4'061–dc20
                                                        91-15364
                                                        CIP

Contents

List of Maps

Preface

This is not a study of blacks during Texas Reconstruction, nor is it an examination of state politics during the era, although both of these topics figure in it. Rather, this book examines a select segment of the military occupation of the State of Texas—the Bureau of Refugees, Freedmen, and Abandoned Lands—in the first three years after the Civil War. It seeks to show how the policies and personnel of the bureau affected Texas in those years. The story is one of a radical program for its day that failed to achieve its idealistic goals because it was administered by white men who acted in an unimaginative, bureaucratic manner, instead of in an inventive, revolutionary fashion. It is a tale of how the peace settlement was not pursued with the same commitment and vigor as the victorious Yankee war effort, which had already overtaxed a weary nation. The war had brought union for the nation and freedom for the slaves; the peace would focus on what kind of liberty emancipation would bring. It was a question of equality, which became what the noted historian, C. Vann Woodward, once aptly called a "deferred commitment." This study might also suggest some public skepticism of those who would reform the nation through underfunded and inadequately committed governmental programs dedicated to lofty goals that elude the usual "quick fix" mentality of American politics.

As a quasi-military organization set up under the auspices of the War Department, the Bureau of Refugees, Freedmen, and Abandoned Lands—called the Freedmen's Bureau—was run as an army operation. At first, all of its officers in Washington were military men, including its commissioner, Brevet Major General Oliver Otis Howard, as were all of the assistant commissioners while in the Texas command. Local bureau headquarters and field offices were staffed by military men or civilians, most of whom had had wartime military experience either as soldiers or as contract employees of the army. Hence, although they may seem quite bewildering and arcane today, military rank and army politics played a key role in decisions that affected the Texas bureau.

Preface

It is necessary, then, for readers to have some basic familiarity with Civil War–era military ranks.

During the conflict, the Federal army expanded rapidly to meet war needs. To facilitate this growth, officers received commissions in either the U.S. Army (USA) or the U.S. Volunteers (USV). While USA commissions were permanent, USV commissions were only for the duration of the war. Professional soldiers often received both USA and USV ranks, since the latter service, which included the majority of enlistments, offered the greatest potential for fast wartime advancement. Civilian soldiers usually received only USV ranks.

Both types of commissions offered the chance for officers to earn brevets, an honorary promotion for meritorious conduct on the field. This allowed those officers to command men who might ordinarily outrank them. Thus an officer might have up to four designations—a USA rank and brevet, and a USV rank and brevet. After the war the USV ranks and brevets gradually disappeared, but the USA ranks and their brevets remained. Jealousy and back-stabbing among officers competing for the relatively few postwar command slots caused much controversy and confusion throughout the postwar army and in the Freedmen's Bureau command in Texas.

I am indebted to many people for their assistance in writing this book. I would like to thank the directors and staffs of the following institutions for their assistance: the Old Military Records Division of the National Archives and Records Service, Washington, D.C.; the Manuscripts Division of the Library of Congress, Washington, D.C.; the Barker Historical Center, Archives, Newspaper Collection, and Library of the University of Texas, Austin; the Archives of the Texas State Library, Austin; the Archives of the Austin, Texas, Public Library; the Department of Manuscripts of the Library of Louisiana State University, Baton Rouge; and the Arizona State Library, Tucson. A special appreciation goes to the staffs of the library of Arizona State University, Tempe, and the Library of the University of Arizona, Phoenix. At Arizona State University, Ellen Welty searched out needed materials while they were still being catalogued. At the University of Arizona, Charles Peters, head of current periodicals and microforms, never flagged in his interest in my work; Virginia Rice in social science reference gave valuable bibliographic help; and Mina Parish and Janice Robrock at the interlibrary loan desk fielded my excessive requests with expertise and enthusiasm.

I would like to thank Carl Moneyhon of the University of Arkansas at Little Rock, and Cecil Harper, Jr., of North Harris County College, Houston, Texas, for reading the initial manuscript with much care and sensitivity in pointing out its shortcomings. Ralph Wooster of Lamar University, Beaumont, Texas, helped me sort out much of the era's politics earlier in another context. Harwood Hinton, John V. Mehring, Conrad Joiner, Kathleen Schwartzman, Robert Hershoff, Margaret Maxwell, and Cecil Wellborn of the University of Arizona, Tucson, and Bruce Dinges of the Arizona Historical Society, Tucson, made suggestions and provided much-needed encouragement. Bertha L. Gable and the Red River County, Texas, Genealogic Society; Thelma Duty McKinney of Fort Worth; Dorthy Schwartz of Buda, Texas; June Tuck of Sulphur Springs, Texas; and Bernardo and Consuelo Velasco of Tucson, Ariz., provided eager assistance. As always a special appreciation goes to James E. Sefton, Burl Noggle, Charles B. Dew, John L. Loos, the late T. Harry Williams, Paul G. Hubbard, Otis E. Young, and Ron Smith for their roles as understanding mentors. The maps included in this volume were expertly drawn by Don Bufkin of Tucson, Ariz. Noel Parsons and the staff of Texas A&M University Press were outstanding in their support. Finally, much thanks to my wife Lynn, and my sister, Jean, who graciously spent endless, boring hours during one summer "vacation," helping me copy list after list of more than twelve thousand Texas Reconstruction political appointments. Many of those men had bureau backgrounds, and all of them helped make the Reconstruction era what it was.

Overreached on All Sides

Introduction
The Post of Greatest Peril

*Mildness and forgiveness make the leading
barbarians of the rebellion only more impertinent.*
−Louis Constant to Provisional Governor A. J. Hamilton,
October 18, 1865

On Tuesday, September 5, 1865, Brevet Brigadier General Edgar M. Gregory, Assistant Commissioner for Texas of the Bureau of Refugees, Freedmen, and Abandoned Lands, stepped ashore at Galveston. He had just completed a long, wearying journey from New York City. The trip had included prolonged stopovers in Washington and New Orleans, which had made a mockery of his superiors' desire that he report for duty "without delay." Now that he had arrived, Gregory could at last begin to implement a process that had its origins in the surrender months before of the Confederate States and their occupation by the triumphant Union armies.[1]

As Gregory proceeded up the street to the Customs House, which would be his headquarters, he reviewed mentally the various conversations he had had recently in Washington with Brevet Major General Oliver Otis Howard, the bureau's chief administrator. Howard had explained how the demise of the Confederacy forced Americans to grapple with one of the greatest social adjustments in their history, the transformation of black slaves into free men possessed of full rights of citizenship. It was to assist in this change that Congress had established the Bureau of Refugees, Freedmen, and Abandoned Lands in March, 1865.[2]

The agency's official title accurately described its functions. Set up under the Department of War, this quasi-military organization was to be governed by the Articles of War and would consist of a commissioner, Howard, and his staff;[3] ten (later twelve) assistant commissioners, men like Gregory, who would control bureau activities in sixteen states and two territories below the Mason-Dixon line;[4] and numerous subassistant commissioners, originally envisioned as Union army offi-

3

cers, but later also including civilians (most of whom had once been military men). These subassistant commissioners were the agents who were to be in direct contact with the blacks at local levels.[5] The bureau was to supervise and expedite the slaves' becoming free men, provide relief for destitute freedmen and loyal white refugees, and administer public and private lands abandoned by unpardoned persons who had aided and abetted the Southern insurrection.[6]

Although Gregory and Howard probably did not realize its full initial implications, the bureau act, like most pieces of legislation, was a series of compromises. Some believed that the bureau would never have been created if it had not also supervised the disposal of abandoned Southern plantations and the resettlement of homeless white refugees. Others may have supported the creation of the bureau on the grounds that the South must be made habitable for the ex-slaves as free laborers, lest the freedmen inundate the North looking for real freedom, as they had in lesser numbers by means of the Underground Railroad before the war.[7]

Since Congress gave Commissioner Howard only a purpose without appropriations or a detailed plan of action, he informed Gregory that the bureau was initially dependent upon the grudging largess of the War Department for funds and personnel, and had to rely on its own ingenuity for a program. As there were no appropriated monies, the bureau often seemed to act more as a coordinating agency for the freedmen's benevolent associations, which abounded in the northern states and whose cooperation Howard earnestly sought. Each assistant commissioner, like Gregory, was to institute a practicable system of compensated labor in his district. Gregory would have to overcome the master's unwillingness to abandon slavery, the freedmen's widespread belief that freedom exempted them from further labor, and the refugees' reliance on the government dole. Finally, Howard emphasized to Gregory that the assistant commissioners were responsible for uplifting both freedmen and refugees through common education and moral instruction, by creating a temporary school system through the aid of the benevolent societies. The temporary system would operate until Southern state governments could be reorganized on a loyal basis.[8]

Six weeks before Gregory's appointment, Howard had assembled the first assistant commissioners as an advisory board to draw up a more detailed program of action.[9] These guidelines called for ready public access to all bureau personnel. The assistant commissioners were to go into the South rapidly and establish their headquarters in places the board deemed most advantageous to bureau business. The assistant commissioners were to "do all in their power to guarantee and direct the industry" of refugees and freedmen. "Great discrimination will be observed in administering relief," continued the board, "so as to include none that are not absolutely necessitous and destitute." The board warned bureau personnel that they were to make every effort to find employment for the destitute, black or white; reminded them that government rations were only temporary stop-gaps; and cautioned that loyal persons regardless of color were to be protected against outrages. Government transportation of refugees could be used "when deemed expedient."[10]

On the local level, Gregory discovered that the board called for a system of subassistant commissioners, usually called agents, who were to supervise the day-to-day contact between blacks and whites. The freedmen were free to choose their employers and jobs, and to negotiate for wages, which, since it was generally assumed that blacks would remain agricultural workers, would constitute a first lien on all crops produced. No wage limits were set, as the bureau believed local market conditions should be allowed to operate freely. The agents were to assist employers and employees to draw up annual labor contracts, a job that became one of Gregory's most important chores in Texas. Should no agent be available locally—a real likelihood in a state as large as Texas—Federal postmasters were to forward contracts to the nearest bureau office for approval. No contract was legal without prior sanction by the bureau. "Simple good faith," suggested the board, would aid in the passing of slavery. Cruelty and corporal punishment were to be avoided, unity of black families guaranteed, and black marriages recognized, recorded, and solemnized by ministers of the gospel.

The board's report instructed Gregory that there would be no binding of labor to the land by any system, nor would any forced labor be countenanced except as punishment for crime. "No substitutes for slavery, like apprenticeship [or] peonage . . . will be tolerated." But as Howard had warned earlier, the "Negro should understand that he is already free, but on no account, if able to work, should he harbor the thought that the government will support him in his idleness."[11] To encourage private, independent agriculture, the bureau should assist refugees and freedmen in gaining title to abandoned or confiscated rebel lands.

Gregory also learned that the board had assumed certain judiciary functions for bureau operatives. In areas that lacked courts or where local officials were prejudiced against equality in the treatment of black litigants, the assistant commissioner was to supervise justice through the use of provost courts, already set up by occupying troops; military commissions, in lieu of existing, prejudiced civil courts; or the adoption of arbitration efforts by the nearest bureau subassistant commissioner. All bureau personnel, however, were subject only to military jurisdiction. Courts-martial and the regulations of the War Department were to guide their actions.

Next, Gregory discovered that all assistant commissioners were to establish a medical department to supervise sanitary conditions of refugees and freedmen, and an educational department to hire teachers and coordinate the educational efforts for the fall term. The assistant commissioner or his subordinates could requisition needed items through the disbursing and receiving system that was standard in all army operations at that time. This meant that the bureau had a definite chain of command, with staff functions duplicated at Howard's office in Washington and Gregory's headquarters at the Galveston Customs House. No item could be used, nor any personnel hired by local agents, without prior approval at all superior levels.[12]

While consulting with Commissioner Howard, Gregory had received the standard legal materials that were to guide his efforts. These included the U.S. Statutes at Large, General Orders of the Volunteer Force (1861–64), the Army Registers (1861–64), Revised Army Regulations, Digest of Opinions of both the judge advocate general and the attorney general, and the Instructions for Officers of the adjutant general's department.[13] "You will not fail to see how exactly their spirit comports with the genius of our free institutions," Howard remarked to Gregory. He instructed Gregory to "seek to harmonize your actions with orders," which the commissioner promised to "dictate from time to time." It was "absolutely necessary to have officers" like Gregory, who were "above corruption and prejudice," and who proposed to do "simple justice" to all, regardless of "color or rank." The key to bureau work, said Howard, was "virtuous intelligence and industry," which would "assure the stability and prosperity" of whites and blacks, refugees and freedmen—that is to say, all those "not tainted by treason or other crimes."

Although Gregory was to explain the bureau's purpose and regulations to his Texas charges by "constant recapitulation," Howard advised against "incendiary" public addresses and "ill-advised schemes." "Consult frequently," he implored. Always keep in mind that "the constraint and exactions of military law are neither normal nor congenial to the American spirit." Gregory would have to walk a fine line, acting, "wisely, faithfully, conscientously [sic], fearlessly," and endeavoring "not to overdo, nor come short of duty." Remember, concluded Howard with a religious flourish, "the Almighty cares for the Nation, and the Nation will care for you."[14]

Undoubtedly Gregory believed in Howard's homily, because he also credited God and the nation for his well-being after surviving four years of battle in a war in which he had played a minor, yet honorable, role. After he was commissioned in 1861 as colonel of the Ninety-first Pennsylvania Volunteer infantry, he and his regiment had served with the famed V Corps of the Army of the Potomac. After a stint of garrison duty in the District of Columbia, Gregory was present at the Battle of Antietam, and was wounded at Fredericksburg. Struck down again at Chancellorsville, Gregory missed Gettysburg as he recuperated from his wound. Breveted and promoted to brigade command for the battles before Petersburg, he fought at Five Forks and was present for the Confederate surrender at Appomattox. Gregory's war record caused Howard to regard him as "fearless of opposition or danger." On July 1, 1865, the commissioner asked the War Department to assign Gregory to duty with the Freedmen's Bureau. Gregory "was well reputed for the stand he always took in the army in favor of clear-cut uprighteous [sic] of conduct," said Howard. A committed abolitionist—the only one among the early assistant commissioners—Gregory received the Texas assignment because Howard thought it to be "the post of greatest peril."[15]

With Howard's words of praise ringing in his ears, Gregory was allotted thirty days in which to settle his affairs, pack his gear, and head for Texas. He evidently took the full time allowed, for he ordered his horse's transportation as late as August 10. He arrived in New Orleans on August 26, only to find the port clogged with soldiers returning from or heading to occupation duties in Texas. It took ten days before Gregory could secure a berth on a Galveston-bound ship.[16]

When Gregory reported to the Customs House, he discovered that the occupation troops and the civilian provisional government had already begun most of the preliminary activity concerning the bureau and the freedmen. The army's district commander, Brevet Major General Horatio G. Wright, was a newcomer like Gregory, who had been in charge less than a month. The provisional governor, Andrew Jackson Hamilton, who had been in Texas since mid-July, was also a late arrival. Each man had different ideas and operated within similar yet different jurisdictions. Hence, Gregory's first problem was to establish a working relationship between the army, the civil government, and the bureau.

Gregory found that Wright's predecessor, Brevet Major General Gordon Granger, had actually begun the process of dealing with the freedmen when the army formally occupied Galveston on June 19. Granger's first act was to issue General Orders No. 3. In it, he informed Texans that "in accordance with a proclamation from the Executive of the United States, all slaves are free." Granger defined freedom as "an absolute equality of personal rights and right of property," and construed the relationship between former master and ex-slaves to be "that between employer and hired laborer." The general hoped the freedmen would stay "quietly at their present homes and work for wages." He forbade them to congregate at military posts, and warned them that they would "not be supported in idleness, either there or elsewhere."[17]

Gregory learned that Howard had informed Granger that he was to handle all bureau matters pending Gregory's arrival. Howard had told Granger to appoint an officer to take charge temporarily and begin the process of appointing local subassistant commissioners, and he had enclosed a packet of bureau directives and regulations for Granger's information. "I wish only to prevent any tendency toward slavery," wrote Howard, "and to encourage everyone concerned in the adoption and maintenance of free labor and good schools."[18]

In his review of earlier policies, Gregory probably had read one of the most widely publicized statements of Granger's attitude towards the freedmen. This document was a speech by the commander of the Eastern District of Texas, Brevet Major General C. C. Andrews, delivered at Brenham on July 20. In his address, Andrews noted that "although the blacks are free, they are not exempt from restraint." The general understood "that after a life of bondage, the blacks should wish to celebrate their emancipation with a day or two of recreation." But even this was not permissible, said Andrews. Army policy would permit no holiday until the crops were gathered.

Andrews urged the Negroes, instead of wandering the roads and gathering at military posts, to "remain on plantations with their former masters, who treat them as freedmen, and engage to pay fair wages, and cultivate and gather the crops." Andrews said that wage rates must be negotiated between employer and employee. The general saw a freedmen's lien on 10 percent of the crop as "reasonable and fair." He promised that the army would supervise the contract process to keep it just.

He warned the freedmen against idleness and the planters against trying to reestablish slavery in any form. No "coercion, or any conspiring
together to thwart the policy of the Government in this matter will
be tolerated," pledged the general. "Let me say to the freed people that
they need have no doubts about their liberty. . . . They may rest assured they will never again be held or sold as slaves."[19]

But while Granger got off to a good start, as demonstrated by Andrews's speech, Gregory was as dismayed as were his superiors to hear
of the Texas commander's erroneous stand on other matters. For one
thing, Granger had a disturbing penchant for working with established
—hence pro-Confederate—officials on the local level. And he, like many
other army commanders in the South, instituted a rigid pass system
for freedmen, which greatly restricted their freedom of movement.
Howard described it as worse than the one used in slavery times. "It
would be well not to issue any orders in regard to blacks," Howard admonished Granger diplomatically, "that are not equally applicable to
whites under similar circumstances."[20]

And although Granger took unnecessary measures to discipline blacks
and restrict their movements, Gregory discovered that the general had
been unable to enforce proper conduct by his own troops toward the
freedmen. Indeed, according to a Galveston Unionist sheet, soldiers
regarded Negroes as suckers to be exploited without mercy. Troops preyed
upon their innocence with con games, beat them up, stole from them,
and ran houses of prostitution staffed with dragooned freedwomen.[21]
The bluecoats were also not above engineering race riots to quell black
protests. Troops who committed depredations on the property of white
Texans, however, were disarmed and quarantined aboard ships or on
desolate sandbars.[22]

Granger's policies were best summed up by an officer at the District
of Texas headquarters, who wrote that the army would keep an eye
on the Negroes and see that they received their freedom and rights
as citizens. But the army would also see to it that the blacks did not
"abuse" those rights in their dealings with whites. The army would strive
to keep blacks at home working until the delayed arrival of General
Gregory. Let him develop the Freedmen's Bureau policy. Until then
very little would change in the lives of Texas blacks. They were no longer
slaves, but they were not yet truly free men.[23] Seen in this light, Granger
evidently never fulfilled Howard's earlier request that he appoint a staff
officer to coordinate Freedmen's Bureau business and begin selecting
subassistant commissioners. It is possible that the continued muster-

out of the Civil War volunteer force made such a course impracticable, but Granger's willingness to work with former Confederates and ex-slaveholders might be a more important factor.[24]

If Granger was a doubtful man to lead the occupation forces in Texas —as indicated by his replacement in August with General Wright—his civilian counterpart, Prov. Gov. "Colossal Jack" Hamilton, left Gregory with no doubts as to his concern for the freedmen. Like Gregory, the governor had had a slow trip from the District of Columbia to Texas. It took him two weeks to sail from the national capital to New Orleans, and another two weeks to get to Galveston. Transportation was indeed hard to come by that summer of 1865.

Upon his arrival, Hamilton told Gregory, he found white Texans to be in three frames of mind about the outcome of the war. The Unionists were understandably happy. The "poor men," mostly former Confederate soldiers, were glad the war was over and ready for amnesty. The planters, however, were a subtle menace. They claimed to be ready to take the oath, but Hamilton suspected the former slaveholders were merely playing for time, and seeking to reestablish slavery or some other "coercive system" of Negro labor. As evidence of this, Hamilton pointed to planters in the interior, out of the army's direct control, who still held their bondsmen by force. Some Texans, it seemed to the governor, expected gradual, compensated emancipation or, better yet, the negation of black freedom by some future Supreme Court decision.[25]

As Gregory later heard, however, many Texans had denied Hamilton's accusations. "By way of posting you in regard to our once *very rebel population*," said one correspondent, they are "shaking off the shackles" of slavery and the "people seem resolved to be true and loyal." Others wrote that a majority in their areas was opposed to secession in the first place, "and that majority has since increased so as to embrace every man. . . ." Granger's order freeing the slaves was greeted without anger in San Antonio, according to a loyal newspaper. In Wharton, a planter wrote that he had not only rehired his 100 ex-slaves, but employed 120 more. This same man read Granger's June 19 proclamation to "his people" shortly after its issuance. In other communications, individuals and groups pledged their support to Hamilton's new Union government.[26]

But the denials seemed insubstantial, in Gregory's eyes, when compared to the dozens of letters Hamilton had received complaining about Texas whites who had "lost all sense of duty; and are still determined to 'rule or ruin'." Many wanted a "military probation" period before

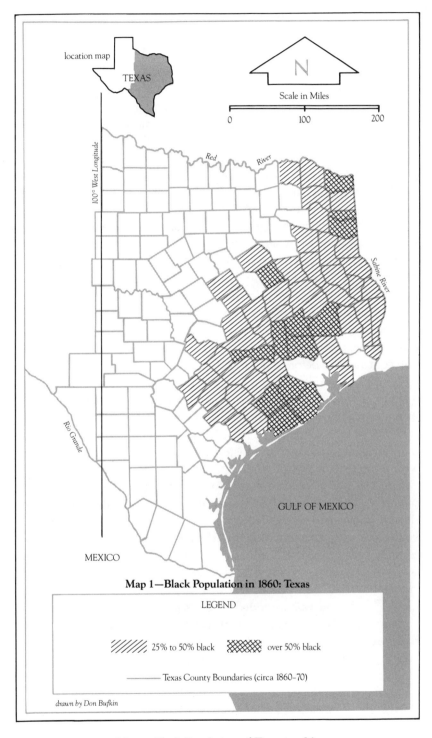

location map

TEXAS

N

Scale in Miles

0   100   200

100° West Longitude

Red   River

Sabine River

Rio Grande

GULF OF MEXICO

MEXICO

Map 1—Black Population in 1860: Texas

LEGEND

///// 25% to 50% black   ⧆⧆⧆ over 50% black

———— Texas County Boundaries (circa 1860–70)

drawn by Don Bufkin

MAP 1: Black Population of Texas in 1860

the restoration of elected government. "The Rebels . . . are still committing outrages, such as *Stealing, Robbing,* and *murdering,*" protested
an Angelina County committee. An Anderson County correspondent
wrote "Jack Hambilton," warning of the formation of secret societies
"all round." Another wrote of how his friends and neighbors, once "seemingly good union men, have become from habit and love of plunder
the most uncompromising Rebels. . . . Nothing but severe handling will
bring such fellows to their sences [*sic*]," he concluded. A German
Unionist bewailed the lack of "forceful measures" by Federal authorities. "Mildness and forgiveness make the leading barbarians of the rebellion only more impertinent," he opined.[27]

Actually, Gregory thought the plight of loyal whites to be of relatively minor concern when Hamilton informed him of the fate of the
former bondsmen. Reports of continued slavery were common, some
very recent. Planters blacklisted other whites who employed their former slaves. Negroes were told they had to work for their old masters,
and no one else. Those blacks who exercised their freedom to seek other
employment were hunted down with "catch hounds." Still other supposedly free persons were being "sold" to new "masters."[28] Use of the
lash continued as before the war. A Colorado County judge complained
to Governor Hamilton that the army would not permit him to execute
a sentence of fifteen lashes apiece on four freedmen who were convicted
of mule stealing. In Van Zandt County, a correspondent begged authorities to send a Freedmen's Bureau agent quickly. A local businessman allegedly had just administered five hundred lashes to a Negro
who refused to work for him![29]

Gregory was pleased to ascertain that Hamilton had gone on the
offensive. The governor had issued his own proclamation abolishing
slavery once again. He called upon the soon-to-be-elected state convention to write emancipation into the new state constitution. He also
recommended that the Negroes receive the right to vote. "No fowler
[*sic*] slander was ever uttered," thundered Hamilton in a speech at
Houston, "than that this is and was intended to be 'a White man's
Gov't'[.] It is and was intended to be 'a *free* man's Gov't'. . . ."[30]

But before the free man's government could be a reality, Hamilton
had to install his own caretaker administration and guide Texans in
creating a loyal government upholding equal rights for the freedmen.
Hamilton hoped to establish the proper loyal atmosphere through his
political appointments. Union supporters backed the governor's estimation of the situation. "All agree that we are not strong enough to carry

an election," wrote one loyalist, "and it [is] desirable you should appoint all officers. . . ." Or as another, still exiled in New York City, put it, "We must rubb out and begin anew."[31]

Gregory was more gratified to see the letters that poured in from nearly every county in the state requesting Hamilton to appoint allegedly loyal men, many of whom were suggested by name. Incumbents begged to be allowed to stay on, claiming to have been Union supporters. Even the army got into the act. For example, the camp commandant at Brenham, Capt. T. S. Post, warned the governor against the current Washington County judge, O. H. P. Garrett. Post had an alternate list of Loyalists drawn up by D. C. McIntyre and Thomas Dwyer. It must have been a good one. For their trouble, McIntyre and Dwyer had been threatened by local "rebels," with loss of property, life, and limb, should the army ever withdraw. In the end, Hamilton made nearly three thousand appointments in the fall of 1865. There were so many offices to fill that the governor was really trusting to luck to find true Unionists, as he admitted to President Johnson. But, by and large, Hamilton did reestablish a form of loyal government in Texas.[32]

The new civil government, however, presented Gregory, the governor, and the army with a real dilemma. If the civil government succeeded, it would not need bureau and army interference. But without this active Federal support, the civil administration could not succeed. There was never enough Federal aid to make Hamilton's regime more than marginally successful. Hamilton came to recognize this problem in his relations with his bureau and army counterparts. In a letter to President Johnson, the governor said that the bureau and army could not keep order in Texas. There were too few bureau agents and troops. Hamilton believed that the extension of the civil court system through his appointments would accomplish this, but, he stressed, it would take time.[33]

Gregory knew that Hamilton had acted on this belief, at least, at first. The governor chastised General Andrews, for example, when the commander of the Eastern District of Texas arrested lawbreakers without giving civil authorities their proper jurisdiction in the matter. Other Texans agreed with Hamilton's course. It was important to organize a pro-Union government, wrote one deputation, so that loyal state authorities could direct the Federals in legal and racial matters and assist them in enforcing state and Federal laws.[34]

One month later, after Gregory's arrival, Hamilton changed his mind. In a letter to General Wright, Granger's replacement in the Texas command, the governor stated that "the freedmen in almost every section of the Country, not occupied with troops are being very badly treated—in many instances murdered. . . . It must be obvious that we cannot depend upon the Civil authority in our State for some time yet, to deal out justice to evil doers." If he were going to complain, it would be about the failure of the army and bureau to assert control, not about overzealousness on their parts. "I not only see no objection to the trial of offenders before Military tribunals, but on the contrary, believe it is a necessity," continued Hamilton. "Unaided by the Military power, the efforts of the Freedmen's Bureau would be nearly fruitless." Anyone who treated the Negro fairly faced threats and actions "which even menaced their lives."[35]

Although Hamilton desired more Federal aid, Gregory found that Wright, following the dictates of his superiors, was reluctant to grant it.[36] The general agreed that he, Gregory, and Hamilton were most "likely to be at cross purposes" in "the relative jurisdiction of civil and military tribunals, and matters connected with the freedmen." But Wright saw a fairly neat three-way division of power between the state and Federal authorities. All matters concerning whites were to be handled by the loyal state civil government, said Wright. Any case involving freedmen was to be adjudicated by the Freedmen's Bureau. Finally, the army would stick to military matters and stand ready to aid the civil government or the bureau, when necessary, upon request.[37]

Admittedly, Gregory and Hamilton thought this approach to be a bit oversimplified, but Wright firmly believed that the civil authorities should handle all criminal cases so long as soldiers were not involved and the freedmen received equal treatment before the bar. If the latter could not be guaranteed, the general would use military commissions and Freedmen's Bureau tribunals. But, Wright emphasized, Reconstruction had as its purpose the establishment of a loyal civil administration and a court system that did not rely on an already strapped military command.[38]

In the meantime, to assist Gregory and Hamilton to the fullest, Wright agreed to institute a series of cavalry patrols in north central Texas to make a show of force and cow the rampant rebel sentiment reported there. At Weatherford, the national flag had allegedly been torn down, pro-Confederate vigilantes roamed the streets, horse stealing was common, and Negroes were still being held as slaves. The deputy town marshal was in sympathy with the mob, and the county sheriff could not raise a posse from fear that its members later be executed one by one.[39] Similar reports came from Belton, where an informed complained that the jail was "not large enough to contain all that ought be to arrested."[40]

Sweeping through Belton to Dallas, Lieutenant Colonel Thomas M. Browne and the 250 troopers from the First Iowa and his own Seventh Indiana, all veteran Civil War volunteer cavalrymen, were stunned by the violence that was plaguing northern Texas. After two days in the Dallas area, they moved on to Sherman, where they set up a base camp and sent out patrols in all directions to pacify the countryside.[41] The troopers had much work to do. Indians raided unprotected homesteads. Gangs of renegade whites roamed the roads. Planters hunted down their former slaves, who refused to work for men who had mistreated them before emancipation. Murders and other atrocities against blacks were common. Every time soldiers showed up in an area, the assaults immediately ceased, only to start up again at an increased tempo upon their departure. Unionists and blacks who cooperated with the Yankees bore the brunt of the renewed violence.[42]

The most important thing the cavalry sweep revealed to the bureau, army, and provisional government was the impossibility of pacifying any area through random military patrols. General Wright recommended a permanent garrison of four mounted companies for the Sherman-Weatherford region. It could not be done. The Civil War volunteers had already been in service long past Appomattox and were due to be mustered out. When Hamilton heard of this, he wrote Wright's superior, Maj. Gen. Philip Sheridan, at New Orleans and begged for more troops. Should Texas be denied adequate protection, Hamilton warned, "there would occur a scene of violence and outrages upon the Union men . . . and . . . the freedmen such as to shock the moral sense of the country." Sheridan offered him "some colored troops," to which Hamilton replied, "In God's name send us help—troops of any sort—and we will be thankful. . . . Violence is everywhere on the increase."[43] But no troops came, for there were none to be had. The black soldiers were being demobilized, too.[44]

This was the situation Gregory faced when he assumed command of the Texas Freedmen's Bureau. His charges, the state's former slaves, had been freed, but were still compelled in ways not befitting truly free persons. He was blessed with a civilian government of a Union character, which could not guarantee to him the loyal actions of many of its members on the local level. He had the open cooperation of the commander of the occupying army, who had too few troops to assist him in all but the most extreme emergencies. And the volunteer officers, from whom Gregory expected to draw his staff and subassistant commissioners, were being mustered out along with their regiments. Their replacements, the men of the regular army, had yet to arrive in force.[45]

PART ONE

Organization: The Gregory Era,
September, 1865–May, 1866

This course will bring the same success on the banks of the Brazos, the Colorado, or the Trinity, as on the Ohio.

—Brevet Brigadier General Edgar M. Gregory to Benjamin Harris,
January 20, 1866

1

To Promote a Mutual Interest

MUCH OF THE INFORMATION that Gregory relied upon to formulate his policies came from personal observations that he or subordinates made on a series of inspection tours in the fall of 1865. That Gregory had great faith in journeys into the backcountry was obvious from the four tours he made personally during his nine short months in Texas. The first took place immediately after his September 5 arrival at Galveston. Visiting over one hundred "East Texas planters," Gregory found them doubtful of their former bondsmen's capacity to work as free men. In spite of their doubts, however, the crops were doing well. Gregory was pleased to discover that the planters expressed a willingness to pay the freedmen for their labor and contract with them for the coming year.[1]

This preliminary scouting foray merely gave Gregory a feeling for the problems he faced in Texas, and whetted his appetite for a more extended intelligence-gathering expedition. But the demands of organizational necessities kept him in Galveston until early November.[2] Then in the last three weeks of the month, Gregory journeyed seven hundred miles, finding a state largely untouched by the war. On his travels, the assistant commissioner spoke to twenty-five thousand freedmen and planters. Gregory praised the blacks for their courteous conduct. He considered them to be extremely moral and religious, qualities he failed to see in most white Texans. Although rumors abounded about a Christmastime revolt, the assistant commissioner discounted them. If any violence were to occur, he believed it would be more a product of white injustice than of black misconduct.

Gregory was greatly surprised to find that many freedmen had no concept of what the end of slavery meant. Others were still held as slaves, especially in areas the Federals had not yet visited. "But few, comparatively, feel and manifest that interest in the advancement of the freedmen they should," he concluded, referring to white Texans. In spite of this disturbing fact, the assistant commissioner discovered few complaints from the planters, and Gregory believed the future of free labor to be generally good. Best of all, he found the freedmen anxious to learn the responsibilities of good citizenship. Unfortunately, they lacked schools, teachers, and books.[3]

Traveling with the assistant commissioner as far as Huntsville was the assistant inspector general of the Freedmen's Bureau, Brevet Brigadier General William E. Strong.[4] An old hand on Howard's wartime staff now serving with the bureau at the commissioner's request, Strong was ordered to Texas via the Gulf coast to "thoroughly examine" conditions there and "form a correct opinion of the condition of the freed people."[5] Upon reaching Huntsville the inspector reported that he and Gregory split up to cover more territory, and not from an alleged disagreement, as gloated over by the local press. Strong had already made inspection tours in the South, but as he traveled up the Trinity and over to the Neches, he was greatly disturbed by conditions in Texas.[6]

The environment around the larger towns—Galveston, Houston, San Antonio, and Austin—the inspector believed to be quite good. But in areas bereft of army protection Strong discovered "a fearful state of things." Freedmen were kept enslaved by force, others had never heard of emancipation until Strong told them of its benefits, murder and maltreatment were common. Texas planters were discouraged, said Strong. They claimed the Negro as a free person was useless for work, demoralized by the responsibilities of freedom, and wandering the roads aimlessly. Strong himself doubted the truth of such charges.

"It is the same old story of cruelty, only there is more of it in Texas than any other southern State that I have visited," Strong lamented. Although the blacks had gathered the 1865 crop, they had not been paid for it. Those planters who did pay wages did so only at the point of a bayonet. What food shortages there were, continued Strong, occurred because planters had hoarded corn and wheat in the hope of forcing prices up. Fair treatment of the ex-slaves, thought Strong, would cure many ills. As badly as blacks were treated, Strong marveled more at the "most intense hatred" shown by Texas whites toward Northerners, soldiers, and the Federal government. Every man was heavily armed. Knives, revolvers, and shotguns were part of everyday dress. Strong believed most of the hostility was shown by men who had not been in the Confederate service. Had his twelve-man escort not been armed with quick-shooting Spencer carbines, Strong feared that his party would have been attacked and destroyed.

"The campaign of an army through the eastern part of the State, such as was made by General Sherman, in South Carolina," Strong concluded, "would improve the temper and generosity of the people." He called for a minimum of fifty subassistant commissioners, each with a small force of troops, for the Texas bureau command. Otherwise, Strong feared that Gregory, whom he called a good capable man, would be unable to provide justice to the newly freed Negroes.[7]

Deeply disturbed by all that he observed, the inspector returned to Galveston to consult with Gregory before going back to Washington by way of Vicksburg.[8] After Strong's departure, Gregory became involved in more administrative duties, as he sought to expand the system of subassistant commissioners throughout plantation areas of the state. He created a five-person staff, and sent out five civilian agents and seven detached army officers to the towns of Marshall, Houston, Victoria, Austin, Brenham, Columbus, Hempstead, Anderson, Courtney, Woodville, Millican, and Leona.[9]

As Gregory busied himself in Galveston, he sent his chief medical officer, Brevet Lieutenant Colonel S. J. W. Mintzer, into the areas north and east of Houston. Knowing Gregory's desire to begin supervising the next year's contract labor system, Mintzer wrote a lengthy review of the conditions he saw, beyond their medical aspects. The surgeon doubted if a dozen planters had more than verbal agreements with their freedmen employees for the period since the "breakup," as freedom was called in that region. Those contracts he did see were not up to Gregory's standards, as they allowed the landowners to dock wages for "damages" and disobedience, rather than using the courts. To the continued accusations by planters that the freedmen were "lazy and will not work," Mintzer noted that blacks were hesitant to contract for the new year because they had yet to be paid for the services rendered in 1865. At the home of loyalist judge Henry C. Pedigo, Mintzer encountered a continual line of freedmen seeking redress for unpaid wages and advice for the future. The judge was a staunch Unionist, and had recently dismissed the county grand jury for failing to credit blacks' testimony.

In nearby counties, the bureau surgeon met planters who openly held their Negroes as bondsmen. One planter said he would free his slaves only at Christmas after the crops were in. Mintzer saw roads east filled with refugees, black and white. One local resident believed an average of three hundred freedmen passed each day. The stream of humanity had flowed unabated for two months or more. The isolated nature of the backcountry provided a perfect breeding ground for rumors. Some folks had heard that England had declared war on the United

States, and when Mintzer asked others about this, the Texans all said they would be more than happy to fight the Federals again. Another story making the rounds was that unnamed parties were shipping abducted freedmen from Texas to Brazil and Cuba for sale into slavery there. Although the doctor did not give credence to the rumor, he heard of secret organizations of whites pledged to hunt down and kill each freedman who left his former master for work elsewhere. He admitted, however, that justice in Texas was a personal and immediate thing, often settled by individuals outside the courts.

All in all, Mintzer characterized the attitude of the former slave-holders in the words of a Tyler County man. "I have not let my niggers go yet," he admitted to Mintzer, "because I don't think the Government wants to take our property without paying us." The planter also maintained that "the Government may yet let Texas have her niggers to conciliate us." After all, he continued, Texas had surrendered without a fight, and the North ought to be willing to do "the fair thing" and "show us that they are a magnanimous people." The man told Mintzer he would await the gathering of the upcoming state convention, "as there are many knotty points to meet and get over." Mintzer concluded, as had Strong, that Gregory had better send more agents into the field quickly.[10]

Gregory agreed with Mintzer's assessment. By the end of January, he had nearly doubled the number of agents and had established new offices at Meridian, Waco, Marlin, Crockett, La Grange, Wharton, Richmond, and Sutherland Springs.[11] The assistant commissioner also had toured the lower Brazos and Colorado valleys, south and west from Galveston. Full of large cotton and sugar plantations, this area teemed with freedmen. Gregory found that 90 percent had signed contracts for the coming year. Most worked for a share of the crop instead of wages, and whites here seemed more willing to pay just compensation than did those elsewhere. In his report, the general denied continued allegations that there was a tax on contracts. All bureau expenses came from fines collected from the many convicted wrongdoers, he said.

As heartening to Gregory as the rich bottom land that promised wealth for all was the decline in violence in areas held by Federal troops. Still, he was dispirited that bureau agents and state courts continued to have upon their dockets hundreds of cases involving the mistreatment of blacks, cases "ranging from downright murder, savage beatings, merciless whippings, [and] hunting men with trained blood hounds" to lesser crimes.[12]

Even before he penned his report on this most recent tour, General Gregory had addressed many of these problems by issuing his first order as the head of the Texas Freedmen's Bureau. In the order, dated October 12, 1865, the assistant commissioner began by stating that he was aware that many Texans continued to hold blacks in involuntary servitude through violence and intimidation that extended even to murder. He warned the planters that he was going to protect the Negroes under Federal law, and to prove his authority he reprinted a circular from his superior, Commissioner Howard. Gregory reiterated, as had General Granger and Provisional Governor Hamilton before him, that all blacks were freed under the Emancipation Proclamation of 1863 and subsequent military orders.

Although the blacks could choose whom to work for, Gregory warned them once again that they were expected to enter into voluntary labor contracts and not to be idle. He also told them that, contrary to rumors spreading around the state, there would be no great Christmastime land allotment. The assistant commissioner promised that his agents in the field would help the planters and their employees adjust to the new free labor system. He cautioned whites against using "corporeal punishment," however, and to treat the freedmen with "the true spirit of Justice and kindness." He admonished them yet again that "slavery is dead" and gave notice that laws and actions in conflict with this principle would not be tolerated. Those who persisted in this course would be arrested and punished.[13]

But Gregory, like Hamilton and Granger before him, found that problems in Texas would not succumb to the injunctions of one order. Since General Granger had announced the emancipation of Texas slaves, most whites suspected that the freedmen would refuse to work without some form of compulsion. Southern whites were not alone in this belief. Commissioner Howard mentioned the need for the Negro to "understand that he is already free but on no account, if able to work, should he harbor the thought that the government will support him in his idleness."[14]

Granger had repeated Howard's injunction in General Orders No. 3 and urged blacks to return home and resume their usual work. Gregory reinforced Granger's stand in his first public statement on October 12, 1865. In his instructions to subassistant commissioners, Gregory said that "freemen should be enjoined to work," although he recognized their right to seek other employers than their former masters.[15] Gregory's conditional statement marked the beginning of a new era in Texas race relations, for the army had not been so understanding. Most army officers seem to have worked in conjunction with planters, doing all in their power to prevent "vagrancy" and little to enforce the new concept of freedom. Granger's emancipation order urging blacks to return home to work had been seen by many planters as a reinstitution of slavery by other means, and they had acted upon it accordingly.[16]

Planters like Thomas Affleck of Washington County, for example, had been quite pleased with the army's conduct of labor relations that summer of 1865 before the arrival of the bureau. The soldiers left the whole problem up to the planters with little interference except by a few officers in selected incidents.[17] But still, the blacks wandered the roads testing their freedom. They threw parties. They danced and sang for joy. They congregated in large towns and near army posts, where freedom seemed more real to them. They sought out lost relatives. Those slaves forcibly shipped to Texas during the war returned home to neighboring states. Blacks often went down the road to the next plantation to work, just to test their rights as free persons.[18]

The jubilation of the former slaves was quite disconcerting to whites, who had prided themselves on their tight control of the Negroes. Blacks were seen as "uppity" and freedom as a "curse."[19] Both Union and Conservative newspapers published Granger's injunction against idleness and noted that the army was rounding up the unemployed freedmen for public works projects.[20] Much of the blame for trouble was foisted upon the black troops who made up about half of the occupation force by Christmas, 1865. The presence of Negro soldiers, cocky, armed, worldly, and free, bothered Texas whites more than any other effect of emancipation. The black troops "demoralized" local Negroes, who flocked to the army posts to see this wondrous sight. In consequence, crops allegedly suffered from neglect.

All decent Texas white folk shuddered in sympathy when the Galveston *Daily News* reported that three regiments of "colored troops" were stationed at Corpus Christi with "nothing to do."[21] Even as ardent a foe of the rebellion as Major General Philip H. Sheridan wondered aloud if mustered-out black soldiers should be allowed to purchase their weapons, as whites were allowed to do. "The purchase will create some uneasiness in this section of the country," he said in a casual understatement.[22]

In reality, however, black troops were well disciplined—more so than white soldiers. The Bellville *Countryman* hit upon the real issue when it deplored "the idea of a gallant and high-minded people being ordered and pushed about by an inferior, ignorant race," which it found "shocking to the senses." The newspaper did admit that Negroes on its side of the Brazos were well behaved and undisturbed by black soldiers stationed many miles away. To his credit, Gregory refused to be buffaloed by the specter of blacks lying about idly to the detriment of normal economic activity. Local governments could use the vagrancy laws against idle Negroes, he said, so long as they were enforced equally against unemployed whites.[23]

Another problem related to idleness was the belief held by many Negroes all over the South, that land would be given them by Christmas, 1865 — the legendary forty acres and a mule. It is hard to pin down the origin of the tale. Northerners blamed disgruntled Southerners, and vice versa. But Congress had mentioned setting aside abandoned lands for freedmen and loyal refugees in the original bureau law, and General William T. Sherman had granted tracts to freedmen in the Sea Islands under his Special Field Orders No. 20, which lent credibility to the rumor.[24]

In any case, the expectation of a land division hit Texas hard. Whites flooded Governor Hamilton's office with complaints. "Negrogogues," said a Danville resident, were stirring up local blacks with tales of a land giveaway at Christmas. Others said that a black rebellion would occur during the holiday season, a common fear during slavery times.[25] Another correspondent warned the governor that blacks were becoming more and more confused by the contradictory promises and denials by whites. "Christmas is coming fast apace," he concluded ominously.[26]

Gregory cautioned bureau employees to discourage the rumor of a land allotment, but his admonition had little effect. Governor Hamilton wrote President Johnson, saying that Texas blacks refused to work. They were instead awaiting the windfall land giveaway at the end of the year. Commissioner Howard sent one of his circular letters and branded the rumors as false. He urged bureau officers to "take whatever steps are necessary" to discourage the notion that blacks would divide up their former masters' property. Instead, Howard suggested that the bureau concentrate on seeing that just labor contracts were drawn up for the 1866 planting season.[27]

Prompted by Gregory, Howard's letter, and the magnitude of the question, Governor Hamilton issued a "Proclamation to the Freedmen" in mid-November, 1865. In it, Hamilton praised the Negroes for their good conduct as freed persons, and expressed sympathy for their hopes of future happiness and prosperity. But, he cautioned them, there were no lands available to be given away at Christmas or any other time. The governor admonished the freedmen to work and save, and purchase land and other property. He also warned them once again against idleness.[28]

Whites acted on their fears by organizing patrols, as in the days of the slave regime, to police the roads and be ready to strike at the first sign of uprising. It was a controversial step, and one which Gregory opposed. Technically, under General Orders No. 90, promulgated by the Adjutant General's Office in May, 1865, any armed group of Southern whites after June 1 was a guerrilla unit whose members would be punished by death, if caught. General Sheridan had reinforced this order with one of his own, which specifically outlawed the use of home guards. He also had made neighborhoods that were infested with bands of brigands responsible for their misdeeds, and ordered citizens to disperse the guerrillas. He never did explain just how disorganized citizens were to enforce law and order against armed desperadoes, a dilemma that had angered many whites.[29]

Nevertheless, the threat of Negro rebellion was an emergency so critical to Texans that temporary home guard units were created and called out despite the bureau and army's protestations.[30] Some of these units actually had the approval of local army commanders,[31] but Gregory's opposition as expressed by the actions of his field agents led one irate Unionist to complain to Governor Hamilton. "The agent of the bureau and the provost marshal commanding at Columbia," he groused, "are far more important functionaries practically than your Excellency and the President."[32]

But the fear of a Negro uprising was a temporary phenomenon. More enduring was the question of how to use the freed people as laborers. Because of the paucity of abandoned lands and refugees in Texas, labor became Gregory's main concern, and a major part of that issue involved fair labor contracts. Freed, but with no lands in their possession and lacking the capital to purchase land or start businesses, Negroes were already doomed to become hirelings. The absence of ready cash in the war-torn South meant that the only payment would be in-kind, a portion of the crops the blacks produced on someone else's land.[33] Gregory knew that the contract labor system was not new to the postwar Southwest. Much of its substance had grown out of the efforts of Brevet Major General Nathaniel Banks during the occupation of lower Louisiana during the rebellion. Banks's system was rather conservative, designed to win over the planters to the free labor ideal and still safeguard certain essential rights of freedom for the black laborers.[34]

Gregory was aware of the labor laws that had been developed by the war's end, as Banks had promulgated them in his General Orders No. 23, which was a revision of earlier experimental rules.[35] The work order called for voluntary contracts between landowners and laborers. The contracts were to be submitted to Banks's superintendents of freedmen (later the bureau agents) for approval. Terms were to include just treatment (the abolition of flogging, in particular), a plot for private cultivation for each black family, wholesome rations, comfortable clothing, living quarters, fuel, medical attention, educational opportunity for the children, and a salary schedule arrived at by mutual negotiation between planter and workers, based upon a ten-hour day. Wages due were protected by a first lien on the crop produced.

Importantly, Gregory knew that Banks allowed the landowner to deduct wages for time lost to sickness, and both wages and rations if the sickness was "feigned." Unemployed blacks were declared vagrants and put to work on public projects. Laborers were free to choose with whom they wished to contract for the year, but once the contract was signed, it was inviolable. No freedman could leave his place of employment "without cause and permission," lest he forfeit wages and be "otherwise punished, as the nature of the case may require." The whole process was to be financed by a general poll tax on each hand hired.[36]

The content of General Orders No. 23, Gregory learned, had provided the basis for the contract procedures used initially upon the army's occupation of Texas in June, 1865. It was quite understandable, since many of the officers, especially in Granger's command, were from the Department of the Gulf, where Banks had operated.[37] Planters generally were pleased with Banks's ideas. Thomas Affleck of Washington County, for example, had been quite happy with the army's early administration of free black labor—almost as pleased as he was disgusted with the bureau's later approach. According to Affleck, the expectations of his 1865 contracts had changed but little from the pre-emancipation rules. Now, however, the employer had less direct control of the laborers and fewer responsibilities for their welfare.[38]

By the time Gregory had arrived and established the first bureau agencies, it was October and the 1865 crop harvest was nearly ended. Hence, the bureau did not actually supervise the contract process for the first time until the preparations for the 1866 planting were being made. All Gregory and his staff could do was examine the year in retrospect and see to it that the freedmen received their just due.[39] On December 9, Gregory ordered the planters to settle with their freedmen for the past year's labor by the end of the month. He generally considered the term of labor under contract to be the six months from July 1 to December 31, 1865. The period of collection would seem interminable to all those involved.[40]

Already there had been problems in getting freedmen's wages from their employers, as Gregory's Houston agent had found. Houston was the central receiving point for everything coming in from the north and west, and General Gregory considered himself fortunate to have as his agent there the provost marshal of the Eastern District, Brevet Lieutenant Colonel Jacob C. De Gress of the Sixth Missouri Cavalry. German-born, speaking English with a heavy accent (*wise* was spelled *wice* in his letters and pronounced *vice*, for example), De Gress had a Prussian stubbornness and penchant for detail that made him well hated by the Texans who ran afoul of him. He also had the courage to ride alone throughout the counties around the city, and the bravado to pull off his patrols without incident. He regularly classified the loosely drawn up contracts as "a damned swindle" and had a tendency to believe the blacks' version of disputes that dismayed former slaveholders.[41]

De Gress reported that planters in the area south and west toward the coast were paying their hands and that by and large all seemed well there. The area to the north and east, however, was festering with discontent. Here, freedmen claimed that planters were harvesting and selling the crops, and then fleeing with the proceeds to neighboring states. De Gress sent John D. Imboden, employed as a special agent, to survey the problem. Traveling with a military escort, Imboden found that many of the planters were refugees from Louisiana, who had moved to Texas to escape the war. Now they were returning home and abandoning the freedmen penniless in the process. De Gress pledged to stop the sale of crops until each planter produced evidence that his employees had been paid. De Gress concluded that "a great many of the planters are treacherous and will bear watching."[42]

De Gress condemned the whites further, declaring that they "had probably forgotten that Rebel Rule had ceased to exist." The planters still held the blacks as slaves, whipped and abused them, and chased down with hounds those who left. When planters did not pay their freedmen for 1865, De Gress seized up to half the crops in some counties, and threatened to chase down those whites who sold out and fled the state without paying their black fieldhands. He sent his agent,

W. D. Whitall, to Alleytown to enforce his edict. To his amazement, Whitall reported that the planters complied rather meekly when confronted by Federal authority. "Everything is working harmoniously," De Gress gloated. It should have. De Gress only demanded that 10 percent of a crop go to the blacks, much less than the third or half that became standard in later years. Like many men of action, however, the provost marshal had problems keeping his accounts current, and he had a lot of paperwork to complete before he headed for Louisiana and his muster-out of the volunteer service in mid-December, 1865.[43]

De Gress's reports were a matter of concern to Gregory. The assistant commissioner had already written glowing letters to Commissioner Howard telling him that the 1865 crop had been "secured and saved to the interests of the state," and that planters were "willing" to pay the wages owed the freedmen. Indeed, Gregory had pledges to that effect from over one hundred East Texas landowners. Now, the problem was becoming worse, not better.[44] To combat those planters who sought to defraud their employees, Gregory instituted as his own the policy referred to by De Gress: that of seizing the crops before or during shipment and holding them until the freedmen's wages were guaranteed. However, he cautioned subassistant commissioners not to overdo the program. All cotton was to be sent forward immediately unless the freedmen made a complaint against the owner, whereupon half of it would be held in lieu of wages owed.[45]

To aid in the process of seizure, the assistant commissioner worked out an agreement with the Galveston cotton merchants, McMann and Gilbert, to deduct any unpaid freedmen's wages from the company's books before paying planters the profits earned. In this way, the merchant could move the crop without attaching individual bales and providing for the storage until the dispute between the bureau, employer, and freedman was solved. If neither the bureau nor the broker could find the crop, or it was already sold, Gregory ordered the closest subassistant commissioner to seize the planter's personal property "in the most summary way possible." But he emphasized the need to get the product first.[46]

In this light, the assistant commissioner was not above making a deal with individual planters to accept personal property instead of the crop as a guarantee to pay freedmen's wages, so as not to delay shipment at the most propitious time for highest prices. Gregory's main goal remained to force every delinquent planter to "do justice to the freedmen," regardless of how this was achieved.[47] Since Gregory's cotton policy was in competition with the Treasury Department, which was still seizing Confederate "tithe" cotton, he figured that if planters could make a bigger profit by going along with the bureau's program they would be more cooperative in the long run.[48]

Gregory also made it his policy to supervise wage payments for periods not under contract, where freed persons were cheated out of salary or mistreated as employees. For those employers unfortunate enough to live in or around Galveston, the general would call them in for a personal reprimand and forced payment on the spot. Judging from the tone of his letters, a forced visit to the assistant commissioner's headquarters could be the low point of a planter's entire month.[49]

Gregory reserved his iciest tone for Federal employees who abused freedmen. When the acting assistant quartermaster of the District of Texas, Major E. O. Farr, impressed freedman George Gilmer for a day's unpaid work unloading a steamship, Gilmer complained to Gregory personally. The general responded with a biting letter addressed to the major. "Feeling that our Generous and noble Government is not only willing but desirous of paying all its employees," snapped Gregory, "this man is respectfully referred to you, who will undoubtedly see that he gets his rights." Things certainly did not bode well for a Lieutenant Reaker of Company C, Tenth U.S. Colored Infantry (USCI), when he was summoned to come in and talk over his refusal to pay another freedman for a week's work as his body servant.[50] Whenever he heard of them, Gregory referred cases occurring outside Galveston to the nearest subassistant commissioner.[51]

If 1865 had been a rough year for freedmen to receive their earnings, Gregory hoped to improve matters in 1866 by addressing the contract problem with closely monitored guidelines. By mid-October, 1865, Gregory had written his agents and outlined his proposed policies, a better supervised version of a plan very much like Banks's program in General Orders No. 23. Gregory told his subordinates that all work contracts lasting more than thirty days had to be made out in triplicate and approved by a bureau representative. He repeatedly warned his subassistant commissioners that only they could approve contracts.[52] The document should be equitable, the assistant commissioner said, and should include "humane treatment, fair and liberal compensation, together with the extension of education facilities to the freedmen." Gregory called his approach "the most direct way to develop and promote . . . mutual interest" between employer and employee.[53]

Any head of family who voluntarily signed a labor contract, continued Gregory, bound himself and his immediate family to its terms. Initially, contracts were to include provisions for food, living quarters, fuel, medical attendance, and a one-acre garden plot. As time passed, however, Gregory seemed to change these regulations, leaving them to the discretion of the contracting parties and the local subassistant commissioner.[54] All contracts, Gregory said, constituted a first lien on the crop produced. No landowner could remove or sell more than one half the crop without the certification of a subassistant commissioner that the freedmen had been paid. The blacks were to labor for a portion of the crop or be paid wages, up to half of which could be withheld until the crop was sold.[55]

Gregory went on to say that laborers were expected to work ten-hour days, five and one half days each week, and not to be absent over one day at a time or five days per month. A laborer's failure to keep to these work standards constituted vagrancy. If his employer testified under oath that a freedman exceeded these limits, the laborer could be put to work on county public projects without pay. "Freedom does not mean living without labor," said Gregory.[56] The "usual" guarantees were to apply to the contracting parties. Planters could forfeit their crop liens or any security deposited with the local bureau agent if they violated contract provisions.[57] The laborers could forfeit wages for violation on their parts. If no preprinted blank contract forms were available (a regular occurrence), the subassistant commissioners could draw up draft contracts, incorporating the stated principles. No contract was to last beyond January 1, 1867, Gregory insisted. And, he concluded, no form of slavery or peonage was permissible.[58]

There is some indication that not all freedmen understood the compulsions surrounding the signing of a contract, or they may have considered its exclusiveness a violation of their rights as free persons. In any case, if a laborer under contract grew disgruntled with his employer, he often did not hesitate to sign a second contract with a landholder down the road. In such instances, Gregory recommended that his agents confiscate the wages earned on the second job and pay them to the first employer as damages. The assistant commissioner warned his subordinates to keep one copy of all contracts on file to protect themselves from damage suits for interference in enforcing the contract process.[59]

Gregory also cautioned the subassistant commissioners not to force the Negroes to comply with any contract provision. The agents, however, were to advise compliance at all times. If the freedman refused, as was his right, the employer could seek redress in court, as was his prerogative.[60] But in no case was a labor contract signed by a freedman to be enforced if he had never understood its provisions in the first place. Subassistant commissioners were allowed to review any contract for its legality, even if it had been approved earlier, and to negate it if the document possessed any provision of a doubtful quality.[61]

It was for this reason that Commissioner Howard had recommended that Gregory set up a "mixed commission" at each agency, consisting of three persons—one elected by the local planters, one elected by local freedmen, and the subassistant commissioner—to adjudicate all questions arising from the labor contract process. Howard told Gregory such a board would involve the freedmen and planters in the work of the bureau, and might make the whole mechanism of contracts more palatable to all. There is no evidence that this procedure ever became widespread among the Texas agents.[62] Indeed troublemakers—"the class you complain of 'who are prowling about the county creating discontent among the freedmen,'" as Gregory wrote to one subassistant commissioner—were to be taken care of by "such steps as may be necessary to put a stop to their evil works."[63]

Besides the issues arising from the contract process, another task that consumed much of the bureau's energy early on was the medical care of the freedmen and refugees. As a general policy, medical officers assigned to the bureau operated under Circular Orders No. 14, issued by the commissioner's office on August 17, 1865. This order required the chief medical officers of each bureau district to note the numbers of freedmen and refugees in need of professional health care, and to provide for their needs by creating hospitals and clinics in key areas. Civilian contract surgeons could be used, provided they could take the ironclad oath that they had never voluntarily rendered aid or comfort to the Confederacy.[64]

The circular also permitted medical officers to draw upon the army for hospital and medical supplies, if the application was made in triplicate, approved by the chief medical officer, and not excessive in the amounts requested. All medical care was to be provided in the "strictest economy," and all requests for equipment and medicines were to be rejected by superiors whenever possible. Of course, the usual reports were to be made regularly.[65]

Like many other bureau officials in Texas, Surgeon Mintzer was a volunteer soldier kept on duty after the war.[66] As chief medical officer,

Mintzer supervised a hospital system that never really developed. At its height, it had hospitals in Houston and Galveston, a clinic at Austin, and some occasional operations at cites along the Texas coast.[67] The bureau hospital system in the state employed in addition to Mintzer two acting assistant surgeons, one of whom lasted only a month before resigning, and another who stayed four months until his muster-out. By the close of Gregory's term as assistant commissioner, it is fair to say the Texas bureau's hospital system was pretty well shut down.[68] The stewards—nurses in a modern context—were men on detached duty from nearby regiments.[69]

Mintzer served Gregory as both a troubleshooter and a medical officer. As such, Mintzer toured eastern Texas and reported general conditions there in December, 1865. The following month, he made another tour of the Gulf coastal plain and reported on the living conditions of the recently freed slaves.[70] Gregory had toured the same area earlier and was quite worried about poor sanitary conditions he had encountered among the freedmen. The assistant commissioner wanted Mintzer's comments from a professional standpoint.[71]

Acceding to Gregory's request, Mintzer found the health of the blacks to be generally good "considering the miasmatic influences of the rich bottom lands, and the quality of the water." Too many relied on river and bayou as water sources. The surgeon discovered marked morbidity differences in the hundred plantations he visited, with those using cistern water being the healthiest. He also considered the freed peoples' shelters to be minimal. Most lived in log huts of about 350 square feet that lacked windows or doors. They were overcrowded, and the roofs leaked. When Mintzer commented on this to one planter, he was told "it was good enough for the nigger while he was worth $1500 to them and ought to be good enough now, as he has no jingle." Rations consisted of varying amounts of pork and cornmeal. Anything else had to be provided by the Negroes themselves.[72]

After his examination of the area south of Galveston along the coast, Mintzer's next assignment was to inspect the habitations and grounds of the freedmen living in and around Galveston. He asked the local army garrison to assist in the task and to issue orders necessary to improve the sanitary conditions and prevent the spread of disease during the approaching season of hot weather.[73] As a result of Mintzer's inspection, the army and the bureau prepared a series of health rules to prevent the entrance of contagious diseases from a tropical port, the most feared of which were yellow fever and Asiatic cholera. Ships arriving from the West Indies were subjected to a twenty-day quarantine and inspection by a health officer. Ships found to be disease ridden were sealed off, and clothing and cargo burned if necessary. The whole vessel was to be thoroughly fumigated, and the crew were not allowed ashore until fifteen days after the last case was cured. The quarantine laws were in effect from March through the end of September.[74]

In addition to the sequestration of diseased ships, the army ordered a general cleanup of all towns and camp areas. Decayed matter was to be burned, sinks and privies filled with dirt regularly, lime used to keep buildings dry, and personal cleanliness enforced. Bureau and army medical officers were to investigate all rumors of disease, especially those involving discharges of the bowels. The Galveston *Daily News,* normally an antimilitary sheet, supported the sanitation orders and suggested that the army command and the city government divide Galveston into cleanup districts to achieve best results. The program was a thorough success.[75]

Closely related to medical care was the bureau's issuance of rations to indigent freedmen and refugees. In Texas, the ration program was tied to the hospitals and local agency offices. The ration program seemed to be one of continual abuse, which Commissioner Howard tried to rectify even before Gregory's appointment to Texas. In June, 1865, Howard told assistant commissioners to estimate the food, clothing, and fuel needed by refugees and freedmen in their districts, and to submit such estimates quarterly to his headquarters for approval before any items were issued to the needy. Howard warned that rations were not to be issued to "teachers and other employees," although they could buy such items according to the rules employed by army command officers who did the same.[76]

The ration in question had been created by the War Department in 1864 and was based upon the individual soldier's allotment employed during the war. It included sixteen ounces of fresh beef or ten ounces of pork or bacon, and sixteen ounces of white flour or cornmeal or twelve ounces of hard bread (hard tack) for each individual. Meat items were issued daily, bread or its substitutes two to five times a week. Also, for each hundred individual rations issued, the bureau could include ten pounds of peas, beans, or hominy; eight pounds of sugar; two quarts of vinegar; eight ounces of candles; two pounds of soap; two pounds of salt; and two ounces of pepper. Women and children were allowed ten pounds of roasted coffee or fifteen ounces of tea per hundred rations. For accounting purposes, children under fourteen years of age received half rations.[77]

The rations for freedmen and refugees were requisitioned on a weekly (later changed to a monthly) basis. Headquarters also recommended that partial rations be issued if freedmen and refugees were able to provide the rest locally on their own. Meticulous records were to be maintained and submitted to Washington each month. In the spring of 1866, Congress asked for a special effort to be made to "prevent actual suffering" among freedmen and loyal refugees. In the South, with the program being directed by local subassistant commissioners or, if none were available, civil authorities or religious organizations.[78]

Congress's concern had no real impact in Texas. By the spring of 1866, there were no commissaries of subsistence listed in the returns of the Texas bureau, and the total number of rations issued was small throughout Gregory's tenure.[79] For example, Subassistant Commissioner Captain Byron Porter reported 15 total rations issued for December, 1865, at Houston. In January, he issued 274 rations at a cost of $29.64. February saw an increase to 397 rations issued, with a peak reached in May of 468 rations issued at a value of $70.20. During the same period, the hospital that issued the rations never had more than thirty patients nor less than sixteen.[80] Galveston Freedmen's Hospital issued an average of 475 rations per month between February and April, 1866, to a patient roster that decreased from sixty in February to only eight in April, of whom one died.[81]

One of the main purposes of rations was to aid in the movement of freedmen and refugees to their homes, from which they had been displaced by the war, or to areas where they could obtain work and no longer be wards of the government. To assist this movement, the original bureau bill had permitted the use of government transportation.[82] Transportation, like the issuance of rations, was an object of abuse. In June, 1865, Howard limited all transportation provided to government vehicles, transports, or the military railroads. By July, even before Gregory's appointment, transportation of refugees had been confined to those cases "where humanity evidently demands it," and then only with the prior approval of headquarters in Washington.[83]

In September, shortly after Gregory's arrival in Texas, Howard limited transportation to destitute refugees and freedmen, civilian employees of the bureau upon receipt of headquarters's permission, stores and schoolbooks to be used by bureau personnel, and any officer traveling under bureau orders from his district or the national headquarters.[84] The only real record of white refugees in the Texas bureau command was a family of seven kept at government expense in Galveston for two months in early 1866, and about twenty miscellaneous persons aided for very short periods of time.[85] By the end of Gregory's term no refugees were reported, and the assistant commissioner strictly enforced all restrictions imposed from above.[86] All in all, Gregory's staff aided 393 freedmen and refugees, who received an average of 20 rations each.[87]

2

The Great Difficulty

THE BUREAU'S WHOLE PROGRAM rested on the abilities, actions, and character of the subassistant commissioners in the field. In Texas, because of its vast size, the number of agents would be even more important than their quality. In a sense, the more Gregory emphasized the quality of his subordinates, the less effective the bureau became. With larger numbers of agents came increased incompetence and corruption. "I find great difficulty in procuring a sufficient number of . . . Sub[.] Asst. Comms. . . . ," Gregory wrote Commissioner Howard in December, 1865. "But few, comparatively, feel and manifest that interest in the advancement of the freedmen that they should." Although Gregory was referring specifically to volunteer military men, the same concern could be applied to all agents, be they volunteer or professional soldiers, or Northern or Southern civilians. It was a problem that had no solution: Gregory and his successors needed to flood the state with capable agents, adequate numbers of whom they were unable to provide.[1]

Although it is tempting to accuse Gregory of being at the same time too sure of the good character of some of his appointments and not sure enough about others, he did realize that he needed more agents. His first request upon arriving in Texas was for fifteen officers to be detached from the local army command.[2] Inspector Strong called for fifty men, and Gregory asked Howard for fifteen more in February, stating that he really needed seventy, for a total of eighty-five agents.[3] But Howard had already asked the army for fifty more subassistant commissioners for the whole South, a figure that many authorities in Washington thought to be astronomical. Few Easterners could believe the size and needs of Texas without actually having been there first. Howard accordingly never really pressed Gregory's case with the War Department or Congress, and he probably would have achieved little success had he done so.[4]

Until January, 1867, the core of the Texas bureau's field personnel consisted of the soldiers from the wartime white and black volunteer regiments that occupied the state in 1865, and the men of the Veteran

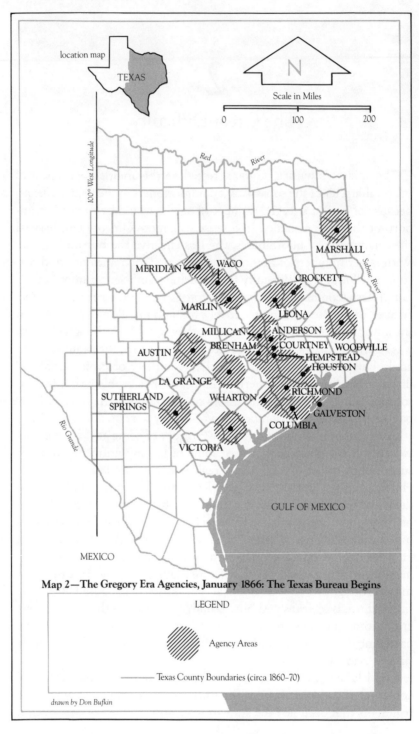

location map

TEXAS

N

Scale in Miles

0   100   200

100° West Longitude

Red   River

Sabine River

MARSHALL

MERIDIAN   WACO

CROCKETT

MARLIN

LEONA

MILLICAN   ANDERSON

AUSTIN   BRENHAM   COURTNEY   WOODVILLE

HEMPSTEAD

HOUSTON

LA GRANGE

SUTHERLAND   WHARTON   RICHMOND
SPRINGS

Rio Grande

GALVESTON

COLUMBIA

VICTORIA

GULF OF MEXICO

MEXICO

Map 2—The Gregory Era Agencies, January 1866: The Texas Bureau Begins

LEGEND

Agency Areas

———— Texas County Boundaries (circa 1860–70)

drawn by Don Bufkin

MAP 2: The Gregory-Era Agencies, January, 1866: The Texas Bureau Begins

Reserve Corps. At least forty-four of the men who served the Texas bureau as field agents came from these units, and a half dozen more volunteer officers served on Gregory's headquarters staff. Many of these continued their tenures into succeeding administrations, but most had been mustered out on orders from the Department of War as an economy measure by early 1867.

As a rule, except for staff assignments, the volunteer soldiers carried out their duties in the interior sections of Texas, and they generally functioned quite well. These field agents fell into three groups – officers from the white volunteer regiments, the Colored Troops, or the Veteran Reserve Corps – based on the military units in which they had served during the Civil War. Since the white Civil War volunteer regiments drew the bulk of the interior occupation duty in 1865, it was natural that General Gregory would turn to their ranks to find some of his first subassistant commissioners. Their greatest disadvantage as agents was that many of them (and particularly the enlisted men under their commands) sympathized with white Texans in their dislike of the free Negro.

Cognizant of this problem, Gregory tended to favor as subassistant commissioners those officers who (unlike the general himself) had transferred to the new black infantry regiments formed in the middle of the war. Such a step had required courage. The Colored Troops had offered capable white enlisted men the chance for quick advancement to commissioned rank, providing they also accepted the onus of being labeled "nigger officers." For the most part, Gregory's assessment of these men's character and interest in the future of blacks as free men proved correct.[5]

The final category of men whom Gregory was able to use as bureau officers came from the ranks of the Veteran Reserve Corps. Set up in 1863, the Veteran Reserve Corps comprised men who had been wounded in battle, yet could offer limited service in behind-the-lines capacities that might free able-bodied men for the front. By 1865, the Veteran Reserves included 24 regiments and 188 separate companies – more than 60,000 men, many of whom now were able-bodied soldiers who wished to continue in Federal service after Appomattox. Still, some of them who were sent to Texas had suffered serious wounds often resulting in amputations, which affected their ability to perform their bureau functions.[6]

If there was one major problem that all these officers faced, it was the fact that they often received their muster-outs within months, sometimes weeks, after their initial bureau assignments. Hence, the volunteer soldiers rarely had time to master the role of subassistant commissioner and learn the character of their subdistricts before they were sent home or rotated to another post that had greater need of their services. With the invasion of Texas in June, 1865, over fifty thousand Federal soldiers inundated the state. Six months later, the number had been reduced to ten thousand, and by June, 1866, the total number available for duty was five thousand. This figure continued to drop day after day, as the far less numerous regulars replaced the volunteers.[7]

As each regiment left, it took the lieutenants and captains on detached duty, many of whom Gregory had used as his subassistant commissioners. Adding in the numerous clerks, orderlies, guards, and teamsters from the enlisted ranks, the Texas bureau's personnel policy resembled a revolving door. Sometimes, Gregory was forced to get rid of personnel on his own volition, as in the case of Private William Johnson of the Thirty-ninth Illinois Infantry. Johnson, a printer at bureau headquarters, had wasted most of his appointment "in a state of beastly intoxication," and was sent back to his regiment after he spent two weeks in the guardhouse.[8] The ongoing muster-out of the Union Civil War armies and the resulting lack of personnel placed Gregory in a real quandary.[9] The shortage became so acute that when Commissioner Howard suggested that all assistant commissioners appoint an officer to be district intelligence officer, Gregory replied that "the demand greatly exceeded the supply" and refused to comply.[10]

It seemed that no sooner did an agent learn his job than he was sent home by the War Department. Although Gregory tried repeatedly to keep officers in the service past their regimental muster-out dates, he was generally not successful. He lost the services of Captain Samuel I. Wright, his indispensable acting assistant adjutant general who ran the headquarters staff, when Wright's commission expired.[11] At Columbus, Captain Eli W. Green of the Twenty-ninth Illinois had become one of Gregory's first field appointments. Dismayed at some whites' brutal treatment of local freed people, Green promised Gregory, "I am determined that the Negroes *shall not* be *imposed* upon by this *class of desperadoes.*" But the captain's regiment left before he had been in office a month, and his pledge went unfullfilled.[12]

First Lietenant George Van De Sande of the Tenth USCI, one of Green's successors at Columbus, stayed two months. His main concern was the health care and feeding of numerous black refugees, who had congregated at the agency for help. Then Gregory was forced to send him like all the others, back to his home-bound regiment. Like Green, Van De Sande barely had time to learn the rudiments of his job before being recalled.[13]

Captain J. B. Bostwick of the Virginia-organized Tenth USCI served twice as long as Van De Sande. Bostwick arrived at the Columbia agency in late December, 1865. As Bostwick began to settle the accounts for 1865 and issue new contracts, he learned of the activities of a Dr. Law, who had been giving speeches to the freedmen and witnessing contracts for a cost. Although Bostwick did not approve of the illegality of Law's actions, he had to admit that the freedmen received whatever they did for the last year's labor because of Law's efforts. Certainly Law did better than one Captain Cochran of the occupying Forty-eighth Ohio. Bostwick reported that the captain had received thirty-five dollars on behalf of a Negro, whom he had never paid. Later, Cochran sent a draft for the sum after Gregory tracked him down.

Bostwick also had several cases of blacks who desired to be reunited with family members. In one case, a freedwoman said that her daughter's husband (who appears to have been white) held the girl prisoner and threatened to give her five hundred lashes if she tried to return to her mother. Bostwick had tried the man before, but the man now defied General Gregory and Bostwick to act again. In another instance, a black teenage girl refused to return to her mother. She said she was well treated by her employer. Bostwick said that he hesitated to act forcibly in this case since he had not done so in the former. His impending muster-out led to his recall to his regiment after just four months on bureau duty.[14]

Realizing that he had to retain key men like Green, Van De Sand, and Bostwick, Gregory attempted to delay the volunteer officers' demobilization. This ploy only led to sharp letters from Washington asking under what authority an officer was being held over, and demanding immediate compliance with previous muster-out orders.[15] The first bureau agent at Victoria, for example, was Captain John Scott of the Twenty-ninth Illinois Infantry. Assuming his position in October, 1865, Scott disclosed that all Federal authorities were cooperating in the area, and the local state authorities were asking many questions to establish the ground rules of bureau control. Gregory insisted on the ten-hour day, but said that contracts did not have to be paid monthly. Scott noted that the 1865 contracts often had the freedmen paid through their old masters, which had caused some complaint. He promised to monitor the settlements closely to prevent fraud.

After Scott had been in office a few weeks, planters and freedmen poured in from all over the surrounding area for advice and adjudication of differences. The freedmen who had gathered at Victoria readily signed contracts and went back to the countryside when the occupying black troops, a novelty to be seen by these former Texas slaves, began to be mustered out. Scott soon joined them, for his own regiment had already left two months before, and the War Department refused to allow any officer to serve beyond his regimental muster-out date, regardless of his competence or the bureau's need. Scott would later serve again briefly as a civilian staff clerk.[16]

Another man who stayed beyond the demobilization of his regiment was Green's successor, First Lieutenant John T. Raper, the adjutant of the Twenty-sixth Ohio. Another of the numerous early subassistant commissioners at Columbus, Raper discovered that labor and crop conditions in the area were good, but that all cotton headed for Galveston had been stopped by the agent from De Gress's provost marshal's office, J. D. Whitall. Gregory ordered Raper to yield his authority to no one, and to forward all cotton without delay, unless the freedmen had not been paid. In such cases, the subassistant commissioner was to hold half the crop and forward the rest.[17]

But his major problem was what to do with black children, said Raper. According to state law all fatherless children were defined as orphans and could be farmed out by the county judge. Raper pointed out that all Negro children born under slavery, by definition, had no legal father. Bureau policy was that Raper was to act as guardian until the state law was changed. Raper really never got the chance to act. He had recently been indicted for swindling, because he had tried and fined a white for assaulting a freedman. The overly enthusiastic interest of the county judge in the case may be an indication that Raper had effectively interfered with his state-granted prerogative to apprentice the black children to local residents.

The harried subassistant commissioner refused to be arrested, the local army post commander backed him up, and the mayor complained to Governor Hamilton. Then came the emphatic confirmation that no volunteer officers were allowed to remain behind after their regiments were mustered out. Gregory was disappointed at the War Department's policy, and seemed ready to challenge it. But Raper pointed out that the contract season was over, and asked to go home to enter private business. Gregory then decided that Raper's muster-out was an easy solution to what promised to be a sticky problem. He sent the controversial lieutenant the usual orders to turn in his records and report to Galveston.[18] Gregory might better have tried to challenge the short-sighted departmental personnel policy over the muster-out of a man like Scott or Green, rather than Raper, even if he had been wrongly accused. Commissioner Howard normally preferred to let go any agent tainted by "immorality, corruption, neglect of duty, [or] incapacity" in any form.[19]

Gregory was plagued not only by men he needed to get rid of, but also by those who wanted to leave, as in the case of Second Lieutenant O. H. Swingley, who opened the Austin agency in late October, 1865. His duties were varied. He contacted Governor Hamilton and obtained a list of loyal county officers he had recently appointed. A tour of his command area found the freedmen to be self-supporting, doing well, and renting land rather than sharecropping, a regional preference throughout Reconstruction. With the aid of Chaplain J. S. Rand of the First Iowa Cavalry, Swingley began a thriving black school system.

The lieutenant was a capable administrator, but after a long war, he was anxious to leave the army and return to Illinois. His parting comment recommended bringing the truth of Yankee victory home to every rebel supporter: "I would like to see Col'd soldiers doing Provost duty in every town in the State."[20] Gregory regretted Swingley's decision to leave, but he understood the lieutenant's desire to go home.[21] Swingley had liked working with Rand so well that before he left, he suggested that the capable chaplain be appointed subassistant commissioner of his own agency. Gregory agreed and sent Rand to La Grange in early 1866. Rand hardly arrived in La Grange before his regiment was shipped home, and he became still another casualty of demobilization.[22]

Others left the bureau's employ but stayed on in Texas for varying amounts of time after their muster-out. Second Lieutenant George Gladwyn of the One Hundred and Twenty-second USCI had been stationed along the Rio Grande, which was considered a boring duty, removed from all amenities. He volunteered for the bureau position at Houston in December, 1865. Gladwyn did not last thirty days before he and his regiment were mustered out by the beginning of February, 1866.[23] But Gladwyn opted to stay behind when his regiment left for home. The lieutenant failed, however, to inform his wife, who awaited her husband's arrival up North. She wrote Commissioner Howard inquiring into her husband's whereabouts. Gregory reported he thought that Gladwyn was in still Houston, working as "a Chief of Police or something."[24]

Like Gladwyn, First Lieutenant Levi Jones of the Tenth USCI stayed on after the termination of his military commission ended his bureau service. Jones had thoroughly enjoyed his position as subassistant commissioner at Hempstead, and when his regiment was mustered out in May, 1865, Jones begged to stay on with the bureau. But civilian agents were not allowed to be hired before the July, 1866, bureau renewal act. So Jones settled in Bellville, southeast of Hempstead, and awaited another opportunity. In December, 1866, he applied for a bureau position but was turned down once again. More than likely, Jones lacked influence at headquarters, as his earlier job performance seemed good.[25]

Not all the volunteer officers who served with the bureau were soldiers. George Abbott, who had preceded Jones at Hempstead, was a boatswain in the U. S. Navy who hailed from New England. But the boatswain found his salary inadequate for his needs, especially when he received no pay for five months and no answers to his pressing questions on this and other official matters. He told headquarters that his job was "a thankless position at best" and "I shall be compelled to resign my position solely from the need of proper encouragement and support." A personal investigation by Gregory in December, 1865, did not help. Abbott asked to be relieved "from a duty which under present circumstances has cessed [sic] to be a pleasant one." But he stayed in the Houston area, where he was "killed by an accomplice in rascality in a personal dificulty." The bureau's epitaph was that Abbott was a "very bad man." His able job performance under very trying conditions indicated that he deserved to be remembered more kindly despite his faults.[26]

Often army unit commanders demanded the return of their detached officers who were serving as bureau agents. As the first subassistant commissioner at Beaumont, Captain Frank Holsinger of the Nineteenth USCI arrived in February, 1866, after several attempts to get through on washed-out roads. He heard of "severe cruelties" being perpetrated against the freed people in Jasper to the north. After receiving an escort from Captain E. H. Pratt of the Twelfth Illinois Cavalry, and Gregory's assurances that he had jurisdiction, he traveled up to investigate. Holsinger found that Pratt's troopers were the cause. With Pratt's approval, the soldiers had been returning Negroes to their former owners and permitting them to be whipped. Pratt admitted that he had been sent to aid the freedmen, "But he'd be G-d d_____d if he would do it."

Holsinger also reported several senseless shootings of blacks in Beaumont, one by a white who did not like the idea of emancipation, and another by a barfly, who shot a Negro "just to see him kick." But Holsinger's regimental and departmental commanders wanted him to return to the Rio Grande valley, where experienced officers were in short supply. The commander of the Sub-District of the Rio Grande, Brevet Major General George W. Getty, called Holsinger's return "an absolute necessity."[27] Leaving Beaumont in April, a disappointed Holsinger resigned his commission shortly afterward for "'Physical Disability'– having lost the use of my right arm (permanently)." He left his unit months before its actual demobilization date, another good agent lost to bureau and army service by poor staff management.[28]

Up in Crockett, the bureau's commitment in the person of Captain Stanton W. Weaver of the Sixty-second USCI was more enduring than Holsinger's term at Beaumont. Arriving in January, 1866, Weaver reported that planters treated their hands well because there was a shortage of labor. But those who had labor complaints told Weaver that it was none of his business and that they would continue to use the local courts. When the blacks were aware of Weaver's purpose, they flocked to his office to see if their contracts were valid and could be changed to better terms. Weaver wondered if they were not really owed salary from the date of the 1863 Emancipation Proclamation rather than Juneteenth, an interesting legal concept that Gregory chose to ignore.

As at other agencies, Weaver saw many methods of reenslavement in use. The planters overcharged their employees and deducted every conceivable item from the end-of-the-year settlement. Blacks were hauled into court on all sorts of minor complaints and trumped-up charges (usually involving petty theft), causing them to spend what meager funds they possessed for legal fees and putting them at the mercy of their employers for the coming year. Their testimony was allowed in court, but juries generally ignored it. Weaver protested these items to local civil authorities. The county judge met Weaver and told the subassistant commissioner to stay out of the way or he would have him indicted for interfering with the court.

Weaver refused to heed the judge's warning, and answered the indictment that followed by correctly referring the judge to the bureau act of 1865 and the various orders under which he acted. He then proceeded to remove the cases involving blacks from county jurisdiction.

His muster-out prevented any further legal squabbles. Weaver later entered the Twentieth Infantry, a white regiment in the regular army, and
briefly served as subassistant commissioner at Jefferson, operating out
of the Department of Louisiana. He also continued to take an interest
in Crockett, informing Gregory of bogus agents he knew of in the area.
If Weaver achieved anything in his short stay, it was to convince certain planters that the bureau provided a worthwhile service. They anx-
iously inquired for the services of a new agent to replace him.[29]

Outlying districts like Crockett could be rather isolated, as First Lieutenant Eugene Smith of the Tenth USCI discovered. Smith had served
the bureau briefly at Indianola, but business was so slow that he recommended the office be moved to Texana or Matagorda. But if Smith
thought headquarters would send him to one of these points, he erred.
He was off to the upper Brazos in a matter of weeks. "In regard to the
inhabitants" of Waco, he grumbled upon his arrival in January, 1866,
"I cannot say much in their favor." In the surrounding countryside things
were worse. Smith heard that "there are some of the Quantral [Quan-
trill] sort of persons," and it was unsafe for a Yankee to move about
without troops.

Confused as to the boundaries under his control, Smith suggested
district boundaries be formed. Gregory, who preferred a more fluid
command structure, refused and told him not to be discouraged but
to carry on. Soon Smith received a request for troop assistance from
the Meridian agency. He complied, but noted that one fourth of the
forty cavalrymen he had were sick or had deserted. Smith visited the
surrounding plantations, encouraged the freedmen to keep working,
"and told them a little of the Yankee way of doing business." In May,
1866, Smith was finally recalled for the muster-out of his regiment. He
had been so far into the hinterland that he had been forgotten by his
embarrassed regimental commander and the bureau staff.[30]

More remote than Smith at Waco was Gregory's first actual field
appointment, Brevet Colonel H. Seymour Hall of the Forty-third USCI,
who became the subassistant commissioner at Marshall. In making Hall's
nomination, Gregory recognized the importance of expanding the bureau into the isolated reaches of northeastern Texas. As Hall tried in
vain to get to Marshall overland from Galveston, he became the first
in a long line of Texas bureau agents who had to take a steamer to
New Orleans and up the Red River to Shreveport, before disembark-
ing and finishing the trip by road. By November, 1865, he had set up
his agency. He had the assistance of the local provost marshal, First

Lieutenant Charles Steelhammer of the Eighth Illinois Infantry (who later served the bureau in Weatherford, Texas, after transferring to the regular army), and a loyal civilian, B. T. Lignowski, who worked out of Tyler.

The first problem Hall faced was one that would plague bureau operations in northeastern Texas for years. Marshall and Jefferson had been placed within the administrative boundaries of the army's District of Louisiana. For bureau purposes, however, they lay in Texas. This meant that army officers stationed in Louisiana treated the area as a poor relative to be ignored, and the army headquarters in Texas had no jurisdiction. The cumbersome process of sending a request for soldiers to Galveston to have it forwarded to the army at New Orleans was next to impossible to coordinate. Hence, when Hall asked for cavalry he got none. The Department of Texas had some available, but the Department of Louisiana did not. Not until 1867 would this counterproductive situation change, and Texas army and bureau boundaries match.

When Hall asked Gregory for subassistant commissioners to place in each of the surrounding counties, he again got nothing. Instead, at Gregory's insistence, Hall had to order Lignowski to cease his operations as an unauthorized agent in Tyler, even though Hall thought that the man was capable and had the interest of the freedmen at heart. In the same breath, Gregory naively told Hall that his command zone included the entire territory around Marshall as far as he could go. That was not far, for Hall's patrols were threatened or ambushed on a regular basis, which confined his influence largely to the town.

The opposition to the bureau and army efforts at Reconstruction was of a special quality in northeastern Texas—violent and pervasive. Killing a Negro was viewed as a public service here, and it was not unusual for the law to support the murderers. Added to this was the fact that the first white occupation troops were Negro-haters from Illinois, who joined in the persecution of blacks. Hall saw, correctly, that it would be impossible to get Texans to change their feeling on race, when the Union Army acted in the same manner toward the freedmen. But he would no longer have to worry about it, since the War Department had slated his regiment for return to its original enlistment point of Philadelphia. By early 1866, Hall had been mustered out of the service. A month later he told his tales of woe to the nation before the Joint Committee on Reconstruction in Washington.[31]

During the twelve months that followed Lieutenant Colonel Hall's departure, Colonel Thomas Bayley of the Ninth Colored Infantry was the subassistant commissioner at Marshall. Possessing an excellent combat record, Bayley had important political influence through his wife's family in Illinois, and came highly recommended by U. S. senator and former Illinois governor, Richard Yates. His appointment evidently made quite a stir among the officers of the black infantry in the Rio Grande valley. Possibly Bayley bragged about his appointment and inflated its importance. In any case, one of the line officers incorrectly addressed Bayley as "Chief of Freedmen's Bureau, Department of Texas," in a letter asking about possible bureau operations at Edinburgh.

Upon his arrival, Bayley was pleased to report that the freedmen were under contract and the planting process well under way. But he desperately needed help to run his large subdistrict. He asked Gregory for several men by name, only to be told that he could neither use soldiers from the Louisiana command nor expect an assistant to be sent from Galveston. The army had ordered all civilians except clerks to be discharged from the service as quickly as could be done without hurting the efficiency of any command, Gregory said. Although this did not seem to affect the use of unpaid civilian subassistant commissioners, it hurt the ability of Texas bureau headquarters to employ civilian clerks. Army personnel were to be used instead.[32] Some subassistant commissioners tried to circumvent the order, but they were brought up short by letters from Gregory questioning their actions. The assistant commissioner warned agents that they had no authority to hire civilian help even if they had sufficient funds from fines to pay them.[33]

But Gregory did realize that Bayley's station at Marshall was so removed from the mainstream of bureau affairs that an exception had to be made in this case. He gave Bayley approval to hire former sergeant Frank Smith of the Eighth Illinois as his clerk. In April, Gregory decided to send him an assistant subassistant commissioner, First Lieutenant Isaac M. Beebe of the Twenty-third Veteran Reserve Regiment.[34] Beebe traveled through New Orleans and Shreveport in order to reach Marshall in the shortest possible time. Even then, the journey took five months.[35]

The fault of failing to obtain enough agents to cover the state was not Gregory's alone. Congress had doomed the bureau's first year's effort when it neglected to appropriate funds specifically for bureau work. This inadequacy meant that civilian agents could not be paid a salary. Hence, Gregory routinely turned away civilian applicants.[36] During his nine-month tenure as assistant commissioner, Gregory turned down at least fifty-five potential candidates for subassistant commissioners' positions. This was fully enough to have covered the state. But following Howard's instructions carefully, Gregory wanted to be sure of all applicants. And while most of the civilian applicants were allegedly loyal Texans (often suspect in Gregory's mind), he also refused men from as far away as New England. Some of the men he turned down had letters of recommendation from members of Congress or Commissioner Howard; from noted Texans like Governor Hamilton, Elisha M. Pease, and James H. Bell; or from important local dignitaries like George Paschal, Colbert Caldwell, J. H. Duval, B. F. Barkley, A. K. Foster, Henry C. Pedigo, and A. P. Delano.[37]

Then in the midst of this mess Gregory received good news. There were Texans willing to serve as bureau agents in their home counties, providing they could do it in addition to their normal employment, which would provide all their salary.[38] Gregory probably suspected that some of these men would use the bureau for their own business advantage. Moreover, they had been so influenced by the attitudes of the slave regime, and the suffering that they had endured at Confederate hands as avowed Union men during the war, that some would be less than ideal bureau representatives. Called Scalawags, these men were often more interested in revenge against the rebel whites who had persecuted them, and in the political patronage available from the provisional governments, than in the intrinsic rights and advancement of the freed people.[39]

But the assistant commissioner was desperate. So Gregory came to rely on Texas citizens for half of his bureau field representatives. These Scalawags were self-confessed loyalists, many were northern-born, and all had made Texas their home well before the Civil War. They offered the advantage of serving without pay at first, and later at reduced salary, their normal occupations supposedly providing the funds they needed to get by. They also knew the area of their operations intimately, and allegedly agreed with the political goals of the victorious Union. Besides, if planters and merchants became subassistant commisisioners, they could forward the contract process in isolated areas or places with large numbers of black farm workers.[40] More important were the judges and lawyers who were willing to serve without pay. A bureau agent would benefit from a legal education, since his duties revolved around contracts and civil rights.[41] A county commissioner and two Federal postmasters also volunteered.[42] Ten of these men were still serving when Gregory left office in May, 1866.[43]

The first civilian agent Gregory appointed was John F. Brown, who worked out of Anderson in Grimes County. Brown contacted Gregory in October, 1865, giving as his sources of recommendation Provisional Governor A. J. Hamilton; the governor's brother, Morgan C. Hamilton; the Federal district judge for western Texas, T. H. Duval; and noted Union man, Swante Palme. Brown received the appointment within ten days and met Gregory on one of the general's fact-finding tours in late November. If no news is good news, Brown's administration must have been excellent. At least Gregory thought so. There was a paucity of communication from the Anderson agency, but no complaints.[44]

The next group of Southern civilian subassistant commissioners came out of Gregory's acquaintance with two men, John T. Whitesides and William H. Farner. Gregory met them in one of his trips into the heavily black-populated planting region, and for some reason or another came to trust them, perhaps more than he should have. Whitesides was a local justice of the peace of the Hamilton regime, whose family had been one of the first to settle the area in the days of Mexican rule. He was the second person picked as a civilian agent for Texas, receiving his appointment at the end of November, 1865, to serve out of his home near Courtney. He wrote Gregory immediately for clearer instructions, and told how all the planters were coming in to see him and promising to abide by the new free labor system. Acknowledging that his appointment was an important trust, he promised to serve in a manner that would not cause Gregory any regret.[45]

Like all the Texans, Whitesides served under the impression that his bureau position was a part-time job, to be done after his normal business hours. Whitesides was soon disabused of this notion. He related to Gregory that his bureau responsibilities were full time, and he could not even leave the house for a moment without someone running down the road after him, begging his advice and assistance. He feared that the job would soon impoverish him, and suggested a system of fees be instituted to give him some income. Gregory sympathized with his Courtney subassistant commissioner, and promised to come up in person to talk over problems. Whitesides was amazed at the great distances freedmen came to lay their grievances before him, most of which involved nonpayment of wages for 1865. "How strange it is," he commented, "that so many men are not willing to do by others as they would wish to be done by, yet it is so."[46]

The work overwhelmed Whitesides so that in April, 1866, he handed in his resignation. Throughout his administration, Whitesides seemed to get along very well with the planters and, he claimed, with the freedmen. But it is disturbing to read of him and his son correcting a former slave sometime later by severely whipping the man while he was staked out on the ground, as reported by a traveling bureau inspector. Perhaps Gregory already knew more than he wished to admit in the spring of 1866. In any case, the new bureau office was established at Navasota.[47]

It was upon Whitesides's recommendation that Gregory appointed F. D. Inge, a loyal refugee, subassistant commissioner for Leon County in early December, 1865. Leaving Galveston, Inge reached Leona and opened his office in mid-January, 1866. Immediately, he quarreled with the county judge, H. B. Pruitt, a Hamilton appointee. Inge said that the judge and his cronies did not relish bureau competition for the freedmen's loyalties. Inge regretted to inform Gregory that now he would need troop support to counter the judge's malevolent influence. The general sent him Company M of the Twelfth Illinois Cavalry.

Inge detailed one of the company officers to be his clerk, with Gregory's promise to persuade General Wright to allow it. One of the soldiers informed Gregory that the freedmen were laboring hard and that Inge was "getting along very well and giving general satisfaction to all parties in matters pertaining to the agency." By May, the troops had to be withdrawn for muster-out, leaving Inge without help. The subassistant commissioner said that it was impossible to protect the Negroes without soldiers. As if to prove his point, Inge was assaulted on the town's main street shortly afterward.[48]

William H. Farner, the other subassistant commissioner whom Gregory had appointed at the same time as Whitesides, would exert much influence, not all of it good, on bureau operations in central Texas throughout 1866. Farner was a physician from Millican, who had once published what he called the first Republican newspaper in the state of Iowa before he came to Texas in the 1850s. After the war, he met Gregory through some officers in the Thirty-fourth Iowa, then stationed at Galveston, and immodestly suggested that the general appoint him as the subassistant commissioner for Brazos County. He quickly launched himself into his work and established numerous churches and schools for the freedmen in addition to his usual business of approving contracts. The amount of contract work he engaged in was prodigious, and he spent much time traveling around and recopying the documents for headquarters.[49]

Farner soon ran into trouble arising from his own conduct. First, his expense account was rejected by the bureau distribution officer. Farner said that he did not know bureau or army regulations or forms, but he asserted that all of the costs were valid. He especially wanted the bureau to pay for the large amounts of stationery he used. His next problem was that he had hired a clerk without prior authorization, and now the unfortunate man was not going to be paid by the government for his services. Finally, Farner seems to have been very understanding of the old slave regime for one who supposedly had abolitionist sympathies. He ignored the pleas of freedmen before him and sided with the planters in disciplinary matters. One complainant hoped that Farner would be replaced with a new man "not so much adapted to the use of whiskey." When they heard of this the outraged Iowa officers who had recommended Farner earlier referred the subject to the always straitlaced Gregory, and Farner was out of office in a matter of days.[50]

Initially heartened by what eventually proved to be illusory successes in securing civilian agents, Gregory decided to make more Scalawag appointments in an area east of the Trinity River. For assistance in making these assignments, Gregory turned to Judge Henry C. Pedigo of Woodville. A staunch Unionist, Pedigo was the judge for the state's Fifteenth Judicial District under appointment by Governor Hamilton and would serve in the State Constitutional Convention of 1868–1869. His home had been the headquarters of Brevet Lieutenant Colonel S. J. W. Mintzer during his tour of eastern Texas. Although the judge did not want the subassistant commissionership for himself, he recommended that Gregory consider his brother, Ira, who was also the Federal postmaster for Woodville. Gregory sent the appointment in early December, 1865.[51]

Ira Pedigo handled his job in workmanlike fashion. He believed that there was little justice for the Negro beyond the confines of the bureau, and kept a close watch on white planters whose schemes to defraud their black employees of wages due were legion, in his mind. The planting business was poor in this area of Texas, and Pedigo estimated that the crop would be half of normal. The freedmen had yet to be paid for 1865. He expected the army's help would be necessary to assist him in guarding the rights of the freed people, and sent a request to Captain E. H. Pratt (the same man Holsinger had criticized), commander of the company of the Twelfth Illinois Cavalry assigned to his district at Jasper. Pratt sent back what Pedigo diplomatically called "quite a crusty note" of refusal. The rest of Pedigo's tenure was uneventful, and he handed in his resignation in November, 1866, wishing to devote himself to his new lumber business.[52]

Judge Henry Pedigo also recommended that Gregory appoint his friend Dr. J. Orville Shelby as bureau representative at Liberty. Shelby was also the county judge under the Hamilton administration, and hence well known to Pedigo, who heard his appeal docket. He was later a justice of the peace and a Federal postmaster. As subassistant commissioner, Shelby was competent, but he had a penchant for riling the wrong people on the headquarters staff. The difficulty probably began when Shelby unwisely sought a salary upon Gregory's departure. The staff officer contacted Gregory about the request, who confirmed that the planter-doctor had agreed to work unpaid.[53]

Judge Pedigo's final recommendation whom Gregory accepted as a bureau employee was James Hogue of Cold Springs. From the beginning, Hogue seemed unwilling to perform his duties capably. Captain W. H. Redman, whose company of the Twelfth Illinois Cavalry was stationed at nearby Livingston, reported that the local freedmen lived in terror, and that Hogue and the planters were in league against the Negroes' rights as free persons. A complaint from a local attorney, O. A. McGinnis, a loyalist, related how freedmen claimed that the agent "suited planters to a T, that they owned the negroes just as much as they ever did." He asked that a more impartial agent be sent.[54]

Less controversial than Hogue was Gregory's appointment (sight unseen) of Philip Howard as the subassistant commissioner for Bosque County. Howard came to Gregory's notice through a complaint he wrote to Governor Hamilton on the treatment of freedmen in his area. One of the original settlers in the region, which was deep in the Texas interior, the fifty-five-year-old Howard was from Kentucky, had fought in the Black Hawk War, and had lived briefly in Louisiana. He was Hamilton's appointee as county commissioner and later justice of the peace. A loyal refugee during the Civil War, he received his bureau position on December 31, 1865. Gregory made a special mention that Howard was the agent for all of northern Texas, as far as he could extend his jurisdiction.[55]

Howard traveled far and wide (and was waylaid and robbed once), encouraging whites to treat the freed people fairly and settle up for 1865. He told the Negroes to continue doing their duty. By February he decided to get tough and resolved by force over one hundred cases of complaint. He reported many "bad cases" on his docket, including the castration of a Negro boy, a vicious whipping, and the buying and selling of slaves after General Granger's proclamation of June 19. Despite all this, he found the freedmen to be in good "sparits," and opined that if the bureau could protect blacks for about two years, they "would not kneed it any morre." There was no unemployment in the areas he had traveled, said Howard, but he was puzzled by the bureau's regulations and the multitude of governmental report forms he had received. "I cannot buy them up here," he cautioned. He had already spent over one hundred dollars of his own to forward bureau business.[56]

Unlike Howard, Gregory's appointment of Asa P. Delano to the Marlin agency in Falls County, also far in the interior of the state, did not turn out so well. A refugee who also had obtained the Marlin postmastership and the right to represent the Galveston commission house of Ranger & Company at its Marlin store, Delano arrived in early 1866 to set up his office. He did all he could to "consil" the local blacks to enter into labor contracts and be gainfully employed. He claimed that the unemployed freed people in his district were mostly freedwomen without contracts. Most of the conflicts he adjudicated occurred between black men and their wives, and he confessed he needed advice on what he should do about them. His only wage settlement case involved the local distillery, whose owner left the country without paying his Negro employees. Delano had to "sees" the remaining "few barrels" of whiskey to pay them off. The Federal tax agent complained that the whiskey belonged to the Treasury Department, but headquarters backed Delano. Whether the blacks ever received the three hundred dollars realized from the process was doubtful, as Delano's successor later reported.[57]

Overwork, too few officers, and the demand that something be done led to improvisations in the field, mostly by the civilian appointees who were ignorant of governmental processes. Their solution was to appoint their own subordinates in contravention of rules of hierarchy and red tape.[58] In November, 1865, for example, in response to citizen inquiry, Gregory wrote to Joseph A. Wright of Houston County and asked him under what authority he operated as a bureau agent. Gregory explained that Wright was not a recognized Federal employee, and instead referred planters to Captain Stanton Weaver at Crockett, the local sub-assistant commissioner appointed by him.[59]

Similar illegal appointments took place in Colorado County and Falls County. In the Colorado County case, Gregory repeatedly told Lieutenant John Raper (the accused swindler) that he was the sole bureau representative in the area, and ordered him to investigate the imposter.[60] In the Falls County incident, the illegal appointment was traced to W. H. Farner, the subassistant commissioner at Millican. Gregory diplomatically told Farner that hereafter all appointments would be made in Galveston.[61]

Part of the problem with illegal actions concerned the lack of prescribed boundaries of jurisdiction for each agent. Even if they possessed valid commissions, local agents did not know the geographical limits of their territory.[62] The reason was simple: Gregory resisted all efforts to define boundaries, preferring a more fluid situation.[63] The result confused military officers used to precise lines of authority. It also bewildered petitioners, who often asked headquarters who their subassistant commissioner was.[64] Many areas of the state went unserved, while the large plantation areas of Grimes County had two agents and needed three. In the meantime, Gregory plodded along, asking "the nearest" agent to handle complaints "perhaps on one of your journeys into the countryside?"[65]

One way to assess the results of Gregory's administration is to peruse the reports of various bureau agents and army post commanders. Required by both bureau and army district headquarters, these reports were supposed to include comments on the loyalty of Texas whites, treatment of the freedmen, and the quality of justice—sort of an analysis of the political results of Reconstruction to date.

The bureau sent out forms premarked for specific information on the status of indigent white refugees and freedmen, abandoned lands, and rations issued. Since most agents had little to do with refugees, most freedmen were employed under contracts, and there was little or no abandoned land, the subassistant commissioners commonly drew the required red line across the report form from one top corner to the opposite bottom one and then horizontally through the "totals" boxes. The bureau was a stickler for format. One agent complained that he had "no red ink to draw a line as directed. These reports has been delayed in hope of being able to procure Red ink."[66]

In the remarks section of these reports, the bureau agents would often write little notes to headquarters. "I have subsisted three and expended of my individual means burial expenses of a freedman—paupers —but cannot report them as subsisted on government forms. Consequently," concluded J. W. McConaughey, the agent at Wharton, "I have nothing to report on this form." William Longworth, Wilson County judge and subassistant commissioner, said the same. "The Bureau not being funded with supplies of any kind," he wrote, "there has been no relief extended except out of the private funds of the Sub Assistant Commissioner." Philip Howard, Bosque County commissioner and bureau representative, ungrammatically agreed. "There is no government farms, . . . neither is there any Hospitals nor rations issued, . . . the freedmen is all employed by the citizens," said Howard, "and doing well [, and] by the assistance of the Bureau will continue to do so." John T. Whitesides wrote bluntly, "Not having any cases to meet the requirements of this report, I take pleasure in forwarding it blank."[67]

Many subassistant commissioners sent in no report at all. Mail service in the backcountry was often nonexistent. "Waco is 45 miles off," complained one agent, "and I have to depend on travelers to obtain my mail matter and to forward my reports." Even General Gregory was forced to admit his frustrations to Washington, calling Texas communications "irregular" at best, and apologizing for his inability to compile the required end-of-the-month reports. He asked his subordinates to send their copies in four or five days earlier than called for, to meet the deadlines put forth in his Circular Orders No. 10, which detailed the reporting procedure.[68]

Volunteer soldiers serving as subassistant commissioners seemed less confused by the need to submit blank pages each month than did their civilian counterparts. "I have the honor to report that I have been six days at my station," replied one officer effectively, "and as yet have no data by which to make my report upon this blank." Others, especially if they were not specifically assigned to bureau duties, objected to the monthly report on political feeling in their command areas. Brevet Brigadier General Samuel D. Sturgis at Austin, for example, called the whole matter "outside the duty of my profession," and refused to cooperate.[69]

Junior officers, of course, did not have the luxury of adopting General Sturgis's attitude. Their reports are important, because they demonstrate that nearly a year's occupation had done little to change Texas civil affairs. Texans were still of "the same unconquered opinion" when it came to "the high crime and treason of which they were guilty." Yet most were willing to distinguish between the government's policy and the soldiers who enforced it, treating Northern men rather well in some areas, particularly those Yankees from the Old Northwest, as opposed to New Englanders and others from the East. This led many officers to feel that their reports were somehow inadequate. They could not express fully the uneasiness that lurked deep in their minds about the professed loyalties of white Texans, even though the freedmen in their areas were treated relatively well.[70]

Other reporters were a little more discerning and discriminating in their statements. These men believed that while a majority of Texas whites were "well-disposed" to the occupying soldiers, and legally loyal to the Union, a small minority acted in a "braggadocio style" and vented their anger on "Yankees and niggers." What puzzled the Federal soldiers the most was how much the vocal haters of blacks associated with the despised race without animosity in their daily contacts. But few observers approached the praise bestowed upon Texans by Lieutenant Colonel R. Kennecott of the Thirty-seventh Illinois stationed at Houston. "I know of no place in the United States where the black man is more kindly treated than here in Texas," he intoned.[71]

When Captain John Moran of the same regiment reported an improvement in the treatment of blacks and the bureau agent at Beaumont, the subassistant commissioner, First Lieutenant Charles C. Hardenbrook, noted that the whole picture changed when Moran's company left for Galveston and its eventual muster-out. Within a day of Moran's departure, Hardenbrook received a half dozen threats, and the heretofore prosperous black school was in danger of being shut down by vigilantes. Hardenbrook begged for a new garrison, but to no avail.[72]

Hardenbrook was not alone in his request for support troops. Brevet Brigadier General James Shaw, colonel of the Tenth USCI, called the area between San Antonio and Victoria a veritable hell-hole of anti-Union, anti-Negro feeling. He singled out Yorktown, Helena, Clinton, and Goliad for racial attitudes that produced conditions "worse than when in slavery" for Texas blacks. The only way to maintain peace and quiet was for the area to be garrisoned by more soldiers, said Shaw.[73] Even though Gregory frequently, and seemingly hardheartedly, turned down those subassistant commissioners who asked for troops, he fully realized that "the presence of troops will enable you to perform the duties of your office without fear of molestation," as he wrote to one agent.[74] The assistant commissioner never stopped asking General Wright for more escorts and detachments for the bureau. But the fact that his requests never stopped and often went unanswered by the army command spoke loudly about the inadequacy of policies and paucity of results of the bureau's operations during Gregory's term as assistant commissioner.[75]

3

Not as Wise as a Serpent

ONE OF THE KEY ITEMS on the bureau's list of what was needed to enable the Negro to compete as a free person was education.[1] Although Brevet Major General David S. Stanley, in charge of the Central District of Texas with headquarters in San Antonio, reported that there were to his knowledge no schools for blacks in Texas during the summer of 1865, by the time of Gregory's arrival in September, at least one had been started in Galveston by Reverend Charles S. Tambling of the American Missionary Association.[2]

Gregory turned the education effort over to his superindendent of schools, First Lieutenant Edwin M. Wheelock of the Seventy-sixth USCI. On detached duty from his regiment, which was stationed in Louisiana, Wheelock had much difficulty with his regimental commander, who wanted the lieutenant's services as a company officer. Hence, Wheelock was absent much of the time until he managed to secure his discharge.[3]

Wheelock's absence made his record all the more remarkable and disappointing at the same time. By the end of Gregory's tenure as assistant commissioner, the numbers of schools had increased to 99, with 4,796 pupils and 53 teachers. The schools were self-sustaining, relying upon a monthly tuition of one dollar and fifty cents paid by the students. "The teachers are effective and competent," said Gregory, "the Scholars orderly, studious, and attentive." Gregory noted that many planters wanted teachers on their lands, an indication that they saw education as a prime drawing card for the employment of a better class of fieldhands.

Gregory happily reported that "while the old proslavery malice is by no means appeased," there were but few outrages perpetrated against teachers or students. He credited the earnest cooperation of General Wright and the army command for the peaceful advance of the black educational system.[4] Although many of the schools were open only part time, and there were on the average less than two per county where blacks represented more than 25 percent of the total population, and less than one teacher per such county, the Texas system compared favorably to those of other Southern states. Texas also operated under many liabilities that other Southern states lacked. The state was geographically isolated from the North, which supplied most teachers, there were too few books for students, there were few educated free blacks from prewar days, and Superintendent Wheelock was absent much of the time. Much more might have been done with a full-time superintendent.[5]

"Nothing can be more cheering than the extraordinary thirst for information which the pupils, both old and young, exhibit," boasted Wheelock, "while the effect which the school has had upon the home in inculcating order, cleanliness, higher hopes and aims, is everywhere apparent." Loyalist and former governor E. M. Pease visited the Austin bureau schools with General Gregory, and seconded Wheelock's opinions. "Our own race here must give more attention to the education of their children," said Pease, "or the rising generation of darkies will outstrip them in knowledge."[6] The assistant commissioner probably had not consulted U. S. District Attorney David J. Baldwin, who wrote to Governor Hamilton that one Houston woman said she would "sooner put a bullet in their heads" than educate the freed people. Baldwin thought her representative of the average citizen's unspoken true feelings on the desirability and efficacy of black education.[7]

As Wheelock had implied in his otherwise glowing education reports, the black family had suffered much dislocation from the throes of the Civil War, and the freedmen of Texas were not exempt from this effect, although they had been spared the passage of fighting armies. Because of the desire of the planters in neighboring states to send their slaves to the relative safety of Texas, the bureau received many requests after the war from freedmen seeking lost relatives, who had been forced to come west during the war. Gregory also sent requests to other states seeking information on people whose loved ones had lost track of them over the passage of time, in some cases as much as twenty years.[8]

In addition, there were also at least two reported cases of black youths shipping out of Galveston for pure adventure, whose parents wanted their return.[9] Moreover, there was the case of Private William Lewis of the Twenty-second USCI. Enlisted at New Orleans during the war, Lewis served in the Red River campaign. The Confederate Army captured him and sent him to a prisoner-of-war camp in Texas from which Lewis was sold back into slavery. Freed by Granger's emancipation order, Lewis was sent back to New Orleans by Gregory, who figured that the

Louisiana assistant commissioner might contact his old regiment and obtain monies and the honorable discharge owed him.[10]

In October, 1865, Commissioner Howard sent out a circular letter informing all of the assistant commissioners of three problems to which he wished them to devote special attention.[11] The first was vagrancy. Many southern states, with army connivance, were using vagrancy laws to obtain black laborers for public works projects. Howard warned the assistant commissioners to watch for this prejudicial enforcement of the law, and to see to it that vagrancy statutes were enforced equally against blacks and whites. As this was the case in Texas, Gregory did little beyond bolstering the army's vagrancy policy with one of his own embodying Howard's principles.[12]

The other two problems were not so easily solved, however. The ending of slavery had also terminated the policy of planters caring for their old and infirm slaves. These blacks were now dumped unceremoniously upon the local governments, which refused to accept the burden. To the inquiry of subassistant commissioners, Gregory referred them to Howard's statement requiring the counties, and not the bureau as southern whites had hoped, to pay for the new public wards. Even with Governor Hamilton's support, it was a problem that Gregory never completely solved during his stay in Texas.[13]

The final problem Howard mentioned in his circular was also of great import in Texas. This was the question of apprenticeship laws. Under this guise, many Texans had hoped to recoup part of the losses derived from emancipation. If they could keep slave children until they reached their majority the former slave owners would get twenty years of free labor. Local judges and army provost marshals often went along with this scheme.[14]

Several Texans, both judges and private citizens, wrote to Gregory to inquire as to the proper course in setting up apprenticeships. The assistant commissioner informed them that he, through his subassistant commissioners, was the guardian of all minor and orphan black children, whenever their parents were unavailable for the task. Until the state legislature acted (it would not meet until August, 1866), current Texas laws were not applicable.[15] Since neither Gregory nor his agents had the time, facilities, or money to provide care for homeless black children, the policy was for the subassistant commissioners to farm out the children to "men you can trust," who would act as temporary guardians. If these persons proved undependable, Gregory would remove the children from their care.[16]

Still, trouble continued over the apprenticeship issue. Claimants on the services of freed children had them kidnapped. Adults were denied access to their children or spouses, requiring orders from Gregory himself to correct the situation. At times, subassistant commissioners neglected to act when requested, and Gregory had to rudely remind them of their responsibilities months later. It was a big problem: In Brazos County alone, the bureau agent said that he had found homes for 500 "orphans" under fourteen years of age, and that an additional 143 aged and infirm individuals, of whom 14 were blind, were "successfully provided for, at no expense to the government."[17]

Another familial matter of interest to the bureau was the legal marriage of freedmen and women. On March 2, 1866, Commissioner Howard sent another of his circular letters to the bureau districts. Referring to his Circular Orders No. 5, which regularized marriage between cohabiting blacks, Howard recommended that all assistant commissioners consult state laws on marriage and divorce, and model their own black marriage edicts upon them. In their orders, Howard recommended that assistant commissioners consider such questions as who was eligible to marry, who should grant certification of marriage, who should solemnize marriages, how should marriage be dissolved, how they should be registered, and what regulations should touch upon those who had lived together without the benefit of marriage vows. Howard suggested that state governors, clergy, and local magistrates might help draft the new rules, which were to be explained to the freed people with "great care."[18]

Gregory acceded to Howard's wishes in his own Circular Orders No. 9, "issued for the information of the Freedmen of the State." No male under eighteen, nor female under fifteen, could contract for marriage without the consent of their parents or guardians, or "the proper officers of the Freedmen's Bureau." All couples had to obtain a license from the clerk of the county court, according to the laws of Texas. Couples could be legally joined by ministers of the gospel, judges of the district or county courts, and justices of the peace. Anyone performing marriages without the proper permission of the state was liable to a fine of five hundred dollars. Marriages could not be dissolved "except by due process of the law." Finally, persons cohabiting or acting as husband and wife were recognized as legally married according to the provisions of the original bureau act, which Congress had passed the previous March.[19] Gregory sent copies of the marriage circular to General Howard and Governor Hamilton, the latter of whom had already issued his own proclamation, ordering state officials to obey the bureau document.[20]

Fully as important to the bureau as the economic and social aspects of black life was the enjoyment by the freed people of the same legal rights as whites. A month before he had appointed Gregory to the Texas headquarters, for example, Commissioner Howard had written to his chairman of the bureau headquarters committee on contracts and put forth this ideal goal he sought for the bureau in its work in the South. "Equally before the law is what we must arrive at," Howard had said emphatically, "I mean a black, red, yellow, or white thief should have punishment for his theft without regard to the color of his skin."[21]

After he came to Texas, Gregory adopted Howard's dictum as his own. When a Houston newspaper accused De Gress's replacement, the one-time Texas bureau acting assistant adjutant general, Captain Byron Porter, of trying to destroy local legal authority, Gregory defended Porter and restated Howard's ideal. Gregory told Porter not to have any "misapprehension" about his duties. The assistant commissioner said that he preferred a little overzealousness to lack of zeal. He told Porter that the bureau had no intention of taking cases from the hands of civil authorities, unless the rights of freedmen were ignored or violated by state officials. But he recommended that Porter send the case in question to the civil courts first, and give them a chance to settle it fairly.[22]

Porter complied with Gregory's request, but the subassistant commissioner said that he had little faith in the Negroes receiving any justice outside the auspices of the bureau. Porter reported that the freedmen were being driven off the land without any pay for their labor in 1865 and that they were being denied rights to their wives and children, and suffering daily assaults. What really embarrassed him, however, was the poor treatment the blacks received at the hands of Federal soldiers. The home-going volunteer troops robbed and assaulted Negroes for sport. Some illegally charged the freedmen for alleged emancipation services rendered during the occupation. By spring, the high demand for labor changed everything. Treatment improved, employment was up, and new contracts were being drawn up daily. But there were still many indigent freedmen, the bureau hospital had been returned to its white landowner, and President Johnson's veto of the bureau bill had caused much openly expressed hatred for the subassistant commissioner, Porter said, which had given rise to the many challenges to his decisions.[23]

It was a tough problem. Even loyal judges complained about bureau interference, and on the face of things, all judges appointed by Governor Hamilton were supposed to be pro-Union. Gregory remained willing to give any judge the benefit of the doubt until the magistrate's actions proved otherwise. He continually admonished subassistant commissioners to turn cases over to civil officials, if they could be trusted, to monitor the trials when held, and to investigate the cases separately from the prosecutor to ascertain the true facts. As he told the chief justice of Leon County, H. B. Pruitt, Gregory wanted to turn over to the state all cases involving freedmen, but he thought at the present time it might establish a bad precedent on any but a case-by-case approach.[24]

Gregory's policy was based on what he saw as sound fact. After all, unrestrained interracial lawlessness had caused Governor Hamilton to comment that "human life in Texas is not today worth as much . . . as that of domestic cattle." One of Gregory's own informants opined "that public opinion would seldom reward the negro his just dues was [*sic*] there no other tribunal" like the bureau. And the Leon County agent's remarks to the general in one report closed with a plaintive, "God help the black man if [the bureau] is not kept up." Texans could not yet be given a carte blanche to handle freedmen in their scrapes with the law.[25]

What troubled Gregory was the signs that racial prejudice and slavery were too deeply ingrained in Texans' hearts to be overcome without a long probationary period. For example, when General Granger had advised freed people to stop traveling the roads and return to their former homes to work, many planters incorrectly seized upon this order as an indication that slavery was to be reinstituted in the state with army help.[26] When President Johnson vetoed the extension of the Freedmen's Bureau Act, Texas whites prematurely seized upon this as the end of the bureau, in spite of Commissioner Howard's assurance to Gregory that he had the president's promise that the bureau would be in operation for at least one more year. And when President Johnson announced that the state of war had terminated, Texans, like other Southerners, leaped at the chance to challenge the right of the jurisdiction of the bureau and the army to administer martial law, and to suspend the right of habeas corpus. Again, explanatory orders from Washington and Galveston restored the situation somewhat. But the harassment of soldiers enforcing Reconstruction was a continual bane to the daily conduct of bureau affairs.[27]

Although most Texans refused to admit it, they knew Gregory's policy had a basis in fact. J. R. Burns of La Grange expressed their secret feelings in a letter to Governor Hamilton, as he commented on an editorial on the subject in the *New Era Extra*, a local sheet. Burns figured the editor understood the problem well. If local, county, and state officials failed to act in a just manner toward the freedmen involved in criminal and civil suits, the bureau would take over all cases, and decide them in favor of the Negro. After all, "they are here for that reason," said Burns, slightly warping Gregory's sense of why the bureau must act.

Burns decried what current Texan stupidity and racial injustice might bring the state. "Would it not be better for the people to have their controversies and difficulties with Freedmen settled by their fellow citizens," queried Burns, "and to have the judgment of the courts, executed by process in the hands of their fellow citizen sheriffs . . . ?" Burns found this scenario far preferable to the execution of the law "by the bayonet in the hands of some military Tom, Dick, or Harry—by perhaps a white soldier," or—the worst of their fears—"perhaps by a black one!"[28]

The bureau subassistant commissioners were not always as aware of the implications of their authority as were bureau officials. J. W. Mc-Conaughey, an attorney recently arrived from Arkansas whom Gregory had assigned to the agency at Wharton in mid-December, 1865, related how he had been "cursed and misrepresented all over the country" when he arrived. McConaughey had ignored his rotten reception and concentrated upon his duties. By February, 1866, he noted that many planters had changed their tune. There were, however, two groups who still hated him. One comprised those who had not yet paid their freedmen for 1865; the other consisted of those who conspired to cheat all those whom they dealt with. As for the freed people, the subassistant commissioner reported that almost all of them had signed contracts for the coming year, which their employers had "cheerfully" altered to bureau standards when necessary. Planters were also in favor of schools on their plantation grounds. At first they had feared that education would "spoil the nigger!" but the ease of obtaining hands when blacks found that their children could receive schooling overcame the whites' reluctance.[29]

Indeed, McConaughey asserted that his biggest problem had become the freed people themselves. Husbands were leaving their life partners "in droves," asserting that they had not been joined "by the book." The black women were outraged and claimed that if they were good enough to be wives as slaves, they were good enough to be free men's spouses, too. McConaughey said that he found the women's argument quite logical, but he regretted that all he could do was advise the families to stay together. The subassistant commissioner much preferred to use some sort of force on the women's behalf. But force had become a rare commodity in Wharton, McConaughey regretted to inform headquarters, because his military garrison had been recalled to Houston.[30]

Gregory nonetheless felt compelled to inform McConaughey that he was not doing his complete duty toward local freedmen, who had complained of abuse and ill-treatment by planters. When one black laborer was struck and then shot at, Gregory remonstrated, McConaughey allegedly did nothing, prompting the freedman to complain directly to Galveston. Gregory warned his Wharton subassistant commissioner to "give justice to freedmen."[31]

In another case, the Sterling subassistant commissioner, Champ Carter, Jr., proved to be as excessively zealous as McConaughey was lax. At first, Gregory had hesitated to appoint Carter, because he had once acted as a bureau agent without proper authority under the tutelage of William H. Farner. Carter, however, wanted the job, and he had influential friends. These included Asa Delano at Marlin, various planters at Sterling, and, more important, the managers of the powerful Ranger & Co. The Ranger firm ran several plantations in Robertson County and a commission house at Galveston, and had favorable contacts with Gregory and his staff. "Carter is a very respectable man and highly thought of by everybody," said one Sterling resident. "It is important that the appointment be made at once," he urged. Under such pressures, Gregory finally complied.[32]

Carter inquired as to the limits of his duties, asking if he could employ an assistant to act as a sheriff, whether he would receive a salary, and what he was to do about indigent freedmen and schools. He said that most of the cases before him concerned freedmen's family problems, especially harsh treatment of wives by their husbands. In one instance, a man broke a three-inch stick over his wife's head. Carter had the man hung by his thumbs, in military style, from a nearby tree. He said that "a former agent" (probably Farner) had told him such punishment was permitted with blacks. Responding to other accusations from headquarters, Carter also denied that he charged planters for his services.[33] Gregory replied that he was sorry that the new agent had been misled and called the dismissed predecessor a "pretender." Gregory also cautioned subassistant commissioners to consider only cases involving freedmen as one or both parties of the dispute. Any problem between whites was to be handled by the civil courts, as usual, and was out of bureau jurisdiction.[34]

Even cases involving freedmen created endless problems between Gregory and his subordinates. One Grimes County agent professed not to have heard of a murder that occurred within two miles of his residence. Gregory was astounded, since he himself had heard of the crime in Galveston. Gregory told the subassistant commissioner to investigate the case, and if the civil authority proved lax, to forward the facts to headquarters for prosecution.[35] Gregory also called the attention of another subassistant commissioner to the case of a freedwoman with the admonishment that he reread the general's Circular Orders No. 1, which defined an agent's powers. "As you are on the scene and have the evidence first hand, you should try such cases like this and report the action to headquarters," Gregory intoned. The assistant commissioner believed that two or three vigorous prosecutions would greatly improve the overall treatment of freed people in any jurisdiction.[36]

Gregory supervised his subordinates' conduct of legal proceedings in many ways. He called for memoranda of facts so that headquarters might prefer charges against defendants, paid expenses for witnesses to appear at hearings, ordered arrests, had defendants sent to military commissions for trial, and decided many cases on his own volition. His penchant for traveling into the hinterland also led him to order subassistant commissioners to delay action in certain cases until he arrived on the scene personally to supervise the proceedings. Many of his delay orders contradicted earlier decisions. No wonder one agent was a bit bewildered to be told by a snappish acting assistant adjutant general to settle a case himself, only to have headquarters decide it before he could act.[37] The only thing worse than being an agent or defendant at the end of a railroad or telegraph line from Galveston was to be a suspected wrong-doer living in the Texas port city, under Gregory's immediate supervision. Allegedly wronged or ill-treated freedmen flocked to the general's office, where a sympathetic ear and a quick pen resulted in orders of redress whose effects were felt all over the community.[38]

Although Gregory could be nosy to the point of exasperation, he generally backed up his subordinates who were in the right, at least as the general saw it. He steadfastly refused to set limits for fines and relied on his agents to use their own judgment as to proper amounts.

When one subassistant commissioner in Crockett assessed a one-thousand-dollar fine against a defendant, Gregory approved the action,
although he thought the punishment a bit excessive. When the defendant threatened not to pay, Gregory ordered the agent to arrest him
and to seize his property, if any, to enforce the edict. "Stand your
ground," he told a subassistant commissioner at Columbus, who was
in a similar predicament. In other cases, the assistant commissioner
suggested that agents fine defendants, or he approved of actions already taken in the field.[39]

An idea of Gregory's personal viewpoint on Reconstruction can be
had from the long letter he wrote to Benjamin Harris, the foreman
of the Panola County grand jury. Gregory's letter was written in response to Harris's inquiry to Colonel Hall, the subassistant commissioner at Marshall, as to the chances of Panola County receiving a
"military provost marshal" to police local blacks charged with violation of their work contracts, vagrancy, insolence, robbery, drunkenness, and "general vicious conduct." Hall referred the matter to headquarters, where Gregory refused to make the sought-after appointment.
Instead, he offered Harris, and through him all Texans, some gratuitous
guidance for the future.

Gregory said evidence in his office showed Texas blacks to be "most
docile, industrious, orderly, free from serious crime, and with all the
substance that goes to make the good citizen." He did not blame Harris or his fellow residents of Carthage for a contrary view. Rather, Gregory faulted the inability of the bureau to penetrate the backcountry
with an adequate number of agents. In time, the assistant commissioner believed, the freedmen "will gain the knowledge of their rights
and duties."

Gregory maintained that the former slaves were moved by "the same
incitements that quicken the industry of other men in free societies."
These included just treatment, adequate wages, and security from the
kind of fraud that characterized their treatment in 1865. Gregory pointed
out to Harris that idleness and theft were unknown in other counties
"where the people are well-inclined" toward the freed people. Indeed,
many of these counties suffered a shortage of labor, said Gregory, which
caused them to seek far and wide for additional black labor.

Gregory spoke of the vicissitudes of slavery and how he found it
"most commendable" that the blacks, who had been "turned headlong
into freedom without preparation" now "exhibit in their industry, docility, and patience, an example beyond the expectation of man." No people

in history had been so tried, claimed Gregory, and not taken "their rulers by the throat and carried carnage into every homestead." Gregory reminded Harris that Governor Hamilton had already praised the freedmen's "forbearance and Christian reliance upon God's providence" to the admiration of the world.

"The wonder is not that disorder, misconceptions, [and] wrongs, should have sometimes occurred," continued the assistant commissioner, "but that they are so few and slight." The purpose of the bureau in Texas was merely to work in cooperation with the civil authorities to "take cognizance of all offences committed by and or against the negro." The bureau had no other desire but the equal treatment of the blacks under the same laws as those for whites. If blacks do wrong, said Gregory, apply the laws as you would in the case of a white. No special legislation or appointments were called for, according to the general.

The new order of things presented problems to the planter as well as the former bondsmen, held Gregory. The planter "still hugs the idea that he had the power to fix wages, restrain personal liberty, and exercise authority over" the Negro. "Past hatreds are still fed and false ideas nurtured." Neither party can "cut loose at a single blow from their past traditions, beliefs, hatreds, and hopes, after the rough schooling of this war." There were still hard lessons to learn, said the assistant commissioner, and "the dominant class must overcome their contempt for the negro."

In conclusion, Gregory recommended to Harris and his fellow Texans "the spirit that has made the great states of the northwest," namely, "the concord" of labor and capital. Offer inducements if you want workers, recommended the general, such as homes, "enhanced wages," schools, and churches. "This course will bring the same success on the banks of the Brazos, the Colorado, or the Trinity, as on the Ohio." Laborers treated with "liberality" and justice, equal before the law, said Gregory, will bring peace to "your locality. . . . The gulf between the two races will be bridged over by a vital sympathy," he ended his letter, that of the voluntary unity of labor and capital.[40]

Unfortunately, Gregory's lofty, idealistic view of Texas's future ran into the baser, unromantic one of the white planter. Typical in this respect were the sentiments of Thomas Affleck, the owner of Glenblythe plantation in Washington County, one of the richest agricultural areas of the state.[41] A month after the Federal occupation of Galveston, Affleck was already angry with the new scheme of things.[42]

He admitted that all was quiet and orderly at Glenblythe, but believed the Negro would not work as a free man without much compulsion. "Already they have, in some instances, attempted rebellion and insolence," he wrote to his uncle, "their instant death being the result. Poor creatures, I do not blame them. But still," he insisted, "they must be kept in their places."

Affleck continued by informing his uncle that he wished to draw up a five-year contract with his freedmen, but feared the Federals would not allow it. "Yankee-like, they will not give up their assured right (the right of might) to interfere between me & the negroes at all times, and that," he thundered, "after a contract is made, I will not tolerate."[43] He offered the blacks an agreement, the preamble of which showed he accepted the ending of slavery with much reservation. He pledged little change in the day-to-day regime from slavery. There would be less direct control of the laborers, and Affleck would take much less responsibility for their welfare. Freedmen would be allowed a voice in crop selection and a right to choose their immediate supervisor.[44] But as he argued in an angry letter to E. H. Cushing, editor of the Houston *Telegraph*, the situation was one "to be *submitted to*, but not *accepted* as you flippantly insist."[45]

In July, 1865, Affleck took his workers to hear the speech delivered by General Andrews. The planter thoroughly enjoyed the sections on labor—those that told the freedmen to go back to work, that freedom was not idleness. "Our negroes are in a terrible stew," he chuckled to his sister. "And it is useless to reason with them." He was not sure if the freedmen understood Andrews the way he did, and grumbled, "from our present prospects, I shall ship the whole of them by Monday morning; or a great portion of them."[46]

But Affleck learned to endure the situation. In September, on the day of Gregory's arrival in Galveston, he hauled an old fieldhand, Henry Carter, before Captain T. S. Post at Brenham. Affleck considered Carter to be dishonest, a troublemaker, and a thief. When Affleck had confronted Carter with stealing flour from the plantation mill, the freedmen readily admitted it. "But, knowing the result of a white man resenting any indignity now from a negro," said Affleck wisely, "I restrained myself."

Instead, Affleck wrote a "paper." It stated that Carter had stolen the flour and had been fired. Anyone who wished could hire him. Then Affleck feared he might have compromised a felony. So he took Carter before Captain Post. Carter told Post that employees, white or black, took all the flour they wanted by custom. Affleck retorted that Carter was a liar.

"If this is allowed to go unpunished," argued Affleck, "not the 'little flour' taken by a negro as something to eat, but the theft of a trusted servant; one whom the other old hands know to have been guilty, in times past of great crimes," but even worse, one "who has placed my authority at open defiance, . . . under the belief that he will be protected by you," then nothing in the neighborhood would be safe from thievery. Still, nothing was done. Post obviously believed Carter's side of the story.[47]

A couple of months later, Affleck was back before the recently appointed subassistant commissioner at Brenham, Second Lieutenant B. J. Arnold of the Twelfth Illinois Cavalry. A black couple had "grossly insulted my wife," growled Affleck. He was furious. "I confess to be under such a degree of excitement that I dare not trust myself to deal with them." He sent a trusted servant in to fetch the lieutenant. "My hands are virtually tied," he complained to Arnold. There was no civil law for dealing with free blacks. Affleck begged the agent, "as the officer in charge of this class of people," to remove the Negro couple from the premises of his plantation, as Affleck feared for his own actions. Although there is no record of the result of his plea, Thomas Affleck did at least call the subassistant commissioner before acting on his own.[48]

The subassistant commissioner at Brenham to whom Affleck had brought his case, Lieutenant Arnold, was a conscientious man who realized that much of what he did would set a precedent for other future bureau agents in the state. Hence he was an avid questioner. He particularly asked confirmation of policies that he obtained from De Gress in Houston. When De Gress told him that policy was to stay out of state court decisions in which blacks were treated like whites, Arnold demurred. Many of the freedmen were being prosecuted for adultery, which Arnold thought was unfair. The state laws had never been enforced against slaves' marital relations, and Arnold thought they should be given time to adjust to the realities of freedom. He noticed that the labor contracts used in the area were either so vague or so complicated that a freedman could not help but violate them unintentionally. Arnold wanted some sort of standard he could follow. When he received Gregory's proposed contract, Arnold altered it so that it did not provide for medical care and raised the salary demands accordingly. Neither freedmen nor planters wanted the planters to deduct for such care, he believed.

Arnold also had charged for his services, a fee that he passed on to a clerk as salary. De Gress had warned him against this policy. But Arnold said he did not have time to write out all documents himself. As it was, he was late in filing most reports, because of the crush of business that confronted him. He did not even have time to leave town, as people of both races piled into his office daily. He farmed out in-digents and minors to other black families and to trustworthy whites, a policy that Gregory had vetoed in favor of county care, as with whites of the same economic circumstances. By spring, Arnold noted that everyone was employed, that the county could use another two thou-sand fieldhands, and that free labor's success defied "the predictions of many croakers," like Affleck.[49] "We are moving along slowly with our business," maintained Gregory when he learned of such cases, "and thus far profitably."[50]

But Gregory had over-estimated his precarious success as assistant commissioner. Affleck was not alone in his dislike of the Freedmen's Bureau. In October, 1865, Mrs. Caleb Forshey, one of Affleck's neigh-bors, wrote a worried letter to President Andrew Johnson. In it, she complained about the activities of an unnamed major who, under the supposed authority of General Gregory, allegedly urged local blacks to assert their civil rights by force of arms, if necessary. She also decried the effects of Gregory's continual declarations that the freedmen were as good as if not better than whites, and the rumors that the former bondsmen would share in their masters' land by Christmas—canards that she claimed Gregory quietly abetted. Mrs. Forshey closed by say-ing that she lived in constant fear of violence and black rebellion.[51]

The Forshey letter was the beginning of a campaign that led to Gregory's downfall. Johnson sent the document over to Howard's office in the War Department, and Howard sent it back to Texas for Gregory's investigation and comment. Gregory asked Lieutenant Arnold, the able subassistant commissioner at Brenham, to check out Mrs. Forshey's facts. Arnold could find out nothing, which led Gregory to inform Howard that the whole story of the alleged major's incendiary speech was either some misunderstanding or a fabrication. Meanwhile Howard also had the army investigate the actions of "Gen. G" through its own separate chain of command in Texas. The army, never happy with the bureau's quasi-independent status within the War Department and in the field, reported that Gregory was so friendly with blacks as to ignore the reasonable competing interests of Texas whites.[52]

Aware of the adverse political implications of the investigation of his Texas assistant commissioner, Howard cautioned Gregory in a letter that advised the Texas bureau head to "be as wise as a serpent, as well as harmless & c." The bureau had to demonstrate a spirit of fairness, continued Howard, and while the commissioner wanted to "commend your zeal and energy," he suggested that Gregory consult often with the army commander in Texas, General Wright, and the civilian executive, Provisional Governor Hamilton, and use the "broadest possible charity" to promote goodwill between blacks and whites.[53]

Gregory responded that criticism of his course of action was not unexpected, but he blamed it on "those who have sought the destruction of our government and . . . would still defraud the freedmen of their just rights." Although Gregory would "confess friendship for the blacks," he also would "claim to have at least an equal one for my own color." The Texas assistant commissioner desired to "seek justice to both," and should he err, one way or the other, he was willing to "amend my judgment on conviction." Gregory asserted that he acted always in conjunction with General Wright, and although he had never met Governor Hamilton nor been to the state capitol at Austin, "confidential friends" had assured him that he and Hamilton were "of one mind" on the matter of the freedmen.[54]

While Gregory and the governor may have been as one in their ideas of the blacks' place in free society, they were at variance with the notions of most whites in Texas. Their objections received public support in the activities of an important antebellum politician and former slaveholder, David G. Burnet. The first president of the Republic of Texas, instrumental in the revolution against abusive Mexican rule, Burnet had been against secession in 1861, although he always had supported the theoretical right of revolution under the proper circumstances. At the war's end he had journeyed north to reestablish former political contacts, and he did not return to the state until January, 1866.

Immediately upon his return, he wrote the editor of the leading Conservative newspaper in Texas, the Galveston *Daily News*, complaining of the "many intolerable" and "unauthorized acts of oppression proceeding from the acts of the Freedmen's Bureau." Burnet found Gregory's policy to be "injurious in many respects and beneficial in none." He accused the bureau of inspiring the "poor negroes with false notions about themselves and a bitter hatred of their late masters, who," according to Burnet, "have ever been their best friends." Burnet feared that bureau policy would "unfavorably affect the industrial pursuits of the planters of the ensuing season," and he invited "gentlemen" to write of their adverse experiences with the bureau, General Gregory, and his agents.[55]

A little over a month later, Burnet was back to inform Texans of the response to his invitation. To no one's surprise, even though he lamented "that our citizens have been so dilatory in forwarding their statements," he had enough material to fill an entire page of the journal with small print. Headlined "The Labor Bureau," Burnet's article listed a half dozen of the choicest complaints against Gregory, his acting assistant adjutant general, Captain Chauncey C. Morse, and the Houston subassistant commissioner, Brevet Lieutenant Colonel Jacob C. De Gress. Burnet said he was horrified at "the manifold abuses . . . from the Freedmen's Bureau in our midst," which he believed had "seldom found a parallel in other States." He charged that Gregory guided his policies "by a manifest hostility to the white man and an inordinate and preposterous partiality for the negro." The former president of the republic asserted that the bureau program had resulted in a "bitter hatred . . . in the minds of the misguided negroes" for all whites, had produced unnecessary racial antagonism, and would eventually cause all whites to withdraw their natural "sympathies" from the freedmen, import foreign labor, and force the blacks into "actual vagrancy."

Burnet went on to describe Gregory's "speeches to the assembled negroes," which he labeled "so injudicious as to excite the dark rabbles to the most vociferous plaudits of the orator, and threatening denunciations to the white man." Burnet thought it possible that Gregory and his agents might not comprehend the effects of their efforts. "But they must be imbued with a singular stolidity," he continued, "if they have not understood the nature and consequences of their extrajudicial proceedings," which he believed indicated "more of fanaticism than ignorance, and less of wisdom than official perverseness."

Burnet maintained that "[f]ew things can be more repugnant to a brave people than subjection to military power." But he heard of no complaints against the army, and believed this was because General Wright, unlike Gregory, was, a "gentleman." Burnet believed that, because Texas had not seceded, it was still in the Union and vested with the rights of all other states according to the Constitution. He branded "the constant repetition of odious oppression and the annoyance of repeated insults by unworthy officials" of the Freedmen's Bureau as lacking in "military and civic virtues," "not consistent with a state of covenanted peace," and "highly arbitrary, malicious, and unwise." In-conclusion, Burnet believed that Gregory's removal from office was "recommended not only by popular aversion, but by justice and hu-manity, and a due regard for the purity which ought to be found in all public administrations." As for General Gregory, Burnet advised that "he return to the land of his progenitors and devote the measure of civilization he has received from us to the redemption of the sons of Ham from their fetish abominations."[56]

The political pressures brought to bear by Burnet's newspaper ac-cusations, compounded by the earlier letter of Mrs. Forshey and what the commissioner referred to as "other sources," and Howard's earlier order warning assistant commissioners to avoid "incendiary public ad-dresses," combined to cost Gregory his job three weeks later. General Howard, however, was not about to abandon Gregory altogether. In-stead he practiced a time-honored bureaucratic tradition and promoted Gregory to a headquarters staff position. Howard also took the "occa-sion to commend General *Gregory* for the marked energy and ability with which he has discharged his duties" in Texas. The commissioner declared that the "new duties to which he is assigned, are deemed at present of paramount duty." Upon his successor's arrival, Gregory's first assignment would be to tour Texas for the commissioner. He then would report to Washington, take twenty days' leave and, upon his return to duty, become the new assistant commissioner for Maryland.[57]

In the month that it took Gregory's replacement to reach Texas, the business of the bureau in the state maintained a sort of stagnant equi-librium. Relieved from duty pending his successor's arrival, Gregory conducted a final tour of western Texas. He made his report a confirma-tion of his prior actions as assistant commissioner. Ignoring the criti-cism that had cost him his job, he stated that the freedmen were "stead-ily at work," and that "[m]isunderstandings between them and their employers are becoming quite infrequent." The general saw "Freedom of the Negro" as a "palpable fact in most of Texas," and noted that plant-ers treated them with "an increasing degree of fairness." Gregory praised the conduct of the freedmen as "loyal and commendable," and believed their "highest ambition" was to "own a little homestead," a desire that kept them "from idleness and excess."

Gregory continued his statement by mentioning that under his ten-ure ninety "satisfactory and flourishing" schools for blacks had been established, with a total enrollment of over forty-five hundred scholars, children and adults. There were also twenty private schools outside the bureau's supervision. The general was proud that the few incompetent instructors were being weeded out, and that, in the larger towns at least, whites were no longer opposed to the education of the former bondsmen. He also praised the blacks' progress as students in many subjects. "It has been my aim," said Gregory, "to cause our schools to conform in discipline and instruction to the best common school system of the north, in the hope that the state Government . . . will . . . continue them on a staple [*sic*] foundation." The general was especially happy that "in no instance has ground been yielded, or a school once organized been suffered to be dispersed, terrorized, or broken up." He deplored the continued withdrawal of Federal troops and the "instances of maltreatment and abuse" it induced in some parts of the state.[58]

Commissioner Howard, who obviously felt badly about giving in to the political realities of the national capital, tried to assuage his uneasy conscience by commending Gregory "for the marked energy and ability with which he has discharged his duties."[59] Gregory seemed to sense that Howard had acted under much pressure, and he took the opportunity presented by his final report in June, 1866, to fire a parting shot at Texans and their Washington supporters, both for himself and Howard. Remarking on the progress Texas had made during the present crop season, Gregory regretted that the "sentiment of Loyalty to the Nation, and Justice to the recently liberated slave, has made no corresponding advance, but is growing weaker day by day."

Texas rebels, whom Gregory characterized as "[t]hese Murder[er]s and assassins, *not one of whom has ever been punished, or even tried,*" were now molding the political future of the state. The retiring assistant commissioner decried the removal of so many U. S. soldiers as to cripple the "moral power of the Bureau" to protect freed persons. Blacks, who "with patient fidelity" continued "their peaceful avocations," still trusted in the Federal government, Gregory believed, but "it is plain that they are beginning to feel a sense of insecurity and alarm." The events of the next few months would show that Gregory, loyal whites, and freedmen had real grounds to be uneasy.[60]

PART TWO
Stalemate: The Kiddoo Era,
May, 1866–January, 1867

Your views, I think, are very different from Gen. Gregory's and much better.

—Champ Carter, Jr. to Brevet Major General J. B. Kiddoo, June 19, 1866

4

A Vigorous System of Labor

G EN. GREGORY LEFT YESTERDAY for New Orleans!"[1] The exclamation point could not begin to impart the joy felt by Texans when they read this one-line statement that appeared in a conservative Galveston newspaper in June, 1866. Nor could it reveal fully the implied change in the relations between whites and blacks in Texas as portrayed by the policies of the Freedmen's Bureau. The Texas assistant commissioner, Brevet Brigadier General Edgar M. Gregory, had just fallen victim to a successful smear campaign mounted by important antebellum state politicians and former slaveholders.

The new assistant commissioner, who would have to cope with the unsolved problems Gregory left behind, was Brevet Major General Joseph B. Kiddoo, a war hero from western Pennsylvania. A young man full of wartime enthusiasm in 1861, Kiddoo had enlisted as a private in a three months' regiment at Pittsburgh. Instead of fighting rebels as he expected, his regiment wound up guarding railroad installations. Upon the expiration of his enlistment, he joined a combat unit, the Sixty-third Pennsylvania, which became part of the III Corps of the Army of the Potomac.

An eager soldier, Kiddoo rapidly advanced through the ranks, earning the rank of first sergeant for meritorious action at Fair Oaks during the 1862 Peninsular Campaign. He then received a lieutenant colonel's commission in the 137th Pennsylvania Volunteer Infantry. Ultimately becoming the regiment's colonel, he led the unit in battle as a part of the I Corps of the Army of the Potomac at Chancellorsville. When this outfit's term lapsed in the summer of 1863, Kiddoo transferred to the new colored infantry service, where he became major of the Sixth USCI. In January, 1864, he received a promotion to the colonelcy of the Twenty-second USCI part of the Army of the James, stationed at Yorktown, Virginia.

In the spring of 1864, Kiddoo's unit joined in the abortive attacks upon Petersburg that resulted in the prolonged siege of that city and the nearby Confederate capital, Richmond. Oddly enough, in October, 1864, as Kiddoo's regiment fought on, it wound up at the old battlefield of Fair Oaks, where its colonel had won honors in the ranks only two years before. In this Second Battle of Fair Oaks, however, Kiddoo did not fare so well. Leading his regiment in a bloody assault, the colonel was wounded severely near the spine.

Afterward, angry regimental subordinates accused Kiddoo of drunkenness on the field, disobedience of orders, and improper leadership of the final attack, all of which had demoralized his black soldiers, and cost unnecessary casualties. Calling him "the finest gentleman and officer" in the division, who had charged enemy works "with an utter disregard for his own personal safety," Kiddoo's superiors rallied to the wounded, beleaguered officer, and quashed the demands for a full investigation. Instead Kiddoo received a series of awards for his service with the colored infantry, which left him a brevet major general of volunteers and a brevet brigadier general in the regular army, but still too ill to enjoy his status as a hero.[2]

Kiddoo's lesion never healed properly. Described as a "lacerated wound of the back by a minié ball" or a "shot wound in the lumbar region, involving the spine," the injury was marked by a "fistulous opening" on his left side, "about the size of a goose-quill," which proceeded "downward, backward, and inward" for "about eight inches," from which "from half an ounce to an ounce of pus discharged daily." Any exercise tended to cramp his left leg painfully, much as with one who has a ruptured disc pressing on a nerve. For the rest of his short life (he died in 1880 at the age of forty) the general was frequently incapacitated from the constant pain of his war injuries. Doctors theorized that much of his discomfort could be stopped by amputation of his left leg, but the back wound was so extensive that they feared the shock of the operation would kill him. As it was, the motion of trains and riverboats caused the wound to suppurate painfully, forcing Kiddoo to pause several times on his trip to Texas in order to regain sufficient strength to continue on his way.[3]

After three days' orientation at the bureau's Galveston headquarters, Kiddoo was ready to assume full command. He told Howard that Gregory had received him "with commendable cordiality" and imparted "his very valuable experience and all the information" that Kiddoo would need to carry on after Gregory left for Washington. The new assistant commissioner said that he found bureau affairs "very encouraging," by which he meant that he was "agreeably disappointed" in all he had heard or seen since his arrival. This was an odd turn of phrase. It leaves one with the impression that Kiddoo and Gregory really did not see eye to eye, but were too circumspect to admit it openly.[4]

There were things for the two generals to disagree about. For instance, whites were bidding against each other to entice away recently hired laborers before the expiration of the terms of their contracts. Black workers, who had spent their lives in the fields, were discovering that railroads and logging companies paid better wages for easier work. "I tell you frankly, General," wrote one informant to Kiddoo, "demoralization" had seized the agricultural industry. If already contracted-for fieldhands were not required to return to work, and planters and other employers were not enjoined from enticing freedmen to disregard contracts, "the whole system will collapse of its own weight."[5]

The day following Kiddoo's assumption of power revealed just how differently he and Gregory viewed the contract labor question. An idealist, Gregory had always viewed the adjustment of blacks to their new status as free laborers with kind understanding that allowed for lots of mistakes as they learned the responsibilities of being free. Kiddoo, who was more of a businessman, ran a tighter ship. Hence he issued Circular Orders No. 14, a page and a half of new labor regulations. Enticement had "become quite prevalent," asserted Kiddoo, and was "not only dishonorable but a flagrant violation of the laws of Contracts, . . . destructive to the energetic system of labor the bureau desires to establish, and detrimental to the agricultural interests of the State."

According to Kiddoo's circular, "any employer, planter, or other person who shall tamper with, or entice laborers to leave their employers, with whom they have contracted in good faith," by the offering of higher wages or other inducements, or by arguing that the contract was illegal in some form even after an accredited bureau agent had authorized it, could be fined a sum of one hundred to five hundred dollars. The fine was set at the discretion of the local bureau representative and became a lien on the crop if not paid at once in cash. Any freedman who allowed himself to be enticed could be fined from five to twenty-five dollars. Again the local bureau agent levied the amount, and the sum became a lien on any wages or share of the crop due the laborer until paid.

If a laborer voluntarily left his place of employment before the conclusion of a legal labor contract, Kiddoo continued, and if his employer was not in violation of the terms of the agreement, he could be fined up to fifty dollars. The assistant commissioner called his order "simple justice" and a part of his duty "to throw such moral influence about the Freedmen in their transition state as will induce them to maintain inviolate the provisions of so solemn a legal document as a written contract." He concluded that if "the employer fills his portion of the contract, as to wages, rations, and treatment, the laborer must fulfill his portion as to time and labor."[6] As Kiddoo explained his position in a letter to Commissioner Howard, "[i]t is my earnest desire to have Such a Vigorous System of labor in the State as will demonstrate the Superiority of free over slave labor."[7]

A month later, Kiddoo reinforced his position on labor with a new pronouncement. Noting that the cotton crop was threatened by the "rapid growth of the grass," Kiddoo ordered all subassistant commissioners to tour the length and breadth of their districts, visit every plantation, and "lecture [the freedmen] on their duties to their employers, who act in good faith toward them, and advise them as to the importance of saving their crops." Kiddoo wanted the Negroes to be told to work "early and late with cheerfulness" and to realize that "the highest enjoyment of their freedom is through the means of labor, industry, dilligence, frugal[it]y, and virtue." Agents were to read and explain carefully the terms of Circular Orders No. 14, and the assistant commissioner especially cautioned the bureau agents in the flooded Trinity River valley "to aid the planters to the full extent of their power, by inciting industry and emulation among the freedmen in this laudable undertaking." Kiddoo emphasized that it was important for the planters, the laborers, and the state "that a large and profitable crop be the result of this year's labor."[8]

The agents in the field quickly reported that Kiddoo's new policy was having good effect. "Your views, I think, are very different from Gen. Gregory's and *much better*," chortled one subassistant commissioner. "All men are anxious for me to stir the *nigger* out with a sharp stick and make him work," stated another. Other agents said that everyone was working well, but the freedwomen. They refused to put in the dawn-to-dusk hours of slavery, preferring to tend to the personal tasks of home and family. But the Clinton operative believed that most complaints came from those who had not worked Negroes before, rather than from experienced planters.[9]

Although some bureau representatives reported that distances or "physical disability" prevented their full implementation of Kiddoo's edicts, Champ Carter, Jr., rode all over a half dozen north central Texas counties. Carter enforced Circular Orders No. 14, which had been ignored by all parties up to now, put all vagrants to work, made numerous contracts among planters and fieldhands, recommended reliable candidates as possible subassisant commissioners, and even paused to close down a house of ill-repute at Milford. The energetic Carter was an exception; so also, in the other direction, was James Hogue of Cold Springs, hired on the recommendation of loyal judge Henry C. Pedigo, who made his district tour, and handed in his resignation. He could do nothing without more military support, he said. But a neighbor told Kiddoo that the area was so flooded as to make communication impossible. Hogue had not been to Livingston in weeks. The neighbor wanted a set of bureau orders so he could "harmonize society to the working of the new order of things," pending a reopening of travel.[10]

By late July, Kiddoo believed that he had been in Texas long enough to understand correctly the bureau's situation there, so he proceeded to make a formal report to Howard on his progress. He began by stating that the crops were in such a bad state upon his assumption of command that he turned to them first. He found few unemployed freedmen in Texas, indeed, the real problem was a lack of labor, which caused unparalleled and unscrupulous competition for those available for work. Although the assistant commissioner blamed much of the problem on the planters and instituted "the heavy discrimination against the employer in the matter of fines," he also believed that the freedmen's "ignorance and shiftlessness . . . in this their transition state from compulsory to voluntary labor" caused a lack of proper respect for the contractual process. The result was the enticement problem and Circular Orders No. 14 which, he justly claimed, "Agents, Planters, and the public press" all lauded for its "happy effect." He did not mention how the freedmen viewed it.[11]

Kiddoo opined that the subject of contracts was critical to the proper supply of labor in Texas. He favored year-long terms of labor in cotton-growing regions to guarantee business the continued labor in the three critical periods—seeding, weeding, and picking. The assistant commissioner wanted labor to offer itself in the "open market," but once both parties had signed a work contract supervised by a subassistant commissioner as "the guardian of the freedmen," both sides should strive to carry out its terms in good faith. According to Kiddoo, this meant the planter paid full wages, provided rations and quarters, and ensured fair treatment, and the Negroes worked a full day and stayed on to the end of the time specified. The assistant commissioner denied that the reason for Circular Orders No. 14 was that the blacks had failed to work with energy in the fields. Rather, it was intended to prevent the unprincipled shifting of hard-working labor from employer to employer "on flimsy pretext," which was "demoralizing the vigorous System of labor that was established by Gen'l Gregory, and damaging the agricultural interests of the State."

Continuing in this vein, Kiddoo saw Texas as having two general classes of planters. The first accepted the results of the war, and determined to get along with the new free labor system as best they could. These planters found the freedmen reasonable, well behaved, and not "carried away by exaggerated ideas of freedom." Indeed, so impressed were they by the economics of the new system that they would never consider slavery as a viable labor alternative again. It cost them much less to contract at from ten to twenty dollars a month and provide certain specifically listed benefits for their hands as freedmen than to invest from one to two thousand dollars in initial purchase and provide them everything from cradle to grave as slaves.

The second class of farmer, said Kiddoo, insisted that the former bondsmen did not, would not, and could not work as free men. Instead, these landowners asserted that the Negroes had become lazy and indolent and insulting in their demeanor, and habitually lied and stole. They also maintained that those of African descent could not be restrained in a state of freedom and were doomed to eventual extinction. They continually reminded the bureau agents, the freedmen's defenders, that the Negroes' "blood would be on the heads of their liberators." Kiddoo breathed a sigh of relief that these vindictive types were a small minority in the state, but events were to show soon that he probably had concluded too much from some unduly optimistic reports of a few subassistant commissioners.

Kiddoo concluded this issue by giving Howard his philosophy as assistant commissioner. He deemed it important to produce a large and profitable crop in 1866 for the good of both the freedmen and the planters, and for the agricultural and financial prosperity of the state. Kiddoo believed that a good crop would vindicate the liberation of the Negro, and provide a prove a moral and social blessing to the whole South. It would, he said, demonstrate to the planter and the free black laborers that they had a common interest, and "[t]he result of my efforts in this direction have so far been very gratifying to me." It was for this reason that the assistant commissioner had issued Circular Orders No. 14.[12]

Unfortunately the picture was not as tidy as Kiddoo portrayed it.

Despite the pronouncements of Circular Orders No. 14, and the sub-assistant commissioners' distribution of it throughout the state under Circular Orders No. 17, planters from many areas complained that contract laborers were not working the crops properly, failing to live up to the terms of contract, and lounging idly about towns. One man wrote "Gen'l Cadoe" that he was satisfied that the assistant commissioner was a gentleman, but that his subassistant commissioner at Waco was a drunk who did little to advance the cause of agriculture as the general had outlined in his circulars. Another feared ruin unless the bureau circulars were better enforced in his area. He asked that a bureau agent be dispatched to Huntsville at once.[13]

Kiddoo was plagued by the vagueness of the contract procedure he inherited from Gregory. Although a printed form was available to all interested parties, in reality there was no standard contract. Each subassistant commissioner was on his own to determine fairness, and in areas without an agent, each planter had to develop his own concept of what a contract should include. Smart planters sent their proposed documents to headquarters for approval, or asked for a pattern to follow. Others merely asked questions about sticky problems that had occurred or that they anticipated might cause problems at settlement time.[14]

In a "confidencial" communique from Fairfield up in Freestone County, for example, J. Q. A. Carter asked Kiddoo a series of questions that bothered him and his neighbors, and which were answered by an assistant adjutant. Could a freedman dispose of his part of the crop as he wished? Many planters preferred to sell the whole crop as a unit. (Yes, the laborer had all rights to dispose of his property when and where he desired.) Does a freedman have a right to bread and corn just like the rest of the white family? (Yes, if the contract calls for it.) If two contradictory contracts exist, which is in force, the one approved by a subassistant commissioner or the other one? (The contract approved by the bureau representative was the only legal document. A nonapproved contract only showed intent. The bureau could invalidate an unjust contract at any time.) Can a freedman take his share of the crop as it is picked, or must he wait until the planter hands it out at the end of the season? (The hands can assume control of their share at any time.) Does the planter have the right to take the better part of the crop for himself and leave the poorer grades for the freedmen? (No, it must be divided equally by quality).[15]

Besides the subject of contracts and how they were honored, Kiddoo's report to Howard addressed the question of the scarcity of labor that caused so many planters and freedmen to sabotage the agreement process. Kiddoo considered the provision of adequate labor to be critical. Planters already were promising one third to one half of the crop, in addition to enticement bonuses, in a vain attempt to attract enough labor to prevent what seemed to be an inevitable crop loss. The assistant commissioner suggested that blacks be imported under bureau auspices from other Southern states that had unemployed hands. He believed that his proposal would lessen the numbers of freedmen on relief in other states.

Kiddoo's plan received much inspiration from the general's misgivings over the activities of the Texas Land, Labor, & Immigration Co. This organization had recently met in Galveston to promote white immigration from Europe to replace the freed blacks. The assistant commissioner knew that many of the society's supporters were individuals who believed that free blacks would not labor reliably, but he thought that the real problem continued to be a shortage of labor of any color. Kiddoo proposed that importers of black labor should have to sign contracts at the point of procurement approved by the assistant commissioner in the state of origin, and that "reliable and just" individuals be allowed to contract for their own use only, to prevent speculation.[16]

After what an excited Kiddoo thought was much delay, Commissioner Howard agreed to the immigration plan on the condition that the freedmen brought to Texas were "dependent or likely to be dependent" on government assistance in the states where they now lived. Howard had started one company to Texas, and said that representatives from Norfolk, Fortress Monroe, and Yorktown, Virginia, and New Berne, North Carolina, were on their way to look over the Texas possibilities for labor. Howard told Kiddoo to have interested Texas planters apply to individual assistant commissioners in the Atlantic coastal states, and he promised that the government would provide transportation, not only to Texas, but also to Mississippi.[17]

Kiddoo immediately began sending planters into the eastern states looking for fieldhands willing to come to Texas. He promised to honor any contract approved by another assistant commissioner providing that it did not last longer than one year. Reflecting Kiddoo's enthusiasm, a bureau staff officer spoke glowingly of the opportunities available in the Southwest. "I deem it greatly for the benefit of the Freedmen and for the interest of the government to place any laborer at a point where there is plenty of subsistence and where labor is required,"

Brevet Major Solon H. Lathrop said. He reiterated Kiddoo's goal "that the Freedmen may not only be self-sustaining, but be able to place himself in a position to be protected and provided for in the future."

Kiddoo himself told one correspondent, "We have bread-stuff enough in this state to last both races two years, but a scarcity of labor." The assistant commissioner frequently used phrases like "personal favor," "especially commended to you," "endorse," "recommend," in seeking approval for the Texas planters who sought laborers to augment their crop production. He recommended at least seventy planters to every assistant commissioner in the Gulf and Atlantic coastal states, and even helped some of them obtain transportation on Texas steamboats and trains for their contract hands.[18]

As the summer progressed, Kiddoo toured the lower Colorado River region and happily reported that the cotton crop looked to be the largest since 1860. Yet in the state's bounty lurked another problem, the fear that the planters might cheat their hands out of their just share of the profits. The planters in general viewed their Negro employees as fair game in this matter to make up for their own lack of compensation from the wartime confiscation and freedom proclamations. Reports from the rest of the state confirmed both a good harvest and the possibility of massive cheating in final crop settlements, and violence toward the freedmen seemed to be on the increase.[19]

To safeguard the contract process and his beloved immigration program, Kiddoo issued three new circulars. The first gave unpaid wages the first lien on the crop in the field. Upon complaint, any subassistant commissioner could attach and hold the whole crop, regardless of prior sale or consignment, no matter who held it when found. Freedmen who worked for monthly wage payments were to be paid in specie at the exchange rate current when the contract was signed. No substitution of paper currency was to be allowed in any contract settlement. A second order commanded bureau agents to supervise the settlement process firsthand in the field. All bureau agents were to make another tour of their areas of influence as called for in Circular Orders No. 17 in June. They were to explain and enforce the enticement provisions of Circular Orders No. 14 and to review all contracts, making sure that the employees received all they had been promised.

Finally, on November 1, the assistant commissioner decreed that no contract could be considered legally settled without the approval of the closest bureau agent. Kiddoo said that the freedmen must be allowed to ship their portion of the crop any way they wished, and prohibited any planter from offering a cash settlement in lieu of the shares promised in the contract. The freedman could sell his share back to the planter, but only if he received the highest market price then current. Once again, the Texas bureau head reminded all planters and bureau agents that the freedmen's portion of the crop constituted the first lien.[20] He repeated the threat to seize and hold any crop without the proper release, no matter where it was found.[21]

Having treated the contract issue to his satisfaction, Kiddoo turned to the question of the blacks' legal position as freed persons. His predecessor, General Gregory, had relied upon bureau courts to fill the gap in dispensing equal justice to the newly freed blacks. Kiddoo expected to do the same. But on the day he took formal command in Texas, Kiddoo received a new order from General Wright, his army counterpart, an order that threatened the notion of an independent bureau court system. In this document, Wright called the attention of all Texas military personnel, including the bureau staff, to General Orders No. 26, issued by the Adjutant General's Office in Washington, which turned over all the court proceedings involving civilian wrongdoers to the state court system. Because President Johnson had declared the Civil War to be over, under existing Federal Supreme Court decisions, the use of any military tribunal to punish a civilian not in the employ of the army or navy was prohibited.[22]

As Texas was the only former Confederate state that had not yet fully complied with the presidential Reconstruction process, Kiddoo asked Howard if there had not been an inadvertent mistake in not exempting Texas from all current proclamations and orders. Howard assured him that there was none. General Orders No. 26 applied to Texas "as well as anywhere else, if the Civil tribunals are in operation." Kiddoo demurred in a lengthy note to the commissioner. He claimed that everyone in Texas—lawyers, judges, and General Gregory—differed with Wright in his stand. So Wright had asked the War Department for clarification, and had issued a new order, repealing the effect of General Orders No. 26 in Texas. Wright had also reconvened the military commission that he had dismissed earlier, said Kiddoo.[23]

The assistant commissioner, at the moment he wrote Howard, was sending six whites before Wright's tribunal on charges arising from murders of Texas freedmen. Kiddoo said he could not get justice for blacks in the restored Texas court system. "I can *trust* some trifling *civil* cases to the State Courts, but the prejudices of this people are so strong against [the blacks'] equality before the law that in criminal cases their trial before Civil Courts is *worse than a farce.*" Surely there had to be a mistake in applying General Orders No. 26 to Texas, insisted Kiddoo. He would gladly turn over all cases to the state courts, maintained the assistant commissioner, but in good conscience he could not. Kiddoo asked Howard, "in a word, have I the power to arrest a white man for the willful, felonious murder of a freedman, when I have the best reason to believe that the Civil Courts will make a farce of trial, and ask for a commission to try him?"[24]

The answer that Kiddoo received was just what he wanted to hear. Howard told him that Wright's repeal of General Orders No. 26 would be put on hold until Texas had completed Johnson's Reconstruction program. The respite was short, however, as the newly elected government was installed in early August, 1866, and Governor James W. Throckmorton moved immediately to secure all justice activities to the state. The subassistant commissioner stationed at Crockett explained to Kiddoo how the state courts functioned. "[T]hey are doing all that they can to strike terror and dismay to the hearts of the freedmen by making arrests for every possible offense. They seem to fully realize that they have now things under their control." Later this same informant characterized Texas justice for blacks in one curt sentence. "They punish them by the law but do not protect them."[25]

Kiddoo knew that the bureau would not countenance this kind of action from the state. Howard already had told him to use state courts only when they consistently admitted Negro testimony and guaranteed blacks the same treatment before the bench as whites. Such conduct was to be administered by the bureau field agents attending individual court sessions. Kiddoo now received a new set of confidential instructions about how the subassistant commissioners were to run so-called bureau courts, which settled mostly contract disputes, civil matters involving sums of less than three hundred dollars, or items that would result in a penalty of fines not over one hundred dollars or thirty days in jail. The army was to enforce the decisions of these tribunals, which were not to be subject to review by normal state courts. All fines collected were to be sent to the chief disbursing officer in Galveston once a month, and records of the proceedings were to be kept by the local agent.[26]

The makeup of the bureau courts was much the same as the ones Gregory had set up toward the end of 1865 under Howard's previous recommendation. The panel had three members, one to be the subassistant commissioner or another bureau employee, the other two to be chosen by the parties to the case. This time, however, the rules were more comprehensive. Should either litigating party refuse to choose a member of the panel, the assistant commissioner could make the choice for him. Panel members who were not Federal employees could receive up to five dollars a day. The panel would operate under the rules established for military tribunals. All cases of capital crime, felony, or real estate were to be referred to the assistant commissioner, the Federal courts, or the state courts. Kiddoo was more than willing to use bureau courts, but Brevet Major General Charles Griffin's accession to power as district commander and assistant commissioner in January, 1867, quashed the habitual use of such bureau courts because of his obedience to General Orders No. 26. He would adopt a different approach to obtain justice for freedmen in state judicial proceedings.[27]

As with the question of justice for Negroes, the issue of their education was one that had its beginnings before Kiddoo came to Texas. But Kiddoo announced that he would make the schooling of the freedpeople "a *speciality*." The new assistant commissioner was quick to deny any implication that Gregory had slighted black education. But Kiddoo appears to have realized that while Gregory, in the words of one historian, "attacked his job with sincerity and industriousness, the task seemed at times too much for him." Kiddoo approached black education on several levels. Because the Northern teachers, especially women, suffered from the lack of provision for their room and board, Kiddoo tried to get more blacks interested in teaching. He supported the black normal school at Galveston and the education of Negro noncommissioned officers from among the regiments along the Rio Grande as sources of instructors.[28]

Kiddoo also realized that Congress would never provide enough money for a proper educational program in Texas. The state was so far away from Washington that, even though it had more students than several other states, it received less money to educate them. So Kiddoo worked primarily with Northern benevolent associations, such as the American Bible Society, the African Methodist Church, and the American Missionary Association, to obtain schoolbooks and teachers with prepaid salaries. The money crunch also hit the Texas freedmen, who could not afford to pay the standard tuition. Kiddoo's solution was to place a fee on contracts, the money collected being used to finance teachers, buildings, and lot procurement. This, he hoped, would allow tuition-free black education. Kiddoo also tightened up the bureaucracy of teaching, making the teachers file monthly reports through the nearest subassistant commissioner. The agents were ordered to survey the educational requirements of their areas, to organize the black population, and to promote the idea of education among the freed people.[29]

During the summer of 1866, Reverend George Honey, ex-chaplain of the Fourth Wisconsin Cavalry and one-time assistant superintendent of schools on Gregory's staff, began to proselytize among the planters to establish schools on their plantations for the contract hands and their families. Now working for the American Missionary Association, Honey held the basic idea that blacks would be more willing to sign on with a progressive white landowner, who was interested in the betterment of the younger generation, than with an old-fashioned, indifferent planter. That such a program could succeed also shows that the Texas blacks prized the educational opportunity especially for their children.[30]

This arrangement was jeopardized, however, by Honey's cynical greed. According to Kiddoo, Honey used his position as a missionary and bureau staff member to sell freedmen pictures of the martyred President Lincoln "at exhorbitant prices." Honey also speculated in real estate, provided fieldhands to planters for a brokerage fee, and took up religious collections, which he used to finance travel expenses home. Kiddoo said that he did "not allow such transactions by the residents of this state," and he definitely would not "allow it with one who comes among the freedmen *as a missionary*." Kiddoo and Honey never got along, probably because the sanctimonious reverend considered Kiddoo to be intemperate. The assistant commissioner did consume much liquor as a medical remedy, but he disliked Honey slandering him to the missionary societies as a drunk. He recommended that Honey be recalled, but the adroit missionary managed to outlast Kiddoo's tour of duty in Texas.[31]

Despite the efforts of Honey and others, there were many reports that freedmen did not seem to appreciate education, but these complaints seem related to the lack of tuition funds or a difference in white and black expectations, rather than representing a dislike of learning. It was also true that the bureau did not appreciate the influence of the crop seasons upon blacks' interest in education. Each new program began in October, when the children were mostly in the fields and their parents too broke to pay tuition. Enrollment improved each winter, only to decrease each spring as the crop matured in the fields. Kiddoo's free tuition approach promised much in the way of ending this cycle of boom and bust, but he left the state before the program could demonstrate success, and his successors did not follow through with it.[32]

As the bureau strove to increase its educational functions, Kiddoo was cutting back in other areas of social assistance. Blacks still requested help in locating missing family members. Most of the queries concerned children who had disappeared during the travails of slavery. Requests also came in for information about one John Henry Edwards, a deranged black soldier reportedly enlisted in the Tenth Virginia Colored Regiment. As no such unit had existed in Federal service, the correspondent suspected that Edwards had been in the Tenth USCI, an outfit that had served in the Texas occupation. In another case a freedwoman wanted information on the whereabouts of her husband who had disappeared in Memphis, Tennessee. She wanted to join him there if he did not plan to return to Texas. Such requests, however, became harder and harder to fill, if they involved the use of government transportation, unless the freedmen in question were disabled, or could prove that they would not be dependent upon government rations in their new domicile.[33]

Kiddoo's administration saw the last of any real help given to refugees. There were a dozen white refugees supported by bureau efforts, three at Houston for the month of June, 1866, the rest for ten days at San Antonio in September. Black refugees received rations at Galveston, Houston, Victoria, Austin, San Antonio, Courtney, Brenham, and Leona. Galveston had as many as sixty freed persons too sick to be moved, a majority of whom were at the infirmary. Houston had about half that many, and again, most were at the bureau clinic. The other agencies averaged less than ten black refugees, with the exception of the station at Leona. Here F. D. Inge reported that freedmen came in from miles away to complain about contract violations, and he felt obliged to provide subsistence for them. Although the Houston clinic continued its operations into the new year, the halting of the issuance of rations on October 1 put an end to the bureau's providing subsistence for refugees elsewhere.[34]

The selling of the buildings comprising the Houston Freedmen's Hospital at the beginning of 1867 marked the return of the ex-bondsmen's social welfare to state control. It was not an easy process. In June, 1866, Provisional Governor Hamilton had approved Kiddoo's issuance of an order compelling the counties to assume the care of all indigent persons, regardless of color—an edict that Gregory had originally promulgated without much success in October, 1865. Kiddoo and Hamilton acted in response to the refusal of the Harris County judge,

Isham S. Roberts, to comply with Gregory's earlier circular. Kiddoo wanted to remove Judge Roberts summarily from office, but Secretary of State James H. Bell pointed out that the newly elected government would be installed shortly and Roberts had not been chosen for another term. But the officials of the new government also objected to caring for black indigents. The Harrison County board of commissioners maintained that "the D____d Niggers should not be allowed the benefits of the poor fund." A cautionary note from newly elected governor James W. Throckmorton quelled this tempestuous revolt.[35]

Besides the hospital at Houston, the bureau under Kiddoo began to sell off other small properties held as abandoned lands or seized for sustaining the Confederate war effort. The town lots held in Brownsville reverted to the original owner, when Francisco Yturria received a presidential pardon. But the rest was slated for sale under orders from Commissioner Howard, the money going to the school fund. Kiddoo reported that he held only the Houston hospital and a tannery at San Antonio, but he may not have known about other small parcels scattered throughout the state. For example, in January, 1867, headquarters began to investigate the rumors that the Waco Manufacturing Co. had been a Confederate government–owned operation. Several small lots and buildings in other areas soon would fall under the same suspicion.[36]

Meanwhile, as Kiddoo tackled these initial problems, he ran head on into the effect of other events in the bureau's field operations and the state's political picture, events that threatened all he had hoped to accomplish as assistant commissioner. These happenings could in no way be blamed on Kiddoo alone. They had their genesis in General Gregory's administration and had been attacked in his usual haphazard, piecemeal fashion, which resulted in their real significance being lost in the command shuffle. The difference was that, in continuing Gregory's casual approach to these field problems, Kiddoo's administration had failed to come to grips with a major change that occurred as the general assumed power—the election of a popular government in June, 1866, whose participants took over the reins of power from the loyal, federally appointed provisional regime of Hamilton two months later.

Led by Governor James W. Throckmorton, the recently installed Conservative Union party represented a new force in Texas politics. It combined secessionist, agrarian Democrats with antisessionist, pro-business Whigs for the first time into a party that found common ground in their experiences during the War for Southern Independence and a general agreement as to the Negroes' place in postwar society. And although Governor Throckmorton was not as enthusiastic in his pro-Confederate and racist assumptions as the new members of the state legislature, he was determined to reassert the traditional powers of the elected civil authority over what he saw as an unwarranted interference by federal authorities in the South based on dubious constitutional principles.

The governor also realized that he would have to work with the legislature to assert the prerogatives of the state government over the Federal policies represented by the bureau and the army. Hence Throckmorton took a harsher stand than he might have done under other circumstances. He rationalized this approach by reference to unwise actions undertaken by bureau field officers, occupying troop garrisons, and unfortunate command changes instituted concurrently at army headquarters, which were, in part, beyond Kiddoo's capacity to influence.[37]

So, as Kiddoo busied himself with bureau matters at Galveston, Throckmorton and the state legislature were putting the finishing touches on a whole new series of laws, generally known as the Black Codes, which redefined the Negro's position in society as a freedman. Historians and contemporaries have simply condemned these laws as discriminatory, but they were more complex than this would imply.[38] For example, the legislature repealed all prewar and wartime provisions regulating slaves and free Negroes, the runaway slave act, the measure prohibiting incitation of rebellion or insubordination among bondspersons, the decree providing for the repelling of the invasion of the state by hostile persons of color, the act to prevent slaves from "exercising the pretended ownership of property," and the law preventing slaves from being in charge of farms or ranches apart from the place of residence of their owner.[39]

Continuing in this mode, the legislative body defined *colored person* as anyone with one eighth or more "African blood." It specifically granted blacks the rights to make and enforce contracts; to sue and be sued; to inherit, purchase, lease, hold, sell, and convey real and personal property; to make wills and testaments; and to enjoy the rights of personal security and liberty. The state also decreed that there was to be no discrimination against blacks in the administration of criminal law. But at the same time, the legislature proscribed interracial marriage, and prevented blacks from serving on juries, voting in state elections, holding state office, or testifying in state courts, unless the offense was committed against a person of color or his property. In another ordinance, the legislature prohibited the carrying of firearms "on the enclosed premises or plantation of any citizen, without the consent of the owner or proprietor." This last could be seen as a measure to disarm black laborers but, as it was not racially specific, it loosely followed bureau directives on such matters.[40]

As the last of the former Confederate states to be reorganized under President Andrew Johnson's suggested plan for readmission to the Union, Texas had learned much from the Black Codes of other Southern states that had already outraged Northern public opinion during the preceding twelve months. Both Kiddoo and President Johnson had cautioned influential members of the state body and Governor Throckmorton to pass carefully drawn laws that would guarantee "equal and exact justice to all persons without regard to color."[41] At Commissioner Howard's request, the Texas bureau headquarters monitored the legislative process continually, relying on reports submitted by the Austin subassistant commissioner, Byron Porter, formerly of Gregory's bureau staff and a one-time Union army captain, acting assistant adjutant general, and former bureau agent at Houston.[42]

Porter discovered that in its consideration of the Black Codes, the legislature sought to stay within or close to announced bureau policy in its pronouncements. Four key parts of the Black Code illustrate this legislative desire.[43] First, the state passed a strict vagrancy law. Colorblind like the firearms prohibition, the law declared a vagrant to be any person living without any means of support and making no exertion to obtain a livelihood "by honest employment." This included prostitutes, gamblers, fortunetellers, habitual drunkards, "or persons who stroll idly about the streets of towns and cities, having no local habitation, and no honest business or employment." Such persons upon conviction could be fined ten dollars. If the fine was not paid "within a reasonable time, to be judged by the officer," a vagrant could be put to work upon the public works at one dollar per day. Those vagrants refusing to work could be held on bread and water until they agreed to work, whereupon their sentences would begin to be computed.[44]

Another measure long awaited by citizens and the bureau alike was the "General Apprentice Law." The bureau had refused to allow any state officials to apprentice black youths before this enactment, reserving the task to the subassistant commissioners. As with the vagrancy law, the apprenticeship law was color-blind, giving the power of indenture to the judge of the county court. Any youth under the age of fourteen could be bound over by his or her parent(s) or guardian or, if older than fourteen, by his own request. The term of service was until age twenty-one. "Indigent or vagrant minors" or orphans could be bound over upon information supplied by any public official. Since many such orphan minors after the Civil War were black, there was great interest in this law. The master or mistress had to give bond to guarantee good treatment, sufficient food and clothing, medical attendance, and compliance with the terms of the indenture. Any person who wilfully enticed, concealed, or harbored a deserting apprentice could be fined five dollars for each day of offence, and held liable for additional damages as determined in a court of law.[45]

A third regulation provided for the punishment of persons enticing away "laborers or apprentices under contract of service to other persons." This measure owed much to Kiddoo's Circular Orders No. 14. The state law provided that anyone who enticed away a laborer under contract to another could be fined not less than ten or more than five hundred dollars and imprisoned in the county jail for up to six months. Anyone who employed a laborer under prior contract to another could be fined the same amount and jailed for up to thirty days. Finally, anyone who discharged a person under contract before or after the expiration of the contract had to give the laborer a letter of discharge upon request. Refusal could incur a fine of up to one hundred dollars.[46]

The final provision the state legislature passed concerned annual labor contracts. It too followed much of the bureau policy practiced by Gregory and Kiddoo. All contracts for more than one month's duration had to be made in writing, in the presence of the justice of the peace, county judge, notary public, county clerk, or two "disinterested" witnesses. The contract had to be read in their presence, assented to, and signed in triplicate, with a copy for the laborer, one for the employer, and one for the county records. A fee of twenty-five cents per contract was to be charged for filing the document.

All laborers had the right to choose their employer, but once they had chosen, the employees had to remain at the place of employment until their contract was fulfilled. To leave before the contract's expiration was to forfeit all wages earned, unless the employer violated the terms by unfair treatment. Such contracts bound the worker's entire family. Wages due were to constitute a lien on one half of the crop, and this half of the crop could not be removed from the plantation until the laborers had been paid. Employers failing to comply with the law could be fined up to twice the amount owed the laborers. Any mistreatment could be punished at the discretion of the court.

Under the stipulations of the contract, the employee was to obey all "proper orders" of the employer or his agent. He was to take proper care of all tools and livestock, with deductions being made from wages for all damages. If an employee feigned sickness, he was to be docked his wages for the time lost. If he refused to work, he could have double time deducted from wages owed. If the employee refused to work for three days and was being given rations as a part of his contract, he could be forced to labor on the public roads until he decided to honor his original labor agreement.

Up to this point, except for the multiple wage deductions and forced public labor provisions, the state action pretty well agreed with prior bureau policies. But from here on, the state document diverged sharply from accepted bureau practices, and even smacked of slavery under another guise. The law regarded "[f]ailing to obey reasonable orders, neglect of duty, leaving home without permission, impudence, swearing or indecent language to, or in the presence of the employer, his family, or his agent, or quarrelling and fighting with one another, [as] disobedience." Such conduct cost the laborer one dollar for each offence.

Other deductions included twenty-five cents for each hour's unauthorized absence from work, or two dollars per day away without leave. Employees were not expected to labor on the Sabbath, except to feed livestock and do other necessary work, without special compensation under a separate contract. Any thefts were to be charged against expected wages at double the value of the item. The same policy was to prevail in cases of wilful destruction of the employer's property. The laborer was not allowed to hold his own animals except by special permission of the landowner. No visitors could be seen during working hours. And for any "gross misconduct," such as disobedience, habitual laziness, or frequent violations of contract provisions or state laws, the laborer could be dismissed from his job. All disputes between laborer and employer could be appealed to a court consisting of the local justice of the peace and two freeholders, one selected by the laborer and the other by his employer. This arrangement paralleled the bureau's court system, except it stacked the process in favor of the white defendant rather than the black plantiff, as before.

Finally, domestic employees were warned to "promptly answer all calls, and obey and execute all lawful orders and commands of the family," with the exception of the hours after ten o'clock at night and all day Sunday, "and it is the duty of this class of laborers," concluded the state edict, "to be especially civil and polite to their employers, his family and guests, and they shall receive gentle and kind treatment."[47]

Kiddoo's response to the state laws was to allow all of them to stand, with the exception of the labor contract law. The latter measure caused the assistant commissioner to call a halt to the contracting process for the coming year (1867) until further notice. Commissioner Howard, however, urged the state assistant commissioners to proceed with the drawing up of new contracts, providing that the mutual interests of the freedmen and planter were guaranteed. Kiddoo then wrote to one of the more influential newspapers in the state, the Galveston *Daily News*, and told the editor that rumors that the contracting process had been terminated were untrue. Kiddoo said that he had placed a temporary ban on contracting until the bureau could fully evaluate whether the new state law complied with the policies of the bureau and the desires of Congress. Kiddoo pledged that he, as assistant commissioner, was dedicated to the advancement of the agricultural business in Texas, as it was best for the interests of the freedmen. He asked the editor to insert his letter in an upcoming edition of the paper to properly inform all interested blacks and whites on the matter.[48]

A few days later, Kiddoo issued Circular Orders No. 25, which nullified his earlier ban on new contracts and established guidelines for the contract process during 1867. The assistant commissioner emphasized that nothing hereafter was to be left to be "understood" in drawing up labor agreements. In the past this had resulted in much litigation and loss for the freedmen. All details were to be specified, down to who would provide what tools and livestock, medical care, clothing, and rations; what standard deductions were to be made; who provided bagging and ginning; the number of hours and days to be worked (the standard workload for men was usually ten hours per day for a five-and-a-half- to six-day week, while women put in ten hours per day for five days, with longer time off in consideration of family and personal domestic responsibilities); the exact time the contract ended (the completion of harvest or end of the year), if fences were to be mended and rails split; and, if an overseer were to be hired, who (employer or employees) would select him. The bureau recommended that all employees contract for a portion of the crop rather than for wages.

The contracts were to be for one year only, and were to be read to the freedmen in the presence of a bureau representative. Contracts not approved by a bureau agent were invalid. The contracts were to be made out in quadruplicate; the original held by the subassistant commissioner and the copies going to the planter, the freedman, and the state bureau headquarters. Appropriate Federal internal revenue stamps had to be affixed to all originals, and if a contract covered more than one freedman's family, each head of household had to have a stamp placed next to his signature. All contracts had to have a clause saying that any violation of the terms would be referred to the nearest subassistant commissioner's office for adjudication.[49]

Other orders soon established further principles. There would be a charge levied of one dollar for each planter and twenty-five cents per employee, all costs to be paid by the employer, and monies collected to go to the general freedmen's school fund. No document drawn up under the terms of the state labor contract law of 1866 was to be valid. The state law was to be ignored in all respects. This abrogation by the assistant commissioner brought on protests from planters, but Kiddoo claimed that the just provisions of the state labor contract code had already been enacted by him in Circular Orders No. 14 the previous summer. The rest of the law would merely reduce the Negro to slavery, he concluded. As if to emphasize his stand, Kiddoo reminded all of his subassistant commissioners to enforce the enticement order to the letter, and to adjudicate all differences with "simple justice."[50]

Of course, it really mattered little what the state legislature truly intended with the passage of the Black Codes. Loyal Texas whites were not about to admit that the laws had any value at all. John Haynes reflected this view when he dismissed the whole legislative package as a conspiracy to reestablish slavery. It would work this way, posited Haynes: The labor contract bill forced all blacks to sign annual contracts by January 10. Those who failed to do so would then be declared vagrants and forced to labor without compensation for the state. In a like manner, young blacks would be given to white guardians until they reached their majority as a payment for what the rebels saw as an illegal, uncompensated wartime emancipation. Meanwhile, continued Haynes, the gun control act disarmed all blacks to prevent any defense of their rights as free persons, and the restriction on visitation at the workplace kept all conspiring meddlers away from the plantation unless they could secure the landowner's permission. The anti-enticement legislation denied labor the natural negotiating advantage it might have secured under ordinary free market conditions. "Is it not more infamous that that of any other state?" asked Haynes, referring to the Texas Black Code. He glumly answered his own question, "I think so."[51]

Unlike Haynes, former provisional governor Hamilton had not even waited for the legislature to go into session before he blasted its character. "We may make due allowance for the provocation of political agitation," began Hamilton, "but still, the men who suffered themselves provoked or excited to adopt violent, mad, and ruinous remidies, are unfit physicians for [the current] political maladies, if not suicides and murders." After all, he concluded, these same men promised a peaceful, safe secession and produced instead the bloodiest war in American history.[52] Men like Haynes and Hamilton were not about to allow the Throckmorton regime to seize without a fight the Federal patronage and the political advantage it signified, even if such a struggle placed them in opposition to present bureau and military policies.

5

Sick at Heart

LIKE THAT OF HIS PREDECESSOR GREGORY, General Kiddoo's program depended upon the numbers and character of his subassistant commissioners. And like the earlier administration, Kiddoo seemed unable
to cope with the size of the state, a factor that was also affected by
the continued demobilization of the volunteer forces of the Union
Army. All in all, although Kiddoo received thirty-one new subassistant commissioners, he lost as many from demobilization and his own
avowed policy of cutting civilians and other undesirables. But while
all but one or two civilian field employees had been Southerners when
Kiddoo assumed power in May, 1866—and they constituted about half
his effective force—only one remained past January, 1867, when Kiddoo left Texas permanently.[1]

These Southerners served without pay, and Kiddoo believed that
their contribution was worth about as much as their nonexistent salaries. He was especially angry when several of the unpaid field operatives inquired as to their chance of obtaining promised back salaries
after the bureau was renewed for another year, beginning in July, 1866.[2]
One of the problems with the Southern subassistant commissioners
was their close experience with slavery. Some of them could not divorce themselves from the habits of the past any more than could their
neighbors, whom they were to supervise. When Kiddoo issued Circular Orders No. 14, several bureau agents took it as a blank check
to get tough with the freedmen in their regions. Throughout Texas,
especially in the area north of Grimes County, disciplinary methods
employed by planters took a turn for the worse, sometimes with the
active participation and supervision of the local bureau officials.

In one instance, several blacks in Robertson County who had left
their place of employment because they believed their employers did
not live up to their contracts, as they understood Circular Orders No.
14 to say, were hunted down and dragged back to their plantation. There,
under the eye of the subassistant commissioner, the freedmen were strung
up by their thumbs. It was an old army punishment, in which the

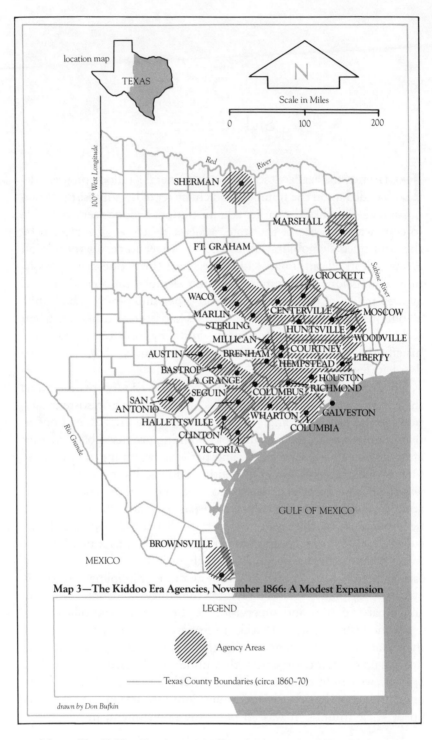

location map

TEXAS

N

Scale in Miles

0   100   200

100° West Longitude

Red River

SHERMAN

MARSHALL

Sabine River

FT. GRAHAM

CROCKETT

WACO

CENTERVILLE   MOSCOW

MARLIN   HUNTSVILLE

STERLING

MILLICAN   WOODVILLE

AUSTIN   BRENHAM   COURTNEY

BASTROP   HEMPSTEAD   LIBERTY

LA GRANGE   HOUSTON

SEGUIN   COLUMBUS   RICHMOND

SAN
ANTONIO

HALLETTSVILLE   WHARTON   GALVESTON

CLINTON   COLUMBIA

VICTORIA

Rio Grande

GULF OF MEXICO

BROWNSVILLE

MEXICO

Map 3—The Kiddoo Era Agencies, November 1866: A Modest Expansion

LEGEND

Agency Areas

———— Texas County Boundaries (circa 1860–70)

drawn by Don Bufkin

MAP 3: The Kiddoo-Era Agencies, November, 1866: A Modest Expansion

offender was suspended just off the ground allowing the tips of his toes to touch the ground tantalizingly, until he grew tired and hung by his thumbs alone. The pain was excruciating, and the punishment could result in loss of the thumbs if overdone. When the subassistant commissioner at Sterling asked Kiddoo to approve of such punishment— he had been doing much the same—Kiddoo wrote back saying that such procedures were not satisfactory. Further investigation showed the practice to be widespread in the region, involving not only legally appointed bureau agents but several without valid appointments.[3] Most lost their positions, but a few lucky ones received sharp reprimands.[4]

After the Robertson County incident, Kiddoo redoubled his efforts to replace bureau representatives of doubtful character. Again, some of the trouble revolved around Circular Orders No. 14. In Liberty County, Dr. J. Orville Shelby had difficulties interpreting the exact meaning of the order. Richard Cole, a planter, complained that Shelby was violating the intent of the order. Some of his fifty fieldhands, he related, had desired to leave months after the contract had been signed. When Cole appealed to Shelby, the agent said that the hands could leave if they were willing to accept a fifty-dollar fine, the maximum he could levy against a black employee under the circular. Shelby defended his action to headquarters. He said that he had returned hands to Cole's plantation before, despite complaints of ill-treatment. Now, however, Shelby had better evidence of the truth of the problem and had decided the hands could leave or stay, as they wished, but he felt obliged to fine those who departed because of Circular Orders No. 14. Later, Shelby lost his position. He claimed that a cabal at headquarters had done him in, but Kiddoo denied this. He said that Shelby had served briefly as a doctor to the Confederate Army, and this precluded him from taking the oath required of all Federal employees. Shelby protested his loyalty, to no avail.[5]

There were several other cases of problem agents, in which Kiddoo also acted. Agent J. W. McConaughey at Wharton left the service for not giving justice to "ill-treated and abused" freedmen. McConaughey denied the charge, although he admitted that he had never heard of the specific case in question, which involved a freedman shot at by a white man. Upon investigation, McConaughey said that the case really amounted to nothing. No shots had been fired. The white had merely threatened the black with a fistfight, and the black had run off. Later, McConaughey vented his anger at the constant meddling of the bureau staff in local affairs. If he had to investigate every little claimed incident, he said, his business for the year would never end. It would be better for the freedman to be permitted to settle his account and leave his employer when irreconcilable differences occur, than to have everyone come running to the subassistant commissioner.

McConaughey said that his major problem now was freedwomen who refused to work in the fields all day long, according to their contract. They preferred to stay at home and tend to housekeeping chores like their white counterparts. He also complained that blacks would go from bureau agent to bureau agent with the same complaint, until they found one who would settle it their way. McConaughey said that this had to stop. It was all too much for Kiddoo. He ordered McConaughey to turn in his books and records to bureau headquarters.[6]

Kiddoo also moved against Agent F. D. Inge of Leon County. A petition signed by thirty-three of his fellow citizens accused Inge of multiple indiscretions. He allegedly charged the freedmen fifty cents each for services rendered, sold them cheap jewelry on the side, and charged planters for approving contracts. The petitioners found Inge "obnoxious and distasteful" and lacked any confidence in him as a reputable official. They claimed that Inge was the cause of all the problems in the county, and that the agent had magnified and even created out of whole cloth the murder, assassination, sedition, rebellion, disloyalty, and outlawry detailed in his reports to headquarters. The signers pledged their loyalty to the Federal and state governments and asked that they be sent a reliable subassistant commissioner. They recommended Captain Joseph H. Bradford, the nearby army troop commander, as the type of individual they could cooperate with.[7]

Inge, of course, was indignant at the charges leveled against him, and made a few good points in his defense. The lies told against him were not unexpected, Inge said, because "there is an antipathy, hatred, prejudice, and malignity arrayed against the Bureau," reinforced by the notion "that no man can hold the position without being vilified, especially one who has been a slave owner, if he undertakes to do justice to the freedmen." Inge maintained that he had discharged his duty "at the risk of my life," and he appealed to Kiddoo in person for fair consideration. The bureau agent reckoned that he faced the same type of smear campaign that had resulted in General Gregory's reassignment.

Inge might have beaten the complaints, except for the fact that a neighboring military subassistant commissioner accidentally found out why the populace hated him so much. Inge, it seems, had been a Confederate commissary officer, in charge of impressing foodstuffs and cotton for the war effort, who had now switched sides. When confronted with the evidence, Inge owned up that he had served the Confederacy for two years, but that he had done nothing "to make me blush." His explanation was irrelevant, however, because Kiddoo had already fired him. Inge simply could not take the required oath. Within six months, Inge, with his family, had been forced to flee to Grimes County for protection, leaving his property behind.[8]

The sad part of Kiddoo's understandable disenchantment with the Scalawag subassistant commissioners was that he lost good agents, too. In Bosque County, Philip Howard noted that bureau activity had come to a near halt, because the "cessationists" paid him little heed after President Johnson vetoed the new bureau bill in February, 1866. "They say it is dead now, that President Johnson has declared the war at an end, . . . and has quit coming forward with their contracts. I have a great deal of trouble with them." By July he concluded that "civil law is a farce up here." He had over one thousand dollars in judgments uncollected, most of which was wages due the freedmen for 1865.

Kiddoo only sporadically answered Agent Howard's continual calls for troops to help him enforce his authority. "If you expect your agents to protect the Blacks," he wrote to General Kiddoo in a mildly scolding tone, "[we] must be invested with some power to enforce [our] orders against Badmen or the Bureau becomes a farce." Receiving little encouragement from headquarters, Howard resigned his position in October, 1866. Kiddoo transferred his case load to the new subassistant commissioner at Fort Graham, whose position was established at Howard's suggestion, and praised Howard by name in orders—an unusual gesture for Kiddoo to make, especially to a nonmilitary man.[9]

As Kiddoo whittled away at the Texas civilians he employed, another problem arose that caused him anxious moments with his subassistant commissioner list. Kiddoo considered volunteer officers to be a prime source for candidates for subassistant commissioner. But upon taking command, he found that the War Department wanted to muster out all volunteer regiments without further delay. Such a policy threatened to gut his entire field force, and Kiddoo correctly claimed that his operations could not continue if he lost them. Many of his agents were members of the Veteran Reserve Corps, and by the summer of 1866, as a cost-cutting measure, Congress began to eliminate the 24 regiments and 188 independent companies, many of whose officers served in the Freedmen's Bureau. With Commissioner Howard's approval, Kiddoo hoped to transfer his Veteran Reserve Corps people to the newly reduced units, thus preserving their use to the Texas bureau.[10]

As the Veteran Reserve Corps represented almost half of his twenty military subassistant commissioners on duty, Kiddoo felt a great urgency to save these jobs. Loosely following Commissioner Howard's guidelines to recommend only "particularly worthy" candidates, "whose characters are not above reproach," and to say "no more than you are willing to be held responsible for at any future time," Kiddoo lauded his agents to the commissioner, using phrases like "one of the best officers of his Rank in the service," and "[i]n addition to being a brave and gallant officer, he is intelligent, competent, and of good moral character." Indeed, said Kiddoo, he needed more such agents, not fewer, but by January, 1867, he had lost fifteen military officers and received eleven replacements.[11] The worst case involved Second Lieutenant H. H. Edelson, who served in the Texas bureau less than one month before he was mustered out in the regular cutbacks in reserve personnel. Gregory had averaged twenty-six people in the agencies between January and May, 1866, the time when he had an effective group of subassistant commissioners. Kiddoo averaged thirty-one over the next nine months, of whom only eleven served during his whole tenure.[12]

Unexpectedly, Kiddoo had trouble with many of his volunteer officers, some of which made the ousted Scalawags look better by comparison. Kiddoo's inspector general, William H. Sinclair, accused First Lieutenant J. Albert Saylor, the subassistant commissioner at Hallettsville of "unjust, unauthorized, and illegal acts." No one in Hallettsville could find anything good to say about him, Sinclair continued. Allegedly, Saylor's goal was to "make a good thing out of the bureau." He did little to safeguard the freedmen's rights. Instead he disarmed them, Sinclair related, fined them for his pocket money, and hobnobbed with the "worst rebels."

Saylor and a male roommate shared sexual favors with a woman who lived with them, causing a public scandal, Sinclair went on. Their landlord evicted all three, and Sinclair was greatly embarrassed to admit that he agreed with the town's assessment of their bureau representative. Recalled to Galveston, Saylor was drummed out of the service for defalcation and malfeasance in office. The only thing that kept him from a court-martial was the time and cost of assembling the board of officers. A speedy muster-out saved him from robbery charges in Galveston and a reaudit of his accounts.[13]

In another case, an informant charged Captain Alex B. Coggeshall at the Bastrop agency of conspiring with his brother-in-law, Julius Schuetze, to provide laborers to planters for a kickback. Coggeshall's replacement uncovered the story, and accused Coggeshall of sloppy record-keeping to hide the evidence. Coggeshall admitted that he had married into the Schuetze family after coming to Bastrop as the bureau representative, that Julius Schuetze provided hands to many planters, and that he and his relatives had plantation interests in common. He conceded that "I was not born a clerk." But he denied any corruption. Later charges appeared in the Galveston *Daily News,* but evidently nothing could be proven. Besides, Schuetze knew Provisional Governor Hamilton, James Bell, and Livingston Lindsay, and was a prominent Unionist and Republican party organizer. After his muster-out, his reputation evidently still intact, Coggeshall would serve as subassistant commissioner again at Hempstead, a year and a half later.[14]

A major problem with Veteran Reserve Corps officers was that many suffered disabling pain from their wartime wounds. Second Lieutenant J. Ernest Goodman of the Second Batallion, for example, had lost his left leg at Ringgold Gap, Georgia, in 1864. In spite of his wound, which still plagued him considerably, he had the enthusiastic recommendations of both General Kiddoo and Commissioner Howard, and received the bureau job at Columbus. But the freed people at Columbus complained when the subassistant commissioner permitted whites to raise the Confederate flag on the Fourth of July, and then asked blacks not to sing "The Battle Cry of Freedom" at school. Goodman's action really did not matter, however, for the schoolteacher, Miss M. Hartwell, ignored him completely. She also ran off Chaplain G. W. Honey, an assistant superintendent of schools, when he tried to assert bureau control over her school. Goodman asked to be retired in August, 1866.[15]

A few months later, headquarters traced Goodman to his home in Germantown, Pennsylvania, and inquired about his illegal sale of military supplies. Allegedly the former lieutenant had disposed of pork, beans, and bread belonging to the Seventeenth Infantry, which had provided his agency guard. Goodman said the stuff was so rotten as to be dangerous to health. He claimed to have told General Kiddoo about the problem, and said the assistant commissioner had told him to destroy it. Goodman did throw out most of the items, but thought he might salvage some of it, despite the weevils and worms. He realized twelve dollars from the sale, said Goodman, and he was about to turn the money over to a local army commissary when the letter of inquiry arrived.[16]

Goodman was not the only agent from the ranks of the Veteran Reserve Corps who was troubled by wartime injuries as well as the hassles of the job. First Lieutenant A. A. Metzner had a smashed thigh, the result of the blast from an exploding shell. Although he did a creditable job when sober, he drank to excess to gain some respite from his still-aching limb.[17] First Lieutenant Charles C. Hardenbrook had been shot through both shoulders at Gettysburg. Like Metzner, he had avoided amputation, but his upper-body mobility was severely limited. He had difficulty writing the endless reports required of a subassistant commissioner, and when his life was threatened he asked for a transfer from his Beaumont position to a safer locale. He preferred Houston, but that position was already filled. Transferred to Richmond, he found it even more inhospitable. When Kiddoo failed to answer his plea for troop support, Hardenbrook resigned and went home.[18]

Other wounded men fared better in their assignments. First Lieutenant James Hutchison had received a gunshot wound in his right hip at Fredericksburg that resulted in partial paralysis of the leg. He served at the Columbia agency, and did quite well despite his handicap. He got "painful tidings" from home that resulted in his resignation. Perhaps it was just as well: His successor died in the yellow fever epidemic of the following summer.[19] Compared to the men with leg wounds, those suffering arm injuries seemed to fare better, perhaps because the effects of the wounds were less debilitating. Edward Miller had lost an arm at Williamsburg and been hit again in the chest by a spent shell fragment at Fredericksburg. Captured by the Confederates, Miller managed to escape and bring back five rebel prisoners with him. An enterprising individual, he did an excellent job at Victoria and Millican, until he refused a chance to reenlist in 1868, probably because he saw the bureau was on its way out of Texas, anyway.[20]

Similarly, Brevet Captain Charles F. Rand, who had lost his left arm during the war, managed to act efficiently as agent at Wharton, Marshall, Gilmer, and Clarksville. He courageously held on at the last post until the Ku Klux Klan ran him out of town for killing a notorious outlaw who preyed on local Negroes.[21] Another agent who had lost his left arm, this time at Chancellorsville while an officer with the famous Berdan Sharpshooters, Captain William H. Horton served the bureau at Wharton, Dallas, and Bastrop. His wound never stopped him from rendering a good account of himself, until his greed got the better of him, and he was forced to resign for accepting bribes.[22]

Regardless of the character of the individual agent, the units that made or broke the effectiveness of the bureau field agencies in their task of protecting the freedmen were the army troops stationed in Texas. Every agent in the field at one time or another needed soldiers to support operations, arrest lawbreakers, or protect his own life. The requests for military help were endless.[23] Army commanders, quite naturally, used detachment requests to rid themselves of troublemakers or dumbbells who hurt the effectiveness of their parent units. Bureau agents, of course, wanted the best troops to increase their chances of accomplishing the job at hand. The result was a running argument between the bureau and the army on the quality of "available" enlisted men. Kiddoo himself led the way, requesting "intelligent and reliable" details, particularly for orderly duty.[24]

The detachment process was never a smooth one. Men on detached duty did not report regularly, took advantage of the looser supervision to desert, were sickly to begin with or took ill while on duty, drank to excess, disobeyed orders, and wound up in the guardhouse commonly for thirty-day stays. Others could not even perform the simple tasks for which they were detailed, like driving wagons, acting as clerks, or running messages.[25]

The problem was not confined to the bureau's Galveston headquarters. When Major L. S. Barnes, the subassistant commissioner at Crockett, asked the army for a noncommissioned officer and some men to assist him, he received a corporal and three men from the Seventeenth Infantry's nearby Company G, posted at Millican. Barnes reviewed the detachment and professed shock. Asking for "men of good character" who would remain sober, he had received a fairly competent corporal, two privates whom he considered "the most inferior men" in the whole company, and one private, Louis Klar, who could not even remember his parent unit without looking at the insignia on his forage cap. One may suspect that Klar did not speak much English, either.

The soldiers' company commander, Brevet Major Louis H. Sanger, did not take kindly to Barnes's complaints to Kiddoo, who had passed them on to army headquarters in Galveston for action. After all, said Sanger, the request did not call for picked men, nor did he really possess any, so he sent "men who would perform their duty to the best of their ability." Brevet Major General Wright opined that Sanger had done all he could under the circumstances, approved the major's performance, and returned the complaint to the bureau. The whole process had consumed a month. Barnes became so disgusted with the lack

The Kiddoo Era

of support from bureau and army headquarters that he asked to be mustered out of the service. He had no transportation; local blacks had ceased complaining to him about injustices, as he could do nothing to help them; the civil courts were unfair to the freedmen; and the planters claimed that he was too pro-Negro to be consulted in any matter. Kiddoo sent him back to his regiment in Louisiana.[26]

Another gripe that permeated the bureau command was the lack of cavalry or, barring that, the inability of a subassistant commissioner to mount himself and a few infantrymen. Horses were expensive luxuries to the War Department, and by January, 1867, it was almost impossible for a subassistant commissioner to have one requisitioned for bureau use. And God save the agent who tried to get the government to pick up the tab on a carriage with two up front for his plantation tours under Circular Orders Nos. 17 and 21! Nonetheless, General Wright tried to answer as best he could the incessant demands for mounted men. He sent ten horses to each of seven infantry posts during the summer of 1866 to fill the gap, but he never had enough to satisfy everyone.[27]

"I might as well have sticks as unmounted men," groused one disgruntled subassistant commissioner. The army commander at San Antonio had sent him a dozen black infantrymen to arrest the alleged murderer of a Gonzales freedman, who was being shielded by his friends. The agent went on to state that the suspect refused to be taken by Negro troops, and that he had specifically asked for white cavalrymen for a purpose—to avoid a fight. Black soldiers were hated in his area. As an "old 3d Michigan boy," the agent asked the post commander to send the dozen white cavalry originally asked for. Brevet Major General Samuel P. Heintzelman, in command at San Antonio, understood the request. But Kiddoo saw it as reflecting the racial aspects of Reconstruction in microcosm, and exploded. "The tone of your communication is disapproved at this office," he said in his scathing rebuttal to Subassistant Commissioner Charles P. Russell. "From the tone and language of this communication this is hardly the proper person to perform such important and delicate duties as are imposed upon him," Kiddoo repeated in a separate message to General Wright. An inspection by Sinclair showed Russell to be a tyrant, hated and distrusted by whites and blacks alike. Union war veteran or not, Russell was on his way home within the month.[28]

Other agents were very happy to receive army help, regardless of the form it took. F. D. Inge, the bureau representative at Leona, feared

110

for his life when the garrison near him was rumored to be ordered to another duty station. An assault against him led to the arrival of Captain J. H. Bradford's company of the Seventeenth infantry. Inge reported that Bradford was very cooperative and willing to move to arrest his attackers on short notice. But Inge wanted him to wait until the subassistant commissioner could develop more "proff," as he spelled it, of the charges. Later Inge queried headquarters about the uses to which he could put Bradford's men. Could the army arrest whites and blacks? Could the soldiers provide a guard for a freedman threatened with violence? Did the subassistant commissioner have to accompany the arresting parties as Bradford desired, even if he had more pressing business elsewhere? Inge said that Bradford wanted written orders before expanding his support role further.[29]

Like Inge, Champ Carter, Jr., the bureau representative over in Sterling, was also more than pleased with his army backup—and so he should have been. The men were B troop of the Sixth Cavalry, one of the rare mounted units in the field. The troop commander worked in close harmony with the subassistant commissioner, sharing duties that allowed each of them to go into the countryside as needed. Later when the captain was absent, Carter and the troop executive officer, First Lieutenant Gus Schreyer, reportedly had some spat, but when confronted by headquarters, Carter denied any problem and said that he and Schreyer handled matters in full cooperation. Carter said that he was off on his tour of the district, and Schreyer would act as subassistant commissioner in his absence.[30]

When Second Lieutenant Lemuel K. Morton, who had been an acting assistant adjutant general at Galveston for only two weeks, took over from Carter in late September, 1866, he found that the cavalrymen had been recalled to another assignment. Morton knew that Carter had been popular with the planters, who greeted him openly with much friendship. But the lieutenant expected that the bureau agent's popularity would end as soon as he began to enforce bureau edicts to the letter and limit physical discipline of black fieldhands, things that Carter had not done. Morton discovered that Carter had permitted the troopers to disarm freedmen for the planters, and had appointed a bogus agent named Shaffer, who had been operating in the area of late. But a worse problem was that the blacks laborers were paid their year-end wages at the plantation stores, which marked up all prices by 100 percent. Other planters took their fieldhands to a cooperative county court where the blacks were sued for property damages to the amount of their wages.

Disenchanted with his ability to affect the situation favorably on behalf of the Negroes, Morton handed in his resignation. He had acted as the bureau representative at Sterling for only three and a half months.[31]

Morton was not alone in his feelings. The agent in Columbia begged Kiddoo to permit his clerk, a private from Company F of the Thirty-fifth Infantry, to stay on when his unit was recalled to headquarters. To be without both soldiers and his clerk he deemed too great a sacrifice. As if to reinforce his subassistant commissioner's estimate, Kiddoo refused to allow the officers of the 114th USCI who were serving as bureau field workers to return to their regiment for muster-out until after the fall picking season had ended. Like the planters, he needed every man he could get in the "field" at that busy time.[32]

But at least these officers were all within the Texas command system. They could appeal to Kiddoo's headquarters, which could go to the nearby army headquarters offices in Galveston to obtain relatively quick action. There was a quirk, however, in the army district boundaries until 1867 that placed northeastern Texas in the District of Louisiana. The Texas bureau officials in Marshall had to appeal to New Orleans for military support, and the commanders in the Crescent City generally forgot about that small sliver of Texas. It was so far away, and staffed by men not of their units. Lieutenant I. M. Beebe wrote his boss, Colonel Thomas Bayley, the subassistant commissioner in Marshall, to plead for Kiddoo to do something about the whites, who "upon the slightest provocation beat, knock down, and shoot" area freedmen, most of whom were being held as virtual slaves a year after emancipation. If something were not done soon, he said, Marshall would need a new hospital just to care for the wounded freedmen.[33]

As expected, the 1866 settlement season around Harrison County was a violent one. Bayley sent in the required report of all murders and outrages committed since the Civil War. He asked that the names of informers be kept secret if the incidents were publicized. Bayley could get little but rumors on most cases, but the subassistant commissioner believed that "where there is so much smoke there must be fire." He did know that bands of regulators roamed the counties around Marshall. He noted that these areas sent few freedmen to the state penitentiary, "because there is a more open and expedicious way of correcting them than by the process of civil law." To void contracts that forbade unauthorized absences, blacks were driven from the plantations by beatings, gunshots, and murder. A few decent whites armed their black workers for self-protection. Since people feared retaliation, grand juries could get no one to testify against the attackers. In those few cases brought to trial, petit juries refused to convict for the same reason. No one, white or black, not even Bayley on official business, dared travel alone.[34]

Bayley's assistant, Lieutenant Beebe, confirmed the system of "knock down and drag out" in the area, and said blacks simply were "not free." Both men said that the Negro soldiers of the two companies of the Eightieth USCI were useless. The men were about to be mustered out, anyhow. They made few arrests. Their officers refused to allow the men to make more than one day's march out and back into the countryside, because they could not camp safely where locals held the black infantrymen in such contempt. It was not safe to go about in town either. The town deputy marshal had murdered two of the Eightieth's black enlisted men without provocation. He was the whites' hero of the hour, as he swaggered about unindicted. In reply to requests from the Marshall office for more troops, the commander of the District of Louisiana said that the muster-out of his regiments would continue as the War Department ordered. "I will not have an armed man on the Red River after the 1st of September," he promised.[35] Bayley had wanted to set up a school system under Beebe, but feared that without military protection in the counties around Marshall it was useless to act. The burning of the schoolhouse at Marshall attested to his wisdom.[36]

Shortly afterward, Beebe was dead from natural causes, and by November, Bayley had been mustered out of the service. General Kiddoo begged Commissioner Howard to intervene and keep Bayley on. Bayley's patron, Illinois governor Yates, did the same. Bayley said that he wished to continue as subassistant commissioner, as his wife's health precluded her going North for the winter. He suggested that he take a leave to go to New Orleans for the termination of his military career, and then return to Marshall. He went instead to Baltimore and returned in such a roundabout fashion that the bureau refused to pay for the journey.

Upon further examination, headquarters discovered it did not like any of Bayley's accounts as subassistant commissioner and wanted a full audit before he received his salary due. His clerk, Frank Smith, went into the planting business in December, forcing Bayley to hire a new clerk, Leonidas Greenleaf. Then, despite glowing praise from Kiddoo, the regular army refused to grant Bayley a commission with the new colored infantry service. To top it off, headquarters refused to endorse Bayley's request to be paid at his old salary rate of colonel of volunteers, higher than that of ordinary subassistant commissioner. The disgruntled Bayley served on, but without much enthusiasm.[37]

When the bureau commander in Arkansas forwarded complaints he had received of continued slavery in northeastern Texas, Kiddoo told the Louisiana command that a token "invasion" of the area by at least one company of cavalry was an "*absolute* necessity." Further, he asked Commissioner Howard to authorize a few traveling subassistant commissioners to be stationed out of Marshall. But to send such men out without mounted escorts was impossible. So Kiddoo turned the whole matter over to Howard. Unfortunately, the bureau would be able to do little in northeastern Texas until the spring of 1867, nor would the area become a part of the District of Texas militarily until December, 1867.[38]

Violence was not limited to northeastern Texas alone, but it seemed more pervasive there than elsewhere. Mrs. L. E. Potts of Lamar County, a Unionist who had recently returned from self-imposed exile in California, wrote straight to President Johnson to voice her concerns. She told how blacks who asserted their rights as free persons were being brutally treated. No one bothered to pay freedmen for their labor. Those who tried to flee were run down with bloodhounds and shot. Indeed, it was no crime for a white to kill any black for any alleged transgression. She concluded that "everything savors of rebellion" in the Paris area. "I wish we could have a few soldiers here just for a while, to let these rebels know they have been whipped." No bluecoats had yet been seen, she said. Her letter went through the channels in Washington, eventually returning to General Wright's desk in Galveston. Wright said that he had no men to spare, but hoped to do better as more regular cavalry arrived. "This section of the State of Texas is very lawless," Sheridan confirmed in relation to another incident, "but I can cover but few of the cases, as I have not the troops to spare."[39]

Kiddoo had seen Mrs. Potts's letter, too. Every report from the interior brought him news of more atrocities committed against freed persons. He believed that his biggest problem as assistant commissioner was providing protection to blacks from indiscriminate white violence in a state so large as Texas. He begged Howard to intercede with the War Department and obtain more soldiers for Texas to "make my duties here a *reality*—instead of a farce." Kiddoo said that he was "*sick at heart*" that the government could free the blacks and leave them so unprotected. Howard felt the same. He informed Kiddoo that he was "reluctant to encourage negroes to go to Texas so long as it is reported that they are killed and outraged, and have so little share of Justice."[40]

In response to Howard's request to all assistant commissioners for a list of murders committed in each of the Southern states, Kiddoo sent a document "of authentic murders and outrages" that was admittedly flawed, both because he had so many areas without subassistant commissioners, and because only half of the agents in the field had yet reported. He believed that his list would demonstrate the "necessity of giving protection to a class of people rescued from slavery by the armies of the republic acting under the 'will of God.'" But five days later, fearing that his report might jeopardize his scheme to bring in needed black laborers from other states, Kiddoo assured Howard that "[g]ood feeling toward the negro is rapidly gaining ground, violent sentiment is on the decrease, and I feel warranted in encouraging emigrants into the state." By January, 1867, however, Kiddoo had forwarded three more collections of reports of horror from the interior, including more tales from the northeastern part, a topic he had discussed with Howard in a recent trip to Washington.[41]

A sampling of the reports Kiddoo sent to Washington shows that crimes against the ex-bondsmen included persons being shot, killed with an axe, killed with a pole axe, knifed, cut to pieces, chained and thrown into a pond, dragged one mile, shot and thrown into a pond. These in addition to victims of wanton, cold-blooded murder. These crimes "punished" such behavior as making a complaint to the bureau, failing to raise one's hat, seeking employment elsewhere, interfering in a quarrel between one's wife and a white woman, reporting a planter for nonpayment of wages, or refusing to allow oneself to be whipped. The motives for other crimes were listed as unknown (a large category). Whites who admitted to murder often claimed to "want to thin out the niggers a little" or "just see him kick." A white who spoke to a black congregation had a visit from a gang who told him if he addressed blacks again, "he would preach his next sermon in hell." As one unidentified informant concluded, "O. What an awful state of affairs we are in the midst of."[42]

By late summer, Kiddoo's bureau field operations had begun to disintegrate, just as the popularly elected government under Governor Throckmorton took office. Eager to assert state sovereignty, Throckmorton moved to take on the bureau's role in Texas, as it was the one Federal institution that typified to white Texans the unprecedented postwar interference with state authority. The chain of events that assisted Throckmorton in his opposition to Kiddoo's bureau administration had begun at the Seguin agency under its controversial subassistant commissioner, the Scalawag county judge, William Longworth. Had he known their ultimate effect, Kiddoo could have pieced together the lamentable story of the bureau field operations from his headquarters files. But these incidents had taken place as Gregory was busy leaving office, and while the general was preoccupied with learning the ins and outs of his new job as assistant commissioner.

Appointed to the bureau agency by General Gregory, Longworth first entered the picture in June, 1865, when he wrote the army command from his home in Sutherland Springs. Claiming to be the most persecuted man west of the Brazos River, after A. J. Hamilton and John Hancock, Longworth wanted to be made the freedmen's representative for Wilson (where he lived), Guadalupe, Gonzales, and Bexar counties. By September, Hamilton had named him judge of the Wilson County court, lending much validity to his assertions of loyalty. In October, Longworth wrote Hamilton and complained that a freedwoman had been carried away from her residence by four whites. He asked that the men be arrested for kidnapping. He followed this letter with another, in which he told how he had observed twenty cases of "high felony," and much continued slavery. Longworth asserted that he lacked adequate popular support as judge, and demanded some kind of concerted action on the behalf of loyal blacks and whites.[43]

Meanwhile General Gregory answered his first note. The general regretted that he could make no civilian appointments at the moment as he lacked funds for their salaries. Longworth wrote Gregory again. He said that his sole object in seeking a bureau appointment was to "ameliorate the condition of the negro," not to garner a salary. He saw the bureau endeavor in Texas as the "last field of action" of the recent war, and was willing to serve "without fee or reward." The "faithful performance of their duties by the agents of the Bureau and the Republican party North" were the only hopes for the freedmen, Longworth continued. He professed astonishment that when loyal whites were given the choice between "Union and peonage (slavery)," they chose the latter. As a lawyer, judge, and businessman, Longworth concluded that he had the capacity to do much good for local blacks.[44]

Gregory agreed with Longworth's immodest self-assessment, and appointed him a bureau subassistant commissioner without pay on December 27, 1865. The general sent the judge blank forms to use as a guide in making the required reports, and asked to hear from the new agent frequently. He would, for Longworth promised to make his district "a model one." His operations would comprise all of Wilson, Karnes, and Guadalupe counties, and Gonzales County west of the Guadalupe River. Longworth asked about requisitions, saying that he would use his own money until government funds were made available. The judge said that the contract blanks were useless, given local conditions. He would insist that the Negroes work for a fair share of the crop, but feared that the planters' tendency to "overreach" would cause problems.

Longworth estimated there were five thousand freedmen in his area who were owed at least twenty dollars each for their labor in 1865, which meant that he would have to collect one hundred thousand dollars in back wages due. He bragged about his Unionism, and asserted that Gregory would have made him the first agent in the state, had he but known how diligently Longworth had worked for the cause. The judge begged Gregory's indulgence when it came to bureau procedure, as he had never worked for the Federal government before. "The only thing I dread is, that there may be an attempt made to poison you against me." Longworth's concluding words proved to be prophetic.[45]

As if to prove how little he understood proper procedure, Longworth sent in a series of complaints about the scope of bureau operations. He had no post, no commissary, no hospital, no surgeon, and no stores to aid the helpless freedmen who were pouring in from all sides. He needed at least fifty soldiers, three clerks, and all sorts of office supplies and furniture. He worried that some would fear he was "flinching in the cause," because his response to the destitution and continued slavery was so limited. "There must not now be any flinching, by anyone in or out of office who wishes well to the United States," he thundered. "For the Cause, I have forgotten everything but my soul's salvation"—a statement that so moved the bureau headquarters clerk that he abstracted it into the summary register of letters received at headquarters.

The subassistant commissioner at Sutherland Springs was not through yet with his want list. He wanted to move his operations to a town with a military garrison, better situated to cover the hundred square miles he estimated his district included. He knew that white Texans would endeavor to hold the Negroes in bondage under other titles and means than "slave" and "slavery." The favored substitute method was "apprenticeship," and Longworth had refused to allow it. Now he faced the hatred of the whole area. "I think I can crush out such feeling," he said. He believed that soon he was going to have the busiest court in the nation, as he sought to move against the residual proslave, rebel sentiment. "Conciliation is wasted on them," he emphasized. Indeed, he hated the very mention of the word. General Gregory unwittingly incited the judge further, when he praised Longworth's "upright and manly course," and hoped that "ere long" everyone in Texas would see it in such a light. Meanwhile, "confident that in right we are, and that the right will triumph," Gregory went on, Longworth should continue his efforts.[46]

Buoyed in spirit by Gregory's assent to his increasingly controversial policies, Longworth also communicated with the army command in San Antonio. In spite of his normal bombast, he knew that he would never get fifty men. So the subassistant commissioner requested that he be sent twenty-five men and a commissioned officer to support his agency operations. The army command demurred. The judge could have ten men and a sergeant, came the reply. The assignment was too insignificant to send an officer without detracting from his status. Worse than that, Longworth could keep the detachment only a week, as they were volunteer infantry scheduled for muster-out. Longworth protested, and managed to secure the services of seven regular cavalrymen, whom he saw as useless. Four of the men were Germans "of the lowest origins," two were "Americans" who cared not at all about their duties, another was an Irishman of the same ilk, and their sergeant could barely write his name.

Although disappointed at the military response, Longworth went ahead with his great plans. He planned a hospital of fifty beds; anything less he saw as doing more harm than good. It would raise false hopes, he thought. He was appalled to report that Negroes were treated like pieces of machinery, incapable of feeling; they were treated as slaves, and their children were seized as apprentices to work off the losses of emancipation. "I have somewhat interfered in this matter," he said, and he promised to end the situation permanently soon. Correctly, Longworth saw the root of most of his problems in the temporary nature of the bureau, which was to last only one year after the termination of hostilities. This seemed to be the case particularly during the spring of 1866, after President Johnson's rejection of the renewal bill and before the congressional override of his veto that July.

Nonetheless, he criticized Gregory for being too slow to appoint more subassistant commissioners. He believed that two were needed at his agency alone. He did grant that men who were adept at business, law, and race relations, with the courage to flout the feelings of the white community, were hard to find. He feared that freedmen at any distance would lose their chance for redress of grievances. To prevent this from happening in his district, the judge decided to move his office to the more centrally located town of Seguin by May, 1866. Echoing what he saw as Commissioner Howard's stance, Longworth admitted that no subassistant commissioner at all was better than an incompetent or corrupt one.[47]

Longworth then proceeded to prove his point in the matter of black minor children. Upon emancipation, many black minors found themselves orphans in fact, temporarily without parents, or with parents who could not care for them because of extreme poverty. As with white children in the same circumstances, the county courts farmed these children out to white guardians, who were allegedly selected for their ability to care for the wards, and who put up a bond to do so under state law. But this system was open to abuse, and black adults poured into bureau offices, complaining that their children had been seized illegally by the courts and apprenticed to their former white owners, the child's labor until he or she reached majority age being intended to pay partially for the economic loss of emancipation. No one caught on to this scheme faster than Subassistant Commissioner William Longworth, probably because he was a county judge who had been approached by many whites for assistance on the matter.

But while many judges cooperated in the practice, Longworth refused. He agreed with the black plantiffs who charged that the scheme was a form of pseudo-slavery, and he moved to crush it in his area of control. His records are filled with cases of black "apprentices" returned to their parents, or to different guardians than the wards' former owners. One such case involved a young woman and man farmed out to James L. Dial of Guadalupe County. Longworth sought out the case, called all parties into his office, and fined Dial sixty-five dollars to be paid to the black male, and twenty-five dollars to go to the female apprentice. He also charged Dial with kidnapping and false imprisonment. Dial resented the proceedings and appealed to headquarters in Galveston. He pointed out that Longworth moved even in cases where there was no complaint by the ward about his or her treatment. Brevet Colonel William H. Sinclair wrote back for Gregory that the subassistant commissioners had complete jurisdiction in these matters on a case-by-case approach without being second-guessed by headquarters.[48]

Longworth's ruling interfered with the prerogative of the Guadalupe County judge, William C. Wiseman, a Hamilton appointee and supposedly a loyalist. Conveniently, the subassistant commissioner had just moved his office into Wiseman's jurisdiction at Seguin. The irritated judge ordered Longworth to free Dial from confinement and desist from all further action. Wiseman asserted that Dial had acted with the court's permission under existing Texas law. Longworth released Dial, then wrote to Gregory and received the general's approval to ignore the county court. "It was a tedious and heavy struggle, the blow being aimed at the very vitals of the Bureau," Longworth said, after a week in court. But he came out a winner. He rearrested Dial and let him out on bail to make his victory clear to local opponents.[49]

But Judge Wiseman was not yet through with the fight. Indeed, the entire legal community at Seguin got together to plot strategy against Longworth. The result was that Dial instituted a suit against Longworth claiming twenty thousand dollars in damages for false arrest. The case was scheduled for a hearing at the next court session in September, 1866. At this moment, President Johnson's proclamation ending the rebellion appeared at Seguin. Longworth protested the confusion the order caused, and the concurrent withdrawal of his soldiers. He said that Wiseman had assaulted him in the bureau office when they left, and he asked for renewed military protection. Judge Wiseman, Longworth asserted, had "sunk the Negro" to a legal level below that of a slave. He asked for clarification of the bureau's stance on apprenticeship, his right to make arrests, and his ability to seize property to compel obedience to his orders.[50]

Meanwhile, Wiseman's position was buttressed by a letter-writing campaign that assailed Longworth as "unnecessarily unpopular with both classes of our people [white and black]," and as "a stranger to us." Samuel Wright, another Hamilton appointee as clerk of the county court, sent documents on other cases similar to Dial's, in which Longworth had negated Judge Wiseman's earlier rulings and levied three-hundred-dollar bail amounts. Judge J. B. McFarland led a petition drive that produced eighty-five signatures calling for Longworth's replacement by Judge Wiseman as subassistant commissioner. The petitioners described Wiseman as antisecession, a man who went with his state during the war but was among the first to accept the war's loss as good, and "a just, Honest, and upright man" who would give satisfaction to whites and blacks alike. Dial himself wrote in his own defense. He claimed to be a Union man and a bureau supporter. But he feared that Longworth's disgraceful, tyrannical, and oppressive course, "which might well stagger the belief of anyone," would jeoparadize the bureau program in Guadalupe County.[51]

Longworth's clerk, a Scalawag named Samuel Gilmore, defended his boss in his own letter to headquarters. Gilmore wrote because he had "an anxiety lest calumnies should, even for a moment, triumph over truth." He told of how "[w]e have got into a perfect Hornet's nest here," with he and Longworth being slandered as "Yankees" and "Radicals," who worked for the "Nigger Bureau" or, at least, a "drawer of the Bureau," according to one local wag. "But, sir," Gilmore said in exasperation, "Christ himself would find persecutors and slanderors here." The real problem was that Longworth "cannot be bought," Gilmore concluded.[52]

Even though Texas was exempted from the benefits of President Johnson's proclamation shortly afterward and Federal troops returned to protect Longworth's person, Judge Wiseman moved to exclude Longworth from further interference in his prior and future judicial rulings. Wiseman wrote Longworth and asked if he would "stop upsetting" the county court rulings on Negro children. "Will you revoke your order instanter?" the judge demanded. He warned Longworth that he would charge the assistant commissioner with kidnapping, if he did not behave himself. "A word to the wise is sufficient," Wiseman threatened.

Longworth shot back a note in which he said that he refused "to tamper with the majesty of the laws of the United States, or the dignity of the office I fill as to comply with your peremptory command." But Longworth promised he would temporarily suspend his actions until his stand was confirmed or modified by headquarters. Wiseman said that he was pleased with the subassistant commissioner's decision. Longworth fired back a missive in which he said he was merely trying to calm matters down, not to please Judge Wiseman. Longworth also wrote the San Antonio garrison commander and asked for more men. The army officer inquired as to Longworth's authority to act against a county court order. Longworth cited bureau orders that made him the guardian of all black orphan children and said he wanted to double his protective force to twenty-five men. Meanwhile Wiseman told the subassistant commissioner that he had given him enough time to ponder his future course of action, and that any further problems between the court and the bureau would be altogether Longworth's fault.[53]

Aware of the program to libel him at headquarters, Longworth blamed the campaign on James Wilcox, the clerk of the district court, whom

Longworth labeled as Wiseman's righthand man and a blatant racist. Wilcox carried on his efforts in the local newspaper's column, "Town Talk." Longworth accused the clerk of misquoting him in the article, and enclosed copies of several issues of the newspaper to prove his point. At this time, the subassistant commissioner received an inquiry from headquarters, containing a dozen charges that dissatisfied citizens had made against him. He dismissed many of the individual charges as rubbish ("Where is the man from Abraham Lincoln down to myself that has not been slandered?"), and focused instead on his overall conduct as bureau agent.[54]

Longworth began by asserting that he asked less than half what was due the blacks in back wages and punitive damages. His major shortcoming, he continued, was that he did not collect everything owed the Negroes from the previous year, for which he apologized. He also refused repeatedly to overlook the law, as whites asked him to do. He denied that he retained any monies from fines, or that he charged fees for hearing cases. He said such notions came from a 10 percent surcharge he levied on all cases to pay for an attorney he hired to cut through all of the legal dodges employed against him and the freedmen.

As for his alleged demoralization of the Negroes, Longworth had to laugh. He merely sent them home with the guarantee of their pay, told them to labor honestly, informed them of their right to schooling, and forced the landowners to pay for the labor of women and children as well of the men. Far from being a stranger to the area, Longworth had lived there for eleven years, and his clerk for seven. He was mystified that the argument was over "orphan" children, because the ones in question all had living parents who wished to care for them. As for the recommendations of Judge Wiseman to be subassistant commissioner, Longworth snorted, "He is the very man I was sent here to counteract and keep in check." Then he so to speak threw up his hands in exasperation and yelled, "Why am I wasting paper?" He asked for a court-martial to clear his name. He had already written Senator Charles Sumner of Massachusetts—a noted Radical Republican who backed a harsher Reconstruction of the South—making the same request.[55]

If there is anything that irritates a lower-echelon bureaucrat, civilian or military, it is when a subordinate bypasses him in the proper chain of command. When Kiddoo received Sumner's inquiry on the Longworth matter, he was just getting acquainted with his new assignment as assistant commissioner, and did not wish to be distracted by local matters in one subdistrict. So he wrote Longworth and told him that his explanations were satisfactory and that no court-martial would be convened. Longworth returned a reply stating that he would have been very sorry to have withstood a formal inquiry, not because he was guilty, but because it would have indicated that Kiddoo had failed to see through the fog of false "rebel" charges against him. He pointed out that none of his rulings had been set aside at headquarters; indeed, only two had even been appealed. Longworth referred to his opposition to secession, a time "when men were scarce, and when I stood almost alone—alone, in the fullest sense of the word. . . . I stood for honor and my country. Now I stand for law and order, and justice to the negro. Those," he concluded, "and the sentiment growing out of them are really my crimes."[56]

The Seguin subassistant commissioner reported that things were relatively quiet now. Not that the bureau was any less hated, but Longworth had very little power left to complete the collection of judgments, most of which totaled less than fifty dollars apiece. He figured that it would take five times the amount owed to collect them, but he suggested that headquarters might consider it worthwhile to do so on principle. Judge Wiseman still toyed with him, trying to entice Longworth into a new confrontation over the problem of orphans and apprentices. But Longworth refused to take the bait. He apologized for accomplishing only a fraction of what he had been hired to do, but was proud that he would "never be called to account for cruelty to, or unfairness towards the negro." He would very much have liked to serve in a more receptive location, but believed that Seguin was destined for him. In early July, Longworth courageously toured his subdistrict under the provisions of Circular Orders No. 17. He was rumored to have been murdered, but nothing out of the ordinary happened.[57]

As things quieted down at Seguin, so did they also at headquarters. Kiddoo had issued most of his initial policy-making orders, and could now turn to matters he had avoided before. One of the matters he addressed was that of Longworth. Kiddoo disliked the distrustful, antagonistic attitude that the Seguin subassistant commissioner had displayed toward him as commander in sending his complaints directly to Senator Sumner, and the disruption of what Kiddoo saw as the bureau's quiet advance under his administration. Besides, Kiddoo did not trust Texas loyalists as bureau agents, and wanted to replace them with soldiers or Northern civilians. The controversial Longworth would be the first to go. On July 26, Kiddoo replaced him with First Lieutenant

James B. Moore of the Tenth USCI. Moore's unannounced arrival placed Longworth "in a most singular position," but the embarrassed subassistant commissioner promised to finish up pending business and to help Moore learn his job.[58]

The citizens of Seguin were pleased that Longworth had been removed, but dismayed to see him stay on as Moore's clerk. As for Moore, a tour of the area convinced him of the truth of Longworth's assertions that "an organized combination" existed against the bureau. The whole population was united against the government, the bureau, and the freedmen, Moore said. The only difference that Moore saw was a change in personnel, for Wiseman had not been reelected as county judge. But the new district judge, of a region that included Guadalupe County, was John Ireland, one of Wiseman's supporters and close friends. He promised to be a thorn in the bureau's side, as had his ally before him. Moore expressed some confusion as to his own jurisdiction in relation to the newly elected state officials. He visited the Dial plantation to settle a labor strike, and complained of the sheriff's refusal to compel witnesses to appear before Moore in an assault case. Then Longworth went back to Sutherland Springs, his job completed, and Moore grew strangely silent.[59]

Kiddoo was puzzled at the lack of news. He sent William H. Sinclair, recently appointed a special-duty agent at headquarters, to check out the entire Seguin situation. Sinclair generally confirmed Kiddoo's suspicions that "many of Longworth's acts while agent of the Bureau were without a shadow of authority." Sinclair had little sympathy for Longworth. He suggested that Kiddoo feed him to the civil courts and let him fight it out on his own. The bureau investigator told of how Longworth had reopened cases that had already been decided to the satisfaction of both sides, compelled parties to appear even when there was no complaint, kept freedmen from work for days until their cases had been heard, once called in every hand and manager of a plantation twenty miles away to testify, charged illegal fees, and persecuted Dial so unfairly that Sinclair thought his fines should be refunded. Longworth made unnecessary, vindictive speeches to freedmen, Sinclair said, which threatened farming efforts in the entire region. Local whites hated Longworth so much that Sinclair believed it a miracle that the subassistant commissioner had not been assassinated.[60]

As for Moore, Sinclair found that he had compelled Longworth to leave town after his business had been completed there. But for the first two weeks in August, Longworth had acted without any authority whatever, since technically he had already been replaced. After Longworth's departure, Moore had changed his policies, much to the acclaim of the white population. But Sinclair found Moore to be a man of little principle. He was drunk much of the time, solicited prostitution from any freedwoman on the street, and was under indictment for gambling within the town limits. Moreover, Moore had financed his hedonistic binge by embezzling bureau money. Kiddoo quickly ordered Moore back to Galveston to face a more formal audit and inquiry, and sent Captain Samuel Craig in his place. Sinclair spoke well of Craig, whom he knew from the latter's earlier experience as subassistant commissioner at Brenham. Craig's loyal service during his difficult tenure at Brenham had impressed Kiddoo, and he was certain that he could trust Craig to deal effectively with the volatile agency at Seguin and to chart a reasonable course of action, somewhere between the extreme ones taken by Longworth and Moore.[61]

6

Gone to the Devil

As GENERAL KIDDOO WORKED to clean up the mess at Seguin, over in Washington County another incident exploded. This was the Brenham fire of September, 1866, and the events leading up to it explain why Captain Samuel A. Craig was transferred to Seguin. An officer of the Seventeenth Regiment of the Veteran Reserve Corps, Craig had originally come to the bureau's attention as its agent in Madison, Indiana, where he had coordinated relief efforts directed toward destitute freedmen in that area immediately after the close of the war. In December, 1865, he was put on the same footing as the other officers of his regiment and ordered to go home. Craig said that he would prefer to continue in bureau service somewhere in the South. By the last of April, 1866, he was in Texas, where he took over the Brenham agency from Second Lieutenant Benjamin J. Arnold of the Twelfth Illinois Cavalry, whose unit had just been mustered out.[1]

Craig's initial experiences at Brenham were normal for a bureau agent at that time. The area was short of the needed labor to work the fields, and hands were promised as much as fifteen dollars in gold a month to get them to change places of employment. Craig's arrival brought many freedmen into Brenham to complain about not receiving last year's wages. The new subassistant commissioner referred all problems to headquarters, which promptly sent them back to Brenham for action. Headquarters told Craig to take notice of all matters between freedmen and whites, between freedmen, and between whites if the issue affected the freedmen, and directed Craig's attention to Circular Orders No. 14, outlawing enticement. Craig said that he had applied the order, and the whites were very happy with its effect.

He also successfully asserted his jurisdiction in cases incorrectly referred to other nearby agents, and promised to get rid of responsibility for the sick and indigent blacks to whom he issued 248 rations in July. This he did, even though the local county government refused to accept its proper responsibility for the old woman, six children, and an old blind man. The Brenham bureau agent then asked for an American flag to mark his headquarters as a loyal building and for a small cavalry force. Although the "sentiment you express and the desire you manifest are highly commendable," Kiddoo regretted that he had no flags available to fly over bureau offices. But the assistant commissioner did send ten horses to the infantry camp outside town, for army and bureau use. By the end of summer, Craig had made a partial tour of his jurisdiction.[2]

Like most Northerners, Craig was amazed at the amount of violence in postwar Texas. When a freedman, Jack Givens, murdered "some white man," Craig had Givens arrested and held in the county jail. Only quick military action prevented a mob from hanging the accused Negro. General Kiddoo had wanted to have Givens tried in the county court, but after the aborted lynching, he ordered the whole matter sent to Houston to be heard by the military commission. Kiddoo disgustedly said that Givens case demonstrated that civil authorities could not yet be trusted to act fairly towards blacks, a sentiment that Craig concurred in completely.[3]

In another incident, Craig discovered that a gang of citizens was committing unprovoked murder, while acting as a vigilante force in Washington County. When Craig sent a couple of mounted men to arrest one of the marauders, who was suspected in the killing of a black man, the gang waylaid the soldiers and beat them up. "This case calls for prompt and energetic action," Brevet Colonel William H. Sinclair wrote Craig, on General Kiddoo's instructions. "Instead of asking instructions, hereafter take immediate steps yourself." Craig dispatched a new, stronger force, which arrested several persons. One of the accused agreed to turn state's evidence for his own reprieve. Kiddoo agreed to drop all charges against the informant and told Craig to send the rest to Houston for trial before a military commission. The informer was shot down on the main street of Brenham before he could testify, but the trial went on without him, despite the protests of the state district court judge against holding a military trial.[4]

So far Craig's tenure at Brenham was pretty much as expected and could have occurred almost anywhere in the state. But in July, 1866, a new issue emerged that ultimately would differentiate Brenham from all other Texas towns staffed by a bureau officer and occupied by an army detachment. It all had begun innocently enough in February, before Craig made his appearance in Brenham. For his expanding program of bureau education, General Gregory had sent Mr. and Mrs. James G. Whann to Brenham to open a school for black children. With the assistance of the bureau agent who had preceded Craig, Lieutenant Arnold, the Whanns' educational efforts were quite fruitful.

Whann found that he had to pay much of the school expenses out of his own pocket, because the students' parents had little ready cash. Within a month the attendance had outgrown the room they had rented. Then the property was sold. Whann suspected that the sale concealed a plot to close the freedmen's school, because soon afterward he was given notice to leave, as the new owner wished to tear down the school building. He asked headquarters to help him raise the two hundred or so dollars he needed to purchase a new site and begin construction of a new church and school. Almost as an aside, Whann mentioned that Captain Craig insisted that the schoolmaster report to him as subassistant commissioner. Whann believed this to be an invasion of his independence and refused, maintaining that he had always reported directly to the bureau school superintendent, E. M. Wheelock. But Whann did agree to give Craig the names and number of his students.[5]

For the Fourth of July, Craig agreed to help the Whanns sponsor a picnic to raise money for the schoolhouse. The affair failed miserably as a fundraiser—Craig complained it cost him eleven-odd dollars—but everyone had a good time. As the function broke up, the freed people announced that they were going to parade through Brenham. Craig and the Whanns were uneasy about the idea, but they knew that the blacks had a right to march. Mrs. Whann warned them, however, to take care and not to be disorderly. Decked out in red, white, and blue, the Negroes, young and old alike, marched on Brenham.

As they paraded through the streets, the children began singing "Up with the Flag, and Down with the Traitor," and "We'll Hang Jeff Davis to a Sour Apple Tree." It was not as if the whites had never heard the songs sung before. But parading freed people on Independence Day signified the loss of the war to them, and the songs seemed designed to rub their faces in the ignominy of defeat. The next day, the Whanns received a letter warning them to take the first train to Houston. It was signed, "A Friend."[6]

The threatening letter was just the beginning. The local newspaper, *The Banner*, took up the fight in its editorial pages. Run by an unreconstructed rebel major, D. L. McGary, the *Banner* was characterized as a "Red Hot Democratic Journal," whose subscription rates were three dollars a year to loyal Southern whites (of the ex-Confederate type), and six dollars annually to "Yankees, Carpetbaggers, and Scalawags."

In a front-page article, McGary irresponsibly tore into the bureau and its school, and turned what might have been an isolated, soon-to-be-forgotten incident into a *cause célèbre*, through a campaign of ridicule. He claimed that the schoolmaster and his wife taught their students to spell the state's name *Texes*. McGary himself was holding out for *Taxes*, referring to the federal policy of collecting back taxes for the Union war effort. He laughed at the bureau's title, "Bureau of Refugees, Freedmen, and Abandoned Lands." The editor was curious as to its reason for existence in Brenham. "We are not a refugee—we are not a freedman," he puzzled in mock bewilderment. "Perhaps," he concluded triumphantly, "we may be an abandoned land."[7]

As McGary kept the white community in stitches with his humorous characterizations, Craig communicated to headquarters his own desire to see the Whanns leave. He may have disliked them for arguing with him over the local chain of command, or he might have wished to avoid a quarrel over what he saw as a trivial matter. But Kiddoo refused to consider Craig's request for transportation for Mr. and Mrs. Whann, their child, and their household effects. Through his adjutant general, Colonel Sinclair, the general ordered Craig to provide the Whanns with protection, and reminded the subassistant commissioner that the blacks had a right to sing Union songs and demonstrate in the public streets. Further, Sinclair told Craig to warn local newspaper editors that "anything pertaining to the school or to Mr. Whann or his wife of the nature heretofore published, or anything else which is untrue and calculated to do injury, will subject them to official action."[8]

Kiddoo would have done better to defer to Craig's desire to avoid a confrontation. Craig had already been kicked out of his office at the county courthouse. He had returned from a trip to Houston to find the bureau sign torn down and his books, papers, and personal effects out in the street. He was told that he could use the courtroom in a temporary capacity, but that his former office was needed by the county court, which had just been elected. Craig had been willing to move, but failed to understand the reason for the rudeness. Now he saw the campaign against himself and the Whanns as a result of the first postwar popular election, and something best put off by ignoring its petty aspects. Besides, a new teacher might cooperate with him as subassistant commissioner better than did Whann.[9]

Unfortunately, McGary did not back off, and Kiddoo knew about it. On August 8, the general ordered Craig to arrest the offending editor and fine him between one and five hundred dollars for his "persistent abuse" of the bureau teachers, and his "libelous and false" statements about the bureau collecting money from the freedmen under false pretenses (probably referring to the Independence Day fund-raising picnic). Craig asked the post commandant, Brevet Major George W. Smith, to help in the arrest of McGary. Smith refused, saying that he did not wish to become involved. Craig persisted, and Smith agreed to lend him a soldier or two, providing that Craig would make a written request and omit any reference as to how the men would be used. Craig did as he was asked. Then the subassistant commissioner returned to town with his detail, and called McGary in. Craig asked McGary to document his charges. McGary replied that they were common knowledge on the town streets. Craig disagreed and fined him two hundred dollars.

McGary told Craig that he did not have such an amount on him. The editor offered to pay the one hundred dollars he had in his pocket and forget the matter. Craig insisted on the whole amount, pointing out that Kiddoo really wanted five hundred. He allowed the editor to go out to fetch the money. Instead of doing so, McGary fled to the army camp for protection. Craig followed, and ordered Major Smith to arrest McGary. Smith said that since the case had now been brought to his official attention, he would take over and report the incident to General Wright for instructions. Meanwhile, he allowed McGary to go free. Craig complained to Kiddoo, who told him to make a new written request and document Smith's refusal. Kiddoo also appealed to General Wright to force Smith to cooperate with the bureau, as required by Wright's standing policy.[10]

Under Kiddoo's orders ("Do not back down!"), Craig re-arrested McGary and demanded payment of the fine. In a brilliant maneuver designed to endear him to his readers, McGary refused, and Craig threw him in the Brenham jail. Townspeople came by to visit the imprisoned editor, encourage him to hold on, and inform him that his case had been taken to Governor Throckmorton, who was writing President Johnson. Of course, McGary was guarded by the local authorities, who allowed the editor to promenade up and down the boardwalk in front of the jailhouse, joke with sympathetic passersby, and write more editorials for his newspaper from this new "American Bastille." Craig was understandably furious. Kiddoo told him to get tough. The subassistant commissioner considered arresting the jailer and deputy sheriff, but feared more and worse trouble. Craig said that the crowd had turned ugly enough as it was, and he had begun to receive the usual anonymous threats against his life. So he threw the jailer and deputy out of the jail and took over the guard duty himself, with McGary securely lodged in a cell in back.[11]

Meanwhile, Kiddoo asked Craig to send him detailed summaries of the whole matter, because Governor Throckmorton had written a "solemn protest" to President Johnson, as promised. Johnson communicated with Commissioner Howard, and told him to clear up the case. Howard wrote Throckmorton that Craig had overstepped his bounds, and that the bureau had no authority to censor newspapers, or to arrest and fine editors. Howard then telegraphed Kiddoo, instructing him to go to Austin and rectify the matter with the governor in person. Throckmorton was pleased beyond all expectations, and took the opportunity to write Kiddoo and refer to the hoped-for meeting. He also asked Kiddoo if he had heard of the president's new proclamation declaring the rebellion ended in Texas, and restoring civil processes. He thought that the case against McGary ought to be turned over to the civil courts.

A disgruntled Kiddoo could read between the lines. On September 3, he reluctantly ordered Captain Craig to release McGary. Kiddoo also praised the subassistant commissioner for his firm adherence to duty and told him to keep an eye on McGary's future conduct. Two days later, however, the general decided that he would have to replace Craig with another man, and ordered the subassistant commissioner to report to Galveston. Two days after that, before Craig had the opportunity to turn his office over to his replacement, a group of soldiers on leave in town got into a tussle with celebrating citizens, a fight that ended in the shooting of a couple of Major Smith's bluecoats. Later that same night, the entire business section of Brenham burned to the ground. Subsequent investigation laid the blame on Major Smith and his men, and suggested that the rest of the town was saved only by Craig's intervention. But the Brenham fire gave the Throckmorton administration another opportunity to rake the bureau and the army over the coals of public opinion. Kiddoo still refused to back down. On September 17, he gave Craig his highest recommendation for reappointment as a Veteran Reserve Corps officer, or to a regular army opening. And two days later he sent him to Seguin as the new subassistant commissioner there.[12]

As Craig left for Seguin, Kiddoo addressed the governor once again. Because of the fire, their planned meeting never took place. Instead, the assistant commissioner sent a firm letter that fully explained his position on the Brenham incident. In it, he said that he had refused to act in the McGary case as long as he could do so and still maintain self-respect, but that the editor had unnecessarily abused the bureau, its agents, and the army officers at Brenham. He took full responsibility for the arrest and the events that followed. He based his action on the military powers delegated to him by Congress in creating the bureau in 1865, and said he had freed McGary, not because he felt compelled to, but because he wished to hear from Washington on his powers under the new bureau act of July, 1866. Kiddoo declared that he had no desire to forestall the operation of civil law, except when necessary to protect the rights of a freedman. The assistant commissioner argued that if the men acting as bureau representatives did not have the right to protect themselves from the vulgar abuse that was heaped on them by McGary, then they clearly had no powers at all.

Kiddoo went on to note that he was aware that the state legislature was in the process of investigating his report of July, 1866, in which he had detailed the outrageous, lawless treatment of blacks in Texas. The general said that he had had no intention of making that report public, as his detractors accused him of doing. This had been done by others without his permission. But he defended the report as revealing only a portion of the magnitude of the problem. He chided the governor and the legislature to require the state courts to give the freed people their rights under state law. Then, Kiddoo said, he could retire and would willingly close down bureau operations in the state. But the governor was unwilling to shift his stance, either. He said that he hoped Kiddoo would investigate and punish the conduct of his officers when they meddled with the liberties of citizens, as Captain Craig had done. And there the matter stood. Neither official had heard or understood the other.[13]

While Kiddoo and Throckmorton exchanged missives, Captain Craig reported to the bureau agency in Seguin. His major problems in Guadalupe County revolved around his two predecessors, Judge Longworth and Lieutenant Moore. Longworth told Craig that he feared for his own safety, because of the actions he had committed while subassistant commissioner. Craig, under Kiddoo's orders, advised Longworth to return to Seguin from his Wilson County home, and face the possibility of arrest. He was to answer all charges with a reference to General Orders No. 3 from the Adjutant General's Office in Washington, as promulgated by General Orders No. 5 of the District of Texas. These measures protected Federal officials from state harassment while performing legally ordered duties, and the assistant commissioner affirmed that Longworth was so acting under General Gregory's appointment as confirmed by Kiddoo. The general also ordered Craig to take personal charge of Longworth's safety, and to request the army to assist him in this task.[14]

Initially, the army refused to cooperate. Brevet Major General Samuel P. Heintzelman, in command at San Antonio, wanted confirmation from his superior, Brevet Major General George W. Getty, the new commandant of the District of Texas, who had just replaced the mustered-out General Wright. Kiddoo knew that a delay could place Longworth and Craig at great legal disadvantage or even in physical danger. "I most respectfully req[uest] *insist* that he [Longworth] receive such protection," Kiddoo demanded. Getty stepped in at once to order Heintzelman to exempt Longworth from any arrest, cancel all of his bonds, return the money to its subscribers, and halt any further prosecution. Craig used this order and the soldiers who accompanied it to prevent further prosecution.[15]

As soon as he had settled the Longworth case, Craig turned to the problem of Longworth's immediate successor, Lieutenant Moore. Moore was under indictment for illegal gambling. He had managed to post bond, so he was not incarcerated. After a few weeks, Craig told of how Moore through some unspecified trick had had his bond money returned to the subscribers. Then he secretly shipped his trunk to Galveston, met the night stage on the road outside town, and made his escape *"clandestinely."* It was well that he moved so quietly. Two men were watching the stage stop to prevent just such a ruse. "He took your slippers (with the posies on) with him," Craig wrote his friend at headquarters, William H. Sinclair. "I hope they will arrive safe[ly]." Craig also said that he and Dr. D. C. Marsh, a local Unionist, had managed by "sharp practice" to intercept Moore's last paycheck for $143. Moore owed money to many people in town whom Craig now endeavored to pay. When Craig visited Longworth, who was residing at Electo in Karnes County, the former agent filed charges for the area's freedmen, whom Moore had bilked like everyone else.[16]

Longworth still was worried and angry about his prosecution. The papers of the case were still in the hands of the Seguin court. "Am I to be annihilated by slow torture, or have I and others in my position no protection from against the Rebel vultures who under the shadow of law are trampling down all law?" he asked. If Longworth had to be tried by a rebel jury for his actions while subassistant commissioner, "then indeed it would have been better for me I had never been born." But he need not have worried. Craig knew how he felt and, if he would not permit a despicable character like Moore to be tried in what he called the "uncivil" courts, he would surely protect Longworth. Indeed, Craig had already acted. He entered the Guadalupe County courthouse, arrested the clerk of court, and "abstracted" the relevant papers in both Moore's and Longworth's cases.[17]

Craig acted under Heintzelman's orders from San Antonio. The old general knew that protection under General Orders No. 3 would soon cease to exist, and Longworth would face trial anew. So he had Craig destroy all the evidence. When he heard the news, Throckmorton blew up. He wrote an angry letter to Kiddoo, demanding to know under whose orders and by what authority Craig had acted. He also complained to General Sheridan in New Orleans, concluding that the new incident involving Captain Craig was "beyond my comprehension."[18]

Craig meanwhile felt a sudden desire to retire, having grown rich by speculating in oil stocks back in Pennsylvania. He wrote a lengthy letter to his friend Sinclair, and vented his feelings. Craig said that he, like Sinclair, was disgusted to see Throckmorton victorious in so many issues or, as he put it, "the country gone to the *devil!*" He cheered "the glorious *radical* Republican party, which fought and whipped Rebels and traitorous copperheads in the beastly battles of this late, miserable war, and again have manhood and pluck to stand up to them and whip them in peace at the ballot box. Bully for the *Rads!*" But with the stock sale, Craig said that he felt like the little boy who stands to one side with a finger in his mouth and a tear in his eye and says, "Oh say, fellers, *I want to go home!*"

He asked Sinclair if he was to be mustered out soon. "Is it possible Gen'l K will succeed in getting me recommissioned and that I shall have to remain in the Booro or resign?" Craig continued. "I am sick and I want to go home. Or to some other seaport anywhere, even to Brenham!" Tongue in cheek, he denied having "oil or some other stimulant on my brain" as he wrote, "but—my night and morning prayer is for muster out." If Kiddoo believed that Craig's actions were embarrassing to his position as assistant commissioner, Craig would back off as much as possible. He wished to bring the freedmen justice, but he said he was willing to be as conciliatory about it as he could. Craig thought that the white citizens of Seguin had finally "succumbed" to his audacious burning of the court records. But they had had to take it with "a wholesome dash of brown sugar(!)," in the form of the mili-

tary force provided by the San Antonio garrison. He chortled cyni-
cally at the thought: "Chuck a cha chuck a cha lunk chalevy!! hi
chuck & c."[19]

Kiddoo was sorry to hear of Craig's desire to leave the service, although he granted the wish, and spoke highly of the captain to Commissioner Howard. But Craig was not out of Texas yet. The district
judge for the area that included Guadalupe County, John Ireland, was
furious that a Federal officer could invade his courthouse, collar his
clerk, and remove and destroy legal records. He ordered a warrant to
be served upon Craig. But the county sheriff dared not move so long
as the platoon of soldiers from San Antonio was in Seguin. The question was whether Kiddoo would replace Craig before the commandant
at San Antonio recalled his men. The troops left first, in early December, 1866. Judge Ireland happened to be in town and saw Craig walking
down the street as the cavalry clattered off on the San Antonio road.
"What!" he bellowed, "Isn't that God damn Yankee thief arrested, yet?"
or "Why isn't that God damn Yankee thief in jail?" (Witnesses differed
in their recollections.) The sheriff arrested Craig immediately, and
lodged him in the county jail, a filthy structure without any heat for
the cold December nights.[20]

Although incarcerated, Craig had friends who managed to transmit
a plea for help to Brevet Brigadier General John Hatch, commander
of the Fourth Cavalry at San Antonio. Hatch sent a lieutenant and
forty-five men back to free Craig. The cavalry galloped into town, surrounded the jail and "suggested" that the sheriff let his prisoner go.
Fortunately, with Judge Ireland away on circuit at Bastrop, the civil
authorities declined a confrontation and released Craig.[21] Governor
Throckmorton did not like it, but by the time he found out, Craig
was out of Texas.[22]

An angry Judge Ireland tried to have General Heintzelman arrested
for ordering the interference, but the gruff old soldier refused to honor
the state warrant. Assisted by the Federal district attorney for eastern
Texas, Unionist David G. Baldwin, Heintzelman cleverly argued his
case using the rationale presented in the prewar case *Ableman v. Booth*—
that the individual states had lost their inherent sovereignty once they
joined the Union.[23] No one regretted Craig's departure more than
William Longworth. "One more meeting between me and Capt. C.
would have left us friends for life," he stated in his epitaph on the affair. "He was beginning to have his eyes opened as to me and my official action."[24]

At the same time Kiddoo was concerned with events at Brenham and Seguin, he had his hands full with the actions of his subassistant commissioner at Houston. Although there had been nothing wrong with the officers who had succeeded Colonel Jacob C. De Gress, General Gregory had known that he needed an extraordinary agent at Houston, and he had asked that De Gress be sent back there as one of the first civilians hired under the second bureau act passed in July, 1866. Ordered by Commissioner Howard to report to Texas, De Gress had proceeded from his Missouri home after a twenty-day leave. By now, Gregory had left for Maryland, and Kiddoo was in charge at Galveston, but he concurred with Gregory's plans for De Gress. Kiddoo sent the reinstated subassistant commissioner off to Houston.[25]

The arrival of De Gress at the height of the picking season signaled a change for the worse for those Houstonians who had had the temerity to think that the relatively mild-mannered interim administrations were tyrannical and unfair. Unlike his predecessors, De Gress cared little about any change in policy as represented by General Orders No. 26. He knew only one way to react to "rebel" actions that threatened to cheat the Negroes—confiscation of the crop. The subassistant commissioner reported that nothing had changed in his absence. Negroes were still being defrauded of the proceeds of their year's work. Planters shipped the crops to market without paying their hands, and those who complained were beaten. When freedmen flocked into Houston to complain to De Gress in person, the local authorities arrested them for vagrancy and put them to work on city public improvement projects.

De Gress found that the cleverer planters had rented their lands to managers, who paid an advance, then collected their costs by cheating the blacks and fleeing the state. Payoffs to Galveston and Houston merchants led to the identifying marks on the bales being changed surreptitiously. Then there was nothing for the bureau to seize. De Gress cooperated with subassistant commissioners from the north and west to intercept all crops not bearing a bureau authorization that the laborers who produced them had been fairly and fully paid.[26]

The planters screamed, the railroad and steamship companies tried unsuccessfully to ignore De Gress's orders, and the commission merchants at Galveston complained that they were going broke. But De Gress bulled ahead with his policies. "I am cursed and abused . . . (not to my face I can assure you)," he told Kiddoo, "and all I can say is, I am proud to have their ill will." Because so little cotton passed Houston, there seems to be some justification in De Gress's suspicion that the planters, carriers, and merchants in the interior were overlooking the proper procedures. But his stubbornness paid off. Within weeks, De Gress proudly announced that new shipments had the proper documents indicating that the Negroes were getting paid, at last.[27]

Operating in cooperation with De Gress was Captain Samuel Sloan of the 116th USCI. Sloan had come to Texas shortly after New Year's Day in 1866, and had been assigned to the agency at Richmond. His policy as subassistant commissioner was to ignore the "technical" aspects of the 1865 documents and settle on the basis of equity for all. He complained about the vagueness resulting from Gregory's insistence on not setting district boundaries. He had approved a contract of a freedman with one planter, only to discover later that the black had already obtained another contract for another plantation from another agent nearby. The planters were amazed at the progress of the free labor system, Sloan said, and many clamored for him to come and address their hands. Sloan settled seventy disagreements between whites and blacks by force of personality alone, never assessing a fine.

Several planters, however, accused him of demanding payoffs and corrupting the labor process. Kiddoo sent his aide, Brevet Colonel J. B. Kinsman, to investigate. Kinsman cleared Sloan of all charges. Kiddoo liked Sloan's ability and sent him to Millican to clean up the situation left by William H. Farner.[28] Making his office at the army's post headquarters in Millican, Sloan found the amount of business there to be staggering. His main task was to assure that the freedmen received fair value for their year's labor. In this, he cooperated with De Gress in Houston in seizing crops suspected to have been shipped without proper releases from the nearest subassistant commissioner. When the planters found that they could not avoid a bureau audit, one of them accused Sloan of fraud and forged the captain's name to certain compromising legal papers. Griffin sent Inspector William H. Sinclair to look into the accusations. Initially "firmly convinced that Captain Sloan was a rascal" who had foiled Colonel Kinsman's earlier investigation, Sinclair completely exonerated Sloan, and all charges against him were dropped. Vindication mattered little in the long run, however, because Sloan soon would be mustered out of the service.[29]

Sinclair was soon off to central Texas and the upper Brazos River region on another tour, which would result in a document of great importance to the bureau's future management, Kiddoo's Circular Letter of December 31, 1866. Sinclair traveled by rail during the height of the cotton-shipping season. In his first letter to Kiddoo, Sinclair praised De Gress and Sloan for allowing the passage of cotton only after the freedmen had been paid. He called them the two most important agents in the field at this time of year.

A few days later, however, Sinclair had second thoughts. He told Kiddoo that De Gress and Sloan had clogged up the whole shipping process with their insistence on certificates of shipment approval. Sinclair understood Kiddoo's policy to be that all cotton was to pass forward unless it had been specifically challenged by the freedmen for lack of satisfactory payment. If Kiddoo preferred the methods of De Gress and Sloan, he said, General Kiddoo needed to inform the public of the need for a certificate of payment to the freedmen before shipment. He suggested that local subassistant commissioners hand these out, since De Gress and Sloan could not cope with the volume of cotton traffic facing them. He especially disagreed with De Gress's halting all rail traffic in cotton.[30]

Kiddoo issued the orders that Sinclair desired shortly afterward. He told De Gress and Sloan to modify his previous orders and allow all products to come to Galveston. They were to inform headquarters of any suspect crops that had eluded the proper payments, so that the produce might be seized at Gulf ports. De Gress denied that he or Sloan had ever stopped any goods in a wholesale manner. But he warned Kiddoo that planters "will move heaven and earth" to avoid paying their freedmen, and sent bureau surgeon Thomas Baird to explain his and Sloan's policy further. Through Baird, De Gress also requested and received permission to hire two extra clerks to handle the increased business at the Houston bureau office.[31]

De Gress also complained to Kiddoo that General Heintzelman had told him that he had to operate under the restrictions of General Orders No. 26, and that such limitations would hurt his ability to protect freedmen. Confirming Heintzelman's assessment, Kiddoo's office warned the Houston subassistant commissioner not to interfere with the state's criminal court system. But the warning came too late: De Gress already had under his protection a freedman named Dick Perkins (also referred to as Richard Harris in some communications), whom he refused to turn over to the state legal authorities. It seems that Perkins had been shot by his employer in an argument. The injured freedman ran into the woods, only to be arrested four days later and charged with assault upon the white man. Perkins's wound went unattended for six weeks as he languished in the Grimes County jail. Finally, he managed to escape and flee to the Hempstead bureau office. The Hempstead bureau agent sent Perkins to De Gress for safety, and the civil authorities now wanted him back.

De Gress told the Houston city marshal that the case was a bureau matter under War Department regulations, General Orders No. 26 notwithstanding. The subassistant commissioner refused to turn Perkins over either to his employer or to the Grimes County courts. With the assistance of his chief medical officer, De Gress had Perkins admitted to the Houston Freedmen's Hospital and placed under a military guard of a sergeant and ten men. De Gress suggested that headquarters allow Perkins to have his wound treated and then arrange to have his case transferred to the Federal courts under the Civil Rights Act of 1866. In the meantime, the subassistant commissioner would refuse all writs and orders not endorsed beforehand by headquarters. Influenced by the personal appearances of De Gress's assistant and his chief medical officer at headquarters to explain the intricacies of the case, Kiddoo approved of De Gress's actions, and sent the matter up the chain of command.[32]

In his answer to Kiddoo's request, Secretary of War Edwin McM. Stanton did order the Perkins case transferred to the Federal courts under the Civil Rights Act of 1866, but De Gress still feared that the influence of Governor Throckmorton might negate any Federal action. The governor had written to the army high command and to President Johnson in an effort to obtain state control of the matter. To checkmate the governor's efforts, De Gress helped Perkins "disappear," which further raised Throckmorton's ire. The furor caused by De Gress's conduct forced Kiddoo to relieve the controversial subassistant commissioner on the last day of the year. De Gress was replaced by a military officer, one who would follow orders to the letter without taking individual initiative.[33]

Upon his return to Galveston, Sinclair anguished over the bureau representatives and their operations in the field as typified by the events of the summer and fall of 1866. Basically he thought the subassistant commissioners to be ill prepared; poorly provided with offices, regulations, and materials; and helpless without the presence of Federal troops. He admitted that since the issuance of General Orders No. 26, the army could do little to assist the bureau, now that the local courts were to be used. But Sinclair thought the civil authorities to be unfair in their treatment of freedmen, who were often arrested without a warrant or charge and sent to prison on a whim. He was especially against the bureau's use of Southern men or Northerners who did cotton business as subassistant commissioners. He thought that the operations of the local agents needed to be clarified and harmonized, and proceeded to suggest how this could be accomplished.[34]

Because the new contract season was about to begin for the year 1867, Sinclair felt that agents in the field needed fuller guidance from headquarters in order to draw up complete documents that left nothing to be "understood" that might be used to the freedmen's disadvantage at settlement time, as had happened in the past. His proposals led to General Kiddoo's Circular Orders No. 25, a call for agents to regulate contracts closely for fairness, but which, unfortunately, lacked Sinclair's desired thoroughness.

The inspector had suggested that all labor contracts should provide for whether the employees were to work on Saturday, and if so should limit the labor to a half day; state when the contract was to terminate, at the conclusion of picking or the end of the year; detail the separate division and storage of corn and other foodstuffs; note whether fences were to be repaired, which fences, and the approximate number of rails to be split; state any medical attention to be provided; specify if there were to be an overseer and how he would be selected; list the crop, land, and tools provided; state who was to pay for animals that died or were injured, and tools that were broken; specify the quantity and quality of rations and quarters; allow a specific deduction for laziness, which Sinclair thought was essential to give planters a way to compel hands to work; state the number of hours of labor per day and whether women and children were to work; note how wages were to be paid (specie or paper); specify the percentage division of the crop, who was to divide it, when it was to be divided (before or after sale), who provided the bagging, and who would provide the ginning, which Sinclair saw as essential to a peaceful settlement time; and state the amount and quality of any clothing provided.[35]

Sinclair also believed that each agent should be required to make out a monthly report that listed his hours of work, the content of his job that month, the hours he was absent from his office and why, the complaints that he received, which complaints he adjudicated and which went to the civil and criminal courts, the action taken in courts on any case involving a freed person, all murders and assaults involving freedmen, the feelings of loyalty of local whites, the treatment of freedmen locally, and the progress of black education in the subdistrict. Sinclair said that subassistant commissioners tended to be too cozy with planters to the exclusion of the blacks, and that all agents needed private transportation so they would not be beholden to the planter who provided conveyance before they even got out to his place to set-tle differences between management and labor. He believed that Texas was short of labor, in general, and that this gave the bureau much leverage to act on the freedmen's behalf. On December 31, 1866, Kid-doo issued a circular letter that placed Sinclair's recommendations in force, although agents never received independent transportation on a regular basis.[36]

As Kiddoo sought to regularize the operations of the various field agents, a series of events took place in the army command during the fall of 1866 that led to the end of his sojourn in Texas. Initially these events revolved around the muster-out of General Wright, the army's District of Texas commander. Wright lost his brevet generalship, re-verted to his old regular army rank of lieutenant colonel of engineers, and went East for assignment. The result was a confusion in the army high command that was to last until the beginning of the new year and adversely affected Kiddoo's position with the Freedmen's Bureau in the long run. As Wright left Texas, his departure aroused the army's traditional jealousy over rank. No one seemed sure who was now the ranking officer in Texas. Brevet Major General Getty had the oldest brevet assignment, and he announced his takeover at the end of Sep-tember. But Getty was located at Brownsville, where he had run the subdistrict of the Rio Grande. He was also in poor health from im-properly healed war wounds.

Kiddoo immediately saw that such confusion could hurt the army's ability to provide the support needed by the bureau field agents and Texas blacks. He stressed that the army needed to command the state from the same town as the bureau, Galveston, to facilitate cooperation on troop matters. In Getty's absence, he offered to run both commands temporarily. Kiddoo probably did not intend it, but such a suggestion was sure to offend the fuddy-duddies in the army high command, for the bureau was a poor stepchild of the War Department. Major Gen-eral Sheridan, in New Orleans, promised Kiddoo that Getty would show up in Galveston in a few days, and asked him to hold off.[37]

Getty never lived up to Sheridan's expectations; his illness instead forced him to decline any command position. Sheridan, in Texas to investigate the Brenham fire, took immediate action. He allowed the still-unfilled army district post to devolve upon the next ranking offi-cer, Brevet Major General Samuel P. Heintzelman. The oldest colonel in the army, Heintzelman was not energetic enough to suit someone of Sheridan's volatile temperament, so secretly he asked the War Department to send Brevet Major General Charles Griffin to Texas. Griffin was a young, enthusiastic officer whom Sheridan had relied on before as a troubleshooter. His brevet rank predated the older man's, which would put him in command upon his arrival in Texas. Kiddoo seemed unaware of the workings of Sheridan's mind at this time.[38]

Because he was serving on a military board, Heintzelman did not arrive in Galveston from San Antonio until October 23. By then, Texas had been without a commanding officer for a month and a half. It was the middle of the picking season, agents needed military escorts, no one had the power to assign them, and the state legislature was passing the Black Codes. Kiddoo was scheduled to leave the state on November 1, to attend the examination board hearings in Chicago for officers for the new black regiments of the regular army. He had recently been promised a permanent lieutenant colonelcy in the Forty-third Colored Infantry. He also wanted to have his back wound re-examined and go on to Washington to consult personally with Commissioner Howard. Realizing the danger of leaving Texas without an assistant commissioner at this moment, he asked that his appearance be delayed at least one month. Howard gave him one week. By November 4, Kiddoo was on his way.[39]

No sooner had Kiddoo left Galveston than the bureau staff unraveled, finally feeling the effects of the shakeup in the army's Texas command. It was not an unexpected occurrence, and Kiddoo had warned his retinue that it might happen. Kiddoo had left behind as his acting assistant commissioner Brevet Lieutenant Colonel Henry A. Ellis. Normally a staff officer in the Seventeenth Infantry, headquartered in Galveston, Ellis had been on detached duty as the bureau's acting assistant adjutant general since September. Now, General Heintzelman informed Ellis that he wished to replace him and Kiddoo's entire bureau staff with individuals of his own choosing.[40]

Heintzelman's action was way out of line, as Kiddoo and Ellis correctly maintained. It was up to Commissioner Howard to replace Ellis, and up to Howard's appointee to select the local staff. Further, there was no good reason to replace Ellis, since no one had accused him of any wrongdoing in office. Ellis refused to accept Heintzelman's communications on the matter, which forced the general to use another approach. Heintzelman happened to be colonel of the Seventeenth Infantry as well as commander of the District of Texas. As Ellis's colonel, he directly commanded Ellis in regimental matters, although Ellis was independent in bureau operations. So Heintzelman ordered Ellis to report to the regiment for orders.[41]

As Kiddoo discovered, the general was able to do this because the War Department was reorganizing the three battalions of the Seventeenth Infantry under congressional mandate into three new and separate regiments. In Texas, the Seventeenth Infantry became the new Seventeenth Regiment (First Battalion) under Heintzelman headquartered at Galveston, the Twenty-sixth infantry (Second Battalion) under Brevet Major General Joseph J. Reynolds at Austin, and the Thirty-fifth Regiment (Third Battalion) under Brevet Major General Charles Griffin at San Antonio. Ellis had been assigned to the Third Battalion, and Heintzelman ordered him to report to his new regimental headquarters for reassignment. Ellis had to obey.[42]

Then, as Kiddoo learned, Heintzelman ordered Brevet Major General Abner Doubleday to head the Freedmen's Bureau in Texas. Doubleday refused to become involved. So Heintzelman made his brother-in-law, Major Solon H. Lathrop (also a Thirty-fifth Infantry officer, but one who had not been sent to San Antonio), the bureau's acting assistant commissioner. As Ellis put it, the entire matter was "unwarranted, not to say rediculous." It was worse than that. It later developed that the situation had been instigated by Lathrop's wife (Heintzelman's sister), who wanted to exile her greatest feminine enemy, Ellis's wife, from her social circles in Galveston. All that remained was for Ellis to fire a futile parting shot at Heintzelman. "I might remark, *en passant*, that the workings of this Bureau have been seriously embarrassed, . . . and it will require the utmost care and attention to prevent its complete demoralization in this state." He surrendered the office on December 11, despite Kiddoo's plea to hold on until he could get back to Galveston.[43]

To complicate matters, Kiddoo later found out that Brevet Major General Charles Griffin had been made the new officer in charge of the army's District of Texas, replacing Heintzelman, the move Sheridan had wanted all along. But Griffin and Sheridan were currently making a tour of the Rio Grande area, which left Heintzelman still in possession of the Galveston office. It is uncertain if Sheridan or Griffin fully understood what had happened to the Texas bureau command, although both seemed to support Kiddoo. But it may be that none of it mattered, because they had other ideas in mind for the Texas bureau in the coming year.[44]

Meanwhile, Kiddoo had proceeded to Chicago and passed his board examination for the lieutenant colonelcy of the Forty-third Colored

Regiment. While there he had doctors reexamine his wound, which was discharging much pus and refusing to heal. The physicians made an incision to enlarge the outer opening, rasped out the crusty duct left by the bullet path, and removed several pieces of dead bone. Next they flushed the canal with a "dilute solution of carbolic acid" and had Kiddoo lie down for several days in such a position as to drain the wound easily. After some recovery he proceeded to Washington, conferred with Howard, and returned to Texas on December 19. Although Kiddoo had planned to ride the rails most of the way to Texas, his wound was still sore and the "jostling of the cars" caused him to change to a steamboat at Cairo, Illinois.[45]

Upon his arrival back in Texas, Kiddoo was pleased to hear of the departure of Heintzelman, who had withdrawn to Pennsylvania, where he complained unsuccessfully to his friends in Congress about his treatment by Sheridan. The returned assistant commissioner moved immediately to get rid of Lathrop, whom he considered a thorn in his side. Lathrop had asked Howard to nullify Kiddoo's Circular Letter of November 22, which, he said, prevented subassistant commissioners from approving any labor contracts. Lathrop said he thought blacks should be able to make any form of contract they pleased, so long as the bureau could annul the objectionable ones later.[46]

Kiddoo scoffed at Lathrop's interpretation of his letter, which had only temporarily halted the contract process in the wake of the passage of the Black Codes. He said that the major had communicated with Howard while intoxicated. Then Kiddoo took the opportunity to nullify the circular letter himself and establish his own new rules of conduct for contracting in 1867. With Griffin still on the Rio Grande, Lathrop used Ellis's old tactics for a couple of weeks and refused to turn over bureau property to Kiddoo's reassigned staff. Griffin's coming to Galveston ended the tomfoolery. Although Kiddoo never did receive the final report he asked Lathrop for, the major was back with his regiment in San Antonio for the new year. There his new commanding officer, Brevet Brigadier John S. Mason, a personal friend of Griffin, shipped him off to Victoria, where he died of yellow fever later that summer. Mason told Griffin that the post life had improved much after the "Lathrop Company" left. "Somehow he has the facility of making a great many enemies amongst officers," Mason concluded, astutely leaving out any mention of the querulous role of Mrs. Lathrop in all of this.[47]

Back in Galveston, Kiddoo soon discovered that he had new problems. He complained to Howard that Griffin's acting assistant adjutant general was asking for reports and sending notices as if Kiddoo were under Griffin's direct command. "I have never had any such trouble, or received such discourtesy before," puzzled Kiddoo. "Gens. Wright and Getty both . . . fully recognized that the Head Quarters of the Bureau was . . . not subordinate." Even Sheridan treated him as an independent officer, said Kiddoo. Griffin's adjutant avowed that he had verbal orders from the commander to exercise control over the Texas bureau. "It would be a complete compromise of the dignity of the Bureau to place the Assistant Commissioner of any state in any such subordination," concluded Kiddoo.[48]

A few weeks later, Kiddoo received a letter from Howard that confirmed Griffin's appointment as assistant commissioner for the Freedmen's Bureau in Texas. Howard's policy of combining the bureau and army commands "to secure prompt and efficient administration" had been announced earlier in August, 1866, but the shakeup in the army's Texas command had prevented its implementation until now. Howard offered Kiddoo the position as chief bureau officer under Griffin's command, as had been done in other states. The day after Griffin announced his assumption of the assistant commissionership, an obviously abashed Kiddoo turned down Howard's offer and asked to be relieved, since his services appeared "no longer necessary." His only expressed regret was that he had not yet solidly established the free school system. He was out of the state by the first week in February, on his way to the Great Lakes to join the Forty-third Colored Infantry as its lieutenant colonel.[49]

Joseph B. Kiddoo did not leave Texas unappreciated. The Galveston *Daily News*, which had vilified Gregory, praised the departing state bureau chief. "That he is a Radical we will not attempt to deny, but the peculiarity about him is that he is an unprejudiced one," said the paper. "Personally, our relations with him have been most agreeable. General Kiddoo had managed the Bureau rather satisfactorily," concluded the Democratic sheet, "which we think is more than can be said of any other of the heads of the Bureau." No matter his faults in promoting the independent bureau court system, supporting the hated black school program, attacking antiblack violence, or negating the state labor laws, to Texans of influence Kiddoo would always be the "unprejudiced" Yankee who created Circular No. 14 and put the Negroes back in the fields, working, where the whites thought they belonged.[50]

PART THREE

Counterattack: The Griffin Era, January–September, 1867

*I should as soon [have] looked to the English crown
to leave the establishment of peace in Ireland to Finians
as to see our Nation leave the reconstruction of the Southern states
to those that tried to destroy the government.*

—Brevet Major General Charles Griffin to Brevet Major General O. O. Howard,
June 17, 1867

7
Forming a New Order

K IDDOO'S SUCCESSOR as assistant commissioner of the Freedmen's Bureau in Texas was Brevet Major General Charles Griffin. A close friend of General Phil Sheridan, the army's departmental commander at New Orleans, who had specifically requested his presence in Texas, Griffin represented a new approach to the issue of the place of the freedman in Southern society. Unlike his predecessors, he held charge of the army and bureau commands simultaneously. This was a cost-saving measure adopted by Howard, which at the same time was designed "to secure prompt and efficient administration" of the state's Reconstruction. Although the commissioner denied that the move reflected any "misdeeds" of the previous state assistant commissioners, one suspects that the turbulent events that had occurred in Texas since the installation of the Throckmorton administration confirmed any doubts that Howard may have had about the feasibility of his officials in that state working independently, yet cooperatively, outside the army's command structure.[1]

Griffin arrived in Texas in December, 1866, ostensibly to take command of the Thirty-fifth U.S. Infantry, headquartered at San Antonio. As Griffin's history showed, Sheridan's confidence in his ability to clear up the myriad problems facing the two Texas commands was not misplaced. Graduated from West Point at the end of the Mexican War, Griffin spent the 1850s in New Mexico Territory. In 1860, as the Civil War threatened, Griffin received an assignment as instructor of artillery at the military academy. There he organized the "West Point Battery," which was designated Light Battery D, Fifth Artillery, and led the unit in the Battle of First Manassas, where it was overrun by rebel infantry after a heroic stand. Escaping capture, Griffin spent the winter in Washington, reorganizing his battery, and courting and marrying Sallie Carroll, a daughter of the famous Maryland family.

Griffin transferred to the infantry in 1862, where the rapid expansion of the army promised a young officer quick promotions. He participated in every campaign with the eastern armies, and rapidly rose to brigade and division command. His spectacular attack at Five Forks won him a battlefield promotion from an admiring Sheridan to command the famous V Corps of the Army of the Potomac. Less than a week later, his men received the formal surrender of General Robert E. Lee's army at Appomattox. After the war, he served briefly in the Military District of Maine. In the army reorganization of 1866, Griffin received the colonelcy of the Thirty-fifth Regiment, then stationed in Texas. Sheridan, however, fed up with the situation existing in Texas, assigned Griffin to serve in his brevet rank as departmental commander.[2]

After the gregarious, cooperative Kiddoo, Griffin brought a new and rancorous spirit to the Texas command. A ramrod-stiff professional man of great ability, Griffin had a basically humorless outlook on life. He was described as an "arrogant, self-confident" man, "often perilously close to insubordinate," one who was "quick to resent insult, fancied or real," and whose overall temperament was "volatile and arbitrary," causing him to be "bluff, bellicose, outspoken, and quick to take offense." Although Griffin rarely attacked those serving under him, and was loved by his men, his temper and lack of tact got him into frequent trouble with his superiors, who were the targets of his sharp tongue. The one exception to this rule was Sheridan, whom he respected and usually agreed with, and who was of a very similar personality.[3]

Griffin knew that his first job was to defuse Governor Throckmorton's assault against military rule by asserting full control over army and bureau field operatives, thereby freeing Sheridan from the onerous chore of having to visit Texas every six weeks to clean up after his previously ineffectual Federal administrators there. Griffin also realized that his operations must be within the limits set by General Orders No. 26, which recognized the elected civil administrations in the Southern states. To accomplish his task, Griffin decided to let the now-departed Kiddoo take the blame for all of the civil-military problems Texas had suffered. In his General Orders No. 5, issued on February 5, Griffin repealed Kiddoo's whole program, including Circular No. 14 (the ban on enticement), Circular No. 17 (subassistant commissioners to enforce the enticement ban), Circular No. 23 (bureau representatives to certify freedmen fairly paid), Circular No. 25 (contract guidelines), General Orders No. 2 (bureau agents to disregard the state labor law), and General Orders No. 4 (reissuing the no-enticement rules). Put another way, Griffin was going to follow much of the system set up in the state labor law that Kiddoo had annulled.[4]

"Having seen the antagonistical spirit of [Kiddoo's policies, and] since the labor act of this state is made to apply without distinction of color, I have formed a new order," Griffin explained. The plan his administration would follow was set forth in his General Orders No. 4. According to the assistant commissioner, all laborers were free to negotiate for the best wage terms available on the open market. Contracts were to be drawn up for the usual one-year terms. But, Griffin said, the contracts could be approved and recorded by any bureau agent, county judge, county clerk, notary public, justice of the peace, or anyone who applied to and received permission from the headquarters of the Texas Freedmen's Bureau to endorse contracts. In all cases the bureau and its representatives reserved the right to challenge unfair or illegal documents. Griffin warned that the bureau was still interested in the rights of the employee and the employer, but asserted that he wished to restore a "natural sense" of free labor to Texas in accordance with justice and normal commercial usage.[5]

One copy of each contract, continued Griffin, would be filed with the local subassistant commissioner, and one copy with the county clerk under the provisions of the Texas labor laws. In any civil dispute, Griffin went on, the bureau agents were to refer the matter to the correct branch of the state courts. Bureau agents should act as legal advisers to freedmen involved, and they could overrule any unfair decision in an emergency. But generally, Griffin wanted any case the agents disagreed with referred to headquarters for review. In all instances, however, Griffin said that the state courts were to be given a chance to act first. This included criminal cases, too. The subassistant commissioners were not to interfere with the operations of any state law so long as it was applied equally and fairly to both races.[6] Griffin did insist that the agents in the field enforce any liens of the 1866 crop on the freedmen's behalf apart from this order.[7]

The new assistant commissioner did not deny that freedmen had suffered many wrongs in prior labor settlements. On the other hand, he believed that the freedmen's "happiness" depended upon the contract process, and he urged his subassistant commissioners to visit freedmen and tell them that, and to urge the laborers to contract only with responsible planters for a share of the crop, as opposed to wages. When Griffin ascertained that the provisions of his edicts were not being fully complied with, he ordered his agents in the field to check up on the contract process. The bureau representatives were not to "disarrange" the labor dispositions in their districts. Rather, said Griffin, they were to use tact and judgment to obtain contracts for all hands,

and to address the blacks concerning the value of adhering to contracts, and laboring industriously. If necessary, Griffin instructed, the
subassistant commissioners could use arrest and force to compel obedience with bureau orders.[8]

Howls of disgust at Griffin's course of action went up from all over
the nation. The New York *Tribune* complained, "The [Texas] Bureau
is virtually withdrawn from all control over the freedmen's interests.
. . . Of course," the paper added hopefully, "its abdicated powers may
be resumed at pleasure." Commissioner Howard sent the *Tribune* article to Griffin with a query as to what was going on in Texas. Griffin
replied that the reason he had issued his orders was that the subassistant commissioners were constantly colliding with the civil authority
to the detriment of the Federal government's ability to enforce its desires, and the national administration was continually losing face. Griffin
believed that the independent stance allowed the bureau field agents
by his predecessors permitted them to act without the judgment and
finesse necessary to deal effectively with the state government.

Previous decisions of the bureau courts, continued Griffin, had been
made on the basis of the subassistant commissioners' likes and dislikes
without regard to law. The army could not provide agents with the
necessary and proper protection for those freedmen and loyalists who
complained, and they were suffering for giving their information to
Federal authorities. Griffin claimed that he was acceding to the use
of the state courts first in all cases because the army had to do so under
General Orders No. 26. He admitted that the state bodies might not
do justice to the freedmen. Then any decision a subassistant commissioner rendered in the absence of correct state action could be enforced
easily by the army. By having to back up only those agents who needed
it, Griffin believed that the army would no longer be overextended,
its influence would increase, and a new respect for its authority would
follow, which would better protect loyal whites and blacks alike.[9]

Griffin was not insensitive to the criticisms leveled against him. He
wrote Howard to say that he realized that the freedmen had not been
paid their wages for 1865 and had been cheated in 1866. But he promised the commissioner that laborers were to be dealt with fairly in 1867
under his administration. Griffin suggested that the problem be approached on two fronts. First, he proposed that the employer's charges
and accounts not be a lien on the freedmen's portion of the crop. Next,
he suggested that a commission merchant be approved and bonded
to handle the crops of all freedmen at a fair price. Griffin said that

this agent would not have sole right to the crops marketed by Negroes, but would be able to set a fair price standard below which others would not dare to fall, at peril of losing business. Too often, Griffin lamented, the corner store and the planter were in league or the same individual. Griffin thought that his plan would finally help free the blacks from slavery by law or economics.[10]

Howard replied that he had no objection to the no-lien proposal, but that he doubted whether giving a monopoly to one company to market the freedmen's cotton was "honest, fair competition." He wondered if any outfit could gather a crop so widely dispersed as that of Texas. He would, however, leave the decision up to Griffin, as the one who was on the spot. The assistant commissioner quickly issued an order forbidding creditors to take a lien on the accounts owed them by freedmen. Negro laborers were to be paid in full the amount agreed upon in the contract, said the Texas bureau head. Subassistant commissioners were to urge the freed persons to pay their debts promptly, Griffin declared, but the freedmen were to be permitted to sell their portion of a crop when and where they pleased to their best advantage.[11]

Both loyal and disloyal planters objected to Griffin's plan. Judge B. W. Gray, who conducted field inspections for Griffin, cautioned that the new edict would severely restrict credit to blacks. He suggested that the subassistant commissioner audit all claims upon settlement at year's end, and negate any deductions that were invalid or unfair. He said the real problem was that the freed people overspent their available cash on nonessential items, and added that they needed education on how to budget their money. Subassistant commissioners were confused over how to enforce the order. The way Griffin had worked the edict implied that freedmen could leave a plantation without first settling their debts. Griffin maintained that its sole purpose was to offset a current Texas law that prevented a lien on the crops of any landowner who held his property in fee simple. Howard agreed with this assessment, but suggested that if either a white employer or a black laborer suffered injustice from the order, it could be easily modified.[12]

Thomas Affleck, the planter from Washington County whom we have encountered earlier and who thought freedom of the Negro to be the ruination of the South, also demurred. He claimed that Negroes contested every item on the bill, and that the result was bad feeling on both sides. To exempt them from a lien would only encourage bad spending habits, Affleck said. He too proposed that the field agents audit accounts at the end of a contract's term, and force the blacks to pay what they owed. Affleck doubted that the blacks would give a fair day's work under any terms at which a white could afford to employ them unless the bureau were more on the side of the landowner. Griffin, however, toughened his order with another one, which warned state tribunals that none of the punitive sections of the Texas labor law were to be used in settlement disputes over labor contracts.[13]

On the second part of Griffin's proposal, the use of a bonded merchant to market freedmen's crops, Howard was so apprehensive that he undertook to consult with Secretary of War Edwin McM. Stanton. Finding him absent from Washington, Howard turned to Lieutenant General U. S. Grant. The army's top general did not like the idea of a monopoly, either. But he understood Griffin's fear about the planters treating the freedmen fairly at settlement time. After consultation, the two men told Griffin that he could have his subassistant commissioners give their black charges "disinterested advice" on business methods and the disposal of their crop shares. Howard suggested that the agents contact black ministers, and let the preachers do the actual advising. The commissioner promised to support whatever course Griffin decided to adopt.[14]

A few days later Howard wrote to his Texas subordinate again. He had spoken to former General Banks and to A. Ruttkey, a commission merchant. Howard told Griffin that he could aid Ruttkey by writing letters of recommendation to local bureau agents and by informing the Texas subassistant commissioners that Ruttkey would guarantee a fair price for the freedmen's cotton, unlike corrupt local merchants. But, Howard cautioned, it all had to be done "quietly." One word in "the wrong place," and the whole scheme was off. Howard left the matter to Griffin's "discretion."[15]

Griffin reassured Howard that no government monopoly would be created in Texas. The commission agents of the Ruttkey firm were merely to set a "full market standard" to which the freedmen and subassistant commissioners could compare the offer of any other merchant. After the bureau eventually left Texas, Griffin grumbled, the whites would return to the old methods of fraud, anyhow. He merely wanted the Negroes to see how an honest business might approach the marketing situation. He had no doubt that many blacks would sell back to the planter. Griffin suggested that Ruttkey send two agents to Texas, one for the interior and another for the coastal areas. On September 3, 1867, Griffin issued a circular announcing that A. Ruttkey Co., operating under a one-hundred-thousand-dollar bond, would help the freedmen realize full profits at a fair market price and prevent fraudulent Texas operators from cheating the blacks of their annual profits. The assistant commissioner recommended the company to all bureau employees.[16]

Griffin felt confident that he could enforce his bureau program, because he had drastically revamped the locations and numbers of subassistant commissioners available in the field. On February 1, the assistant commissioner demonstrated the value of combining the bureau and army commands in one position, when he issued Circular Orders No. 3. Acting as army district general "and with a view to a more efficient and economical administration of [the] Bureau," Griffin decreed that hereafter at all military posts lacking a subassistant commissioner the local military commander would assume that task in addition to his other duties. These officers were to report to the bureau headquarters as well as the army command, unless they were specifically detached from the army and formally assigned as bureau agents. The officers formally assigned to the bureau were to report to it alone. Those post officers not specifically detached to the bureau hierarchy were instructed to use enlisted men under their commands as clerks, as needed. The others were to apply to bureau headquarters for a civilian clerk. Civilians would be hired if headquarters determined they were necessary to the local agency's efficiency.[17]

At the same time, Griffin received from Howard a circular letter instructing all assistant commissioners to better organize their commands bureaucratically. Each position was to have a uniform title and accurate job description of the duties to be performed. Each subassistant commissioner (the title was applied formally for the first time here) had all powers of the assistant commissioner, less those reserved specifically to the head of the state organization. Those bureau employees not assigned to a subdistrict were deemed agents, with the exception of staff members and clerks, who now received the titles descriptive of their jobs. Howard recommended that each assistant commissioner divide his state into specific districts to prevent overlapping jurisdictions, like those that had plagued the field operations of the Texas bureau in previous administrations.[18]

Griffin asked to delay the division of Texas into bureau subdistricts. He said that he had only thirty-six hundred soldiers available, but that he expected reinforcements momentarily. In truth, the general was busy shifting troops to the state's northwestern frontier in response to Governor Throckmorton's successful criticism of army Indian policy. By

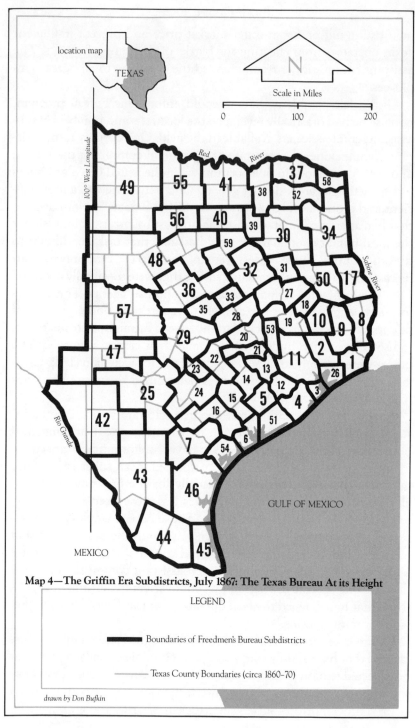

location map

TEXAS

N

Scale in Miles

0   100   200

100° West Longitude

Red   River

49   55   41   37
                 38   58
                 52
      56   40
           39   30   34

            59
48
           32   31   50   17
   36   33   27   18
57   35   28   19   10   9   8
            53   2
29   20   11   26
   47   22   21   13
         23   14   12   3
25   24   15   5   4
         16   51
42   7   54   6

Rio Grande

43
      46   GULF OF MEXICO

44   45

MEXICO

Sabine River

Map 4—The Griffin Era Subdistricts, July 1867: The Texas Bureau At its Height

LEGEND

━━━ Boundaries of Freedmen's Bureau Subdistricts

──── Texas County Boundaries (circa 1860–70)

drawn by Don Bufkin

Map 4: The Griffin-Era Subdistricts, July, 1867: The Texas Bureau at Its Height

April 1, however, Griffin was ready to act. Already, in a piecemeal fashion through Circular No. 3 and individual appointments of civilians, Griffin had increased the field force to forty-eight. Now he organized the state into forty-nine subdistricts staffed by fifty-eight people. In May, the assistant commissioner reorganized Texas into fifty-three subdistricts, staffed by sixty people. In June, he added four more subdistricts, and eight more officers.

By July 10, Griffin had the bureau at an all-time high, with fifty-nine subdistricts and seventy people in the field. But in mid-September, fiscal realities caused Commissioner Howard to warn that it was "very desirable" to reduce the number of bureau employees to "the lowest practical limit." He recommended that traveling agents replace the more stationary subassistant commissioners, and that more regular army officers be used in dual capacities. The commissioner also suggested that any remaining hospital employees be discharged (there were none in Texas), and that any bureau employees being used as voter registrars could be let go, too.[19]

Although in theory the subassistant commissioners were in Texas for the purpose of serving the black population, the amount of paperwork routinely called for gives the impression that many acted as glorified clerks. Those who were more conscientious performed as clerk, diplomat, sheriff, lawyer, judge, labor negotiator, and auditor. Reports were expected on the fifth of each month, and slackers were severely reprimanded in follow-up letters. Of course, there never were enough blank forms for the agent to use, and new employees floundered on as best they could. The chain of command was jealously guarded, and official correspondence had to be sent to the correct staff officer.[20]

Field operatives usually had to provide their own transportation and, although they were told they could requisition a saddle horse and fodder, such requests were usually ignored, which further restricted their mobility. Many subassistant commissioners were afraid to leave the town where they were stationed, horse or no horse; eventually, some were actually shot at and a few were killed. On top of all of this, the good bureau agent was expected to eschew excessive use of alcohol and to encourage his black charges to do the same. The frustration was enough to drive a temperance advocate to drink, not to mention an intemperate subassistant commissioner.[21]

Griffin's agents did have one advantage that no previous Texas subassistant commissioners could claim: He consistently protected them from all forms of violence through the aggressive use of U.S. soldiers, which was more than the assistant commissioners before or after him were able to do. Every subassistant commissioner received an escort of at least five men. Military post commanders serving as bureau representatives, of course, had the support of their commands, ranging in size up to several companies. But it was not merely the numbers that were important, it was an attitude. Griffin did not expect his bureau representatives to go unprotected into potentially threatening situations. Nor did Griffin allow petty interservice rivalries. He issued specific orders that all officers were to render full cooperation and safekeeping to subassistant commissioners.[22]

Of the men who served the bureau under Griffin's tutelage, over half were army officers or members of the Veteran Reserve Corps. The rest were civilians, of whom about one third were Texas citizens. For the first time, Griffin found and appointed some future important Republicans to office—Albert Latimer, Hardin Hart, Anthony M. Bryant, and the sole representative of the black race on Texas bureau rosters, George T. Ruby. Griffin suggested all civilian appointments to Howard who, in turn, issued commissions to those he thought acceptable. These agents were paid from $75 to $150 a month, depending upon their jobs (and sometimes on their nerve in demanding a raise). They came from places as diverse as Prussia, Ireland, Canada, and various Northern and Southern states.[23]

One of Griffin's principal sources of subassistant commissioners was the officer corps of the occupying forces of the U.S. Army. Although Kiddoo had been the first to employ regulars as bureau agents in Texas, Griffin was the first assistant commissioner to use them in an organized fashion. All of the Texas assistant commissioners naively believed that the professional soldiers would provide them with a constant source of unimpeachable officer material. In truth, the army men were no more moral or capable than their counterparts from the civilian world and the volunteer army.

General Kiddoo had employed the first regular army men as bureau officers during the summer of 1866, and he was surprised by their lack of character. In Robertson County for example, Second Lieutenant Robert McClermont of the Fourth Cavalry, the subassistant commissioner out of the nearby Millican office, strung up several freedmen by their thumbs for supposed violations of Circular Orders No. 14. McClermont allegedly cursed one freedman as he trussed him up, "You Son of a B____h, this ought to be around your neck." But the lieutenant evidently did not do the horrible job well. "You do not understand the Texas way of throwing the rope," said Dr. W. H. Farner, whom McClermont had replaced in office a short time earlier. Farner retied the thongs, and the labor contractor, Mrs. E. H. Mitchell, took the opportunity and slapped one of the freedmen as he hung there.[24]

After the hanging, McClermont found a neighboring planter, William B. Anderson, guilty of enticing the hands away. Farner, acting as the agent's clerk (without salary), told Anderson the fine was six hundred dollars. Anderson, flabbergasted, protested. Farner told him to fork over the cash, or he would jack up the amount to twenty-five hundred. Anderson paid up. As he left the bureau office at Millican, he heard McClermont tell Farner to take a pistol and fetch the next victims, who had not reported as scheduled. Anderson went home and wrote to headquarters about the incident, and McClermont soon lost his bureau position. Even though McClermont wrote to Commissioner Howard and promised to behave himself in the future, Kiddoo refused to have anything more to do with the unscrupulous officer.[25]

McClermont's replacement was Brevet Major Louis H. Sanger of the Seventeenth Infantry. Shortly after his assignment, Sanger sent a telegram to headquarters asking that someone else be made subassistant commissioner at Millican as his position there was "insufferable." Millican was an important railhead and receiving point for cotton from the area to the north, and Kiddoo felt obliged to comply immediately with the major's request. He sent Captain Samuel C. Sloan, a volunteer officer, to take Sanger's place. Sloan found out that Sanger had had a run-in with the female teachers at the Negro school at Millican. Sanger had committed an unnamed "grave indiscretion," for which he had later apologized. General Wright reportedly was satisfied, and so were the teachers. Sloan examined Sanger's term as agent and found the officer to have been fully competent in spite of his gaffe, more so than those who had preceded him.[26]

Kiddoo had more bad luck with a pair of McClermont's fellow Fourth Cavalry officers. The first regular soldier detailed to bureau duty at San Antonio, First Lieutenant D. R. Porter, asked to be relieved because he disliked the duty. General Kiddoo called him "impudent and insubordinate" and "unsoldierly and unmanly." Kiddoo told Porter's commander to relieve the lieutenant immediately, "as none but intelligent, capable, and faithful officers are needed" as subassistant commissioners. Porter received a reprimand in orders for his "ignorance and presumption." Kiddoo was especially angered that the lieutenant was not only a fellow Pennsylvanian but also had a West Point education, which the assistant commissioner thought should have taught him better. Porter's successor, Second Lieutenant William C. Hemphill, a Virginia loyalist, was a bit cleverer. Still, he never seemed able to get the hang of the job, even though Kiddoo had detailed a civilian agent to guide him and teach him his responsibilities. Hemphill soon joined Porter on the frontier, where Reconstruction duty was a remote encumbrance.[27]

If one man did measure up to Kiddoo's expectations of regular army officers, it was First Lieutenant S. C. Plummer of the Seventeenth Infantry. General Wright had sent Plummer on a tour into east Texas to assess the conditions in the summer of 1866. Plummer reported that had he not been accompanied by ten cavalry troopers armed with quick-shooting carbines, he surely would have been murdered. Most of the persons he met were "of the Southern blustering type." Those who had served the Confederacy had rarely left the state, and had never seen Yankee power. Indeed, along the Sabine River bottoms, he was the first Yankee that the people had ever seen. Although Plummer was not well acquainted with bureau policy, he wrote General Kiddoo that he had cautioned several planters about honoring contracts and treating freedmen fairly. Plummer concluded that no subassistant commissioner could accomplish much without at least one mounted company in support.[28]

Kiddoo was impressed enough by Plummer's report to appoint him to his personal staff. Later when Governor Throckmorton specifically asked General Griffin to place an army garrison in Caldwell County to protect freedmen from local toughs, the general sent Plummer to the scene. Plummer reported that the whites were orderly and that his only opposition came from a disgruntled freedman, whom he shot down. The usual investigation cleared Plummer of all charges in the shooting.[29]

Nothing was done to implement the lieutenant's suggestions for East Texas until Griffin expanded the number of bureau agencies, and sent the rehabilitated Major Sanger and Company G of the Seventeenth Infantry to Woodville. Before Sanger's arrival, most of the east Texas agents were Scalawags with varying abilities to handle the job of protecting the interests of the freedmen. Sanger reported their shortcomings to Griffin and was rewarded with his own appointment as bureau representative for the Ninth Subdistrict. Sanger maintained that sharecropping was inadequate for the blacks' needs, required too much bureau supervision to be successful, and ought to be replaced with a wage system that would encourage freedmen to rent their own farms.[30]

Griffin used regular officers in a wholesale manner, and the men he picked tended to be more competent than earlier appointees. One reason may have been the fact that the military subassistant commissioners tended to be troop garrison commanders in addition to their bureau duties. They usually had a lot of help to subdue troublemakers, which other subassistant commissioners had lacked. Another reason was that two out of five army subassistant commissioners served on the frontier, where Reconstruction was a relatively minor problem. Even in those frontier places that had freed persons, like Weatherford, Lampasas, Fort Inge, and Fort Mason, they were so few and scattered as to be impossible to monitor (or harass) on a regular basis. At Fort Griffin, for instance, the only freedmen present were employed as body servants by the fort's officers.

The Weatherford subassistant commissioner, First Lieutenant H. H. Humphries, had more blacks in his area than did other frontier agents. He said that the voter registrars would be threatened with death whenever the army should be withdrawn; he had arrested two men already for firing upon them and their escort. His successor, Captain Charles Steelhammer, managed to set up a black school only to see the project fail because the only person willing to teach was a former secessionist who could not take the oath. But Steelhammer got further than the agent at Laredo, who complained that not only were there no blacks living in his subdistrict, there also was no English school. The local Hispanic population refused to send their children to any institution that did not conduct classes in Spanish. Steelhammer also had the distinction of being the only frontier bureau agent who was complained of to headquarters for arresting a citizen until he paid past wages owed a freedman. The defendant alleged that he had already paid, but that Steelhammer refused to credit the payment in full.

Frontier settlers generally treated each other on the basis of other factors than skin color—unless it happened to be red—and blacks out west tended to receive justice in the courts just like white folks. The biggest problem, besides an unforgiving environment and Indian raids, was the presence of white renegades. They were so prevalent at Fort Mason that the bureau subassistant commissioner, Captain John A. Thompson of the Fourth Cavalry, lost his life in a gun battle with the outlaws. Frontier officers tended to be lackadaisical in their attitude to reports and bureau procedure. When headquarters asked Brevet Major General Alexander McD. McCook at Brownsville for a missing report, the general replied that the area needed no subassistant commissioner and that he had no report to make. This is surprising because the local

The Griffin Era

newspaper, the Brownsville *Daily Ranchero*, was one of the most un-compromising pro-rebel sheets in the state, and repeatedly baited the black soldiers who garrisoned the area.

As if to underscore the insignificance of Reconstruction issues on the frontier, each time the revolving fort garrisons were changed, the new commandant had to write headquarters and ask for a copy of the orders and manuals under which the bureau operated. Few comman-dants kept these items, if indeed they ever received them by the un-certain mails. Headquarters finally decided to accept reality and in-structed most of these isolated subassistant commissioners on the frontier to make no report unless something special happened. Nothing did. When the bureau went out of business in December, 1868, the frontier agents generally stated that they had no records, books, or papers of any kind to forward to Austin. There never had been any bureau busi-ness to transact.[31]

But troops were a critical element in other subdistricts in making for an easier execution of bureau mandates. When the notorious Brevet Major George W. Smith, remembered from the Brenham fire incident, was transferred to Seguin, he observed a marked change in the attitude of the whites there, who had pestered every subassistant commissioner who had served before him. He had one difference in his administra-tion—he was the first bureau agent who brought an infantry company with him. His reputation from Brenham probably did not hurt, either.

In addition to his efforts on behalf of the freedmen, Smith helped local Republicans draw up a list of loyalists for future political rewards. Outlaws abounded in the area, and headquarters authorized Smith to "resort to extreme measures, if necessary" to clean them up. "You will be sustained in any course you take to accomplish the desired ef-fect." To carry out his mission, the major was forced to divide his com-mand to garrison the town of Gonzales. He asked for an assistant to run the office there, but headquarters refused. Denied help, Smith split his time between the two posts. Business went briskly, however. There were nearly one hundred cases of contract violation in August, 1867, alone, and numerous contract settlements pending for over a year were rapidly completed. But it all ended when local planters complained that Smith was using military force to extort bribes. An investigation confirmed the charges. The major had to face a court-martial for mis-appropriation of bureau funds, after which he resigned his commission.[32]

Other areas also noticed the difference that troop support made in the ease of handling Reconstruction. Waco, for example, had the worst crime rate for the whole state, but Captain James Jay Emerson thought he could manage bureau affairs adequately, backed up by his infantry company. The civil authorities acted to assist him only because they feared the troops more than they feared those who attacked local freedmen, said Emerson. Blacks, however, said Emerson's influence with local officials was based on his policy of not allowing Negroes to hold public political meetings. Emerson denied the charge, saying that he offered to protect all loyal political gatherings with soldiers. But, he continued, he believed that the Negroes' plan to come into town armed with pistols and to parade with a red flag was a bit inflammatory and contrary to his order that no weapons be carried by anyone in town. Shortly after, headquarters reduced his troop contingent to fifteen men, and reprimanded him for his incomplete reports on abandoned lands like those of the Waco Manufacturing Co. Emerson thought that the reduction in soldiers was foolish, given the reign of terror "after the '66 troop withdrawal."[33]

Almost as bad as Waco was Kaufman. The military subassistant commissioner, First Lieutenant S. H. Lincoln, reported that the civilian who held the job before him had done little because he lacked soldiers to back him up. As it was, the lieutenant had only a part of his infantry company; the rest had been detached under orders to Dallas. White hatred of the loyal blacks and whites was so bad, and Lincoln's powers so limited, that he advised the Negroes to leave the county for safety. The freedmen had yet to be paid since the war, Lincoln said. Although the lieutenant settled many accounts while he was in Kaufman as bureau agent, the planters routinely warned the freedmen that the army would have to leave someday, and that racial killing would then begin anew. As if to emphasize their point, several whites constituted themselves a self-appointed court and hanged two freedmen. When they were found not guilty by civil authorities, Lincoln had the suspects arrested and sent to Marshall for military trial.[34]

As in Waco and Kaufman, everything was fine in Goliad so long as the soldiers stayed there in force. Brevet Major P. E. Holcomb, however, probably unintentionally hit the mark when he stated that all went well so long as the freedmen "behaved themselves"—a remark that carried possibly ominous implications for his actions as subassistant commissioner. Holcomb thought the greatest danger threatened loyal whites, not blacks. When the soldiers were withdrawn, the local teacher of the freedmen's school left with them, under threats against his life. Goliad was not the only place where the subassistant commissioner may have had less trouble because he agreed with local whites about the acceptable behavior allowed the freedmen. In Freestone County, Captain T. M. K. Smith noted that the local black fieldhands were lazy, bickered among themselves over petty issues, and generally wasted his time. He thought the disgust of planters was justified.

Although he was not as quick to credit white testimony, First Lieutenant Phineas Stevens at Hallettsville saw the same attitude among planters, who called the freedmen lazy. He also questioned a list of loyal names for political appointments submitted to General Griffin by his predecessor, W. H. Heistand. Griffin had ordered the list drawn up in March, 1867, which clearly demonstrates the general's early start on political involvement. Griffin told Stevens to revise it as he saw fit. When the lieutenant complained that local courts had released one landowner who maltreated his fieldhands, headquarters ordered him to rearrest the culprit and fine him five hundred dollars. The agent evidently did not accomplish the task, because he was told three months later to get on with the job. He probably was hindered by the fact that both whites and blacks habitually wore revolvers strapped on their hip, even to church services.[35]

Sometimes the army bureau agent created his own problems, and in such cases, the availability of soldiers could make an unwise course of action even worse. This had happened at Brenham under General Kiddoo's regime, and it occurred under Griffin's administration again in 1867 at Hempstead. Situated at the junction of the rail link to the great cotton-producing districts in central Texas where troops could be loaded on cars and sped at a moment's notice north to Millican or west to Brenham on the main route to Austin, Hempstead occupied a strategic location.

The Hempstead bureau agents before Griffin's takeover at Galveston were Captain H. W. Allen and First Lieutenant S. F. Hathaway from the Thirty-sixth Colored Infantry. They operated at a time when Hempstead had no troop support beyond a headquarters guard of a half dozen men, a fact about which Allen complained bitterly. But their real problem was the restrictions imposed upon them by General Wright's strict enforcement of General Orders No. 26, which limited the use of military arrests, and by Kiddoo's failure to provide them with an office and equipment, which forced them to carry out their bureau functions from a tent. After the demobilization of the Thirty Sixth USCI, Griffin garrisoned the post with two companies of the Seventeenth

Infantry, under the command of Captain George Lancaster, who also acted as the subassistant commissioner.[36]

Although Lancaster's men, like all infantry units, suffered from a lack of mobility, the captain diligently sent regular foot patrols out into the far reaches of his district to guard Negro rights. Even though he usually listed from forty to eighty "effectives" on his rosters, Lancaster feared that he had too few men to stop a mob action. Given the hostile racial feelings of his area, the captain said, the slightest spark might trigger a riot. In reality, much of the tension in Lancaster's Thirteenth Subdistrict came from his roving patrols and the captain's loose discipline. These men would ransack isolated farms, scare the very Negroes they were assigned to protect, and raise general havoc in Hempstead, which they threatened to burn like Brenham. Lancaster allegedly warned his subalterns that "if they didn't quit their deviltry somebody would kill them." But he did little else to stop the practice.

As Lancaster feared, after one of the ill-advised raids, the plantation managers pursued the soldiers and made a retaliatory attack. In the exchange, the two mounted Texans emptied their six-guns at the column and hit two of the infantrymen. The surprised soldiers, armed with single-shot, muzzle-loading rifles, were no match for the riders, who galloped away unharmed. Lancaster sent out another unit to arrest the attackers, but they had already fled the area. The captain may have been more meticulous about his disciplinary methods after the incident, but the 1867 yellow fever epidemic shut down all operations from August to December, anyhow. From then on, Lancaster kept busy supervising settlements, and his force was reduced to a single company.[37]

Sometimes the soldiers available for bureau use were not well enough equipped to force obedience to bureau edicts. William H. Horton, the subassistant commissioner from Dallas, came up to the military post at Sherman to see if he could find troop support there. First Lieutenant Thomas Tolman, the post commander, said he had sixty men, but only eighteen carbines. Still, he offered to send a squad armed with sabers back to Dallas to help Horton. Tolman had repeatedly reported his plight to headquarters, to no avail.[38]

But the events in no other region in the state could compare to what went on in northeastern Texas in the valleys of the Red and Sulphur rivers. The military outpost for the region was Mount Pleasant which belied its name. The post was staffed by two companies of the Sixth Cavalry, whose commander also acted as the subassistant commissioner for the Fifty-second Subdistrict. Brevet Colonel S. H. Starr told of how most whites there considered all freedmen as "personal enemies." His criminal docket was full of rapes, floggings, assaults, and murders. Without the cavalry, Starr believed that the whole region would suffer an even greater reign of terror than currently existed.

The situation at Mount Pleasant was complicated by the presence of Cullen Baker's outlaw gang. Baker relished attacking lonely army supply wagons and their escorts. Egged on by Baker, local whites told Starr that they would soon reenslave the Negroes and declare another rebellion. Judging from the bureau reports common to the region, Baker's war was already in progress. Starr tried to protect the rights of freedmen and loyalists in his subdistrict, while detaching units to guard surrounding bureau agencies manned by civilians. At the same time, he refused to waver from the principle of unity of command, so dear to army manuals. The result was a constant conflict between bureau and army needs that helped no one but the brigands and vindictive planters.[39]

East of Mount Pleasant lay Marshall, one of the earliest occupied bureau agencies in Texas, its first subassistant commissioner having been appointed in October, 1865. The first bureau agents stationed at Marshall were hampered not only by their isolation but also by the fact that they had to cover the whole of northeastern Texas alone until Griffin's expansion in the spring of 1867. Their military support came from the District of Louisiana's Shreveport post until December, 1867. The first regular army officer to run the bureau operation, First Lieutenant Adam G. Malloy, arrived in May, 1867.

Lieutenant Malloy was appalled at what he encountered. There was no law and order. Local officials shot it out with their enemies on the streets. The collector of internal revenue, a Unionist, killed his deputy, an alleged rebel. When Unionists tried to hold a meeting, it was attacked by rioters led by public officials. The local sheriff who was to protect the gathering had conveniently "disappeared" for the evening. His deputy joined the rioters and fired upon the principal speaker, Judge Colbert Caldwell. When Malloy arrested and fined the riot leaders, the local troop commander (from the Department of Louisiana) informed him that the action was contrary to the policy of the New Orleans command.

As bad as conditions were in the city, they were good compared to those in the backcountry. Malloy could protect blacks in Harrison County but not in surrounding counties. Rusk and Davis counties were run by outlaw gangs led by the notorious Cullen Baker. When Malloy sent a trooper to arrest a man charged with shooting a Negro's eye out, the soldier made the arrest easily. On the way back to Marshall the man asked to answer a call of nature. When the soldier considerately turned his back to allow the prisoner a little privacy, the arrested man produced a pistol, fired at the astonished trooper, and escaped. All Malloy could do was seize a prized horse belonging to the man's nephew. Malloy admitted this was a bit high-handed, but he could do little more. Over in Panola County, no one paid any attention to his orders. Outrage was the order of the day.[40]

Malloy also had problems with Thomas Bayley, the man whom he had replaced as subassistant commissioner at Marshall. A former colonel of colored troops, Bayley had served in Marshall both as a military man and a civilian. Disgusted with the bureau's refusal to pay him at his higher former salary of colonel of volunteers, Bayley became sullen. He also was irritated by the presence of Brevet Captain Charles Rand, recently arrived from Wharton. Rand was to take the place of Lieutenant I. M. Beebe, who had died suddenly in September, 1866. Bayley did not think that Marshall needed two bureau representatives, and suggested that Rand be sent to Jefferson or to one of the counties to the west.

Bayley's uncooperative attitude annoyed Griffin, who ordered Bayley to Carthage and turned the Marshall office over to Malloy, a regular army man. Rand and Malloy hit it off right away. When Bayley delayed his departure, claiming that he was ill and that his wife was too frail to travel, Malloy and Rand refused to back him up. A personal appeal from his wife to Griffin failed to change the general's mind. Faced with a journey to a place where he did not wish to serve, condemned by Griffin's inspector general as "not the kind of man we want," Bayley handed in his resignation and returned North, ostensibly for his wife's health.[41]

When headquarters ordered Rand to make a dangerous tour of Davis [Cass], Bowie, Lamar, Red River, Hopkins, Wood, Titus, and Upshur counties, however, Malloy helped Rand postpone his departure long enough (ten weeks) to arrange to have the trip canceled. After all, unlike those at headquarters, Rand and Malloy knew that without cavalry their jurisdiction and safety ended about fifteen miles (a day's march for infantry) from Marshall. In fact, this was the reason Bayley had been reluctant to accept the assignment to Carthage.

Next, Malloy tried to get a leave of absence for Rand, who was chronically ill, but he failed. Malloy then intervened to keep Rand at Marshall instead of sending him out to Gilmer as Griffin had ordered. When the weather permitted, Rand traveled to Gilmer with an infantry escort and quickly reported that it had too few blacks to warrant an agency. But Griffin made him stay until after the picking season, convinced that Rand, like Bayley, was a coward. Inspector Sinclair interviewed Rand and Malloy and decided that Rand was a brave man (he had won the medal of honor during the war)—indeed, one of the best agents the Texas bureau had. Sinclair recommended that Rand be sent to a critical area like Jefferson, but headquarters wanted him at Clarksville, instead. So Rand happily rode off to the Red River County seat in the fall of 1867. Little did he know that he would need all the courage any man could muster in his new job.[42]

Unlike the agents at Marshall, most volunteer officers who served with the Texas bureau did not have the luxury of a military garrison to back them up. True, military support was not necessary at all agencies, but its lack could cause many problems. A case in point was that of Captain Albert Evans of the 116th USCI, who served the bureau at Austin, Sherman, and Kaufman. Evans had specifically asked to be transferred to the bureau, and upon arriving in Austin, found the situation to be pretty good. Blacks were doing well as free laborers; the education system was expanding. Evans protested to no avail that the abandoned property used as a school and clinic was going to be returned to a man who had fled to Mexico in 1865. He failed to get a list of landowners for bureau headquarters. The land office records were such a mess as to preclude any search. He evidently was quite popular with the black population, because thirty of them petitioned Kiddoo to keep him at Austin, when Kiddoo sent him up to Sherman as the first subassistant commisioner there and to expand the bureau's influence in northern Texas.[43]

At Sherman, Evans found a radically different environment from Austin. He told of massive fraud and violence being perpetrated against the freed people, who were not allowed to contract freely or to leave their old plantations. His position there was secure only because of the presence of Lieutenant Tolman's troop of the Sixth Cavalry. Indeed, the planters had actually welcomed his arrival, which pleased Evans—until he found out why. Having just received news of Kiddoo's Circular Orders No. 14, they expected him "to stir the *nigger* out with a 'sharp stick.'" Before he could begin to attack the massive problems he faced, his regiment was mustered out. Evans asked to be reemployed as a civilian agent, and Griffin agreed. But upon Evans's return from the muster-out center at Louisville, Kentucky, Griffin sent him to Kaufman instead of back to Sherman.[44]

Evans found the situation at Kaufman to be even worse than in Sherman, complicated by the absence of any soldiers. Civil authorities refused to act on any bureau request, or even to promote general law and order. In one murder case, a disbelieving Evans told how one "Jerry Nash required the crowd to stand back, saying, 'I will fix the D____d nigger,' which he gracefully did according to the tactics of this section [i.e., with a pistol shot]." The grand jury found no true bill. Evans angrily recommended that local authorities be removed, although this was long before Griffin had the congressional sanction of the Third Reconstruction Act to do so. In July, Evans had had enough, and he resigned to enter private business. It took a full company of the Twenty-Sixth Infantry to reoccupy Kaufman safely some months later.[45]

At times, the army's mere presence was not enough. Lack of support for his vigorous policies from Griffin soured Second Lieutenant Alfred F. Manning of the Second Battalion of the Veteran Reserve Corps on bureau service. Manning had lost his right leg at Chancellorsville, but now hobbled about on an artificial limb with no apparent trouble. Coming to Waco as the bureau representative in July, 1866, Manning toured his district on horseback. He found that the planters believed that the freedmen were too lazy to pick cotton. The lieutenant discovered that the real problem was a bumper crop and not enough labor. Hands were being paid one dollar per hundred pounds picked, nearly twice the going rate in the rest of Texas. He managed to get everything straightened out, but noted that there was a great animosity toward all Negroes, Unionists, and Yankees. He also said that he had heard stories from loyalist Judge Thomas Ford of Bosque County that would "make your flesh creep."

One of Ford's stories chilled Manning as no other incident had. He told of the castration of a young black boy in Bosque County during the summer of 1865, after the initial breakup of the slave regime. Allegedly the Negro had tried to rape his former owner's daughter. According to the mutilated victim, however, he had merely gone to the white children's bedroom (boys and girls slept together), to visit with the planter's son, his friend. In the dark, the girl screamed, and the planter came running and cried rape. He gave the young black a choice: get cut or die. The "operation"—there were a couple of doctors present in the mob that gathered to witness the act—was done with a dull knife.

Manning checked wtih Philip Howard, the Scalawag subassistant commissioner at Meridian. He, too, knew of the story and had already reported the incident to headquarters. Manning returned to Waco and launched an extensive investigation. In January, 1867, he arrested the main perpetrators of the deed, J. C. McCrary and doctors Bell and Irving. Refusing to honor a writ of habeas corpus from a local court, Manning said that McCrary was in league with men sworn to kill "every nigger, Union man, and Yankee" they encountered. The lieutenant employed a whole company of the Sixth Cavalry to guard the jail and prevent mob action to free the men. The citizens reported Manning's "tyranny" to Throckmorton.

At first supportive of the complaints, Throckmorton backed off when he learned the truth of the incident. He and General Griffin agreed to let the civil courts handle the case, with Manning monitoring the trial. If the matter was not handled fairly, Manning was to report to headquarters. Griffin would then transfer the case to Federal court under the Civil Rights Act of 1866, although there was some doubt that he could do so, since the castration had taken place before the law was enacted. Besides, the white girl, pressured by her father, was willing to testify to the attempted rape, which pretty much decided the matter. Griffin saw the case as a lost cause. To keep the angry Manning from interfering, since his personal pride and interest in the matter were already too great, the general ordered him to Dallas. Griffin then changed his mind, however, and recalled the lieutenant to Galveston.[46]

A month later, however, the general returned Manning to Cotton Gin, thirty or forty miles east of Waco in Freestone County. Manning's approach to his job seems to have changed during the intervening period he spent in Galveston. Maybe he was simply disappointed at the lack of support that his vigorous administration in Waco had received, especially in hunting down and holding the castration conspirators. It is possible that he was more interested in the charms of a local woman in his new location. In any case, Manning sent in no reports from Cotton Gin, and when he applied for a leave, Griffin refused the request, citing Manning's inattention to work. The argument became moot, for Manning was shot down on his way to visit a "friend" on a private matter, when he "had occasion to step into the bushes." Hearing the cocking of a weapon behind him, Manning turned. An unidentified man fired two revolver shots, hitting the subassistant commissioner in the thigh and calf of his good leg. Manning returned fire with his Derringer to no effect. Unable to mount his horse, the wounded agent had to crawl into town for help.[47]

Manning asked for and received permission to return to Galveston to convalesce. Griffin wanted to see him, anyway. The general had received complaints of the lieutenant's conduct as subassistant commissioner at Cotton Gin. Manning had allegedly seized "Negro cotton" from a planter and sold it for his own enrichment. In another case, the beleaguered officer was charged with pocketing a bribe exacted from three men charged in a murder case, who were allowed to go free. Manning denied all charges and produced a letter from a Unionist to back him up. Meanwhile, the lieutenant had run up a healthy hotel bill in Galveston, which he tried to skip town without paying. He also began to appear in public quite drunk. Griffin, in exasperation, threw him out of the service and sent him home for muster-out.[48]

Still other volunteer officers continued to serve the bureau, despite the absence of military support or staff encouragement. Transferred from Clinton to a new post at San Augustine in March, 1867, First Lieutenant Albert A. Metzner found the Seventeenth Subdistrict ruled by what he referred to as "lynch law." One suspect was in jail for killing an old man so that he could rape his daughter. There were at least eleven homicides during Metzner's first nine months in the subdistrict. In another instance, reminiscent of Manning's Waco experiences, Metzner learned of a white planter who during the days of the breakup had castrated a black man for leaving the plantation without permission. The white was so rich and powerful that Metzner saw little hope of arresting him, much less of obtaining a guilty verdict. He did, however, examine the Negro physically and found the tale to be true. Headquarters ordered the army to arrest the offender, but he fled to Mexico. Afterward, Metzner found out that the same man had committed two similar outrages on other blacks.[49]

In general, Metzner said, the population was crazed over two topics, politics and cotton. Politically, Metzner himself was active in the local Republican party. He belonged to the Union Loyal League, and served as one of the votor registrars. Metzner tried to get a leave to take the registration records to New Orleans, but the army recalled his clerk to his company, and Metzner could not find another to act as subassistant commissioner in his absence. He had to trust a local carpetbagger to file the registration records for him. Blacks outnumbered whites in the registration, and the Republican ticket carried the day in the convention election.

The day was marred by a white, who shot one black voter and threatened others. The sheriff refused to intervene. A justice of the peace encouraged the activity by shouting to the crowd, "Go ahead boys, drive those d____d Yankees out." A few days earlier, Metzner had been talking quietly to a group of men, including the same judge. Suddenly they all drew their revolvers and trained them on him. They laughed, but said that they would have him soon. The black voter registrars had to sleep in the woods for safety.[50]

To tour the district and bring some semblance of bureau control to the planters, Metzner tried to get headquarters to furnish him a horse, but there were none available for subassistant commissioners. Griffin told him to hire one animal and send the bill to the distribution officer. Metzner also hired a teacher and set up a fledgling school system. But the bureau agent neglected to tell headquarters of his actions, probably because he mistakenly thought he had the proper authority. So when the teacher tried to collect his promised salary, headquarters refused to pay it. Metzner was mustered out of the Veteran Reserves in December, 1867, but he accepted a civilian appointment to continue on at the San Augustine agency. With his acceptance of civilian status, Metzner joined the ranks of a group that would from here on constitute between 40 and 50 percent of the bureau force in the field—civilian employees from the North and South.[51]

8

To Make the Devil Blush

ONE OF THE MOST IMPORTANT SOURCES of bureau field representatives was the Northern states. Fifty-nine Northern civilians were hired after congressional passage of the second bureau act in July, 1866. The second largest group of bureau employees, after the regular army men, these men served terms as short as one month and as long as twenty-nine months, and included some of the best and worst employees of the Texas bureau. In many ways, the Northern civilians were the most dedicated to the accomplishment of the political and social goals of Reconstruction, the admission of the freedmen into the ranks of free persons with the legal and civil rights of all citizens at that time.

Although it may be stretching the accepted definition to call these men carpetbaggers, a term usually applied to Northerners who came south and entered politics, white Texans certainly considered bureau appointments to be political jobs and Northern civilian bureau appointees to deserve the appellation. And by their own admission, the Northern bureau appointees acted in a political manner in conjunction with the army and the provisional government to reconstruct the state. They reported on the loyalty of local residents; pointed out men to be disfranchised; called for military support to make arrests when authorities refused or could not act; monitored the trials of Negroes and those accused of violating black rights; organized freedmen into the political arm of Reconstruction, the Union Loyal League; served on boards of voter registration; recommended the men that the military commanders removed from or appointed to local political positions; and ran for and held political office.[1]

The appointment of civilians to bureau positions in the South was made possible by new clauses in the renewal of the bureau act in July, 1866. The use of Northerners was not an innovation by Griffin; General Kiddoo had engaged nineteen Northern subassistant commissioners, of whom a dozen still were in office when Griffin took over. The latter continued to use Northerners, hiring nineteen more, most of whom had served with the Union volunteer forces during the war. Some of the carpetbaggers did not serve very long, but few passed through as rapidly as the eight-day tenure of W. H. McClune, who was to replace Champ Carter, Jr., at Sterling. McClune asked for an appointment on the basis of his Federal service from 1861 to 1865. Kiddoo responded, offering him a position at twelve hundred dollars a year, the top salary available at that time. But it is doubtful that McClune ever left Galveston. His name made the monthly muster roll only once, before Kiddoo revoked the original order for unspecified reasons.[2]

A. M. Sperry was another unusual Texas bureau employee, although for more substantial reasons than McClune's. A representative of the Freedmen's Savings Bank, Sperry had followed the course of the XXV Corps to the Rio Grande, where he had assisted the black soldiers with their financial affairs, and shipped their muster-out money home for safekeeping. It was not uncommon for Sperry to handle fifteen thousand dollars or more per regiment. He was carried on the Texas bureau muster roll as a traveling agent after January, 1867, a position he resigned four months later. His branch banks in Houston and Galveston were not doing well, probably because the only blacks in Texas with money were the home-going soldiers. The last of them were ready to leave in the spring of 1867, which ended Sperry's usefulness as a banker. He also was soured on the unsupportive Texas command when he got into a vicious argument with E. M. Wheelock involving religious matters and Wheelock's alleged poor treatment of freedmen while subassistant commissioner at Galveston.[3]

Sperry was not the only agent to fall victim to headquarters politics. Mathew Young opened the Belton agency in June of 1867. But Young had had a drinking problem before becoming an agent, which continued to plague him. And the situation in Belton was tension-filled. His subdistrict was dominated by "ultra secessionists" and outlaws, who shot up the town nightly. A vicious murder of a white woman and child in the countryside, allegedly committed by a freedman whom Young protected, had the local whites in an uproar. The infantrymen sent to assist him were "mutinous and disorderly," Young said, and more of a problem than the populace. He relied on three cavalrymen also detailed to the agency, and recommended that the foot soldiers be sent back to their regiment. Nonetheless, Young managed to quiet the place down by disarming the townsmen. He also instituted the voter registration process. But in the end, liquor got the best of him, and he was replaced by Charles Stiles, a superfluous assistant subassistant commissioner, whose brother was the troop commander and subassistant commissioner at nearby Waco. Young was told that he had been removed to reduce the number of employees.[4]

As Young's case illustrated, it took a tough man to act as a bureau agent in Texas. Such a man was William H. Horton, the subassistant commissioner at Wharton. Horton's fearless manner led General Griffin to send him to another hotspot, Dallas. The area had never had an agent before, and Horton encountered abominable conditions in Dallas and Tarrant counties. Unionists and blacks were shot down "like dogs," nightriders abounded, and civil law "was a sham," Horton reported. Whites "dislike to pay men that were once property, and there seems to be a general combination to get their labor for nothing," he continued. Horton was threatened daily. He marveled at the "deep and malignant hate displayed towards Union men," who suffered even more than Horton himself or the Negroes. Horton recommended a general removal of all current officeholders, particularly District Judge John J. Goode of Dallas, and Tarrant County judge, W. B. Tucker. Despite an attempted assassination, Horton managed to obtain a general registration of voters by working with Dr. B. F. Barkley, the leader of loyal forces in the area. But by March, 1868, even after the rejuvenation of a forty-day leave, he asked for a transfer to another duty station.[5]

Another carpetbag bureau agent, James Lowrie at Jasper, received treatment almost as harsh as Horton's, but under vastly different circumstances. Lowrie was stationed in east Texas for twenty-one months. A former lieutenant in the Eighth U. S. Colored Artillery, he found most of his bureau career tainted by an incident that took place shortly after he arrived at Jasper in March, 1867, after serving six months at Moscow. Lowrie and G. W. Hewitt, the local teacher of freedmen, were asleep in their room about midnight, when the quiet of the night erupted in gunfire. Somewhere between fifteen and thirty shots were fired, mostly to no effect, but Lowrie was hit in the thigh. He told Hewitt, who was unharmed, to go and fetch the army at Livingston. Hewitt jumped from the window and ran. Out on the road, Hewitt panicked. He headed in the opposite direction, and did not stop running until he reached Alexandria, Louisiana. Major Louis Sanger's men finally arrived from Livingston, and all was quiet for awhile.

As Lowrie healed slowly, he made the mistake of arresting the sheriff for killing a freedman at a political meeting. The town went crazy, with mobs roaming the streets, and rabblerousers calling for an attack on Major Sanger's force. A neighboring county offered one hundred

men to help in the assault. As a way to quiet the mob, Lowrie agreed
to let the sheriff go free. The man promptly violated his parole and
disappeared into the woods. Any further attempts to enforce the law
were met with the same hostility. To show who really had the power
in the area, local thugs "arrested" Lowrie and the former agent M. H.
Goddin and held a kangaroo court session, during which their "crimes"
were assessed, and the two men warned to "go straight" or die.[6]

Death could appear in many forms during Texas Reconstruction.
One of the strangest incidents happened to bureau representative John
Williamson, the subassistant commissioner at Corsicana. Williamson
was returning from a tour of his district when his horse shied, reared
up, and fell back, pinning the bureau agent beneath him. When the
horse was pulled off, it was discovered that Williamson had broken
both bones in his left calf about three inches above the ankle. Medical
personnel noticed that he was not mending well, and closer examination revealed that he had internal injuries. Despite all the doctor could
do Williamson died three weeks later from tetanus. The government
paid a Negro nurse and the white doctor $371 for their care of the hapless
agent. His death was ruled an accident, but when Charles E. Culver
came over to investigate, he rode a colt so green that he feared that
he would be thrown and have his neck broken. There was more than
one way to get rid of an agent.[7]

Culver, the subassistant commissioner at Cotton Gin, also lost his
life while serving the bureau. Succeeding Alfred F. Manning, who himself had survived a shooting, Culver attacked his job with a reckless
vigor and thoroughness designed to aggravate those opposed to Reconstruction. Everyone tried to throw obstacles in his way, Culver said.
He could not find a "broke" horse to rent. He managed to ride a "half
broke" colt over to Corsicana, where he addressed blacks and whites.
The freedmen were quite receptive to his speech, but the whites walked
out, laughing at his "damned Yankee" notions of justice and fairness
toward all men. One man said that the bureau "would be swallowed
up before they allowed a nigger to be equal." Culver found much slavery continuing under the title of "apprenticeship," which he worked
to eradicate.

Whites complained to headquarters that Culver was "a zealous, dangerous fanatic." He was accused of arming black vigilantes to enforce
his edicts, a charge that Culver called "a lie from beginning to end."
When headquarters sent him a squad of picked men, Culver character-

ized them as "not worth H_____ Room." In one outburst, he accused other bureau agents of interfering with his district. But headquarters cautioned him to back off and be less provocative in his actions. It was too late. On November 15, 1867, Culver and an orderly tried to arrest a white man for carrying firearms in Cotton Gin in violation of the subassistant commissioner's antigun law. The offender was quicker on the draw, and shot and killed both Culver and the soldier right out on the main street. The killer rode off without opposition and was never caught. Culver had been in office exactly five months.[8]

Other agents also died while serving in Texas, but from disease. In addition to taking the lives of several teachers and clerks, the yellow fever epidemic of 1867 cost the bureau three men who had served it in the field, L. J. Warren at Houston, P. F. Duggan at Columbia, and James C. Devine, a traveling agent who died at Brenham. Warren had · been a traveling agent in the field for two months at the end of 1866 before he transferred to the Houston office as an assistant subassistant commissioner and clerk. He inspected the agencies at Columbia, Wharton, and Richmond. Upon his return to Galveston, Warren got into a quarrel with the chief disbursing officer concerning trip expenses. Soured on the notion of traveling at short pay, he asked for and received the transfer to the position at Houston. A Michigan native, Warren, like all bureau employees, had to fill out a personnel information sheet in September, 1867. Just coming down with the first symptoms of yellow fever, he wrote sarcastically that at "the time of my appointment, I had the misfortune of having to acknowledge Texas as my place of residence." He died within a month, along with his post commander, Colonel J. D. O'Connell.[9]

A similar fate awaited James C. Devine, a former captain of the Twenty-eighth Pennsylvania Infantry, who had settled at Brenham after the war. Applying for a bureau position, Devine was appointed to the Brenham office after the tragic fire in 1866. Within two weeks, however, Devine was sent to Huntsville, where he was the bureau agent for seven months. Then he took a brief leave of absence, before accepting a transfer to headquarters at Galveston as a traveling agent in May, 1867. His only complete inspection tour was a lengthy one that covered the Neches and Trinity river valleys. On his way back to Galveston, Devine arrived at Brenham in August, 1867, feeling sick to his stomach. He took a stuffy hotel room, until Captain Edward Collins removed him to his headquarters in the army camp outside town. Devine died from the advanced symptoms of yellow fever five days later. He was twenty-seven years old. Collins buried him near the camp, and sent his effects to a sister living in Philadelphia.[10]

Another bureau agent who died in the 1867 epidemic was P. F. Duggan, the subassistant commissioner at Columbia. A former officer of the Tenth USCI, Duggan was born in Ireland and claimed Minnesota as his home, although he was living in Galveston when appointed to the bureau. At Columbia he handled several assault cases, and was visiting a plantation to speak to the freedmen, when he came down with "congestion of the stomach." Three days later he was dead. During his illness, Duggan displayed all the classic symptoms of yellow fever. He was delirious, his extremities were cold and clammy, he had black vomit, and his skin was yellow. His personal effects were catalogued and sent to a sister, his only known relative. He was buried in a local churchyard.[11]

Given such risks, it is not hard to understand why some agents simply tired of the vicissitudes of the job. Arriving in Hallettsville in the fall of 1866, William H. Heistand found horrible conditions facing the freedmen and their few supporters. He said that the blacks were treated worse than slaves. They were ruled by the revolver and the Bowie knife. Upon his arrival in town, several men had entered the bureau office, Heistand related, and threatened him with death. The town jail was burned. A traveling Yankee had to flee for his life from nearby De Witt County. Then Bob Harper, a local tough, cussed out the bureau policy, and ordered Heistand to leave town or die. Heistand ignored the threat against his life until a freedwoman came in and told him the murder attempt was planned for that evening. The terrified agent hid in his darkened room all night. He stayed, awaiting the arrival of troops, and lasted out the winter until he was relieved by a full company of infantry. He then resigned, happy just to be alive.[12]

Although he lasted longer in his position, Captain Byron Porter came to feel much as Heistand did. Once Gregory's acting assistant adjutant general, Porter had gone into the field as the Houston subassistant commissioner. Porter reported that the freedmen were being driven off the land without any pay for their 1865 labor, that they were being denied rights to their wives and children, and were suffering daily assaults. What really upset him, however, was the poor treatment the blacks received at the hands of Federal soldiers. The home-going volunteer troops robbed and assaulted Negroes for sport. Others illegally charged the freedmen for alleged services rendered during the occupation.[13]

On September 11, the Harris County sheriff tried to arrest Porter at the office of the post commandant, on charges of illegally fining a local citizen fifty dollars for disparaging and threatening the life of President Johnson seven months earlier. Porter had heard that the arrest was imminent, and had sought the protection of the army post commander, Brevet Major Salon H. Lathrop, who had refused to allow the sheriff to act. Described by Kiddoo as "one of the most efficient officers on duty in the Bureau of this state," the general was not about to allow Porter to be harassed as other officers had been. Since Porter's military commission had just expired, Kiddoo had recommended that he be retained as a civilian and reassigned him to Austin.

Arriving in the Texas capital, Porter reported that all was quiet, not only in Austin, but along the railroad and highway from Houston to there. The freedmen were working diligently in the fields. He was surprised to find few records from those who had preceded him. He suggested that all subassistant commissioners be required to keep a docket of complaints, a book of letters sent, a book of letters and endorsements received, and a file of all official monthly reports. He expected much trouble during the settlement season, but his main task that fall was monitoring the progress of the Black Codes through the legislature.[14]

A friend of William H. Sinclair, a fellow volunteer officer of the adjutant general's corps who also had been recently reappointed as a civilian subassistant commissioner at Galveston, Porter easily kept up with affairs at headquarters. He reminded Sinclair that the plan had been for Porter to come up to Austin for one month, prior to a staff reassignment. He had been there over two months now, and all of his personal baggage was still in storage at Galveston. He had yet to receive any pay, and his funds were growing light. He really needed to know if he had a more permanent posting. He got one all right, but not in Austin. Just before his resignation as assistant commissioner, Kiddoo sent Porter on an inspection tour of Columbus, La Grange, and Bastrop. Griffin so liked Porter's report on matters at the Bastrop office that he gave Porter the troubled agency for his own.[15]

Porter had a rough time at Bastrop. He faced a prolonged hassle with a local tough, William J. A. Bell, and his son, Willis, over their shooting of a Negro. No one would arrest the Bells, and the elder man rode about town defying Porter to act. When Bell threatened twice in one day to shoot the subassistant commissioner, Porter managed to get some soldiers to arrest him. He fined the old man fifty dollars. Bell refused to pay, said Porter later, until he spent two hours in jail thinking it over.

Since Bell quarreled with everyone, local authorities decided to appoint him deputy sheriff, much to Porter's disgust. In his new job, Porter said, Bell assisted the persecutors of Unionists to escape. Bell still maintained that he would force Porter to refund his fine or else kill the subassistant commissioner. Yet he was defended by a large portion of the town, including ex-agent Alex B. Coggeshall and Throckmorton's lieutenant governor, George W. Jones. Porter figured that Bell gave him more trouble than all the rest of his subdistrict combined. When the subassistant commissioner was taken to court on a matter growing out of the Bell case, he decided that he had had enough. After receiving immunity from prosecution as a Federal employee doing his assigned job, Porter resigned his commission and went North.[16]

Unlike Porter and Heistand, who left at their own volition, headquarters intentionally cut F. B. Sturgis from the rolls after fourteen months' service proved him to be too much in league with the planting class at one station, and unable to administer effectively at another. Sturgis, appointed from Pennsylvania, asked to be assigned to the La Grange agency after Isaac Johnson went home for his muster-out. In the two months before Johnson returned, Sturgis completely changed the planters' conception of the bureau, by himself assisting in the picking of a bumper cotton crop. A petition arrived in headquarters asking that Sturgis be made the permanent bureau agent for Fayette County, because "we know and appreciate Mr. Sturgis and desire his residence among us." Even Governor Throckmorton sang his praises in a letter to General Kiddoo.

Probably hoping that Sturgis was more capable than most rather than in league with the white landowners against the freedmen, Kiddoo sent him to open the post of Fort Graham, which had been suggested by Scalawag Philip Howard as a central location for the area southwest of Dallas. But the fort proved to be too far from the main black population of the district, and in addition the area was infested by vicious anti-Union outlaws. Kiddoo withdrew Sturgis to Waco in December, 1866.

At Waco, Sturgis found that no kind of personal charm or sympathy for the planters' point of view could soothe the hatred felt toward the bureau. Planters refused to allow any stranger on their land, probably because they held their freedmen in pseudo-bondage. Other men arrived from the "old states" to take advantage of the forced labor situation. Few blacks had been paid for their past labor. Sturgis had infantry to support him, but only four horses for transportation, so he could do little. He suggested that the whites be closely monitored and their crops seized when they tried to evict their laborers without payment. Sturgis spent much of his time on the road between Waco and Austin, operating as a traveling agent in places like Marlin, Belton, and Salado. Because of the numerous cases he encountered there, he recommended that Bell County have an agent of its own.[17]

In January, 1867, Kiddoo ordered Sturgis to go up to Marlin and relieve A. P. Delano as subassistant commissioner. On one of his inspection trips, during which he traveled disguised as a cotton broker to milk the public of information on bureau agents' operations, William H. Sinclair had discovered that the planters liked Delano's regime in Falls County, because he acted as "a general overseer for the planters." Sinclair noted that Delano had delegated his functions illegally to a man known only as "Jones." Slaves were whipped, hung up by their thumbs, and docked wages—all under alleged bureau supervision. Sinclair entered Delano's store at Marlin unannounced and actually witnessed Jones defend a planter who had whipped a freedman. Jones told the complaining Negro that if he did not get back to work, worse punishment could be devised for him. Their operations were more efficient than the old slave regime, the inspector said, and he did not marvel that the 1866 cotton crop was a bumper one. Sinclair believed that such "dead wood" ought to be cut out and opined that Delano's "conduct has been atrocious and most damnable."[18]

But there was evidently some white displeasure at Delano's operations, because Jesse Howard came into Delano's store with a "cocked pistol." Delano escaped by running into the back room and locking the door. The attempt on his life was unnecessary, because Kiddoo had already relieved Delano of his bureau job a week earlier. As the bureau's representative on the scene, Sturgis became involved with Delano's indictment for mail fraud and incitement of soldiers to desert. In addition, Delano faced state charges revolving around his management of the general store's profits. It is possible that his money problems arose from not having the ironclad oath properly on file at headquarters, which led to his not being paid for his "Servisis," as Delano phonetically put it, on a regular basis.[19]

Sturgis seemed to have a real disgust for Delano, which the local population sensed. Since Delano had been a popular agent, Sturgis received the brunt of their hatred against what they saw as Delano's persecution. Sturgis seems to have replied in kind. He quarreled with local elected officials, and called for military aid to prevent mob action

against him. As fall approached, Sturgis became more and more lackadaisical in his paperwork and responsibilities. At the end of the picking season, his job was cut, allegedly for reasons of economy.[20]

Many of the men appointed by Griffin left office, not out of weari-
ness with the job or because Griffin demanded it, but so they could
influence Reconstruction in a more active political manner. Representative of this class of employees was William Garretson, the civilian
brother of one of Griffin's acting assistant adjutant generals, Lieutenant Charles Garretson. William Garretson received the Refugio agency
in May, 1867. He spent his summer growing disgusted with blacks who
would not work as he thought they should, and with planters who
lied about their Unionism and mistreated their laborers. He survived
the yellow fever that swept the region, promoted voter registration, and
complained to headquarters about the lack of transportation and incessant rains. Griffin recalled Garretson in late August, as the agent
really had little to do. While in Galveston, Garretson accepted the post
of financial agent at the state penitentiary at Huntsville under the
new Pease government, and resigned his bureau commission shortly
afterward.[21]

George T. Ruby had a bureau career that paralleled Garretson's fairly
closely. Appointed as a traveling agent in June, 1866, Ruby was a black
carpetbagger—a Negro born and educated in the North who came south
after the war to write newspaper columns and to work for black education and civil rights. Described by General Griffin as "a very intelligent
mulatto" who was "energetic" and possessed "great influence" with the
freedmen, Ruby toured the state touting schools and temperance, operating out of Galveston. But his main interest was politics, and with
the inauguration of the Pease administration, Ruby resigned his bureau
job in October, 1867, to influence the course of Reconstruction in the
upcoming state convention and as a state legislator.[22]

A third bureau representative who cut his tenure short to take a
political role in Reconstruction was Ira H. Evans, who served in the
Wharton agency from June to December, 1867. Evans had served in
a black volunteer regiment along the Rio Grande, and remained in
the state after his muster-out. He learned the bureau ropes under De
Witt C. Brown, whom he soon replaced. Evans found Wharton to be
a hostile area for bureau operations. He constantly needed troops to
enforce his policies and protect his life. The soldiers sent him kept deserting, and Evans found them to be of doubtful quality. He did the
usual tasks assigned to a bureau agent. He approved contracts and set-

tlements, protected the freedmen's civil rights, encouraged Negroes to register as voters, seized property to collect debts owed black workers, and supported black education. After the 1867 crops were harvested and divided up properly, Evans resigned to enter the internal revenue service. He later served in the state legislature.[23]

Another subassistant commissioner who reisgned to enter state politics was James P. Butler, who served at Brownsville and Huntsville. In Brownsville, Butler had little to do but manage a few small pieces of abandoned land, which were ultimately returned to their owners. To fill up his time, Butler started an education program among the black soldiers who occupied the border area to guard against French incursion from Mexico. Griffin thought that Butler's talents were being wasted in the frontier zone, and brought him to Galveston for reassignment. At first the general thought to send Butler to Sumpter, but decided to give this agency to the Scalawag, Hiram S. Johnson. Butler instead was sent to Huntsville to replace James C. Devine, who wanted to take the job of traveling agent.[24]

At Huntsville, Butler settled the usual disputes over contracts, salaries, and treatment, and kept an eye on the operations of the state penitentiary. He thought that whites treated the freedmen fairly well physically, but that they tried to cheat their black employees "out of every dime." He asked for a few soldiers so that he would have "the unavoidable pleasure of arresting" those whites who openly defied bureau policy. He received eight men, but five of them died when yellow fever brought all operations to a halt in the subdistrict until November, 1867. As cooler weather approached, Butler pushed the organization of schools. He also noticed a rise in the number of assaults against both blacks and white loyalists. "The old spirit of slavery is so deeply engraved into the dark recesses of their hearts," Butler said, "that nothing but death can ever eradicate their animosity against the colored man." Crop settlements occupied most of Butler's time until the new year. He spoke of the civil authorities "annoying and harassing me," and called for the military appointment of new county officials. But he realized that if he really wanted to influence Reconstruction further, he would have to become a politician. He stood for election and won a seat in the state convention. So Butler resigned his bureau job and later was elected to the new legislature as a Republican representative for the district of Walker, Grimes, and Madison counties.[25]

A final example of a subassistant commissioner who resigned to enter another position was P. B. Johnson of Woodville, a man with connections to the Pedigos. It is possible that Johnson had already done some bureau work in the area, as he received a communication from headquarters concerning his ability to act at Jasper without troops, and sent one in listing loyal men available in Livingston, Moscow, and Woodville. But he did not accept the formal appointment to the Woodville agency until early April, 1867, when he sent in his oath of allegiance. Even then he begged James Lowrie, who brought the commission to him—and who had great difficulty in locating Johnson's whereabouts as he was never home—to take it back. Lowrie persisted, and Johnson reluctantly caved in.

Johnson toured the subdistrict, although he was much delayed by heavy rains, and reported that the area was sparsely settled, mostly by small farmers. Unionists were a "small and dispisable" minority, Johnson said, and the free blacks were viewed as worthless. When Johnson sent in his requisitions, the distribution officer noticed that his office rent was double the going rate of others nearby and challenged it. Johnson was outraged at the implication of fraud. He had already spent sixty dollars a month in personal funds and resented the bureau's niggardliness.

Johnson had already asked for troops, which arrived that same June. Like Lowrie earlier, their commander, Brevet Major Louis H. Sanger, noted that he could not find Johnson anywhere about. The following month, Johnson handed in his resignation. He had been in Galveston putting his time to good use, and was now the new assistant assessor of internal revenue for east Texas, a much safer job. Major Sanger became the new bureau agent. Johnson suggested that Sanger coordinate all agents in east Texas from here on, a brilliant idea for a man who seemed so uninterested in bureau affairs. Unfortunately, the idea was never put into effect.[26]

Griffin needed more agents than these northern civilians and military men to staff fully his program to increase the number of field agents. His needs caused him to reverse Kiddoo's hiring policy and revert to Gregory's expedient one of using Texans to fill out the subassistant commissioner ranks. His first such appointment was Oscar F. Hunsaker, a Galveston attorney, who acted as a legal adviser to harmonize bureau edicts with state law and to set up a fee schedule used by the bureau for notaries public. In addition, he acted as a political adviser and recommended the appointment of several subassistant commissioners on the basis that they "would augment us in the coming campaign," that is, the elections for a state constitutional convention.[27]

Hunsaker also investigated the conditions facing prisoners at the Galveston city jail, and discovered that many prisoners had already served longer sentences awaiting trial than they would have received if they had been convicted. He recommended their immediate release. On other occasions, Griffin utilized Hunsaker's talents in the field. The attorney visited Brazos County to investigate the activities of George Linder, a former member of the Twelfth Illinois Cavalry, who was accused of acting as an illegal bureau representative. He charged Linder with expropriating cotton profits from area freedmen and accepting bribes from planters to alter already approved contracts.[28]

In another expedition into Robertson County, Hunsaker found local blacks persecuted by whites, whom he described as "arrogant and ignorant and rebel to the core." Hunsaker said that "the condition of the Freedmen is as abject now as when slaves," and that to hold an election under such circumstances would be "humbug." Hunsaker also rounded up a posse of blacks and, along with the subassistant commissioner at Sterling, dispersed a gang of outlaws who threatened the Ranger & Co. plantation. He asked that the two outlaws captured in the fight be tried by military commission ("it will have a good affect"), and concluded that there was probably not one loyal white in the entire county. He returned to Galveston, where he resigned his position to accept another as the Galveston city recorder.[29]

Another Scalawag agent of importance was John Dix, the Nueces County judge who worked out of Corpus Christi. As soon as the city was occupied by Negro troops, the Massachusetts-born Unionist had returned from wartime exile, arriving on July 4, 1865. He had been in communication with General Gregory early. He favored using Southern men like himself as subassistant commissioners, because he thought Northern soldiers and civilians could not "be so well acquainted with the wants of the emancipated, or so interested in providing for their wants as some of our own citizens."

Unfortunately, however, not all Southern residents were as trustworthy and dedicated to emancipation and Reconstruction as John Dix. He made several recommendations for a Corpus Christi bureau representative, only to be told the Southern men could not be paid and the Northern men were about to be mustered out of the service. Using his Hamilton-inspired appointment as county judge, Dix attempted to do what he could to protect blacks in their freedom. Impressed, Griffin made him the subassistant commissioner of the Forty-sixth Subdistrict in April, 1867, as a part of his expansion program.[30]

Dix was an active supporter of black education—his wife taught at no pay—and he earnestly believed that his role was to give advice and suggest alternative modes of action to freed people with problems. He gave them weekly lectures in moral principles, so that they might develop the skills to go their own way without depending on the bureau in the long run. He was not loath to use his judicial position to intervene in any instance of fraud against the freedmen. In fact, he had to be warned about confusing his roles as judge and subassistant commissioner, which he often combined in such a manner as to trouble headquarters, especially when he arbitrarily jailed troublemakers. But the dual roles of judge and agent did give Dix a real flexibility in his approach. If a case did not come under the bureau jurisdiction, it probably could be considered as a state matter. And he did not have to worry about a lack of support from the county court, as did so many other subassistant commissioners. He also had the active support of the army, at first in Corpus Christi, but after the yellow fever scourge of 1867, from Lake Trinidad, about fifty miles to the interior.[31]

As a devout Unionist, Dix was active in local politics. Along with Edmund J. Davis, later elected Reconstruction governor of Texas, he recommended a full slate of county officials to Griffin, and saw to it that the general's successor used the list to replace those less enthusiastic than Dix in protecting the rights of freedmen and loyalists. He believed that "a few bayonets in the hands of a judicious person" would counter the malevolent activities of the "Rebels, Copperheads, and Democrats," whose slogan was "White Supremacy or Another War." Dix called their program the "assassin's war," although he had to admit, despite the inflammatory rhetoric on both sides, that his opponents really sought to "break down" the voting rights of the Negro, whom they characterized as "half human-half beast," by every means short of violence.

The Corpus Christi whites opposed to Reconstruction used economic pressures—not hiring, not paying—to get their way, which prompted Dix to call for a restoration of Griffin's get-tough policies in October, 1868, a year after the general's death. He wanted the right to seize the property of whites who refused to pay their black employees, "as nothing but vigor will do for mean, refractory rebels who are disposed to carry their Ku Klux dispositions into every act of their lives."[32]

Naturally Dix's aggressive defense of black rights caused complaints to headquarters. A group of petitioners from Corpus Christi griped that Dix was a part of "a dangerous combination amongst certain officeholders" who wished to reconstruct the county to satisfy their "personal rancor and enmity," to control county tax monies for their own use, to raise more money by litigation costs and fees assessed in Dix's court, and to promote their tyrannical and arbitrary course in settling Yankees and Negroes in town to inflate the Republican vote. They accused Dix of interfering with the area's prosperity, making arbitrary arrests, imprisoning accused people without trial, and intimidating citizens by force to settle claims and suits without regard to merits of the cases or the law.

Further, the petitioners charged Dix and the county officeholders with engaging in pro-rebel activities during the war, supplying food to the Confederate service, outfitting Confederate gunboats (accusing Dix by name here), running the blockade, and even serving in the Confederate Army. They asked that Dix be replaced as a state officeholder and subassistant commissioner by impartial Federal military men of "moral integrity and qualifications and capacity."

Interestingly, cases of false imprisonment, claiming of expenses without proper vouchers, and illegal property seizure were traced to Dix in later months. But he had one big ace in the hole: He was a crony of Edmund J. Davis, whom the petitioners accused of running for office under the Confederate government and running cotton through the blockade before joining the Union army. And Davis was too important to the future of the Republican party to be attacked in this manner or to allow Dix to be attacked in his home political base, be the charges true or false. Dix served on to the bureau's end in Texas, and then as a militarily appointed county official until his death in 1870.[33]

Dix was not alone in his beliefs among the Southern civilian subassistant commissioners. His feelings were shared in large part by Griffin appointee John H. Morrison of Palestine. Originally from Iowa, Morrison had been a refugee during the war. Upon his return to his Texas home, he applied to the Marshall agency to become the agent in Palestine. But General Gregory was not hiring at that time. Morrison did some contract work for the Marshall office, and made several voluntary reports on the evil conditions facing the freed people in Anderson County. "O what an owful state of afares is now the case under the presant Administration," he wrote during the days of the Throckmorton regime. "What will we do. Can you tell me? iff so do so." Just keep headquarters posted, came the reply.[34]

Evidently Morrison made a good impression on the indefatigable inspector, William H. Sinclair, because the bureau staff officer recommended him to Griffin as an "out and out Union man" and "the only man that ought to be appointed" as the Palestine bureau representative. Griffin readily complied with Sinclair's suggestion. Morrison opened his office on April 10, and promptly suggested all of his close friends for bureau positions: post doctor, clerk, and freedmen's teacher. Headquarters warned him to hire no one without prior permission. Morrison then got down to business. He described the feelings of the local whites toward the freedmen as "desperately wicked and bad," "desperately bad," "intolerant," "very bitter," "bitter," and "indifferent." One time he said that he could not find the words to characterize the feelings of whites. "The feelings of the whites towards the freed people by Words is a curse and a damn," he said in another report, "'and actions' is a *knock down* with a stick or a *Shot* with a *pistol*. Neither the *freed people* or *Union white men* could live in *Anderson County* in Peace without U.S. Soldiers."[35]

Violence was a way of life in Anderson County, continued Morrison. The county clerk had had five shots fired through his closed office door, just missing his head. Morrison himself received daily threats from the Ku Klux Klan. Petitioners condemned him before headquarters as a vindictive, unfair tyrant, while others called him an unrepentant rebel. Morrison saw the results of terrorism frequently, and in March, 1868, he reported twenty-two murders and outrages to headquarters as having occurred since the end of the war. He believed that many more went untold; "I have colected this infermation heredly in order to be as prompt as posable," he wrote. Then he took a tour into Freestone County, and came back more mortified than ever. The murderer of bureau agent Charles E. Culver roamed unmolested. The Ku Klux Klan left a notice on his buggy one night. Freedmen begged him not to make a public display of helping them lest he wind up a dead man. It was the harshest anti-Negro feeling he had ever experienced, Morrison said. As in Palestine, Democratic clubs threatened not to hire any black who voted Republican.[36]

"There is not a local[it]y in the state," continued Morrison, "where the spite of antagonism to the Government, and its authority, and its officials, is so rampant as in the town of Palestine and the Circle of its influence." When Griffin's successor refused to let him use general orders to increase his powers and ordered him to turn all cases over to the local judges, he was especially disappointed. "I have to be lenant on Rebellious people," groused Morrison, as he defended the Unionists' and freed people's right to impartial legal treatment. But "two or three [rebels] come into my office and raise a row at a time and the crowd refuse to obey any sumons of officers to quell disturbances." He maintained that "the Civil Authorities, such as *Rebel Jurors*, is but a farce and give them no *protection* and *justice.*"[37] Nonetheless Morrison struggled on. He served concurrently as subassistant commissioner, county treasurer, and voter registrar. Later he was county judge under military appointment and state representative by election (confirmed by military appointment).[38]

Another outspoken Scalawag whom Griffin hired was Mortimer H. Goddin of Livingston. Like many of his contemporaries, Goddin had property and influence in several counties between the Trinity and the Sabine valleys. Born in Virginia in 1828 and "a long time" Texas resident, Goddin had served as a justice of the peace under the Hamilton regime, and would continue to take an active part in Reconstruction after his bureau appointment expired. He was a delegate to the state constitutional convention of 1868–1869, postmaster at Huntsville, newspaper editor, clerk of the district court, and a delegate to the 1875 state constitutional convention.

So swarthy was Goddin that some historians have erroneously identified him as a Negro, and many contemporaries thought him a bit insane. He was, if nothing else, very much in the mold of Agent Longworth at Seguin—outspoken and dedicated to the destruction of the Rebellion, or as Griffin thought him, "a proper man" to be a subassistant commissioner. At first he refused to accept the job, thinking that a military man or Northerner would be preferable. Griffin, however, refused to take no for an answer, and Goddin took office in April, 1867. Goddin thought the Negroes to be the loyalists' only friends, and repaid their fealty with his full support. He was one of the few subassistant commissioners to support openly Griffin's jury order to guarantee black justice (he admired Griffin and invited the general to stay with him during the yellow fever "fleeing spell"), and he did his utmost to ensure fair labor contracts. But his true mission was to punish the Livingston rebels for the persecution the loyal whites had suffered during the war in what he called "the worst hole in the county. . . . How I do want a chance at them!" he concluded grimly.[39]

Goddin got his chance, and he made the most of it. He was proud to be one of "a well tried few . . . white livered, sand gizzard, Dirt eating Unionists" who had steered clear of treason even though they "were threatened with hemp." But then, "unflinching National men are jewels here," he continued. Goddin said that he had resigned his political office when Sam Houston did, and he never took "the oath to support Jeff Davis' Wheel Barrow concern." The agent told Griffin that he was "ashamed to sent you the few names capable . . . of Holding office among the whites, who can take the iron clad," but he did so. After a successful voter registration (802 blacks and 324 whites), he thought "the vote of Polk [County] is now in loyal hands" providing they could keep the blacks from being "hoodwinked."

Goddin believed that the loyalists had to protect the newly freed blacks to prevent the "scenes of '60 and '61." As to the local rebels, "the devil is in some of them as big as Hell itself," he wrote. "They are making as little business as possible, so the freedmen get the benefit and I get the cussing." He believed the words he heard would "make the Devil blush though he be as black as Hell." But, he concluded, "we will be able after a while to ask them no odds." He then issued a poignant warning: "if the Military power of the government fails at this juncture to carry out its designs, the freedom of the negro will prove to be the worst calamity that has befallen him or his race."[40]

A voter registrar cautioned headquarters to avoid the notion that Goddin "is in some respects non compus mentis [sic]," saying that his orders were enforced and that he was a real terror to the rebels. But his Federal soldier guards believed he was crazy, and two of them even tried to kill the subassistant commissioner. Brevet Major Louis H. Sanger voted with his men. He reported that he had received a note from Goddin claiming that the whole subdistrict was in rebellion. It was the third such note he had received, and Sanger said the violence and revolution were figments of Goddin's imagination. He said that Goddin was so injudicious with his judgments as subassistant commissioner that he caused his own troubles. Goddin's bitterness towards the whites in his jurisdiction was unbelievable, said Sanger. His want of discretion eventually would cause him to need Federal protection, the major concluded, and he recommended that Goddin be relieved "at once." He was, in favor of Sanger, and he later fled to Huntsville to avoid assassination.[41]

Not all of the Scalawags hired on by Griffin proved to have been as circumspect as Goddin, Morrison, and Dix had in eschewing any association with the Confederacy. Dr. D. S. Hunsaker (no relation to Oscar F. Hunsaker), a Trinity County resident assigned to the Crockett agency, was a case in point. After its good experience with prior agents, the Houston County white population fairly exploded at Hunsaker's appointment. They complained that he was a former secessionist who, in 1861, had made much of shooting at an effigy of Abraham Lincoln and had brutally whipped a Negro he had recently bought to show his alleged support of the slaveocracy. During the war, he led a vigilance committee to search out Unionists, and he hired a substitute to avoid the Confederate military draft, whom he refused to pay as promised. In fact, rumor had it that Hunsaker's rebel support was merely a guise by which he hoped to cancel a heavy prewar debt owed to a New York firm. In 1863, Hunsaker fled to Mexico to avoid retaliation from his neighbors, and called himself a Union refugee—the only part of his past that Griffin had been aware of.

The Crockett *Sentinel* wondered how the man could begin to take the ironclad oath, as the newspaper exposed him to the world. Hunsaker stupidly sent the newspaper to headquarters, as a part of his defense, figuring a "rebel" newspaper would never be believed by the bureau staff. But the sheet was not alone in its condemnations. Captain Joseph H. Bradford, the local army commander, reported that Hunsaker had been drunk and disorderly in town, where his outrageous conduct nearly precipitated a riot. Despite the petition of three hundred freedmen that Hunsaker be kept on, he was summarily fired forty days after his appointment, one of the most disappointing choices Griffin ever made.[42]

More reputable in his conduct, but with the same Confederate liabilities, was Edwin Finch of Milford. A New Yorker who had lived in Texas for years, Finch has asked for a consideration before Christmas, 1866. He had the recommendations of Milton Stapp, the Federal collector of internal revenue, and the Kirkman brothers, one of whom (Joel T.) was Griffin's acting assistant adjutant general while the other (William G.) was the subassistant commissioner at Boston, Texas. "I have been a strong, out and out Union man and an almost penniless [one], rendered so by this . . . rebellion," Finch said in his application, referring to his refugee status.[43]

Finch's district included Ellis and Hill counties, and he noted that the arrival of a corporal's squad from the Thirty-fifth Infantry quieted things down quite a bit. Hill County was the worst, however, and the subassistant commissioner heard lots of mutterings against the bureau and recommended that Griffin purge the county government of all but the clerk of the district court. Finch was conscientious in his job, because he took "great pleasure in thus being able to secure Justice to the poor Freedmen." Most of his problems arose from the vicious persecutions and murders of Union men and their families. He was happy to report that the murderers of J. W. P. Doyle and his son had been captured by his soldiers and a posse, and hanged. The jails were too "unsafe" to hold such men, concluded Finch.[44]

While Finch was confident he was doing a good job, bad news arrived. John Lippard, the chief voting registrar, had accidentally found mention of Finch in the Confederate records at the Hill County courthouse. He had served Confederate Texas as a justice of the peace, and had even put up a five-hundred-dollar bond. The witness was none other than William H. Farner, the former bureau agent, who had been the clerk of the Confederate county court! Adherents begged headquarters to keep Finch on the job because he was a good subassistant commissioner and the only one courageous enough to serve. But an appeal to Washington only led to his outright removal by Commissioner Howard under General Grant's orders. Finch later served as a military appointee as constable, justice of the peace, county commissioner, voter registrar for the 1869 state elections, and Federal postmaster for Milford. This wealth of appointments indicates not only that the appointment pool in this area was down to a few hardy souls, but also that he truly was one of the few men willing to aid the provisional government at this time.[45]

But the worst mistake that Griffin made in a bureau appointment had to be naming Hiram S. Johnson subassistant commissioner at Sumpter in Trinity County. A native of Tennessee, Johnson had lived in Texas for some time before the war, and was A. J. Hamilton's selection as justice of the peace in Trinity County in 1865. Griffin wrote him in February, 1867, and asked him to serve as the bureau representative for his area, claiming that Johnson's legal background and ability to take the oath would make him "a particularly successful Sub. Asst. Comsr." Johnson accepted the offer, sent in his oath, and received his appointment in the massive Special Orders No. 35, as had the other Scalawags. There was a brief mixup when headquarters revoked his appointment, but he was reappointed three days later.[46]

At first a very vigorous subassistant commissioner, Johnson arrested outlaws with a citizen posse when his military guard proved too infirm to be of service (one died from disease). He fined planters so heavily for violating the terms of freedmen's labor contracts that headquarters had to step in and temper his zeal, confiscated rebel government property anew, made numerous political suggestions that even predated Griffin in the question of removals, investigated the wartime anti-Unionist activities of the home guard and recommended the arrest of

115 of its members by a sudden cavalry raid, supervised vigorously the fall crop division, and enforced liens upon landowners and not on freedmen. He communicated at such length with headquarters on each issue that the staff asked him to shorten his letters and confine them to a single topic. Johnson said in reply that "were it not for *fear* of the *Military Authorities*" brought on by his dedication to duty, "the woods would *Stink* with the carcasses of *dead Freedmen.*"[47]

Johnson seemed to be all that the bureau could want in a field agent. Upon hearing "the mournful intelligence" of the death of General Griffin, Johnson "draped our flag in mourning and suspended it at half mast in token of our respect for his many eminent qualities and gallant deeds." He expressed his desire that "Gen'l Griffin may be Succeeded by another as honest and as just and as fearless to do right." But the warning signs already had appeared. In mid-August, 1867, a planter in Houston County complained that Johnson had settled his freedmen's accounts unfairly and taken a portion of the crop from the employer and employee in exchange for services rendered. When the men protested, Johnson threatened to jail them for contempt.

The Crockett *Sentinel*, the same pro-rebel sheet that exposed Hunsaker, continued the assault. First it exposed his war record to the public. His activities as an impressment agent for the Confederate military draft were carried out with such glee, claimed the newspaper, that Johnson had to take to the bush himself until the rebel army came to his rescue. He had run for his judgeship in 1866, and received fewer than twenty votes in the county. As bureau agent, the newspaper asserted, Johnson had armed a large group of freedmen to support him in his quarrels with the local county government. He also was charged with confiscation of the money entrusted to him by local blacks to deposit in the Freedmen's Savings Bank at Galveston.

The *Sentinel's* story was corroborated by O. A. McGinnis, a respected attorney and loyalist who had kept the bureau informed over the years of events in eastern Texas, and who had recommended Johnson's appointment to Griffin in the first place. McGinnis now called Johnson one who "Glories in human misery!" and said he feared that whites in Trinity County would "smell Hell before he is done with them." When another planter swore out a complaint in the presence of Captain Joseph H. Bradford at Centerville, Bradford had to admit it only confirmed numerous rumors flying about his district.[48]

That was enough. Although the yellow fever epidemic delayed a response, the intrepid inspector, William H. Sinclair, came to look into the Johnson affair. He was too late. When Sinclair arrived in Sumpter, he found that Johnson had skipped town. Sinclair ordered his arrest—rumor had him headed toward Waco—and recommended that he be dismissed from the service with a loss of all pay and allowances. Years later, the vouchers were so messed up that McGinnis still had not collected from the government what little Johnson owed him alone.[49]

Griffin fared much better with the rest of his Southern appointments. When he noticed that one section of the state southwest of Dallas was particularly isolated, because of Kiddoo's withdrawal of the Fort Graham agency, he turned to a Scalawag of impeccable reputation, Philip Howard. Howard, who had resigned his position a few months before, agreed to serve as subassistant commissioner for the new Forty-eighth Subdistrict, providing he could operate out of his home at Meridian. Griffin promised Howard the assistance of a sergeant and six men and, although the soldiers were infantry and were sick most of the time, Howard cleared up a prodigious fifty-case backlog. By late fall, Howard said he no longer needed the soldiers, "as the people here believes I aim to do right," and they were withdrawn. Howard served on into January, 1868, when he was let go as part of an economizing measure. He had to submit to the usual audit before he was paid, a process that somewhat irritated the veteran agent.[50]

Two other Griffin appointees acted as bureau representatives for only a short period, preferring to resign their posts and seek elected political positions. There are few records to reveal the activities of Hardin Hart as subassistant commissioner at Greenville. A neighboring agent, Anthony M. Bryant, claimed that Hart ignored blacks' problems and said the freedmen came to Sherman to see him instead. But Hart did tour his district and make political recommendations to Griffin as requested. He also investigated a brutal multiple rape. Hart's ability to act may have been limited by the lack of military aid. When he did get a squad from Tyler, the men were sickly and useless much of the time. It cannot be said that the subassistant commissioner lacked courage. He also served as county judge, and had the guts to shoot down a member of the notorious Bob Lee gang in his front yard, after the armed man cursed and threatened him. But Hart, too, had state political aspirations, and the agency was transferred to the army post at Kaufman in late September, 1867.[51]

Hart's neighbor, who had reported the judge's alleged lack of interest in freedmen's problems, was Anthony M. Bryant. Originally from Kentucky, Bryant was an outspoken Unionist who had written Governor Hamilton early to expose the horrible conditions facing freed people in his area. He had served as a receiver of Confederate property under the authorization of Lieutenant Colonel Thomas Browne when he led the Seventh Indiana Cavalry into Grayson County in late 1865, and had been county judge for the Hamilton provisional government. Both he and Hart had signed petitions complaining about the lack of bureau supervision in northern Texas in early 1867. Griffin had already recommended Bryant for the subassistant commissioner's petition, and he took office at the end of March. There was some doubt if Bryant could take the ironclad oath, since he had run on the Union ticket for the first state legislature under Confederate rule. But Griffin believed that Bryant's action had been pure in its intent (unlike Finch at Milford he lost the election and did not serve), and his local post commander swore Bryant in.[52]

Considering the number of outlaws who populated the backcountry, the hostility of the white residents in general, the fact that only eighteen of the seventy-four cavalrymen on duty at Sherman had proper arms, and Bryant's preoccupation with state politics, he did rather well as the bureau representative for the Forty-first Subdistrict. Bryant made two thorough tours of his district, often announcing his itinerary weeks in advance. But he seems to have accurately estimated the situation, maintaining that the threats against his life were mostly bravado. He set up schools and adjudicated freedmen's complaints. But state politics beckoned, and he announced that he would resign his position on November 1 to seek a seat in the upcoming state convention. He won the election and was off to Austin. His subassistant commissionership went to the army post commander with whom he had shared bureau responsibilities since July.[53]

Like the professional and volunteer soldiers Griffin appointed to be subassistant commissioners, the Northern and Southern civilians embodied a wide range of talents and motives that makes characterizing the average agent a difficult task. For this reason, the general, and all of the other assistant commissioners, had to rely on an often inadequate system of inspections and monthly reports to keep track of the varying conditions that field agents faced within this very large bureau command area. But the actual chore of checking up on the bureau's work in Texas fell on the shoulders of the acting assistant inspector general, whom we have already encountered at several points in our account of the Texas bureau, William H. Sinclair.

9

The Meanest Republican in Texas

WHEN GENERAL GRIFFIN ASSUMED CONTROL of the bureau in February, 1867, one of his first acts was to give William H. Sinclair the title of acting assistant inspector general. A former brevet colonel of volunteers in the adjutant general's department, Sinclair had served as a bureau staff officer since March, 1866, under various titles. Sinclair had handled the inspector's duties as a civilian appointee for General Kiddoo after his discharge from the volunteer service in September, 1866, so he had experience. He was the author of Kiddoo's Circular Letter of December 31, 1866, which set the standards for the field agents' monthly reports. He also possessed the ability to discharge his duties faithfully under anyone's leadership, a quality that gave him unusual permanence and much influence in the ever-changing bureau command structure.[1]

Sinclair's important role as a staff officer was demonstrated early on, when Griffin ordered him to inspect the counties that ringed Houston. In his report, Sinclair discoursed widely on subassistant commissioners, the freedmen, and life in Reconstruction Texas in general. Although most freedmen had signed contracts for 1867, Sinclair noted that they did so reluctantly. He blamed three factors: a late picking season that lasted into February, 1867, in many places, in which the fieldhands made good wages; the freedmen's general dislike of the contract system, which the blacks astutely saw as an extension of slavery, a notion that the bureau could not disabuse them of; and poor treatment, which found its expression in the forms of deceit and cruelty practiced in 1865 and 1866.

Sinclair believed, despite the blacks' dissatisfaction with the contract system and his own critical reports, that the subassistant commissioners had done well as a group. He asserted that much of the evasion of bureau edicts was made possible by the size of the state, and the ease with which agencies could be bypassed by violators. Without the beneficial influence of the field agents, Sinclair said, "the results may be easily imagined." As it was, everything that went wrong was charged up to the freedmen by the planters' system of deductions. Sinclair told how planters regularly charged items against the freedmen's accounts at double price. The end result was that the blacks were broke at the end of the year, instead of being entitled to wages for their annual work. He admitted that some planters treated the blacks fairly, but said they were the exception in Texas, not the rule. Worse yet was the practice of the landowners to rent the land to a white contractor, who cared not at all about humane conditions, so long as a crop was produced. These men were especially prone to sell the crop and abscond with the profits.

Whatever land lay fallow was the result not of poor work habits among the Negroes, but of the shortage of hands that plagued much of the Texas cotton region. This led to much competition between whites from the hills and the bottom lands, which in turn resulted in much bickering among whites and enticement attempts, with the Negro caught innocently in the middle. The big plantations were doomed in the long run, Sinclair said, because the blacks tended more and more to favor renting small plots and running family farms. The inspector agreed with Texas whites that the freedmen's plots were economically unproductive, but Sinclair held that the freedmen had the right to try a new method of production.

What amazed Sinclair the most was that the blacks were so willing to contract with the very men who had cheated them in years past. "The freedpeople are as yet children," he continued. The Negroes fell for every false and outlandish promise that the labor contractors could dream up. "I see no hope for them," Sinclair concluded. In the last analysis, Sinclair agreed with the planters that the freedmen's own laziness and neglect of labor responsibilities had cost everyone "thousands of bales" of potential profit. On the other hand, the freedmen fully realized that their only white friends were the subassistant commissioners, who worked to assure them a fair contract. Sinclair advised the bureau representatives to favor the old slaveholders as the most responsible employers with whom the freedmen could sign on. Most responsible planters insisted that the bureau agent review all transactions to prevent quarrels and misunderstandings. Renters and nonslaveholding whites were the cruelest employers and the ones least likely to pay at year's end.

Above all, Sinclair warned that the punitive sections of the state labor laws must be abrogated by the field agents. To allow the blacks to be charged such deductions, Sinclair said, would cost them any chance of a cash settlement. In fact, he went on, about the only thing the state laws did not do to ensure peonage was give the planters a lien on the freedman's person until they were satisfied with the year-end settlements. But the blacks would be safe until the fall, the inspector maintained. Then the subassistant commissioners' services would be indispensable, because of the injustice of the civil law, the hatred felt toward blacks by local administrators, the child-like nature of the freedmen themselves, the inability of the freedmen to hire proper legal assistance, and the ability of the rich planters to stretch the cases out until the poverty-stricken freedmen had to settle for a fraction of what they were due just to have something to live on.[2]

Sinclair called for the field officers to be fully supplied with furniture and stationery supplies. He said that the supplies specified in bureau regulations were inadequate and that one lengthy contract could exhaust the subassistant commissioner's stock of ink and paper. He also recommended that all contracts be held in the agency, not at headquarters, since the local bureau agent, the blacks, and the planters would need to refer to them often. And although contracts could be authorized by any subassistant commissioner, county judge, justice of the peace, notary public, or clerk of the county court, Sinclair pointed out that documents agreed to before Griffin established this rule had to be filed in the local clerk's office in order to be recognized by state law. He suggested that all documents agreed to before January 30, 1867, be enforced only by bureau representatives.[3]

During the summer of 1867, Sinclair made an extensive fact-finding tour of the whole state. The inspector thought he had already seen all the evils Reconstruction Texas had to offer, but nothing had prepared him adequately for Clarksville. The local agent was a loyal Texan, Albert H. Latimer. As subassistant commissioner, Latimer was not an aggressive agent, probably because of his advanced age and poor health. He also was more interested in statewide office, and would later serve, despite his age, under military appointment on the state supreme court.[4]

Sinclair found conditions at Clarksville to be the worst in the whole state. Indicted men entered and left the town at will. Freedmen were brutalized daily. Whenever the bureau agent, Latimer, or the county court tried to get the sheriff to act, the peace officer had to face not only the suspect, but a gang of his friends and supporters. It was an uneven fight that the sheriff could not hope to win. When the lawman called upon the citizens to form a posse to assist him, they refused. The county judge would fine the slackers, lecture them sternly, and quietly remit the fines a few days later. Sinclair called for the appointment of a new judge.

It was no wonder that Latimer feared for his own life and had asked to be relieved, Sinclair continued. Latimer was not safe in his own home, and the stress of the bureau job had aged the old man ten years since Sinclair had last seen him in Galveston. Sinclair recommended that a full company of cavalry be stationed at Clarksville. The inspector believed that the post at Mount Pleasant ought to be transferred to Clarksville, as the need for the troops was much greater in Red River County. He also suggested that a younger man with "plenty of backbone," a man who would "do his duty" without hesitation, be sent to replace Latimer.

Meanwhile, Sinclair said that he feared for the success of voter registration. He had already been warned that the local registrars would be killed. All had been threatened, and he had no doubt that at least one would resign that very day. South Texas with all of its shortcomings was a paradise compared to Red River County, Sinclair said. "I am now afraid I have written so earnestly that you will think me wild," he cautioned. "If you . . . were here, though, it would not take long to convince you that to the Union men and the freedpeople, this northern part of the state is pandemonium, itself."[5]

Evidently, Sinclair still worried that the men isolated from reality back in the Galveston headquarters would discount the horrible tale he related in his official communiqué from the field, because he also wrote an impassioned personal letter to the bureau's acting assistant adjutant general, Second Lieutenant Joel T. Kirkman, whose brother had just been assigned to the agency in neighboring Bowie County. "You have no idea of the kind of people there are here," Sinclair began. If anyone from Galveston were to come up to Red River County to speak to the Negroes, Sinclair said, he would never leave town alive. Civil law was a dead letter, the inspector asserted. "My God, how your heart would bleed for the Union men of this country if you knew what they have suffered and are yet suffering from this Rebel rule."

Slipping into a bitter caricature, Sinclair related how being in Red River County was like being taken back in time to the harrowing days of the recent war. The inspector had naively assumed that the war was over when he was in Galveston. "It isn't," he emphasized. What northeastern Texas needed was for a fleet of Union gunboats to come up the Red River and defeat the unrepentant Texans once and for all. As for the freedmen, Sinclair referred to them as "slaves," whom local planters held by force, fearing that the bureau agents might carry them off to "Yankee lines" and freedom.

Sinclair said he thought at first he was having a nightmare. He had pinched himself to awaken, but found the dreadful dream was indeed harsh reality. "Hasn't Throckmorton been relieved or kicked out yet? Why don't Gen'l Griffin or Sheridan put the political demagogue out?" demanded Sinclair, outraged. The governor's idea that the "civil law reigneth" was absurd here. Even Throckmorton would have to start telling the truth if he came up to Clarksville, thought the disheartened inspector. "Send [Brevet Captain Charles F.] Rand or some other young man with blood in his eye up here and a good officer to command the troops. *A man who is up to the times*" was needed, Sinclair concluded.[6]

But of all Sinclair's inspections, the most noted at that time was his visit to the state penitentiary at Huntsville in February, 1867. The issue was one that had bothered bureau agents for a long time—the equal treatment of blacks in the justice system. Sinclair had had the issue brought home to him a month earlier, when he wrote Governor Throckmorton on behalf of General Kiddoo to complain of the treatment of two black prisoners held at Marlin in a small room, chained together, with no heat or basic creature comforts. He also believed that many other blacks jailed in Texas were victims of white persecution, as opposed to legal prosecution. Griffin agreed, and Sinclair went to the largest repository of prisoners in the state, the penitentiary at Huntsville, to check out the truth of his hypothesis.[7]

Sinclair visited the state prison in the company of the Huntsville bureau agent, James C. Devine. They were received cordially by the warden, James Gillespie, who cooperated in the investigation. Sinclair thought that Gillespie and his staff ran the institution well. The prisoners were "well fed, well clothed, and kindly treated," Sinclair said. Many had work furloughs to jobs outside the prison walls, and many of these were totally unsupervised leaves, with the prisoners coming back voluntarily each night. There was, of course, a pack of hounds and catch dogs for those who sought to stay away prematurely, before the completion of their sentences.

Examining the prison records, Sinclair found that there were 411 persons held, of whom 225 were black. Of the Negroes, 211 were male and 14 female. Although no white women were imprisoned, two of the women were so high-yellow that Sinclair disbelieved they were Negroes; but everyone swore they had been held as slaves. The records revealed that the majority of the blacks were incarcerated on charges of theft. Little more was indicated. So Sinclair received permission to interview the prisoners to learn more of their circumstances of arrest. It was a moving experience for the inspector. The thefts usually turned out to be "trivial" in nature, often of food or clothing, crimes that would have been "during times of slavery punished with the lash." Sinclair never intended to question the whole prison population, "but the statement of the few whom I first examined so impressed me of the injustice of the treatment these unfortunate creatures had received at the hands of justice (?) that I felt . . . I must examine and record the statement of each particular case."

With the help of Agent Devine acting as clerk, Sinclair went through the prison population. He found that most were serving a three-year term, plus about six months in the county jail while their cases had been tried. He admitted that he realized convicts' tendency to assert their innocence, but he thought that this time the claim rang true. "I am fully convinced," he wrote, "and any person listening to their simple, frank statements and looking into the[ir] black and ~~apparently~~ honest faces could not believe otherwise." The circumstances of the prosecution showed that the spirit of the charge was revenge and malice, and frequently the black victims had committed no real crime. It was a situation that "cannot but excite in the heart of any man who sees them as I did sympathy for their fate and a resolve to make the effort for their relief."[8]

The bureau inspector suggested that Texas follow the example of the state of Alabama and issue a mass pardon of all those not held for rape or murder. The laws under which they had been convicted had been changed in the most recent Texas legislature, and the new punishments were much lighter, Sinclair said. The inspector believed that three fourths of the freed persons now held at Huntsville could be let go with no harm to society.[9]

When the proposal reached the desk of Governor Throckmorton, the state's chief executive expressed profound shock that Sinclair could make such a proposal. He lectured the bureau for eight long pages about law, morality, and the need of society to prevent and punish crime. The governor refused to change his current policy of a case-by-case approach on the individual merits of the case and the criminal. The whole question soon became moot, for by the time the matter had been fully discussed, nearly two thirds (61 percent) of the blacks held at Huntsville and interviewed by Sinclair had been freed by completing their terms or pardoned by Governor Throckmorton, according to the bureau's own figures. But Throckmorton's attitude would be remembered. Griffin stored such perceived transgressions in the back of his mind for a future, final reckoning.[10]

Even though Griffin had given way to Throckmorton's assault on military rule, he was merely biding his time, consolidating his position, and awaiting a new opportunity to attack the "rebel" civil government from a different approach. His chance came in March, 1867, when Congress passed the first of the Military Reconstruction acts. These measures made Texas and Louisiana into the Fifth Military District, under the command of General Sheridan in New Orleans. Griffin still controlled Texas at Galveston.[11] It was his responsibility to protect the civil and property rights of all persons, to suppress insurrection, disorder, and violence, and to punish, or cause to be punished, all criminal actions. The general could use the civil courts or, if he believed it necessary, military tribunals. In the latter instance, Griffin was to review all sentences and pass on death sentences to the president for approval. General Orders No. 26, which turned all court proceedings over to civil government in Texas, no longer applied.

In addition to his expanded judicial responsibilities, Griffin received new political duties. Texas was to call a new constitutional convention. Should Governor Throckmorton fail to do this, Griffin could issue the call. The convention delegates were to be elected by all males, white or black, over the age of twenty-one, who had lived in the state for one year, and who had been registered by the boards of registration composed of three persons appointed by General Griffin. No one barred from holding office under the proposed Fourteenth Amendment could register to vote or serve in the convention. The convention was to provide for universal male suffrage and bring the Texas organic document into agreement with the Constitution of the United States in all respects. Once the new constitution had been ratified by a majority of the registered voters (later amended to a majority of those voting), the new government elected was to ratify the Fourteenth Amendment, whereupon Congress could readmit the state into the Union.[12]

Griffin made his first move on April 5. He issued Circular Orders No. 10, which allowed any post commander to take charge of any case in a local court, when he believed the proceedings to be unfair, and to present the case to Griffin's headquarters for review. Under this edict, the general ordered stays in proceedings, reversed state court decisions in cases settled during and after the war, and freed state prisoners whom he thought were unfairly convicted, as he expressed it, "in a spirit of malicious prosecution fostered by vindictive and disloyal sentiments."[13]

Later that same month, Griffin committed the most celebrated act of military interference with civil courts during Reconstruction. When General Orders No. 26 had been in effect, Griffin and other loyalists found cases in Texas courts to be decided more on the basis of race and wartime politics than on that of justice. In his Circular Orders No. 13, designed to prevent "persons disqualified by law" from serving as jurors, Griffin required that all potential jurors take the "ironclad oath" that they had not voluntarily given "aid, countenance, counsel or encouragement" to the Confederacy or its agents. In the same order, Griffin printed a portion of the Civil Rights Act of 1866, which provided that anyone who "under color of any law, statute, ordinance, regulation or custom" deprived any citizen of his civil rights was guilty of a misdemeanor, subject to a fine of one thousand dollars or one year in jail, or both.[14]

The effect of the jury order was to exclude the great majority of white Texans from courtroom juries, which produced howls of rage throughout the state.[15] Angered by Griffin's actions, Governor Throckmorton placed the plight of his constituents before President Johnson, but at the same time he advised all judges to comply with the circulars. Throckmorton then sent Griffin a copy of his letter to Johnson because he feared that the document might be misrepresented to the general. Privately, Throckmorton was convinced that Griffin has issued the jury order to force him to oppose it, thus giving the general cause to remove him from office. For the same reason, the governor sent copies of his communications with Griffin to the president.[16]

The massive attack on his Circular Orders No. 13 put Griffin on the defensive. He justified the order in a letter to General Grant by stating that its purpose was not to foist black jurors on Texas, as had been charged, but rather to ensure that loyal whites and blacks were able to serve and protect themselves from injustice. The oath was the same that Congress required of Federal officeholders, said Griffin. He further maintained that he had not interfered with the state requirements that a juror must be a qualified voter, a householder of the county, or a freeholder of the state. These existing regulations, continued the general, could exclude nearly every black in Texas from being a juror.[17]

Griffin labeled as untrue the many complaints of a shortage of jurors in many counties because of Circular Orders No. 13. Griffin accused state judges of concealing the actual number of qualified jurors in their counties merely to embarrass him. The general reiterated that the purpose of the jury order was to protect "loyal residents in their lives, liberties and property." He believed Unionists were all for it and would rather be tried by blacks, regardless of their level of education, than by disloyal whites, whose motto seemed to be "rule or ruin."[18]

Sheridan agreed with his subordinate. He adopted as necessary the idea of removing the "disaffected element," as he and Griffin liked to characterize the white majority in Texas, from the juries because of its opposition to equal justice for blacks. He told Griffin that if Texas officials tried to embarrass him by including unqualified blacks on juries, Griffin should report them and Sheridan would remove them from office. One officer was so pleased with the effect of the jury order in his command area that he recommended its adoption throughout the entire Fifth Military District. This move was opposed by Grant, however, who said that the rules for selecting juries should assure "equal justice for all classes." Grant insisted that if a man could be considered loyal enough to vote he was loyal enough to be a juror. This policy became standard by the end of September, 1867, after Griffin's death, and the jury lists were revised accordingly.[19]

In his solution to the jury problem, Grant touched upon one of the most important questions facing Griffin—who was loyal enough to vote and hold office? If a loyal government could be elected in Texas and other Southern states that would guarantee fairness in the treatment of black and white loyalists, the bureau and the army of occupation would be unnecessary and could be withdrawn. Reconstruction would be a success. The first step in organizing Republican strength was the registration of voters who would select delegates to a new constitutional convention. Griffin's search for qualified registrars began in March, when he ordered his subassistant commissioners to examine their districts for the best located polling places in each county, and for the names of "undoubted Union men" and qualified blacks to act as registrars. Actual registration did not start until May. Griffin had feared that Throckmorton would oppose the registration effort, but to his surprise, the governor cooperated fully in obtaining the names of qualified registrars.[20]

Registration was carried out under a series of orders that Griffin issued in April, May, and June. Although Griffin issued these orders as army commander of the District of Texas, he relied on his bureau field representatives to coordinate the registration process. In these edicts, Griffin established fifteen registration districts that corresponded to the state's judicial districts. Each registration district was entitled to two registration supervisors and a clerk appointed by Griffin from Galveston. All three men had to take the ironclad oath. The supervisors were to provide the books and stationery, organize the actual registration boards (consisting of three men appointed by the supervisors who could subscribe to the ironclad oath), adjust causes of complaint, detect fraud, and forward the returns to Griffin with a report. Each county was to be a registration precinct.[21]

Griffin announced a target date of September 1 for the completion of registration. He ordered each voter to take an oath that he was not excluded by law from voting through actions committed during the war. This oath pledged future loyalty to the United States and affirmed that the individual had not sworn allegiance to the U.S. government and then seceded and supported the Confederacy through service in any army, state, or national institution. The precinct registrars gave each voter a certificate of registration upon enrollment. Griffin cautioned the registrars to take special care in signing up black voters. Their registration certificates were to be marked "colored voter" in red ink on the back. The general warned planters not to use the contract terms to deny any freedman the time necessary to come in and register. Because Griffin correctly suspected that many blacks had been discriminated against anyway, he reopened the registration process for six days in September. This late registration after the announced deadline caused much ill-feeling among whites about the whole process.[22]

Griffin had the boards keep separate lists of registered voters and those rejected for enrollment, with the cause of rejection, because the Reconstruction Acts were ambiguous as to disqualifications. At Griffin's request, Sheridan wrote General Grant to clear up the question. Grant told the generals to make their own policy until he could get a ruling from the attorney general. Sheridan told Griffin to "exclude from registration every person about whose right to vote there may be doubt."[23] Shortly thereafter, Attorney General Henry Stanbery recommended a more liberal approach, but Griffin and Sheridan got Grant's permission to proceed with their stricter interpretation. They rationalized their stand by noting that the will of the people as expressed by Congress's overriding the president's vetoes of the Reconstruction Acts was superior to the wishes of the executive branch.[24]

The result of Griffin's query was Sheridan's famous "secret memorandum" to him on voter registration. This notice, kept from the press to avoid "intricate questions as to the restrictions imposed," allowed Griffin and his registrars to disfranchise anyone who had served as a civil officer before 1861 on the Federal or state level, from senators to sextons of cemeteries. Registrars were to use their own judgment and disfranchise anyone they suspected of giving false answers to a half dozen key questions used to determine loyalty.[25] Griffin saw the tough line as critical to building a loyal biracial political party.[26]

As registration progressed, Griffin ordered the boards to make weekly reports to the nearest military commander, who was to forward them to headquarters. When they failed to do this faithfully, the general turned again to his bureau subassistant commissioners, whom he asked to supervise the weekly reporting process. When the registration was completed, Griffin ordered the registrars to make out full returns. These reports were to show the total number of voters registered, the number of black voters registered, and the number of applicants rejected and the reason for their rejection, and should contain a full statement by the board on whether it believed the returns were complete, or if not, why not. Griffin warned the registration personnel that the performance of their duties would be subject to his review, and that any irregularity would be adjudicated by a military tribunal.[27]

In spite of Griffin's promised military supervision, the registration boards' subjective exercise of power caused a great deal of dissatisfaction among white Texans. Numerous letters arrived at Griffin's headquarters accusing board members of arbitrary action. Other writers complained that they had to stand in long lines while black applicants, many of whom were under voting age or could not fulfill residency requirements, were passed on through. Some complained that blacks had been registered ahead of the registration period.[28]

The result of these complaints was continual violence at the registration sites. Dr. B. F. Barkley, a Tarrant County registrar whom Confederate authorities had once jailed and who needed the job now to support his large family, was "grossly insulted" by one rejected white applicant. Barkley "promptly replied to it in such language as to preclude its repetition." One of his fellow board members, Anthony Rucker, was black, and received so many assassination threats that everyone lost count. These were not idle threats. Two registrars were shot within fifteen miles of Brenham. A disgruntled white rejected by the Clarksville board assaulted its black member. He had to flee into Indian Territory to avoid military arrest. A Marion County registrar believed that his acceptance of the position had ruined his chance of ever making a living there again. He charged local newspapers with inflaming public opinion against the registration process.[29]

Anticipating such trouble, Griffin had all boards operate initially out of county courthouses. Then, as they moved into more rural areas, the general promised that he would send escorts of ten soldiers with each registration team. On June 1, he ordered all post commanders to afford full protection to the registration boards. Escorts often were infantrymen, who rode in a wagon behind the registrars who traveled in classier ambulances. Often the soldiers were not needed. When white applicants saw black board members at the registration tables, they frequently walked off in disgust. This caused one registrar to remark, "[T]he more I think of the folly of men refusing to act because of a freedman being on the local board—the more I am convinced of their unfitness to give a helping hand in the reconstruction." He, like Griffin and others, thought that registration was a serious obligation of any qualified citizen, and one not to be spurned flippantly. Griffin admitted that "it will look a little funny to see the former Master's application for registration rejected by the old black servant, but such is the law and it shall have full force here."[30]

Having moved to secure justice for blacks in court and to guarantee their entrance into the political system, Griffin turned next to getting rid of his main obstacle in reconstructing the state, the elected government headed by Governor Throckmorton. Griffin was not about to wait out the lengthy and intricate process of election, convention, reelection, and readmission called for by Congress. If he did that, the wily governor would make the general into an impotent figurehead as he had Sheridan and Kiddoo before him. Instead Griffin would force the governor into a stance of opposition and have him removed from office. Sheridan was doing much the same in Louisiana at that very moment. Griffin requested that his bureau subassistant commissioners draw up a list in each county of the names of "thoroughly competent men of position and decent character," who could take the ironclad oath, and were pro-Union. He asked them to hurry.[31]

But Throckmorton refused to fall into Griffin's trap. He was too cooperative to checkmate, yet too obstructionist to allow the loyal whites and blacks to win the electoral process. After all, Throckmorton's men held the local offices and patronage. As one disgruntled Unionist had phrased it, "a Union man has no more chance of getting elected to office than Satan has of getting to heaven." The election of the previous summer had proven that. The loyal whites and blacks, in the process of organizing a Republican party, needed assistance in the form of an active interference in the current political situation by the bureau commander.[32]

But when Griffin turned to his superior, Sheridan, he was surprised to have his plan of partisan political removals and appointments rejected out of hand. Sheridan himself was under fire from Washington for his aggressive policies in Louisiana. He told Griffin that, as a matter of principle, he would not act except in specific cases for due cause. Rebuffed, Griffin snorted, "Give me assistance by removals, soon as possible." To Elisha M. Pease, the Unionist candidate who had lost the 1866 election to Throckmorton and whom Griffin slated to be his new provisional governor at the proper moment, the general wrote, "It comes back to what I remarked to you, whilst in Galveston, that no reason should be assigned for removals." In his emphasis upon actual cause, "Sheridan makes a great mistake," concluded Griffin.[33]

The Texas bureau commander now realized that unless Congress acted to modify the Reconstruction Acts to allow specifically for removals and replacements of obstructionist local officials, he would have a tough time with the governor. Yet Throckmorton's removal was crucial to the success of the bureau and other Reconstruction programs. Griffin kept deluging Sheridan with letter after letter describing the officials in Texas as "rebels" who allowed "lawless" actions against blacks. He threatened to strip the frontier garrisons to protect blacks in the interior. Griffin blamed every problem directly on Throckmorton's attitude. "I trust so soon as the law will permit," he reiterated to Sheridan, "there will be changes in the civil affairs of this state."

Sheridan dutifully forwarded all communications from Texas to Washington. By the end of July, Grant informed Sheridan that military commanders could remove local officials who hindered Reconstruction. Sheridan moved immediately. "A careful consideration of the reports of Brevet Major General Charles Griffin," stated Special Orders No. 105, "shows that J. W. Throckmorton, Governor of Texas, is an impediment of the reconstruction of the State, under the law; he is therefore removed from office." Elisha M. Pease was to be the new provisional governor.[34]

The response to Sheridan's act was for President Andrew Johnson to reassign him to a new military command on the Great Plains fighting Indians. Sheridan would be replaced by Major General Winfield S. Hancock, a known Democrat. Meanwhile, however, because of the complexities of the transfer, Griffin would become the *ad interim* head of the Fifth Military District. The irony of the man who had cost Sheridan his job being rewarded with the same position drew a few chuckles, as Texas Republicans rejoiced. Colbert Caldwell, a noted Republican judge, explained the new arithmetic made possible by Griffin's political support. Last year sixty thousand persons voted for governor, he said. The totals were twelve thousand for Pease, and forty-eight thousand for Throckmorton. Now, a year later, through the activities of the general and his bureau-led political crusade, eight thousand whites had been disfranchised, and the local patronage given to the Republicans. Caldwell thought that the repoliticized white electorate would split, twenty-four thousand for Pease, and twenty-eight thousand for Throckmorton.

Add the new thirty-four thousand black votes, Caldwell continued, and the totals would be fifty-four thousand for Pease and forty-two thousand for Throckmorton. If the "rebels" had any sense, concluded Caldwell, they would let the election go by default. The loss of the hesitant Sheridan would be a great gain for the Texas Republicans. The deposed Throckmorton agreed. He saw Griffin as a much worse district commander than Sheridan. "He is a dog—mangy—full of fleas," he declared of Griffin, "and as mean as the meanest Radical Republican in Texas, and that is saying as mean a thing of a man as can be said."[35]

While Griffin busied himself with fair justice, voter registration, and politics, more mundane bureau matters also occupied his attention. Although interest in the scheme had dropped off drastically, the assistant commissioner still continued the importation of black labor begun so enthusiastically by General Kiddoo the previous year. Bureau policy was to move indigent freed persons or white refugees, who were dependent upon government support, to places where they might receive employment. Only the assistant commissioners, like Griffin, could authorize transportation requests. These orders became more and more expensive, and less frequent, with the removal of wartime controls upon the fares railroads and steamship companies could charge.[36]

The cause of labor transportation was not helped any by the tale of J. B. Darby of Montgomery County. He claimed that one Levi King of Alabama had brought seven minors to Texas against their will. The children were apprentices under Alabama law, but Darby asserted that the law had been an attempt by the Alabama legislature to reestablish slavery under a new guise, and had been annulled by the bureau there. King reputedly had stolen the two youngest from their mother as she fled to the protection of a Mobile subassistant commissioner. King had promised the older children fifty dollars each to come to Texas, said Darby, but now they feared that King would not pay them. Darby called the whole deal a kidnapping, and begged Griffin to act quickly. The general promised to compensate Darby, who continued his investigation and located King and the children in Smith County, Texas. When Darby pressed for payment, Griffin told him to hold on, as the case was still under investigation.[37]

As with the Darby case, Griffin was loath to pay out government funds for any item not truly essential. He merely followed headquarters policy in this matter. Griffin's tenure saw the closing of the Houston Freedmen's Hospital,[38] the ending of rations being dispensed to the needy,[39] and the corresponding interest in the proper amount of correct paperwork on all accounts.[40] Field agents were expected to act as quartermaster clerks when no army personnel were available,[41] brand bureau animals,[42] and feed them from army forage stocks.[43] Griffin preferred that his men purchase all bureau supplies from the army quartermaster stocks, as he considered the army price to be the cheapest he could obtain.[44] Meanwhile, Griffin's staff supervised the collection and deposit of the claims of black soldiers from the war occupation,[45] and the general himself took time out to issue the only Texas Reconstruction order, bureau or army, demanding equal treatment of blacks using public accommodations.[46]

Although the Griffin administration saw the winding down of many bureau activities, the topic of abandoned lands actually assumed new dimensions. The Texas bureau had returned the lots seized in Brownsville when their owner obtained a presidential pardon. But it still held property in Austin and Houston, which it was in the process of selling. In addition, the bureau received much opposition from the pro-Union city government in its attempts to sell the sawmill and tannery at San Antonio to private parties. Threatened with a city-sponsored lawsuit, potential purchasers declined to bid on the property. In the end, the city made its own bid, which the bureau decided to accept, and the funds received were used to help finance the freedmen's normal school at Galveston. The Waco Manufacturing Co. had been returned to its owners by the U. S. Treasury Department, but further investigations caused the bureau to retake it and hold it for sale as a Confederate enterprise. The bureau also seized property in Milam County (a sawmill and two cabins), Lamar County (a blacksmith shop), Smith County (a storehouse), and Anderson County (an office and two dwellings once used as a machine shop).[47]

The other area in which Griffin expanded bureau concern was education. Indeed, his first measure upon assuming the joint control of the bureau and army commands had been to abolish the charges for contracts by which Kiddoo has wished to finance free schools for blacks. The next thing Griffin did was to reinstate tuition payments for all students except the children of widows and orphans, who still attended free of charge. The rest of the families paid fifty cents a month for one scholar attending school, seventy-five cents for two pupils, and one dollar for three or more students. He also guaranteed that bureau teachers would be paid forty dollars a month beyond tuition collections, less any funds they might receive from a benevolent association.[48]

As far as the benevolent associations were concerned, Griffin offered to subsidize the American Missionary Association to the amount of twenty-five dollars a month for ten teachers' salaries. He also proposed that up to one hundred army enlisted men stationed with white and black regiments in Texas be detailed as bureau teachers of freedmen. This plan, however, was refused by the Adjutant General's Office in Washington. Still requests poured in for more teachers to establish schools, not only in towns, but on individual plantations. One planter described how the freedmen working for him had raised over one hundred dollars to pay the bureau to send them a teacher, and would pledge the same amount each month as tuition. The planter asked for a sober, Protestant man of "mild and even disposition," who would be "agreeable and not officious or medlesome." The plantation owner promised to treat such a person with the respect due a gentleman.

The planter's cautions were well founded. From San Antonio came a letter written by the army post commandant, Brevet Brigadier General John S. Mason, complaining about the schoolteacher there. Mason's letter related how the teacher abused the local subassistant commissioner, an officer on Mason's staff; bragged that he had more influence at Griffin's headquarters than any of the military men in San Antonio (Mason's letter was addressed to "Dear Griffin" and closed with Mason's regards to Mrs. Griffin, which took care of that debatable point); and ran after "the wenches," which caused him to be disliked by the local blacks, who eagerly reported the teacher's every fault to Mason's office. Mason wanted to fire the teacher outright, but since the topic had been referred to Griffin, Mason now wanted the general to know his preferences in the matter. He believed that a new teacher could be had by the fall term, and that the summer session could be handled by the town's second teacher of freedmen, a woman of unquestioned moral conduct.[49]

With the demand for schoolteachers at a new high, the need for schools also became critical. Griffin next issued Circular Orders No. 3, which provided for freedmen to begin construction of a school on their own volition and then apply to the bureau for funds to "repair" the building into a usable state. He sent his assistant superintendent of schools, D. T. Allen, and the school inspector, G. T. Ruby, to coordinate the program through visits to teachers and local subassistant commissioners, and to expedite the process. Trustee associations of freedmen were encouraged to purchase land and to begin to erect buildings. New and used lumber was obtained from bureau sources, abandoned buildings, or other stocks on the lists of the state distribution officer. Occasionally a public-spirited citizen would donate land, building use, or materials. In rare cases all three came free.[50]

Much of the success of Griffin's school expansion was made possible by his dual role as bureau and army commander. His expansion of the military occupation and the corresponding creation of new bureau subdistricts gave the school effort the protection it needed in outlying areas to be safe from brigandage. He also made the bureau representatives responsible for the success of educational efforts in their subdistricts. Already the agents were to report the feeling of whites and blacks as to Negro education in their areas, and to encourage a positive outlook on the matter. Now Griffin ordered his subassistant commissioners into the field to visit each school monthly, impress the value of education upon the freedmen, coordinate rental and purchase of land and buildings, apply for teachers at headquarters, and provide for their physical wants and safety once they arrived. The agents were also to evaluate each teacher's job performance. Finally, Griffin provided bureau transportation to the job site for teachers, according to regulations established in Washington.[51]

The advances in black education were marred by a bitter quarrel between Reverend Jacob R. Shipard of the American Missionary association, Superintendent of Schools E. M. Wheelock of the Texas bureau, and General Griffin. Shipard intensely disliked Wheelock, who was a Unitarian. Both men refused to compromise their perceived truths, and Griffin wound up in the middle with a few notions of his own about the need for a central command system. Griffin objected to the independent position that the missionary societies had held with regard to his predecessors. Gregory and Kiddoo had let the benevolent associations run the whole educational system with minimal bureau supervision provided by Wheelock. Griffin now wanted to control the entire bureau program directly. Like his predecessors, Griffin also found Wheelock more interested in arguing fine points of religious doctrine than in teaching black students. In his arguments, Wheelock was assisted by his sister Lydia, a local teacher, who possessed an extremely sharp tongue. Neither brother nor sister appreciated the benefits of a private discussion of differences.

Griffin decided to neutralize the Wheelocks first. Allying himself with Shipard, Griffin removed Wheelock from his position as superintendent, and exiled his sister to teach at Alleytown in Colorado County. Then he reported his actions to Howard. Howard was a receptive audience, since he had problems of his own in Washington with one of Wheelock's friends, B. Rush Plumbley. Howard accused Wheelock, the "liberal Christian," of possessing an "illiberal spirit." According to Howard, Wheelock sat in his room doing little for bureau educational efforts, plotting his own little pedantic religious victories, and scattering his teachers about the state with no regard to their protection or effectiveness. If nothing else, Howard said, Wheelock "certainly writes bad letters" about bureau personnel. Griffin wanted to make Wheelock a school inspector and get him out of Galveston into the countryside, away from the press, but both Howard and Shipard demurred. They wanted him where they could watch him closely. Finally, Griffin demoted him to subassistant commissioner at Galveston where the general could keep an eye on him.[52]

After taking care of Wheelock, Griffin turned upon Shipard, accused him of claiming too much "special privilege." He made his bureau command's acting assistant adjutant general, First Lieutenant Joel T. Kirkman, the new superintendent. Griffin told Howard that Shipard supplied only sixteen teachers in Texas, and if the reverend could not cooperate with the command system and follow Griffin's orders, he should end his association with the bureau's educational efforts. Griffin asserted he could not abide "false men" like Shipard in his employ. The general now had centralized the bureau educational effort in his own hands as assistant commissioner. By the time schools were let out for summer vacation, enrollment had reached a new high of over five thousand day and night students.[53]

Throughout the summer, Griffin worked to expand the school effort for the coming fall by recruiting eighty more teachers from benevolent associations other than the American Missionary Association, whose leader, Shipard, Griffin found "so unreliable and untruthful." He sent his assistant superintendent, D. T. Allen, to New Orleans, but Allen continued to cooperate with Shipard, overstepped his bounds, and went on to Chicago and then to his home in Kalamazoo, Michigan. Allen kept asking for thirty-day extensions of a supposed leave of absence. Griffin declared him away without leave, and fired him.[54]

His other effort promised little more success. Griffin sent his army command's acting assistant adjutant general, Second Lieutenant A. H. M. Taylor, to the east coast to secure teachers. Stopping in Washington, where he conferred with Howard, Taylor discovered that most military officials did not care if the freedmen got even " a few crumbs of knowledge." Taylor went on to say, "I feel very sad at the want of consideration given to the Freedmen in their present ignorant condition." He presented Griffin's plan to use military men to teach in Texas, only to be refused. He went on to New York City to gain support from the societies headquartered there. Suddenly, Taylor's trip was cut short by unexpected news. General Charles Griffin was dead.[55]

PART FOUR
Abandonment: The Reynolds Era, September, 1867–December, 1868

I have a thorough knowledge of the people,
know what they say in the recesses of their dwellings,
and know that their hatred of the government
is as deep and damning as perdition itself.

—First Lieutenant Gregory Barrett, Jr., to Second Lieutenant Charles A. Vernou,
July 27, 1868

10

Willful and Benign Neglect

Y ELLOW FEVER: The very mention of the disease caused normally brave persons to shudder in fear. The epidemic of 1867 was one of the worst ever to hit Texas. By July, Griffin reported that the fever was at Indianola, Corpus Christi, and Brownsville. By August, the scourge had passed through the rest of the Texas Gulf coast and reached New Orleans. Business and daily life came to a halt, as all efforts turned to the one necessary goal—survival. In Texas the fever moved deep inland, hitting normally safe places like Chappell Hill and Anderson. "Sickness at these Headquarters has caused the delay in forwarding these reports," the general appended by way of apology to an August 26 message. He sent his acting assistant adjutant general, First Lieutenant Joel T. Kirkman, home to Chicago. Kirkman carried with him the dead body of his young wife. Many urged Griffin to move his headquarters to a safer place. No, said the general, "to desert Galveston at such a time was like deserting one's post in the time of battle." His family fell ill. His son died. Still Griffin refused to withdraw. Then the general himself contracted the disease. Three days later he was dead.[1]

Griffin's death hit the command hierarchy hard. Howard called the "sad intelligence" of the general's passing a "heavy loss." He said that Griffin had conducted his duties "with marked ability" characterized by "fairness and justice" that resulted in "beneficial results" for Reconstruction. He was seconded by the bureau's national superintendent of schools, John W. Alford, who said that "one of the highest tributes to his memory is the record of what he accomplished in the educational interests of Texas." Alford agreed with Howard's benediction, "I mingle my heart felt sympathies with those who are mourning him."[2]

Without Griffin, the command structure of the Texas bureau collapsed. Even with his presence, the yellow fever epidemic would have severely limited bureau programs. As it was, the command of the bureau devolved onto the shoulders of the only staff officer able to get on his feet, Second Lieutenant Charles Garretson. The lieutenant had assumed job after job all summer until he now rolled the entire headquarters staff into one. He telegraphed Howard and begged relief from the incessant paperwork. Howard excused him from the monthly reports and informed him of his replacement on October 23. The weary soul was returned to his regimental duties shortly thereafter.[3]

Late summer was never a good time to be in Galveston, and especially so in that summer of 1867. The town was filled with yellow fever victims, and the disease spread daily. Within a month, the bureau and army commands had been devastated. Several officers had died, besides General Griffin. Army doctors were in short supply, and Inspector Sinclair obtained permission from Commissioner Howard for the bureau agents (but not their families) to employ civilian doctors (but not nurses) and bill the government. Sinclair asked that, because of the scope of the epidemic, the ordinary rules be waived, so that nurses would be allowed and the cost of caring for family members could be absorbed by the government. He forwarded the expenses for himself and his family, which totaled $312 (two months' salary of a well-paying job at that time). Under Howard's intercession, the government paid all legitimate medical bills of surviving bureau personnel and their families, but continued to disallow the amounts Sinclair and others claimed "for Ice, Brandy and Lemons, and Nurse hire, &c."[4]

The Galveston staff of the bureau never recovered from the blow dealt it by the yellow fever. The bureau lost its assistant commissioner, two chief medical officers, eight subassistant commissioners, three clerks, and three teachers. Uncounted others were ill, and in addition nine of the Texas loyalists serving as subassistant commissioners resigned to enter Republican politics at this same time. The fever caused school enrollment to fall 90 percent from the high of sixty-seven hundred in June.[5]

As the remaining Galveston staff recovered from the effects of yellow fever, another problem surfaced. With Griffin's death in September, the Texas assistant commissionership had gone to Brevet Major General Joseph Jones Reynolds, who set up his headquarters in the safety of Austin on September 17. Reynolds immediately appointed a new staff, based on men he knew from the Twenty-sixth Infantry, the regiment he commanded. Griffin had favored men from the Seventeenth Regiment, whom Reynolds now returned to their ordinary regimental positions. But Garretson also continued to run the bureau operation from Galveston until late October. The duplication and delay in unification of staffs further complicated bureau operations in Texas.[6]

Inspector General William H. Sinclair and the other civilian employees of the Galveston headquarters were left in limbo as to their job status. Sinclair wrote to the new Austin group in early October, and offered to assume the post of superintendent of bureau schools in Texas, which had been held by Second Lieutenant Charles Garretson, along with nearly every other staff position, when the yellow fever laid everyone else low. But Reynolds's acting assistant adjutant general replied that Sinclair's services were not needed in the education department.

Sinclair then asked Reynolds for orders, suggesting that he come up to Austin as bureau inspector. Reynolds replied that he had no orders, but inquired about what Sinclair was doing at the moment. Sinclair stated that he was the inspector and ought to report to Austin. Somehow, in the crush of the movement of the headquarters, Reynolds temporarily forgot about Sinclair and the Galveston clerks, perhaps assuming that they had died of yellow fever. He was not well served by his acting assistant adjutant general, Second Lieutenant J. P. Richardson.

Unknown to Reynolds, the lieutenant was part of a movement headed by bureau field agents like George T. Ruby and E. M. Harris and disenchanted radical Republican politicians, who disliked certain compromises they had had to make recently to get General Reynolds to appoint their men to office. These disaffected elements blamed army and bureau staff officers in Galveston, like Sinclair and Garretson, for Reynolds's course of action, and they sought to isolate Reynolds from what they saw as the Galvestonians' pernicious advice. Because of Sinclair's timely inquiries, Reynolds personally ordered him and several other civilian employees to report to Austin along with the old headquarters' records in November, which thwarted the Radicals' plans. Once there, the dedicated Sinclair continued to act as the bureau's inspector general.[7]

A Kentuckian by birth, Sinclair's new boss, General Reynolds, had graduated from West Point in 1843. Reynolds had served in various frontier and eastern garrison positions and had taught mathematics at the military academy. He resigned his commission to teach at Washington University at St. Louis in 1857. At the beginning of the war, he was in Indiana assisting in the family grocery business. He accepted an assignment as colonel of the Tenth Indiana Volunteers, was quickly promoted to brigadier general, and fought in the early campaigns in western Virginia. In 1862, his brother's death back in Indiana caused him to resign and go home to settle family affairs. He took time to recruit for the Union Army, and received a new commission as major general. Returning to the front, Reynolds was a division commander in the Army of the Cumberland at Chickamauga and chief of staff at Missionary Ridge. He finished the war as corps commander in Arkansas.

Because of his war record, Reynolds was one of the volunteer officers who received a commission in the postwar regular army. He was appointed colonel of the Twenty-sixth Infantry, and served as commander of the Subdistrict of the Rio Grande. In December, 1866, he had been considered as a candidate for the then vacant position of assistant commissioner of the Freedmen's Bureau in Georgia. Commissioner Howard wrote that "there is no better officer in the Army better fitted to fulfill the troublesome duties of Assistant Commissioner. . . . He is a man of high character and good judgment." But the War Department had considered Reynolds too valuable an officer to remove from a critical area like the international border. Now as senior officer in Texas after Griffin, he assumed command in this emergency with everyone's blessing.[8]

With Reynolds's accession to power came a series of subtle changes, not all of them his responsibility, that marked the beginning of the end of the bureau's protection of the Negro in postbellum Texas. The first issue Reynolds attacked was Griffin's Circular No. 7, which had set up A. Ruttkey & Co. as a safe place for blacks to dispose of their crop shares in the fall of 1867. Griffin's order had caused confusion among other cotton merchants, who wished clarification as to their role in the coming harvest season. Did all freedmen's cotton have to go through Ruttkey? Was there any discretion available to laborers, their employers, or other commission merchant houses? Did all freedmen have to ship their cotton solely through subassistant commissioners?

Reynolds answered these queries with his General Orders No. 17. In it, he said that freedmen could sell their crops the same as anyone else, without prior restraint, relying on their own good judgment. Subassistant commissioners could operate only in an advisory capacity when asked, but no single merchant house could be recommended to the exclusion of others. After the trouble he had taken to set up the Ruttkey deal for Griffin, Howard now wanted Reynolds to explain why his estimate of the situation differed so markedly from that of his predecessor. Reynolds replied that Griffin's concept would be impossible to carry out. Bureau agents could see to it that the freedmen received a fair price from their crop shares, Reynolds continued, but they could do little else legally. Reynolds pointed out that those freedmen who had sold their cotton on the spot in 1866 had made more profit than those who dealt through any commission house. He could not see his way clear to eliminate the freedmen's chances to sell to anyone at any time to their advantage.

Reynolds asserted that it was time for the bureau to encourage the Negroes to act like anyone else in money matters, profiting or suffering by their own decisions. If anyone wished advice, he could consult with his local bureau representative. Reynolds said he had consulted with attorneys who assured him that Ruttkey's bond was meaningless. No merchant could bond himself to see to it that he paid his own commissions. Besides, Reynolds continued, Ruttkey had sent Texas subassistant commissioners a notice that implied that this firm alone could handle freedmen's cotton, and that the bureau agents were obligated to help secure it for them. This was not so, even under Griffin's orders, the general maintained, and besides it gave the subassistant commissioners an interest in the disposal of the crop.

All Griffin's Circular Orders No. 7 did, according to Reynolds, was give Ruttkey an unfair advantage in the Texas cotton market. It did nothing to benefit Texas blacks or the bureau. Reynolds apologized for denigrating Griffin's policy, but he said he was compelled to be frank because of Howard's inquiry. Howard evidently was won over by Reynolds's argument, which paralleled many of his own initial objections to Griffin's plan, because he gave the general his approval of the new approach.[9]

At the same time that he changed Griffin's arrangement with Ruttkey & Co., Reynolds cancelled his predecessor's General Orders No. 11, which prevented liens of the freedmen's share of the crops. Reynolds found this principle to be confusing and unfair, echoing planters' objections to it when Griffin established it the previous summer. He said that such a lien could be created with the approval of a subassistant commissioner, and held that bureau agents were to enforce "fair" debt settlements for "necessaries" furnished according to labor contracts. He also dropped for the coming year Griffin's requirement in General Orders No. 4, which ordered copies of all labor contracts to be sent to headquarters for review. Instead they were to be filed in the offices of the nearest county clerk.[10]

The next problem that Reynolds needed to address was the War Department's desire to muster out all remaining volunteer officers still serving with the bureau as members of the Veteran Reserve Corps. Although Reynolds had only four such officers left in Texas, they were important employees, since all of them had served eighteen months or more as subassistant commissioners. Reynolds agreed that these men ought to be reinstated as civilian employees under Howard's suggested policy, but he believed that he could manage without them, if necessary. Howard offered them the highest salary paid at that time, $150 a month, and all but one accepted the new appointments.[11]

Reynolds's solution to the lack of subassistant commissioners arising from a shortage of government monies for salaries, was sent to Howard at the same time he was threatened with the loss of the four Veteran Reserve officers. Reynolds, who was in Washington on official business, wanted to replace the system of subassistant commissioners with local loyal officials not on salary. Instead, the general wanted these officials to finance themselves through charging and collecting the same fees as notaries in the state. Howard was not so sure of the scheme's merits. He said that the system suggested by Reynolds was one of "considerable risk" and had been tried already in Georgia, resulting in "great oppression and wrong" to the freedmen. The commissioner said that Reynolds could attempt his plan if he could find "true and loyal men" friendly to the interests of the Negro, but that the general ought not do it in an "indiscriminate" fashion. Reynolds, probably wisely, decided to let the matter ride.[12]

Reynolds also issued the usual orders concerning the proper paperwork procedures that subassistant commissioners were to follow. Griffin had submitted most of these matters to the field agents in detail already, but Reynolds repealed these circulars and issued new instructions of his own. All reports were to go to the staff officer in charge of the department with which they were concerned. No persons or articles could be hired, nor purchases made, without the permission of the assistant commissioner. If no statement was to be made in a particular report category, the subassistant commissioner had to note this, not just leave the item blank. Field representatives were warned to leave rented buildings in good condition upon vacating them.

In addition, civilian agents were to send a statement of all monies collected on behalf of the bureau, which the distribution officer would then deduct from their salaries. Subassistant commissioners could purchase rations from the army quartermaster stores, like any other military officer, with the proper requisition papers. Finally, all agency employees were expected to keep a full file of pertinent documents to guide their actions as bureau representatives. These included the act creating the bureau in 1865, its extension in 1866, the Civil Rights Act of 1866, the bureau officer's manual, and all the circular orders and letters for 1865, 1866, and 1867 from both the Texas headquarters and Commissioner Howard's office, and all general orders from the Texas bureau for 1867 and 1868.[13]

Exactly what the jurisdiction of these subassistant commissioners would be in the coming months became the focus of a prolonged argument between Reynolds and Sheridan's successor to the command of the Fifth Military District in New Orleans, Major General Winfield S. Hancock. Appointed by President Johnson to leaven the unwarranted radicalism he perceived in Sheridan's policies under the Reconstruction, Hancock was a war hero with future Democratic party presidential pretensions. The yellow fever epidemic had delayed Hancock's arrival in New Orleans until the last days of November, a fortuitous circumstance that allowed Reynolds a free hand in Texas to strike a deal with the militarily appointed provisional governor, Elisha M. Pease.

Pease's Republican provisional government had feared that Reynolds might not cooperate with it in the matter of patronage as Griffin had promised to do before his untimely death. But these fears proved groundless. Reynolds, in exchange for Pease's statement of his government's subordination to the Federal military administration of the state (which Hamilton and Throckmorton had refused), appointed a Republican administration before Hancock could assume command and stop him. Now, Hancock moved to limit the scope of Reconstruction in the Fifth Military District, an operation that would materially affect the functions of the Freedmen's Bureau in Texas.[14]

Immediately upon his arrival in New Orleans, Hancock stated his philosophy in his General Orders No. 40. The general declared that he regarded "the maintenance of the civil authorities in the faithful execution of the laws as the most efficient [approach] under existing circumstances." The war was over, said Hancock, and it was time for the civil authorities to exercise full power. "The right of trial by jury, the habeas corpus, the liberty of the press, the freedom of speech, the natural rights of property must be preserved," the proclamation continued. If the civil authorities proved unequal to the task before them, Hancock pledged military action to ensure "the liberties of the people." In another statement, Hancock also attacked those who assumed that he as military commander had the right to make arbitrary law. Not so, averred the general. He was there solely to enforce the existing laws, and not to aid any party in any specific complaint.[15]

After his general statement of principles, Hancock got down to particulars. He canceled Reynolds's ability to make political appointments under a grant of power Sheridan originally had given Griffin in September. He reissued an order confirming the suspension of Griffin's Circular Orders No. 13 on using the ironclad oath for jury selection. And he sent an inquiry to Reynolds asking the Texas commander to detail the authority under which bureau subassistant commissioners operated in Texas. The assistant commissioner replied that his field representatives functioned under orders from Commissioner Howard, Reynolds himself, and previous orders and circulars kept on file at each agency and the Texas bureau headquarters. Howard also made all bureau appointments upon Reynolds's recommendations.

Reynolds asserted that the bureau chain of command went directly from him to Howard in Washington, and not through New Orleans. Only the military command, which Reynolds held jointly, involved Hancock's headquarters in New Orleans, maintained Reynolds. Hence, he really did not need to inform Hancock of bureau matters, but the Texas assistant commissioner would send the Fifth Military District commander a full file of documents as a matter of courtesy, and would continue to do so in the future. Meanwhile, Reynolds told Hancock that he had made a proposal to phase out bureau operations through the use of civil officeholders, a scheme he thought the commander in New Orleans might favor. Reynolds reglected to mention, however, that Howard had already rejected his proposal. He probably hoped that the idea of phasing out the bureau would help Hancock see the necessity for his appointments of loyal state officials, or would further confuse the issue.[16]

For a month, Reynolds heard no more about bureau operations. Then, in early February, 1868, Hancock wrote again. This time the major general claimed to have in his possession letters that proved that the Texas subassistant commissioners were "in the habit" of sitting as judges, adjudicating cases brought before them, imposing fines and other penalties, and receiving monies for services performed. Such activities violated the principles stated in General Orders No. 40, and Hancock wanted to know who had authorized this.[17]

Reynolds replied that Texas bureau agents were "in the habit" of consulting upon matters brought before them in which the freedmen were concerned. Texans merely referred to these proceedings in common parlance as "courts" and to the agents as "judges," but he denied that his subassistant commissioners sat as judges or held court in any formal, legal sense. The assistant commissioner went on to admit that bureau representatives had imposed fines, but pointed out that such monies went to the bureau's school fund for freedmen. He then listed as the authority upon which the Texas bureau functioned the two Freedmen's Bureau Acts, the first Military Reconstruction Act, four circulars issued by Howard, and seven circulars and general orders issued by his predecessors as assistant commissioners in Texas. Once again, Reynolds enclosed copies of all documents except the congressional acts.[18]

But Hancock, operating under the recommendations of his judge advocate for civil affairs, told Reynolds that he doubted whether President Johnson still extended the powers of military protection or jurisdiction into Texas, and whether the normal operations of state or federal courts should be "disturbed" by bureau usurpations. He believed that the bureau had to use the existing courts just like any other person or legal entity, and recommended that subassistant commissioners be limited to recommending freedmen's cases to the Federal courts under the Civil Rights Act of 1866. Hancock bluntly informed Reynolds that his rationale might have satisfied earlier district commanders, but that Reynolds had offered nothing new from previously rejected arguments, and his position was now inconsistent with that of the major general commanding and was no longer to be allowed.[19]

Reynolds was dismayed to see that Hancock intended to enforce his viewpoint by stripping the Texas bureau of the troop support that Griffin had worked so diligently to establish. As military commander of the district that included Texas, there was no doubt that Hancock possessed the power to act and that Reynolds would have to obey the orders. On February 5, Hancock sent Reynolds a letter instructing him to recall all separate detachments not under direct orders. The Texas commander was specifically to remove all troops from the direct authority of subassistant commissioners or other bureau personnel. Hancock told Reynolds to move all his infantry "to the points most likely to be required for the performance of its legitimate duties," and the cavalry to the frontier where no duty should be required of it but fighting Indians. Hancock did allow Reynolds to keep one squadron (two companies) in reserve for the interior.

Reynolds recalled the bureau agencies' guards, but he did not fully comply with the spirit of Hancock's desire to concentrate all troops on the frontier. Hancock sent a new order, demanding that Reynolds concentrate all of his troops not presently on the frontier at Houston, Brenham, Tyler, Woodville, and Jefferson. The Fifth Military District commander told Reynolds that he was not to move any soldiers from these posts without his approval, except on a temporary, emergency basis.[20]

In an attempt to preserve some future role for the bureau and get around Hancock's objections, Reynolds wrote his supervisor and proposed that they issue a new general order defining the behavior of subassistant commissioners. Reynolds reminded Hancock that the bureau had a legal existence guaranteed by Congress, which had to be recognized. Freedmen were still applying to it for aid, he continued, and no one could prevent that. So Reynolds suggested that since the bureau field agents were not to have the continuous support of U.S. soldiers, they would have to rely upon assistance from state officials—the very men whom Reynolds had appointed to office a couple of months earlier.

Reynolds proposed that the new order should state that the bureau had been created by acts of Congress, and that this order was to ensure uniformity of action among the many subassistant commissioners. He wanted to limit the duties of the bureau agents to cases relating to freedmen, refugees, and abandoned lands. The subassistant commissioners were to be cloaked with the powers of justices of the peace and county judges according to existing state law. All sheriffs and constables, said Reynolds, were to honor the writs issued by bureau representatives as if they came from a Texas court. All fees allowed under state law would be charged and collected by state authorities operating under bureau auspices.

The subassistant commissioners, however, would not charge for their own services. They were to handle any case valued under the sum of five hundred dollars. All other cases were to originate in civil courts, with the bureau agents acting as advisers to the freedmen involved. No subassistant commissioner could levy a fine of more than one hundred dollars, and fined were to be collected only for violations of the law. Reynolds saw all appeals from the bureau agents as going directly to his office. And, concluded the general, any state official who refused to obey this order could be replaced in office.[21]

Hancock refused to consider Reynolds's plan. He said that he wanted all cases in the Fifth Military District to go directly to the state courts. He also stated that he would prefer that Reynolds stop interfering with his prerogatives as superior officer. Hancock pointed out that the Reconstruction acts reserved to him as district commander the right to decide on the treatment of all legal proceedings in the Fifth Military District. He saw no reason why the Freedmen's Bureau Act or the Civil

Rights Act of 1866 were germane to this situation, or should override the Reconstruction acts.[22]

Reynolds denied that his position was "an interference with the authority of the District Commander." It was not so intended, said Reynolds, nor should such a course ever be allowed. He said that the object of his proposal was to bring about a degree of uniformity that most agreed was missing from the actions of Texas subassistant commissioners. He merely wished to maintain their legitimate authority and prevent oppressive acts. The assistant commissioner claimed that the records, reports, complaints interviews, and previous orders of the Texas bureau demonstrated that the bureau administration there—before Reynolds's takeover, of course—was in utter confusion. The Texas commander hoped that his suggestions would begin a gradual process of placing the freedmen's affairs in the hands of the civil authorities, rather than dumping the whole matter in their laps at once.[23]

Suddenly, the whole matter was moot. Hancock had been alienating more important men than Reynolds, and these influential Republicans, with the connivance of General Grant, had backed Hancock into a corner where he was denied the right to remove Louisiana officials, just as he had denied the same right to Reynolds in Texas. In a huff, Hancock resigned his position. Reynolds could hardly believe his own luck. He was the senior officer next in line to take over the whole Fifth Military District on an *ad interim* basis. He quickly traveled to New Orleans to assume command. To his disgust, however, he found that President Johnson had already assigned Brevet Major General Robert C. Buchanan to assume Hancock's old position.[24]

Returning to Austin, Reynolds issued General Orders No. 4, as assistant commissioner of Texas. The new order defined the position of subassistant commissioner in Texas exactly as he had proposed to Hancock two weeks earlier. Reynolds took a calculated risk that Buchanan would be so involved with the readmission of Louisiana to statehood that he would not pay Texas much heed. He was correct. When Howard asked what was going on, Reynolds sent him an argument similar to the one he had used earlier with Hancock. Since the withdrawal of troops from the agencies, Reynolds began, the question he faced as assistant commissioner was how to proceed without them. The result was General Orders No. 4, designed to guarantee uniform and satisfactory action by bureau agents in Texas.[25]

Reynolds asserted that before General Orders No. 4, the field agents had done many illegal things, which had greatly embarrassed him as assistant commissioner. Now, he could send out inspectors who had standards by which to measure the performance of all subassistant commissioners. Reynolds denied that he was criticizing any officer's plan that had preceded his. The general said that he was just stating the facts. Results before now had been unsatisfactory. Reynolds went on to assert that one had to experience Texas to appreciate what the bureau was up against. There existed an unusual failure to execute the criminal law that the general labeled appalling.

While there were good people in Texas, Reynolds continued, "it is a remarkable fact that the aggregate sentiment of the people, generally, regardless of party or politics, is averse to punishing men for murder and other great crimes." The Texas commander expressed his hope that his plan would gradually solve this "attitude problem." Reynolds had brilliantly appealed to Howard's worries and desires while, at the same time, he had indirectly insulted the departed Hancock, and subtly reassumed complete and very nearly independent command of Texas from Buchanan at New Orleans.[26]

This independence in command was important to Reynolds. Although Commissioner Howard had been opposed to the assistant commissioner's earlier plan to allow loyal civil authorities to engage through a fee system to carry out bureau responsibilities to protect the Negroes' rights as freed people, the commander of the Texas bureau realized that ultimately elected officials would have to assume the burden of guaranteeing civil rights to loyalists, black or white. Reynolds, like Griffin before him, decided that his best contribution to a reconstructed Texas government was to cooperate with the nascent state Republican party to place Unionists in office. Unlike Griffin, however, Reynolds was located in Austin, where he could be in daily contact with the state's Republican political leadership.[27]

The first step was to work out an alliance with Provisional Governor Pease. This was completed by the end of October, 1867, when Pease issued a proclamation recognizing the U.S. Army as the supreme authority in Texas. No other previous state executive had been willing to make such a concession. Pease also recognized the validity of all laws passed since secession except those that conflicted with the Union victory in the Civil War. This denied the theory held by most Republicans that all laws passed since secession were null and void *ab initio*, from their inception. All in all, Pease stated that his government had only the legality that Reynolds wished to accord it, and that ideological considerations were to be played down in reconstructing Texas. In more common terms the general was "now the law-maker, law-giver, judge, jury, pettifogger, and teazer over the whole state of Texas."[28]

In exchange for Pease's proclamation, Reynolds issued nine special orders, removing Democrats from office in county after county and replacing them with about six hundred Republican loyalists. The arrival of Hancock in New Orleans stopped further movement in this direction, but by and large Reynolds had completed his political task. He would rely upon loyalists to enforce the results of the war. For black Texans, however, this was a doubtful approach. Prejudice was not limited to former secessionists, but pervaded the whole of Texas white society. If the loyalists became impotent to act, through their own inertia or the withdrawal of the bureau and its army support, Reynolds's Reconstruction would collapse. Worse than that, if the Republicans' opposition could register enough white voters (very likely, given the state's racial demography of the time), the system could be voted out of office legally, with or without the intimidation of loyal black and white voters.[29]

The problem of abandoned lands continued to grow under the Reynolds administration. It was an issue that Commissioner Howard wished to do away with. In November, 1867, Reynolds received a circular letter in which the commissioner indicated that any abandoned property in various Southern states reoccupied but not refiled on by its former owners by January 1, 1868, would be seized and rented to freedmen. He indicated that six town lots in Texas fell under this category. He also stated that he wished Reynolds to settle the matter of the sawmill and tannery at San Antonio, and he sent two men, Brevet Major General A. P. Howe and Mr. J. P. McMehaffey, to help solve this problem.[30]

Reynolds notified Howard that he had received a thirteen-hundred-dollar advance toward the purchase of the property, but that the sale had "not consummated" and the buyer, Isaac Moses, now wanted the money returned. The assistant commissioner said that the money had been advanced without interest or penalty. The problem was that the Texas bureau had placed the cash into the freedmen's school fund, and it had already been spent. Howard's distribution officer ordered Reynolds to take the money from the refugees and freedmen's fund and pay Moses off. Shortly afterward, Reynolds notified Howard that he had new bidders, a partnership of S. A. Wray and E. C. Dewey. The general urged that their offer be accepted, but soon he reneged, claiming to have received a better offer. Howard ordered Reynolds to proceed with the new deal, as the Wray-Dewey agreement had not yet been processed. The new agreement was with the City of San Antonio, which offered to pay forty-five hundred dollars in five installments by August, 1868. Since the city had threatened a lawsuit against any other purchaser, this was an ideal arrangement, and the sale was made.[31]

The next biggest piece of property once owned by "the so-called Confederate States," as the bureau liked to list such things, was the Waco Manufacturing Co. General Howe advertised it for sale in December, 1867, but no bids were received. The ownership of the firm was so confused that the bureau had to finance extensive title searches to substantiate that it had been a Confederate holding. These investigations were made by a loyal Unionist who could not take the oath, Judge B. W. Gray, and another loyalist who could take the oath, A. J. Evans. Griffin allegedly agreed to pay the men 10 percent of the asking price of about thirty thousand dollars.

Evans accepted $500 in salary and $300 in expenses without any problem (he had a written contract), but Gray's claim of $3,000, later increased to $5,000, was rejected by the bureau as excessive (he had no written contract, only an oral agreement). Reynolds countered with a bureau appointment as subassistant commissioner at $150 a month for four months, which Gray took, although he probably never really acted in that capacity.[32]

The bureau had already spent several thousand dollars investigating titles, and still was unsure of who owned what at the manufacturing plant. When a local attorney, William T. Clark, asked for another $1,150 for more legwork, Howard blew up. He told Reynolds that for $3,000, the bureau would get rid of the actual part of the Waco firm, Barron's Mill, that produced cotton cloth for the Confederacy, and free the current owner, J. B. Earle, of all Federal claims to the rest of the property. Earle agreed to buy back the mill for the sum in monthly installments of $500. The deed was done, although by December, 1868, only two thirds of the asking price had been collected.[33]

Other properties allegedly belonging to the Confederate government consisted of town lots in Brownsville, Austin, San Antonio, and Tyler. All but the half dozen Tyler pieces, several of which contained buildings used as army troop quarters, eventually reverted to their original owners. The Tyler land was sold at auction in late 1868, along with several acreages in Anderson County, which had been turned in by John Morrison, a local Scalawag who served as subassistant commissioner, and who had informed upon his neighbors. Many of these plots are of interest because they had been occupied by black farmers, who were later evicted when the land was returned to the white owners. The bureau also sold a property called the Brazos Manufacturing Co. in Robertson County near Sterling.[34]

Besides alienating seized property, Reynolds had a group of minor issues concerning freedmen to handle. He informed petitioners that former slaveholders were no longer liable for the care of the old and indigent ex-bondsmen from their plantations. This was a responsibility for the counties.[35] He also became involved in several cases of black minors, one of whom he refused to send back to her mother from her place of apprenticeship, another of whom he refused to return to her white guardian, while a third, who had been left to a white woman as an apprentice in her dead mother's will and was now wanted by the natural father, he turned over to the local subassistant commissioner for investigation.[36]

Reynolds continued to attempt to locate missing relatives of freed persons, and investigated a case of fraud involving the plan to import black laborers from another state. The importer had taken the hands to Mississippi to work his own plantation using provisions bought on misappropriated credit from his Texas employer.[37] The assistant commissioner also authorized the care of two black refugee families at the Austin agency in the late summer of 1868 under guidelines Howard had established for "soup houses" for the extremely destitute.[38] Finally, Reynolds authorized the final transportation orders Howard allowed in Texas.[39]

Much more substantial was Reynolds's concern with Negro education. When the general assumed control of the bureau at Austin, headquarters was still at Galveston. Reynolds solved this problem by setting up his own staff at the Texas capital and phasing out the veteran personnel at Galveston. This created a period of six weeks when neither staff really did much. The Austin staff members were learning the job and trying to amass the headquarters records, while the Galveston people were still sick with yellow fever and mystified about their authority to act. On October 7, 1867, when Inspector William H. Sinclair inquired specifically what to do about the fall educational plans, Reynolds told him that affairs would continue in limbo, with Second Lieutenant Charles Garretson acting as superintendent as well as temporary assistant adjutant general.[40]

Garretson was not pleased with this arrangement. Indeed Sinclair may have made his inquiry at Garretson's behest, since the inspector had been a colonel in the wartime volunteers, knew the ins and outs of military etiquette, and was well-respected among bureau personnel. Dissatisfied with Reynolds's answer, Garretson wrote another note himself, explaining that Griffin had planned to have freedmen's schools opened by October 1. The acting assistant adjutant general mentioned that teachers were still owed salary from the past term, and that the school fund was totally empty. In addition, he informed Reynolds that the bureau school fund owed another $1,325 to Isaac Moses, money advanced to the school fund on the purchase of the Waco Manufacturing Co., the sale of which had since fallen through by no fault of Moses's. The businessman wanted his loan repaid. The freedmen's schools were to be funded in part by the sale of abandoned lands, continued Garretson, but none had yet been sold.[41]

Meanwhile, Garretson and the Galveston staff heard to their amazement that E. M. Wheelock had been in to see Provisional Governor Pease and had secured an appointment as state superintendent of schools. Seeing this as his opportunity to have the school issue resolved or at least placed beyond his responsibility, Garretson intimated to Reynolds that he ought to appoint Wheelock as bureau superintendent also, since Griffin had wanted one person to hold both positions. Reynolds thought this a capital suggestion and followed through. He then told Garretson to forward all school records to Wheelock, and to step down as temporary head of bureau schools. Garretson happily complied.[42]

Reynolds's elevation of Wheelock to the superintendency, of course, was not what Griffin and Howard had had in mind. Howard irritably demanded that the Texas assistant commissioner assign the troublesome Wheelock to some other bureau duty. He also informed Reynolds that he wanted R. D. Harper of Xenia, Ohio, to assume the directorship of the bureau school effort. Harper, however, never seems to have arrived. Wheelock resigned his bureau clerkship, the one Griffin had placed him in the summer before, and continued on in state service. Ultimately, Reverend Joseph Welch took over the bureau school program in the middle of March, 1868.[43]

Along with transferring the superintendent's office to Austin, Reynolds moved to secure the freedmen's school finances and teacher supply. In General Orders No. 19, the assistant commissioner informed teachers that all bureau salary support would cease as of December 1, 1867. The general set up a new tuition system of one dollar a month for families with one student attending, seventy-five cents a month each for a family with two students attending, and two dollars a month for families with more than two students in school. Reynolds would list only those qualified teachers who agreed to these terms. He also called the attention of all bureau personnel to Griffin's school circulars requiring monthly reports, the purchase of school lots, and the repair of buildings. He ordered all subassistant commissioners to make the creation and maintenance of schools a paramount duty of their agencies, and later required them to collect and forward all reports made by teachers within their agency boundaries.[44]

Having covered the problem of school finances, Reynolds next turned to the teacher supply. He wrote the American Missionary Association in New York concerning Lieutenant Taylor's visit. Reynolds asked that the association provide Texas with nine teachers, two for Galveston, and one each at Houston, Columbus, Millican, Indianola, Huntsville, Marlin, Hempstead. He promised them free room and board in Galveston, transportation to inland duty points, a guaranteed student population, and military protection. Their salary was to be funded through tuition, and all teachers would have to agree beforehand to serve under bureau control. Despite Reynolds's caution to the benevolent associations as to bureau control of education, he had a run-in with Reverend J. R. Shipard over the placing of schools, particularly inside the city of Galveston. Reynolds reminded Shipard of the bureau's leadership authority and the association's support role. He said further that the bureau would operate on the reports of its subassistant commissioners to promote the expansion of schools in the state.[45]

Reynolds's efforts to expand the educational program for Texas blacks were only partially successful. He had only brought back enrollment to eighteen hundred students, well below the highest level that Kiddoo had attained in 1866, of around four thousand students, and also Griffin's acme of achievement in 1867. When Howard inquired about the reason for this, Reynolds detailed the problems faced by the bureau school program in Texas. In 1865 and 1866, Reynolds said, the freedmen's schools had been self-supporting, operating on tuition, which limited the attendance of the children as their families were too poor to pay. Then, the general continued, the bureau offered to guarantee the teachers forty dollars a month and to help finance the program from fines and the sale of abandoned lands. Attendance soared, but the program was paralyzed by the yellow fever epidemic, which reduced schools' attendance by 90 percent, killed several teachers, and drove many of the rest from the state. Most of the departed teachers refused to return. Moreover, the school fund was exhausted, so Reynolds was not trying to start from nothing, with a new self-supporting program, and he expected much from it—if the price of cotton did not fall again.[46]

Realizing the precarious condition of the bureau's education program in Texas and the rest of the South, Commissioner Howard arranged with the benevolent associations to send more teachers for the next term. He asked each assistant commissioner to communicate with the associations on his own to meet his state's needs. Howard also ordered that school reports be more methodical, and include the name of the teacher, number of students, number of buildings occupied by schools, and the name of the owner.

Reynolds remarked that while he was happy with the expansion program, he was bothered by the notion that Northern young ladies should be enlisted to teach. Women were hard to house and difficult to protect from outrage and assault, said the general. He believed that the problems would become more acute after January 1, 1869, when the bureau would go out of operation. No one would help bureau employees in Texas, Reynolds warned, and each subassistant commissioner was on his own for protection. Reynolds said that he would find positions for any women teachers interested in working under these harsh conditions but, for the moment, he recommended that only men who could face up to much opposition and insult be sent instead.[47]

Reynolds knew whereof he spoke. As Goliad's harried teacher testified after being threatened and shot at and denied military protection, all he wanted was one month's salary, "with that, I can get away from this nest of d____d traitors, horsethieves, and assassins." The army post commander (who was also the subassistant commissioner) at Goliad had warned headquarters a year earlier that the area was one of the most violent in Texas and had earned its reputation well. When the army withdrew the occupation soldiers, this officer had doubted that a black educational program could be maintained without military protection, a prediction that was now borne out. At Paris, which had a freedmen's school taught by a black couple, the local subassistant commissioner told of how several "young ladies" had entered the vacant schoolhouse, and "emptied filth from their bodies" over parts of the building. The still-shocked agent stated that the "ladies" had "actually shit over the floor, and upon the benches, and in the water bucket."

The anti–Negro-school sentiment continued. In Bowie County, for instance, the Freedmen's Bureau agent was absent from a scheduled

Negro school meeting. It was well that he did not show up, because two whites with shotguns did. They told the crowd that if they ever caught the agent out alone he was a dead man. The school continued to receive threats on a daily basis, but the black instructor bravely carried on. When unidentified men burned the schoolhouse at Circleville —a fairly commonplace occurrence when opponents wanted to end black education in their area—Reynolds posted a five-hundred-dollar reward for their arrest and conviction. The money went uncollected.[48]

But there was worse violence to come as anti-Reconstruction forces began to gather to help close down bureau efforts in Texas once and for all. During the summer of 1868, the energetic Inspector Sinclair undertook one of the most dangerous trips of his career. This was his thousand-mile journey "to ascertain the condition of affairs" involving Ku Klux Klan activities in eastern Texas in the sixteen counties comprising the Trinity, Neches, and Sabine river valleys and their headwaters. Returning to Austin, the bureau inspector made a full report of his trip.[49]

Sinclair began by saying that the blacks were fairly helpless when left to their own devices and the state court system, for there was so much fraud that the judges ignored. Even worse, the judges merely had to follow the dictates of state law to conspire legally with the planters to cheat the freedmen out of all they were owed at year's end. Texas law reserved the first lien on a crop to secure the rent of the land. The second lien was to obtain any money owed by the freedmen to the planters in the form of advances, tools, rations, quarters, and clothing. Admittedly there was a second lien in the old labor law of 1866, which reserved to the freedmen who worked for wages a lien on half the crop after the rent had been paid. But those who sharecropped received no money until the third round at settlement time. Sinclair called for a new order granting the freedmen first lien on the whole crop in 1868. Otherwise, he feared that the blacks would be cheated legally out of another year's work.[50]

The inspector next recommended several changes to General Orders No. 4 of the previous spring. He thought that the subassistant commissioners should not try any cases in a judicial fashion. Rather they should present all cases to the county courts, and act as the freed people's legal adviser and counsel. After all, Sinclair continued, General Reynolds had the right to remove any civil officer from office who failed to give the blacks justice. The subassistant commissioners could monitor the civil authorities to assist the general, Sinclair said. Eventually the inspector hoped that the fear of removal would force local authorities to accept the new order of things. Besides, the bureau was soon to be phased out, and it was best for all that this should be taken into account now, and a head start obtained. Sinclair suggested that his plan be adopted quietly, with no order given but with personal letters sent out to the agents to inform them of the scheme. The local agents could then act under the pretense of giving the civil authorities a chance to act responsibly on their own. Many whites would rather settle fairly with Negroes than involve the Federal government through the bureau, Sinclair opined.

Barring this, Sinclair wanted to exclude juries from deciding any case heard before a subassistant commissioner, as the planters used this provision to secure long delays filled with legal technicalities. Sinclair wanted the bureau agent to decide all cases with no appeal except to the office of Assistant Commissioner Reynolds in Austin to provide quicker justice without the legal tricks used by whites to wear out black plantiffs. Juries were too prone to cut the just claims of blacks in half, if they granted their validity at all, Sinclair noted. If the subassistant commissioner's ruling was appealed to the assistant commissioner, Sinclair suggested that the whole crop could be frozen in place on the plantation until the case was settled. In an earlier letter, Sinclair had already persuaded Reynolds to issue an order preventing any bureau agent from leaving his post without permission from headquarters in Austin, to prevent them from being unavailable at a time when they were needed most.[51]

Finally, as Sinclair traveled, he had catalogued the usual series of atrocities, outrages, and murders. Many of these crimes were racially inspired, but the general scope of violence affected everyone regardless of race. A freedman and his son, who were taking their cotton to Shreveport, had been killed and robbed; a white man, who murdered two other whites, was shot and killed for resisting arrest for stealing a horse; a Negro was found dead along the roadside; two whites shot it out and killed each other in Anderson County; the same occurred in Montgomery County, where the first white shot another white, who stabbed his assailant to death before dying himself; a white witness to a horse theft was found dead in the woods; a known murderer was killed on the streets of Huntsville, when he quarreled with a man quicker on the draw than he.

Sinclair's litany went on and on. So many blacks had died and disappeared that an accurate body count was impossible. Sinclair's report so dismayed General Reynolds that he sent it on to Commissioner Howard in full. Reynolds also informed the army high command that the law had ceased to exist east of the Trinity River. To combat illegal activities, Reynolds ordered that anyone caught wearing a mask or disguise was subject to indefinite military arrest. Commanders were to send such prisoners from post to post, seeking witnesses to identify them as perpetrators of crimes. Of course, under such conditions it became increasingly difficult at best for the bureau field officers to discharge their responsibilities adequately.[52]

11

Care and Circumspection

THE MEN WHO HAD TO HEED these disintegrating conditions changed from predominantly military officers to civilians during Reynolds's tenure as assistant commissioner. When Reynolds came to Austin, two thirds of his subassistant commissioners were military officers. Military men dominated the field agencies until March, 1868, when the ratio first tipped in favor of the civilian representatives. Three out of five subassistant commissioners were civilians until the field offices closed in December, 1868. Of the civilians employed at the beginning of the Reynolds administration, one third had not been in the war. But by late 1868, almost all of them were men who had seen some kind of service with the Union volunteers during the war. Reynolds had a multitude of men to choose from who wished to serve as agents. He even hired one at the suggestion of a member of Commissioner Howard's staff to pay off a claim he had against the Texas bureau.[1]

Reynolds averaged fifty agents in the interior throughout his term, fluctuating from a high of sixty-one when he took command to a low of forty-three in June, 1868. In general, the assistant commissioner let the tally decrease during the growing season, then increased the number during harvest and settlement time. Reynolds constantly shifted the district boundaries in response to perceived need and available manpower. The ninety-six special orders devoted to personnel gave fifty boundary changes in fourteen months.[2]

Many of Reynolds's commissions were issued for short-term appointments. This was because the two-year bureau extension act of 1866 was scheduled to expire in July, 1868. Congress, however, yielding to complaints that the bureau would close down before the completion of the growing season, extended the field operations until December, 1868. But the subassistant commissioners found that their effectiveness was limited by the impending deadline, and some of them refused to stay on. First limited by Hancock's interference in late 1867, and then by Reynolds's General Orders No. 4, and hampered by planters who sought to drag out even the simplest quarrels until July, then December, 1868,

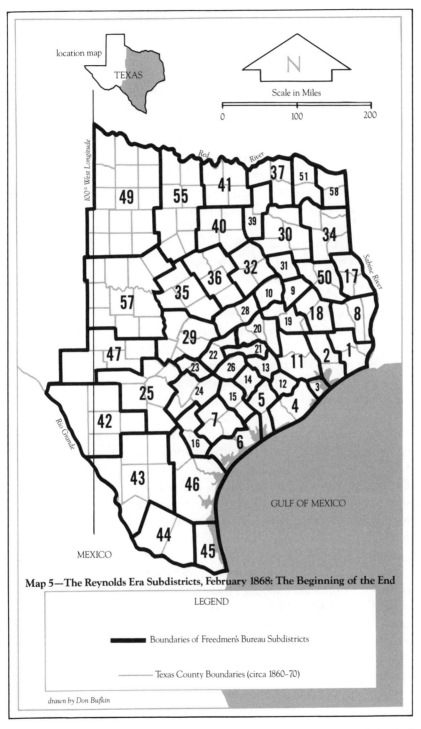

dedicated agents recoiled at duping blacks and abetting what they now saw as a futile cause.[3]

Typical in this respect was A. H. Mayer, the man who replaced J. Orville Shelby at Liberty. An Ohioan who came to Texas on business in May, 1866, Mayer bluntly asked for and received the Liberty position in August. He went to work immediately. He toured his subdistrict monthly, talking to planters and freedmen and notifying them of their responsibilities under General Kiddoo's circulars. He refused to allow freedmen to gather idly in Liberty and forcibly ejected them from their shantytowns. He spoke to them frankly, refusing to make what he derisively called "buncum speeches." Mayer told freedmen of their responsibilities to work and reminded the planters of their obligations to treat the blacks fairly and settle fully. He read Kiddoo's Circular Orders Nos. 14, 19, 21, 23, and 25, which explained bureau policies. On his own volition, he distributed one hundred fifty copies of Circular Orders No. 23, on the necessity of paying the freedmen before shipping the 1866 crop to market.[4]

The planters, however, had to test Mayer to see if he was serious in his intentions. The result was that Mayer seized tons of cotton that had been shipped without a bureau certification to attest that the black workers had already been paid their shares. One large confiscated cargo belonged to former bureau agent Orville Shelby. Mayer was also angry with Shelby for interfering with his prerogatives by acting illegally as a bureau representative behind Mayer's back. Mayer used men to closed off all wharves, but the planters devised many ingenious schemes to evade detection. The army cooperated most of the time, but refused to send soldiers during the yellow fever contagion in the summer of 1867, since traveling soldiers might help spread the disease. Mayer also enforced the provisions of Griffin's jury order and tried to establish new schools for black children, but had little success in obtaining teachers.[5]

Mayer was finally worn out by his diligence. He worked sixteen to nineteen hours a day, most of it dedicated to writing documents, letters, and contracts. The rest of the time, he traveled throughout his territory, monitoring conditions of the freedmen. He wanted to hire a clerk, but could find no one who could take the oath. It was no wonder that Mayer fell sick during the summer of 1867, although he seems to have contracted a simple flu and not yellow fever. He went back to his rigorous schedule too soon and suffered a relapse. Exhausted, Mayer took a thirty-day leave in late November, 1867. He returned to work by Christmas, but found new problems to exacerbate him. When Hancock's orders came out, Mayer was told to obey them. He refused, and quarrelled with several headquarters staff officers, whom he accused of trying to undercut him with General Reynolds. Finally, rather than submit to what he saw as an injustice, Mayer resigned his position, too sick and tired to fight on.[6]

Like Mayer, Captain Edward Miller declined to stay on in the bureau ranks. Miller had arrived in Millican at the end of February, 1867, after a 160-mile stage trip from his prior posting at Victoria. During his tenure at Millican Miller emphasized the creation of a black school system and the settlement of old accounts, still unpaid from the end of 1866. He investigated several murders of freedmen and one of an ex-sailor who had served in the Union Navy. Miller also uncovered a half dozen cases in which soldiers of the Seventeenth Infantry garrison at Brenham had been bribed to "stir up" Negro workers whom planters deemed of "lackadaisical" work habits. The blacks' actual "crime" had been wanting to go into Brenham to register to vote. The infantrymen had tied them up by their thumbs for a couple of hours, and the planters reported all hands were working diligently now.

During the summer of 1867, yellow fever laid Miller low and caused him to send his wife into the countryside for safety. He estimated that 10 percent of Millican's population died during the epidemic. Transferred to Bryan that fall, Miller was one of the four volunteers Reynolds recommended for reappointment as a civilian agent at the end of 1867. He was the only one to refuse a commission. Although Miller never made public his reasons for declining a reappointment, he probably believed that Hancock's and Reynolds' new policies did not warrant risking his life to the perils of assassination and yellow fever any longer. He returned to New York, and Captain Nathan H. Randlett was called over from Anderson to assume the combined agencies of Brazos and Grimes counties which now operated out of Bryan.[7]

The tentative existence of the bureau law affected other agents. The Sherman bureau agency had been staffed by civilians, but the unsettled nature of its surroundings called for real military strength; the area abounded with the remnants of Quantrill's wartime guerrilla force. When the Sixth Cavalry company holding the town left for the frontier in the spring of 1867, the district exploded with anti-Negro violence. The town was reoccupied immediately, but six months later, after the local politician, Anthony M. Bryant, resigned the subassistant commissioner's post and went on to bigger things at Austin, only a squad of twelve cavalrymen remained.

Their commander, First Lieutenant Harvey E. Scott, tried to get capable Republicans appointed to office to enforce the laws for loyal whites and blacks, but had to admit that only three or four likely applicants could be found. He condemned as useless the men Reynolds appointed in the fall of 1867. He and the man who followed him in office, Second Lieutenant E. C. Hentig, endeavored to obtain more men to cover their district, and failing in that, attempted to get the district divided up, with additional garrisons at Pilot Grove and Pilot Point. They failed here, too. Both officers condemned the local newspaper, the Sherman *Courier*, for stirring up opposition. The depressing nature of their reports to headquarters never changed during the bureau's ineffective existence there.[8]

Another bureau agent stymied by the bureau's coming demise was M. E. Davis. Originally from New Hampshire, Davis had served with his state's white volunteers and then transferred to the Colored Troops. He came to Texas in 1866 at the behest of his wife, who was the sister of Brevet Major George W. Smith, the post commander responsible for the Brenham fire, who was later court-martialed for embezzlement of government funds while serving as bureau agent at Seguin. As a loyalist readily available on short notice, Davis was Captain Samuel Craig's replacement at Brenham in September, 1866. His basic duty as the Brenham subassistant commissioner was to keep a low profile, which he did quite well. Griffin tried to transfer Davis to Anderson in Grimes County and Wharton, but Davis refused to go and resigned when his office was burned out in early 1867.

After the Brenham experience, Davis moved to Houston, where Reynolds asked him to serve out the seven remaining months of the bureau's existence. He moved the bureau office to his home, over the protests of the Union Loyal League, and got rid of a Scalawag clerk who was prejudiced against blacks. Bereft of troop assistance, however, Davis could do little but record the outrages committed against blacks in town, and the poor response of local authorities to them. To cure the lack of concern by local officials through personal service may have been one reason he accepted the military appointment as city marshal in February, 1869.[9]

Ineffective local authorities plagued many bureau agents besides Davis at Houston, but often the problem could be traced back to Reynolds himself. Inspector Sinclair, for example, reported that he had been pleasantly surprised by Charles Schmidt as the new subassistant commissioner at Sumpter, who was "doing exceedingly well." Sinclair believed that Schmidt was knowledgeable about his duties, industrious, and temperate. But Sinclair suggested that Schmidt might assert more authority than he had. The inspector suggested that R. A. Clifton be made the local sheriff. Sinclair liked the way that Clifton worked with the bureau as town marshal, and thought that Clifton would be the best sheriff that the county ever had. But Reynolds waited nearly a year before putting Sinclair's recommendation into effect, and then Clifton failed to qualify for the position by not submitting the proper affidavits.[10]

Louis W. Stevenson, just out of the regular army having served the bureau during the occupation of Virginia, found his new civilian bureau posting at Columbus to have similar problems to Schmidt's agency with ineffective local officeholders. Unlike Schmidt, however, Stevenson aggressively cleaned out the incompetents, recommending new appointees to take their places. The agent got rid of four justices of the peace, a deputy sheriff, and the Columbus town marshal. The following year, Reynolds also moved to oust the county judge and sheriff, whom Stevenson had wanted removed from the beginning. The subassistant commissioner also had the town constable at nearby La Grange superseded. Stevenson suggested that all justices of the peace be placed under Reynolds's General Orders No. 4, which gave the bureau agents the power to act as justices for the freedmen. Then lines of authority would be clear to all, maintained Stevenson. He also wanted specific penalties created for civil authorities who failed to do their jobs.

Meanwhile, Stevenson asked for twenty-five soldiers to help him "induce" the county and city officials to do their duty by the freedmen. Stevenson found that the mere threat of asking for soldiers was enough to cause a change for the better in the administration of many officials. It also caused the Ku Klux Klan to be circumspect in its activities, disciplining just enough blacks and loyal whites to satisfy adherents, yet not so many as to cause bureau headquarters to send troops on a permanent basis. But after a month's occupation, the soldiers were recalled to Galveston, and local authorities soon proved as reluctant to act as before.

Stevenson spent the rest of his time clearing up the accounts of Enon M. Harris, his predecessor, and organizing an effective school system for black children. He found his most serious problem in education to be the itinerant teachers, who would stay on a few months, earn pocket money, and move on. Stevenson raised money, repaired buildings, and hired a permanent teacher. His success in revamping local government and the school program did much to promote his continued employment with the bureau after December, 1868, as an assistant superintendent of schools, stationed out of Jefferson.[11]

A. B. Homer, who assumed control of the Columbia agency, had a fairly easy eleven months as subassistant commissioner. Outside of a riot on the Caney, which he easily suppressed, Homer reported improving conditions between the races and no need for soldiers. Labor was scarce, so planters had to treat their hands fairly or go without. He spent his time making contracts, negotiating settlements and wage disputes, registering voters, and visiting plantations. He negotiated a deal whereby whites and blacks avoided violence during the national election campaign and agreed to discuss matters quietly and openly. His only regret was that he could not find sufficient teachers and money for black schools. After his bureau position expired, Homer continued to work for the Reconstruction regime, serving as county commissioner, voter registrar, and Federal customs agent.[12]

More typical than Homer's situation was that of a former sergeant in the Sixth Cavalry, William Holt, the subassistant commissioner at La Grange. No one paid much attention to his orders, Holt said. Although the whites "profess to entertain the kindliest feeling for the freedmen," Holt continued, this sentiment was valid only if the black was humble, deferred to the white's desires, and took his hat off in the presence of white people. But if a black should stand up for his rights, Holt went on, he was labeled a "saucy nigger" who "should have his head shot off." As in other agencies, Holt discovered that the Negroes' worst enemies were the local justices of the peace, who selected white juries and stacked court procedure against justice for any black plaintiff or defendant. The subassistant commissioner tried to establish schools for black children, but was hampered by one group of blacks, who preferred to have nothing to do with the bureau and went off on their own to establish an independent school.[13]

Illustrative of the inherent ineffectiveness of the short-term appointments were the tenures of two men Commissioner Howard's office sent down to Texas for the settlement season in 1868, Thomas H. Browning and Henry C. Lacy. Browning went to Jasper to replace James Lowrie, and found conditions there still poor. He reported that he had heard of a former Confederate military man who bragged that he had killed three Union soldiers at the Battle of Atlanta. But no arrest was made. Lacy served at Crockett. He was surprised that the planters thought that a requirement for a "proper" vote should be a part of all labor contracts. Reynolds quickly disabused him of that notion. Lacy asked for troops to improve the moral quality of the civil administration. Failing in that he asked for the replacement of various state officials. Again, nothing was done. Both Browning and Lacy took government-paid transportation back to Washington following their tenures in office.[14]

Commissioner Howard's office could be a liability as well as an asset to the Texas command during the last days of its field operations, as in the case of William J. Neely, the last subassistant commissioner at Victoria. Reynolds had appointed Neely in July, 1868, sending his application to Washington for approval, a standard procedure. Meanwhile, Neely reported that outwardly everything was quiet at Victoria. Reynolds had defined Neely's position as having the same legal status as a justice of the peace, but he told Neely to advise the freedmen "as a kind of guardian" or an attorney, rather than become bogged down in litigation.

Neely, who had already been appointed county collector and assessor on August 20, was actively involved in local politics. Electioneering for the constitutional convention went on peaceably, he reported, but blacks had been threatened with death if they failed to support the Democratic ticket in the next elections. To counter this ploy, he recommended a change in his fellow civil officials of the town and county. As far as his bureau job was concerned, Neely seems to have had trouble with the paperwork requirements. He made the requisite number of reports, but he failed to place them in separate envelopes addressed to proper individual staff officers. He also had a penchant for granting freedmen divorces, something that annoyed headquarters. But, all in all, Neely carried out his responsibilities creditably.[15]

While Neely was serving as subassistant commissioner, his application made the rounds of the various staff officers in Washington. Howard's office sent the document back, along with several others, asking for more specific information on the applicant's war record. Neely sent in his whole dossier, and several new letters of recommendation. In October, Reynolds had to revoke Neely's appointment, Howard's office having refused approve it. Inspector Sinclair suggested that Neely be replaced by Hiram Clark, the current agent at Clinton. Neely was understandably angry. He claimed that he had done a good job, and labeled his successor a "mere cypher." Reynolds agreed that Neely had been good agent, and successfully sought to get him his three months' back pay.[16]

Clark, as the subassistant commissioner at Clinton for twenty months in 1867 and 1868, was a more active agent than Neely had implied, but his initial enthusiasm for the job had declined by the time he reported to Victoria. Clark had emphasized educational programs for the black children and hard work in the fields for their parents. Whites were opposed to education, because it might raise blacks out of peonage, and many swore that they would never again hire free Negroes after the less than satisfactory harvest of 1867. But under Clark's leadership, blacks subscribed to a school fund and built schools, and the planters rehired their black fieldhands, rather than allow their fields to lie fallow.

But Clark said that the Radical Republican victory in the contest for the state convention had caused nothing but bitter feelings. This bitterness carried over into the fall contest for the presidency, which took place even though General Reynolds declared Texans' votes inadmissible, since they had not completed Military Reconstruction. By the time Clark was transferred to Victoria in the fall of 1868, the only blacks who received a modicum of fair treatment were the ones who had voted Democratic, and there were few of those. He made the yearly settlements, closed down his office, and left, with matters pretty much unchanged from the beginning of his term to the end.[17]

More than the supplanting of Holt by Clark, the situation at the Huntsville agency showed the confusion that resulted from the urgent need for new short-term personnel in the final months of the bureau's operations in Texas. Reynolds's first candidate, James Burke, was discovered to have run for office under the Confederate regime, and was disqualified, even though Provisional Governor Pease vouched for his loyalty.[18] The next, William H. Stewart, took the oath, but within a month, Inspector Sinclair reported him to be less competent than desired. Stewart possessed lots of "animal force," Sinclair said, but he was "mentally imcompetent" and could barely read and write. Stewart also spent too much money on liquor and cigars, as far as the inspector was concerned. The inspector thought that Stewart would do better as a police officer. Even though there was some suspicion of Stewart as a former rebel, Reynolds chose to ignore it, and Stewart would later serve as town marshal of Huntsville and as Walker County sheriff.[19]

Sinclair then recommended William H. Howard, a local lawyer and newspaper editor, to replace Stewart. It turned out to be a less than auspicious choice. Howard fouled up his oath, tried to get a forage voucher paid that predated his assignment, and missed sending in his monthly reports for August, September, and October, 1868, in spite of reminders to do so. Howard did inform Reynolds in separate letters that outrages against the freed people were increasing daily. Black laborers were driven off the plantations to place them in violation of their contracts. Planters dragged their feet at settlement time, knowing that the bureau would close its doors at the end of the year and that they would then be able to settle in more understanding state courts.[20]

Agent Howard sought to combat this by preventing the shipment of all cotton that did not carry his endorsement that the employees had already been paid. Reynolds refused to allow this approach and told the agent to turn to the local courts. When Howard asked in exasperation what he was to do, the general told him to keep a list of all infractions, and await the arrival of troops. Howard did as he was told, but he was shocked to discover, when the soldiers arrived, that they were in sympathy with the hostile whites and their officers were "good Democrats." "*Don't* take them away unless you should send them into New England," he commented sarcastically in a message to Reynolds. The subassistant commissioner also asked that the county judge be replaced, a job to which Reynolds would appoint Howard himself, ten months later.[21]

When Howard printed atrocity stories in his newspaper, a party of whites threatened to shoot him. His newspaper was a source of trouble to him in other ways, too. He had sold it to his partner, M. H. Goddin, the former bureau agent in Livingston, who had fled to Huntsville at the threat of losing his life. Goddin, however, had not honored his note, and Howard went to court. In retaliation, Goddin had several local freedmen challenge Howard's administration as subassistant commissioner at Huntsville.

Goddin also induced the Federal troop commandant, Howard's "good Democrat," to prefer charges of fraud against the subassistant commissioner. Howard exploded, asserting in a letter to headquarters that the accusations "*are most hellishly false* and *I can prove them so.*" He believed that he should warrant as much consideration as Goddin, whom he called a "relentless miscreant," a common drunk, and patently dishonest. Moreover, Howard said, according to a freedwoman who had quit his employ in disgust, Goddin "slept with his daughter as a husband" would his wife. Howard said that when he presented Goddin with a writ to return the publishing plant, Goddin told him "that he did not care a '*damn*' for the law," and he would hold the newspaper by force of arms, if necessary. In the end, the bureau was probably glad to be rid of both of them.[22]

In an attempt to get local authorities wedded to bureau policies, General Reynolds often moved to appoint local law enforcement officials as bureau agents. After all, General Orders No. 4 made the subassistant commissioners adjunct officers of the state courts. Reynolds also hoped to be able to pay a county officer half the going rate, but the wary appointees usually insisted that the paperwork and dangers of a subassistant commissionership merited full pay. In one instance, the general tried to persuade the county judge of Dallas County, A. Bledsoe, to take the bureau job there or recommend another county official to be subassistant commissioner. He did suggest that his son, Willis, would take the proper oath and perform the job, if he could serve out of Lancaster, instead of Dallas, where W. H. Horton had been sorely tried as a civilian agent.

Reynolds accepted Bledsoe's conditions, and the young man did well, by Reynolds's own admission. The arrival of Company G of the Seventeenth Infantry brought order to the racial relations of the subdistrict, and the general then decided to transfer the bureau position to the commander of the post of Dallas, who was more centrally located and would serve at his regular army pay rate. First Lieutenant Henry Norton and his superior, Brevet Major Louis H. Sanger, found the attitude of local whites good—so favorable, in fact, that Sanger sent in his last report totally blank.[23]

Although Reynolds failed to persuade Judge Bledsoe to act for the bureau in Dallas County, he was more successful elsewhere when Frank P. Wood, the chief judge in Washington County, took over the post at Brenham in March, 1868. But Wood immediately asked Reynolds to double his salary to one hundred dollars a month. Reynolds refused, pointing out that Wood had a state income, and noting that he could obtain Federal money to forage his horse. But Wood was adamant—and in the end he got his raise, as no one else wanted the position.[24] Entering upon his job at the increased salary rate, Wood specifically mentioned his ability to carry out bureau mandates while acting as Washington County judge at the same time. He had the support of the army, commanded by Captain Edward Collins, who had held the bureau position for some months before at Brenham, and who understood his support duties well. But Collins's replacement, First Lieutenant A. H. M. Taylor, was not so cooperative, and he and Wood argued much as to jurisdiction. Meanwhile, the freedmen grew confused, wondering who was supposed to exercise legal power on their behalf.[25]

Besides a rumored jail-break plot at Brenham, the only major difficulty Wood faced was a riot at Hempstead, which was caused by the unwillingness of blacks to put up with nightly Ku Klux Klan raids. According to Wood's own account, the freedmen armed themselves, marched into town, and freed two black prisoners held for alleged cattle stealing. Wood talked everyone back into calmness, then tried the suspected Negro rustlers and found them not guilty. He left a squad of soldiers to police the area and returned to Brenham.[26] An investigation by the omnipresent Sinclair soon revealed that the disturbance had taken place over the Fourth of July, and that Wood had taken a vacation to his plantation, rather than go to Hempstead and cool the situation there. The inspector recommended that someone be made subassistant commissioner at Hempstead, an area he found to be full of "murder and outrage." Reynolds responded by appointing Alexander B. Coggeshall, a former agent at Bastrop, to the bureau position at Hempstead. Coggeshall acted ably to defuse the situation and prevent further violence.[27]

Another county law enforcement official who also functioned as bureau subassistant commissioner was Abner K. Foster. Foster had been A. J. Hamilton's appointment for county sheriff in the summer of 1865, and had applied to Gregory for a bureau position, only to be refused. Elected Lavaca County judge in 1866, Foster continued his Union support, and obtained a bureau agency for the region. Reynolds followed the recommendation of Inspector Sinclair and appointed Foster to the job at Hallettsville, which had previously been held by a volunteer officer, a Northern civilian, and a regular army officer. Foster immediately suggested that the bureau operations be extended in scope to guarantee the freedmen their rights.[28]

Foster was particularly interested, as was Wood at Brenham, in obtaining the same exemption privileges for black laborers that only landowners had in Texas. State law permitted the landholding employer to escape crop seizure to pay the salary of hired hands, but allowed the employer to attach what crop share the freedman received to satisfy accounts contracted by the laborer during the growing season. Both agents suggested that the law give the same privileges to both classes. Unlike others, however, Foster did not see his position as a guarantee that the freedmen would receive greater justice. Foster recognized that the better educated, wealthier whites could always tie up any litigation through the use of attorneys, legal delays, and prejudicial juries to escape the rightful claims of the freedpeople. He left office at the bureau's close, still calling for a fast, cheap method for freedmen to have their claims adjudicated beyond the state court system. He would later serve in the Reconstruction state senate.[29]

Like Foster, Thomas H. Baker at Lockhart was simultaneously a judge of the county court and a bureau agent. Baker reported that race relations deteriorated as the national presidential election approached in the fall of 1868. Anti-Reconstruction whites burned Negro schools and attempted to poison headquarters against his administration, but without success. Baker's appointment reflected the scarcity of men in his area who could take the oath. His major difficulty was that local justice courts interfered with his bureau decisions, which forced the blacks to go through a lengthy and expensive appeals process to reach his court and obtain a fair ruling. He asked Reynolds to prohibit interference with any subassistant commissioner's orders by a state court, but got nowhere.

As with all agents who served in the latter days of the field offices' existence, Baker noted that whites bided their time, waiting for the bureau's announced demise. The judge expected much trouble in the fall during settlement time, but Inspector Sinclair thought that he was merely unnecessarily jumpy. As county judge, Baker had all the power he needed to handle the situation under state law, without having to worry about the obstructionist tactics county courts usually threw in the path of other subassistant commissioners. He felt strongly enough about the Reconstruction effort to act later as mayor of Lockhart and state senator.[30]

Thomas C. Griffin, "one of Sherman's Bummers," according to one of his letters of recommendation, had a rougher time than Baker. He lacked a sheriff to enforce his edicts, for the former sheriff had resigned. When Agent Griffin went over to Hunt County, part of his bureau subdistrict, he said that he was lucky to escape alive. He asked for troops, but none were sent. Night riders and outlaw gangs appeared to be on the rise, who were waylaying, shooting, and beating blacks on the roads, and burning their schools. Although things seemed to have calmed down by December, he still lacked a sheriff and other men who could take the oath and were courageous enough to serve in political positions. To emphasize his point, Griffin agreed to act as a justice of the peace as well as county judge.[31]

Although there were numerous problems with those who served short terms, the Reynolds administration also saw the culmination of the careers of the men who had served the bureau the longest. First Lieutenant William H. Rock, Thirty-sixth USCI line officer, had the distinction of serving as subassistant commissioner for the longest time in the same post of all bureau agents. Born in Canada, Rock enlisted from the state of Kansas. A lawyer by trade, he had made a good impression on the bureau and army commands when he served on a court-martial board with distinction. General Kiddoo asked General Wright to detail Rock to the bureau in June, 1866. He went to Houston for a month on special duty, and then received the Richmond agency.

Rock served twenty-eight months at Richmond, until the bureau's close in December, 1868, with only a brief hiatus in the fall of 1866, necessitated by his regiment's muster-out process. Upon Rock's return, Kiddoo employed him as a civilian with the pay of a first lieutenant, since he had been in bureau service when his enlistment had expired and was entitled to the extra benefits of a military salary. Rock then went back to Richmond, because the current bureau representative there, Lieutenant Hardenbrook, had not worked out.

Rock was a vigorous agent and a good abolitionist, and he conducted his office responsibly in full agreement with the Republican party's desire to change Southern institutions. He was a voter registrar, and an advocate of equal rights for the Negro. He spent so much time touring his district that headquarters had to admonish him to visit only those plantations on which there was trouble reported. The exhausted subassistant commissioner was laid up with fever much of the summer of 1868. Rock liked to address the freedmen on their responsibilities as good citizens, read the newest bureau edicts, discourse on freedom, and offer gratuitous advice and counsel. He jealously guarded the fieldhands' first right to their share of the crop, and seized planters' property when they did not cooperate. He was disgusted and dismayed by General Hancock's orders, which forced him to use the state courts to obtain justice for his black charges, but he believed that Reynolds's General Orders No. 4 restored much of the subassistant commissioners' legal power.

Although race relations in Fort Bend County and the surrounding area were generally good enough for Rock to brag that he had the most orderly subdistrict in the state, there was a lapse in the fall of 1868, brought on by the canvassing for the presidential election. And there was the usual violence, perpetrated by a few hard cases. Rock especially did not get along with the county sheriff, J. W. Miles, and the two men had an altercation in Rock's office that led him to request troops. Rock was very willing to draw on the Houston garrison for soldiers at the slightest hint of opposition, which caused the post commandant to complain to headquarters that Rock was draining his manpower pool too often. This was probably also the reason why Rock's subdistrict was relatively quiet, despite the occasional political murder and some desultory Ku Klux Klan activity primarily against the local white teacher of Negro children. Upon the bureau's demise in 1868, Rock asked for transportation home to Kansas, but received travel expenses only to Galveston, his place of duty when he joined bureau ranks.[32]

The man who served the longest term as subassistant commissioner in a series of posts, twenty-nine months in all, was Fred W. Reinhard, who would later act in a state judicial capacity. The bureau agent at various times in Leona, Crockett, and Centerville in Leon and Houston counties, Reinhard had served three years in the volunteers before writing to Inspector Sinclair to request a bureau position in August, 1866. Kiddoo immediately sent the Prussian-born agent to the upper Brazos region at Leona. Reinhard went to work and soon had visited every plantation in the area, informing the planters of his presence. Although he generally considered the treatment of the freedmen by the planters to be good and believed that the civil authorities at least tried to be fair to the Negroes, it took him until June of 1867 to settle the troublesome 1866 plantation accounts.[33]

At the same time, Reinhard helped investigate the incident on the Cessna plantation in Robertson County. G. K. Cessna had allowed several freedmen and their families to work his land unsupervised by a white overseer, a liberal attitude that annoyed his neighbors. One night, after they allegedly held an antiwhite political meeting, the freedmen were attacked by gunmen. Two blacks died, another was wounded, and the buildings were burned. Working in conjunction with Dewitt C. Brown, a traveling agent, and Captain Joseph H. Bradford, the army troop commander in the area, Reinhard identified the marauders and had them jailed and tried for murder and assault. The jury refused to find the men guilty. General Griffin ordered that the men be rearrested, but Reinhard found that they had fled. The bureau seized some property of the men to pay off the freedmen's survivors but, in the end, Reinhard believed that little else could be done. Reinhard's resigned attitude led to much criticism from the local U. S. commissioner, Judge John K. Potts.[34]

Reinhard managed to survive Potts's criticism, and he outlasted other critics, too. On his way to join General Gregory's staff in Maryland,

Captain Samuel I. Wright stopped in New Orleans to write Inspector Sinclair that he had overheard on the steamboat that Reinhard and A. P. Delano were in the habit of "tasking" fieldhands at the rate of two hundred pounds of cotton a day. Those workers who failed to meet the quota had been tied up to tree limbs by their thumbs, as examples to the others. Reinhard allegedly had disarmed all blacks in his area, also. Reinhard denied these charges. He investigated and learned that the incidents had occurred before his arrival and the actions were those of a sergeant in the Seventeenth Infantry. Headquarters professed to be satisfied with his explanation, and dropped the matter with a reminder that Reinhard should see to it that freedmen were treated the same as whites before the law. Yet a local resident repeated these charges in a book written some years later, asserting that Reinhard had been trying to impress the family of a woman he was courting, and to assist them with their labor problems.[35]

But there was more. Reinhard weathered accusations that he apprenticed out black children to selected planters, charges that he unfairly favored blacks in debt disputes, and assertions that he wrongly or unfairly seized property. When Ned Wingate shot loyalist Henry Driskoll, "a good citizen," on Centerville's main street, Reinhard disgustedly reported that the defendant was acquitted by a jury in county court. "So much for the civil authority in this county," he said, viewing the verdict as an admonition for everyone else "to go forth and do likewise." When Reinhard threatened to pursue the case further, Wingate complained to headquarters. Reynolds told Reinhard to leave the Wingates alone. Wingate's brother Frank, however, soon was charged with the murder of a freedman, and Reinhard seized and sold some of the accused's property for bond. Headquarters disapproved the action and wanted the property returned, if possible. Reinhard said it was not possible.[36]

Soon after, the intrepid inspector Sinclair came to Crockett to investigate the murder of a deputy U. S. marshal by Frank Wingate and his son over the same bureau-ordered property seizure. Sinclair now endorsed Reinhard's seizure, saying that the refusal of the Wingates to pay their freedmen had caused the seizure and sale to be made. The murder of the marshal was a result of the Wingates' desire to get even with the law officer for merely doing his duty. The Wingates now threatened to sue Reinhard and the county sheriff for their parts in the seizure. "A bigger set of scoundrels than this tribe, I never knew," Sinclair concluded wearily.[37]

In the midst of all this, the county's Republican delegation to the state convention had the gall to accuse Reinhard of being anti-Union and unprotective of freedmen and loyal whites. This charge exasperated Reinhard. The first item stemmed from when he had fined the county sheriff for accepting a bribe from a freedman, only to have headquarters disallow the action. When Reinhard suggested that the sheriff at least be removed from office, he lost out again. As to the second, Reinhard had asked headquarters to remove Judge Kenneth Murchison from office for failing to protect Unionists upon Reinhard's complaint. Once again, Reynolds said that he could do little to remove anyone, now that General Hancock was in command at New Orleans. Hancock was a good excuse, but Reynolds characteristically failed to move against either man until over a year later, long after Hancock was gone.[38]

With all of the complaints, it seems miraculous that Reinhard could endure for twenty-nine months. But most of the accusations were strung out over the whole period, and they often were mutually contradictory. Moreover, Reinhard was the one individual who was able to get along with all sides, black and white, loyal and rebel, and still retain the respect of everyone. He was always available to assist in introducing new agents to the bureau policies, to take over when another agent died or resigned, and to move without a quarrel to the next town or county whenever headquarters desired. He also had the important support of Inspector Sinclair, who praised Reinhard for his ability to work with blacks and whites alike to make his subdistrict one of the most progressive in the state. His flexibility continued to be an asset, when he moved to Freestone County after the bureau's close and accepted appointment as county judge, a position to which he won election a year later. But his moderate Republicanism failed him in 1870, when General Reynolds removed him from office for a more Radical Republican. He returned to Prussia shortly afterward.[39]

A third man who served as bureau agent at several posts for nearly as long as Reinhard (almost twenty-eight months) was Captain Nathan H. Randlett of the Sixteenth Regiment, Veteran Reserve Corps. Assigned to Grimes and Brazos counties, the area where the Scalawag agents, William H. Farner and John T. Whitesides, had served, Randlett arrived in late April, 1866. New to the area, he had no room, and gratefully accepted temporary lodgings at Whitesides's plantation near Navasota. Headquarters angrily rebuked him. It would not do at all for a new agent to fall under the influence of the former agent. Randlett quickly found a place in town, and began work.

Much of the new subassistant commissioner's business initially had been held over from earlier agents. He forwarded Whitesides's claim for 1,188 rations for indigent freedmen originally paid out of his own pocket. He handled the usual contract disputes, abuses, and assaults. Randlett made the tour of his district that Kiddoo demanded of all agents in the summer of 1866, but headquarters refused to pay for the team of horses and carriage he hired for the job. Randlett reported that all went well in his subdistrict, except that there was a large class of unpredictable white "roughs," which necessitated troops at the agency. Headquarters sent him a squad of cavalry to give some force to his decisions. But generally Randlett operated without soldiers, once he obtained the appointment of a capable sheriff. He made several political recommendations, including the pardons of prominent citizens whom he believed to be "good men."[40]

In the middle of all, he found time for a forty-five-day leave, which gives some indication of his success as bureau representative in Grimes County. His office was moved from Navasota (two months) to Courtney (nine months) to Anderson (ten months) as circumstances demanded. In the summer of 1867, he was struck down by yellow fever and lay ill for four weeks. He moved his office out of town briefly to prevent the spread of the contagion to and from those who visited the agency. That fall, he was one of four volunteer soldiers (Randlett, Edward Miller, Charles F. Rand, and A. A. Metzner) in Texas due for muster-out whom General Reynolds recommended for reappointment as civilians.[41]

The main problem faced by Randlett during his tenure at Bryan was the so-called Millican Riot of July 15, 1868. The incident was caused by the Ku Klux Klan parading through a Negro village called Freedmen's Town near Millican. Rather than hide, the blacks fired on the Klansmen, who retreated hastily. Both sides armed and organized for a fight. Randlett went down to Millican and negotiated an agreement whereby both sides would disband. All was quiet for a couple of weeks. Then the black community heard that a freedman, Miles Brown, had been hanged. The whole community turned out to seek his body, but it was not found.

Angrily the blacks marched upon the house of a white man, Andrew Halliday, who had had a previous altercation with Brown, and had threatened to hang him. Panicked, Halliday sent to town for help. The mayor and a deputy sheriff raised a posse that marched in relief of Halliday. Meanwhile the blacks had rethought the situation and begun to disperse. As ill luck would have it, the two armed remnants of the white and black mobs met on a narrow road in the woods. Words were exchanged, and someone was the first to fire a shot. When the smoke cleared, there were several dead and wounded, primarily among the freedmen. The white rampage continued until Randlett arrived and summoned Federal troops from Brenham.

By the time the army arrived, all was quiet. Counting their losses, blacks discovered that their leaders, Harry Thomas and George E. Brooks, had been killed. Thomas and two other black leaders died on July 15; another black lost his life the following day; and Brooks, a preacher, voter registrar, and defender of black civil rights, disappeared a day later. All that was ever found were his clothes and a few personal possessions scattered in the woods. Within a month, Randlett had modified his report to blame the first shot on the freedmen. The army inspector, Brevet Lieutenant Colonel W. T. Gentry, who was once secretary of civil affairs under Griffin—the chief staff person in charge of Texas Reconstruction—endorsed the alteration, although he had black testimony to the contrary. And without its leaders, the Brazos County black opposition was much less threatening to the unreconstructed white population. Recognizing the futility of it all, Randlett, who had been transferred back to Anderson, resigned his position in October and went back North for reasons of business, health, and family.[42]

North of Randlett's subdistrict in Grimes County, Joshua L. Randall was the subassistant commissioner at Sterling. He was determined to make a favorable impact on the Reconstruction of Robertson County. Randall arrived at his station in April, 1867, and entered upon his work. His first case concerned one of the biggest planters in the area, Dr. E. H. Mitchell, who was accused of owing wages from 1866 to one of his hands, Charles Brandon. The employee testified that former bureau agents, Second Lieutenant Robert McClermont and William H. Farner, had strung up him and two others by their thumbs for leaving the plantation, in violation of Kiddoo's Circular Orders No. 14. Allegedly Mrs. Mitchell had slapped one of the men as they dangled, writhing in pain. Randall was determined to sift to the bottom of the dispute. Mrs. Mitchell came into his office one day with her lawyer and assured Randall that he could come out and inspect the account books, which would verify that Brandon had no grounds for complaint.

The next day Randall went out to the plantation and was greeted hospitably. Mrs. Mitchell said that she could not find last year's books, but would look again. She returned with the accounts, and as Randall

looked at them, he was astonished to note that the ink was not yet
dry. Randall, a lawyer by training, did an immediate audit that showed
the Mitchells owed Brandon over one hundred dollars from 1866. The
Mitchells refused to pay. Randall scheduled a hearing at his office a
week later. Meanwhile Mrs. Mitchell put a one-thousand-dollar price
on Randall's head, which her husband said was too small. He believed
that ten thousand dollars was a more accurate value. Attempted bribes,
and threats of being hanged from a post oak or shot down like a rabid
dog did not deter Randall from his course. Griffin sent cavalrymen
to back Randall up, but still the subassistant commissioner said that
he mailed his letters and reports only at the risk of his life.

The dislike of the agent among whites was countered by his popularity with blacks. Randall said that only the wholesale removal of local
officials would improve the situation, and Griffin ordered him to document every inadequacy he saw in county administration to facilitate
the process. Yet outside of replacing the sheriff a couple of times, Randall did little to change the personnel in county offices. As he helped
to register voters, however, Randall bragged that the blacks would vote
as he told them, and he himself ran at the head of the Republican convention candidates to prove it.

He set up a posse composed of his soldiers and armed blacks ("every
freedman has a revolver and a pony," he said), which did not improve
his image among whites. "No southern man is going to take impudence
from a nigger," one man warned Randall. "If a nigger insults me, I will
shoot him dead every time." At the same time he was using the black
posse to subdue such whites, Randall decried the "deplorably ignorant"
freedmen and their lack of enthusiasm about education, and remarked
on the "great care and circumspection" it took to break up unwanted
"combinations" among them. He feared a Christmastime revolt among
blacks, but the 1867 holiday passed without incident. Random racial
violence and cheating on wages continued until Randall closed the
bureau office on schedule a year later.[43]

One agent who had an easier time than Randall was John H. Archer,
who was a second lieutenant from the Seventh USCI when he wrote
the Texas bureau headquarters in June, 1866. Born in England, Archer
enlisted from New York City and had eighteen months left of a three-
year enlistment when he asked for duty with the Freedmen's Bureau.
"I would respectfully ask to be assigned any where except in the state
of Texas," he implored. Three months later Archer had changed his
tune. He was to receive an early muster-out with the rest of his regi-

ment. "I propose to make my home in the South," he said, and he asked for a military or civilian appointment to the bureau. General Kiddoo made him a civilian agent at Hempstead. Later Archer would ask to be paid at the higher military salary. General Reynolds refused, reminding the subassistant commissioner that he had been mustered out before receiving his bureau job and hence he was not qualified for a military pay rate.[44]

Archer reported to Hempstead, where he spent the 1866 settlement season. He regularly seized cotton shipments to guarantee the freedmen their fair share of the crops. Everyone tried to cheat the blacks, said Archer, and his presence was "positively necessary (and if President Johnson will only take his seat in my office for a week, I will undertake to convince him of the fact)." Archer pledged to use "every endeavor to deal out justice" during the drawing up of contracts for 1867. Satisfied with his performance, General Griffin sent Archer to Beaumont in his reorganization that spring, where Archer would stay for the rest of Reconstruction.[45]

Compared with the arduous activity that he had faced in Hempstead, Archer found the situation in Beaumont to be relatively quiet. Indeed it was hard to believe that this was the same violent Beaumont that Charles Hardenbrook had refused to serve in. Archer attempted unsuccessfully to organize a school system, he tried the few cases brought to his knowledge, and he recommended a few civil officers to be removed from office. And he found time for a thrity-day leave. He also remarked on the notion prevalent among whites that the newly freed blacks were to be allowed to work as hirees but denied the right to set up businesses for themselves. But in general, his reports were a dull litany of "nothing new," and "nothing to report." Archer turned in his papers in December, 1868, as the bureau closed down all of its field offices. He then returned to Beaumont and accepted a military appointment as the county judge. It seems that Texas was not such a bad place to make a home, after all. His twenty-six-month tenure as subassistant commissioner was one of the longest and quietest of the era.[46]

Matters were relatively quiet over in Seguin, too, although C. C. Raymond thought that troops were needed in neighboring Gonzales County to stop Ku Klux Klan–style organizations from their nightly activities. Raymond had received his appointment at the request of the Unionists at Seguin. Although his own life and the lives of blacks and white loyalists were rarely in danger, he maintained, no Negro could expect justice from any court. The reason was that all-white juries refused to convict any white defendants. The local judges allowed this condition to flourish, Raymond said, even though they were all General Reynolds's military appointees and allegedly loyal men.

In this light, Raymond asked Reynolds to clear up some questions concerning the authority of a subassistant commissioner to act. Can he force payment of debts owed blacks? (Only under Texas law and in state courts, came the reply.) Can he order a sheriff to seize a portion of a crop and turn it over to the freedmen? (Yes.) Can a landowner be arrested until he pays the freedmen what he owes? (No, use state courts and debtors' laws.) Can the subassistant commissioner disallow or discount charges made against the freedmen's accounts by a landowner? (No, freedmen must pay for all items bought on account.) Can he interfere in cases and seize property if a freedman is physically injured by a white? (No property may be seized except as provided for by state law.) In effect, as the responses made clear, all the bureau agent could do was advise the blacks how to proceed under state laws that were unfairly enforced by racially prejudiced, yet technically loyal, local judges and juries. This did not inspire Raymond with confidence about the future of the free labor system.[47]

While Raymond might get away with expressing his doubts about the bureau's course in Texas, the same privilege was not reserved to army officers like the outspoken captain, Edward Collins. The new bureau agent for Brenham arrived in March, to find the town plagued by a series of fires that gutted his office building. Collins was from the first dismayed that he could find no enlisted man in his command with enough education and discretion to assist him as a clerk. Worse than that, however, was his opinion of the contract labor system. He maintained that the cancellation of the state labor law was a mistake that had thrown the system into an unstructured mess. He found the freedmen unduly contentious and unbelievably lazy. He thought that the inclusion of black women in the contracts was ridiculous. The terms were meant for strong males, and he was reluctant to enforce them in the case of women and children.

Collins declared that the freed people were too dependent upon the bureau and reluctant to take the necessary risks to forge ahead on their own. He believed that education in self-reliance was the answer, but deplored the lack of Northern male teachers who, he said, were more respected by the black students than were white women or black teachers of either sex. Most of all, Collins wanted the freedmen to be employed like laborers in the North, for cash wages paid on a regular monthly basis. He believed that blacks should have the unmitigated right to quit any employer, and that planters should be able to fire any unproductive employee at will.

For this reason, the captain thought that Griffin's order forbidding crop liens was a step in the right direction. The idea that Negroes were to be paid from a percentage of the crop raised, said Collins, meant that in a poor year they received too little to pay the debts they had incurred. He condemned the Texas contract labor system as the worst system he had ever seen. When Hancock issued his General Orders No. 40, Collins said that the edict made the position of subassistant commissioner superfluous. But he also stated that if blacks were left to the state courts, he feared that they would see a lot of law, but very little justice.[48]

When Commissioner Howard heard of these complaints, he wrote Hancock and asked what was going on. Hancock replied that Collins was merely an ill-disciplined sycophant of General Reynolds, who personified the lack of control exercised by Reynolds over the bureau representatives in the state. Hancock said that he had passed through Brenham twice on his recent Texas tour and that Collins had said nothing to him then. He retorted that what the Texas bureau needed was a definite order specifically delineating the rights and duties of the field agents and requiring that they work in cooperation with, not in opposition to, the civil authorities. Hancock continued that neither Reynolds nor Collins had yet given him a specific instance where his policy had interfered with the proper execution of Federal laws. Rather their whole opposition was "vague and indefinite," the general concluded. Needless to say, Collins was soon on his way to a new posting.[49]

Few of the other subassistant commissioners were as verbose as Collins. But nearly a year later, as the bureau was being shut down, Brevet Major James Gillette, who had seen Reconstruction as an officer in the Fifteenth Infantry in both Alabama and Texas, seconded the emphasis that Collins had placed upon educating the freed people as to the need for self-reliance. At the same time, he incorporated many of Hancock's notions about the primacy of civil government. But Gillette thought that before the state was turned over to its own administration, bureau subassistant commissioners, post commanders, or special bureau inspectors ought to analyze the capabilities of the county governments and recommend men who could be trusted to act as fair justices of the peace to all parties, black or white, who might appear in a court of law. In a sense, when one ignores all of the unfortunate political machinations that infected his policies, this is what General Reynolds tried to do. The tragedy was that without the presence of the bureau, backed up by the power of the army, the process collapsed even before the state was redeemed.[50]

12

The Grand Cyclops Has Come

G ENERALLY, INSPECTOR GENERAL WILLIAM H. SINCLAIR liked to travel incognito. It was safer, and it allowed him to pump local tongue waggers about the activities of the bureau in their areas. But this time the news of his journey had preceded him. As Sinclair rode into San Augustine, a crowd was waiting. "The Grand Cyclops has come," someone shouted. "Oh, Hell no," came another cry, "he is only one of the Grand Cyclops Reynolds' cyclops[es]." The crowd laughed and hooted. Sinclair ignored them and rode on. "I know how to excuse ignorance and ill-breeding," he sniffed to General Reynolds in his report of the incident.

But to subassistant commissioners like Albert A. Metzner at San Augustine, about whom many complaints had been received, a visit by Sinclair could have all the effect of a visit from a Grand Cyclops of the Ku Klux Klan. True, it was not deadly in a personal sense, but an adverse inspection by General Reynolds's "Grand Cyclops" could wreck an agent's career. Metzner knew it, too. He had arrived from the Clinton agency about a year past, had been well received, but had had several problems, which Sinclair attributed to Metzner's "bad habits."

The subassistant commissioner was "given to swagger, braggadococia [sic], and indolence equal if not superior to any I have seen in the state," Sinclair elaborated. Numerous charges had been placed against Metzner months earlier by William C. Philips, an important local politician and friend of Governor E. M. Pease. Philips had claimed that the assistant commissioner was a habitual drunkard and was pro-rebel in his operation of the agency. Metzner had denied the charges at the time and had been backed up by other citizens. Everyone knew that the lieutenant liked his bottle after hours. But now, Sinclair was not convinced that Metzner's drinking was so limited, and his accounts were all muddled, as usual.

The inspector proceeded to describe in his report Metzner's incredible bar bill that filled one side of thirteen legal pages and totaled over five hundred dollars (he liked to buy drinks for the house). The subassistant commissioner owed money to others, as well. The inspector was saddened by the Metzner situation because, "in spite of his disgraceful conduct," the agent was still generally well respected. Sinclair asked that Metzner be replaced by Michael Butler, whose brother had been a subassistant commissioner at Huntsville earlier. But Reynolds had heard enough. He fired Metzner for drunkenness and neglect of duty, and confiscated all of his back pay. It was a bit rough on a man who probably drank to forget the constant pain in his damaged thigh.[1] It mattered little that when Butler arrived, he could not travel safely in most of his district. But then neither could anyone else. The area was infested with outlaws. Murder was an everyday affair. Butler called for troop support. Not receiving any, he did little beyond survive.[2]

Of course, Sinclair was in San Augustine not to worry about Butler's future, but about Metzner's past. Metzner had done little bureau business, Sinclair went on. Not only had Metzner been drunk much of the time, but the area was filled with Yankee-hating, anti-Negro rebels, who refused to allow any public political meetings beyond religious services addressed only by local parsons. Since his soldier guards had been withdrawn, the lieutenant noticed that few blacks came in to see him anymore. Small wonder, since one daring Negro complainant was actually shot at in Metzner's own front yard. Then the agent was hauled into local court on a trumped-up charge of horse stealing. At Metzner's request, General Reynolds intervened and blocked the prosecution.

Sinclair told of "Munchausen stores" about the supernatural powers of the Ku Klux Klan which circulated about town, "and with the inclination [of] ignorant people to believe all things of a supernatural nature," he continued, "nothing is now necessary over there but to *say* Ku Klux and almost anything might be accomplished." There were men who don sheets and "ride about the country in this *gostly* style," Sinclair admitted, but he doubted that any organized body of regulators existed. But blacks wisely did not go out at night, and Unionists were almost "as cowered and hushed."

There could be no fair vote in the area without the presence of a large body of Federal troops, the inspector said. On the first day Sinclair interviewed witnesses, for example, a mob assaulted the registration board, and the black registrar fled in terror out of town. The local black preacher could not even attend church services, because white gunmen awaited his appearance to kill him for "dabbling in politics." As Sinclair returned to his hotel room that night, he heard someone make a clicking noise three times from the bushes nearby. He was warned that it was the mimicking of the sound made by the cocking of a revolver or rifle hammer—a Ku Klux warning. Sinclair also heard the whites say that they would vote in defiance of the Reconstruction laws because President Johnson's amnesty gave them that right, and they would enforce their right with shotguns.[3]

Sinclair also had to investigate and clear up other cases of a more ignoble nature. The one at Columbia began when First Lieutenant A. H. M. Taylor of the Seventeenth Infantry, Griffin's acting assistant adjutant general, had recommended his brother-in-law for a bureau position, during the lieutenant's trip to the east coast on educational matters. Taylor said that his relative, A.F.N. Rolfe, a graduate of Oxford University, had had much experience in teaching and school administration, and sought a position with General Gregory at Baltimore or Griffin in Galveston. Arriving in Galveston, Rolfe found Griffin had died and the headquarters had been transferred to Austin. General Reynolds, however, appointed Rolfe to the vacant bureau post at Columbia. After a brief visit with Lieutenant Taylor at Brenham, Rolfe traveled to Richmond to meet with William H. Rock for an orientation session. But Rock was ill from yellow fever, and Rolfe stayed on to handle Rock's case load.[4]

After a prolonged delay at Richmond, Rolfe arrived in Columbia in early December. He was in office only two weeks before he received a visit from Inspector Sinclair, who relieved him from duty for being "addicted to intemperance." Sinclair said that Rolfe had taken nineteen days to reach Columbia from Austin, normally a five-day journey. He had been drunk much of the time since his arrival, Sinclair went on, and Rolfe's "associates have been the vilest of rebels and the vilest of men—barroom loafers and common drunkards." He had addressed the freedmen while drunk, called himself a "southern man," and done no real business. It would be better to have no subassistant commissioner at Columbia, than to put up with Rolfe, whom Sinclair called a "rascal" and an embarrassment to all loyal persons.[5]

Rolfe professed shock at the charge. He protested that he was twenty-five hundred miles from his home, without his wife and three children, and suspended without a chance to defend himself. He asked for all pay until the first of January, 1868, as all of his expenses had been paid out of pocket up to now, and he owed the government nothing. He complained that he had "not made _no money, as other agents have,_ who preceded me." He said he was willing to stay on to assist the bureau in any way. Lieutenant Taylor also wrote his contacts at headquarters, asking that Rolfe be given a chance to defend himself. Rolfe was supposed to work on schools, and had been made a subassistant commissioner for salary purposes only, Taylor said.[6]

Second Lieutenant J. P. Richardson replied for Reynolds. Richardson commiserated with Rolfe's "unhappy condition of your wife and children, but I have my duty to perform to you and not to them." He said that Rolfe was due no back pay. He had drawn salary advances in New Orleans and Houston, and had spent the money in a drunken binge at Galveston, which forced him to borrow from bureau agents to continue his travels. He had inquired at headquarters on how agents could make extra money, implying that the subassistant commissioner's position was a source of ill-gotten wealth. Richardson accused Rolfe of being drunk the whole time he spent with Rock at Richmond. Rolfe had forged orders, signed Rock's name to liquor purchases, associated with known rebels, and announced that he was a Southern man at heart. Rolfe had been investigated at the request of loyal and disloyal men, both equally fed up with his public spectacle. Richardson concluded that Rolfe was a disgrace to the bureau, himself, and his family. Taylor also turned against Rolfe, thanked Richardson for his frankness, and apologized for his family's embarrassing relation.[7]

Rolfe was not the only agent who had serious problems. When Otto F. Steinberg applied for a bureau position in late 1868, Reynolds sent him to Gonzales to supervise the crop settlements there. But when Steinberg's name was sent through Howard's headquarters, some clerk remembered the name and investigated it. Sure enough, Steinberg had been dismissed from a bureau job in Alabama two years earlier for embezzlement of government funds. He had been dismissed from the service, fined two thousand dollars, and confined to the state penitentiary until the fine was paid. Reynolds dismissed Steinberg at once without pay after thirty-five days at his post.[8]

Although Steinberg was caught rather quickly, Reynolds was not so lucky in the case of William H. Horton, the one-armed subassistant commissioner at Bastrop. Horton suffered the same fate as his predecessor, Byron Porter, at the hands of the same men, led by the notorious William J. A. Bell. By now, Bell's reputation was so bad at headquarters that Horton could not accept a ride out to Bell's plantation to inspect the conditions of the freedmen without being accused of consorting with a known felon. Bell continued his reign of terror against blacks and Union men. His arrest in one case led to a guilty verdict and a one-cent fine, much to Horton's disgust.

Bell was not alone in his misdeeds. Justice of the Peace W. T. Allen was rumored to have raped a freedwoman who worked for him. Nothing was done. Horton protested, but not even Governor Pease thought the case could be prosecuted successfully. Murders were common on the county roads. Prisoners escaped from the jail regularly. Concerned by Horton's troubles, Reynolds sent Sinclair to nearby Bastrop to assist him in two sticky cases. The first involved a murderer and cattle rustler whose friends threatened to break him out of jail. Reynolds wanted the man transferred to Austin, but Sinclair thought the trip too hazardous to attempt. Instead, the inspector had a troop detachment sent to Bastrop to secure the jail for the civil authorities.

In the second matter, a defendant would not pay a fifty-dollar fine for contempt of court, involving his refusal to be arrested by the local sheriff. Horton said that the sheriff had been lackadaisical in his duties or the incident could not have occurred. The sheriff wanted the support of the army to arrest such a dangerous fugitive. Sinclair placed the sheriff on probation for his refusal to act and ordered the army to assist him in the arrest. After the matter was successfully concluded, Sinclair released the sheriff from his bond.[9]

About this same time, Horton was greatly embarrassed on a personal level when Commissioner Oliver O. Howard's ambulance broke down opposite town as the general was going back to Washington on his only trip to Texas during Reconstruction. Howard's driver could not rouse the ferryman, and the general and his driver had to spend the night in the ambulance. Horton said that the real problem was that the general's driver had pushed the horses too fast and they both played out. One never recovered from the trip and died. Horton took Howard personally to the steamboat wharf at Columbus to continue his journey. Shortly after this incident, Horton was told to turn his records over to the despised Judge Allen, and report to Austin.[10]

There, he was stripped of all back pay and dishonorably discharged from the service for accepting bribes and pocketing the salary of a bureau schoolteacher while subassistant commissioner at Dallas. Horton was mortified by General Reynolds's "bitter comments" after all his faithful service at rough duty stations. "The Rebels here swore that they would ruin me," he continued, "and I think they will succeed." Horton said that his wife was on her way to Texas, and now he would have to send her back, which would take every cent he had. He begged Reynolds to keep the case out of the newspapers, until he could blow his brains out. "The humiliation is too great to bear," Horton confessed gloomily. He also noted that he was being sued for ten thousand dollars' damages for false arrest in a Dallas court, and asked Reynolds to quash the charges. The general readily complied. In fact, the taking of Horton's back pay was all that Reynolds felt he could do. A court-martial was in order, but the costs were too prohibitive for it to be set up.[11]

Much like Horton, Agent Enon M. Harris gave the bureau eighteen months' service before his fraudulent activity was established. Technically appointed as a bureau clerk, Harris acted as subassistant commissioner at Columbus during his entire tenure. He supervised contracts, collected debts owed to blacks, arrested a few murderers, recommended taking part of the Buffalo Bayou, Brazos, and Colorado Railroad as rebel-built public property, and seized much cotton since his station was a central receiving and shipping point for both rail and riverboat traffic. Harris's tour of duty was marred only by his poor relations with the often drunken and deserting soldiers who served as his guard, whom the subassistant commissioner neglected to provision properly.[12]

The incident that did Harris in was his conduct in the settlement of the Crisp estate. Dr. John Crisp had read General Granger's emancipation order to his 130 slaves in the summer of 1865. He asked them to stay on and help bring in the crop at ten dollars a month. Most had agreed. Crisp then had second thoughts about the loss of the Confederacy and went to Brazil. He left the plantation in the hands of his son James, who tried to change the terms of the contracts. The freedmen, advised by the commander of the Union occupation force in the area, refused to allow it. Dr. Crisp returned at Christmas, and told the freedmen that he had no cash to pay them. But the Negroes knew that the doctor had bragged in town about harvesting and selling at big profit fifty bales of "sea island quality" (the best) cotton.

The following year was one of confusion. The freedmen's claim was lost amid the constant changes in subassistant commissioners. Then Dr. Crisp sold his plantation for ten thousand dollars. To make matters worse, the buildings and land were sold to one buyer, while the crop in the field and farming implements were conveyed to another. The fieldhands now had a new contract, approved by the bureau. By the time Harris got the whole matter organized, it was late 1867, another year had passed, and the blacks wanted settlement for 1865, 1866, and 1867. Harris admitted that he was confused and asked headquarters to send up Subassistant Commissioner William H. Rock, a former lawyer, to work things out. Meanwhile, Harris seized the plantation and its crop in lieu of debts amounting to nearly $4,900. The buyers refused to pay Crisp, and Crisp protested the matter to headquarters.[13]

Reynolds backed up Harris, so Crisp went to General Hancock at New Orleans, accusing Harris of stealing his property from him. Hancock ordered the plantation returned to the Crisp family, and all complaints settled in court. To block the case, Crisp got the local judge to rule that all court costs must be paid up front, or the freedmen's suit would be dismissed. Of course, the Negroes had no money to meet this demand, but Harris managed to have the ruling overturned by Governor Pease. Reynolds then refused to allow the subassistant commissioner to come to Austin to plead his case in person. Harris argued that his life was in danger and he needed protection.[14]

Meanwhile, in Austin, Inspector Sinclair was drawn into the Harris case during a tour of inspection that took him into the area around Houston. On the way, he met and spoke at length with Mrs. James J. Jameson, the former schoolteacher at Columbus, who wanted to bring Harris up on charges of murder. But Sinclair thought she exaggerated the circumstances of the case. Her husband had died from yellow fever the previous summer while they were employed as bureau teachers. The couple had fled to the countryside, a standard practice, to avoid the disease. But Mr. Jameson contracted it and died, after lingering on for two and a half weeks in agony.

Although they were only four miles from town, Harris refused to send them a doctor or any medicine, beyond a dose of quinine. Mrs. Jameson had some freedmen take her to town, where she confronted Harris, although she herself was sick. Harris put her in a room on the floor with a pillow and blanket, which he removed when he thought she was dying. Only the assistance of a few brave Negroes saved her life. Now she lived in Galveston on public charity. Harris denied the story, explaining that there was no medicine or doctor available at Columbus, as all were busy treating other cases closer at hand. He described Mrs. Jameson as being out of her head with fever and raving all the time in her grief.

Nonetheless, Harris's attitude disturbed Sinclair. He distrusted Harris even more for "traducing the character" of two women teachers from the American Missionary Association, who were as pure "as my own sister," Sinclair said. Harris had never been able to get along with any of the teachers sent to the town, the inspector discovered. He also recommended an audit of the medical bills that Harris had submitted to the bureau for yellow fever care, as he suspected they were much inflated. Sinclair questioned other charges in Harris's bureau accounts. The inspector had talked to a former Union Army officer who claimed that he could "knock him higher than a kite" with stories of Harris's corruption. Sinclair concluded that Harris had not the confidence of local blacks, Unionists, or rebels, and ought to be removed from office. General Reynolds concurred in Sinclair's estimate and fired Harris.[15]

Further investigation by Sinclair indicated that Harris had cut corners in several cases during his term at Columbus. Sinclair admitted that his charges were guesswork, because Harris had destroyed most of his financial records before returning home to Pennsylvania. Harris was suspected of pocketing two thousand dollars subscribed for the building of a schoolhouse for the freedmen. He probably kept over one hundred dollars in fines collected while he was at Columbus. He also charged illegal fees to draw up contracts and took bribes to settle debts owed to freedmen on a basis favorable to the white debtors. Finally, the subassistant commissioner had kept the proceeds from an estate sale of a dead freedman that amounted to another one or two thousand dollars. Harris's pay was stopped to cover the sums, but he never was brought to justice. Sinclair reckoned that the pay represented about thirty-seven cents on the dollar of the actual amount in question.[16]

Angered by Sinclair's success in taking his job and impugning his character, Harris sought to get even. He contacted Robert K. Smith, the editor of the Galveston *Republican,* and told him that Sinclair and his brother-in-law were part of a cabal of evil men who, under the coat of philanthropy, had worked to destroy the bureau's image with the public. Sinclair, said the newspaper, "together with a relative who has been and still is, employed as a clerk in the Department," opposed the full impact of the Reconstruction process. "Those men have done their utmost to defeat in every possible way, the reconstruction of the state," the sheet continued, referring to Sinclair's selection of supposedly inept voter registrars. Editor Smith then asserted that General Griffin had been onto Sinclair and E. C. Bartholomew, and was going to sack both of them. Only the general's untimely death from yellow fever had prevented him from completing this plan.

Of course, a copy of the article reached the commissioner's desk in Washington. Howard asked Reynolds to look into the story. Reynolds and Governor Pease quickly rallied to Sinclair's defense. Reynolds said there was no truth in any of the assertions, and appended a letter to him from Sinclair, which referred to Smith as a "political demagogue and trickster." The inspector related that he had said this to Smith and his friends publicly, which was the reason behind the attacks. Sinclair also knew of Enon M. Harris's role. Ever since he had suspended him from office, Harris had been spreading lies about him, Sinclair said. His reports against Harris were on file, the inspector continued. What else was one to expect, he concluded, when his job forced him to concern himself with "swindling, lying, drunken, worthless, and inefficient Bureau agents" like Harris. Pease called Sinclair one of the best agents in the state and defended his political selections as loyal "by word, look, or act," and the best for the Republican party's future in Texas.[17]

But as devastating as a visit from Sinclair could be, nothing could match the stifling influence of the Ku Klux Klan or outlaws on bureau operations in 1868. Isolated centers of violence seemed to exist in all parts of the state, but it was concentrated in the depths of eastern and northeastern Texas. Retired sergeant Nesbit B. Jenkins of the Fourth Cavalry, for example, served his bureau time in hostile Wharton County. Attacks against freedmen ran on unabated. When Reynolds removed his troop escort, Jenkins said that the blacks would be totally unprotected and that he would also be the target of threats and abuse. Reynolds apologized but referred to General Hancock's policies. No troops were to be detached from their units to serve under the command of any officer but those from their companies. Jenkins threatened to resign, but stayed on when Reynolds told him that no one else would take the job. The outrages continued. When several assaults and a vicious murder followed, in which one black victim's corpse was mutilated by having the penis cut off, Jenkins asked for soldiers once again. This time Reynolds sent him an entire company, whose presence Jenkins found "indespensible."

As the fall presidential election approached, the racial attitudes hardened on all sides. At a Democratic political meeting, one speaker referred to Jenkins as a "God-damned son of a bitch," and a "God-damned liar." He came into the agent's office and repeated the statements to be sure Jenkins would get them correct in his report to headquarters. Jenkins disgustedly told headquarters, "I believe it was never the interest of the Government to appoint me to a Post in the midst of a hostile community like this, and to an office which is particularly hated with no other protection than what my own personal Strength can afford me." Jenkins was physically and mentally sick of the whole matter. He warned Reynolds that since the bureau was finished in December, 1868, it was of the greatest concern that loyal men be appointed to all county offices to carry on the protection of the freedmen. Reynolds was obliged to agree, and the general appointed Jenkins to be sheriff of Goliad County the following year.[18]

On a par with Wharton was Cotton Gin in Freestone County. By the time First Lieutenant James F. Hill arrived in late 1867, Cotton Gin had already seen one subassistant commissioner wounded from ambush and another killed on the town street. Hill said that he had met only two possibly loyal whites. All the others were decidedly hostile to the bureau presence. Planters refused to give the freedmen their shares of the crops, and dared them to report it to the bureau. Hill was at a loss what to do. Headquarters quickly sent Brevet Major Robert P. Wilson and a full company of the Thirty-fifth Infantry to quiet things down. Wilson did his job well—so well that Reynolds decided that his company could be one of those sent to the frontier under Hancock's new policy. Wilson warned that although there now appeared to be justice in the civil administration for blacks, everything depended upon the continued presence of his soldiers. His caution, however, carried no weight in Austin. The Cotton Gin bureau office was closed on March 2, 1868, and its functions were shifted to the already overextended Waco agency.[19]

But Wilson's warning was prescient. Before the summer was out, Reynolds had to send another retired sergeant, David S. Beath of the Sixth Cavalry, to Cotton Gin. Beath reported that freedmen in the area were still unpaid and that the hills were full of outlaws. Beyond that, Beath was shocked at the numbers of blacks living in adultery. He instituted a vigorous policy of identifying these miscreants and assessing fines. Reynolds had to explain the realities of slavery and its aftermath to the sergeant and order him to remit the money collected.[20]

After Beath grumpily complied with Reynolds's orders, the general sent him to Bastrop, which needed an agent more desperately even than Cotton Gin. When Beath arrived, the town believed that it had run off Byron Porter and Horton before him, and now it was Beath's turn to fly. But Beath was a tough man with seven years' military experience behind him, and he fought instead of running. Reynolds warned Beath that he could not have military assistance and to stay out of matters that should have been settled by his predecessors, but Beath bulled ahead with what he thought was right. He set a black defendant free from the city jail, because he thought him wrongly accused and unfairly denied bail. Judge W. T. Allen, the man Horton had accused of raping a freedwoman, threatened Beath in public, and loudly damned Congress, General Reynolds, and the bureau. Beath refused to fight him, although many blacks said that they would back up the subassistant commissioner, because he feared a race riot was exactly what the judge wanted.

A few nights later, Allen's carriage house went up in smoke. The fire was prevented from spreading throughout the town only by a providential rainstorm. Allen accused Beath of starting the fire. The judge said that Beath was so objectionable as the bureau representative in Bastrop that he and other allegedly loyal military appointees to civil office would resign in protest. Allen and his friends claimed that Beath had threatened to burn the town, and spent most of his time drinking in a saloon with an army buddy. Beath, for his part, denied that he had started the fire. He begged Reynolds to remove Allen and his cronies from office and give Bastrop a decent local government. Reynolds refused to back Beath, who resigned his position. But the end of the bureau a week later made the whole argument moot. Beath left Bastrop and secured an appointment as the Federal postmaster at Weatherford, close to his old Sixth Cavalry stamping grounds.[21]

In Waco, a perennial trouble spot, First Lieutenant D. F. Stiles ran afoul of Hancock's General Orders No. 40, when he held a civilian prisoner charged with shooting a freedman on behalf of the Waco sheriff. Stiles had no guardhouse, so he put the prisoner in leg irons in a tent. When the defendant's lawyer got a writ of habeas corpus, Stiles released him for the sheriff, and then placed him under military arrest. The lieutenant put him back in irons, and held him incommunicado a day and a half, before letting him out on two thousand dollars' bond to keep the peace for one year. Reynolds, in violation of Hancock's orders, approved Stiles's actions. Stiles, an aggressive subassistant commissioner, who characterized the townsmen as "anything but friendly," also caused a protest when he seized cotton on behalf of a freedman, whose employer asserted that the five bales belonged to him for debts the Negro had incurred during the growing season.[22]

In late March, 1868, Stiles's company was reassigned elsewhere, and the new subassistant commissioner, Charles Haughn, formerly from the Fifty-first USCI, arrived. Haughn wanted to be paid at his old military rank of first lieutenant and quartermaster, but Reynolds informed him that since he came to the Texas job as a civilian well after his muster-out, he would have to accept the same pay—$125 a month—as others. Haughn agreed to this, only to have his job increase in difficulty when his troop garrison left a few weeks later for points west. Haughn saw a turn for the worse in his relations with local whites. Outlaws returned to the region, and two gangs of the Ku Klux Klan, known locally as "the Families of the South," roamed McLennan County's byways with impunity. Blacks who had not been run off the land already (making them away without permission and in violation of their contracts) went unpaid.

It irked Haughn to see Brazos valley planters riding fine horses, flashing big gold watches, toting fancy revolvers in tooled leather holsters, and claiming that they made no money and could not afford to pay fieldhands who failed to produce a good crop. His only recourse was to seize the landowner's properties. But county officials refused to act after the soldiers left. The planters laughed at the freedmen who asked for their wages. "You went and voted, God damn you!" they shouted. "Now let's see what the Yankees can do for you." Those Negroes who refused to comply were cut, shot, and hanged all over the county. It was not uncommon to find a dozen bodies at the site of a single atrocity. Haughn believed that the only thing that prevented an all-out race riot in Waco proper was the whites' fear that their own property and businesses would be destroyed.

The truth was that Haughn could do very little without a massive military presence, and everyone knew it. Whenever the subassistant commissioner issued an order, the town's legal talent would meet and figure a way around it. He wanted to make planters responsible for any depredations the freedmen suffered. After all, Haughn said, they had hired ruffians to come in and discipline and run off their hands at settlement time, and now this "Disloyal Rabble" claimed to be innocent of any wrongdoing. But headquarters refused to take any such course. Planters, on the other hand, offered certificates of protection to any black who would join the Democratic Club, just as they had protected them from nonslaveholding whites before the war.

Haughn wanted to remove the McLennan County sheriff from office, but no one else would take the job. The situation improved somewhat in November, 1868, when a company of infantry returned to town. But the infantry could do little outside Waco because of its limited mobility against mounted opponents. "The Bureau has played out," whites reminded Haughn, "we now have things our own way and we will put those damned niggers through" the county legal system. In December,

Haughn closed down his office and moved to Nacogdoches, where he accepted a bureau appointment as an assistant superintendent of education. He later shifted his residence to Marion County, where he served as a voter registrar and was elected justice of the peace.[23]

Yet Haughn and the others were lucky that the outrages in their subdistricts had not involved them personally, as the careers of other bureau men aptly demonstrated. When a vacancy opened up at Dallas, for instance, Reynolds appointed George F. Eber, the Federal deputy collector of internal revenue at Canton, to take the job. Eber traveled west to Dallas, reaching Kaufman on April 3, 1868, where he stayed with the local subassistant commissioner. The bridges on the Trinity were out, so Eber proceeded to Rockwell to cross. He never made it. On the morning of April 5, he was shot down and robbed. Authorities arrived "at the body while it was yet warm and the blood oozing out." They followed the tracks in the mud to a nearby farmhouse. There they found a man who possessed a double-barreled shotgun, one barrel of which had been recently fired. The wadding found in Eber's body matched that in the loaded barrel, and the man was arrested. It seemed a simple case of robbery-murder, so very common in that time and place, and not a political assassination.[24]

As bad as individual locations could be, outrage against blacks and the bureau agents rose to a height of horror in the arc along Texas's eastern and northern borders. At Nacogdoches Captain T. M. K. Smith disclosed that not only had attacks increased against blacks who asked acting subassistant commissioner Alexander Ferguson for help, but they were abetted by the refusal of the local sheriff to step in. Griffin ordered Smith to remove the peace officer and recommend a replacement. But cooperation with the civil authorities continued to deteriorate. A new low was reached when a white shot in the head a freedman who had reported him to the bureau. Then, as the Negro lay on the ground, the gunman coolly and deliberately shot him in each arm and the shoulder. The criminal was never caught.[25]

When Smith's troops were sent to Marshall in 1868, Reynolds made Ferguson subassistant commissioner in his own right. The planters in his subdistrict refused to contract with their hands or to pay for back services rendered. They were waiting for the bureau to go out of existence, an event first expected in July and then confirmed for December. To aid their subterfuge, someone broke into Ferguson's office one night and destroyed all of his records. Tattered papers were strewn from one end of town to the other. He received four threatening letters "cowardly" shoved under his door. He had the support of the sheriff, Ferguson said, but the removal of the soldiers had emboldened bad men who had fled the county to return.

Murders of black leaders rose alarmingly. When Ferguson hauled suspects into court, he had to abandon the cases from lack of evidence. But the subassistant commissioner said that he knew he had the right men when the defendants arrived with two high-priced lawyers to defend them. One Negro was murdered by a shot in the back of his head and the "Civil Authority declared it *Suicide!*" a disbelieving Ferguson wrote. The Ku Klux Klan rode nightly. One planter came in and asked Ferguson to help him. His fieldhands were so afraid of Ku Klux Klan raids that they slept in the woods. He asked Ferguson to come out, but warned him to stay off the public roads, for they were unsafe. Ferguson wisely decided that he could do nothing. He knew that he could not stay alive if he traveled one mile from town on business. He did offer to stay on to protect Negroes as best he could, but Reynolds pulled him out at the end of the year when the bureau closed down. Later Ferguson settled in Fort Bend County where he served as the local constable and Richmond town marshal.[26]

But while Ferguson merely lived in fear, James Lowrie, the bureau agent at Jasper, had already been shot in his sleep by unknown assailants. As Lowrie healed slowly, he made the mistake of arresting the sheriff for killing a freedman at a political meeting. The town went crazy, with mobs roaming the streets, and rabble-rousers calling for an attack on Major Louis Sanger's occupying force of infantry. A neighboring county willingly offered one hundred men to help the assault. As a way to quiet the mob, Lowrie agreed to let the sheriff go free. The man promptly violated his parole and disappeared into the woods. Any further attempts to enforce the law were met with the same hostility. To show who really had the power in the area, local thugs "arrested" Lowrie and former agent M. H. Goddin and held a kangaroo court session, during which their "crimes" were assessed, and the two men warned to "go straight" or die. Violence against Unionists and soldiers, and fraud against the freedmen, had become such a routine that a weary Sanger merely wrote the word, "same," after all the questions in his printed monthly report forms.[27]

The rest of Lowrie's term was marked by constant threats on his life, which made his job not only hazardous but ineffective as well. Headquarters had always considered his conduct a bit hesitant, but Lowrie claimed that his post was so isolated that without constant troop support he could do little. But General Reynolds spurred Lowrie on (as had Griffin before him), and even asked the subassistant commissioner to act as a deputy U. S. marshal in addition to his bureau duties. Lowrie refused to accept the added responsibility. Instead he showed up in Austin in June, 1868. Lowrie claimed that he was there to avoid assassination, but Reynolds ordered him back to his post at Jasper and sent the reliable inspector Sinclair out to check on Lowrie's story.[28]

When he got to Jasper, Sinclair found that Lowrie was rarely at his post. Instead, the agent spent most of his time at Woodville, under the protection of Sanger's infantry company. He had followed Sanger's men to their reassignment to Bryan, and had just returned when Sinclair arrived. The inspector thought the reason Lowrie had left was that the bureau was to "play out" in July, 1868. When Congress extended this to December, however, Lowrie had decided to return and finish his tour. Although Sinclair sympathized with Lowrie's danger at Jasper, the harried subassistant commissioner had failed to follow correct procedure and report his predicament to headquarters. So Sinclair advised that Lowrie be fired from his job.

Despite Lowrie's failure to do his job, Sinclair admitted that a "certain kind of quiet exists," but he attributed it to the freedmen working diligently in the fields in a form of quasi-slavery. "It is not strange that in the intoxication wrought by sudden emancipation they should have done many strange, wild, and foolish things—that they became restless, discontented, and unreliable," Sinclair explained, referring to the freed people. Now, however, good crops tended to make for "jubilant" feelings on all sides, he said. Besides few blacks dared risk the consequences of reporting violations to the bureau, Sinclair went on, since bureau agencies were more than fifty miles apart, and Federal troop garrisons were spread even thinner. "Rebel sentiment is rampant and intolerance of anything savoring of loyalty or support of the reconstruction laws is fully developed and openly expressed," the inspector asserted. And although the whites were not cheating the blacks so much, the freed people were still viewed by white Texans as "legitimate plunder." Sinclair feared that the settlements would be unfair in 1868, once again.[29]

Lowrie was not alone in being the object of hostile attack. First Lieutenant Gregory Barrett, Jr., the agent at Tyler, was a junior officer in the Twenty-sixth Infantry battalion stationed in Smith County and commanded by Brevet Lieutenant Colonel D. L. Montgomery. Although Montgomery and, during July, 1867, Brevet Colonel Levi Bootes, were listed as subassistant commissioners on paper, Barrett seems to have handled the actual duties. But Montgomery as post commander still influenced the nature of these duties. The colonel's inadequacies as an administrator had led to a written argument between him and Second Lieutenant Charles Garretson, the bureau's erstwhile staff coordinator at Galveston, who despised Montgomery's "great carelessness" as a bureau representative in Tyler.[30]

In March, 1868, Tyler was discontinued as the station for the three infantry companies there. Left behind to protect the freedmen, contrary to Montgomery's wishes, were Lieutenant Barrett, a dozen men, and two noncommissioned officers. Barrett noticed an immediate change for the worse in his relations with the white community at Tyler. The talk was "to clean the blacks out as soon as *all* of the 'Yankees' leave." Barrett referred to the "pretended" loyalty of local officials, the way in which local officials ignored the numerous cases involving freedmen's rights and wages that Montgomery had referred to them, and the uselessness of his operations as subassistant commissioner there. All Barrett could do was just protect himself and his men, he said. In the surrounding counties that made up his Thirtieth Subdistrict, sheriff's deputies often warned suspects of Barrett's interest in them, judges refused to cooperate, and freedmen received continual legal harassment.[31]

The tenuous nature of Barrett's position was aptly demonstrated in July, 1868, over what at first seemed a trivial incident. On the morning of the nineteenth, Barrett arrested George Kennedy, a local white, for pushing a freedwoman off the sidewalk. The black woman had bumped into his female companion, or been bumped into, as the white woman and Kennedy strolled down the walk. The next day, Barrett held a trial in the county courthouse, found Kennedy guilty of assault and battery, fined him fifty dollars, and ordered him to post a bond to keep the peace for one year. Kennedy yelled he would not pay, drew a concealed revolver, and jumped toward the door. Two soldier guards tried to stop him, and Kennedy opened fire.

The gallery was full of Kennedy's friends — Barrett estimated about fifty men — of whom about ten joined in the shooting. Barrett drew his Derringer and fired at and hit Kennedy, who fled, with his companions covering his withdrawal. The shooting continued in the courtyard, with two soldiers being hit, before Barrett could assemble his whole squad and clear the streets. One man, drunk old Thomas Meador, was arrested and held for urging the shooters on and yelling for a shotgun so that he could help "clean the damned Yankees out." Several days later, Barrett recognized some of Kennedy's pals in town, and tried to arrest them. The result was another brief shootout as the men fled town.[32]

The situation in Tyler and the rest of the subdistrict disintegrated into a guerrilla war, with the freedmen suffering the brunt of the action. Barrett asked for replacement of the Smith County sheriff and authority to prohibit the carrying of firearms. General Reynolds got him a new sheriff, but refused to disarm all persons, as he said it would unfairly discriminate against those who were law-abiding citizens. Local townspeople sent the general petition. They pledged to obey the laws fairly enforced, but called Barrett a tyrant and asked that he be superseded by a man with a different "temper and views."[33]

Reynolds, naturally, sent Sinclair to investigate the whole affray. "Barrett seemed to lead a charmed life," Sinclair related, which was just as well, because had the agent been killed, Sinclair believed Tyler's blacks would have joined in the fray, and "there would have been one of the bloodiest times that has transpired since the riot at New Orleans." As it was, Unionists lived in great fear, loyal newspapers were afraid to print the true story of the gunfight, and Barrett stayed on, forted up in the courthouse with his squad of bluecoats. Sinclair asked that a full company of infantry be sent to bolster the white and black loyalists' security. Reynolds agreed with Sinclair's assessment, but it would take time to get the troops moving.[34]

Meanwhile, Reynolds told Barrett to hold on until he was relieved by the full company of the Fifteenth Infantry sent in from Marshall to restore order. Barrett's replacement, Second Lieutenant W. T. Hartz, reported that he found most of the whites to be reasonable in their conduct toward the freedmen, and local law enforcement officials willing to act in any case "properly presented"—a great contrast to what Barrett and even Montgomery had faced. After a petition drive by over one hundred local citizens, Reynolds ordered Hartz's superior, Brevet Major Horace Jewett, to release Meador from jail in October, 1868. In his communications to headquarters, the major had confirmed that he thought that the civil authorities would act in a responsible and fair manner to all.[35]

Unlike Barrett and most subassistant commissioners, who served in one or two bureau agencies, DeWitt C. Brown had a bureau career that included seven assignments, as he was shunted from subdistrict to subdistrict, much to his disgust. A former colonel of Colored Troops, Brown became a bureau agent in January of 1867. His first assignment was in Courtney, a locale that Brown found quite congenial. He traveled much of the time in Grimes County, without an escort and with few problems from planters. Promised a permanent posting at Palestine, Brown learned that the job had gone instead to a Scalawag, John Morrison. Brown was moved to Navasota, a short distance from Courtney, but a world of difference. Here, the white population was decidedly hostile to the bureau, and Brown thought troops would be necessary to enforce his edicts. Then he was sent to Robertson County, where he helped investigate the Cessna plantation attack, and handled general matters until Randall arrived to take over.[36]

After the four months he had just spent going from place to place on bureau business, Brown received the Wharton agency, which he hoped would be a permanent job. Wharton was a locale hostile to all bureau agents, and Brown was no exception. But he no sooner had gotten acquainted with its problems than Ira H. Evans arrived, with instructions from General Griffin to Brown that he should teach Evans the intricacies of the job of a subassistant commissioner. Brown did so with a sinking heart. Sure enough, as soon as he had taught Evans the job, he received new orders to head for Tyler, an army post of some size. Brown found Tyler to be the worst posting he had had. There were at least three military men who acted as subassistant commissioner, and they did not like civilians, especially one who had been a volunteer colonel during the war. Brown was made the visiting agent for the post, and he rode all over northern Texas until he was physically exhausted. He threatened to quit unless he received an agency of his own.[37]

General Reynolds agreed to Brown's conditions for continued employment, and sent Brown to the just created position at Paris. Located in Lamar County, Paris was surrounded by outlaws and Ku Klux Klan klaverns. The streets of the town rang with gunfire, night and day. The harried subassistant commissioner set up his office and bravely began to hear cases, issue contracts, and bring persecutors of Negroes to justice. He also toured his district and set up a fledgling school system. All went comparatively well until the spring of 1868, when General Hancock withdrew his troop escort. Outlaw and Ku Klux Klan activity then arose with a vengeance, and Brown heard that he was marked for an early hanging. Local authorities, even those appointed by General Reynolds, refused to get involved in Brown's problems. Brown decided to retreat to a plantation he had bought in nearby Fannin County. He stayed here all summer until he was ambushed by Cullen Baker's gang.

Escaping the shootout, Brown found that Baker had destroyed his farm and run off all of his freedmen. Retreating to Paris, Brown forted up in the bureau office and waited for Reynolds to send the soldiers he had promised. The outlaws and Ku Klux Klan men swarmed into town, each wanting to be the first to shoot down the hated bureau agent. Brown saw them coming, slipped out the back way, and rode through the woods, escaping minutes ahead of the mob. Reynolds sent him on to Dallas for the 1868 settlement season, but Brown soon resigned his post and went back to Ohio. It had been an arduous twenty-two months. He had lost all of his property, but he still was alive and well.[38]

A similar fate awaited Brevet Captain Charles Rand, who arrived in Clarksville in late 1867. His first assignment was to compile a list of the various crimes committed against freedmen in Red River County, which he determined to include eighteen murders.[39] His normal workday ran from eight in the morning to six in the evening, and he spent this time in his courthouse office negotiating settlements for freedmen who had been cheated out of past years' wages. He also supervised the drawing up of contracts between white employers and their black laborers. In enforcing these contracts, Rand was not hesitant to seize a planter's property, if the white employer failed to pay the wages agreed upon.[40]

Yet in this and other areas, Rand was severely limited in what he could do for the freedmen, because he could not travel safely into the countryside. Indeed, if his reports and communications are accurate, he was away from Clarksville only two days during his nine-month tenure. This trip was to Mount Pleasant to pick up the records of the newly defunct Fifty-second Subdistrict in March, 1868, which added Titus County to his original responsibilities. There is no evidence that he ever did any more work in that county after this first foray, and he gives very little information on criminal or civil cases brought before him.[41]

Rand blamed his difficulties, quite rightly, on the lack of troop support. Without some military aid, Rand warned, he could not travel three miles from town and live.[42] As if to illustrate his problems, Rand suffered a public assault at the county courthouse in broad daylight,[43] had his schoolteacher run off by the Ku Klux Klan,[44] and had his life threatened by a local outlaw, Ben Griffith. When Griffith rode into town, he was lightly armed (only three revolvers instead of the five or six normally carried in the area), but he kept his double-barreled shotgun cocked and ready, resting across his saddle, and pointed down the street.

Griffith was well known about Clarksville, and a curious crowd formed to listen to his story. Griffith told how Cullen Baker, Ben Bickerstaff, and Bill English were awaiting him outside town. The gang had recently murdered two Yankees and four freedmen, and burned an army commissary train. He claimed twenty-five men in the gang, and said that they were headed out to destroy another wagon train that supplied the western forts. Cautiously, never putting down his cocked shotgun, Griffith went into a nearby store and bought a canteen of whiskey. Remounting, he said he would be on the Boston road if anyone wanted to see him. Then Griffith yelled, "Look out niggers!" and, amidst the rebel yells and laughter of bystanders, he rode off. Informed of Griffith's appearance in town, Rand organized a small posse and set off in pursuit. He and his men caught up to Griffith, who was about to kill a Negro youth. Rand shot the brigand dead on the spot.[45]

Griffith's death confirmed Rand's worst fears about his tenuous position in Clarksville. The whole region rose up against him. Clarksville was in a state of siege. Reinforcements were rumored on the way from Griffith's family in Arkansas. Rand ate and worked with a cocked six-gun on the table. He was afraid to trust anyone. He reported that even men he once considered his friends would now be among the first to kill him. For ten days he toughed it out, forted up in the courthouse by day, hiding after dark, hoping for military assistance. At night, the streets were filled with strangers who shot up the town and cheered for Jefferson Davis and Andrew Johnson. They cursed Rand and dared him to come out of hiding. He slept in a different spot each night to thwart attempts to burn him out or assassinate him.

Finally, on August 1, an escort of soldiers arrived from Marshall. Disguised in civilian clothes, they surreptitiously made contact with Rand at the courthouse. That night, the whole party slipped out of town and rode twenty-eight miles before daybreak. Reaching Marshall safely, Rand stated that had the escort come one day later, he would have had to take to the woods. Fifteen gunhawks had come in from Arkansas the next morning, he later learned. "I am worn from exhaustion and constant anxiety day and night," he wrote.[46]

Actually, Rand was lucky: he escaped death. William G. Kirkman at Bowie did not. Serving sixteen months, Kirkman possessed a real thoroughness and devotion to duty. As subassistant commissioner, Kirkman tackled Reconstruction on three fronts—the mistreatment of blacks, the problem of labor contract disputes, and the issue of black education. Although he was a diligent worker, he was opposed at every step by the local white power structure. So he also worked to remove it from office. When whites refused to obey his orders, Kirkman sent out his soldier guards to make arrests. He fined those planters who did not draw up bureau-approved contracts with their fieldhands.

The planters had an ace in the hole, however, which they played without mercy. The plantation owners had an army of their own, a force of Civil War riff-raff led by the premier gunfighter of his day, Cullen Baker. For a small fee, Baker would exert his own style of six-gun discipline against recalcitrant blacks, and drive them from the field after harvest had been gathered, so their wages were forfeit for unauthorized absences. Kirkman tried to stop Baker. He courageously pursued the outlaw, with and without army assistance. Finally, harried by lawsuits, threatened by assassination, and worn out by a year and a half of constant bickering, Kirkman received Reynolds's orders to return to Austin and save his life. On the night he was preparing to leave, however, Baker and his gang shot him down outside the bureau office. Another agent had been lost from lack of military support.[47]

But even the bureau offices staffed by the army were not safe in northeastern Texas. At Mount Pleasant, Brevet Colonel S. H. Starr tried to protect the rights of freedmen and loyalists in his subdistrict, while detaching units to guard surrounding bureau agencies manned by civilians. At the same time, he refused to waver from the principle of unity of command, so dear to army manuals. The result was a constant conflict between bureau and army wishes that helped no one but the brigands and vindictive planters. Starr, like so many subassistant commissioners, ran up against General Hancock's new policies, when he fined two planters five hundred dollars for enticing away contract fieldhands from another plantation. Upon further investigation, Starr discovered that the original white contractor had abused the freedmen and hence voided the original contract. Starr confiscated the fine money, which had been paid the aggrieved planter and, rather than returning it to the two innocent defendants, he placed it in the bureau school fund with General Reynolds's approval. The defendants' complaint to Hancock was referred to Reynolds for readjustment. But the Texas assistant commissioner merely approved of his own actions once again. Hancock left New Orleans, the Mount Pleasant agency closed down, and Starr's men went to the frontier before any further action could be taken.[48]

To replace the Mount Pleasant office, Reynolds reopened a post and bureau agency at Sulphur Springs in the fall of 1868. But if Starr and his cavalry could not cover the region, Brevet Lieutenant Colonel W. B. Pease (no relation to the governor) and his infantry could do even less. Besides the bureau was on its way out, and everyone knew it. Pease said it would be unsafe to make a tour of the backcountry, but that he had heard many rumors of outrages committed against the freedmen. Reynolds reinforced him with another infantry company and a troop of cavalry.

Using the new men, Pease spent most of his time out chasing desperadoes, to the detriment of his bureau business. He had no books, records, or orders, and fairly hated "this especially disagreeable Post," as he characterized Sulphur Springs. In nearby Clarksville, Brevet Major George Shorkley and his company of the Fifteenth Infantry (who had replaced the hapless DeWitt C. Brown) could not do as much as Pease. He concentrated on holding the town. The "best, or rather, the most influential men in the county," he said, made no effort for law and order. There were no courts. The freedmen had been left to "all evil disposed persons" to butcher, so he asked for martial law and wanted to hold all leading citizens responsible in person and property for the violence of the outlaws.[49]

Unlike the outlying towns, the major urban areas in northeastern Texas, Marshall and Jefferson, had plenty of troop support. But it made little difference, for it was all immobile infantry. By the time Captain T. M. K. Smith came up from Nacogdoches to take over Marshall, freedmen were no longer coming in to report the numerous outrages that were still occurring, but rumors of them filled the city, said Smith. In May, 1868, Smith reported things were improving—yet no black in Marshall could get a job without a certificate of political cleanliness from the Democratic Club. Smith suggested that Reynolds order any Negroes who had been denied jobs be made wards of the county. Violence continued unabated in the rest of the subdistrict, especially in Upshur County. The following month, black families were being driven off the land in the backcountry by night riders. People killed black men just for the sake of killing, Smith said.[50]

When the Fifteenth Infantry arrived to bolster the occupying forces, First Lieutenant Henry Sweeney could not believe what he saw. He claimed that conditions in Texas were far worse than his last posts in Arkansas or Alabama, and that whites routinely practiced all sorts of petty revenge schemes against any freedman at random. Those who were cursed at were the lucky ones, the lieutenant said. Whippings, murder of whole families, and the driving of freedmen off the land to void their contracts were all common. Smart blacks slept in the woods where the Ku Klux could not find them. Sweeney called for martial law.[51]

When Sweeney's commanding officer sent him to establish a new bureau office at Jefferson, First Lieutenant Edward C. Henshaw took over in Marshall. He found eighty-two unsettled civil and criminal cases on the books. The Ku Klux controlled the countryside. Of all those appointed to office by General Reynolds on the advice of loyalists, only one civil official, Judge George R. Hill, acted to protect the civil rights of blacks and Unionists. Henshaw called for a law to exempt the attachment of up to three hundred dollars in property of any man for a judgment. The whites' houses were exempt under Texas law, but the freedmen's cotton was not. Negroes did not own houses, said Henshaw. The lieutenant turned all of his unsettled business over to "Squire" Hill, as the bureau closed down for good in December, 1868.[52]

Meanwhile Sweeney was at Jefferson, where he arrived in the wake of one of the more embarrassing episodes to befall the bureau and army during the era, the murder of state convention member George W. Smith (unrelated in any way to the Brenham Smith). The town had been garrisoned by twenty-five men of the Fifteenth Infantry led by Brevet Major James Curtis at the end of August, 1868. Curtis noted that "unblushing fraud and outrage" were perpetrated upon the freedmen of the area, and that "[n]o more notice is taken here of the death of a Radical negro than of a mad dog." He called for cavalry armed with double-barreled shotguns to "scour the country." The primary contenders for loyalty of the blacks and whites respectively were George W. Smith, a former Union Army captain and storekeeper, and the Knights of the Rising Sun, the local Ku Klux organization. When the Knights tried unsuccessfully to ambush Smith, he shot back, hitting two of the attackers. The Knights brought trumped-up charges in court against him and a black compatriot, Anderson Wright, for assault. They were arrested and taken to the city jail.

The next night, October 4, an armed, disguised mob surrounded the jail and captured the sixteen soldiers Curtis had placed there to guard against such an assault. Before Curtis could arrive with the balance of his command, the mob had killed two black prisoners. Wright and another Negro prisoner had managed to escape in the confusion. Curtis and his relief column were intercepted and disarmed. Then as some of the mob held back the enraged Curtis, the rest broke into the jail (the city marshal helped to lead the mob and had the keys) and shot Smith dead. As Smith's body lay twitching on the floor, the members of the mob came into the cell, one by one, and pumped him full of lead.

After the murders, Curtis was recalled, and Sweeney and Company H of the Fifteenth infantry were sent to reinforce the soldiers already there. Eventually the whole regiment would garrison the town, thirty-seven citizens would be arrested, and others would flee as far as Canada to escape the nationwide dragnet. Reynolds issued an order that anyone caught hereafter anywhere in Texas wearing a mask or disguise was to be arrested and tried by a military commission exclusively. Nonetheless, Sweeney reported that both Baker and Bickerstaff allegedly had been seen "prowling about" town, and little changed for the better.[53]

Finally, on October 12, Reynolds issued an order to all military and civil officers to arrest persons wearing any disguise or mask, and hold them for the army and military trial. He also noted that so many freed persons had been killed in eastern Texas that the army could no longer keep track of the numbers. Reynolds then sent an elite squadron from the Sixth Cavalry to Sulphur Springs. Led by Brevet Major Adna R. Chaffee and Captain Thomas W. Tolman, the troopers swept through the Sulphur River region with heretofore unknown viciousness. Few prisoners were taken. Reports listed suspects "lost in the swamp" or "shot while trying to escape." Local farmers who misled troopers or refused to inform on outlaws were strung up by their thumbs. One column logged over one thousand miles while pursuing brigands. Its tactics in combating outlaws and their sympathizers were so brutal that the column earned the nickname, "Chaffee's Guerillas." Tolman's activities in Sulphur Springs led to his eventual punishment for undue cruelty toward civilians.[54]

The Sixth Cavalry's methodical scourging of northeastern Texas cleaned the area of outlaw gangs within six months. But they never found Cullen Baker. He was murdered by his own henchmen, who feared for their lives at the hands of their psychotic leader. Appropriately, Baker was shot from ambush, while he was in a drunken stupor, by Thomas Orr and three compatriots. As befitted a man of action, Baker died carrying four six-shooters, two double-barreled shotguns, three Derringers, and a half-dozen assorted knives, a graphic illustration of the kind of opposition bureau agents had to face in Texas.[55]

Unfortunately the onslaught of Chaffee and Tolman came too late to help the bureau in Texas; it had already disbanded according to plan at the end of December, 1868. But the campaign indicates what the army might have done earlier, with a commitment to protecting the bureau personnel and expediting their programs, had it recognized the difference between the exigencies of war and occupation, revamped the command structure, stationed infantry in the towns, and used roving cavalry units to provide mobility and offensive power in the hinterlands. Although General Reynolds sent out the Chaffee squadron of the Sixth Cavalry and the detached companies of the Fifteenth Infantry in this fashion, it remained for his successor, Brevet Major General E. R. S. Canby, to put this concept into permanent effect through his General Orders No. 4, in January, 1869.[56]

Conclusion
"Almost" Never Made a Stew

Self reliance should be taught the Freedmen
& the Bureau discontinued.

—Captain Edward Collins to First Lieutenant J. P. Richardson,
February 1, 1868

ON DECEMBER 31, 1868, according to the act of Congress passed the previous July, the operations of the Texas Freedmen's Bureau came to an end. Actual field offices suspended their functions on December 15, and the subassistant commissioners packed up their books and records and arranged for their shipment to headquarters. Judging from the numerous letters in the coming months questioning the agents as to the whereabouts of their documents, many records were either lost in transit or nonexistent. Reynolds called in early the eighteen civilian subassistant commissioners, who served in places other than their hometowns. Military officers who served as agents concluded their bureau transactions on January 1, 1869. Only the educational functions of the bureau were to continue until their termination in 1870.[1]

At the same time that the bureau concluded its operations in Texas, General Reynolds was replaced as military commander by Brevet Major General Edward R. S. Canby. The latter was President Johnson's troubleshooter for Reconstruction problems in states that seemed doomed never to complete the congressional requirements for readmission into the Union—a category that Texas fell into because of the raucous first session of its constitutional convention. Because Reynolds was more familiar with the bureau operations in Texas, General Canby allowed him to conclude the field operations, pay off the agents, sell bureau-administered lands, and balance the books.[2]

On January 1, 1869, Canby assumed control of the bureau's remaining educational functions. He appointed Reverend Joseph Welch as superintendent of schools, with a staff that included former bureau inspector William H. Sinclair as assistant superintendent for the Second District at Galveston, and previous subassistant commissioners Louis W. Stevenson and Charles Haughn as assistant superintendents for the Third District at Jefferson and the Fourth District at Nacogdoches, respectively. Welch would handle the First District at Austin along with his overall supervisory functions. His clerk and chief aide would be Sinclair's brother-in-law, E. C. Bartholomew.[3]

In analyzing the role of the bureau in Texas Reconstruction, it would be hard to deny its notable contributions in guardianship of the former slaves during their first years of freedom. The bureau was instrumental in securing freedom itself; the notion of black legal rights to contract, sue, and be sued; security of marriage and family; education, and the vote. It is true that the bureau did not introduce these concepts alone — the Federal and state governments had a hand in it, too, as did the blacks themselves through their own demands as citizens — but the bureau saw to it that these rights of freedom were instituted on the local levels in day-to-day life. That these ideas were not fully guaranteed and would have to be reasserted in the twentieth century does not detract from the bureau's importance in their introduction for blacks in Texas and the South.

Yet at the same time, the failure of Negroes to enjoy rights guaranteed by the state and Federal constitutions and enunciated in the Declaration of Independence was not exclusively the fault of Southern white racism. Here the bureau must take part of the blame. Although its national and local administration was hindered by the quarrels between Congress and the president, the individuals who ran the Texas branch of the Freedman's Bureau, the assistant commissioners, and their erstwhile employees, the subassistant commissioners, contributed to the less than perfect outcome of its efforts. In their administration of the state agencies, two questions might be asked: How competently did these men act as bureaucrats? How effectively did they conduct themselves as publicists for the new social order?[4]

The first Texas assistant commissioner, Brevet Brigadier General Edgar M. Gregory, fell short on both counts. It was not that Gregory lacked decency. Of all of the Texas assistant commissioners, he was undoubtedly the most upright in his own conduct and the strongest in his feelings of sympathy for the freed people. With his Christian, abolitionist background, Gregory was the only Texas bureau head who viewed the blacks as adults of political, if not social, equality. Moreover, Gregory had the courage to stick to his beliefs, regardless of any opposition. He saw the blacks as deeply religious, hard workers, and noble, patient sufferers who had ably survived a crushing system of bondage. Unlike most nineteenth-century individuals Gregory believed that property rights should be mitigated by personal rights, and he understandingly allowed his black charges many mistakes and personal foibles as they learned the responsibilities of freedom.

But Gregory could not talk to the white Texans, whom he considered inferior to the former bondsmen. He and the Texas white leadership had no common ground on which they could meet. Both sides adopted rigid ideological positions and talked past each other, neither one hearing anything the other said. Indeed, whites saw Gregory as so much a representative of the hated victorious Union that they failed to see his shortcomings in running the bureau. After nine months in office, Gregory's administration was falling apart, and the general seemingly could do little to change this. Part of the blame lay with the absurdities of the original bureau law, which made no provision for hiring large numbers of civilian employees. Part lay with the rapid demobilization of the volunteer army. There was no way Gregory could reconstruct Texas without force, and this he did not have.

But the truth seemed to be that Gregory could not run an operation so large as the Texas bureau. He never divided the state into subdistricts with defined zones of control for his subassistant commissioners. He failed to attract the type of staff officer who could assist him in his bureaucratic functions. The general had a horrible penchant for employing allegedly loyal Texas civilians who talked a good line, but who accomplished little for the freed persons whose livelihood they were supposed to safeguard. He also liked Northern men, who like himself theorized the proper results for Reconstruction, but could not bring it off. They were easy marks for David G. Burnet's slick smear campaign, which cost Gregory his job and revealed the vulnerability of bureau employees to political highjinks inspired by nationwide racism. Moreover, had Burnet not attacked Gregory it is likely that Gregory's inept administration would have reached a crisis shortly, anyhow. Burnet merely kicked in an already rotten door. Indeed a cogent argument could be made that Burnet could have done the bureau more harm if he had left Gregory undisturbed in his bumbling ways.[5]

On the other hand, Gregory's successor, Brevet Major General Joseph B. Kiddoo, was an affable man, who revealed in his demeanor many of the character faults Gregory assiduously avoided. He was warmly gregarious, like to drink (perhaps too much, because of the discomfort of his still-open war wound), and was less interested in individual rights than property rights, like most nineteenth-century white Texans. He saw the Negroes, by and large, as deprived children, who had to be led by the hand into adulthood by their betters. Dismayed by what he saw as the collapse of the contract system under Gregory, the planters greedily outbidding each other for laborers and the laborers jumping from one contractor to another at whim, he issued an order to prevent these practices. He also sought to import unemployed black labor from eastern states to satisfy the insatiable demands for harvesters of abundant Texan crops.

To guarantee that the laborers would be paid rather than exploited, Kiddoo instituted a policy whereby labor became the first lien on production, and he ordered his agents into the fields to explain the program to the planters and their employees. The general also established a vigorous court system that threatened to cost him his popularity with the planter class, until they realized that rigorous bureau supervision could work to keep laborers in the fields as well as to monitor kind treatment and fair payments. Numerous admonitions by headquarters personnel to the field agents to protect black rights as well as planters' production schedules, and to desist from corporal punishment demonstrated that many subassistant commissioners were implementing the new labor policies, often with too much enthusiasm.

Clearly Kiddoo had great possibilities if he could be "guided" by the proper people, and the newly elected state governor, James W. Throckmorton, was such a person to Texas whites. He and the Eleventh Legislature gave a resounding vote of approval to Kiddoo's labor policies by enshrining them in the Black Codes. True, they could not resist adding a little more vigor to the state laws than the bureau edicts had provided for, but the resemblance was too close to be coincidental. The horror the new laws aroused in Union ranks was probably more the product of who wrote them than what they said, although some farsighted loyalists realized that a black population controlled by peonage could not deliver a reliable bloc vote in the future.

Throckmorton also pressured Kiddoo to assume a more moderate approach by attacking the assistant commissioner's critical crime report after it had been leaked to the press by Radical Republicans in Washington. The governor attacked field agents who zealously protected Negroes and loyalists in their rights of free speech and assembly. Kiddoo had already indicated his desire for a tighter, more moderate administration when he fired William Longworth of Seguin. When the Brenham subassistant commissioner, Captain Samuel Craig, got caught up in a feud with a local newspaper that helped cause the fire of 1866, Throckmorton used the incident to force Kiddoo to replace the now controversial agent. Kiddoo's angry defense of himself and Craig was too little, too late.

Transferring Craig to Seguin, Kiddoo had to fire the vigorous agent, after he burned court records relating to Longworth's previous administration. Kiddoo also succumbed to Throckmorton's pressure to get rid of Brevet Lieutenant Colonel Jacob C. De Gress at Houston, after he interfered with the state courts by freeing a black prisoner, Dick Perkins, before a trial. The real issue, of course, was not Perkins, but De Gress's prosecution of the complaints of unpaid black fieldhands through crop seizures. Kiddoo's position was further weakened by his need to leave the state to take an officer's examination and have his still painful wound operated on, and by an abortive attempt by army officers to displace the independent bureau staff with their own men.

On top of all this, the army command disintegrated through ineffective leadership, which left Kiddoo without a responsive form of military support to counter Throckmorton's attacks. Major General Philip Sheridan, the overall army district commander, sought to rectify this problem and bolster Kiddoo's bureau policies by placing the army in Texas under Brevet Major General Charles Griffin, a man who understood congressional aims in Reconstruction and had the drive to put them into operation. Griffin edged Kiddoo out of the bureau position, and for the first time both bureau and army commands were issued from one office. Kiddoo's day-to-day administration of the bureau was more able than Gregory's, and he expanded its operations within the limits of the military demobilization. But like Gregory he failed to organize the state into defined jurisdictions with precise zones of responsibility for each subassistant commissioner. His ability to operate in the Texas environment was better than his predecessor, because his hope for black aspirations as free people was more in line with the prevailing prejudices of the country. But he also demonstrated how thoroughly a moderate man could be chewed up when caught in the middle of state, national, and military politics in a volatile situation.[6]

As the next assistant commissioner of the Texas bureau, Griffin had some real advantages over his predecessors. At first, Griffin seemed to be as much under Throckmorton's spell as Kiddoo had been. But the new bureau head was merely biding his time until the advent of the Military Reconstruction acts. Once he received this sanction from Congress, Griffin tackled Reconstruction on two levels, administrative and political. As combined army commander and bureau head, Griffin had immediate access to and control over two commands that were previously separate and uncoordinated. He used this valuable power to make all post commanders the bureau agents in their areas of control, which helped expand the bureau into all parts of Texas for the first time. The general made each subassistant commissioner responsible for an exact zone of operations. He detailed the small troop detachments so critical to a subassistant commissioner's success in outlying areas. In short, he stopped the bickering and competition between the two chains of command. He also perfected the uniform system of inspections and monthly reports that Kiddoo had inaugurated to keep track of the activities of local agents.

Griffin also expanded the bureau system throughout the state. Although he found it necessary to charge a tuition fee to finance education, the general divorced the school fees from the fines and contract system. Unlike Gregory and Kiddoo, Griffin did not work well with the benevolent associations because he did not tolerate their incessant doctrinal quarrels, which he deemed petty and divisive. He also did not relate well to Texas politicians, whom he considered to be traitors and lawbreakers. But he impressed loyal whites with his willingness to lead the state into a new political environment, dominated by the growing Republican party. Although Griffin did not think much better of the blacks than Kiddoo had, he did act in a more balanced manner toward them, and he was the only bureau head who thought to issue and enforce a public accommodations order. He also set up an authorized bonded commission merchant to provide a standard that blacks could use to help set fair prices for their share of the state's staple crops.

Griffin was the first assistant commissioner to make use of all possible sources for his subassistant commissioner appointments. He reinstituted the placement of Texas loyalists in select agencies, and he tended to appoint well-known prewar politicians of considerable merit. He expanded the numbers of Northern civilians in the bureau ranks, tending to prefer former Union soldiers. Although most volunteer regiments had been sent home, Griffin kept as many Veteran Reserve officers as he could in bureau posts and liberally reinforced them with regular army officers. The whole system was buttressed with troop detachments. He was able to do this even as he garrisoned the frontier in force for the first time, a remarkable fact in light of his own and his successor's complaint that they could not do both.

On the political front, Griffin registered black males as voters and sought to guarantee equal justice by instituting the ironclad oath for all jurors. He moved to neutralize Throckmorton and his adherents in the governing process by a vigorous policy of removals of allegedly disloyal elected officials and appointments of loyal men to office. This culminated in the removal of the governor himself and the appointment of Elisha M. Pease in his stead. But just as Griffin's program seemed to be invincible, yellow fever swept the state. The army and bureau commands were devastated, and many officers, including Griffin, lost their lives. The educational system ground to a halt. And the whole process had to begin again under a new regime.[7]

After Griffin's death the bureau never recovered its former vigor. The officer who superseded him in office, Brevet Major General Joseph J. Reynolds, was perhaps the best assistant commissioner in dealing with the public; indeed, one observer described him as the most "affable or oily man" he had ever seen in public life. But as far as administering the bureau on a daily basis, Reynolds seemed inclined to see it as a nuisance that interfered with his political Reconstruction responsibilities of producing a loyal state government. Reynolds quickly repealed many of Griffin's intended safeguards to guarantee black rights as freed persons. He ended the cozy arrangement with Griffin's bonded commission merchant to give blacks a fair price for their crop purchases, and he canceled the jury order allowing a simple oath of future loyalty to determine the qualifications for jurors. Both of these actions were endorsed by the bureau and army high commands in Washington, which showed a very complaisant, nonconfrontational attitude that did not bode well for the success of future Reconstruction demands for Negro rights.

It is true that Reynolds faced a very difficult situation in the arrival of Major General Winfield Scott Hancock to command the departments of Louisiana and Texas at New Orleans after Sheridan. An outspoken advocate of President Johnson's concepts on readmission of the South to the Union, Hancock attacked the bureau as an uncontrolled, independent Radical Republican institution that needed to be curbed, regardless of the effect on the position of the blacks as freed people. Reynolds realized this, and moved rapidly to clean out the remaining Throckmorton men holding office on the local and state levels, before Hancock could arrive and assume control. Somehow, the bureau got lost in the political machinations to entrench the Republican party. Reynolds's belief that the Negro was doomed to an uncertain position in American society ("their ignorance, their idleness, and their follies," he maintained, were a constant theme of all "better" persons) did not help; neither did the impending demise in July, 1868, of the congressional act under which the bureau functioned.[8]

The extension of the bureau field operations to the end of 1868 was a mere formality. Reynolds behaved toward the bureau much as the Texas planters did—he would wait out the bureau's short remaining life until it no longer mattered. The arrival of General Hancock at New Orleans assured the bureau's impotence. Hancock's first action was to issue General Orders No. 40, which ordered the army and bureau to support the Texas civil authorities in the maintenance of law and order. The general curtailed the use of independent military or bureau actions without giving the civil authorities the chance to proceed first, even if Federal officials had any doubt that local officials would act to protect blacks or Unionists. He re-registered whites excluded by Griffin, and he temporarily ended Reynolds's appointment of Republicans to Texas political positions.

Tired of complaints from bureau field agents and General Reynolds (not to mention civilians like Governor Pease), all of whom he considered as insubordinate, Hancock withdrew the separate troop detachments Griffin had supplied as bureau guards. He also shifted troops toward the frontier to guard against Comanche and Kiowa raids. He told the bureau agents first to contact local civil authorities in all incidents and, if they refused to grant equal protection to blacks or loyalists, only then to make an application to Austin for assistance on a specific case.

But the bureau's decline in vigor was not all Hancock's fault, as Reynolds and Texas Republicans averred, although his conservative political stance reinforced local army commanders' reluctance to cooperate with the bureau. Hancock left office in mid-March, 1868. His successor at New Orleans, Brevet Major General Robert C. Buchanan, left Reynolds and Pease a free hand in governing Texas, and by the end of July of that year, Texas was made an independent command area under Reynolds's exclusive control. Yet Reynolds voluntarily entrenched Hancock's system in an order that made the bureau agents part of the state judicial system under a limited basis, and he did next to nothing to protect his agents in the field (or his black charges) from white violence.

Even at the height of Hancock's control, Reynolds always had available the one troop of cavalry from which to detach men to critical bureau agencies in need of military aid. As Griffin had realized earlier, most agencies needed only a half dozen men to ensure their successful operation. All Reynolds had to do to get a force in the field was report actual, specific incidents to conform to Hancock's announced procedures, and call his superior's bluff. This Reynolds never did, although individual agents filled their reports with likely examples. Reynolds continually preferred to speak only in the general terms that Hancock had already denounced. The impression is that Reynolds really did not care about the bureau functions. He was more interested in the constitutional convention, voter registration, political removals and appointments, and state Republican factional politics. He saw the blacks' salvation coming through education and the vote, and he ignored their devastating economic plight, which would work to negate the other factors, as a product of their own ignorance.[9]

The story of the bureau activities in Texas, then, reveals a problem common to the whole Reconstruction effort, a lack of commitment to a potentially imaginative program. Somehow, Congress through its inadequate funding, headquarters through its optimistic edicts from Washington, and the assistant commissioners in Texas, with the possible exception of Griffin, through their haphazard operations in the field and short tenures of office (only Reynolds served longer than nine months), never understood the commitment necessary to transform a system of racial servitude that had been sanctified by centuries of practice. Since about half of the bureau subdistricts were not established until Griffin's accession to power in 1867, bureau influence, particularly in northeastern Texas, was of short duration.

But the Texas problem was national in scope. The North erred in thinking that Appomattox was a peace treaty, rather than a temporary cease-fire. There was a bit of smugness that attached to the Northern victory in the field. Agent Mortimer H. Goddin in Livingston epitomized this feeling for bureau agents in Texas, when he sneeringly referred to the Confederacy as "Jeff Davis' Wheel Barrow concern." Goddin and men like him were surprised and dismayed when defeated Southern whites refused voluntarily to adopt the stance that Unionists determined to be reasonable and necessary for the ultimate peace.[10]

The pervasiveness of Goddin's attitude among bureau agents becomes obvious when it is compared to that of William Longworth over in Seguin. Longworth demanded a commitment to Reconstruction that paralleled the war effort in time, men, and resources. He is a unique case, and his request for troops, equipment, doctors, medicines, and legal talent stands out to this day as an outrageous aberration. But as Longworth's poor reception at bureau headquarters shows, the real

"Wheel Barrow concern" was the Northern attempt to Reconstruct the South, not the Southern bid to divide the Union.[11]

As for the subassistant commissioners, they reflected the attitudes of their superiors. Agents settled some wage disputes from 1866 and many from 1867 (often at a fraction of what was promised), and instituted the first fair contracts in 1868; but the field agents that spring lost the military force needed to compel planters to honor them, and the agencies were closed down before they could even pretend to supervise their collection that fall. Planters simply waited out the bureau's demise in 1868 before settling with their contract hands. As for 1865, after the June 19 emancipation, even the enthusiastic William Longworth merely tried to collect a fraction of what was owed black laborers, and he generally failed. Others did less. Ultimately, bureau actions on behalf of the freedmen amounted to little more than a brief nuisance to local labor contractors, and an unachieved promise to black workers.[12]

It is not that subassistant commissioners ignored their Bureau duties (they did not), but rather that they were restricted to their agencies, unable to move about the countryside freely, powerless to enforce their edicts, and inundated by a sea of red tape. It is very difficult to describe a "typical" bureau agent. Regardless of whether they were detailed from the ranks of the professional or volunteer soldier, or employed from Northern or Southern civilian sources, they ranged from good to indifferent to bad.

But the lack of support and unrealistic approaches from Washington that the higher command felt in its position at Galveston or Austin became a stifling influence when it reached the individual agencies. Only during the Griffin months, and then only after the passage of the Military Reconstruction acts (five months of the bureau's forty months in Texas), did the field agents receive unquestioning support from headquarters. But it is fair to say that through very difficult circumstances most agents risked their lives to carry out their responsibilities as honestly and as effectively as they could. The indifferent and the corrupt were spectacular oddities, not the norm. That the former have been emphasized in historical accounts merely demonstrates the innate human appeal of the sensational over the ordinary in daily life.[13]

Perhaps the fault lay with using military men and organizations to effect social change. The army was too rigid, relied on a deference to the chain of command, and was an instrument of the status quo, not a creator of racial reform. It mirrored too closely the society it served. The subassistant commissioners were constantly moved, left out of communication, not given local autonomy, and denied military force.[14] Through it all, Texas bureau headquarters seemed more interested in having all of the correct forms on file than in establishing and supporting a viable field operation. For instance, the acting assistant adjutant general continually wrote to field officers reminding them that such and such a report was late, and demanding that the agents do their paperwork on time according to the eight or nine orders governing the procedure. Usually the really active subassistant commissioners were too busy carrying out their responsibilities in the field to meet these paperwork demands. On the other hand, their necessary requests for troop support routinely went unfilled, even though the soldiers were available.[15]

Some idea of the paperwork done in an individual agency office can be gained by examining the records of William G. Kirkman at Boston. Kirkman kept a more meticulous account of his field work than the average agent, and his papers are among the most complete of any subassistant commissioner in Texas. He misfiled only two monthly reports during the fifteen months he was at Boston, although they probably were lost in the mail, which was chancy in that remote northeastern part of the state.

Appointed during the halcyon days of the Griffin administration, Kirkman received authorization to purchase office furniture (a desk and six chairs), and a temporary troop garrison of eight men. He soon moved his office from the courthouse to a separate building on the town square to maintain an image of independence of the local civil authorities. He lacked revenue stamps to make his documents legal (none were available anywhere in north Texas), asked for missing orders and circulars to keep his knowledge of bureau policy up to date (and was rebuked for acting on his own when he failed to receive them), begged for two different Texas law treatises to familiarize himself with local procedure that differed his native Illinois (only to be refused these legal aids as too expensive, then to receive a set after all), received only a partial copy of the 1866 Civil Rights Law (which lacked the section he needed, so he asked for another complete copy), and was denied the right to hire a clerk to assist him in the dozens of contracts and summonses he laboriously wrote each month.

Besides the office routine, Kirkman went into the field regularly to supervise a half dozen freedmen's schools, chase outlaws, and force appearances before his own judicial proceedings. In addition, he had to travel to a neighboring county to answer to criminal charges brought

against him in state district court by local planters for being too enthusiastic about his responsibilities. Each action had to be communicated
to headquarters for approval. Many were turned down, which entailed
starting a particular proceeding all over again. All of it took time. Opponents often fired upon him from ambush and threatened him in the
open streets. No wonder Kirkman collapsed from fatigue during the
summer of 1868 and just went fishing for a couple of weeks.[16]

Kirkman was not alone in his frustration and fatigue. No one expressed these symptoms to headquarters better than A. H. Mayer, the
agent at Liberty in 1866 and 1867. Mayer was angered that he could
not submit travel expenses from touring his district to assist freedmen
and planters after the trips, even when the tours were in response to
direct orders. He found it ridiculous to let a problem fester while he
awaited approval from headquarters for the trip and its purpose. He
was harassed by headquarter clerks, who returned packets of letters
for minor corrections. His requests were not answered and, Mayer suspected, not even read. Approvals arrived so late as to be no longer relevant to the changing field situation. He was denied a clerk when the
only suitably educated man could not take the ironclad oath.

Denied many of his travel requests, Mayer was furious when his
vouchers for postage, rent, fuel, and lighting oil were disallowed or paid
only in part. He drew up 123 contracts in 1867—each one had to be
written out, a process that occupied him late into the night. When
headquarters refused to pay his vouchers, he demanded an audit by
inspector Sinclair. Mayer finally collapsed from the frustrations of doing unnecessary paperwork, wrangling with headquarters, and feeling
unable to assist the freedmen properly. His recovery was followed by
a relapse that led to his resignation.[17]

Mayer and Kirkman did not have unique problems with headquarters; such problems were commonplace. Office rents had to be sent
to headquarters for approval by a board that met regularly for that
purpose. Meanwhile the subassistant commissioner had to rent the place
out of his own pocket and pray that his choice was not too expensive
for the board's taste. A refusal meant the process had to begin again
and, of course, the agent was out the money already paid, for it was
now an unauthorized expense.[18] Revenue stamps, blank books to record
transactions in, and blanks to make reports on were always in short
supply. Smart field operatives kept a copy of all forms and copied them
longhand when new forms were not forthcoming.[19] Headquarters was
not above denying permission to hire a clerk and telling the agent to

send the reports late instead. Then headquarters would send an angry missive asking where the late report was. The same technique was used with answers to specific letters, where facts had to be investigated before the subassistant commissioner could reply.[20]

Everything had to be exactly right for the officials at headquarters. Papers not folded correctly were sent back to the offending subassistant commissioner for his attention. Field agents who wrote the wrong headquarters clerk, did not address him by his full and proper title, and failed to sign themselves with their own correct title of subassistant commissioner ("the Bureau knows none of its Agents as Minister, Doctor, farmer, or Attorney at Law"), received their communications back to be recopied, along with a formal reprimand.[21] Oaths of allegiance were returned for unspecified corrections. Army officers could not draw a fuel or quarters allowance from the bureau. They had to go through their army command, which was reluctant to pay any expenses for detached personnel. Traveling agents, who by their job description were to journey about, could not go where they were needed without prior permission. Anyone expecting to be paid had to submit the correct forms in duplicate, sign the blank receipt, enclose a full accounting, and affix the proper canceled revenue stamp.[22]

Some of this was understandable for accounting purposes, but headquarters itself was constantly losing papers, books, records, and documents, and sending orders to the wrong agents. No wonder field representatives asked headquarters to rule on every nonsensical issue and make corrections when staff used the wrong titles to address junior employees. Initiative in the field was rarely rewarded with anything other than rebukes.[23]

Unlike many others, however, Agent John Archer at Beaumont understood how the system really worked. He never wrote more than the minimum of required letters in answer to specific questions. He sent in his reports religiously by the fifth of the month. He never received the reprimands so common to the others. The strange thing is that Archer's reports did not say anything—he merely wrote "same" in each of the blanks on the forms provided, month after month. Headquarters did not query him as to what exactly "same" meant, and Archer never volunteered to tell them. But he met the requirement, his files were up to date, and he did not rock the bureaucratic boat. He was smarter than Major J. W. Eccles, who had the audacity to write "I don't know" in his form blanks, which brought an instant rebuke from the headquarters clerk. It was all a matter of proper attitude. Of course, the freedmen, the objects of the bureau's existence, got lost somewhere along the trail in this unfortunate bureaucratic jungle.[24]

The bureau also wasted its personnel's abilities to serve in a fuller capacity. Strangely, the staff often assigned agents in a random fashion, failing to realize the size of Texas (understandable for those from smaller Northern states), even to the extent of not consulting a map. Sloppy coordination by the staff meant that men in outlying subdistricts got lost in personnel records, and were alienated by their seeming uselessness in the overall picture. Admittedly, transportation and communication difficulties kept most communities far apart in the nineteenth century, but the field agents suffered more, and isolation affected the carrying out of their duties.[25]

Because the subassistant commissioners' attitudes nicely paralleled those of their superiors, blacks, who had flocked to the agencies early on, soon saw no need to take the risk of a beating or death by reporting alleged wrongs to a nonsupportive bureau. The lack of commitment by the Federal power structure was deadly because of the ingrained hostility Negroes faced as free persons in Texas from all whites, even loyal Republicans. When it came to Reconstruction, very few whites could openly espouse the new Yankee-imposed free labor system without great personal reservations based upon racial animosity, or upon fear of violent retaliation from their neighbors. It seems safe to conclude, from the support received by those who persecuted the freed blacks and their Northern and Southern allies, that the white population as a whole acted on the former reason more than the latter.[26]

Some of the fault can be traced to Hancock, for limiting the ability of the army and bureau to operate outside the state legal code as military governors. But all along, the real problem was that the army had two and a half squadrons (five troops or almost one fourth of all cavalry in the Fifth Military District) on display in headquarters duty in New Orleans and Austin. The army commanders in the field were still mentally fighting the glorious Civil War with its concentrated, massive armies commanded by generals led by flashy cavalry escorts. The aftermath for those who stayed on after the war had been disillusioning. Reconstruction was, like the Indian campaigns, a time for isolated, small-unit action.[27] Nor was the situation assisted by the beginning of Congress's reduction of the army's manpower in the summer of 1868, in the midst of the crisis of lawlessness in northeastern Texas.[28]

So Reynolds stayed in Austin, surrounded by his paper-shuffling staff and a generous four-company escort (half infantry, half cavalry), as befitted an important district commander. He turned his attention to more immediate political problems, such as the break in the Republican party that threatened to destroy the activities of the State Constitutional Convention. In cahoots with Governor Pease, Reynolds used the enormous political patronage he possessed to appoint numerous state officials whose main claim to office was their stance on often esoteric political philosophies arising from the war, not their effectiveness in local government. Texas was a big state with nearly 130 organized counties. And individual bureau subassistant commissioners were a long way off when the whole process of writing a loyal constitution for the State of Texas seemed in jeopardy at Austin.[29]

Obviously the local civil authorities, even those appointed by the army upon the recommendation of staunch Unionists, saw no need to jeopardize their lives for the likes of ineffectual army and Yankee bureau men, or the hated free blacks. They had warned all along that the Yankees should show the flag and get tough. They, like the former rebels, already sensed a lack of long-range commitment in the Federal program.[30]

Troubles with local officials were compounded by two factors that were unknown or misunderstood in the North: a personal code of behavior based on violence, and a well-armed force of gunmen dedicated to massive violence against both whites and blacks who favored the Federal Reconstruction program. Texans believed in a personal code of individual response to all wrongs, real or imagined, which had its origins in the days of the prewar slavocracy. A real man never retreated from any confrontation, he stood and fought it out by any means available—the more violent, the better. This "code of the west," as some historians have labeled it, added to the availability of a wide variety of weapons, an overindulgence in liquor (every settlement had a grog shop), and the racial hatred compounded by the loss of the war and the social changes that followed, created a powerful force that reached its epitome in Reconstruction Texas before it spread into the Far West as part of an all-consuming national drive for money and power in what Mark Twain characterized as the "Gilded Age."[31]

Individual violence was bad enough, but it soon took on an organized flavor typified by the bandit gangs that roamed postwar Texas. First Lieutenant Cyrus S. Roberts, who served as subassistant commissioner out of Clarksville in 1867, was well acquainted with the outlaws' prowess. "God knows," he had informed his superiors, "that there is no other region in these United States so cursed with crime, so filled with lawless men, who have done their lawless acts so unblushingly as in this North Eastern Texas." Roberts believed that local officials, no matter what their political affiliation, could not handle the situation. Fear of the outlaw gangs, who Roberts said numbered over one hundred members and roamed from Kansas to the Rio Grande, undercut the normal operation of the testimony and evidence rules of ordinary courts. It was up to the army to declare martial law and institute the use of trials by military commission, Roberts insisted, not to rely on isolated bureau agents and gutless civil courts.[32]

To achieve proper military control of the northeastern corner of Texas, Roberts had suggested to headquarters that the Thirty-seventh, Fifty-second, and Fifty-eighth Bureau Subdistricts (comprising the counties of Fannin, Lamar, Red River, Hunt, Hopkins, Titus, Bowie, and Davis) be consolidated under the control of Brevet Brigadier General James Oakes, the commanding officer of the Sixth Cavalry, then at Mount Pleasant. All neighboring subassistant commissioners ought to report to Oakes for coordination of operations, continued Roberts. He recommended that two companies of infantry join the two troops of cavalry stationed at Mount Pleasant, with the parceling out of infantry to key towns in the area.

Roberts suggested that Mount Pleasant be made merely a small outpost and that the major troop concentration be at Paris, which Roberts considered a more centrally located, larger, and more important community. But even Clarksville should have not less than twenty to eighty men, Roberts concluded grimly. Similar plans were proposed by agents William G. Kirkman of the Boston agency, Brevet Major George W. Shorkley, one of Roberts's successors at Clarksville, and P. B. Johnson of the Livingston office. None of these proposals ever received any real consideration. Once again, the staff had failed the agents in the field.[33]

Although the brigands were not above attacking anyone who got in their way, they saw to it that freedmen and loyal whites bore the brunt of the assault. Cullen Baker, for example, cleverly used the propaganda of the "New Rebellion," fighting to avenge the dead heroes of the Lost Cause, to gain the public support necessary to make his guerrilla war viable. He, Ben Bickerstaff, "Indian Bill" English, and Ben Griffith also adopted the garb and tactics of the Ku Klux Klan, although the Klan also existed independently of the outlaw bands.[34]

Despite numerous repeated pleas for assistance, Reynolds waited much too long to initiate his successful campaign to subdue the outlaws and Ku Klux Klan in northeastern Texas. Such a program as had been proposed by Lieutenant Roberts, Kirkman, Shorkley, and Johnson was finally put in place throughout the state by Reynolds's successor, Brevet Major General Edward R. S. Canby, in January, 1869, and did much to quell lawlessness and violence. But the bureau was gone by then. Indeed, with the sole exception of General Griffin briefly in 1867, no bureau commander had been able or willing to challenge the army's reluctance to divide its troop contingent to provide some military power on the local level.[35]

It is fair to ask whether a more thorough military occupation would have solved the racial problem in selected rural areas of Texas. The conditions in these zones mirrored rather closely those that existed in the Kansas-Missouri border country before and during the Civil War. The activities of organized guerrilla units there were to be curtailed by the draconian measure of removing the whole civilian population to areas controlled by the Union Army. But the result had been merely to cause the guerrillas to transfer their base of operations to nearby counties. Given the criticism that followed the institution of the wartime removal policy, a program characterized by one historian as "the harshest treatment ever imposed on United States citizens under the plea of military necessity" with the exception of the mass incarceration of Japanese-Americans in World War II, it seems doubtful that a Federal government unwilling adequately to support morally and monetarily the Reconstruction of the South could have resorted to more peacetime force than it actually used.[36]

The success of Chaffee's column in suppressing the Texas outlaws who plagued Brown and other agents, however, would seem to suggest that Reynolds was lax in not trying something on the order of Lieutenant Roberts's proposal sooner. The troops were available within the Texas command despite any reductions in force or changes in duty stations. Yet perhaps General Reynolds was more realistic in his assessment of the situation, no matter how mercenary his actions may seem one hundred years later. In the words of the chronicler of the army's role in Reconstruction, "the melancholy fact was that no amount of troops could have prevented assaults on Negroes when the crimes took place on remote stretches of country roads by disguised men."[37] Brevet Lieutenant Colonel D. L. Montgomery, for one, would have agreed. In his reports on the bureau operations at Tyler, he continually characterized the effort in one phrase—the bureau and its allies were "overreached on all sides."[38]

Colonel Montgomery was correct. A successful Reconstruction required the same commitment and innovation that the Union put out to win the Civil War. But the war itself had exhausted the nation, which had tired of hearing about the "infernal" race issue. The nation wanted peace. More than that, the whole racial philosophy of nineteenth-century American society worked to deny the necessity of thorough Reconstruction. Those who comprehended the complexity of the problems of race and strove to implement legal equality were dismissed as oddballs. The government had established no social relief programs up to that time for any group but veterans.

Although the bureau attempted initially to transcend the racist beliefs of the nation, it wound up embodying them in its very soul. Its programs, by their uniqueness, were reserved for blacks and became a vital precedent in the segregationists' separate-but-equal philosophy that would be enunciated so forcefully by the U.S. Supreme Court by the end of the century. Chattel slavery administered by Southern whites was replaced by a wage slavery acquiesced in by Northern whites who ran the Freedmen's Bureau. The bureau, founded in a burst of innovation, had been tempered by the conventional thoughts and actions of its white administrators.[39]

All of this spelled a critical difference between the "reconstruction" of the nation and the "Reconstruction" of the South. It is tempting—since the bureau began by breaking new ground in the epic journey of the American black as free person—to see the ledger containing the bureau's achievements as half full, rather than half blank. Many historians have done so.[40] But a gnawing sense of what might have been continues to haunt the history of the bureau's field operations, as it has all of Reconstruction.[41] As if to accentuate this feeling, from deep in West Africa, the former homeland of so many of the slaves brought to Texas and the American South, comes an eery refrain, an old Yoruba proverb that catches the dilemma of Reconstruction and the role of the bureau: "I almost caught a bird," the exuberant youth said. "*Almost* never made a stew," the wise elder answered.[42]

General Griffin understood this fine point, too, better than most. "I should as soon [have] looked to the English crown to leave the establishment of peace in Ireland to Finians," the general had snorted in a statement to Commissioner Howard during the summer of 1867, "as to see our Nation leave the reconstruction of the Southern states to those that tried to destroy the government."[43] Yet in the end, the enshrinement of Griffin's foreboding is exactly what it took to obtain the illusion of peace in Ireland and in the American South. When

Northern and Southern whites met at Washington's Wormley Hotel in 1877 to put Reconstruction formally behind them, Griffin's apprehension and the old saw of the Yoruba became an American reality.[44] And what General Granger's adjutant had said in the summer of 1865 became the epitaph of the entire Texas bureau program. The state's blacks were no longer slaves, but neither were they truly free.[45]

Abbreviations Used in Notes

AAAG	Acting Assistant Adjutant General
AAC	Acting Assistant Commissioner
AADO	Acting Assistant Distribution Officer
AAG	Assistant Adjutant General
AAIG	Acting Assistant Inspector General
AAQM	Acting Assistant Quartermaster
AC	Assistant Commissioner
AGO	Adjutant General's Office, Washington, D.C.
APL	Austin History Center, Austin Public Library
ASCA	Acting Secretary of Civil Affairs
C	Commissioner
CA	Office of Civil Affairs
Circ.	Circular Orders
Circ. Letter	Circular Letter
CO	Commanding Officer
C/S	Chief of Staff
DO	Distribution Officer
D of G	Department of the Gulf Headquarters
DT	Department of Texas Headquarters
ES	Endorsements Sent
FB	Freedmen's Bureau Headquarters, Washington, D.C.
FMD	Fifth Military District Headquarters
GCMO	General Court-Martial Orders
GO	General Orders
KIA	Killed in action
LC	Archives Division, Library of Congress
LR	Letters Received
LS	Letters Sent
LSU	Department of Archives and Manuscripts, Louisiana State University
MDSW	Military Division of the Southwest Headquarters
Ms.	Manuscript
NA	National Archives

OR   *The War of the Rebellion: The Official Records of the Union and Confederate Armies* (128 vols., Washington, D.C.: Government Printing Office, 1889–1903). All citations to Series I, unless otherwise noted.

RG   Record Group

ROC   Reports of Operations and Conditions

RR   Received and Retained Reports Relating to Rations, Lands, and Bureau Personnel

SAC   Subassistant Commissioner

SCA   Secretary of Civil Affairs

SO   Special Orders

SS   Superintendent of Schools

T   Texas

TAGO   Texas Adjutant General's Office Papers

TFB   Texas Freedman's Bureau Papers

TR   Telegrams Received

TS   Telegrams Sent

TSL   Archives, Texas State Library

USA   U.S. Army

USCI   U.S. Colored Infantry

USOR (1869)   *Register of Officers and Agents, Civil, Military, and Naval, in the Service of the United States, on the Thirtieth of September . . .* (Washington, D.C.: Government Printing Office, 1870). Also known as the *U.S. Official Register.*

USV   U.S. Volunteers

UT   Archives, Barker Texas History Center, University of Texas

VRC   Veteran Reserve Corps

Notes

INTRODUCTION

1. Howard to Stanton, July 1, 1865 (without delay), LS, C, RG 105, NA. Hereafter manuscript documents cited will come from RG 105, NA, unless otherwise stated. Details of the trip in Gregory to Howard, September 21, 1865, LS, AC, T.

2. Secretary of War Edwin M. Stanton seemingly handed Howard a "basket case," as the new bureau's papers had been thrown haphazardly into a bushel basket before his acceptance as commissioner. See Howard, *Autobiography*, vol. 2, 208. Howard's leadership of the bureau has been looked at favorably by Carpenter, *Sword and Olive Branch*; Olds, "The Freedmen's Bureau as a Social Agency," 72–109; and John and La Wanda Cox, "General Howard and the 'Misrepresented Bureau'," 427–56. A less sympathetic view is that of McFeeley, *Yankee Stepfather*.

3. Howard's appointment is in GO 91, May 12, 1865, AGO, RG 94, NA; the staff appointments are in Circ. 1, May 15, 1865, unnumbered Circ., May 19, 1865, Circ. 6, June 13, 1865, Ms. Orders, C. A detailed report is in Howard to Cpt. R. Brinckerhoff, May 31, 1865, LS, C. For the organization and activities of the Freedmen's Bureau on the national level, see Bentley, *History of the Freedmen's Bureau*; Pierce, *Freedmen's Bureau*; Olds, "Freedmen's Bureau as a Social Agency," 110–54, and DuBois, "Freedmen's Bureau, 354–65. See also Litwack, *Been in the Storm So Long*; Berlin, *Slaves without Masters*; and Groff, "Freedmen's Bureau in High School History Texts," 425–33.

4. The original appointments of the assistant commissioners are in Circ. 6, June 13, 1865, as revised by Circ. 16, September 19, 1865, Ms. Orders, C. Various state studies on the bureau include Alderson, "Influence of Military Rule and the Freedmen's Bureau on Reconstruction in Virginia, 1865–1870"; Abbott, *Freedmen's Bureau in South Carolina*; Richardson, "Evaluation of the Freedmen's Bureau in Florida," 223–38; Thompson, "Freedmen's Bureau in Georgia in 1865–1866," 40–49; Hasson, "Medical Activities of the Freedmen's Bureau in Reconstruction Alabama, 1865–1868"; Bethel, "Freedmen's Bureau in Alabama," 49–92; Ganus, "Freedmen's Bureau in Mississippi"; J. Thomas May, "Medical Care of Blacks in Louisiana during Occupation and Reconstruction, 1862–1868"; Englesman, "Freedmen's Bureau in Louisiana," 145–224; White, *Freedmen's Bureau in Louisiana*; Low, "Freedmen's Bureau in the Border States," 245–64; Everly, "Freedmen's Bureau in the National Capital"; Fields, *Slavery and Freedom on the Middle Ground*; Fuke, "Reform Mentality," 214–35; Howard, *Black Liberation in Kentucky*; Phillips, "History of the Freedmen's Bureau in Tennessee"; Stealey, "Freedmen's Bureau in West Virginia," 99–142.

5. The continual muster-out of volunteer officers caused havoc with the system. See Howard to Stanton, July 25, 1865; Howard to Maj. Thomas F. Eckert, September 14, 1865; and Howard to Brig. Gen. E. D. Townsend, December 12, 1865; all in LS, C. See also Olds, "The Freedmen's Bureau as a Social Agency," 111–12.

6. See "An Act to Establish a Bureau . . . ," 13 *Statutes at Large*, 507–509 (March 3, 1865). Also of interest is Pierce, *Freedmen's Bureau*, 34–54.

7. Pierce, *Freedmen's Bureau*, 48–52; Belz, "Freedmen's Bureau Act of 1865 and the Principle of No Discrimination according to Color," 197–217; Woodward, "Seeds of Failure in Radical Race Policy," 214–47. Wartime federal efforts in emancipation, which preceded the bureau's activity, are detailed in Pierce, *Freedmen's Bureau*, 1–33; Gerteis, *From Contraband to Freedman*; Rose, *Rehearsal for Reconstruction*; Mohr, *On the Threshold of Freedom*; Ripley, *Slaves and Freedmen in Civil War Louisiana*; Messner, *Freedmen and the Ideology of Free Labor*; Cimprich, *Slavery's End in Tennessee, 1861–1865*; Wagandt, *Mighty Revolution*; Olds, "Freedmen's Bureau as a Social Agency," 29–71.

8. Circ. 2, May 19, 1865, Ms. Orders, C.

9. SO 2, May 25, 1865, Ms. Orders, C.

10. The temporary nature of bureau relief measures is emphasized in Carpenter, *Sword and Olive Branch*, 93.

11. Circ. Letter, May 15, 1865, Ms. Orders, C.

12. Circ. 5, May 30, 1865 (signed by President Andrew Johnson, June 2, 1865), and reissued as Circ. 11, July 12, 1865, (without Johnson's signature), Ms. Orders C. Gregory issued Howard's Circ. 5 as a part of his own Circ. 1, October 12, 1865, Ms. Orders, AC, T.

13. Howard to AAG-AGO, June 9, 1865, LS, C, defines these guidelines.

14. Howard to all ACs, June 14, 1865, LS, C. See also Circ. 11, July 12, 1865, Ms. Orders, C. The independent nature of the assistant commissioners is emphasized in Pierce, *Freedmen's Bureau*, 51–52.

15. Gregory's war record is in Boatner, *Civil War Dictionary*, 358, and Heitman, *Historical Register*, vol. 1, 477. Howard's comments are in *Autobiography*, vol. 2, 218. Bentley, *History of the Freedmen's Bureau*, 60, calls Gregory one of two assistant commissioners not personally known to Howard. Howard, *Autobiography*, vol. 2, 217, however, mentions three others as unknown to him personally, implying that he was acquainted with Gregory at least casually. The commissioner's request for Gregory's services is in Howard to Stanton, July 1, 1865, LS, C.

16. Gregory's travel orders and appointment are in SO 25, July 10, 1865, Ms. Orders, C; horse transportation is in Bvt. Maj. Gen. D. H. Rucker to AAAG-C, August 10, 1865, and the trip details in Gregory to Howard, September 21, 1865, LS, AC, T. The standard study of the bureau in Texas has been Claude Elliott's too brief article, "Freedmen's Bureau in Texas," 1–24. The most recent related comprehensive study is James Smallwood, *Time of Hope, Time of Despair*. See also his articles, "Freedmen's Bureau Reconsidered," 309–20; "Charles E. Culver, a Reconstruction Agent in Texas," 350–61; and "G. T. Ruby," 24–33. On education, see Hornsby, "Freedmen's Bureau Schools in Texas 1865–1870," 397–417. Some of the better writings on the Texas bureau come from the pen of Barry A. Crouch. See his "Freedmen's Bureau and the 30th Sub-district in Texas," 15–30; "Black Dreams and White Justice," 255–65; "Self Determination and Local Black Leaders in Texas,"

344–55; and "Spirit of Lawlessness," 217–32. See also Crouch and Schultz, "Crisis in Color," 34–49; and Crouch and Madaras, "Reconstructing Black Families," 109–22. A brief but excellent analysis of the state headquarters personnel is in Sinclair, "Freedmen's Bureau in Texas." See also Neal and Kremm, "'What Shall We Do with the Negro?'" 23–33. The literature and certain bureau problems are surveyed in Crouch, "Hidden Sources of Black History," 211–26, and "Freedmen's Bureau Records," 74–94. Also of interest is Pitre, "Note on the Historiography of Blacks in the Reconstruction of Texas," 340–48; Crouch, "'Unmanacling' Texas Reconstruction: A Twenty Year Perspective." *Southwestern Historical Quarterly* 93 (1989–90), 275–302; Sneed, "A Historiography of Reconstruction in Texas: Some Myths and Problems," *Southwestern Historical Quarterly* 72 (1968–69), 435–48.

17. GO 3, June 19, 1865, DT, RG 94, NA.

18. Howard to Granger, July 17, 1865, LS, C.

19. Bvt. Maj. Gen. C. C. Andrews, "Speech at Brenham, Texas, July 20, 1865," in *Early Steps in Reconstruction*, 2–3, printed copy in TSL.

20. Quote from Howard to Granger, July 21, 1865, LS, C. See also Granger's pledge to local government, *Flake's Tri-Weekly Bulletin* (Galveston), June 17, 1865; GO 9, August 4, 1865, Post of Galveston, and O. H. P. Garrett to Hamilton, August 7, 1865, Governor's Papers (Hamilton), TSL; Howard to Stanton, July 18, 1865, LS, C. For a typical city ordinance limiting the free movement of the former slaves, endorsed and enforced by the occupying federal army, see Palm, "Slavery in Microcosm," 122–24.

21. *Flake's Daily Bulletin* (Galveston), July 10, 1865.

22. AAAG-IV Corps to [Bvt. Maj. Gen. Thomas T. Wood], August 6, 1865, OR, vol. 48, pt. 2, 1169–70. See also, David Thompson (free men of color) to Hamilton, August 26, 1865, Governor's Papers (Hamilton), TSL.

23. AAAG-DT to Col. John Kelly, June 28, 1865, OR, vol. 48, pt. 2, pp. 1017–18.

24. The lingering effect of Granger's influence can be seen in Bvt. Brig. Gen. Loren Kent to Hamilton, October 27, 1865, Governor's Papers (Hamilton), TSL, in which Kent asks the governor to reappoint Galveston's former Confederate officials as the loyal government was supported by only a small portion of the city's white population. For Granger's removal, see Sheridan to Grant, July 15, 17, 1865, and Grant to Sheridan, July 13, 1865, Grant Papers, LC. To what extent army occupation orders, which regulated Negroes' activities as free persons, locked the Texas bureau administrators into a predetermined, pro-southern-white policy is open to question. These attitudes, however, do reappear in Texas bureau work throughout Reconstruction. Penelope K. Majeske postulates that such early military influences markedly influenced President Johnson's Reconstruction program and laid the groundwork for the Compromise of 1877 as early as 1865. See her "Virginia after Appomattox," 95–117. See also May, "Continuity and Change in the Labor Program of the Union Army and the Freedmen's Bureau," 245–54; and O'Brien, "Reconstruction in Richmond," 259–81.

25. Hamilton to Andrew Johnson, July 24, 1865, Johnson Papers, LC. A good statement of these options made before Hamilton's arrival is in "Pacificus" to Pendleton Murrah, May 1, 1865, Governor's Papers (Murrah), TSL. Murrah was the last Confederate governor of the state. The Supreme Court decision scheme

is noted in Nat Hart Davis to Hamilton, August –, 1865, Governor's Papers (Hamilton), TSL.

26. S. Wright to Hamilton, September 16, 1865; Amos Clark to Hamilton, July 22, 1865, Governor's Papers (Hamilton), TSL; San Antonio *News*, June 22, 1865; O. L. Batchelder to Hamilton, August 4, 1865, R. S. Hunt to Hamilton, July 6, 1865; Resolutions of the Citizens of Belton, July 20, 1865; J. Patrick to Hamilton, September 2, 1865; Governor's Papers, (Hamilton), TSL.

27. J. M. McAlpine to Hamilton, August –, September 4, 1865 (rule or ruin); Kidder Walker to Hamilton, June 5 (military probation), July 15, 1865; N. U. Gunn et al. to Hamilton, October 8, 1865 (rebel outrages); John E. Thompson to Hamilton, October 8, 1865 (Jack Hambilton); A. A. Deavalon to Hamilton, July 10, 1865 (love of plunder); Louis Constant to Hamilton, October 18, 1865 (leading barbarians); all in Governor's Papers (Hamilton), TSL.

28. Reports of slavery after emancipation are in Citizens of Lockhart to Bvt. Maj. Gen. George A. Custer, January 24, 1866; Thomas Ford et al. to Hamilton, September 6, 1865; W. Longworth to Hamilton, October 10, 1865; D. J. Baldwin to Hamilton, November 7, 1865; all in Governor's Papers (Hamilton), TSL.

29. "Fifteen lashes" is in William B. DeWees to Hamilton [Summer 1865]; the best summary of the whole problem and the five hundred lashes story are in S. J. Richardson to Hamilton, September –, 1865; Hamilton to Wright, September 27, 1865, Governor's Papers (Hamilton), TSL. That the army and later the bureau knew about these and other incidents is evident from C. C. Andrews, "Speech at Brenham, Texas, July 20, 1865," in *Early Steps in Reconstruction*, 2; Gregory to Howard, December 9, 1865, LS, AC, T; Gregory to Howard, January 31, LR, C; and Circ. 1, October 12, 1865, Ms. Orders, AC, T.

30. All spelling as in the original. Proclamation to the People of Texas, July 24, 1865, Governor's Papers (Hamilton), TSL; undated speech, 1865, Hamilton Papers, UT.

31. F. Flake to Hamilton, July 30, 1865, Governor's Papers (Hamilton), TSL; S. M. Swenson to Pease, June 17, 1865, Pease-Niles-Graham Papers, APL.

32. Both the Governor's Papers, TSL, and the Pease-Niles-Graham Papers, APL, are full of petitions seeking favors for loyal men and warning of disloyal tricks. The Brenham incident is described in O. H. P. Garrett to Hamilton, August 7, 1865, and Cpt. T. S. Post to Hamilton, August 30, 1865, Governor's Papers (Hamilton), TSL. Hamilton's defense of his actions is in Hamilton to Johnson, September 23, 1865, Johnson Papers, LC.

33. Hamilton to Johnson, August 30, 1865, Johnson Papers, LC.

34. Hamilton to Bvt. Maj. Gen. C. C. Andrews, August 17, 1865, RG 307, TSL, James H. Bell et al. to Johnson, Johnson Papers, LC.

35. Hamilton to Wright, September 27, 1865, Governor's Papers (Hamilton), TSL.

36. Sheridan to C/S, October 7, 1865, OR, vol. 48, pt. 2, 1238; Stanton to Sheridan, October 10, 1865, copy in Governor's Papers (Hamilton), TSL; Wright to Sheridan, Sheridan Papers, LC.

37. Wright to Hamilton, September 22, 1865, October 10, 1865, Governor's Papers (Hamilton), TSL.

38. Wright to Hamilton, October 10, 1865, ibid. Wright's policy was graphically

demonstrated in a Williamson County case in which the army arrested two men and later apologized to the civil government for interference in its domain. See Anon. to Hamilton, August 11, 1865; Bvt. Col. A. S. Bager to Hamilton, August 10, October 23, 1865; Governor's Papers (Hamilton), TSL.

39. D. B. Lucky to Hamilton, October 16, 1865; D. O. Norton to Hamilton, October 17, 1965; B. F. Barkley to Hamilton, October 30, 1865; Governor's Papers (Hamilton), TSL.

40. Quote from H. Christian et al. to Hamilton, October 9, 1865, ibid. See also, H. Christian to Hamilton, November 14, 1865; and John Flint to Hamilton, January 6, 1866, ibid.

41. The troopers' orders are in Bvt. Maj. George A. Custer to Hamilton, November 23, 1865, Governor's Papers (Hamilton), TSL; their arrival in Dallas in Dallas *Herald*, December 9, 1865.

42. Lt. Col. Thomas M. Browne to Bvt. Brig. Gen. Samuel Sturgis, February 12, 1866; C. B. Binkley et al. to Sturgis, February 12, 1866; Wright to AAAG-D of G, March 2, 1866, Sheridan Papers, LC.

43. The recommended cavalry garrison is in Wright to AAAG-D of G, March 2, 1866, Sheridan Papers, LC; quotes from Hamilton to Sheridan, January 17, 1866, Johnson Papers, LC; Sheridan to Hamilton, February 5, 1866, Sheridan Papers, LC; Hamilton to Sheridan, February 26, 1866, *House Executive Documents*, 40th Cong., 2nd Sess., No. 57, 26.

44. Wright to Hamilton, March 3, 1866; Sturgis to Hamilton, March 19, 1866; Governor's Papers (Hamilton), TSL.

45. See William L. Richter, "'It Is Best to Go in Strong-handed'," 113–42.

1: TO PROMOTE A MUTUAL INTEREST

1. Gregory to Howard, September 21, 1865, LS, AC, T.

2. See Circ. 1, October 12, 1865, Ms. Orders, AC, T.

3. Gregory to Howard, December 9, 1865, *House Executive Documents*, 39th Cong., 1st Sess., No. 70, 374–77.

4. Elliott, "Freedmen's Bureau in Texas," 5–7, incorrectly has Strong making the trip in December. See Gregory to Howard, December 9, 1865, House Executive Documents, 39th Cong., 1st Sess., No. 70, 375, who says Strong went with him in November.

5. SO 84, October 6, 1865, Ms. Orders, C.

6. See Howard to Strong, June 13, July 15, 1865, LS, C.

7. Strong to Howard, January 1, 1866, *House Executive Documents*, 39th Cong., 1st Sess., No. 70, 308–13.

8. For Strong's itinerary, SO 84, October 6, 1865, Ms. Orders, C.

9. Circ. 2, December 5, 1865, Ms. Orders, AC, T.

10. S. J. W. Mintzer to Gregory, December 1, 1865, RR, AC, T. The tales of freedmen being sold into Cuban slavery disturbed Congress enough to cause a full investigation. See *Senate Executive Documents*, 39th Cong., 1st Sess., No. 30.

11. See Ms. Rosters, January 31, 1866, AC, T. See also Gregory to Howard,

January 31, 1866, *House Executive Documents*, 39th Cong., 1st Sess., No. 70, 306. There were now twenty agents in the field and five staff officers.

12. Gregory to Howard, January 31, 1866, *House Executive Documents*, 39th Cong., 1st Sess., No. 70, 304–306.

13. Circ. 1, October 12, 1865, Ms. Orders, AC, T.

14. Circ. Letter, May 15, 1865, Ms. Orders, C.

15. GO 3, June 19, 1865, Printed Orders, DT, RG 94, NA; Circ. 1, October 12, 1865, Ms. Orders, AC, T.

16. Ira P. Pedigo to Gregory, [January 31, 1866], RR, AC, T.

17. See Cole, "Texas Career of Thomas Affleck," 200, 214.

18. Smallwood, "Black Texans during Reconstruction," 9–23.

19. C. W. Binckley to Hamilton, August 22, 1865, Governor's Papers (Hamilton), TSL.

20. Galveston *Daily News*, June 28, 1865; *Flake's Daily Bulletin* (Galveston), June 29, 1865.

21. Galveston *Daily News*, September 18, 30, 1865. Black soldiers had an exaggerated effect on Texans' fears. They were blamed for problems even in counties where they were never stationed.

22. Sheridan to C/S, October 24, 1865, Grant Papers, LC.

23. Bellville *Countryman*, August 9, 18, 1865; Gregory to Benjamin Harris, January 20, 1866, LS, AC, T.

24. 13 *Statutes at Large*, 507–509 (March 3, 1865); Ramsdell, *Reconstruction in Texas*, 70–74; Rose, *Rehearsal for Reconstruction*, 327–28.

25. J. O. Thally to Hamilton, November 6, 1865; Citizens of Liberty County to Hamilton, November–, 1865; Charles B. Stewart to Hamilton, November 27, 1865 (negrogogues), Governor's Papers (Hamilton), TSL.

26. F. W. Grassmeyer to Hamilton, November 22, 1865 (Christmas is coming), Governor's Papers (Hamilton), TSL. For more on the land question, see DuBois, *Black Reconstruction*, 600–604; Lynd, "Rethinking Slavery and Reconstruction," 198–209; La Wanda Cox, "Promise of Land for the Freedmen," 413–40; Oubre, *Forty Acres and a Mule*; Magdol, *Right to the Land*, 139–73; Abbott, "Free Land, Free Labor, and the Freedmen's Bureau," 150–56; Hoffnagel, "Southern Homestead Act," 612–29; and Bentley, *History of the Freedmen's Bureau*, 89–102, 144–46; Pierce, *Freedmen's Bureau*, 129–32. Doubt as to the effect of a land grant to freedmen changing the role of blacks in Southern economic history over the long run is expressed in Degler, "Rethinking Post–Civil War History," 255–56.

27. Circ. 1, October 12, 1865, Ms. Orders, AC, T; Hamilton to Johnson, October 21, 1865, Johnson Papers, LC; Howard, Circ. Letter, November 11, 1865, LS, C.

28. Hamilton, "Proclamation to the Freedmen," November 17, 1865, Governor's Papers (Hamilton), TSL. Individual bureau agents issued the same warnings, or read Hamilton's proclamation. The proclamation was sent to all county judges for distribution. See 1 Lt. O. H. Swingley to Gregory, November 25, 1865; Judge Ira P. Pedigo to Gregory, [January 31, 1866], RR, AC, T.

29. GO 90, May 11, 1865, Printed Orders, AGO; and GO 5, June 30, 1865, Printed Orders, MDSW; RG 94, NA; *Flake's Daily Bulletin* (Galveston), July 10, 1865; Bellville *Countryman*, July 15, 1865.

30. See W. B. Price to Hamilton, December 23, 1865, Governor's Papers (Hamilton), TSL.

31. For local police organized by the army with cavalry pay, see *The Standard* (Clarksville), August 5, 1865; and Cpt. Robert Hathdorf et al. to Hamilton, August 14, 1865, Governor's Papers (Hamilton), TSL, for approval of loyal home guards by Bvt. Maj. Gen. Wesley Merritt. The Clarksville unit was dispersed by black soldiers sent in from the Louisiana command, and who disobeyed their officers in order to defend local freedmen from persecution (see *Flake's Daily Bulletin* [Galveston], January 11, 1866).

32. A. P. McCormick to Hamilton, November 13, 1865, Governor's Papers (Hamilton), TSL.

33. Historians have not yet arrived at a consensus concerning the role of the Federal government in revolutionizing the relations between Southern blacks and whites or in merely confirming the dominance of the old order. The ideal of cooperation between the three elements (freedman, planter, Federal official) is explored in Bigelow, "Vicksburg," 28–44; and Hermann, "Reconstruction in Microcosm," 312–35. In defense of the bureau's policies are Abbott, "Free Land, Free Labor, and the Freedmen's Bureau," 150–56; Belz, *Emancipation and Equal Rights*, 71–72, Alderson, "Influence of Military Rule and the Freedmen's Bureau on Reconstruction in Virginia, 1865–1870," 44–46, 98–101; Olds, "Freedmen's Bureau as a Social Agency," 174–81; and Fuke, "Reform Mentality," 235. Less sure of the bureau's assistance to blacks are Nieman, *To Set the Law in Motion*; Novak, *Wheel of Servitude*; Ransom and Sutch, *One Kind of Freedom*; Daniel, *Shadow of Slavery*; Richardson, "Freedmen's Bureau and Negro Labor in Florida," 176–84; Wynne, "Role of Freedmen in the Post Bellum Cotton Economy of Georgia," 309–21; Humphrey, "Failure of the Mississippi Freedmen's Bureau in Black Labor Relations," 23–27; May, "Continuity and Change in the Labor Program of the Union Army and the Freedmen's Bureau," 245–54; Smallwood, "Perpetuation of Caste," 5–23; and Carper, "Slavery Revisited," 85–99. Davis, "U. S. Army and the Origins of Sharecropping in the Natchez District," 60–80, points out there was no official policy that led to sharecropping; rather, it was the result of a vast interplay of economic and social forces. Compare Degler, "Rethinking Post–Civil War History," 253–54; Bentley, *History of the Freedmen's Bureau*, 148–51; and Pierce, *Freedmen's Bureau*, 32–43. Cimbala, "'Talisman Power'," 153–71, admits that less than perfect results flowed from the bureau programs. But he holds that bureau officials worked diligently to avoid them, only to be thwarted by the mores of the existing society. See also McDonald and McWhiney, "South from Self-sufficiency to Peonage," 1095–1118; Wagstaff, "'Call Your Old Master–Master'," 323–45; Cohen, "Negro Involuntary Servitude in the South," 31–60; Schlomowitz, "Origins of Southern Sharecropping," 557–75.

34. Dawson, *Army Generals and Reconstruction Louisiana*, 14. Critics of Banks's lack of daring include Gerteis, *From Contraband to Freedman*, 5, 7, 82–83; and Ripley, *Slaves and Freedmen in Civil War Louisiana*, 48–49, 200–202. See also May, "Continuity and Change in the Labor Program of the Union Army and the Freedmen's Bureau," 245–54; Kassel, "Labor System of General Banks," 35–50; Olds, "Freedmen's Bureau as a Social Agency," 47–51; and the discussion in Pierce, *Freedmen's Bureau*, 1–33.

35. See GO 12, January 29, 1863, D of G, OR, vol. 15, 666–67.

36. GO 23, March 11, 1865, D of G, OR, vol. 48, pt. 2, 1146–48. By this time, Banks had been relieved for the botched Red River campaign, and the order contained the signature of his successor, Bvt. Maj. Gen. Stephen Hurlbut.

37. Custer, *Tenting on the Plains*, 111. Andrews, "Speech at Brenham, Texas, July 20, 1865," in *Early Steps in Reconstruction*, 2–3, is a good example of this carryover.

38. Cole, "Texas Career of Thomas Affleck," 201–202, 205, 220.

39. Although the first agents were announced in SO 2, October 9, 1865, the first public statement of their supervising the contract process was not made until Circ. 2, December 5, 1865. See Ms. Orders, AC, T.

40. Circ. 3, December 9, 1865, Ms. Orders, AC, T, AAAG-TFB to Cpt. Stanton Weaver, January 23, 1866, LS, AC, T, for the term of contract. Some freedmen were still trying to collect their 1865 wages in 1867, which leads to the suspicion that some were never paid. See Griffin to Howard, June 12, 1867, LR, C.

41. SO 2, October 9, 1865, Ms. Orders, TFB; Lt. Col. J. C. De Gress to AAAG-TFB, November 13 (damned swindle), 30, December 1, 1865, LR, AC, T. See also De Gress to Gregory, November 3, 1865 (*wice*), RR, AC, T; Gregory to De Gress, December 4, 1865, January 20, 1867, LS, AC, T; Gregory to AAAG-C, February 2, 1867, LR, C. Gregory asked Commissioner Howard to send De Gress back after muster-out, as he was needed in the "upper counties." See Gregory to Howard, February 26, 1866, LS, AC, T; SO 19, December 28, 1865, Ms. Orders, TFB. See also Dyer, *Compendium of the War of the Rebellion*, vol. 3, 1306–1307.

42. De Gress to Gregory, November 1, 3, 1865; De Gress to John D. Imboden, November 3, 1865; RR, AC, T.

43. De Gress to AAAG-TFB, November 13, 1865 (had probably forgotten), and December –, 1865 (everything is working), LR, AC, T.

44. Gregory to Howard, October 12, 1865, LR, C; Gregory to Howard, October 31, 1865, LS, AC, T.

45. See Gregory to all SACs, December 6, 1865, LS, AC, T.

46. AAAG-TFB to Messrs. McMann and Gilbert, December 5, 1865; AAAG-TFB to J. W. McConaughey, February 15, 1866 (summary way), May 9, 1866, LS, AC, T.

47. See, for example, Gregory to Bvt. Lt. Col. J. C. De Gress, October 2, 1865 (do justice); AAAG-TFB to Messrs. J. T. and W. Brady, January 15, 1866; AAAG-TFB to 2 Lt. B. J. Arnold, January 3, 1866; AAAG-TFB to W. H. Farner, February 14, 1866; AAAG-TFB to A. P. Delano, May 3, 1866, all in LS, AC, T.

48. On the cotton pledged to the now defunct Confederacy, see GO 3, June 1, 1865, MDSW, OR, vol. 48, pt. 2, 713–14. U. S. occupation forces refused to become involved in the issue; GO 5, June 18, 1865, DT, ibid., 929–30. Granger hurried all crops to market before Treasury agents could intercept them. But Grant told his subordinates to cooperate in holding up tithe cotton (Grant to Sheridan, June 26, 1865, ibid., 1035). Bvt. Maj. Gen. Francis J. Herron warned Texan Charles Stokes of Crockett that the Federals would hunt down anyone who interfered with public property coming under the provision of the surrender documents. Undated letter in the Bellville *Countryman*, June 17, 1865. For agents seizing the part of an 1865 crop formerly pledged to the Confederate government, see Thomas Affleck to his wife, December 10, 1865, Affleck Papers, LSU.

49. AAAG-TFB to Mrs. Haig, October 7, 1865; Gregory to Col. Walters, October 25, 1865; Gregory to Captain of the Steamer *Arizona*, October 26, 1865; Gregory to Mr. Bosch, October 27, 1865; Gregory to Captain of the Steamer *Era No. 3*, October 27, 1865, AAAG-TFB to Mr. Croft, [November 10, 1865]; AAAG-TFB to Wilson Sweeney, December 1, 1865; AAAG-TFB to Captain of the Brig *Prince of Wales*, April 19, 1866, LS, AC, T.

50. AAAG-TFB to Major E. O. Farr, February 15, 1866; AAAG-TFB to 1 Lt. [N. H.] Reaker [*sic*], March 10, 1866, LS, AC, T. The lieutenant's surname, "Ricker," is correctly given in *Official Army Register of the Volunteer Force of the United States Army, 1861–1865*, 8, 180.

51. See, for example, AAAG-TFB to De Gress, October 10, 1865; AAAG-TFB to Cpt. J. B. Bostwick, March 8, 1866; AAAG-TFB to J. W. McConaughey, April 6, 1866; LS, AC, T.

52. On this point, see AAAG-TFB to James L. Green, October 12, 25, 1865; AAAG-TFB to E. A. McCracken, January 19, 1866; AAAG-TFB to Cpt. S. W. Moon, March 13, 1866; AAAG-TFB to A. P. Wheeler, March 19, 1866; LS, AC, T. All of these men wished to approve or had approved contracts, many of which met Gregory's standards, but all of which were invalidated since they were not countersigned by a subassistant commissioner.

53. Circ. Letter, October 17, 1865, LS, AC, T; Circ. 2, December 5, 1865; Circ. 3, December 9, 1865 (quoted); Ms. Orders, AC, T; AAAG-TFB to Cpt. Stanton Weaver, February 12, 1866 (fair on its face), LS, AC, T.

54. Circ. Letter, October 17, 1865, Ms. Orders, AC, T; as modified by letters, AAAG-TFB to 1 Lt. O. H. Swingley, December 22, 27, 1865; AAAG-TFB to Cpt. Stanton Weaver, January 15, 1866, LS, AC, T.

55. Circ. Letter, October 17, 1865, Ms. Orders, AC, T; as modified by AAAG-TFB to Cpt. John Scott, December 9, 1865; AAAG-TFB to Cpt. Stanton Weaver, January 15, 1866; LS, AC, T. Gregory told his agents to use their own judgment in advising freedmen to work for wages or a share of the crop. See AAAG-TFB to 1 Lt. O. H. Swingley, January 16, 1866, LS, AC, T.

56. Quotation from Circ. Letter, October 17, 1865, Ms. Orders, AC, T. See also Gregory to Isaac Dennis, October 21, 1865 (on vagrancy); AAAG-TFB to Cpt. Stanton Weaver, January 15, 1866; AAAG-TFB to 2 Lt. B. J. Arnold, January 25, 1866 (on the ten-hour day), LS, AC, T.

57. Security deposits were used whenever freedmen rented land. See AAAG-TFB to John E. George, February 9, 1866, LS, AC, T. Few freedmen rented, but it was done in Travis County. See AAAG-TFB to 1 Lt. O. H. Swingley, November 25, 1865, LS, AC, T.

58. Circ. Letter, October 17, 1865, Ms. Orders, AC, T; AAAG-TFB to Cpt. Stanton Weaver, February 12, 1866 (no slavery or peonage), LS, AC, T.

59. AAAG-TFB to J. W. McConaughey, January 19, 1866; and AAAG-TFB to Cpt. Samuel C. Sloan, January 22, 1866; LS, AC, T.

60. AAAG-TFB to J. O. Shelby, March 12, 1866; AAAG-TFB to Cpt. Samuel C. Sloan, April 28, 1866; LS, AC, T.

61. AAAG-TFB to Cpt. John Scott, February 8, 1866, LS, AC, T; AAAG-TFB to Cpt. I. Johnson, May 12, 1866, ES, AC, T.

62. AAAG-C to Gregory, November 24, 1865, LS, C.

63. AAAG-TFB to Cpt. Stanton Weaver, February 12, 1866, LS, AC, T.

64. Circ. 14, August 17, 1865, Ms. Orders, C. The ironclad oath requirement is in AAAG-C to all ACs, October 23, 1865, LS, C. The difficulty in obtaining a medical appointment is revealed in Gregory to AAAG-C, November 6, 1865; Gregory to Surgeon M. P. Thomas, October 17, 1865, LS, AC, T; and Gregory to Howard, January 25, 1866, LR, C.

65. Circ. 14, August 17, 1865, Ms. Orders, C.

66. Mintzer's appointment is in SO 33, July 24, 1865, Ms. Orders, C.

67. See, for example, Gregory's report, May 7, 1866, RR, AC, T. The bureau's medical activities nationally are surveyed in Raphael, "Health and Medical Care of Black People in the United States during Reconstruction"; and Olds, "Freedmen's Bureau," 218–20, 225–26. Medical activity in Texas never approached that of Virginia, Louisiana, Mississippi, Alabama, Georgia, or South Carolina, but was similar in scope to that of Kentucky. At best, most bureau medical services could be described as haphazard. See Alderson, "Influence of Military Rule and the Freedmen's Bureau on Reconstruction in Virginia, 1865–1870," 41–43, 97–98, 285–86; White, *Freedmen's Bureau in Louisiana*, 86–100; May, "19th Century Medical Care Program for Blacks," 160–71, and his "Louisiana Negro in Transition," 29–36; Legan, "Disease and the Freedmen in Mississippi during Reconstruction," 257–67; Hasson, "Health and Welfare of Freedmen in Reconstruction Alabama," 94–110; Savitt, "Politics in Medicine"; Abbott, *Freedmen's Bureau in South Carolina*, 37–52; Raphael, "Health and Social Welfare of Kentucky Black People," 143–57; and Foster, "Limitations of Federal Health Care for Freedmen," 349–72.

68. The acting assistant surgeons were J. E. Painter and H. W. Wadsworth. The latter lasted for one month. See Ms. Rosters, March 2, April 2, May 1, June 1, 1866, AC, T. Orders to condemn equipment for sale are in Howard to all ACs, March 22, 1866, LS, C. See also Circ. 7, April 23, 1866, Ms. Orders, C.

69. See Gregory to AAAG-C, February 3, 1866, LS, AC, T.

70. Mintzer to Gregory, December 1, 1865, RR, AC, T.

71. Gregory to Howard, January 31, 1866, *House Executive Documents*, 39th Cong., 1st Sess., No. 70, 304–306.

72. Mintzer to Gregory, January 31, 1866, RR, AC, T.

73. AAAG-TFB to AAAG-DT, March 9, 1866, LS, AC, T.

74. GO 10, March 7, 1866; GO 12, March 19, 1866; GO 13, March 21, 1866; SO, 11, September 11, 1866; Printed Orders, DT, RG 94, NA.

75. GO 16, April 14, 1866, Printed Orders, DT, RG 94, NA; Galveston *Daily News*, May 28, 1866.

76. Circ. 7, June 13, 1865, Ms. Orders, C.

77. Circ. 8, June 20, 1865, Ms. Orders, C. This ration was standard as long as it was permitted to be issued in Texas. See Kiddoo to Howard, July 11, 1866, LS, AC, T. The bureau followed regular army procedures, although the ration was not the same one soldiers received, but a "contraband ration." See, for example, Circ. 18, October 6, 1865, Ms. Orders, C.

78. Circ. 8, June 20, 1865, as modified by Circ. 19, November 27, 1865; Circ. 21, December 11, 1865, Ms. Orders, C. For the congressional request, see AAAG-C to all ACs, May 4, 1866, LS, C.

79. AAAG-TFB to AAAG-C, April 9, 1866, LS, AC, T.

80. Cpt. Byron Porter to Gregory, January 5, February 2, March 2, March 31, 1866, RR, AC, T.

81. Gregory to AAAG-C, March 6, March 31, May 7, 1866, RR, AC, T. It is possible that earlier periods for which records do not exist had more.

82. Circ. 5, May 30, 1865, Ms. Orders, C.

83. Circ. 9, July 6, 1865, Ms. Orders, C.

84. Howard to Stanton, September 7, 1865, LS, C.

85. Gregory to AAAG-C, March 6, 31, 1866, RR, AC, T.

86. Gregory to AAAG-C, May 7, 1866, RR, AC, T. See also Circ. 8, March 14, 1866, Ms. Orders, AC, T; and Circ. 2, April 10, 1866, Ms. Orders, C.

87. Bvt. Maj. Gen. J. B. Kiddoo to Howard, July 11, 1866. Kiddoo, Gregory's successor, blamed rations issued on the refusal of local county government to support the aged and infirm freedmen, who had been cared for by their masters in slavery times, and now had no whites interested in their welfare. Federal relief programs in Texas do not begin to approach those in other states; see, for example, Abbott, *Freedmen's Bureau in South Carolina*, 37–51; White, *Freedmen's Bureau in Louisiana*, 64–85; Alderson, "The Influence of Military Rule and the Freedmen's Bureau on Reconstruction in Virginia, 1865–1870," 37–41, 95–97, 282–84; Pierce, *Freedmen's Bureau*, 87–104; Olds, "Freedmen's Bureau as a Social Agency," 196–226; and Bentley, *History of the Freedmen's Bureau*, 136–44. None of the assistant commissioners in Texas had the temerity to order former masters to care for the aged and infirm until the counties were willing to assume the burden, as described in Alderson, "Influence of Military Rule and the Freedmen's Bureau on Reconstruction in Virginia, 1865–1870," 43.

2: THE GREAT DIFFICULTY

1. Quotation in Gregory to Howard, December 9, 1865, LS, AC, T. Personnel appointments are in SO 1–75, 1865–1866; Circ. 2, December 5, 1865; Circ. 4, December 27, 1865; Circ. 5, February 1, 1866; Circ. 6, March 5, 1866; Circ. 11, May 8, 1866; all in Ms. Orders, AC, T. See also Ms. Rosters, January 31, 1866–May 1, 1866.

2. Gregory to Howard, September 21, 1865, LS, AC, T.

3. Strong to Howard, January 1, 1866, *House Executive Documents*, 39th Cong., 1st Sess., No. 70, 313; Gregory to AAAG-C, February 10, 1866, LS, AC, T.

4. Howard to E. D. Townsend, February 5, 1866, LS, C.

5. The best statement of this feeling is in Bvt. Maj. Gen. J. B. Kiddoo to Howard, January 3, 1867, ES, AC, T, which is quoted, but all whites who served with Negro soldiers shared the onus and saw themselves as a brotherhood apart. For black soldiers and their white officers, see Cornish, *Sable Arm*, 197–228; and Glatthaar, *Forged in Battle*, 35–60, 108–109, 159, 195–96.

6. Boatner, *Civil War Dictionary*, 870; Johnson and Buel (eds.), *Battles and Leaders of the Civil War*, vol. 4, 767.

7. Richter, *Army in Texas*, 11–31.

8. AAAG-TFB to AAAG-C, December 13, 1865, LS, AC, T.

9. AAAG-TFB to AAAG-C, May 11, 1866, decrying the lack of enlisted men for bureau needs.

10. Gregory to AAAG-C, January 29, 1866, LS, AC, T.

11. For the example of Cpt. S. I. Wright, see Gregory to AAAG-C, February 20, 1866; Gregory to AAAG-D of G, February 21, 1866; Sheridan to AAAG-DT, March 3, 1866 (endorsement), LS, AC, T.

12. See SO 5, October 10, 1865, Ms. Orders, TFB; Cpt. E. W. Green to AAAG-TFB, October 24, 1865 (quotation), LR, AC, T. See also Dyer, *Compendium of the War of the Rebellion*, vol. 3, 1057–58.

13. For Van De Sande, see SO 34, February 8, 1866; SO 67, April 23, 1866; Ms. Orders, TFB; Van De Sande to AAAG-TFB, March 31, April 30, 1866, RR, AC, T. See also, Dyer, *Compendium of the War of the Rebellion*, vol. 3, 1725.

14. SO 17, December 12, 1865; SO 69, April 30, 1866; SO 75, May 10, 1866; Ms. Orders, TFB; Bostwick to AAAG-TFB, December 23, 1865, January 16 (two letters), March 26, 1866, LR, AC, T; Gregory to AAAG-C, October 13, 1865; AAAG-TFB to Bostwick, March 6, 8, 16, 26, 1866, LS, AC, T. See also Dyer, *Compendium of the War of the Rebellion*, vol. 3, 1725.

15. AAAG-TFB to AAAG-C, February 27, 1866; AAAG-TFB to Cpt. John Scott, March 2, 1866; LS, AC, T. Compare Bentley, *History of the Freedmen's Bureau*, 72–73.

16. SO 2, October 9, 1865; SO 55, March 20, 1866, Ms. Orders, TFB; Scott to AAAG-TFB, November 12, 30, 1865, January 18, 26, February 15, 26, 1866, LR, AC, T; Gregory to AAAG-C, October 3, 1865; AAAG-TFB to Scott, November 30, December 9, 1865, February 27, March 2, 1866, LS, AC, T; Sinclair to AAAG-TFB, May 19, 1866, ES, AC, T. Scott's regiment in bureau orders is listed as the Twenty-fifth Illinois, but it never served in Texas. A correct reference to the Twenty-ninth is in Cpt. E. Miller to AAAG-TFB, September 17, 1866, LR, AC, T. See also Dyer, *Compendium of the War of the Rebellion*, vol. 3, 1057–58.

17. Whitall, an agent of Provost Marshal Bvt. Lt. Col. Jacob C. De Gress, was formerly a lieutenant in the Second Illinois Battery. He operated out of Houston and saw that freedmen received their pay under De Gress's orders of November 19, 1865. See De Gress to AAAG-TFB, December–, 1865; L. C. Cumham & Co. to AAAG-TFB, November 20, 1865, LR, AC, T. General Kiddoo employed Whitall again, this time officially as a traveling agent, during the 1866 settlement season. See SO 116, October 3, 1866; SO 144, December 1, 1866, Ms. Orders, TFB.

18. SO 8, November 5, 1865, Ms. Orders, TFB; SO 55, October 14, 1865, Printed Orders, DT, RG 94, NA, Raper to AAAG-TFB, November 24, 29, December 26, 1865, January 15, 1866; Raper to Gregory, January 15, 1866, LR, AC, T; Gregory to AAAG-C, October 14, 1865; AAAG-TFB to Raper, November 28, 29, December 6, 1865, January 3, 20, 1866, LS, AC, T. See also Dyer, *Compendium of the War of the Rebellion*, vol. 3, 1508–1509. Years later Raper tried unsuccessfully to collect a salary; see AAAG-TFB to AAQM & DO-TFB, July 21, 1868, LS, AC, T; AAAG-TFB to AAAG-DT, July 21, 1868; Reynolds to Howard, November 28, 1868, ES, AC, T.

19. Gregory to AAAG-C, October 14, 1865; AAAG-TFB to Lt. John T. Raper, January 20, 1866, LS, AC, T; Mayor Fred Barnard to Hamilton, December 26, 1865, Governor's Papers (Hamilton), TSL. The policy on suspect subassistant commissioners is in Howard to Gregory, February 28, 1866, reprinted for the agents' own information in Circ. 7, March 6, 1866, Ms. Orders, AC, T.

20. SO 4, October 14, 1865; SO 49, March 10, 1866, Ms. Orders, TFB; Swingley to AAAG-TFB, November 25, 1865, RR, AC, T; Swingley to AAAG-TFB, November 1, 1865, January 11, February 28, 1866 (quotation), LR, AC, T. See also Dyer, *Compendium of the War of the Rebellion*, vol. 3, 1029.

21. AAAG-TFB to Lt. O. H. Swingley, January 17, 1866, LS, AC, T.

22. On J. S. Rand, see SO 29, January 1, 1866; SO 32, February 6, 1866; Ms. Orders, TFB. See also Dyer, *Compendium of the War of the Rebellion*, vol. 3, 1158–59.

23. See SO 16, December 15, 1865; SO 25, January 11, 1866, Ms. Orders, TFB; Dyer, *Compendium of the War of the Rebellion*, vol. 3, 1740.

24. Gregory to Howard, April 17, 1866, ES, AC, T.

25. SO 43, February 23, 1866, Ms. Orders, TFB; Jones to AAAG-TFB, February 21, 29, March 7, 13, April 5, 10, August 5, 1866, LR, AC, T; AAAG-TFB to Jones, March 7, 10, April 17, 1866; Gregory to AAAG-C, January 27, 1866, LS, AC, T; AAAG-TFB to Jones, May 2, December 13, 1866, ES, AC, T; SO 72, May 5, 1866, Ms. Orders, TFB. See also Dyer, *Compendium of the War of the Rebellion*, vol. 3, 1725.

26. Abbott to AAAG-TFB, [October–], October 25 (already proven, Nigger Driver), 31 (no amount), November 2 (thankless position, compelled to resign), 6, 16, 23, December 16, 1865, January 16, February 19, 1866, LR, AC, T; AAAG-TFB to Abbott, October 25, December 22, 1865, January 2, 22, February 14, 1866; Gregory to Abbott, November 4, 1865, LS, AC, T; SO 69, September 18, 1865, Ms. Orders, C; SO 6, October 19, 1865; SO 43, February 23, 1866; Ms. Orders, TFB; Kiddoo to Howard, August 29, 1866 (killed, very bad), ES, AC, T.

27. AAAG-TFB to Cpt. F. Holsinger, April 4, 1866, LS, AC, T; endorsements on letter of Holsinger to AAAG-TFB, March 13, 1866, ES, AC, T. Holsinger's own account of his military career is in "How Does One Feel under Fire?" 290–304.

28. SO 39, February 15, 1866, Ms. Orders, TFB; Cpt. F. A. Holsinger to AAAG-TFB, February 19, March 5 (severe cruelties), 19, 30, April 5, 1866, (but he'd be); Holsinger to AAAG-TFB, April 29, 1866 (permanent disability), LR, AC, T; AAAG-TFB to Holsinger, March 8, 1866; AAAG-TFB to Holsinger, April 4, 1866, LS, AC, T; Holsinger to Kiddoo, October 20, 1866 (to see him kick), LR, C; Gregory to AAAG-DT, April 17, 1866, ES, AC, T; SO 63, April 16, 1866, Ms. Orders, TFB. See also Cpt. John Moran to AAAG-DT, March 25, April 10, 1866, *House Executive Documents*, 40th Cong., 2nd sess., No. 57, 117–18; and Dyer, *Compendium of the War of the Rebellion*, vol. 3, 1726–27.

29. SO 21, January 2, 1866, Ms. Orders, TFB; Cpt. Stanton Weaver to AAAG-TFB, January 17, 22, 27, 31, February 28, 1866, March 20, April 5, LR, AC, T; AAAG-TFB to Weaver, January 29, February 12, 1866, LS, AC, T; AAAG-TFB to W. H. Cardiff et al., April 9, 1866, ES, AC, T; SO 44, February 25, 1866, Ms. Orders, TFB. See also Dyer, *Compendium of the War of the Rebellion*, vol. 3, 1733.

30. SO 17, December 17, 1866; SO 29, January 18, 1866, Ms. Orders, TFB; 1 Lt. E. Smith to AAAG-TFB, January 1, February 23, March 12, May 1, 1866, LR, AC, T; AAAG-TFB to Smith, March 2, 1866, LS, AC, T; AAAG-TFB to Smith, April 19, 1866, ES, AC, T; SO 72, May 5, 1866, Ms. Orders, TFB. See also Dyer, *Compendium of the War of the Rebellion*, vol. 3, 1725.

31. SO 1, October 6, 1865; SO 22, January 4, 1866, Ms. Orders, TFB; Hall to AAAG-TFB, November 1, 4, 6, December 9, 26, 30, 1865, LR, AC, T; Hall to

AAAG-TFB, December 9, 26, 1865, RR, AC, T; Gregory to AAAG-C, September 10, 1865; Gregory to Hall, October 17, 1865; AAAG-TFB to Hall, December 20, 1865, LS, AC, T. See also testimony of Bvt. Col. H. S. Hall in *House Reports*, 39th Cong., 1st sess., No. 30, 46–50. The record of the Forty-third USCI is in Dyer, *Compendium of the War of the Rebellion*, vol. 3, 1731. The rapport on racial issues between the men of the Eighth Illinois Infantry and white Texans is in Johnson Roney III, "Marshall, Texas," 165–77. But the regiment had the usual record of robbery, rape, and rowdiness associated with occupation troops. See Lale, "Military Occupation of Marshall, Texas," 39–47. Also of interest is Campbell, *Southern Community in Crisis*, 251–52, 257.

32. On Bayley, see note 34 below. GO 1, January 1, 1866, DT; GO 4, January 25, 1866, D of G, Printed Orders, RG 94, NA.

33. AAAG-TFB to Cpt. Byron Porter, February 14, 1866, LS, AC, T; AAAG-TFB to W. H. Farner, May 14, 1866, on letter of A. C. Hinton to AAAG-TFB, May 10, 1866, ES, AC, T. Headquarters refused to pay Hinton for services claimed as Farner's clerk.

34. Bayley's appointment is SO 22, January 4, 1866; Beebe's appointment is SO 64, April 17, 1866, Ms. Orders, TFB; Yates to Howard, October 7, 1865; Cpt. C. F. Ingersoll to Bayley, January 15, 1866; Bayley to AAAG-TFB, January 15, 17, February 28, March 25, 29, July 31, undated order [1866]; 1 Lt. I. M. Beebe to AAAG-TFB, June 6, July 16, 1866; LR, AC, T; Gregory to AAAG-C, December 6, 1865; AAAG-TFB to Bayley, January 29, April 17, 1866, LS, AC, T; AAAG-TFB to Bayley, June 1, July 21, 1866; Kiddoo to AAAG-DT, June 5, 1866; AAAG-TFB to Beebe, June 8, 1866; Kiddoo to Bvt. Maj. Gen. A. Baird, June 19, 1866; Kiddoo to Howard, July 20, 1866, ES, AC, T.

35. AAAG-TFB to Col. Thomas Bailey, January 29, 1866, April 17, 1866, LS, AC, T; SO 64, April 17, 1866, Ms. Orders, AC, T. Upon Beebe's arrival, the first thing Bailey did was to apply for a leave of absence. See Bailey to AAAG-TFB, May 1, 1866, LR, AC, T; endorsement of Gregory to Howard, May 8, 1866, ES, AC, T.

36. Gregory asked Howard for guidance on a plan to use these applicants, but got none. See Gregory to Howard, September 21, 1865, LS, AC, T.

37. See, for example, AAAG-TFB to A. K. Foster, September 21, 1865 (Texas), LS, AC, T; G. M. Marin to Hamilton, August 1, 1865 (Texas), Governor's Papers (Hamilton), TSL; Sam Earle to James H. Bell, October 13, 1865, Bell Papers, UT; and AAAG-TFB to J. H. Duval (re: Sam Earle), October 30, 1865 (Texas), LS, AC, T; AAAG-TFB to Martin K. Ryan, October 23, 1865 (Texas; also included recommendations from Pease and Paschal); AAAG-TFB to Joseph A. Wright, October 25, 1865 (Texas, with recommendation of Bvt. Maj. Gen. Joseph A. Mower); AAAG-TFB to John S. Blinn, February 16, 1866 (Illinois, with recommendation of Howard); AAAG-TFB to George L. Barnes, December 4, 1865 (Vermont); AAAG-TFB to W. P. Pray, December 4, 1865 (New Hampshire); AAAG-TFB to Frank G. Hayne, December 5, 1865 (Connecticut); AAAG-TFB to T. B. DeWees, March 22, 1866 (Pennsylvania); AAAG-TFB to E. H. Brier, April 10, 1866 (Illinois); AAAG-TFB to B. F. Barkley, March 7, 1866 (Texas); AAAG-TFB to A. P. Delano, March 7, 1866 (Texas), all in LS, AC, T.

38. The best example of this is AAAG-TFB to W. Longworth, December 27,

1865, LS, AC, T. It is not surprising that Gregory should turn to the Scalawags, as Texas had one of the largest such populations in the South. See Trelease, "Who Were the Scalawags?" 445–68, especially 458. See also Donald, "The Scalawag in Mississippi Reconsidered," 447–60; Olsen, "Reconsidering the Scalawags," 304–20; Alexander, "Persistent Whiggery in the Confederate South," 305–29; and Mehring, "Persistent Whiggery in the Confederate South," 124–43.

39. When he replaced Gregory as assistant commissioner in May, 1866, Bvt. Maj. Gen. Joseph B. Kiddoo remarked that he agreed with Gregory that the civilian subassistant commissioners could not be trusted. Kiddoo to Howard, May 14, 1866, LR, C. See also Gregory to Howard, September 21, 1865, where Gregory refers to certain "classes to be suspect" desiring subassistant commissioner positions. Broadly defined, Scalawags were generally those who were born in or came to the South before the war and were loyal to the Union cause, regardless of their war records. They were a very diverse group. A good study is Wetta, "Louisiana Scalawags." His inclusive use of the term is confirmed in a related work, Current, *Those Terrible Carpetbaggers*, 121, 437n.16. Also of interest are Ellem, "Who Were the Mississippi Scalawags?" 349–72; and Lancaster, "Scalawags of North Carolina."

40. Six planter-businessmen volunteered for the bureau: J. F. Brown, Grimes County, SO 3, October 11, 1865; W. H. Farner, Brazos County, SO 14, December 4, 1865; F. D. Inge, Leon County, SO 15, December 5, 1865; J. W. McConaughey, Wharton County, SO 16, December 10, 1865; James A. Hogue, Polk County, SO 41, February 21, 1866; Champ Clark, Jr., Robertson County, SO 53, March 17, 1866, all in Ms. Orders, AC, T.

41. Agents' duties were similar to those of the county judge. The subassistant commissioner handled any matter involving freedmen's affairs, while the county judge was restricted to whites' legal problems. See AAAG-TFB to Champ Carter, Jr., April 28, 1866, LS, AC, T. The three judges who served as agents were: J. T. Whitesides, Grimes County, SO 10, November 28, 1865; William Longworth, Wilson (later Guadalupe) County, SO 18, December 27, 1865; J. Orville Shelby, Liberty County, SO 35, February 9, 1866; all in Ms. Orders, AC, T. These state officers are also listed in "Election Register, 1865–1866 (2-1/7, 2-1/8)," vols. 261 and 262, Ms. copy, TSL.

42. The county commissioner was Philip Howard, Bosque County, SO 20, December 30, 1865. The postmasters were A. P. Delano, Falls County, SO 20, December 30, 1865; and Ira P. Pedigo, Tyler County, SO 12, December 3, 1865. The bureau appointments are all in Ms. Orders, AC, T. The county commissioner appointment is in "Election Register (2-1/8)," vol. 262, Ms. copy, TSL. The postmasters are listed in "Postmasters Appointment Record, 1858–1867," Texas Registers of Appointments, RG 28, NA.

43. Any of these men who questioned the no-salary policy later were told to accept the terms or resign. See AAAG-TFB to Champ Carter, Jr., April 25, 1866, LS, AC, T.

44. John F. Brown to AAAG-TFB, October 2, December 1, 1865, February 28, July 25, August 30, 1866, LR, AC, T; AAAG-TFB to Brown, March 8, 1866, LS, AC, T; SO 3, October 11, 1865 (appointment); SO 107, September 5, 1866 (removal); Ms. Orders, TFB.

45. SO 10, November 28, 1865, Ms. Orders, TFB; J. T. Whitesides to AAAG-TFB, November 29, December 1, 1865, LR, AC, T.

46. AAAG-TFB to Whitesides, December 11, 1865, LS, AC, T; Whitesides to AAAG-TFB, December 8, 1865, January 25, March 8, 1866 (quotation), LR, AC, T.

47. Whitesides to AAAG-TFB, April 24, 1866, LR, AC, T; AAAG-TFB to Whitesides, April 28, 1866, LS, AC, T; DeWitt C. Brown to AAAG-TFB, March 7, 1867, ROC, AC, T.

48. For Whitesides's recommendation, see Gregory to Whitesides, December 4, 1865, LS, AC, T. See also SO 15, December 5, 1865, Ms. Orders, TFB; F. D. Inge to AAAG-TFB, January 25, February 17, May 12, June 17, July 13, 30, August 5, 1866; 1 Lt. C. H. Bussom to AAAG-TFB, March 22, 1866 (getting along); LR, AC, T; and AAAG-TFB to Inge, February 22, 1866, LS, AC, T.

49. SO 14, December 4, 1865, Ms. Orders, TFB; W. H. Farner to AAAG-TFB, November 25, 1865, January 22, February 1, March 11, April 12, 1866, LR, AC, T.

50. Farner to AAAG-TFB, May 1, 1866; Charles Harrison to AAAG-TFB, May 5, 1866 (quotation), LR, AC, T; AAAG-TFB to Farner, May 14, 1866; AAAG-TFB to A. C. Keaton, September 11, 1866; Reynolds to Howard, April 27, 1868, ES, AC, T; SO 75, May 10, 1866, Ms. Orders, TFB. General Reynolds later made Farner the clerk of the district court in Freestone County; see SO 149, June 24, 1869, Printed Orders, FMD, RG 94, NA.

51. H. C. Pedigo's positions are listed in "Election Register (2-1/7)," vol. 261, Ms. copy, TSL; SO 206, November 11, 1867; SO 78, April 13, 1868; SO 144, August 18, 1868; Printed Orders, DT, RG 94, NA. Ira P. Pedigo's postmastership is in "Postmasters Appointment Record, 1867–1877," Texas Registers of Appointments, RG 28, NA; his bureau office in SO 12, December 3, 1865, Ms. Orders, TFB.

52. AAAG to W. L. Gordon, March 22, 1866, LS, AC, T; I. P. Pedigo to AAAG-TFB, March 1, August 6, November 19, 22, 1866, LR, AC, T. See also H. C. Pedigo to AAAG-TFB, December 15, 1866, LR, AC, T. Ira Pedigo was asked to investigate one other case of nonpayment of wages after his resignation as a special assignment. See AAAG-TFB to Pedigo, December 21, 1866, LS, AC, T. The resignation is in SO 143, November 30, 1866, Ms. Orders, TFB.

53. On Shelby's job record, see "Election Register (2-1/7)," vol. 261, Ms. Copy, TSL; "Postmasters Appointment Record, 1867–1877," Texas Registers of Appointments, RG 28, NA; GO 18, February 1, 1870, Printed Orders, FMD, RG, 94, NA; and SO 35, February 9, 1866, Ms. Orders, TFB. See also H. C. Pedigo to AAAG-TFB, January 27, 1866; Shelby to AAAG-TFB, July 18 ("incarserated," Radical), 20, 1866 (malcontents); Ira P. Pedigo to AAAG-TFB, August 20, 1866; LR, AC, T; Shelby to AAAG-TFB, May 6, 1866, ES, AC, T; AAAG-TFB to Shelby, August 16, 1866, LS, AC, T; SO 98, August 10, 1866, Ms. Orders, TFB.

54. See H. C. Pedigo to AAAG-TFB, January 25, 1866, LR, AC, T; SO 44, February 21, 1866, Ms. Orders, TFB; Cpt. W. H. Redman to Lt. Col. E. H. Powell, April 16, 1866, *House Executive Documents*, 40th Cong., 2nd Sess., No. 57, 124; Redman to AAAG-TFB, May 1, 1866; O. A. McGinnis to AAAG-TFB, August 22, 1866 (to a T); G. W. Davis to AAAG-TFB, June 15, 1866; James Hogue to AAAG-TFB, July 13, 18, 1866; LR, AC, T; SO 100, August 16, 1866, Ms. Orders, TFB.

55. SO 20, December 30, 1865, Ms. Orders, TFB; Thomas Ford, Philip How-

ard, and S. S. Nichols to A. J. Hamilton, September 6, 1865; Governor's Papers (Hamilton), TSL; AAAG to Howard, December 30, 1865, LS, AC, T. Howard's governmental appointments are in "Election Register (2-1/7)," vol. 261, Ms. copy, TSL.

56. Howard to AAAG-TFB, March 22 (sparits; kneed), April 1, 1866 (I cannot buy), LR, AC, T.

57. SO 20, December 30, 1865, Ms. Orders, TFB; A. P. Delano to AAAG-TFB, March 26 (consil) April 24 (sees, few barrels), 28, 1866, LR, AC, T; AAAG-TFB to Delano, May 3, 1866, LS, AC, T; AAAG-TFB to F. B. Sturgis, July 13, 1867, ES, AC, T. See also Delano to AAAG-TFB, January 6, 1867, ROC, AC, T.

58. One agent tried to appoint his own sheriff, but Gregory told him to call on the army instead. AAAG-TFB to Champ Carter, Jr., April 25, 1866, LS, AC, T.

59. Gregory to J. A. Wright, [November 9, 1865]; AAAG-TFB to A. D. Elam, January 25, 1866, LS, AC, T; AAAG-TFB to W. H. Cardiff et al., April 9, 1866, ES, AC, T. Weaver's muster-out is in SO 44, February 25, 1866, Ms. Orders, AC, T. His replacement's arrival is in Maj. L. S. Barnes to AAAG-TFB, April 11, 1866, RR, AC, T.

60. There were probably two agents loose illegally in Colorado County. See AAAG-TFB to Fred Miller, January 17, 1866; AAAG-TFB to Lt. John Raper, November 28, 1865; LS, AC, T. Miller received his appointment from Boatswain George Abbot. Raper was to look for a "Whithall." It is not clear if he ever found the man, who appears to have been the agent De Gress sent out from Houston to enforce cotton payments to the freedmen.

61. AAAG-TFB to W. H. Farner, January 22, 1866, LS, AC, T. Farner's appointment, Champ Carter, Jr., later received an agency in his own right from Gregory. See SO 53, March 17, 1866, Ms. Orders, AC, T.

62. AAAG-TFB to Philip Howard, December 30, 1865, AAAG-TFB to F. W. Grassmeyer, February 7, 1866, LS, AC, T.

63. AAAG-TFB to Lt. Eugene Smith, March 2, 1866, LS, AC, T.

64. AAAG-TFB to John R. Shackleford, February 17, 1866; AAAG-TFB to William P. Booth et al., March 12, 1866; AAAG-TFB to Martin W. Wayne, March 23, 1866, LS, AC, T.

65. AAAG-TFB to Lt. S. P. Hines, December 5, 1865, LS, AC, T.

66. Philip Howard to AAAG-TFB, April 30, 1866, RR, AC, T.

67. J. W. McConaughey to AAAG-TFB, May 2, 1866; W. Longworth to AAAG-TFB, April 30, 1866; Philip Howard to AAAG-TFB, May 1, 1866; J. T. Whitesides to AAAG-TFB, March 31, 1866, RR, AC, T.

68. Philip Howard to AAAG-TFB, April 30, 1866, RR, AC, T; Gregory to Howard, January 3, 1866; and AAAG-TFB to all SACs, October 17, 1865, LS, AC, T.

69. Bvt. Cpt. Charles F. Rand to AAAG-TFB, May 1, 1866, RR, AC, T; Bvt. Brig. Gen. S. D. Sturgis to AAAG-DT, April 13, 1866, *House Executive Documents*, 40th Cong., 2nd Sess., No. 57, 123.

70. Reports of Maj. A. H. Longholy, March 25, 1866; 1 Lt. A. J. Norton, March 25, 1866; Cpt. William C. Wilson, March 25, 1866; Cpt. John C. Cashen, March 29, 1866; Cpt. Gallis Fairman, March 26, 1866 (high crime); Cpt. A. W. Evans, April 3, 1866; Cpt. J. P. Gillespie, April 26, 1866; Cpt. H. Lossberg, March 25,

1866; Cpt. George H. Merrill, March 25, 1866; Lt. Col. E. H. Powell, March 25, 1866 (unconquered opinion), Bvt. Maj. Gen. George W. Getty, May 1, 1866; Cpt. Thomas McCarty, April 25, 1866, in *House Executive Documents*, 40 Cong., 2nd Sess., No. 57, 98, 99, 102, 109, 114–15, 117, 118–19, 121, 125.

71. See reports of Lt. Col. R. Kennecott, March 21, 1866 (legally loyal, kindly treated), Cpt. John J. DeLacy, March 25, 1866 (braggadocio style, Yankees and niggers); Lt. Col. James R. Lynch, March 25, 1866 (well-disposed); 1 Lt. L. C. Mayer, April 10, 1866, all in ibid., 98, 99–100, 103–104, 120.

72. Report of Capt. John Moran, March 25, 1866, April 10, 1866, ibid., 117, 118; 1 Lt. Charles C. Hardenbrook to AAAG-TFB, LR, AC, T; AAAG-TFB to Hardenbrook, April 27, 1866, LS, AC, T.

73. Report of Bvt. Brig. Gen. James Shaw, Jr., April 16, May 1, 1866, *House Executive Documents*, 40th Cong., 2nd Sess., No. 57, 96–97.

74. AAAG-TFB to Cpt. Samuel C. Sloan, May 5, 1866, LS, AC, T.

75. A good example is Gregory to AAAG, DT, February 21, 1866, LS, AC, T.

3: Not as Wise as a Serpent

1. For Howard's commitment, see Carpenter, *Sword and Olive Branch*, 154; Bentley, *History of the Freedmen's Bureau*, 169–84; Pierce, *Freedmen's Bureau*, 75–86; Olds, "Freedmen's Bureau as a Social Agency," 85–86. Gregory's pledge is in Gregory to Howard, September 21, 1865, LS, AC, T. The standard study of bureau education efforts in Texas is Hornsby, Jr., "Freedmen's Bureau Schools in Texas," 397–417. In addition to Hornsby's work, black education in Texas from the freedmen's perspective is studied by Smallwood, "Education and Black Self-Help," in his *Time of Hope, Time of Despair*, 69–95, a shorter summary of which appeared as "Early 'Freedom Schools'," 790–93. Also relevant here is Thompson, "Influence of the Freedmen's Bureau on the Education of the Negro in Texas"; and Chunn, "Education and Politics"; Christopher, "History of Negro Public Education in Texas"; White, "History of Education in Texas"; Davis, *Development and Present Status of Negro Education in East Texas*; Erby, *Development of Education in Texas*; Heintzen, *Private Black Colleges in Texas*, Drake, "American Missionary Association and the Southern Negro"; and Bullock, *History of Negro Education in the South from 1619 to the Present*.

2. Stanley's testimony is in "Report of the Joint Committee on Reconstruction," *House Reports*, 39th Cong., 1st Sess., No. 30, pt. 4, 40; Gregory to Howard, September 21, 1865, LS, AC, T.

3. Wheelock's appointment is in SO 2, October 9, 1865, and confirmed in Circ. 2, December 5, 1865, Ms. Orders, AC, T. His absence is noted in AAAG-TFB to George W. Grant, October 25, 1865; AAAG-TFB to 1 Lt. O. H. Swingley, December 4, 1865; AAAG-TFB to H. W. Sharp, March 22, 1866, LS, AC, T. Wheelock is a controversial figure in Texas Reconstruction, a man who could be combative, arrogant, and smug in both his opinions and his actions. A very favorable biographical sketch of him appears in the series of essays by Kassel: "Edwin Miller Wheelock and the Abolition Movement," 166–75; "Edwin Miller Wheelock: A Prophet of the Civil War Times," 116–27; "Interpreter of Destiny,"

406–18, "Herald of Emancipation," 230–42; "Knight Errant in the Department of the Gulf," 563–76; "Educating the Slave," 239–56; and "Edwin Miller Wheelock," 564–69.

4. E. M. Wheelock to Gregory, January 31, 1866, RR, AC, T; Gregory to Howard, February 28, April 18, 1866, LR, C. See also Elliott, "Freedmen's Bureau in Texas," 10 n. 22.

5. Hornsby, "Freedmen's Bureau Schools in Texas," 398–400. The topic of the bureau and black education has received much attention. See, for example, Alderson, "Freedmen's Bureau and Negro Education in Virginia," 64–90; Alexander, "Hostility and Hope," 113–32; Jackson, "Educational Efforts of the Freedmen's Bureau," 1–40; Abbott, "Freedmen's Bureau and Negro Schooling in South Carolina," 65–81, Jones, *Soldiers of Light and Love*; Owen, "Negro in Georgia during Reconstruction"; Drago, "Black Georgia during Reconstruction"; Thornberry, "Northerns and the Atlanta Freedmen," 236–51; Rosen, "Influence of the Peabody Fund," 310–20; Proctor, "Yankee 'Schoolmarms' in Post-war Florida," 275–77; White, "Alabama Freedmen's Bureau and Black Education," 107–24; Campbell, "Exploring the Roots of Tougaloo College," 15–27; Smith, "Ohio Quakers and the Mississippi Freedmen," 159–71; White, *Freedmen's Bureau in Louisiana*, 166–200; Pearce, "Enoch K. Miller and the Freedmen's Schools," 305–27; and his "American Missionary Association and the Freedmen's Bureau in Arkansas," 123–44, 246–61; Christensen, "Schools for Blacks," 212–35; Kimball, "Freedom's Harvest," 272–88; Putney, "Baltimore Normal School for the Education of Colored Teachers," 238–52; Halstead, "Delaware Association for the Moral Improvement and Education of the Colored People," 19–40; Parmet, "Schools for the Freedmen," 128–32; West, "Peabody Fund and Negro Education," 3–21; Brown, "Lyman Abbott and Freedmen's Aid," 49–92; Wesley, "Forty Acres and a Mule and a Speller," 113–27; Swint, *Northern Teacher in the South*; Morris, "Reading, Riting, and Reconstruction"; Small, "Yankee School Marm in Southern Freedmen's Schools"; Butchart, *Northern Schools, Southern Blacks, and Reconstruction*.

6. E. M. Wheelock to Gregory, January 31, 1866, RR, AC, T; Pease to Carrie [his daughter], March 30, 1866, Pease-Niles-Graham Papers, APL. One wonders whether Pease's somewhat condescending praise held the ultimate seeds of failure for the whole program.

7. D. J. Baldwin to Hamilton, November 7, 1865, Governor's Papers (Hamilton), TSL.

8. A few examples will suffice. The letters are numerous. See Gregory to Messrs. Holman Brothers, October 30, 1865; Gregory to AC-Georgia, September 19, 1865; Gregory to AC-Louisiana, February 7, 1866; AAAG-TFB to A. P. Delano, April 17, 1866; Gregory to AC-Tennessee, May 8, 1866, LS, AC, T; Gregory to AAAG-C, May 8, 1866, LR, C.

9. Gregory to AC-Louisiana, September 15, October 3, 1865, LS, AC, T.

10. AAAG-TFB to AC-Louisiana, April 14, 1866, LS, AC, T.

11. Howard, Circ. Letter, October 4, 1865, LS, C.

12. See Circ. 1, October 12, 1865, Ms. Orders, AC, T; the army policy was in GO 3, June 19, 1865, Printed Orders, DT, RG 94, NA.

13. Gregory to 2 Lt. B. J. Arnold, November [4], 1865, January 25, 1866; AAAG-

TFB to J. W. McConaughey, May 9, 1866, LS, AC, T; W. H. Farner to AAAG-TFB, May 1, 1866, RR, AC, T.

14. AAAG-TFB to J. W. McConaughey, February 5, 1866; AAAG-TFB to Cpt. Samuel C. Sloan, April 6, 1866; AAAG-TFB to 2 Lt. A. A. Metzner, May 2, 1866; LS, AC, T.

15. See AAAG-TFB to G. W. McMahon, December 4, 1865; AAAG-TFB to James R. Dial, March 19, 1866; AAAG-TFB to Dr. R. C. Nelson, March 22, 1866; AAAG-TFB to Judge Edward Austin, March 22, 1866, LS, AC, T. See also Austin to AAAG-TFB, March 21, 1866, LR, AC, T.

16. Gregory to 2 Lt. B. J. Arnold, November [4], 1865; AAAG-TFB to J. W. McConaughey, February 5, 1866; AAAG-TFB to Philip Howard, April 17, 1866; AAAG-TFB to Ira P. Pedigo, April 17, 1866; AAAG to 2 Lt. A. A. Metzner, May 2, 1866; LS, AC, T; AAAG-TFB to 1 Lt. Levi Jones, May 2, 8, 1866, ES, AC, T. In one case, the freed child's mother asked the bureau to find a home for her eight-year-old daughter. See AAAG-TFB to John Robertson, May 14, 1866, LS, AC, T.

17. Kidnapping in AAAG-TFB to W. Longworth, March 27, 1866; denial of access to spouse or child in AAAG-TFB to Provost Marshal at Houston, October 1, 1865; Gregory to Judge ____ Chambers, October 27, 1865; inaction by agent in AAAG-TFB to Cpt. J. B. Bostwick, January 2, March 6, 1866; AAAG-TFB to Cpt. Samuel C. Sloan, April 6, 1866; all in LS, AC, T. The Brazos County Report in W. H. Farner to AAAG-TFB, May 1, 1866, RR, AC, T.

18. Howard, Circ. Letter, March 2, 1866, LS, C. For more on this topic, see Crouch, "Black Dreams and White Justice," 260–63; Crouch and Madaras, "Reconstructing Black Families," 109–22; Scott, "Battle over the Child," 101–13; Moran, "Negro Dependent Child in Louisiana," 185–86.

19. Circ. 9, March 23, 1866, Ms. Orders, AC, T.

20. AAAG-TFB to AAAG-C, April 11, 1866; AAAG-TFB to Hamilton, April 11, 1866; LS, AC, T. Hamilton's edict is appended to Circ. 9, March 23, 1866, Ms. Orders, AC, T. See also Crouch and Madaras, "Reconstructing the Black Family," 109–22; Smallwood, "Emancipation and the Black Family," 849–57; Everly, "Marriage Registers of Freedmen," 150–54; Gutman, "Slave Family and Its Legacies," 183–211; Olds, "Freedmen's Bureau as a Social Agency," 182–85.

21. Howard to Cpt. Charles C. Soulé, June 21, 1865, LS, C.

22. AAAG-TFB to Cpt. Byron Porter, January 26, 1866, LS, AC, T.

23. AAAG-DT to AAAG-C, February 17, 1866, LR, C; Porter to AAAG-TFB, September 12, 1866; De Gress to AAAG-TFB, July 31, 1866, LR, AC, T; AAAG-TFB to Porter, September 25, 1866, LS, AC, T; SO 102, July 25, 1866, Ms. Orders, C; SO 115, September 25, 1866, Ms. Orders, TFB.

24. For a loyalist's protest of bureau interference, see Judge B. W. Gray to Hamilton, November 30, 1865, Governor's Papers (Hamilton), TSL. Gregory's policy is in Gregory to Cpt. ____ Grew, October 30, 1865; AAAG-TFB to Maj. L. S. Barnes, April 19, 1866; and Gregory to Judge H. B. Pruitt, January 19, 1866; LS, AC, T. For an army officer interfering with a local court decision, see Col. Edward Colyer to J. L. Cunningham, March 5, 1866; Cunningham to Hamilton, March 8, 1866; Governor's Papers (Hamilton), TSL.

25. Hamilton to Sheridan, February 26, 1866; Lt. Col. E. H. Powell to AAAG-DT, March 27, 1866. *House Executive Documents*, 40th Cong., 2nd Sess., No. 57, 26, 100; AAAG-TFB to F. D. Inge, March 27, 1866, LS, AC, T.

26. See Ira F. Pedigo to Gregory, [January 31, 1866), RR, AC, T.

27. See GO 5, January 27, 1866; Circ. 3, April 17, 1866, Printed Orders, DT, RG 94, NA; Circ. 7, March 6, 1866; Circ. 10, April 23, 1866, Ms. Orders, AC, T, AAAG-TFB to Maj. L. S. Barnes, April 24, 1866; AAAG-TFB to W. Longworth, May 2, 1866, LS, AC, T.

28. J. R. Burns to Hamilton, November 15, 1865, Governor's Papers (Hamilton), TSL.

29. SO 16, December 15, 1865, Ms. Orders, TFB; J. W. McConaughey to AAAG-TFB, February 24, 1866 (all quotations), LR, AC, T.

30. McConaughey to AAAG-TFB, March 28 (all quotations), May 2, 1866, LR, AC, T.

31. AAAG-TFB to J. W. McConaughey, May 11, 1866, LS, AC, T.

32. C. M. Garrett and fourteen others to AAAG-TFB, February 12, 1866; A. P. Delano to AAAG-TFB, [late February, 1866?], J. T. Garrett to Messrs. Ranger & Co., March 7, 1866; J. Norris to Gus ___, March 17, 1866 (quotations), LR, AC, T; AAAG-TFB to Delano, March 7, 1866, LS, AC, T; SO 57, March 17, 1866, Ms. Orders, TFB.

33. Champ Carter, Jr., to AAAG-TFB, April 19 (former agent), May 1, 1866, LR, AC, T.

34. AAAG-TFB to Champ Carter, Jr., April 25, 1866, LS, AC, T; AAAG-TFB to 2nd Lt. B. J. Arnold, April 19, 1866; and AAAG-TFB to Cpt. J. Ferguson, May 7, 1866, ES, AC, T.

35. AAAG-TFB to J. T. Whitesides, January 29, 1866, LS, AC, T. Gregory continually referred cases to his agents for investigation locally. See AAAG-TFB to J. O. Shelby, April 18, 1866, ibid.

36. AAAG-TFB to W. H. Farner, March 12, 1866, LS, AC, T.

37. See AAAG-TFB to W. H. Farner, December 15, 30, 1865, February 17, April 3, 1866; AAAG-TFB to 1 Lt. Levi Jones, March 7, 10, April 17, 1866; AAAG-TFB to Lt. Col. Jacob De Gress, October 16, 1865; AAAG-TFB to 1 Lt. Eugene Smith, December 27, 1865; AAAG-TFB to Cpt. Edward Miller, May 9, 1866; AAAG-TFB to AAAG-DT, May 10, 1866; all in LS, AC, T. See also AAAG-TFB to 1 Lt. Eugene Smith, April 19, 1866, ES, AC, T.

38. The examples in LS, AC, T are endless. See, for example, AAAG-TFB to Captain of the Steamer *Peabody*, [December] 2, 1865; Gregory to Mr. ___ Thompson, November 4, 1865; AAAG-TFB to Sheriff of Galveston County, May 12, 1866; AAAG-TFB to J. G. Sewall, May 11, 1866, all in ibid.

39. See AAAG-TFB to Cpt. Stanton Weaver, February 19, 1866; AAAG-TFB to Cpt. John T. Raper, January 3, 1866; AAAG-TFB to Cpt. Samuel C. Sloan, January 15, 1866; AAAG-TFB to CO, Post of Brenham, October 9, 1865; LS, AC, T. See also AAAG-TFB to AAAG-C, February 17, 1866, LR, C.

40. Gregory to Benjamin Harris, January 20, 1866, LS, AC, T.

41. The best account of Affleck is Cole, "Texas Career of Thomas Affleck." For Affleck as a typical Texas planter, see ibid., 201. Planter reactions to emancipation and free labor are covered in Roark, *Masters without Slaves*. Also of interest

is the reaction of Northerners who came South to manage plantations after the war in Powell, *New Masters.*

42. Affleck to E. H. Cushing, July 24, 1865, letter book, Affleck Papers, LSU.

43. Affleck to Alexander Hannay, July 14, 1865, ibid.

44. Cole, "Texas Career of Thomas Affleck," 201–202.

45. Affleck to E. H. Cushing, July 24, 1865, letter book, Affleck Papers, LSU.

46. Affleck to his sister, July 22, 1865, ibid.

47. Affleck to Cpt. T. S. Post, September 5, 1865, ibid.

48. Affleck to Lt. B. J. Arnold, November 12, 1865, ibid.

49. Arnold to AAAG-TFB, October 20, 28, December 2, 1865, January 16, April 28 (quotation) 1866, March 22, 1868, LR, AC, T; AAAG-TFB to Arnold, December 27, 1865, January 25, March 13, 1866, March 18, 1868, LS, AC, T; Gregory to Howard, April 16, 1866; Gregory to AAAG-DT, May 3, 1866; ES, AC, T; SO 4, October 14, 1865; SO 69, April 30, 1866, Ms. Orders, TFB. See also Dyer, *Compendium of the War of the Rebellion*, vol. 3, 1029. Arnold was the man who received the task of investigating the letters that ultimately resulted in Gregory's recall as assistant commissioner. When his regiment was demobilized, Arnold stayed in Washington County and went into farming. He was offered another bureau position, but he refused to move to Cotton Gin and leave Brenham. He also declined to serve Washington County as a voter registrar under military appointment, but he later agreed to be assessor and collector of taxes for the county. His political activity is in SO 179, October 8, 1869, and SO 195, April 24, 1869, Printed Orders, FMD, RG 94, NA, and "List of Registrars and Clerks in Texas, October–November 1869," Ms. vol. 85, AC, T, under "Post of Brenham, Washington County."

50. Gregory to W. J. Jones, September, 1865, LS, AC, T.

51. Mrs. Caleb G. Forshey to Andrew Johnson, October 19, 1865, LR, C.

52. The bureau investigation can be traced in Gregory to Howard, April 16, 1866, ES, AC, T; the army inquiry is in Howard to Maj. Gen. Philip H. Sheridan, December 2, 1865; and the results presented in Howard to Gregory, March 3, 1866, LS, C.

53. Howard to Gregory, March 3, 1866, LS, C.

54. Gregory to Howard, March 17, 1866, LR, C.

55. Burnet to Editor, January 26, 1866, to Galveston *Daily News*, January 28, 1866.

56. Burnet to Editor, March 3, 1866, in Galveston *Daily News*, March 3, 1866.

57. Howard to Gregory, March 3, 1866, LS, C, spoke of the anonymous informants; Circ. 11, July 12, 1865, Ms. Orders, C, FB, warned bureau personnel against making controversial speeches, Gregory's relief is in SO 46, March 30, 1866; and the praise quoted appears in SO 48, April 2, 1866; both in Ms. Orders, C, FB. Gregory's ensuing career is from SO 115, August 7; SO 129, August 29, 1866; ibid. Gregory later had Delaware added to his new district, SO 7, January 16, 1867, ibid. Gregory also had his defenders in Texas. See, for example, C. Caldwell and A. P. Wiley to Howard, n.d. [1866], LR, C.

58. Gregory to Howard, April 18, 1866, LS, AC, T.

59. Gregory was the only Texas assistant commissioner so praised by Howard; see SO 48, April 2, 1866, Ms. Orders, C, FB.

60. Gregory to Howard, June 18, 1866, LR, C.

4: A VIGOROUS SYSTEM OF LABOR

1. Galveston *Daily News*, June 20, 1866.

2. Kiddoo's wartime career is listed in Heitman, *Historical Register*, vol. 1, 596; and Boatner, *Civil War Dictionary*, 458–59. For the record of the regiments in which Kiddoo served, see Dyer, *Compendium of the War of the Rebellion*, vol. 3, 1582–83 (Twelfth Pennsylvania), 1595–96 (Sixty-third Pennsylvania), 1615 (137th Pennsylvania), 1724 (Sixth USCI), 1727 (Twenty-second USCI). The charges against Kiddoo are in Cpt. Arthur P. Morey and six others to AAAG-Army of the James, October 30, November 30, 1864, *OR*, vol. 42, pt. 3, 442, 762–64; the defense of Kiddoo is in Col. Alonzo G. Draper (his division commander) to AAAG-XVIII Corps, October 30, 1864; the endorsements to Morey's complaint of Col. Draper, November 3, 1864; and Bvt. Maj. Gen. G. Weitzel (his corps commander), November 3, 1864, in ibid., pt. 1, 814–17 (utter disregard); and ibid., pt. 3, 443 (finest gentleman).

3. Kiddoo's injury is described in Otis (ed.), *Medical and Surgical History*, vol. 2 (Injuries to the Pelvis), pt. 2 (Surgical History), 234 (all quotations). See also Custer, *Tenting on the Plains*, 305, whose husband described Kiddoo's wound and problems to her. Kiddoo's birthdate is given as 1840 by Boatner, *Civil War Dictionary*, 458–59, but doctors listed his age as thirty in 1864; see Otis, *Medical and Surgical History*, vol. 2, pt. 2, 234. He died on August 19, 1880; see Heitman, *Historical Register*, vol. 1, 596. Kiddoo's assignment to Texas is SO 48, April 2, 1866, Ms. Orders, C, FB, reissued as part of Circ. 13, May 14, 1866, Ms. Orders, TFB; the difficult trip to Texas is in Kiddoo to Howard, May 14, 1866, LR, C. For a recommendation of Kiddoo, see Bvt. Maj. Gen. Wager Swayne to A. J. Hamilton, April 20, 1866, Governor's Papers (Hamilton), TSL.

4. Kiddoo to Howard, May 14, 1866, LS, AC, T. Kiddoo's assumption of command is Circ. 13, May 14, 1866, Ms. Orders, AC, T.

5. 1 Lt. I. M. Beebe to AAAG-DT, May 26, 1866, LR, DT, RG 393, NA; Champ Carter, Jr., to AAAG-TFB, May 26, 1866 (quotations), LR, AC, T.

6. Circ. 14, May 15, 1866, Ms. Orders, AC, T.

7. Kiddoo to Howard, May 28, 1866, LR, C.

8. Circ. 17, June 19, 1866, Ms. Orders, AC, T.

9. Maj. L. S. Barnes to AAAG-TFB, June 14, 1866; Champ Carter, Jr., to AAAG-TFB, June 19, 1866 (your views); 1 Lt. C. C. Hardenbrook to AAAG-TFB, June 29, 1866; J. W. McConaughey to AAAG-TFB, July 8, 1866; Cpt. H. W. Allen to AAAG-TFB, July 12, 1866; 1 Lt. A. A. Metzner to AAAG-TFB, August 14, 1866; Cpt. Albert Evans to AAAG-TFB, October 31, 1866 (sharp stick), all in LR, AC, T.

10. 1 Lt. J. Ernest Goodman to AAAG-TFB, July 31, 1866 (physical disability); Champ Carter, Jr., to AAAG-TFB, September 13, 1866; H. C. Pedigo to AAAG-TFB, January 12, 1866; James Hogue to AAAG-TFB, July 17, 18, 1866; G. W. Davis to AAAG-TFB, June 15, 1866, ibid.

11. Kiddoo's estimation of his action is confirmed in Cpt. Byron Porter to AAAG-TFB, June 8, 1866; Maj. L. S. Barnes to AAAG-TFB, June 14, 1866; Champ Carter, Jr., to AAAG-TFB, June 30, 1866, ibid.

12. Kiddoo to Howard, July 23, 1866, LR, C.

13. J. H. Thomason to AAAG-TFB, June 26, 1866; James M. Alexander to

AAAG-TFB, September 12, 1866; and J. G. Sanderson to "Gen'l Cadoe," October 31, 1866, LR, AC, T.

14. Kiddoo to AAAG-C, August 29, 1866, LR, C, for an example of an approved Texas contract. AAAG-TFB to J. M. Roak, July 28, 1866, LS, AC, T, for a disallowed contract drawn up by a private party that extended over a year in length, and provided insufficient compensation for freedwomen, and a legal statement that the bureau could not compel anyone to keep a contract, but merely adjudicate complaints as they were raised.

15. J. Q. A. Carter to Kiddoo, October 16, 1866, LR, AC, T; AAAG-TFB to Carter, November 5, 1866, LS, AC, T.

16. Kiddoo to Howard, July 23, 1866, LR, C. On the Texas Land, Labor, & Immigration Co., see Cole, "Texas Career of Thomas Affleck," 227–46.

17. Howard to Kiddoo, September 11, 1866, LS, C. Kiddoo had written Howard a second time on August 24, 1866 (LS, AC, T), and sent his own agent, L. M. E. Ricks, to Washington to coordinate immigration efforts, even before receiving Howard's approval. See Kiddoo to Howard, August 30, September 30, 1866, LS, AC, T.

18. See, for example, Kiddoo to AC-Georgia, August 28, November 7, December 21, 22, 24, 1866, January 5, 1867 (bread-stuff enough); Kiddoo to AC-Alabama, August 28, November 21, 1866; AAAG-TFB to AC-South Carolina, November 21, 1866, January 5, 1867; Kiddoo to AC-North Carolina, October 11, December 20, 1866; Kiddoo to AC-Louisiana, August 13, 1866; Kiddoo to AC-any Southern state, October 11, December 29, 31, January __, 1867 (two letters); all in LS, AC, T. See further AAAG-TFB to R. F. Flewellen, September 14, 1866; AAAG-TFB to Cpt. Edward Miller, October 20, 1866; AAAG-TFB to J. L. Throp, October 27, 1866; AAC to all ACs, December 27, 1866 (greatly for the benefit), all in ES, AC, T. See also Kiddoo to Agent, Houston Steamers, January 7, 1867; and Kiddoo to Agent, Texas Central Railroad, January 7, 1867; LS, AC, T. Even Commissioner Howard intervened upon Kiddoo's behalf; see Howard to Maj. Gen. P. H. Sheridan, September 16, 1866, LS, C. The whole system was promulgated in Circ. 24, December 20, 1866.

19. Kiddoo to Howard, August 8, 20, 1866, LS, AC, T. Kiddoo gracefully gave most of the credit for the good harvest to Gregory's earlier administration, although planters credited Kiddoo and Circular Orders No. 14. See Cpt. Albert Evans to AAAG-TFB, October 31, 1866, LR, AC, T.

20. Circ. 19, August 20, 1866; Circ. 21, October 1, 1866; Circ. 23, November 1, 1866; all in Ms. Orders, TFB. There were many questions as to the form (gold, specie, or paper) in which wages could be paid. See AAAG to 1 Lt. L. K. Morton, October 2, 1866, ES, AC, T. But already the country store was becoming the creditor and receiver of all wages, with the freedmen seeing no money, just a chit book full of overcharged goods received. See Morton to AAAG-TFB, November 6, 1866, LR, AC, T.

21. Kiddoo kept his word on crop seizures, holding most crops at the merchants' houses. See, for example, Kiddoo to Messrs. McMann & Morris, November 5, 1866; AAAG-TFB to all SACs, November 23, 1866; AAAG-TFB to Messrs. R. & D. G. Mills, November 27, 1866; AAAG-TFB to Cpt. S. P. Christian of Steamer *Whitelaw*, December 1, 1866; AAAG-TFB to Bould, Baker & Co., December 5,

1866; AAC to Messrs. Sealan & Lipscomb, December 14, 1866; AAC to Messrs. J. F. & William Brady, December 16, 1866; AAC to Messrs. McMann & Co., December 17, 1866; Kiddoo to Messrs. Nichols & Bros., December 19, 1866, all in LS, AC, T. Kiddoo also continued Gregory's policy of personally reprimanding Galveston-area residents, regardless of their influence, who were lax in paying wages owed black employees. See AAAG-TFB to William McKenzie, May 18, 1866, AAAG-TFB to S. Jones, June 12, 1866; AAAG-TFB to Mr. Wolf, Vice Consul of Russia, October 1, 1866, ibid.

22. GO 19, May 14, 1866, DT; GO 26, May 1, 1866, AGO, Printed Orders, RG 94, NA.

23. Kiddoo to Howard, May 23, June 26, 1866, LS, AC, T; AAAG-C to Kiddoo, June 7, 1866 (as well as anywhere else), LS, C.

24. Kiddoo to Howard, June 26, 1866, LS, AC, T. For the proclamations and their effect, see Richardson, *Messages and Papers of the Presidents*, vol. 6, 429–32, 437–38; and Sefton, *Army and Reconstruction*, 74–82; Thomas and Hyman, *Stanton*, 498–99.

25. Howard to Kiddoo, July 10, 1866, LR, AC, T; Throckmorton to Heintzelman, September 8, 1866. Throckmorton Papers, UT; the quotations are from Maj. L. S. Barnes to AAAG-TFB, September 1, 11, 1866, LR, AC, T.

26. Circ. 8, July 5, 1866, Ms. Orders, C; AAAG-C to Kiddoo, September 19, 1866, LR, AC, T.

27. AAAG-C to Kiddoo, September 19, 1866, LR, AC, T; the prior rules were in AAAG-C to Gregory, November 24, 1866, LS, C. Kiddoo's willingness to act independently is in AAAG-TFB to D. W. Barziza, December 8, 1866, LS, AC, T; Griffin's more restrictive view is in Circ. 1, January 12, 1867, Printed Orders, DT, RG 94, NA. A good examination of the judicial activities of bureau agents and the types of cases litigated before them is in Crouch, "Black Dreams and White Justice," 255–65. See also Crouch, "A Spirit of Lawlessness," 217–32. Agents in Texas and the rest of the South continually tried to enforce the concept of equality before the law, which was a central aspect of the Federal Reconstruction effort. Unfortunately for freed people, the effort was not always successful, particularly after the bureau was disbanded and the army withdrew from the South. See Flannigan, "Criminal Law of Slavery and Freedom," 375; Nieman, "Andrew Johnson, the Freedmen's Bureau, and the Problem of Equal Rights," 399–420; Oakes, "Failure of Vision," 66–76; and Kaczorowski, "To Begin the Nation Anew," 45–68, esp. 58–59. For more on the bureau's legal processes during Reconstruction, see Pierce, *Freedmen's Bureau*, 143–60; Bentley, *History of the Freedmen's Bureau*, 152–68; Olds, "Freedmen's Bureau as a Social Agency," 187–94; Morris, "Equality, 'Extraordinary Law,' and Criminal Justice," 15–33; Abbott, *Freedmen's Bureau in South Carolina*, 99–113, passim; St. Clair, "Judicial Machinery in North Carolina," 415–39; and "Military Justice in North Carolina, 1865," 341–50; White, *Freedmen's Bureau in Louisiana*, 134–66; Howard, "Kentucky Press and the Negro Testimony Controversy," 29–50; and Volz, "Administration of Justice"; Alderson, "The Influence of Military Rule and the Freedmen's Bureau on Reconstruction in Virginia," 58–64, 92–95, 280–81. The tragedy of the Reconstruction court system was that bureau courts tended to become centers for punishing whites, while state courts tended merely to perpetuate the slavery system. The two never came together in one sys-

tem of equal justice. See Alderson, "The Influence of Military Rule and the Freedmen's Bureau on Reconstruction in Virginia," 114, and DuBois, "Freedmen's Bureau," 362.

28. The subject of education and the bureau has been looked at by Hornsby, "Freedmen's Bureau Schools in Texas," 397–417, especially 399 n. 6 (the quotation on Gregory), 402–405; Elliott, "Freedmen's Bureau in Texas," 12–13; Smallwood, *Time of Hope, Time of Despair,* 68–95, esp. 68–71, 74–76; and Smallwood, "Early 'Freedom Schools'," 790–93. See also Kiddoo to Mrs. H. E. Binckley, July 26, 1866, LS, AC, T; AAC to AAAG-C, November 13, 1866, LR, C; D. T. Allen to AAAG-TFB, January 2, 1866, LR, SS, T.

29. Circ. 4, May 29, 1866, Ms. Orders, C; AAAG-C to all ACs, June 16, 1866, LS, C; Kiddoo to Howard, May 14, July 23, August 20, 1866, January 7, 15, 1867, LR, C; Circ. 20, August 31, 1866, Ms. Orders, TFB; AAAG-C to all ACs, September 12, 1866; Howard to Kiddoo, July 16, 1866; Howard to all ACs, November 26, 1866; LS, C; Kiddoo to AAAG-C, September 28, 1866; Kiddoo to all SACs, January 10, 1867, LS, AC, T.

30. Smallwood, *Time of Hope, Time of Despair,* 75–76. Honey served as assistant superintendent of schools until Gregory left Texas in May, 1866. His regiment left Texas that same month to be mustered out. See *Union Army,* vol. 4, 46–47. Honey continued to serve as a citizen bureau employee until he was replaced by D. T. Allen (SO 153, December 22, 1866, Ms. Orders, TFB), who assumed all of Honey's bureau functions (Kiddoo to all SACs, January 10, 1867, LS, AC, T).

31. AAAG-TFB to Kiddoo, November 10, 1866; Kiddoo to Rev. J. R. Shipard, January 2, 1867; LS, AC, T; Jacob De Gress to AAAG-TFB, October 1, 1866, LR, AC, T; Griffin to Howard, May 14, 1867, LR, C.

32. Asst. Surgeon Thomas Baird to AAAG-TFB, September 12, 1866, LR, AC, T; J. M. Avarne to AAAG-SS, January 5, 1867, LR, SS, T; Sinclair to D. T. Allen, January 5, 1867; Kiddoo to all SACs, January 10, 1867, LS, AC, T.

33. Cases of search for family members include Kiddoo to Bvt. Brig. Gen. J. W. Sprague, May 19, 1866; Sinclair to AC-Mississippi, June 22, 1866; AAAG to G. W. Grant, September 17, 1866; Sinclair to Mr. Brussom, November 5, 1866; Sinclair to Clarissa Scott, January 4, 1867; all in LS, AC, T; Sinclair to Chief Justice, Collin County, August 14, 1866, ES, AC, T. The missing husband is in Sinclair to SAC-Memphis, November 5, 1866, LS, AC, T; the deranged soldier is in AAAG-TFB to Howard, November 5, 1866, LR, C. On transportation, see Kiddoo to Howard, November 3, 1866, December 25, 1866, LR, C; Kiddoo to Howard, October 16, 1866, January 19, 1866, LS, AC, T; Circ. 24, December 21, 1866, Ms. Orders, TFB. Kiddoo also aided in the establishment of branches of the Freedmen's Savings Bank; GO 3, January 11, 1867, Ms. Orders, TFB. See also Osthaus, *Freedmen, Philanthropy, and Fraud,* 27–29, for the activities of Special Travelling Agent Anson M. Sperry in Texas. More general information is in Bentley, *History of the Freedmen's Bureau,* 146–48.

34. Refugee Reports (Kiddoo to AAAG-C, June 7, July 1, August 8, September 7, October 11, November 15, December 6, 1866, January 21, 1867), RR, AC, T; Freedmen's Reports (Kiddoo to AAAG-C, June 7, July 9, July 31, August 8, September 7, October 11, November 15, December 6, 1866, January 21, 1867), ibid.; F. D. Inge to AAAG-TFB, July 31, 1866, ibid. See Howard to Stanton, August 17,

1866, LS, C; Circ. 10, August 22, 1866, Ms. Orders, C; AAC to W. F. Laird, December 13, 1866, RR, AC, T, for the general stoppage of rations, October 1, 1866.

35. On the Houston clinic, see Kiddoo to Bvt. Maj. Gen. H. G. Wright, August 8, 1866; AAAG-DT to AAQM-TFB, September 5, 1866; Sinclair to Surg. S. J. W. Mintzer, December 27, 1866; Sinclair to Cpt. W. B. Pease, January 5, 1867; Kiddoo to Griffin, January 10, 1867, all in ES, AC, T. Howard had already warned all medical officers to cut back. See Circ. Letter, December 5, 1866, LS, C. Kiddoo's order is Circ. 16, June 21, 1866, Ms. Orders, TFB. The Roberts case is in Kiddoo to Hamilton, May 27, 1866, ES, AC, T; Kiddoo to J. H. Bell, July 24, 1866, ES, AC, T; Bell to Kiddoo, August 2, 1866, LR, AC, T; Kiddoo to Bell, August 10, 1866, LS, AC, T. The Harrison County case is in Bvt. Cpt. Charles Rand to AAAG-TFB, February 11, 1867, "Transcript of Records," TAGO, UT; Throckmorton to Griffin, March 4, 1867; Throckmorton to Harrison County judge, March 4, 1867; RG 307, TSL. When the Galveston County judge complained that he was having to provide subsistence for a freedwoman from another county, which he thought should have to care for her, he was referred to Circ. 16 and told to pay anyhow. Edward J. Austin to AAAG-TFB, June 22, 1866, LR, AC, T; AAAG-TFB to Austin, June 22, 1866, LS, AC, T. Kiddoo refused to conduct a general survey on the destitute in Texas, fearing undue expense. See Howard to Gregory, May 4, 1866, LR, AC, T; Kiddoo to Howard, June 4, 19, 1866, LS, AC, T; Kiddoo to Howard, July 23, 1866, ES, AC, T; Howard to Stanton, July 3, 1866, LS, C. Cases of insane freedmen were also handled by the state, AAAG-TFB to James F. Camp, July 28, 1866, LS, AC, T; John A. Green to AAAG-TFB, January 19, 1867, LR, AC, T; Gammel, *Laws of Texas*, vol. 5, 1125.

36. Report of Abandoned Lands (Kiddoo to AAAG-C, June 7, July 9 [including President Johnson's pardon to Yturria, also in SO 87, June 26, 1866, Ms. Orders, TFB], August 8, September 7, October 11, November 15, December 6, 1866, January 21, 1867), RR, AC, T. AAAG-C to all ACs, August 17, November 9, 1866, LS, C (inventory and disposal); Kiddoo to Howard, September 14, 1866, LR, C (tannery and hospital); Kiddoo to Griffin, January 10, 1867, LS, AC, T (discovery of Waco Mfg. Co.). Unlike Virginia, for example, where abandoned lands decreased in scope as Reconstruction progressed, in Texas the issue of abandoned lands tended to increase in importance as more and more were found later in the era. But the amount of abandoned lands never approached the quantities located in other states. See Alderson, "Influence of Military Rule and the Freedmen's Bureau on Reconstruction in Virginia," 46–58, 281–82.

37. On the political changes wrought by the 1866 state elections, see Carrier, "Political History of Texas during the Reconstruction," 84–167; Ramsdell, *Reconstruction in Texas*, 108–15; Elliott, *Leathercoat*, 147–60, passim. The military picture is in Richter, *Army in Texas*, 50–57, 62. Throckmorton's political philosophy was an accurate replica of President Andrew Johnson's as portrayed in Trefousse, *Andrew Johnson*, 214–33, 378–79. Although Throckmorton was a prewar Whig and Johnson was a Democrat, their careers are remarkably similar, particularly as regards their Unionism. Johnson stayed with the Union, whereas Throckmorton served Texas (fighting Indians) but not the Confederacy. More on the Texas governor in Marten, "Lamentations of a Whig," 163–70; and Richter, "General Phil Sheridan," 134–35.

38. On the Black Codes, see Albrecht, "Black Codes of Texas"; Wilson, *Black*

Codes of the South; Richter, "Army and the Negro," 7–19. See also Richardson, "Florida Black Codes," 365–79; and, although somewhat dated, Mecklin, "Black Codes," 248–59; Wood, "Black Codes of Alabama," 350–60.

39. Gammel, *Laws of Texas*, vol. 5, 976–77.

40. Gammel, *Laws of Texas*, vol. 5, 177, 988–89, 1049–50; Albrecht, "Black Codes of Texas," 85–87. During Reconstruction, bureau policy on disarming citizens was that it was permissible so long as the edict made no specific reference to race and was enforced impartially. See, for example, AAAG-TFB to Bvt. Cpt. Charles F. Rand, February 14, 1868, LS, AC, T.

41. Kiddoo to M. L. Dunn, August 21, 1866; Johnson to Throckmorton, October 30, 1866 (quotation); Johnson Papers, LC.

42. Kiddoo to Howard, October 8, 1866, LR, C; Porter to AAAG-TFB, October 9, 1866, LR, AC, T; AAAG-TFB to Howard, December 10, 1866, LR, C; Sinclair to Porter, December 20, LS, AC, T; Howard to Stanton, December 21, 1866, LS, C; Kiddoo to Howard, December 25, 1866, LR, C; Howard to all ACs, January 25, 1867; Howard to Griffin, January 25, 1866, LS, C; AAAG-C to Kiddoo, January 25, 1867, LR, AC, T.

43. This thesis was first presented in regard to the South in general by Wilson, *Black Codes of the South*; and in regard to Texas, by Richter, "Army and the Negro," 7–19. The failure of the bureau to respond to the defense of freedmen against the effects of the Black Codes is noted in Oakes, "Failure of Vision," 70–71; for the bureau's ready endorsement of the compulsory work ethic, see Morris, "Equality, 'Extraordinary Law,' and Criminal Justice," 25–33; and on the whole problem of Presidential Reconstruction, consult Dan T. Carter, *When the War Was Over: The Failure of Self-Reconstruction in the South, 1865–1867*, and Michael Perman, *Reunion without Compromise*.

44. Gammel, *Laws of Texas*, vol. 5, 1020–22. The provost marshal of Galveston had placed all "idle" Negroes to work on the city streets within two weeks of the army's arrival; Galveston *Daily News*, June 28, 1865. See also Circular Letter, October 17, 1865; and Gregory to Benjamin Harris, January 20, 1866; LS, AC, T; Albrecht, "Black Codes of Texas," 92–94. Local communities followed the state legislature's lead with similar laws of their own. See Tausch, "Southern Sentiment among the Texas Germans," 81; Dobie, "History of Hays County, Texas," 77. An excellent discussion of the problems of post–Civil War labor-management relations as revealed in the Black Codes, and their implications for the twentieth century, is in Cohen, "Negro Involuntary Servitude in the South," 31–60. Also of interest is Carper, "Slavery Revisited," 85–99; also Wynne, "Role of Freedmen in the Post Bellum Cotton Economy of Georgia," 309–21.

45. Gammel, *Laws of Texas*, vol. 5, 979–81; Albrecht, "Black Codes of Texas," 91–92. The bureau had held up all apprenticeships by state authorities before the law's passage, and monitored it afterward. See W. H. Farner to AAAG-TFB, May 1, 1866, RR, AC, T; AAAG-TFB to Cpt. Isaac Johnson, May 12, 1866, ES, AC, T; 1 Lt. L. K. Morton to AAAG-TFB, December 27, 1866, LR, AC, T; W. H. Sinclair to Fred W. Reinhard, January 29, 1867, LS, AC, T.

46. Gammel, *Laws of Texas*, vol. 5, 998–99; Albrecht, "Black Codes of Texas," 91–92.

47. Gammel, *Laws of Texas*, vol. 5, 994–97; Albrecht, "Black Codes of Texas,"

94–98. Some of the rationale for these clauses in the laws can be gleaned from Friedman, "Search for Docility," 313–23; and more specifically from Ledbetter, "White over Black in Texas," 406–18.

48. Circ. Letter, October 4, 1865, LS, C, outlined the procedure on state laws and their validity; see also Circ. Letter, November 22, 1866, Ms. Orders, AC, T; Circ. 3, December 9, 1866, Ms. Orders, C; Kiddoo to Mr. Richardson, December 19, 1866, LS, AC, T.

49. Circ. 25, December 21, 1866, Ms. Orders, AC, T, which was drawn up from the state bureau inspector's recommendations, in W. H. Sinclair to AAAG-TFB, November 30, 1865, LR, AC, T. All contracts, to be valid, had to be completely clear to the fieldhands at the moment of signing; hence the emphasis on their being read in the presence of the bureau agent and all contracting parties. See AAAG to Cpt. Isaac Johnson, May 12, 1866, ES, AC, T. In spite of the orders, many field agents were confused as to what was really legal that fall, bureau edicts or state legislature pronouncements. See, for example, 1 Lt. James Hutchinson to AAAG-TFB, November 30, 1866, LR, AC, T.

50. The charges are in GO 1, January 1, 1867, Ms. Orders, AC, T. Howard's confirmation of the charges is in Howard to all ACs, January 24, 1867, LS, C. The Texas state laws are nullified in GO 2, January 3, 1867, Ms. Orders, AC, T. A typical protest of Kiddoo's actions and rationale is in G. W. Chilton and A. M. Branch to AAAG-C, January 10, LR, C. The reminder of the enticement prohibitions is in GO 4, January 20, 1867, Ms. Orders, AC, T.

51. Haynes to Pease, October 4, 1866, Pease-Niles-Graham Papers, APL.

52. Hamilton, speech at Washington, D.C., July –, 1866, Hamilton Papers, UT.

5: Sick at Heart

1. Appointments and removals by group are in Circ. 15, June 1, 1866; Circ. 18, August 1, 1866; Circ. 22, October 9, 1866, Ms. Orders, TFB. See also SO 77-150, series 1866, and SO 1-10, series 1867, ibid., for individual appointments and removals.

2. For back salary requests, see Kiddoo to Howard, October 8, 1866; Bvt. Maj. Joseph J. Reynolds to Howard, April 11, 1868; ES, AC, T. For refusals to appoint civilians, from North or South, Sinclair to James Young (New York), September 5, 1866, LS, AC, T; 2 Lt. George A. Albee to Kiddoo (New Hampshire), LR, AC, T; AAC to Levi Jones (Texas), December 13, 1866, ES, AC, T. Some of the agents could not take the oath, which precluded any Federal payments, as in the case of F. D. Inge (Reynolds to Howard, April 11, 1868, ES, AC, T; others had neglected to take the oath, as with A. P. Delano (AAAG to Delano, April 14, 1866, ES, AC, T; some had illegal appointments, as did F. E. Miller (Kiddoo to Howard, October 8, 1866, ES, AC, T. For a promise to pay, pending congressional action, see Sinclair to Cpt. Charles P. Russell, June 26, 1866, LS, AC, T.

3. The thumb-tying story is in W. B. Anderson to AAAG-TFB, May 30, 1866, LR, AC, T. Farner is characterized in a prior complaint, which helped to cost him his job, by Charles Harrison to AAAG-TFB, May 5, 1866, LR, AC, T. A stunned Kiddoo asked Cpt. Louis Sanger to check out Farner's activities after the doctor was fired; Kiddoo to Sanger, June 6, 1866, LS, AC, T. See also Champ

Carter, Jr., to AAAG-TFB, June 6, 11, 1866, LR, AC, T; and AAAG-TFB to Carter, June 7, 1866, ES, AC, T; AAAG-TFB to Farner, January 22, 1866, LS, AC, T; and Farner to AAAG-TFB, January 29, 1866, LR, AC, T. This assistant may have been Carter, but there were also a Jones and a Schaffer functioning as unauthorized agents in this general area. On the illegal Carter appointment, see Carter to AAAG-TFB, January 21, 1866, LR, AC, T; and AAAG-TFB to Carter, January 25, 1866, LS, AC, T. 1 Lt. L. K. Morton to AAAG-TFB, September 30, 1866, LR, AC, T; Morton, who replaced Carter, mentioned that the planters would turn on him as soon as he stopped Carter's unapproved practices, the origin of which he blamed on an illegal agent named Shaeffer. Other self-appointed subassistant commissioners abounded in this area, many of whom could be traced by Farner. See F. D. Inge to AAAG-TFB, July 30, 1866; Cpt. Samuel C. Sloan to AAAG-TFB, December 18, 1866, LR, AC, T; AAAG-TFB to A. C. Keaton, September 11, 1866; Kiddoo to Howard, April 23, 1868; Sinclair to Farner, April 14, 1866, ES, AC, T.

4. The case ran on forever; see W. B. Anderson to AAAG-TFB, May 30, 1866, LR, AC, T; Dr. E. H. Mitchell to AAAG-TFB, May 28, 1867; J. L. Randall to AAAG-TFB, June 7, 1866, LR, AC, T; AAAG-TFB to Randall, June 1, 1867, LS, AC, T. One officer, 2 Lt. Robert McClermont, was removed from office and severely reprimanded. McClermont to AAAG-TFB, May 13, August 30, 1866, LR, AC, T; Sinclair to McClermont, May 21, 30, 1866, LS, AC, T; Sinclair to McClermont, May 28, 1866, ES, AC, T. For other related actions, see also Kiddoo to Bvt. Maj. Gen. H. G. Wright, June 2, 1866; Sinclair to Cpt. Samuel C. Wright, July 30, 1866, LS, AC, T; Kiddoo to Howard, August 17, 1866; Howard to McClermont, August 14, 1866, ES, AC, T. McClermont managed to keep his Fourth Cavalry commission, probably because he was a personal friend of Lt. Gen. Grant, with whom he had served during the Mexican War. See, for example, Grant to Stanton, May 8, 1865, in Simon, *Papers of Ulysses S. Grant*, vol. 15, 25.

5. Richard Cole to AAAG-TFB, June 26, 1866; J. O. Shelby to AAAG-TFB, July 8, 18, 20, 1866, LR, AC, T; Sinclair to Shelby, July 25, August 16, 1866, LS, AC, T. Shelby had been recommended as a Union man who had been jailed by Confederate authorities. See H. C. Pedigo to Gregory, January 27, 1866, LR, AC, T.

6. AAAG-TFB to McConaughey, May 11, 1866, LS, AC, T; McConaughey to AAAG-TFB, May 19, 23, July 8, 14, 1866, LR, AC, T; SO 97, August 8, 1866, Ms. Orders, TFB.

7. A. B. Newsome to AAAG-TFB, July 23, 1866, LR, AC, T.

8. Inge to AAAG-TFB, August 13, 1866 (all quotations); Maj. L. S. Barnes to AAAG, July 9, 1866; Thomas J. Mortimer to AAAG-TFB, January __, 1867; LR, AC, T. See also Bvt. Maj. J. J. Reynolds to Bvt. Maj. Gen. O. O. Howard, April 11, 1868, ES, AC, T; SO 96, July 28, 1866, Ms. Orders, TFB.

9. Howard to AAAG-TFB, April 30, July 10 (civil law), September 19 (if you expect), 1866, LR, AC, T; Howard to AAAG-TFB, June 2, 1866 (cesationists, they say), RR, AC, T. Kiddoo's praise is in SO 128, October 27, 1866.

10. AAAG-C to Kiddoo, August 6, 1866, LR, AC, T. A short history of the Veteran Reserve Corps is in Boatner, *Civil War Dictionary*, 870.

11. Kiddoo to Howard, May 14, 1866, LS, AC, T. Kiddoo would lose two of his five employees to muster-outs, a third to become subassistant commissioner

at Austin, and another, who already had been sent into the field at La Grange, to General Gregory's personal request for an aide de camp in Maryland. AAAG to Kiddoo, May 18, 1866, LR,.AC, T; Kiddoo to Howard, May 21, 1866; Kiddoo to Gregory, October 1, 1866, LS, AC, T; AAAG to Kiddoo, October 5, 1866, LS, C. Compare "Rosters of Officers and Civilians on Duty . . . ," May–December 1866, Ms. vol. 9, AC, T. He had no volunteer officers whose regiments had been mustered out left behind by midsummer; AAAG to all ACs, July 13, 1866, LS, C; Kiddoo to Howard, July 15, 1866, LS, AC, T.

12. AAAG-C to Kiddoo, August 6, 1866 (quotation), LR, AC, T; Kiddoo to Howard, August 15, 1866, for a list of the men in the Texas bureau who were affected; Howard to Stanton, August 18, 1866, LS, C; Kiddoo to Howard, August 22, 1866, ES, AC, T, for quotations on a typical recommendation (1 Lt. I. M. Beebe). At the end of the year, Howard ordered a recapitulation of the events with a final personnel list to be repeated monthly thereafter. See Circ. 12, December 1, 1866, Ms. Orders, C; AAAG-C to all ACs, December 4, 14, LS, C; complied with in Kiddoo to Howard, January 3, 1867, LS, AC, T. The officials from whom the figures are derived are listed in "Rosters of Officers and Civilians on Duty . . . ," January–December 1866, Ms. vol. 9, AC, T. There were plenty of places requesting an agent. Huntsville received its first bureau agent, James C. Devine, in September 1866; the initial request had been made in April. See Sinclair to J. F. Rodes, August 24, 1866, ES, AC, T; SO 112, September 17, 1866, Ms. Orders, TFB. On Edelson, see SO 113, September 19, 1866; SO 119, October 11, 1866; SO 132, November 6, 1866, Ms. Orders, TFB; Edelson to AAAG-TFB, October 1, 1866, LR, AC, T; AAAG-TFB to Edelson, October 1, 1866; AAAG-TFB to AAAG-C, October 11, 1866, LR, C. His wartime service was with the Excelsior Brigade (Seventieth New York Infantry), and is noted in Phisterer, *New York in the War of the Rebellion*, 2717, 4228, 4236 (because this five-volume series is paginated consecutively, no reference to volume number will be made).

13. On Saylor, see Sinclair to AAAG-TFB, September 22 (all quotations), October 7, 1866, LR, AC, T; Kiddoo to Howard, October 11, 1866; AAAG-TFB to 1 Lt. J. Albert Saylor, November 19, 1866; ES, AC, T. See also SO 68, April 4, 1866; SO 113, September 19, 1866; SO 119, October 11, 1866; SO 126, October 24, 1866; SO 132, November 6, 1866; Ms. Orders, TFB. Other relevant information is in Saylor to AAAG-TFB, July 12, September 10, 1866; AAAG-TFB to Saylor, May 23, 1866; AAAG-TFB to Maj. Turney, November 9, 1866, LS, AC, T; AAAG to Saylor, August 9, October 29, November 19, 1866; AAAG-TFB to AAAG-DT, April 25, 1866; Kiddoo to Howard, October 11, 1866; AAAG-TFB to AAQM and DO-TFB, October 25, 1866, ES, AC, T.

14. Cpt. A. B. Coggeshall to AAAG-TFB, January 18, February 25 (quotation), 1866; Julius Schuetze to AAAG-TFB, January 22, 1867, LR, AC, T. Coggeshall was appointed SAC by SO 42, February 22, 1866 (Ms. Orders, TFB), mustered out with his regiment, 114th USCI, in early 1867 (Dyer, *Compendium of the War of the Rebellion*, vol. 3, 1739), and reappointed in SO 42, July 13, 1868 (Ms. Orders, TFB). His Bastrop replacement, Byron Porter, received his investigation orders in SO 6, January 11, 1867, Ms. Orders, TFB. For more on Coggeshall, see SO 42, February 22, 1866, Ms. Orders, TFB; Mark W. Wagner to AAAG-TFB, December 11, 1865; Julius Schuetze and three others to AAAG-TFB, n.d. [1865];

Arthur E. Eddy to AAAG-TFB, August 18, 1866; Coggeshall to AAAG-TFB, April 18, June 6, July 2, 7, 26, August 2, December 5, 27, 1866, January 2, 18, 1867, LR, AC, T; AAAG-TFB to Coggeshall, July 11, December 10, 1866, January 15, 1867, LS, AC, T; Kiddoo to Griffin, December 21, 1866, ES, AC, T; AAAG-TFB to AAAG-D of G, March 2, 1867; C. V. Schafer and forty others to AAAG-TFB, n.d. [1867], LR, AC, T; Sinclair to Coggeshall, January 15, February 18, 1867, LS, AC, T; Galveston *Daily News*, January 13, 1867; SO 15, February 7, 1866; SO 22, February 20, 1867; Ms. Orders, TFB.

15. On Goodman, see SO 67, April 12, 1867; SO 106, August 18, 1867; Ms. Orders, TFB; Goodman to AAAG-TFB, July 31, 1866, LR, AC, T; AAAG-TFB to Goodman, July 19, 1866, LS, AC, T; AAAG-TFB to Goodman, May 28, July 9, August 17, 1866; Kiddoo to Howard, June 19, 1866; Kiddoo to Wright, July 13, 1866; AAAG-TFB to Miss M. Hartwell, August 29, 1866, ES, AC, T; Kiddoo to AAAG-C, June 19, August 27, 1866; LR, C. His wound and military career are described in *Field Record of Officers of the Veteran Reserve Corps*, 28.

16. 1 Lt. C. A. Dempsey to AAAG-TFB, August 29, 1866, and endorsements, LR, AC, T. See also, SO 101, August 18, 1866, Ms. Orders, TFB.

17. SO 63, April 16, 1866; SO 35, March 25, 1867; Ms. Orders, TFB; Metzner to AAAG-TFB, April 23, 26, August 14, 1866, April 3, 1867, LR, AC, T; AAAG-TFB to Metzner, May 2, 1866, March 7, 1867, LS, AC, T; Metzner's reports, December, 1866–January, 1867, ROC, AC, T. His wound and military career with the Forty-sixth New York Infantry are described in *Field Record of Officers of the Veteran Reserve Corps*, 35; Phisterer, *New York in the War of the Rebellion*, 4229, 4242.

18. SO 63, April 16, 1866; SO 87, June 26, 1866; SO 90, July 14, 1866; SO 122, October 16, 1866; SO 149, December 17, 1866; SO 150, December 19, 1866; Ms. Orders, TFB; Hardenbrook to AAAG-TFB, May 1, 7, 10, June 22, 29, July 8, 18, October 10, November 13, 17, 22, 1866; De Gress to AAAG-TFB, October 2; AAAG-TFB to AAAG-C, November 26, 1866, LR, AC, T; AAAG-TFB to Hardenbrook, April 27, May 29, October 3, 24, November 22, 1866, LS, AC, T; Kiddoo to Wright, June 6, 1866; Kiddoo to Howard, September 5, 1866, ES, AC, T; Kiddoo to Howard, August 22, 1866, LR, C. For Hardenbrook's wounds and sterling career in the Sixty-sixth New York Volunteers, see *Field Record of the Officers of the Veteran Reserve Corps*, 23; Phisterer, *New York in the War of the Rebellion*, 2656, 4227, 4239.

19. SO 69, April 4, 1866; SO 56, May 20, 1867; SO 57, May 26, 1867; Ms. Orders, TFB; Hutchison to AAAG-TFB, November 30, 1866, January 19, 21, April 22, May 1, 1867, LR, AC, T; AAAG-TFB to Hutchison, November 27, December 28, 1866, February 28, March 12, 21, April 12, 1867; Maj. S. H. Lathrop to W. C. Wagley, December 14, 1866; Sinclair to Hutchison, January 2, 10, 14, 24, 1867, LS, AC, T; Griffin to AAAG-C, April 19, 1867, LR, C; Hutchison's reports, December, 1866–April, 1867, ROC, AC, T. His wound and military career are described in *Field Record of Officers of the Veteran Reserve Corps*, 25.

20. SO 63, April 16, 1866, Ms. Orders, TFB; Miller to AAAG-TFB, April 28, May 9, 30, July 10, October 2, December 1, 16, 1866, January 24, February 5, 1867, LR, AC, T; Miller to AAAG-TFB, May 31, June 30, July 27, August 27, 1866, RR, AC, T; AAAG-TFB to Miller, August 2, 17, September 11, 1866, ES, AC, T; Kiddoo to Griffin, January 17, 1867, ES, AC, T; Miller's reports, December, 1866–January, 1867, ROC, AC, T; SO 13, February 2, 1867, Ms. Orders, TFB. Miller's wound and

military service with the Thirty-eighth New York Regiment are not described in *Field Record of Officers of the Veteran Reserve Corps*, but can be found in Phisterer, *New York in the War of the Rebellion*, 2184, 4230, 4242.

21. SO 66, April 17, 1866; SO 128, October 27, 1866; SO 146, December 9, 1866; SO 146, December 9, 1866; SO 45, April 17, 1867; SO 100, November 21, 1867, Ms. Orders, TFB. Rand's wound and military career are not described in *Field Record of Officers of the Veteran Reserve Corps*, but his wartime service is in Phisterer, *New York in the War of the Rebellion*, 416, 2459, 3181, 4231, 4244.

22. 1 Lt. I. M. Beebe to AAAG-TFB, August 8, 1866; Col. Thomas Bayley to AAAG-TFB, August 8, 1866 (quotations); Horton to AAAG-TFB, December 31, 1866, January 24, February 1, March 8, 25, 1866; LR, AC, T; reports of Horton, December, 1866–March, 1867, ROC, AC, T; Sinclair to Horton, December 21, 1866; AAAG-TFB to Horton, January 29, 1866, LS, AC, T; Sinclair to Horton, December 26, 1866, January 5, 1867; Sinclair to Henry George, January 4, 1867; Kiddoo to Griffin, January 10, 1867, ES, AC, T; SO 103, August 8, 1866; SO 142, November 26, 1866, Ms. Orders, TFB.

23. See, for example, AAAG-DT to Kiddoo, August 13, October 1, 1866; AAAG-DT to AAAG-TFB, December 22, 1866, LR, AC, T; AAAG to Bvt. Col. E. C. Mason, October 23, 1866; Kiddoo to Bvt. Maj. Gen. S. P. Heintzelman, October 15, 31, 1866; LS, AC, T; Kiddoo to AAAG-DT, January 31, 1867, ES, AC, T; SAC-Moscow to AAAG-TFB, January 4, 1867, LR, C.

24. Kiddoo to Bvt. Col. E. C. Mason, May 15, 28, 29, June 8, 1866, LS, AC, T.

25. Kiddoo to Mason, May 28 (two letters), July 16, September 27, 1866; Kiddoo to AAAG-DT, May 31, 1866; Kiddoo to Bvt. Lt. Col. Henry A. Ellis, July 21, 1866; Kiddoo to Howard, January 24, 1867; all in LS, AC, T. Kiddoo became angry enough to prefer charges against Col. Mason, the post commander at Galveston, but nothing came of this either; Kiddoo to Wright, August 11, 1866, LS, AC, T.

26. Maj. L. S. Barnes, March 19, 26, April 2, 4, 5, May 6, 17, 29, September 1, 11, October 20, 1866, LR, AC, T; AAAG-TFB to Barnes, April 24, 1866, LS, AC, T; AAAG-TFB to Barnes, June 28, 30, October 20, 1866, ES, AC, T; SO 51, March 12, 1866; SO 134, November 9, 1866; Ms. Orders, TFB. See also, Dyer, *Compendium of the War of the Rebellion*, vol. 3, 1725.

27. Bureau policy of no horses if possible is in Howard to Stanton, January 24, 1867, LS, C. Complaint of the use of carriage in AAC to Cpt. Nathan H. Randlett, December 15, 1866, ES, AC, T. Wright's policy is in Wright to Cpt. Byron Porter et al., May 30, 1866, LS, AC, T. The use of mounted infantry is in Kiddoo to Wright, June 20, 1866, LS, AC, T. Some SACs refused to make the tours requested in Circs. 17 and 21, because they lacked transportation and could not get a government requisition for any. See Maj. L. S. Barnes to AAAG-TFB, October 20, 1866, LR, AC, T.

28. Charles P. Russell to AAAG-TFB, June 5, July 24, August 4, 12, 14, 1866, LR, AC, T; Kiddoo to Wright, August 22, 1866, ES, AC, T. AAAG-TFB to Russell, June 26, July 30, August 4, September 5, 1866, LS, AC, T; Russell to AAAG-TFB, August 31 (two letters), 1866, RR, AC, T; SO 113, September 19, 1866, Ms. Orders, TFB; Sinclair to AAAG-TFB, September 22, October 7, 1866, LR, AC, T. Russell was not on the October list, "Rosters of Officers and Civilians on Duty . . . ," October 1, 1866, Ms. vol. 9, AC, T.

29. F. D. Inge to AAAG-TFB, May 12, June 17, July 13, August 5, 1866, LR, AC, T.

30. Champ Carter, Jr., to AAAG-TFB, June 6, July 10, 30, August 25, 1866; 1 Lt. Gus Schreyer to AAAG-TFB, July 30, 1866; LR, AC, T; Sinclair to Carter, July 1, 1866, August 17, 1866, ES, AC, T; AAAG-TFB to Carter, July 1, August 17, 1866, ES, AC, T.

31. 1 Lt. L. K. Morton, September 30, November 6, 1866, LR, AC, T; Kiddoo to AAAG-C, December 20, 1866; Griffin to AAAG-C, March 22, 1867; LR, C; SO 108, September 4, 1866; SO 113, September 19, 1866; SO 8, January 18, 1867, Ms. Orders, TFB.

32. AAAG-TFB to CO, DT, December 1, 1866; Kiddoo to Heintzelman, October 26, 1866, ES, AC, T.

33. 1 Lt. I. M. Beebe to AAAG-DT, May 26, 1866, LR, DT, RG 393, NA; Beebe to AAAG-TFB, June 6, 1866 (knock down), LR, AC, T.

34. AAAG-TFB to Bayley, September 11, 1866, AC, T; Bayley to AAAG-TFB, October 9 (quotations), November 15, 28, 1866, LR, AC, T.

35. Kiddoo to Bvt. Maj. Gen. Absalom Baird, June 19, 1866; Kiddoo to Howard, July 20, 1866 (quotations), ES, AC, T; Beebe to AAAG-TFB, June 6, 1866 (not free), LR, AC, T. The murder of the black soldiers is in Sheridan to C/S, October 1, 1866, Sheridan Papers, LC. See SO 217 (December 23, 1867, Printed Orders, FMD, RG 94, NA) for the combining of the posts of Marshall and Jefferson with the rest of the army's Texas command.

36. Bayley's appointment is SO 22, January 4, 1866; Beebe's appointment is SO 64, April 17, 1866; Ms. Orders, TFB; Yates to Howard, October 7, 1865; Cpt. C. F. Ingersoll to Bayley, January 15, 1866; Bayley to AAAG-TFB, January 15, 17, February 28, March 25, 29, July 31, 1866, undated order [1866]; 1 Lt. I. M. Beebe to AAAG-TFB, June 6, July 16, 1866; LR, AC, T; Gregory to AAAG-C, December 6, 1865; AAAG-TFB to Bayley, January 29, April 17, 1866, LS, AC, T; AAAG-TFB to Bayley, June 1, July 21, 1866; Kiddoo to AAAG-DT, June 5, 1866; AAAG-TFB to Beebe, June 8, 1866, ES, AC, T. For more on Beebe's wartime career with the Ninty-fourth New York Volunteers, see Phisterer, *New York in the War of the Rebellion*, 4231, 4233, 3065. He had received fractures of the left arm and the knee from bullet wounds received at the Battle of Fredericksburg, *Field Record of Officers of the Veteran Reserve Corps*, vol. 25.

37. Bayley to AAAG-TFB, December 6, 28, 1866, LR, AC, T; AAAG-TFB to CO-Post of Marshall, December 8, 1866; Sinclair to Bayley, December 31, 1866 (two telegrams), January 5, 1867, LS, AC, T; Kiddoo to Howard, October 11, 1866; January 3, 1867; Griffin to Bayley, February 2, 1867; AAAG-TFB to Bayley, May 3, 1867, ES, AC, T; Yates to Howard, September 25, 1866; Kiddoo to AAAG-C, January 5, 1867; LR, C; SO 137, November 18, 1866; SO 150, December 31, 1866, Ms. Orders, TFB.

38. Kiddoo to Bvt. Maj. Gen. A. Baird, June 19 (absolute necessity), 1866; Kiddoo to Howard, July 20, 1866, ES, AC, T.

39. Mrs. L. E. Potts to Johnson, June 21, 1866; Wright to AAAG-D of G, July 21, 1866; Sheridan to C/S, October 1, 1866; in *House Executive Documents*, 40th Cong., 2nd Sess., No. 57, 28–32. The Potts letter and Wright's reply are also in *House Reports*, 39th Cong., 2nd Sess., No. 61, 1–4. The progress of the letter can be seen

from Kiddoo to Sheridan, July 20, 1866, ES, AC, T. On an inspection tour, Commissioner Howard referred to the section of Louisiana along the northeastern Texas border as being the most unruly part of that state, too. See Howard to Stanton, January 19, 1867, LS, C.

40. Kiddoo to Howard, August 8, 1866, LR, C; Howard to Kiddoo, September 11, 1866, LS, C.

41. Howard to all ACs, September 24, 1866, LS, C; Kiddoo to Howard, October 25, 1866 (authentic murders, giving protection), LR, C; Kiddoo to Howard, October 30, 1866 (good feeling), ES, AC, T. See also Kiddoo to Howard, January 2, 8, 25, 1867, LS, AC, T.

42. See the enclosed letters, many without identified author, in Kiddoo to Howard, October 25, 1866, LR, C. For a more or less complete list of crimes committed against freedmen during the period, see "Record of Criminal Offenses Committed in the State of Texas" (3 vols., Mss. in AC, T).

43. Longworth to AAAG-DT, June 30, 1865, LR, AC, T; Longworth to Hamilton, October 9, 10, 1865, Governor's Papers (Hamilton), TSL. Longworth's appointment as judge is in "Election Register (2-1/7)," vol. 261, Ms. copy, TSL. He was later also made a justice of the peace, "Election Register (2-1/8)," vol. 262, Ms. copy, TSL.

44. AAAG-TFB to Longworth, October 23, 1865, LS, AC, T; Longworth to AAAG-TFB, December 15, 1865, LR, AC, T.

45. See SO 18, December 28, 1865, Ms. Orders, TFB; AAAG-TFB to Longworth, December 27, 1865, LS, AC, T; Longworth to AAAG-TFB, January 15 (quotations), 19, 1866, LR, AC, T. Longworth received the normal reprimands for failing to turn in his scheduled reports, although he wrote so frequently that such reports were largely superfluous. See Longworth to AAAG-TFB, April 16, 1866, LR, AC, T. An example of the reports required (freedmen, abandoned lands, refugees) is in Longworth to AAAG-TFB, April 30, 1866, RR, AC, T. On estimated expenses, much of which was financed from fines levied (he considered himself far too lenient in this matter), and the rest from his own pocket, see Longworth to AAAG-TFB, March 17, April 30, May 16, 1866, LR, AC, T; AAAG-TFB to Longworth, February 19, March 23, 1866, LS, AC, T.

46. Longworth to AAAG-TFB, January 29 (flinching in the cause, crush out all such, conciliation wasted), February 10 (there must not now, for the cause), March 9, 28, 1866, LR, AC, T; AAAG-TFB to Longworth, March 22, 1866, LS, AC, T.

47. Longworth to AAAG-TFB, March 28, 1866, LR, AC, T. The politics of the bureau renewal bill, the president's veto of it, and the congressional override of the veto are presented in Bentley, *History of the Freedmen's Bureau*, 103–35; Pierce, *Freedmen's Bureau*, 55–69.

48. James L. Dial to AAAG-TFB, February 10, 1866, LR, AC, T; Sinclair to Dial, March 19, 1866; Sinclair to Longworth, March 23, 1866, LS, AC, T. The testimony in the case is filed under "Randel Brooks," the original complainant, in LR, AC, T.

49. Longworth to AAAG-TFB, April 25, May 1, 1866, LR, AC, T; Sinclair to Longworth, May 2, 1866, LS, AC, T.

50. Longworth to AAAG-TFB, May 8 (two letters), 14, 17, 1866, LR, AC, T.

51. L. P. Hughes and seventy-three others to AAAG-TFB, April 30 (stranger), 1866; Samuel Wright to AAAG-TFB, May 18, 1866; J. B. McFarland and eighty-five others to AAAG-TFB, May–(unnecessarily unpopular, just, Honest, upright), 1866; Dial to AAAG-TFB, June 6, 1866, ibid.

52. Samuel Gilmore to AAAG-TFB, May 18, 1866, ibid.

53. Longworth to AAAG-TFB, May 17 (stop upsetting), 25 (all other quotations and the exchange of messages appended), 1866, ibid.

54. Longworth to AAAG-TFB, May 27 (quotation), June 4, 1866, ibid.

55. Longworth to AAAG-TFB, May 18, 30 (quotations), 1866, ibid.

56. Sinclair to Longworth, June 9, 1866, LS, AC, T; Longworth to AAAG-TFB, June 21, 1866, LR, AC, T.

57. Longworth to AAAG-TFB, June 13, 25 (quoted), July 16, 1866; Cpt. Joseph Ferguson to AAAG-TFB, July 25, 1866; LR, AC, T; AAAG-TFB to Ferguson, July 24, 1866, LS, AC, T.

58. SO 95, July 26, 1866, Ms. Orders, TFB; Sinclair to Longworth, July 27, 1866; LS, AC, T; Longworth to AAAG-TFB, July 29 (quotation), 31, 1866; Moore to AAAG-TFB, July 29, 1866, LR, AC, T.

59. Moore to AAAG-TFB, August 6 (quotations), 12, 31, 1866, LR, AC, T; AAAG-TFB to Moore, July 30, August 24, 1866, ES, AC, T.

60. Sinclair to AAAG-TFB, October 7, 1866, LR, AC, T.

61. Sinclair to AAAG-TFB, October 7, 1866, ibid; SO 113, September 19, 1866, Ms. Orders, TFB; Kiddoo to Heintzelman, October 25, 1866; AAAG-TFB to Maj. Gen. P. H. Sheridan, November 10, 1866; LS, AC, T. Moore's activity even attracted the castigation ("a drunkard and a debauchee are not fit to be officers of our government") of Commissioner Howard in Washington. Howard to Kiddoo, August 21, 1866, LR, AC, T, quoted in Carpenter, *Sword and Olive Branch,* 151.

6: GONE TO THE DEVIL

1. Cpt. S. A. Craig to AAAG-C, September 15, 20, December 8, 20, 1865, January 31, March 19, 1866, LR, C; AAAG-C to Craig, September 20, October 4, 1866; Howard to Rev. J. W. Blythe, September 20, 1865, LS, C; SO 119, December 26, 1865; SO 46, March 30, 1866; Ms. Orders, C; SO 69, April 30, 1866, Ms. Orders, TFB.

2. Craig to AAAG-TFB, May 3, 15, 18, 25, 26, June 1, July 15, August 2, 1866, LR, AC, T; Sinclair to Affleck, July 28, 1866, LS, AC, T; Sinclair to Craig, May 23 (two letters and quotation), 30, June 1, June 7 (two Letters), July 19, July 28, 1866, ES, AC, T; Criag to AAAG-TFB, June 30, August 1, 31, 1866, RR, AC, T.

3. Craig to AAAG-TFB, June 14, 1866, LR, AC, T; Sinclair to Craig, May 29, June 1, 1866, LS, AC, T; Kiddoo to AAAG-DT, June 20, 1866, ES, AC, T.

4. Craig to AAAG-TFB, May 28, June 7, 20, 27, 1866, LR, AC, T; Sinclair to Craig, May 31 (quotation), 1866, LS, AC, T; Kiddoo to Wright, June 25, 1866; Sinclair to Craig, June 29, 1866, ES, AC, T.

5. AAAG-TFB to 2 Lt. B. J. Arnold, February 2, 1866, LS, AC, T; J. G. Whann

tiff's attorney), January 2, 1867; ES, AC, T; AAAG-TFB to De Gress, December 15, 1866, LS, AC, T; Bvt. Maj. S. H. Lathrop to AAAG-C, December 18, 1866, LR, C. Terrell became so disgusted with the bureau and army's interference in state law that he retired within six months to plantation management, finding it "more congenial with my nature to direct negroes in the field than to bow before them. See Wallis, "Life of Alexander Watkins Terrell," 70–71.

33. Howard to Griffin, February 26, 1867, LR, AC, T; Kiddoo to Stanton, December 28, 1866; Kiddoo to Throckmorton, January 3, 1867, LS, AC, T; Throckmorton to Stanton, February 18, 1867, Throckmorton Papers, UT; SO 156, December 31, 1866, Ms. Orders, TFB. Later, when asked if he wanted De Gress back as subassistant commissioner, General Charles Griffin delayed his reply until the fall of 1867. Then he agreed to send De Gress, who had just become a first lieutenant in the new Ninth (Colored) Cavalry, to Henderson in northeastern Texas, an area where De Gress's kind of toughness as an agent was demanded. But De Gress never got there. He had managed to alienate the entire Department of Louisiana with his bluntness. So General Sheridan intervened and sent the controversial officer to the western frontier to criticize the barren plains. See Howard to Sheridan, March 25, July 29, 1867, LS, C; AAAG-TFB to AAAG-DT, July 4, 1867; AAAG-TFB to De Gress, September 1, 1867; LS, AC, T. See also SO 85, August 7, 1867; SO 93, October 7, 1867; Ms. Orders, TFB. De Gress later became state superintendent of public education under the E. J. Davis regime (Shook, "Federal Occupation and Administration of Texas," 249).

34. Sinclair to AAAG-TFB, December 10, 23, 1866, LR, AC, T; AAAG-TFB to John M. Schaffer, January 10, 1867, ES, AC, T.

35. SO 139, November 19, 1866; Circ. 25, December 21, 1866, Ms. Orders, TFB; Sinclair to AAAG-TFB, November 30, 1866, LR, AC, T.

36. Sinclair to AAAG-TFB, December 10, 23, 1866, LR, AC, T; Circular Letter, December 31, 1866, Ms. Orders, TFB. The monthly reports instituted by Sinclair's inspection tour eventually became regularized in a printed format and are in ROC, AC, T.

37. Kiddoo to Sheridan, September 5, 16, 1866, LS, AC, T; Sheridan to Kiddoo, September 28, 1866, LR, AC, T. Sheridan was in Texas from September 24 to October 1; see Sheridan to C/S, September 24, October 1, 1866, Grant Papers, LC. See also AAAG-DT to AAAG-D of G, September 3, 1866; Kiddoo to AAAG-D of G, September 16, 1866; TR, D of G, RG 393, NA. Getty's assignment is in GO 2, September 24, 1866, DT, RG 94, NA.

38. Heintzelman's assignment is in GO 5, October 9, 1866, DT, RG 94, NA. He did not arrive in Galveston until the end of October; GO 6, October 24, 1866, ibid. Sheridan to Grant, November 10, 1866, Grant Papers, LC, for the request of Griffin. The ranks of the superior officers in Texas and Louisiana are explained in Brig. Gen. E. D. Townsend to Sheridan, October 25, 1866, Sheridan Papers, LC.

39. Heintzelman to AAAG-D of G, TR, D of G, RG 393, NA; Howard to Kiddoo, October 15, 1866; AAAG-FB to Kiddoo, November 2, 10, 1866, LS, C; Kiddoo to AAAG-C, October 26, November 5, 10, 1866, LR, C; Kiddoo to Howard, October 23, 1866, LS, AC, T, SO 172, November 24, 1866, Ms. Orders, FB, C. Kiddoo had wanted to see Howard in August, but had missed the session of the bureau boards. See Kiddoo to Howard, August 8, 1866, LS, AC, T; AAAG-C to

346

Kiddoo, August 11, 1866, LS, C. A typical board's membership and agenda can be found in SO 96, July 11, 1866, Ms. Orders, C.

40. Ellis was assigned to the bureau in SO 111, September 14, 1866, Ms. Orders, TFB; Kiddoo requested him in Kiddoo to Bvt. Lt. Col. E. C. Mason, September 11, 1866, LS, AC, T. Doubleday replaced Mason as commandant of the post of Galveston, SO 27, November 4, 1866, DT, RG 94, NA; Kiddoo's warning to Ellis and the latter's refusal to accede to the army coup are in AAAG-TFB to CO-DT, November 6, 1866, ES, AC, T; AAAG-TFB to Doubleday, November 21, 1866, LS, AC, T.

41. Ellis held on to his position, basing his action on the technicality that he could not legally sign over the bureau property. But Heintzelman and Lathrop receipted him for it, thereby putting an end to this approach. See Ellis to Kiddoo or Howard, November 20, 1866; Ellis to Kiddoo, November 20, 1866; Ellis to Howard, November 22, 1866; Ellis to AAAG-DT, November 22, 1866; Ellis to Heintzelman, November 22, 1866, all in LS, AC, T.

42. The command intricacies are in Richter, *Army in Texas*, 29–30. See also Ellis to Kiddoo, November 20, 1866, LS, AC, T.

43. The best general accounts are Ellis to Howard, December 18, 1866, and Kiddoo to Howard, December 21, 1866, LS, AC, T. The quotations are in Ellis to AAAG-DT, November 23, 1866 (unwarranted), and Ellis to Heintzelman, November 24, 1866 (en passant), LS, AC, T. See also Kiddoo to Ellis, December 3, 1866, LR, AC, T; Ellis to Kiddoo, December 8, 11, 12, 1866; Ellis to AAAG-DT, December 11, 1866, LS, AC, T; Lathrop to AAAG-FB, December 14, 1866, LR, C.

44. A short description of the whole army leadership picture from Sheridan's point of view is in Richter, "General Phil Sheridan," 134–35. See GO 10, December 1, 1866, and GO 11, December 1, 1866, DT, RG 94, NA, for the change in command. Sheridan's support of Kiddoo is in AAAG-DG to AAAG-TFB, November 23, 1866, LR, AC, T.

45. Kiddoo to Howard, December 21, 1866, LS, AC, T. The account of the operation is from Otis, *Medical and Surgical History*, vol. 2, pt. 2, 234.

46. The view of Kiddoo and his men on Griffin is in W. H. Sinclair to Byron Porter, December 7, 1866, LR, AC, T. See also Lathrop to Howard, December 17, 1866, LS, AC, T.

47. Kiddoo to Howard, December 19, 1866; Kiddoo to Sheridan, January 3, 1866; Kiddoo to Griffin, January 10, 27, 1866, LS, AC, T. Sheridan finally prohibited Lathrop from engaging in any staff activity in the bureau or army headquarters, and ordered him to turn over all papers to Kiddoo, who evidently never received them. See AAAG-D of G to Griffin, January 6, 1867, LR, AC, T. Lathrop's exile is mentioned in Mason to Griffin, July 8, 1867, LR, AC, T; his death is in Heitman, *Historical Register*, vol. 1, 617.

48. Kiddoo to Howard, December 24, 1866, LR, C.

49. Howard to Kiddoo, January 14, 1867; Howard to Griffin, January 14, 1867, LS, C; GO 1, January 24, 1867, Ms. Orders, TFB; Kiddoo to Howard, January 25, 28 (letter, quoted), 28 (telegram), 1867, LS, AC, T; SO 19, January 29, 1867, Printed Orders, DT, RG 94, NA; Howard to Griffin, February 4, 1867, LR, AC, T; Howard to Stanton, February 5, 1867, LS, C; Griffin to Howard, February 7, 1867 (letter and telegram), LS, AC, T. The commissioner's policy of combined army and bureau

commands had been announced in Circ. 4, August 24, 1866 (quotation), Ms. Orders, C. Howard had not projected keeping independent assistant commissioners past November, 1866. See Howard to Stanton, August 24, 1866, LS, C. The combining of the positions of army and bureau commander had taken place by now in several states, including Louisiana; for the details, see Howard to Sheridan, August 22, 30, September 18, 27, 1866, LS, C. Griffin had already been in communication about the feasibility of using army post commanders as adjunct bureau subassistant commissioners to increase bureau control in Texas. See Griffin to Howard, December 18, 1866, LR, C.

50. Galveston *Daily News*, February 5, 1867.

7 : FORMING A NEW ORDER

1. Circ. 4, May 24, 1866, Ms. Orders, C. The placing of bureau and army authority in the hands of one officer was not new. The top officer in the army, Lt. Gen. U. S. Grant, in his report of a tour of the south Atlantic states, had already suggested combining bureau and army commands in the South immediately after the war, as well as making post commanders automatically the bureau subassistant commissioners for their command area. See Grant to Johnson, December 18, 1865, in Simon, *Papers of Ulysses S. Grant*, vol. 15, 434–37.

2. For Griffin's life, see Heitman, *Historical Register*, vol. 1, 478; Cullum, *Biographical Register*, vol. 2, 196–97; Boatner, *Civil War Dictionary*, 360–61; *Dictionary of American Biography*, vol. 7, 617–18; *National Cyclopaedia of American Biography*, vol. 4, 337–38.

3. *Dictionary of American Biography*, vol. 7, 618; Cullum, *Biographical Register*, vol. 2, 331; William A. Russ, "Radical Disfranchisement in Texas," 40; Catton, *Stillness at Appomattox*, 63–66.

4. GO 5, February 5, 1867, Ms. Orders, TFB. Upon Kiddoo's departure, Griffin began a new series of orders and circulars, and hence it is possible to have duplicate numbers for 1867 in General Orders Nos. 1–4, differentiated only by date. Examples of "cooperation" between Throckmorton in Austin and Griffin in Galveston — the two never met — can be seen in the letters listed below. The communications are full of little snide remarks and commentary, especially on Throckmorton's side. Griffin's brusque replies, however, give the impression of a cauldron ready to boil over. See Throckmorton to Griffin, February 7, 22, March 5, 7, June 28, 1867, LR, AC, T; Griffin to Throckmorton, February 7 (two letters), 28, 1867, LS, AC, T.

5. GO 4, January 30, 1867 (natural sense), LS, AC, T. See endorsements, Kiddoo to G. W. Chilton and A. M. Branch, Members of Congress from Texas [sic], January 29, 1867; Griffin to Chilton and Branch, February 4, 1867 (having seen), ES, AC, T. Examples of persons sending in contracts for approval include John Matthews to AAAG-TFB, March 19, 1867; John Stiehl to AAAG-TFB, March 16, 1867, LR, AC, T. Approval notices include AAAG-TFB to J. A. Gray, February 19, 1867; AAAG-TFB to George McKinney, February 19, 1867; AAAG-TFB to John Pace, March 1, 1867; AAAG-TFB to Charles W. Austin, March 13, 1867;

AAAG-TFB to John C. Stiehl, March 20, 1867; AAAG-TFB to John Matthews, March 23, 1867; AAAG-TFB to Z. M. French, April 23, 1867, all in LS, AC, T.

6. GO 5, February 5, 1867, LS, AC, T. Griffin, like Kiddoo, expected blacks to honor a contract. See J. R. Robertson to AAAG-TFB, April 11, 1867, LR, AC, T; AAAG-TFB to J. N. Waul, July 25, 1867, LS, AC, T.

7. Griffin kept his word. See, for example, Sinclair to Shropshire, Henderson & Co., January 29, 1867; AAAG-TFB to J. L. Gay, March 2, 1867; AAAG-TFB to Cpt. William H. Rock, July 26, 1867, LS, AC, T.

8. Circ. 1, February 2, 1867; AAAG-TFB to all SACs, June 21, 1867 (quotation), LS, AC, T.

9. Howard to Griffin, February 9, 1867, LR, AC, T; Griffin to Howard, February 12, 18, 1867, LR, C. For an example of the bureau refusing to intervene in a case without prior application to the state courts, see Sinclair to D. E. Haynes, January 17, 1867, ES, AC, T. See also Bentley, *History of the Freedmen's Bureau*, 161.

10. Griffin to Howard, June 12, 17, 1867, LR, C.

11. Howard to Griffin, June 25, 1867, LS, C; GO 11, July 8, 1867, Ms. Orders, TFB.

12. Gray to AAAG-TFB, August 10, 1866, LR, AC, T. The questions and answers pertaining to the enforcement of GO 11 are in Cpt. J. H. Bradford to AAAG-TFB, September 11, 1867, and the endorsements in AAAG-TFB to Bradford, October 1, 1867, and AAAG-C to Bradford, October 15, 1867, LR, AC, T.

13. Affleck to Griffin, August 26, 1867, LR, AC, T; GO 25, August 3, 1867, Printed Orders, DT, RG 94, NA.

14. Howard to Griffin, July 2, 1867, LS, C.

15. Howard to Griffin, July 6, 1867, LR, AC, T.

16. Griffin to Howard, July 11, 1867, LS, AC, T; Circ. 7, September 3, 1867, Ms. Orders, TFB.

17. Circ. 3, February 1, 1867, as modified by SO 22, February 1, 1867, Printed Orders, DT, RG 94, NA.

18. Circ. Letter, February 12, 1867, LS, C; repeated as GO 9, April 11, 1867, Ms. Orders, TFB.

19. See personnel return for February 1, March 1, April 1, May 1, June 5, July 10, August 10, September 10, 1867; "Rosters of Officers and Civilians on Duty . . . ," Ms. vol. 9, AC, T; Griffin to Howard, March 4, 1867 (delay); Circ. Letter, April 1, 1867 (first 49 subdistricts), LS, AC, T. The personnel appointed can also be followed individually in the SO series (beginning with SO 13, February 2, 1867 and ending with SO 89, September 2, 1867) for 1867, Ms. Orders, TFB. See Circ. Letter, September 13, 1867, LS, C, for Howard's admonition to cut employees.

20. An idea of the perennial red tape is in Circ. Letter, December 31, 1866; Circ. Letter March 8, 1867; AAAG-TFB to all SACs, May 23, July 26, 1867, LS, AC, T; Circ. 4, February 5, 1867; Circ. 25, July 20, 1867, Ms. Orders, C; and Bvt. Brig. Gen. Lewis R. Brown to AAAG-TFB, June 6, 1867, LR, AC, T.

21. Horse policy in Circ. 23, July 17, 1867, Ms. Orders, C; Williamson's death in Judge John Miller to AAAG-TFB, May 5, 29, 1867, LR, AC, T. For the deaths of three other agents after Griffin's administration, see "Report of Agents and Clerks," November, 1867, in RR, AC, T (for the murder of Cpt. J. B. Thompson, SAC–Ft. Mason); Smallwood, "Freedmen's Bureau Reconsidered," 309–20; and

Smallwood, "Charles E. Culver, a Reconstruction Agent in Texas," 350–61. The morality emphasis in Circ. Letter, May 15, 1867, LS, C; AAAG-C to Griffin, July 5, 1867, LR, AC, T; Griffin to Howard, July 13, 1867, LS, AC, T.

22. Griffin's policy was based on GO 102, May 31, 1865, AGO, which Wright had reissued in his command as GO 21, June 23, 1866, DT, and Griffin reconfirmed as Circ. 25, DT, all in Printed Orders, RG 94, NA. The big difference was that Griffin followed up and saw to it his order was more fully obeyed. See Circ. Letter, April 2, 1867; AAAG-TFB to AAAG-DT, July 5, 1867; LS, AC, T. The best single example of Griffin's approach is AAAG-TFB to AAAG-DT, May 2, 1867, LS, AC, T, where he orders seven separate detachments to secure various bureau agencies.

23. See "Rosters of Officers and Civilians on Duty . . . ," AC, T, for months from February to September, 1867. For future Republicans, consult: Robert H. Taylor to Howard, February 11, 1867; B. W. Gray to Griffin, July 25, 1867; LR, AC, T; Howard to Griffin, February 25, April 3, 1867, LS, C; Smallwood, "G. T. Ruby," 24–33. Appointment policies are in Howard to all ACs, April 4, 1867, LS, C; Griffin to Howard, April 13, 1867, LS, AC, T; and Circ. 24, July 19, 1867, Ms. Orders, C. Salary information is in Circ. Letter, July 24, 1867; Howard to all ACs, August 1, 1867; LS, C; and Griffin to Howard, August 17, 1867, ES, AC, T. Places of origin are from Circ. Letter, August 28, 1867, LS, C; and Texas list for September, 1867 (T-413), LR, C.

24. The story in this and the following paragraph with the quotations from McClermont and Farner is in W. B. Anderson to AAAG-TFB, May 30, 1866, LR, AC, T.

25. See also 1 Lt. L. K. Morton to AAAG-TFB, September 30, 1866, LR, AC, T. Morton, who replaced Carter, mentioned that the planters would turn on him as soon as he stopped Carter's unapproved practices, the origin of which he blamed on an illegal agent named Shaeffer.

26. Sanger to AAAG-TFB, July 23, 1866 (insufferable), LR, AC, T; AAAG-TFB to Sanger, July 23, 1866, LS, AC, T; Cpt. Samuel C. Sloan to AAAG-TFB, August 8 (grave indiscretion), 31, 1866, LR, AC, T.

27. See Porter to AAAG-TFB, October 17, 1866, LR, AC, T; AAAG-TFB to Hemphill, November 28, 1866, LS, AC, T; and AAAG-TFB to Bvt. Maj. Gen. S. P. Heintzelman, November 24, 1866, ES, AC, T. See also "Rosters of Officers and Civilians on Duty . . . ," Ms. vol. 9, AC, T; Heitman, *Historical Register*, vol. 1, 521, 799.

28. 1 Lt. S. C. Plummer to Bvt. Maj. Gen. J. B. Kiddoo, August 14, 1866, LR, C.

29. See reports of 1 Lt. H. C. Peterson, August, 1867–May, 1868, ROC, AC, T; and Peterson to AAAG-TFB, July 29, 1867, LR, AC, T, where he investigates the shooting of the freedman by Plummer, which had caused Plummer's replacement and exoneration. See also Plummer to AAAG-TFB, February 21, July 5, 1867, LR, AC, T; AAAG-TFB to Plummer, May 18, 1867, LS, AC, T. Evidently Peterson was no angel in his conduct towards Texans, either. He was later court-martialed and dismissed from the service for a poolhall altercation in which he threatened the life of 1 Lt. Gregory Barret and several civilians at Laredo. See Heitman, *Historical Register*, vol. 1, 786; and GCMO 25, April 16, 1870, Printed Orders, AGO, RG 94, NA. It also turned out that Peterson, whose real name was E. D. M. Hamilton, had served his entire military career under a pseudonym

for unexplained reasons (Bvt. Lt. Col. T. M. Anderson to AAAG-DT, May 10, 1870, LR, DT, RG 393, NA).

30. Reports of Bvt. Maj. L. H. Sanger, August, 1867–March, 1868, ROC, AC, T; Sanger to AAAG-TFB, August 6, 14, 1867, LR, AC, T; Sanger to AAAG-DT, April 15, 1868, LR, DT, RG 393, NA; AAAG-FMD to CO-Jefferson, December 25, 1867, LS, FMD, LR, DT, RG 393, NA.

31. On the various western bureau operations or the lack of them, see the following:

Brownsville: Brown to AAAG-TFB, June 6, 1867; Morse to AAAG-TFB, February 11, April 23 (two letters), 1867; Bvt. Cpt. H. M. Hutchins to AAAG-TFB, May 12, 1867; LR, AC, T; Morse's reports, April–July, 1867, ROC, AC, T; reports of Bvt. Maj. Gen. J. J. Reynolds, August, 1867; of Bvt. Gen. R. S. Mackenzie, September, November, 1867; of Cpt. A. M. Randol, December, 1868; of Bvt. Maj. Gen. A. McCook, April, August 1868; ROC, AC, T; and McCook to AAAG-TFB, July 22, 1868, LR, AC, T.

Camp Verde: reports of Bvt. Brig. Gen. John P. Hatch, March–November, 1867; of Maj. G. C. Cram, January–February, 1868; of Bvt. Cpt. W. W. Clemens, March–July, October, 1868; of Bvt. Lt. Col. H. A. Ellis, September–October, 1868; ROC, AC, T; and 2 Lt. J. W. Bean to AAAG-TFB, January 26, 1869, LR, AC, T.

Camp Wilson (Fort Griffin): reports of Bvt. Brig. Gen. Samuel D. Sturgis, September, 1867–March, 1868, ROC, AC, T.

Laredo: reports of Cpt. J. A. Wilcox, April–May, 1868; of 2 Lt. A. F. Bayard, August, 1868; of 1 Lt. J. B. Cole, November, 1868, ROC, AC, T; and Cole to AAAG-TFB, January 29, 1869, LR, AC, T.

Fort Duncan: report of Bvt. Col. W. R. Shafter, April, 1868, ROC, AC, T.

Fort Griffin: reports of Bvt. Maj. A. R. Chaffee, April, 1868; of Bvt. Col. S. B. Hayman, June–December, 1868, ROC, AC, T.

Fort Inge: reports of 1 Lt. N. J. McCafferty, September–October, 1867; of Cpt. E. J. Conway, November, 1867–February, 1868, ROC, AC, T; Cpt. J. P. Gillespie to AAAG-TFB, April 26, 1866; *House Executive Documents*, 40th Cong., 2nd sess., No. 57, 117; 1 Lt. N. J. McCafferty to AAAG-TFB, March 21, [July–], 1867, LR, AC, T; AAAG-TFB to Cpt. D. M. Sells, August 28, 1868, LS, AC, T; AAAG-TFB to Sells, June 16, 17, 1868; Sinclair to Sells, June 25, 26, 1868, ES, AC, T.

Fort Mason: reports of Cpt. J. A. Thompson (KIA), September–October, 1867, ROC, AC, T; and Thompson to AAAG-TFB, September 9, 1867, LR, AC, T; reports of 1 Lt. John Murphy, November, 1867–March, 1868; of Bvt. Maj. P. E. Holcomb, April–July, 1868; of 1 Lt. Phineas Stevens, November, 1868, ROC, AC, T.

Fort Richardson: reports of Bvt. Col. S. H. Starr, March–November, 1868, ROC, AC, T.

Lampasas: reports of 2 Lt. C. F. Roe, October–November, 1868, ROC, AC, T.

Ringgold Barracks: reports of Bvt. Col. W. R. Shafter, July, October, December, 1867, February, 1868; of Cpt. J. H. Bradford, April, June–August, 1868; of Bvt. Maj. R. P. Wilson, May, November, 1868, ROC, AC, T.

Weatherford: reports of 1 Lt. H. H. Humphries, July–August, 1867; of Cpt. Charles Steelhammer, September, 1867–February, 1868, ROC, AC, T; and Humphries to AAAG-TFB, August 31, 1867; A. J. Bell to Maj. Gen. W. S. Hancock, March 1, 1868, LR, AC, T.

32. On Seguin, see reports of Bvt. Maj. George W. Smith, January–September, 1867; of Bvt. Maj. E. W. Whittimore, October, 1867–January, 1869, ROC, AC, T; Smith to AAAG-TFB, July 4, 24, 1867, LS, AC, T; and AAAG-TFB to Smith, July 16, 1867 (quotations), ES, AC, T. Smith's political activities are in Smith to AAAG-TFB, September 16, 1867, LR, AC, T; Nat Benton and others to AAAG-FMD, February 15, 1868, LR, CA, FMD, RG 393, NA; and Alex Rossy to E. M. Pease, October 23, 1868, Pease-Niles-Graham Papers, APL.

33. See the reports of Cpt. J. J. Emerson, May–November, 1867, ROC, AC, T, Emerson to AAAG-TFB, July 19, 1867, LR, AC, T; and AAAG-TFB to Emerson, December 13, 1867, LS, AC, T.

34. On Kaufman, see reports of 1 Lt. S. H. Lincoln, September, 1867–August, 1868, ROC, AC, T, Lincoln to AAAG-TFB, September 5, December 10, 1867, LR, AC, T; AAAG-TFB to Lincoln, November 30, 1867, LS, AC, T; and AAAG-TFB to Lincoln, July 18, August 27, 1867, ES, AC, T.

35. For Goliad, see reports of 2 Lt. J. D. Vernay, November–December, 1867; of P. E. Holcomb, May, July–August, 1867, January, 1868; of J. W. Wham, February, 1868; of 2 Lt. J. A. Hopkins, March, 1868. For Woodland, see report of Cpt. T. M. K. Smith, October, 1868. On Hallettsville, see reports of 1 Lt. P. Stevens, May, 1867–February, 1868, ROC, AC, T. See also Stevens to AAAG-TFB, February 8, 1868, LR, AC, T; Griffin to Stevens, August 30, 1867; AAAG-TFB to Stevens, February 4, 1868, LS, AC, T; AAAG-TFB to Stevens, June 7, November 8, 1867, ES, AC, T. Stevens was the one officer who seems to have been the most successful in getting army horseflesh, although the reason for his success is not apparent; see AAAG-TFB to Stevens April 9, April 24, June 3, 1867, ES, AC, T. For the political list, see AAAG-TFB to Stevens, April 29, 1867, ES, AC, T.

36. SO 77, May 14, 1866; SO 101, August 18, 1866; SO 125, October 22, 1866; TFB; Allen to AAAG-TFB, June 3 (if the bureau), 13, July 12 (some embarrassing exceptions), August 14 (calamity), November 26, December 12, 1866, LR, AC, T; AAAG-TFB to Allen, May 30, July 5, 1866, LS, AC, T; AAAG-TFB to Allen, June 7, July 18, 1866, ES, AC, T. See also Dyer, *Compendium of the War of the Rebellion*, vol. 3, 1729–30, where the muster-out date is given as October 28, 1866.

37. See reports of Cpt. George Lancaster, March, 1867–January, 1868, ROC, AC, T; SO 19, March 12, 1868, Ms. Orders, TFB. For the shootings, see also Graber, *Life Record of H. W. Graber*, 272–75, 280 (quotation).

38. Sinclair to AAAG-TFB, July 18, August 1, 24, 1867, LR, AC, T. See also Sinclair to AAAG-DT, LR, CA, DT, RG 393, NA.

39. Reports of Bvt. Col. S. H. Starr, September, 1867–January, 1869, ROC, AC, T. On the activities of the Baker gang, see Bartholomew, *Cullen Baker: Premier Texas Gunfighter*, which includes a copy of Thomas Orr, *Life of the Notorious Desperado, Cullen Baker, from His Childhood to His Death, with a Full Account of All the Murders He Committed*, first published in Little Rock in 1870; Al Eason, "Cullen Baker: Purveyor of Death," *Frontier Times* 40 (August–September, 1966), 6–12, 44–47, 67; James Allen Marten, "Drawing the Line: Dissent and Loyalty in Texas, 1856 to 1874" (Ph.D. diss., University of Texas, 1986), 264–67; and Boyd W. Johnson, "Cullen Montgomery Baker: The Arkansas-Texas Desperado," *Arkansas Historical Quarterly* 25 (1966), 229–39.

40. Reports of 1 Lt. A. G. Malloy, May, 1867–March, 1868, ROC, AC, T; Malloy

to AAAG-TFB, January 19, 1868, LR, AC, T. Unlike most post commanders, Malloy did manage to get a few mounted men through the personal intervention of William H. Sinclair, the bureau inspector. See AAAG-TFB to Malloy, May 20, 1867, ES, AC, T; and Sinclair to AAAG-TFB, June 22, 1867, LR, AC, T. On the shooting involving the internal revenue officers, see Campbell, *Southern Community in Crisis*, 248–49, 254, 281–83; and Dimick, "[Davis B.] Bonfoey Murder Case," 469–83.

41. Sinclair to AAAG-TFB, June 21 (he is not), 22, 1867, LR, AC, T; Bayley to AAAG-TFB, February 28, May 9, June 21, 1867; Mrs. Thomas Bailey to Griffin, June 4, 1867, LR, AC, T; Griffin to Howard, May 28, 1867; AAAG-TFB to Bayley, June 29, 1867, LS, AC, T; Howard to Griffin, June 6, 1867, LS, C. On Bayley, see SO 45, April 17, 1867; SO 70, June 6, 1867; SO 53, May 13, 1867; SO 54, May 16, 1867, Ms. Orders, TFB. For Beebe's death, see Circ. 22, October 9, 1866, Ms. Orders, TFB. See also Dyer, *Compendium of the War of the Rebellion*, vol. 3, 1725; for Rand's award, see Phisterer, *New York in the War of the Rebellion*, 416.

42. SO 146, December 9, 1866; SO 45, April 17, 1867; SO 100, November 21, 1867, Ms. Orders, TFB; Rand to AAAG-TFB, December 31, 1866, March 28, July 1, 20, 1867; Bayley to AAAG-TFB, April 10, 1867; 1 Lt. A. G. Malloy to AAAG-TFB, May 8, July 20, 1867; Sinclair to AAAG-TFB, June 21, 1867, LR, AC, T; AAAG-TFB to Rand, February 25, April 11, 1867; LS, AC, T. See also Rand's report, November, 1867, ROC, AC, T; SO 53, May 13, 1867; SO 54, May 16, 1867; Ms. Orders, TFB; Sinclair to AAAG-TFB, June 21, 22, 1867, LR, AC, T.

43. SO 49, March 10, 1866; SO 122, August 21, 1866; Ms. Orders, TFB; Evans to AAAG-TFB, April 1, May 1, June 1, 1866, RR, AC, T; Evans to AAAG-TFB, January 18, 1866; Thomas Mary and twenty-nine others to Howard, July 26, 1866; LR, AC, T; Kiddoo to Howard, July 23, 1866, LR, C.

44. SO 102, August 8, 1866; SO 13, February 2, 1867, Ms. Orders, TFB; Evans to AAAG-TFB, September 20, October 31, 1866, February 17, 1867, LR, AC, T; Evans's reports, December, 1866–February, 1867, ROC, AC, T. See also Dyer, *Compendium of the War of the Rebellion*, vol. 3, 1739.

45. Evans never really got a correct appointment, which raised problems later when he tried to collect his salary. See AAAG-C to Griffin, July 1, 1867, LS, C; AAAG-TFB to AAQM & DO-TFB, August 10, 1868, LS, AC, T; Evans to AAAG-TFB, May 1, June 9, 22, 24, 25 (two letters), 1867, LR, AC, T; AAAG-TFB to Evans, May 25, 1867, ES, AC, T; Evans's reports, May–June, 1867, ROC, AC, T.

46. SO 91, July 21, 1866; SO 15, February 7, 1867; SO 18, 1867, Ms. Orders, TFB. Manning to AAAG-TFB, February 28, 1867 (all quotations), LR, AC, T, is a summary of his administration at Waco. His wound and military career are described in *Field Record of Officers of the Veteran Reserve Corps*, 28. See also Richter, *Army in Texas*, 90; Crouch, "Spirit of Lawlessness," 225. Of great interest and some eery relevance is Savitt, "Use of Blacks for Medical Experimentation," 331–48.

47. SO 38, April 4, 1867, Ms. Orders, TFB, for the Cotton Gin assignment; Manning to AAAG-TFB, May 30, 1867, LR, AC, T; AAAG-TFB to Manning, May 28, 1867, for the leave refusal; describing the shooting, AAAG-TFB to Charles E. Culver, June 28, 1867 (all quotations), ES, AC, T.

48. Griffin to Howard, June 15, July 13, 1867, LS, AC, T; Manning to AAAG-TFB, February–, July 1, 1867; E. A. McCrackin to AAAG-TFB, June 25, 1867; Glenn R. Waters and twenty-one others, June–, 1867; Charles Delair, July 9, 1867,

LR, AC, T; SO 62, June 15, 1867; SO 78, July 23, 1867; SO 80, July 25, 1867; SO 85, August 17, 1867, Ms. Orders, TFB.

49. SO 35, March 25, 1867, Ms. Orders, TFB; Metzner to AAAG-TFB, April 26, May 31 (two letters), July 16, August 14, November 23 (lynch law), 1867, LR, AC, T.

50. AAAG-TFB to Metzner, July 31, 1867, LS, AC, T; Metzner to AAAG-TFB, January 30, February 3, 21, June 19 (quotation), 1868, LR, AC, T.

51. AAAG-TFB to Metzner, June 17, 20, July 27, 1867; Sinclair to AAAG-TFB, August 15, 1868, ES, AC, T. The reappointment is in AAAG-TFB to Metzner, December 21, 1867, January 20, 1868, LS, AC, T; Metzner to AAAG-TFB, January 6, 1868, LR, AC, T; Metzner's reports, June–December, 1867, ROC, AC, T.

8: To Make the Devil Blush

1. On the carpetbaggers and definitions of the term, see Current, *Those Terrible Carpetbaggers*, xi, 72, 91, 156, 171, 261–62, 387, 422–25. The carpetbagger agents in the Texas bureau were fully as diverse a group in character, motive, and ability as the ten men whom Current examined (none of whom was based in Texas), but with a slightly greater tendency toward what might in the twentieth century be seen as corruption. Such an attitude, however, was more often viewed as entrepreneurial imagination in the era after the Civil War. Also of interest are Current, *Three Carpetbag Governors*; Current, "Carpetbaggers Reconsidered," 139–57; and Powell, "Politics of Livelihood," 315–47. Powell maintains that the carpetbaggers had greater difficulty than Current implies in divorcing their noble idealism from the petty hunger for the spoils of office. On the latter point, see also Summers, *Railroads, Reconstruction, and the Gospel of Prosperity*; and Summers, *Plundering Generation*.

2. W. H. McClune to AAAG-TFB, August 28, 1866, LR, AC, T; SO 105, August 29, 1866; SO 109, September 5, 1866, Ms. Orders, TFB. See also "Roster of Officers and Civilians on Duty . . . ," September 1, 1866, Ms. vol. 9, AC, T.

3. SO 13, December 12, 1865; SO 48, March 8, 1866; SO 2, January 2, 1867; SO 6, January 11, 1867; SO 13, February 2, 1867; SO 50, April 30, 1867, Ms. Orders, TFB; Sperry to Gregory, September 2, 1865; Sperry to AAAG-TFB, December 28, 1865; April 30, May 4, 1867; 1 Lt. Thomas Price to AAAG-TFB, September 6, 1866, LR, AC, T; Griffin to Howard, May 1, 1867, LS, AC, T; Griffin to AAAG-C, May 2, 1867, ES, AC, T. Sperry's career with the Freedmen's Savings Bank is detailed in Osthaus, *Freedmen, Philanthropy, and Fraud*, 27–29.

4. SO 87, August 19, 1867; SO 90, September 28, 1867, Ms. Orders, TFB; Stiles to AAAG-TFB, August 2, October 8, 24, 31, 1867, LR, AC, T; Griffin to Howard, August 17, 1867, LS, AC, T.

5. SO 20, February 18, 1867; SO 93, October 7, 1867; SO 21, March 29, 1868, Ms. Orders, TFB; Horton to AAAG-TFB, May 13, 19, June 19, 30, August 10, 23, 1867, March 4, 21, 1868, LR, AC, T; Citizens of Dallas to Pease, February 25, 1868, Pease-Niles-Graham Papers, APL; reports of Horton, May–September, December, 1867, January, 1868 ("dislike to pay" from September, 1867; "malignant hate" from December, 1867; "sham" from July, 1867; "like dogs" from May, 1867), ROC,

AC, T. For the replacement of the local governments, see SO 195, November 11, 1867; SO 206, November 18, 1867; Printed Orders, DT, RG 94, NA.

6. SO 124, October 19, 1866; SO 35, March 25, 1867, Ms. Orders, TFB; Lowrie to AAAG-TFB, July 29, August 12, September 13, October 22, 1867; Bvt. Lt. Col. J. C. Bates to AAAG-District of Louisiana, August 3, 1867; H. C. Pedigo to AAAG-TFB, September 17, 1867, LR, AC, T. Lowrie, a friend of Agent Enon M. Harris, came highly recommended. See Kiddoo to Howard, August 25, 1866, LR, C; AAAG-TFB to Lowrie, September 10, 1866, ES, AC, T.

7. SO 35, March 25, 1867, Ms. Orders, TFB; J. H. McCormack to AAAG-TFB, February 21, 1867; C. P. Kerr and forty-three others to AAAG-TFB, April 25, 1867; John Miller to AAAG-TFB, May 5, 29, 1867; Cpt. Edward Miller to AAAG-TFB, June 1, 1867; Culver to AAAG-TFB, June 30, 1867; LR, AC, T; AAAG-TFB to Williamson, March 26, April 2, 1867, LS, AC, T; Griffin to Howard, May 28, June 1, 1867, LR, C.

8. SO 62, June 15, 1867; SO 63, June 18, 1867; Ms. Orders, TFB; Culver to AAAG-TFB, June 26, July 13, 22, 31 (swallowed up), August 8, September 22, 28, October 11 (H___ Room), 21, 26 (lie from beginning to end), 1867; Arthur H. Eddy to Cpt. J. H. Bradford, September 28, 1867 (zealous, dangerous fanatic); Corsicana *Observer*, October 4, 1867, copy in LR, AC, T; AAAG-TFB to AAAG-DT, August 17, 1867, LS, AC, T; AAAG-TFB to Culver, November 12, 1867, ES, AC, T; reports of Culver, June–October, 1867, ROC, AC, T. See also Dallas *Herald*, December 7, 1867; Smallwood, "Charles E. Culver, a Reconstruction Agent in Texas," 350–61.

9. SO 127, October 26, 1866; SO 133, November 8, 1866; SO 145, December 7, 1866, Ms. Orders, TFB; L. J. Warren to Kiddoo, October 20, 1866; Warren to AAAG-TFB, December 6, 1866, September 13, 1867 (quotation), LR, AC, T; AAAG-TFB to Warren, November 5, 1867; AAAG-TFB to Howard, October 11, 1867, ES, AC, T.

10. SO 54, May 16, 1867; SO 83, August 8, 1867; Ms. Orders, TFB; Devine to AAAG-TFB, June 8, 10, 27, July 22, 1867; Cpt. E. Collins to AAAG-TFB, August 11, 13, 1867; LR, AC, T; AAAG-TFB to AAAG-FMD, November 25, 1868, ES, AC, T.

11. SO 59, June 1, 1867, Ms. Orders, TFB; Duggan to AAAG-TFB, May 29, June 26, September 1, 16, 1867; Harry Lesser to AAAG-TFB, October 22, 1867; Hennell Stevens to AAAG-TFB, October 15, 1866; A.F.N. Rolfe to AAAG-TFB, December 9, 12, 1867, LR, AC, T; Griffin to Howard, May 31, 1867; AAAG-TFB to Duggan, June 1, July 5, 10, 1867; Reynolds to Howard, November 14, 1867, LS, AC, T; Griffin to Wheelock, August 6, 1867, ES, AC, T; reports of Duggan, June–July, 1867, ROC, AC, T.

12. SO 120, October 10, 1866; SO 121, October 13, 1866; SO 46, April 4, 1867; SO 47, April 22, 1867, Ms. Orders, TFB; Heistand to AAAG-TFB, November 13, 1866, April 10, May 10, 1867; Howard to AAAG-TFB, May 9, 1867, LR, AC, T; AAAG-TFB to Heistand, April 3, 1867; Griffin to Howard, May 1, 1867, LS, AC, T; reports of Heistand, December, 1866–February, 1867, ROC, AC, T.

13. AAAG-DT to AAAG-C, February 17, 1866, LR, C; Porter to AAAG-TFB, September 12, 1866; De Gress to AAAG-TFB, July 31, 1866, LR, AC, T; AAAG-TFB to Porter, September 25, 1866, LS, AC, T; SO 102, July 25, 1866, Ms. Orders, C; SO 115, September 25, 1866, Ms. Orders, TFB.

14. SO 115, September 28, 1866, Ms. Orders, TFB; Porter to AAAG-TFB, October 5, 9, November 2, 5, 1866, LR, AC, T; Sinclair to Porter, December 20, 1866; Kiddoo to Howard, December 28, 1866 (quotation), LS, AC, T; Porter to AAAG-TFB, January 1867, ROC, AC, T.

15. Porter to Sinclair, December 7, 1866; Porter to AAAG-TFB, January 25, 1867, LR, AC, T; Kiddoo to Howard, December 28, 1866, LS, AC, T; Kiddoo to AAAG-C, December 24, 1866, LR, C; SO 15, February 7, 1867, Ms. Orders, TFB.

16. On Porter's career, see SO 15, February 7, 1867; SO 24, April 1868, Ms. Orders, TFB; Porter AAAG-TFB, September 17, 1867; March 21, 1868, LR, AC, T. On the Bell matter and related incidents, see Porter to AAAG-TFB, April 2, May 28, November 17, 1867, February 7, 10, March 28, 1868; C. C. McGinnis and others to AAAG-TFB, January 27, 1868; E. M. Pease to Reynolds, January 31, 1868; C. G. Jungmichel to AAAG-TFB, March 6, 1868; Caesar Bell (free man of color) to AAAG-TFB, May 9, 1868; William J. Allen and twenty-eight others to AAAG-TFB, n.d., LR, AC, T; AAAG-TFB to Porter, April 25, November 22, 1867, January 24, February 10, 1868, LS, AC, T; AAAG-TFB to Porter, June 7, 1867, ES, AC, T; Porter's reports, February, 1867–April, 1868, ROC, AC, T.

17. SO 104, August 27, 1866; SO 122, October 10, 1866; SO 128, October 27, 1866; SO 152, December 21, 1866, Ms. Orders, TFB; Sturgis to AAAG-TFB, August 25, September 18 (two letters), October 29, December 27, 1866; Thomas F. McKinney and eleven others, October 22, 1866, LR, AC, T; Throckmorton to Kiddoo, October 25, 1866, Throckmorton Papers, UT; AAAG-TFB to Sturgis, October 17, 1866, LS, AC, T; report of F. B. Sturgis, December, 1866, ROC, AC, T.

18. Sinclair to AAAG-TFB, December 2, 4, 10 (their conduct), 23 (all other quotations), 1866, LR, AC, T; AAAG-TFB to De Gress, December 7, 1866, ES, AC, T.

19. Delano to AAAG-TFB, January 10, 1867 (cocked pistol), LR, AC, T; AAAG to Delano, August 14, 1866, ES, AC, C; Delano to AAAG-TFB, November [30], 1866 (Servisis), RR, AC, T; Delano to AAAG-TFB, January 6, 1867, ROC, AC, T; SO 3, January 3, 1867, Ms. Orders, TFB.

20. SO 3, January 8, 1867; SO 98, November 13, 1867, Ms. Orders, TFB; Sturgis to AAAG-TFB, February 16, April 1, May 8, July 8, 16, August 26, 31, October 24, 1867, LR, AC, T; AAAG-TFB to AAAG-DT, June 27, 1867; AAAG-TFB to Sturgis, July 3, 1867; Reynolds to Howard, November 22, 1867, LS, AC, T; AAAG-TFB to Sturgis, April 5, 13, June 13, July 11, 15, September 24, October 15, 1867; Griffin to Sturgis, August 8, 24, 1867, ES, AC, T; reports of F. B. Sturgis, February–August, 1867, ROC, AC, T.

21. SO 52, May 3, 1867; SO 88, August 24, 1867; SO 91, October 1, 1867, Ms. Orders, TFB; Garretson to AAAG-TFB, May 18, 21, June 6, 14, November 23, 1867, LR, AC, T; AAAG-TFB to Garretson, April 12, May 23, July 16, 1867; Griffin to Howard, May 1, 1867; AAAG-TFB to Howard, September 27, 1867; AAAG-TFB to AAAG-DT, August 24, 1867, LS, AC, T; AAAG-TFB to Garretson, July 5, August 23, 1867, ES, AC, T; reports of Garretson, May–August, 1867, ROC, AC, T. Garretson's political job is in "Election Register (2-1/9)," vol. 263, Ms. copy, TSL.

22. SO 63, June 18, 1867; SO 77, July 17, 1867; SO 92, October 2, 1867, Ms. Orders, TFB; Ruby to AAAG-TFB, July 24, 25, October 24, 1867, LR, AC, T; Griffin to Howard, May 24, 1867 (quotations); AAAG-TFB to Ruby, June 7, 1867; AAAG-

TFB to Howard, October 1, 1867; Reynolds to AAAG-C, November 13, LS, AC, T. For his election confirmations, see SO 78, April 13, 1868; GO 5, January 11, 1870, Printed Orders, FMD, RG 94, NA. See also Smallwood, "G. T. Ruby," 24–33; Woods, "George T. Ruby," 269–80; Merline Pitre, "George T. Ruby: The Party Loyalist," *Through Many Dangers, Toils, and Snares: The Black Leadership of Texas, 1868–1900,* 166–75; Moneyhon, "George T. Ruby and the Politics of Expedience," 364–78.

23. SO 60, June 3, 1867; SO 66, June 21, 1867; SO 5, January 23, 1868, Ms. Orders, TFB; reports of I. H. Evans, June–July, 1867, September, 1867–January, 1868, ROC, AC, T; Evans to AAAG-TFB, June 3, 22, July 9, August 9, 14, 28, September 17 (two letters), November 13, 1867, LR, AC, T; Gregory to AAAG-C, March 14, 1866; Griffin to Howard, June 3, 1867; AAAG-TFB to Evans, June 3, 6, July 3, September 24, November 4, 1867, January 15, 1868; Reynolds to AAAG-C, January 15, 1868, LS, AC, T; AAAG-TFB to Evans, August 21, September 3, November 16 (two letters), 1867, January 6, 1868; Griffin to Evans, August 28, 1867, ES, AC, T. For his political appointment to the legislature, see GO 18, January 11, 1870, Printed Orders, FMD, RG 94, NA.

24. SO 105, August 29, 1866; SO 31, March 11, 1867; SO 42, April 8, 1867; SO 43, April 11, 1867, Ms. Orders, TFB; reports of J. P. Butler, January–February, 1867, ROC, AC, T.

25. Butler to AAAG-TFB, June 14, 26, 29, August 13, 27, September 16, December 2, 28, 1867, January 22, 24, May 25, 1868; C. H. Marriott to AAAG-TFB, June 16, 1867; H. M. Ellmore to AAAG-TFB, Match 12, 1868; L. B. Hightower to AAAG-TFB, April 16, 1868; LR, AC, T; AAAG-TFB to AAAG-DT, April 8, June 29, 1867; AAAG-TFB to Butler, May 8, June 29, 1867, January 31, April 24, June 5, 1868, LS, AC, T; AAAG-TFB to Butler, June 21, July 29, 1867, ES, AC, T; reports of J. P. Butler, April, 1867–May, 1868 (every dime, unavoidable pleasure [May 1867], old spirit [November]), ROC, AC, T; SO 34, May 30, 1868, Ms. Orders, TFB. For Butler's political career, see SO 78, April 13, 1868; GO 5, January 11, 1870, Printed Orders, FMD, RG 94, NA.

26. See AAAG to Johnson, March 26, 1867, LS, AC, T; Sinclair to Johnson, December 26, 1866; AAAG-TFB to Johnson, May 7, 18, 1867, ES, AC, T; reports of P. B. Johnson, April–July, 1867 (small and dispisable [April]), ROC, AC, T; Johnson to AAAG-TFB, March 15, April 1, June 7, July 6, 1867, LR, AC, T; AAAG-C to Griffin, July 16, 1867, LS, C. See also Lowrie to AAAG-TFB, April 29, 1867; Bvt. Maj. L. H. Sanger to AAAG-TFB, July 8, August 6, 14, 1867, LR, AC, T.

27. SO 21, February 19, 1867, Ms. Orders, TFB; Hunsaker to AAAG, April 27, June 2, 1867, LR, AC, T; AAAG-TFB to [O. F.] Hunsaker, May 11, 1867, LS, AC, T.

28. Hunsaker to AAAG-TFB, February 26, March 29, 1867, LR, AC, T; AAAG-TFB to Hunsaker, February 19, 1867, LS, AC, T.

29. AAAG-TFB to Hunsaker, June 27, 1867, LS, AC, T; Hunsaker to AAAG-TFB, July 9, 16, 31, 1867, LR, AC, T. Griffin seems to have planned for Hunsaker's city appointment for almost a month; see Griffin to Howard, July 3, 1867, LS, AC, T; AAAG-C to Griffin, July 9, 1867, LS, C; SO 82, August 1, 1867, Ms. Orders, TFB; SO 145, August 1, 1867, Printed Orders, DT, RG 94, NA.

30. John Dix to AAAG-TFB, [December ?] 1865, September 25, 1866; September 27, 1867, March 10, 1868; 1 Lt. James Downing to AAAG-TFB, September 22,

1866; Cpt. W. H. Howard to Bvt. Maj. Gen. O. O. Howard, April 25, 1866; LR, AC, T; AAAG-TFB to Dix, October 3, 1866, ES, AC, T; AAAG-TFB to Dix, December 9, 1865; AAAG-TFB to Dr. [Horatio] Taylor, March 2, 1866; LS, AC, T. See also Galveston *Daily News*, September 30, 1865, for the makeup of the occupation forces. Dix states that he returned from "exile" on July 4, 1865 (Dix to AAAG-TFB, March 10, 1868, LR, AC, T), probably to escape his trial for treason to the Confederacy, although local tradition has him raising the national banner upon the landing of Federal troops the month before.

31. For Dix's policies, see his reports, April, 1867–December, 1868, ROC, AC, T. See also Dix to AAAG-TFB, April 23, May 22, 1867, August 17, February 3, 1868; Cpt. W. H. Howard to Bvt. Maj. Gen. O. O. Howard, April 25, 1866, LR, AC, T; AAAG-TFB to Dix, April 10, May 15, 1867, January 31, 1868, ES, AC, T; SCA-FMD to Reynolds, May 12, 1868, LS, CA, FMD, RG 393, NA. His bureau appointment is in SO 41, April 16, 1867, Ms. Orders, TFB.

32. E. J. Davis to AAAG-TFB, August 2, 1867, LR, AC, T; reports of John Dix, February (a few bayonets), April (white supremacy, assassin's war, half human), May (break down), August (Rebels, Copperheads, and Democrats) October (nothing but vigor), 1868, ROC, AC, T.

33. R. J. Denney and forty others to AAAG-TFB, June 5, 1867 (all quotations), LR, AC, T; see also AAAG-TFB to Dix, July 16, December 4, 1867; Reynolds to AAAG-C, May 27; LS, AC, T; AAAG-FMD to Reynolds, May 21, 1868, LS, C; Dix to AAAG-TFB, December 16, 1867; E. J. Davis to Reynolds, December 16, 1867; Dix to AAAG-TFB, March 26, 1868 (including letter to Alice Hawkins [free woman of color]); Margaret E. Love to AAAG-FMD, January 27, 1868, LR, CA, FMD, RG 393, NA. His military political appointment as justice of the peace for county precinct no. 1 is in SO 48, February 2, 1869, Printed Orders, FMD, RG 94, NA. For his county judgeship, see "Election Register (2-1/7)," vol. 261, Ms. copy, TSL.

34. John H. Morrison to AAAG-TFB, June 9, October 3, 1867, September 21, 1867, LR, AC, T; AAAG to Morrison, June 23, 1866, LS, AC, T.

35. Sinclair to AAAG-TFB, March 19, 1867; Morrison to AAAG-TFB, April 7, 10, 1867, LR, AC, T; AAAG-TFB to Morrison, March 28, April 19, 1867, LS, AC, T; SO 36, March 28, 1867, Ms. Orders, TFB; reports of J. H. Morrison, May, 1867–November, 1868 (the feelings [November]), ROC, AC, T.

36. George R. Spaulding to AAAG-TFB, April 15, 1867 (Morrison a rebel); William V. Tunstall to AAAG-TFB, July 3, 1867, April 16, 29 (defends Morrison), 1868; John Reagan and fifteen others to Hancock, January 10, 1868; E. Pettit to Hancock, January 24, 1868; Morrison to AAAG-TFB, February 18, March 18 (I have collected), April 29, May 18, 1868, LR, AC, T; report of J. H. Morrison, May, 1868, ROC, AC, T.

37. Reports of J. H. Morrison, February, 1868 (not a local[it]y), March, 1868 (I have to be lenant), [November 1868] (the Civil Authorities), ROC, AC, T; AAAG-TFB to Morrison, April 16, May 27, 1868, ES, AC, T.

38. AAAG-TFB to Morrison, September 26, 1868, ES, AC, T; SO 71, December 7, 1868, Ms. Orders, TFB; for his political appointments, see SO 195, November 1, 1867, Printed Orders, DT, RG 94, NA; SO 179, October 10, 1869; SO 251, October 26, 1869; GO 5, January 11, 1870, Printed Orders, FMD, RG 94, NA.

39. SO 35, March 25, 1867, Ms. Orders, TFB; M. H. Goddin to AAAG-TFB, April 1, May 9 (fleeing spell), 13, June 12, 20, July 20, August 31, September 25, 1867, LR, AC, T; AAAG-TFB to Goddin, March 26, 1867 (proper man), LS, AC, T; AAAG to Goddin, April 13, 1867, ES, AC, T; reports of M. H. Goddin, April–September, 1867 (worst hole [July], chance at them [May]), ROC, AC, T. For his political career, see "Election Register (2-1/7)," vol. 261, Ms. copy, TSL; SO 78, April 4, 1869; SO 18, January 24, 1870, Printed Orders, FMD, RG 94, NA; "Postmasters Appointment Record, 1867–1877," Texas Registers of Appointments, RG 28, NA. See also Webb et al., *The Handbook of Texas*, vol. 3 (Supplement), 342–43.

40. Goddin to AAAG-TFB, April 19 (hoodwinked, be ashamed, unflinching National men, Jeff Davis), 20 (Devil blush, well tried few, threatened with hemp, white livered), June 30 (devil is in some of them, making as little business), August 31 (scenes of '60), [September 4] (ask them no odds), September 16 (we think the vote), 1867, LR, AC, T; AAAG-TFB to Goddin, July 30, 1867, ES, AC, T; reports to M. H. Goddin, September, 1867 (but will add), ROC, AC, T.

41. Thomas L. Westbrook to AAAG-TFB, August 30, 1867; Bvt. Maj. L. H. Sanger to AAAG-TFB, September 10, 1867; Goddin to AAAG-TFB, October 8, 13, 1867, LR, AC, T; report of M. H. Goddin, July, 1867, ROC, AC, T; SO 90, September 28, 1867, Ms. Orders, TFB.

42. Griffin to Howard, August 17, 1867, LS, AC, T; SO 87, August 19, 1867, Ms. Orders, TFB; Joseph A. Wright to Howard, October 3, 1867; Hunsaker to AAAG-TFB, October 3, 1867; Hunsaker to AAAG-TFB, n. d. (enclosing the Crockett *Sentinel* for October 4 and 23, 1867), LR, AC, T; SO 90, September 28, 1867, Ms. Orders, TFB. AAAG-TFB to Hunsaker, October 12, 1867, LS, AC, T, indicates that Hunsaker was never paid because of "no oath."

43. General Howard recognized the need of an agency here; see Howard to Griffin, April 3, 1867, LS, C. See also Milton Stapp to AAAG-TFB, December 17, 1866; W. G. Kirkman to Joel T. Kirkman, June 17, 1867; Finch to AAAG-TFB, December 18, 1866 (strong, out and out), January 20, September 21, 1867, LR, AC, T; AAAG-TFB to [Finch], July 1, 1867, LS, AC, T; SO 70, July 1, 1867, Ms. Orders, TFB.

44. Reports of Edwin Finch, July–September, 1867 (great pleasure [September]), ROC, AC, T; Finch to AAAG-TFB, August 6 (unsafe), October 9, 1867, LR, AC, T; AAAG-TFB to Finch, July 1, 1867, April 2, 1868, LS, AC, T; AAAG-TFB to Finch, September 5, 1867, ES, AC, T.

45. See John Lippard to AAAG-TFB, August 31, 1867; Alvin Wright to AAAG-TFB, October 18, 1867; Finch to AAAG-TFB, October 9, 22, 1867, LR, AC, T; AAAG-TFB to Finch, October 19, 1867, LS, AC, T; SO 90, September 28, 1868, Ms. Orders, TFB. For Finch's later officeholding (requiring the same ironclad oaths), see SO 73, November 3, 1868; SO 136, June 9, 1869; SO 218, September 16, 1869; GO 179, October 8, 1969, Printed Orders, FMD, RG 94, NA; and "Postmasters Appointment Record, 1867–1877," Texas Registers of Appointments, RG 28, NA.

46. AAAG-TFB to H. S. Johnson, February 12 (quotation), March 26, 1867, LS, AC, T; Johnson to AAAG-TFB, February 18, April 3, September 18, 1867, LR, AC, T; SO 35, March 25, 1867; SO 42, April 8, 1867; SO 43, April 11, 1867, Ms. Orders, TFB. For his earlier political appointment, see "Election Register (2-1/7)," vol. 261, Ms. copy, TSL.

47. On law and order, see AAAG-TFB to Johnson, April 20, May 27, 1867, LS, AC, T; Johnson to AAAG-TFB, April 26, June 13, July 21, August 20, September 17, October 1, 16, November 22, 1867, LR, AC, T. On fines, see Johnson to AAAG-TFB, October 12, 1867, LR, AC, T; AAAG-TFB to Johnson, October 22, 1867, LS, AC, T. Confederate property seizures are in Johnson to AAAG-TFB, May 18, 1867, LR, AC, T. Political considerations are in Johnson to AAAG-TFB March 19, October 15, 17, November 12, 18, 1867, LR, AC, T; AAAG-TFB to AAAG-DT, April 20, 1867, ES, AC, T; SCA-DT to SAC-Sumpter, June 7, 1867, LS, CA, DT, RG 393, NA. The home guard issue is in Johnson to AAAG-TFB, April 16, October 28, 1867, LR, AC, T; AAAG-TFB to Johnson, May 18, 1867, LS, AC, T. Johnson's crop settlement policy is in GO 2, October 1, 1867, Ms. Orders, SAC-Sumpter, copy in LR, AC, T. The request to limit correspondence is from AAAG-TFB to Johnson, October 18, 1867, LS, AC, T. Other similar topics are in reports of H. S. Johnson, March–November, 1867 (dead carcasses [November]), ROC, AC, T.

48. On the several quotations concerning Griffin's death, see Johnson to AAAG-TFB, September 28, 1867, LR, AC, T. The complaints against Johnson's crooked policies are in W.H.H. Brazier to AAAG-TFB, August 16, 1867; L. L. Skeins to Cpt. J. H. Bradford, October –, 1867 (including Bradford to AAAG-TFB, November 2, 1867); O. A. McGinnis to AAAG-TFB, November 13, 1867 (Glories, smell Hell); LR, AC, T; Crockett *Sentinel*, October 23, 1867 (copy in D. S. Hunsaker file for 1867), LR, AC, T; AAAG-TFB to S. F. Robb, December 10, 1867, LS, AC, T.

49. The investigation is in Sinclair to AAAG-TFB, December 7, 13, 1867, January 10, 11, 1869, LR, AC, T; unnumbered order of W. H. Sinclair, December 7, 1867; AAAG-TFB to Cpt. J. J. Emerson, December 20, 1867; Reynolds to Howard, January 9, 1868, LS, AC, T. The McGinnis claim is in Bvt. Maj. Gen. E. R. S. Canby to Howard, March 22, 1869, LS, AC, T. Johnson's relief is SO 3, January 11, 1868, Ms. Orders, TFB.

50. Griffin made no formal order putting Philip Howard in as subassistant commissioner, but Reynolds did reconfirm the appointment in SO 96, October 31, 1867, Ms. Orders, TFB. See AAAG-TFB to P. Howard, May 2, 3, 1868; Griffin to Bvt. Maj. Gen. O. O. Howard, June 3, 1867, LS, AC, T. See also the reports of Philip Howard, May, 1867–January, 1868, ROC, AC, T; AAAG-TFB to Howard, May 18, June 10, 1867, February 28, 1868; Reynolds to P. Howard, January 28, 1868, LS, AC, T; P. Howard to AAAG-TFB, July 30, 1868, LR, AC, T; SO 6, January 28, 1868, Ms. Orders, TFB.

51. On Hart, see SO 35, March 25, 1867, Ms. Orders, TFB; reports of Hardin Hart, May–September, 1867, ROC, AC, T; A. M. Bryant to AAAG-TFB, September 11, 1867; Hart to AAAG-TFB, September 28, 1867, LR, AC, T; AAAG-TFB to Hart, July 20, September 24, 1867, LS, AC, T; Thomas Griffin to AAAG-TFB, July 30, 1868 (story of the shooting), LR, C; SO 90, September 28, 1867, Ms. Orders, TFB. His county judicial appointment is in "Election Register (2-1/7)," vol. 261, Ms. copy, TSL. He left office to become the judge of the Seventh Judicial District, see SO 206, November 11, 1867, Printed Orders, DT, RG 94, NA. Another account of the shooting from Hart's front porch is in the Austin *Republican*, July 25, 1868.

52. A. M. Bryant and others to AAAG-TFB, September __, 1865; Robert H. Taylor and six others [including Bryant] to AAAG-TFB, February 11, 1867; J. C. Richards and fourteen others [including A. M. Bryant] to AAAG-TFB, February 15, 1867; Bryant to AAAG-TFB, September 23, 1867, LR, AC, T. See also, Lt. Col. William S. Abert to AAAG-DT, October 20, 1866; Bryant to Bvt. Maj. Gen. George W. Getty, n.d., in *House Executive Documents*, 40th Cong., 2nd Sess., No. 57, 32–33, 104–105. The oath problem is in Bryant to AAAG-TFB, June 5, 1867, LR, AC, T; AAAG-TFB to Bryant, June 14, 1867, LS, AC, T. His judgeship is in "Election Register (2-1/7)," vol. 261, Ms. copy, TSL.

53. Reports of A. M. Bryant, May–October, 1867, ROC, AC, T; Bryant to AAAG-TFB, May 14, July 16, August 2, September 12, 30, 1867, LR, AC, T; AAAG-TFB to [Bryant], March 7, 1867, LS, AC, T; AAAG-TFB to Bryant, May 8, 1867, ES, AC, T; Bryant to AAAG, June 8, 1867, RR, AC, T; SO 96, October 31, 1867, Ms. Orders, TFB. On the army assumption of duties, see AAAG-TFB to AAAG-DT, July 13, 1867, LS, AC, T; 1 Lt. Thomas Tolman to AAAG-TFB, July 28, 1867, LR, AC, T; report of A. M. Bryant, September, 1867, ROC, AC, T. His election is in SO 78, April 13, 1868, Printed Orders, FMD, RG 94, NA.

9 : The Meanest Republican in Texas

1. On Sinclair's life and career, see Sinclair to AAAG-TFB, October 2, 1867, LR, AC, T; Heitman, *Historical Register*, vol. 1, 889; Galveston *Daily News*, January 12, 1897, 8. For a detailed study and suggestion about the importance of his Reconstruction contributions, see William L. Richter, "Who Was the Real Head of the Texas Freedman's Bureau?: The Role of Brevet Colonel William H. Sinclair as Acting Assistant Inspector General," *Military History of the Southwest* 20 (1990), 121–56.

2. This was the reason for Griffin's GO 11, July 8, 1867, Ms. Orders, TFB, which prevented the planters from making deductions until after the freedmen received their share of the crop and sold it as they pleased, as guaranteed in their contracts.

3. SO 13, February 2, 1867, as modified by SO 27, March 4, 1867, Ms. Orders, TFB; Sinclair to AAAG-TFB, February 26, 1867 (quotations), 28, March 1 (two letters), LR, AC, T.

4. SO 35, March 25, 1867, Ms. Orders, TFB; Howard to Griffin, February 25, 1867, LS, C. On Latimer, see AAAG-C to Latimer, February 25, 1867, LS, C; Latimer to AAAG-TFB, May 1, 21, September 27, 1867, LR, AC, T; Latimer to AAAG-TFB, June 20, 1867, RR, AC, T; Latimer to AAAG-TFB, June 1, 1867, ROC, AC, T; AAAG-TFB to Latimer, May 11, 1867, ES, AC, T; AAAG-TFB to Howard, September 27, 1867, LS, AC, T; and Latimer to E. M. Pease, July 25, 1867, Pease-Niles-Graham Papers, APL. His military appointments to the bench may be followed in SO 169, September 10, 1867; SO 171, September 12, 1867; Printed Orders, DT, RG 94, NA; SO 254, October 29, 1869; SO 279, November 27, 1869; Printed Orders, FMD, RG 94, NA. His earlier appointment is in "Election Register (2-1/8)," vol. 262, Ms. copy, TSL.

5. Sinclair to AAAG-TFB, July 2, 1867, LR, AC, T.

6. Sinclair to 2 Lt. J. T. Kirkman, July 2, 1867, ibid.

7. Sinclair to Throckmorton, January 17, 1867, LS, AC, T. Blacks were not the only ones to suffer from the effects of an inadequate jail at Marlin. When bureau agent A. P. Delano was arrested for mail fraud, he also was chained and at the mercy of the elements. One suspects that most county facilities were sadly inadequate, regardless of the race of the prisoner. See Mrs. E. A. Delano to Griffin, July 7, 1867, LR, AC, T.

8. The crossed-out word was in the original, and all quotations from Sinclair to AAAG-TFB, February 26, 1867, Box 21, RG 105, NA. The problem with Sinclair's stand is that he also interviewed Sergeant John Ross of the Fourth Cavalry, who received a seven-year sentence from a Gonzales County court for horse stealing. Ross claimed that he had rented the animal and had been railroaded by the court because he was a Union soldier. Sinclair said that the sergeant appeared to be a good man, his story reasonable, and that he himself had no doubt that a Texas court would act in such a manner. But upon further investigation, the charge against the sergeant was sustained. See Sinclair to AAAG-TFB, February 26, 1867; Bvt. Maj. George W. Smith to AAAG-TFB, March 25, 1867, LR, AC, T.

9. All quotations from Sinclair to AAAG-TFB, February 26, 1867, Box 21, RG 105, NA. Sinclair's communication includes his prison report, a tabular account of the prison interviews, and an extract from a report by Alabama assistant commissioner of the Freedmen's Bureau, Bvt. Maj. Gen. Wager Swayne.

10. Throckmorton to Bvt. Brig. Gen. James Oakes, March 18, 1867, Governor's Papers (Throckmorton), TSL. Just when the prisoners were released and whether it was by pardon or completion of term of incarceration is not clear. See tabular report in Sinclair to AAAG-TFB, February 26, 1867, Box 21, RG 105, NA. The governor did pardon prisoners in some number, but not in the wholesale manner that Sinclair had recommended. His policy, which never changed, is stated in Throckmorton to AAAG-DT, December 29, 1866, LR, AC, T. For more on the perception of the governor by the army and bureau, and of the Federal authorities by the governor, see Richter, "General Phil Sheridan," 131–54. Quote from SO 105, July 30, 1867, Printed Orders, FMD, RG 94, NA. Sinclair continued to have an interest in blacks jailed in Texas. See Sinclair to AAAG-TFB, March 3, 1867, LR, AC, T, where he looks into conditions in the city jail at Galveston.

11. GO 1, March 19, 1867, Printed Orders, FMD, RG 94, NA. See also Sheridan to Griffin, March 28, 1867, LS, FMD, RG 393, NA.

12. Griffin's role is paraphrased from 14 *Statutes at Large*, 428–29, and 15 *Statutes at Large*, 2–4. For a scathing attack on the congressional policy of favoring dictatorial military over loyal civilian republican rule, by ex-provisional governor A. J. Hamilton, see his "Speech of February 9, 1867," Hamilton Papers, UT.

13. Circ. 10, April 5, 1867, Printed Orders, DT, RG 94, NA. Quote from SO 155, July 16, 1867, ibid. See also GO 71, April 20, 1867; SO 155, August 20, 1867, ibid; and Bvt. Brig. Gen. James Oakes to District Judge–2nd Judicial District, May 26, 1867, Governor's Papers (Throckmorton), TSL.

14. Circ. 13, April 27, 1867, Printed Orders, DT, RG 94, NA. A good statement of the loyalist interpretation of "rebel" justice is in Judge John C. Watrous to Griffin, February 25, 1867, LR, AC, T. Watrous was the Federal judge for the Eastern District of Texas at Houston. Griffin continued the policy of collecting reports of

racial "outrages"; AAAG-TFB to all SACs, March 7, July 3, September 11, 1867; Griffin to Howard, June 15, 1867, LS, AC, T. He also reintroduced the so-called "bureau courts." See printed form, "Monthly Statement of Fines Imposed in Cases Adjudicated by the Freedmen's Court at _____, County of _____, State of Texas, during the Month of _____, _____, with Amounts Collected and Unpaid," LR, AC, T; Griffin to Howard, July 1, 1867, LS, AC, T. This particular statement was for Wharton County in June, 1867. Smarter state officials consulted with the bureau beforehand when arresting blacks; see Georgetown *Watchman*, August 24, 1867.

15. For some of the complaints, see M. S. Huson to Andrew Johnson, April 30, 1867; A. H. Shanks to Johnson, May 8, 1867; Johnson Papers, LC; M. D. Ector to Throckmorton, May 10, 1867, Governor's Papers (Throckmorton), TSL; and H. S. Thomas to AAAG-DT, June 24, 1867, LR, DT, RG 393, NA. For Griffin's insistence that the order be followed, see Griffin to Throckmorton, May 7, 1967, LS, DT, RG 393, NA.

16. Printed form addressed to all judges, May 2, 1867; Throckmorton to Johnson, May 2, 1867; Throckmorton to B. H. Epperson, May 7, 1867, Throckmorton Papers, UT; Griffin to Throckmorton, May 7, 1867; Griffin to Judge J. C. Watrous, May 16, 1867, LS, CA, DT, RG 393, NA; Throckmorton to Johnson, May 20, 1867; Throckmorton to Griffin, May 20, 1867; Johnson Papers, LC.

17. Sheridan to Grant, May 22, 1867; Griffin to Sheridan, May 29, 1867; Sheridan Papers, LC.

18. Griffin to Sheridan, May 29, 1867, Sheridan Papers, LC. See also Griffin to SCA-FMD, June 10, 1867, ibid.

19. Sheridan to Griffin, May 25, 1867, in *House Executive Documents*, 40th Cong. 1st Sess., No. 20, 72; Bvt. Brig. Gen. F. T. Dent to AAAG-FMD, August 8, 1867, LR, FMD, RG 393, NA; Grant to Sheridan, August 15, 1867, Grant Papers, LC; SO 151, September 28, 1867, Printed Orders, FMD, RG 94, NA.

20. AAAG-TFB to all SACs, March 30, 1867 (quotations), LS, AC, T. See also Griffin to SAC-FMD, March 27, 1867, LS, CA, DT, RG 393, NA; Sheridan to Grant, April 12, 1867, Grant Papers, LC; Griffin to Throckmorton, March 26, 1867, LS, AC, T; Throckmorton to Griffin, May 3, 1867, Throckmorton Papers, UT.

21. Circ. 12, April 17, 1867, as modified by Circ. 16, May 16, 1867, Printed Orders, DT, RG 94, NA.

22. Circ. 12, April 17, 1867; Circ. 14, May 1, 1867; Circ. 16, May 16, 1867; SO 163, September 2, 1867; ibid. The oath was also included in AAAG-TFB to all SACs, March 30, 1867, LS, AC, T.

23. For the quotation, see SO 15, April 10, 1867, Printed Orders, FMD, RG 94, NA. For other correspondence, see Sheridan to Grant, April 1, 1867; Grant to Sheridan, April 7, 1867; Grant Papers, LC; Sheridan to Grant, April 6, 1867, Johnson Papers, LC; Grant to Sheridan, April 21, 1867, Sheridan Papers, LC.

24. Sheridan, *Personal Memoirs*, vol. 2, 253, 270.

25. The memorandum was reproduced later in GO 3, January 3, 1868, Printed Orders, FMD, RG 94, NA; for the secrecy statement, see AAAG-DT to AAAG-FMD, December 27, 1867, LS, DT, RG 393, NA.

26. 15 *Statutes at Large*, 14–16; Griffin's view is in Circ. 12, April 17, 1867, Printed Orders, DT, RG 94, NA.

27. Circ. 12, April 17, 1867; Circ. 16, May 16, 1867; Circ. 23, June 21, 1867, Printed Orders, DT, RG 94 NA; AAAG-TFB to all SACs, July 10, 1867, LS, AC, T.

28. There are numerous letters on this topic in National Archives Film Publication M619, roll 634. The men rejected and various letters and figures are in "Protests," Registration Papers, Box 1, RG 393, NA.

29. On B. F. Barkley, see W. H. Horton to AAAG-TFB, August 10, 1867; Barkley to Griffin, February 6, 1867; Barkley, Lewis H. Brown, and Anthony Rucker to AAAG-TFB, August 10, 1867; Hamilton Hunt and sixty others to AAAG-TFB, August 22, 1867, LR, AC, T. Other incidents from Griffin to Sheridan, July 15, 1867, Sheridan Papers, LC; J. W. Wilbarger, *Indian Depredations in Texas*, 128; A. Grigsby to AAAG-TFB, August 1, 1867, LR, AC, T.

30. Circ. 19, June 1, 1867; Circ. 20, June 1, 1867, Printed Orders, DT, RG 94, NA; Griffin's promise is in William Alexander to E. M. Pease, April 12, 1867, Pease-Niles-Graham Papers, APL. See also AAAG-AGO to all COs-MDs in the South, May 22, 1867, *House Executive Documents*, 40th Cong., 1st Sess., No. 20, 12. A registration convoy is described in Speer, *History of Blanco County*, 46. On the duty of whites to register, see J. T. Allen to Dr. Musgrove Evans, June 21, 1867 (the more I think), Registration Mss., box 1, RG 393, NA. Compare Griffin to Harris Greene and others, July 15, 1867, LS, AC, T; Griffin to Howard, May 4, 1867 (it will look), LR, C.

31. AAAG-TFB to General Davis and others, July 20, 1867, LS, AC, T. The Texas situation is in Richter, *Army in Texas*, 79–115, passim. For the situation in Louisiana, see Dawson, *Army Generals and Reconstruction Louisiana*, 46–62.

32. W. B. Thompson to AAAG-DT, August 12, 1867, LR, CA, DT, RG 393, NA. For examples of black voters consulting the bureau for advice, see Green Harris and eight others to AAAG-TFB, July 12, 1867; Colored Republicans of Navasota to AAAG-TFB, August 5, 1867, LR, AC, T. Also of interest on bureau Republican political involvement is Bentley, *History of the Freedmen's Bureau*, 185–202; Pierce, *Freedmen's Bureau*, 161–71.

33. Griffin to Sheridan, July 20, 1867, Sheridan Papers, LC; Griffin to Pease, August 15, 1867, Pease-Niles-Graham Papers, APL. A good example of how Griffin had to await a change in the laws is SCA-DT to SAC-Sumpter, June 7, 1867; Sam T. Robb to AAAG-TFB, July 27, 1867; Z. Norton to AAAG-TFB, [July, 1867?], LR, AC, T.

34. Griffin to Sheridan, July 15, 20 (quotation), 1867, Sheridan Papers, LC; Sheridan to Grant, July 25, 1867; Grant to Sheridan, July 30, 1867, Grant Papers, LC; SO 105, July 30, 1867, Printed Orders, FMD, RG 94, NA. The new law is in 15 *Statutes at Large*, 14–16.

35. C. Caldwell to Pease, September 3, 1867, Pease-Niles-Graham Papers, APL. The quotation is from Throckmorton to B. H. Epperson, September 5, 1867, Epperson Papers, UT. For the command change, see Richter, *Army in Texas*, 112–15.

36. Griffin to N. A. Radgate, May 27, 1867; Griffin to AC-any southern state, July 25, 1867, ES, AC, T; Circ. 3, February 3, 1867; Circ. 9, March 18, 1867; Circ. 14, April 10, 1867; Ms. Orders, C; Circ. Letter, February 24, May 21, 1867, LS, C. See also Circ. 12, December 31, 1868, Ms. Orders, C.

37. See Darby to AAAG-TFB, June 11, August 5, 1867, LR, AC, T; AAAG-

TFB to Darby, August 17, 1867, LS, AC, T; Griffin to Darby, March 15, 1867, ES, AC, T.

38. Report on Freedmen, March 12, 1867, RR, AC, T.

39. Report on Freedmen and Report on Refugees, February 13, 1867; Report on Freedmen, April 10, 1867; Report on Freedmen, May 9, 1867, ibid. Governor Throckmorton pleaded poverty on behalf of several counties in the care of indigent whites and blacks, but Griffin refused to assume any burden given to the state. See Throckmorton to Griffin, April 10, 1867, LR, AC, T; AAAG-TFB to J. J. Thornton, ES, AC, T. The Federal government declared destitution ended in the South. See Circ. 11, April 3, 1867; Circ. 26, July 26, 1867, Ms. Orders, C.

40. Circ. 7, March 9, 1867; Circ. 13, April 10, 1867; Circ. 20, June 6, 1867; Circ. 21, June 27, 1867; Circ. 27, August 9, 1867, Ms. Orders, C; GO 10, June 6, 1867, Ms. Orders, TFB.

41. SO 35, March 11, 1867, Ms. Orders, C.

42. Circ. 17, 1867, ibid.

43. Circ. Letter, June 27, 1867, LS, C.

44. Circ. 2, February 1, 1867, Ms. Orders, C; Griffin to Howard, February 20, 1867, LS, AC, T.

45. Circ. 8, March 12, 1867; Circ. 12, April 7, 1867; Circ. 16, April 17, 1867; Circ. 19, May 27, 1867, Ms. Orders, C; AAAG-TFB to Hasner, Chapman & Co., June 1, 1867, AAAG-TFB to President–First National Bank, Galveston, June 24, 1867; Griffin to Howard, June 24, 1867; AAAG-TFB to William C. Carroll, August 20, 1867, LS, AC, T.

46. SO 155, August 20, 1867, Printed Orders, DT, RG 94, NA. This measure was a response to the state law setting aside separate railroad accommodations passed the previous fall; Gammel, *Laws of Texas*, vol. 5, 1015.

47. Report on Abandoned Lands, June 16, 1867, RR, AC, T. See also Circ. Letter, February 8, 1867; AAAG-C to Griffin, July 22, August 29, 1867; LS, C; AAAG-TFB to AAAG-C, June 25, 1867, ES, C; B. W. Gray to AAAG-TFB, August 18, 20, 1867, LR, AC, T; Griffin to Howard, February 19, June 15, 1867; Griffin to Chairman Newton, February 27, 1867; AAAG-TFB to 1 Lt. A. B. Bonnafon, June 10, 1867; Griffin to Colonel Jones, July 25, 1867; Griffin to Gray, July 27, 1867; all in LS, AC, T.

48. GO 3, January 29, 1867; Circ. 2, February 7, 1867; Ms. Orders, TFB.

49. Griffin to Rev. J. R. Shipard, February 6, 1867, LS, AC, T; Howard to Bvt. Brig. Gen. E. D. Townsend, July 26, 1867, LS, C; 1 Lt. A. H. M. Taylor to Griffin, August 6, 1867; Joseph Beavers to Griffin, March 20, 1867, LR, AC, T. The San Antonio incident is in Mason to Griffin, July 8, 1867, LR, AC, T.

50. Circ. 3, February 12, 1867; GO 6, February 12, 1867, Ms. Orders, TFB; AAAG-TFB to E. M. Wheelock, June 27, 1867, LS, AC, T; D. T. Allen to AAAG-TFB, March 21, 1867; Thomas Mortimer to AAAG-TFB, April 1, 1867, LR, AC, T; SO 129, August 27, 1867, Ms. Orders C.

51. Circ. Letter, December 31, 1866; Circ. Letter, March 8, 1867; Circ. 4, March 30, 1867; Circ. 5, March 29, 1867; Ms. Orders, TFB; Circ. 5, February 20, 1867; Circ. 22, July 1, 1867, Ms. Orders, C. The best understanding of the interdependency between the bureau and the army under the Griffin administration

is Smallwood, *Time of Hope, Time of Despair,* 71. Various transportation orders are in the SO series for 1867, Ms. Orders, TFB.

52. See GO 7, March 1, 1867; GO 12, August 1, 1867; SO 82, August 1, 1867, Ms. Orders, TFB; Howard to Griffin, March 26, April 23, 1867, LS, C; Griffin to Howard, May 1, 1867, LR, C; Howard to Griffin, April 12, 1867; 2 Lt. A. H. M. Taylor to Griffin, August 1, 1867, LR, AC, T; Griffin to Howard, May 25, June 19, 1867; AAAG-TFB to Mrs. Julia G. Allen, March 22, 1867, LS, AC, T; Shipard to Howard, April 19, 1867, ES, C. One historian described Wheelock as a "profane, indolent, scoffing" man whose career embodied "one continuous narrative of malfeasance and misfeasance." See Carpenter, *Sword and Olive Branch,* 163–64.

53. Griffin to Howard, May 1, 1866, LR, C; GO 6, June 19, 1867, Ms. Orders, TFB. See also Sinclair, "Freedmen's Bureau in Texas," 12. Smallwood correctly assesses Griffin's contribution to the program, *Time of Hope, Time of Despair,* 71. His view is in contrast to Hornsby, "Freedmen's Bureau Schools in Texas," 405–406.

54. SO 73, July 9, 1867; GO 12, August 1, 1867, Ms. Orders, TFB; Griffin to Howard, August 12, 1867, LS, AC, T; Allen to AAAG-TFB, August 16, September 6, 1867, LR, AC, T. Quotation in Griffin to 2 Lt. A. H. M. Taylor, July 15, 1867, LS, AC, T. Allen tried to get his job back with Shipard's help, but failed. See Reynolds to Shipard, November 16, 1867, LS, AC, T.

55. Howard to Griffin, July 2, 1867, LS, C; Griffin to Taylor, July 15, 1867, LS, AC, T; Taylor to Griffin, July 15, 23, 27, August 1, 6, 1867; Taylor to Bvt. Maj. Gen. Joseph J. Reynolds, September 17, 1867, LR, AC, T. Taylor returned to his regiment in Texas since Reynolds did not wish to use him as a staff officer. AAAG-C to Reynolds, October 16, 1867, LS, C; Reynolds to AAAG-C, October 25, 1867, LR, C.

10: WILLFUL AND BENIGN NEGLECT

1. Griffin to Howard, August 26 (sickness), 1867, LS, AC, T; Howard to Griffin, August 23, 1867, LR, AC, T; SO 130, August 24, 1867 (Kirkman's wife), Ms. Orders, C; *National Cyclopaedia of American Biography,* vol. 4, 338 (to desert). See also Brownsville *Daily Ranchero,* August 3, 13, 21, 1867; Griffin to AAAG-FMD, July 3, 1867, TR, FMD, RG 393, NA; Sheridan to Grant, August 10, 20, 23, September 3, 1867; AAAG-DT to Grant, September 13, 15, 1867; Doubleday to Grant, [September 15, 1867]; Grant Papers, LC; AAAG-TFB to Howard, September 15, 16, 1867, LR, C; AAAG-DT to Pease, September 15, 1867, Governor's Papers (Pease), TSL. For various military and bureau deaths, see GO 28, August 26, 1867; GO 29, September 5, 1867; GO 30, September 9, 1867; Unnumbered Circular, September 15, 1867; GO 37, October 9, 1867, Printed Orders, DT, RG 94, NA; Bvt. Maj. Gen. J. J. Reynolds to Howard, November 20, 1867, LS, AC, T. For Griffin's death, see Unnumbered Circular, September 15, 1867, Ms. Orders, TFB; transportation home for Mrs. Griffin and the general's body in SO 173, September 16, 1867, Printed Orders, DT, RG 94, NA. See also AAAG-AGO to Bvt. Maj. Gen. J. Mower, No-

vember 11, 1867, Grant Papers, LC. There were no messages out of Texas from August 31 to September 13 (LS, AC, T).

2. Howard to Grant, September 16, 1867, LS, C; Alford, *Fifth Semi-Annual Report on Schools*, 38. Hornsby's criticism of the decline in school attendance because of yellow fever in the statistics for Griffin's administration is not appropriate, as he had the highest attendance levels of any assistant commissioner so far by several thousand. There is no reason to believe Alford's praise, which Hornsby calls "perfunctory," to be anything but sincere and deserved. See the figures in Reynolds to Howard, November 20, 1867, LS, AC, T; Hornsby, "Freedmen's Bureau Schools in Texas," 406.

3. Garretson to Howard, September 17, 18, 1867, LR, C; Garretson to Howard, October 10, 1867, LS, AC, T; AAAG-C to Garretson, September 18, 1867, LS, C; AAAG-DT to Garretson, October 23, 1867, LS, AC, T; GO 15, October 23, 1867, Ms. Orders, TFB.

4. Sinclair to AAAG-C, September 18, October 30, 1867, LR, C; Sinclair to AAAG-C, October 28, 1867 (plus endorsements), LR, AC, T; AAAG-C to Sinclair, October 1, November 22 (quotation), 1867, ES, C.

5. Much of this material is from Reynolds to Howard, November 14, 20, 1867, LS, AC, T. For the effect of the fever on the headquarters staff, see AAAG-TFB to Bvt. Maj. C. Bacon, November 30, 1867, LS, AC, T. For the effect of the fever on selected individuals, see also E. C. Bartholomew to AAAG-TFB, October 28, 1867, LR, AC, T; AAAG-TFB to AAAG-C, October 29, 1867, LR, C; Max Mobbins to Reynolds, December 30, 1867, LR, AC, T; AAAG-TFB to AAAG-C, October 25, 1867; Reynolds to AAAG-C, December 31, 1867; LR, C; Reynolds to AAAG-C, December 7, 1867, January 24, 1868, ES, AC, T; (Thomas Waldron) Reynolds to AAAG-C, November 14, 1867, LR, C; AAAG-C to AAAG-TFB, December 5, 1867, ES, C; Reynolds to Howard, January 31, 1867, LS, AC, T. For resignations, see AAAG-TFB to Howard, September 27 (two letters), 30, 1867, LS, AC, T; SO 90, September 28, 1867; SO 91, October 1, 1867; SO 92, October 2, 1867; SO 96, October 31, 1867, Ms. Orders, TFB. Private surgeons had difficulty in getting all their pay for attending to sick Federal personnel; see AAAG-TFB to AAAG-DT, December 20, 1867, ES, AC, T; Circular Letter, March 15, 1868, LS, C; AAAG-C to AAAG-TFB, September 12, 1868, ES, C; Reynolds to AAAG-C, October 19, 1868, LR, C. The fever caused a delay in sending new recruits to Texas (AAAG-DT to AAAG-FMD, September 30, 1867, LR, FMD, RG 393, NA), prevented officers from rejoining their regiments (Bvt. Brig. Gen. E. D. Townsend to AAAG-FMD, ibid.), and stopped all pay for troops for six months (Townsend to AAAG-FMD, December 20, 1867, ibid.). The army paid for the transport of all Federal dead and their families (AAAG-FMD to Reynolds, October 21, 1867; Townsend to Bvt. Maj. Gen. Joseph Mower, October 22, 1867; LS, FMD, RG 393, NA), but Reynolds suggested that all dead lie buried in Texas at least one year as a type of quarantine (Reynolds to AAAG-FMD, March 9, 1868, LR, FMD, RG 393, NA).

6. The details of the transfer to Austin and the promotion to district command are in SO 444, September 16, 1867, AGO; SO 141, September 17, 1867, DT; GO 36, October 14, 1867, DT, Printed Orders, RG 94, NA; GO 14, September 21,

1867, GO 15, October 23, 1867, Ms. Orders, TFB; AAAG-C to Garretson, September 20, 1867; Howard to Bvt. Col. W. G. Moore, February 10, 1868, LS, C; Reynolds to AAAG-FMD, October 4, 1867, TR, FMD, RG 393, NA; AAAG-FMD to Reynolds, November 13, 1867, TS, FMD, RG 393, NA.

7. Sinclair to AAAG-TFB, October 7, 1867, ES, AC, T; Sinclair to AAAG-TFB, October 25, 30, 1867, LS, AC, T; Sinclair to AAAG-TFB, October 31, 1867; AAAG-TFB to Sinclair, October 31, 1867, LR, AC, T; SO 101, November 22, 1867, Ms. Orders, TFB. The headquarters quarrel is in G. T. Ruby to E. M. Harris, November 1, 1867, LR, AC, T. The political compromises exacted from the Texas Republicans included formally recognizing military supremacy over the provisional government (something that all previous governors had refused to do), and repudiating the notion of *ab initio* (that all laws passed since the 1861 secession were null and void at their conception). Reynolds preferred merely to negate laws in conflict with the results of the war. See Richter, *Army in Texas*, 120–24.

8. Heitman, *Historical Register*, vol. 1, 825; Cullum, *Biographical Register*, vol. 2, 78; Warner, *Generals in Blue*, 397–98; Boatner, *Civil War Dictionary*, 649. See also AAAG-C to Howard, December 27, 29, 1866, January 2 (two letters), 1867; Howard to Stanton, December 20, 1866 (quotation), LS, C.

9. Arthur Eddy & Co. to Reynolds, October 1, 15, 1867, LR, AC, T; GO 17, October 29, 1867, Ms. Orders, TFB; AAAG-C to Reynolds, November 29, 1867, LS, C; Reynolds to Howard, December 3, 1867, LS, AC, T; AAAG-C to Reynolds, December 18, 1867, LR, AC, T.

10. GO 18, November 17, 1867; GO 20, November 27, 1867; Circ. Letter, December 8, 1867; Ms. Orders, TFB; AAAG-TFB to Howard, October 1, 1867, ES, AC, T. Records were really unsafe anywhere but in the headquarters files. For a reward of one thousand dollars for information leading to the arrest and conviction of those who destroyed the records of the Nacogdoches agency, see GO 5, April 27, 1868, Ms. Orders, TFB.

11. Reynolds to Howard, December 3, 1867, January 3, 1868; AAAG-TFB to Howard, December 9, 1867, LS, AC, T; Grant to Reynolds, December 10, 1867; Howard to Reynolds, January 7, 1868, LR, AC, T; Circ. Letter, November 28, December 9, 18, 1867; January 27, 1868, LS, C; AAAG-C to AAAG-TFB, January 22, 1868, ES, C. The problem of the volunteer officers was destined to be repeated eight months later; see Howard to Reynolds, August 19, 1868, LR, AC, T. At that time, these retained volunteer officers were paid at their old in-service grade; Circ. Letter, September 29, 1867, LS, C.

12. Reynolds to Howard, December 17, 1867, LS, AC, T; Howard to Reynolds, December 27, 1867, ES, C.

13. The paperwork requirements are in GO 21, December 5, 1867; GO 1, March 12, 1868; and the files of documents needed in GO 2, March 18, 1868, Ms. Orders, TFB. See also Circ. 29, December 13, 1867, Ms. Orders, C; Circ. Letter, December 18, 1867, LS, C; which treat bureau rights in the army subsistence system and disposal of bureau property. AAAG-TFB to Bvt. Maj. G. M. Bascom, March 24, 1867 (warning against sending documents in lieu of written reports), ES, AC, T; AAAG-TFB to William Holt, October 9, 1868 (warning about addressing the wrong man at headquarters), LS, AC, T. A good example of rents

paid for offices (ranging from ten to thirty dollars a month, depending upon the town) is in Reynolds to AAAG-C, July 16, 1868, LR, C. The only civilian agent who tried to defraud the government in his accounts was Hiram H. Johnson of Sumpter; AAAG-TFB to Bvt. Lt. Col. Warren Webster, February 3, 1868, ES, AC, T. Ignorance of these procedures could cost one his job; see James W. McGreal to AAAG-TFB, August 9, 1868, LR, AC, T.

14. On the agreements between Reynolds and Pease, see Richter, *Army in Texas*, 119–24.

15. GO 40, November 29, 1867, Printed Orders, FMD, RG 94, NA. See also GO 1, January 1, 1868, ibid. Hancock referred special requests back to Texas; see, for example, AAAG-TFB to E. Pettit, February 20, 1868, LS, AC, T. See also Bentley, *History of the Freedmen's Bureau*, 166.

16. For the exchange on political removals and appointments, see SCA to Reynolds, December 4, 1867, TS, CA, FMD, RG 393, NA; Reynolds to Hancock, December 30, 1867; Reynolds to SCA, December 31, 1867; File 57M1868, RG 94, NA. The reconfirmation of the cancellation of Griffin's jury order is in SO 203, December 5, 1867, Printed Orders, FMD, RG 94, NA. The bureau matters are in AAAG-FMD to Reynolds, December 23, 1867, LS, FMD, RG 393, NA, Reynolds to AAAG-FMD, December 30, 1867, LR, C. To protect himself from any possible repercussions, Reynolds forwarded all communications to Howard; Reynolds to Howard, December 31, 1867, LR, C.

17. ASCA to Reynolds, February 4, 1868, LR, AC, T.

18. Reynolds to ASCA, February 12, 1868, LS, AC, T. Once again, Reynolds sent all papers to Howard. See Reynolds to Howard, February 12, 1867, LR, C. A description of subassistant commissioners' procedures according to Reynolds is in Reynolds to Howard, April 14, 1868, LR, C.

19. ASCA to Reynolds, February 27, 1868; Bvt. Lt. Col. G. Norman Lieber to ASCA, [February __, 1868], LR, AC, T.

20. AAAG-FMD to Reynolds, February 11, 1868, LS, FMD; Reynolds to AAAG-FMD, February 19, 1868, LR, FMD; Hancock to Reynolds, March 14, 1868, TS, FMD, all in RG 393, NA.

21. Reynolds to AAAG-FMD, February 20, 1868, LS, AC, T.

22. ASCA to Reynolds, March 3, 1868, LR, AC, T.

23. Reynolds to ASCA, March 11, 1868, LS, AC, T.

24. See GO 14, March 16, 1868; GO 15, March 18, 1868; GO 16, March 25, 1868; Printed Orders, FMD, RG 94, NA; AAAG-FMD to Reynolds, March 16, 1868; Reynolds to AG-USA, March 24, 1868, TS, FMD, RG 393, NA.

25. GO 4, April 7, 1868, Ms. Orders, TFB; Howard to Reynolds, March 28, 1868, LR, AC, T.

26. Reynolds to Howard, April 14, 1868 (two letters), LS, AC, T. The assessment of the independent nature of the Texas command under Buchanan is by his own admission in Buchanan to C/S, July 18, 1868, LS, CA, FMD, RG 393, NA. All Buchanan ever asked of Reynolds was the letter he sent to Hancock in February, 1868, detailing the laws, circulars, and orders under which the Texas bureau command operated; see AAAG-FMD to Reynolds, May 12, 1868, LR, AC, T; Reynolds to ASCA, May 19, 1868, LS, AC, T. Reynolds consistently referred

all policy questions to GO 4; see AAAG-TFB to W. G. Kirkman, April 11, 1868; AAAG to L. B. Hightower, April 22, November 4, 1868, LS, AC, T; W. Tate to AAAG-TFB, June 17, 1868, LR, AC, T.

27. See Richter, "'We Must Rubb Out and Begin Anew'," 334–52, esp. 336–37; Richter, "'Devil Take Them All'," 5–30, esp. 20–21.

28. Proclamation of October 25, 1866, Secretary of State's papers, RG 307, TSL. The quotation is from Brownsville *Daily Ranchero*, December 11, 1867.

29. The whole Reynolds period is revealed in "Letters Received by the Office of the Adjutant General (Main Series), 1866–1890," File 57M1868, Microcopy 619, Roll 634, which contains the pertinent letters, removals and appointments, and general orders and special orders. Removals and appointments are listed in the Mss. "Election Register, 1866–1870," TSL, and "Civil Officers, Texas," RG 393, NA.

30. Circ. Letter, November 5, 1867; AAAG-C to Reynolds, November 9, 1868; LS, C; SO 178, November 18, 1867, Ms. Orders, C.

31. See Reynolds to Howard, January 28, 30, 1868, LR, C; AADO-C to Reynolds, January 21, 1868, ES, C; AAAG-C to Reynolds, March 16, September 30, 1868, LS, C; Reynolds to Howard, March 14, December 12, 1868; AAAG-TFB to James P. Newcomb, March 20, 1868; Reynolds to William R. Thielepape, April 10, 1868; AAAG-TFB to Thielepape, October 13, 1868; LS, AC, T; Bvt. Brig. Gen. John Mason to AAAG-TFB, April 16, 1868, LR, AC, T; SO 54, September 12, 1868, Ms. Orders, TFB. See also Reports on Abandoned Lands, October 5, December 27, 1867, December 21, 1868, RR, AC, T.

32. The Gray-Evans payments are in 2 Lt. Joel T. Kirkman to AAAG-TFB, September 26, 1867, LR, AC, T; Reynolds to Gray, November [25], 1867; AAAG-TFB to Gray, February 15, March 9, 1868; Reynolds to Howard, March 7, April 9, 1868, LS, AC, T; Reynolds to Howard, April 29, 1868, LR, C.

33. The Clark matter is in Reynolds to AAAG-C, September 18, 1868, LR, C; AAAG-TFB to William T. Clark, October 12, December 12, 1868, LS, AC, T; William T. Clark to AAAG-TFB, May 28, 1868, LR, AC, T. The purchase is discussed in Howard to Reynolds, January 22, 1868, LS, C; Reynolds to SCA-FMD, January 4, 1868; AAAG-TFB to Hancock & West, Attorneys, February 3, 1868; Reynolds to Lyman Mallory, April 17, 1868, LS, AC, T; Lyman Mallory to AAAG-TFB, April 13, 1868, LR, AC, T. See also Reports on Abandoned Lands, October 5, December 27, 1867, December 21, 1868, RR, AC, T.

34. Reports on Abandoned Lands, October 5, December 27, 1867, December 21, 1868, RR, AC, T; AAAG-C to Reynolds, September 18, 1868; Circ. Letter, October 9, 1868, LS, C; Reynolds to Howard, August 28, 1868; AAAG-TFB to AAAG-FMD, August 29, 1868; Reynolds to Bvt. Brig. Gen. Ranald S. Mackenzie, November 16, 1868, LS, AC, T; Reynolds to Howard, June 9, 1868, ES, AC, T; Bvt. Maj. W. Hartz to AAAG-TFB, November 10, 1868, LR, AC, T. See also SO 10, February 21, 1868; SO 11, February 22, 1868; SO 37, June 12, 1868; SO 63, October 26, 1868, Ms. Orders, TFB.

35. AAAG-TFB to George F. Harris and others, January 13, 1868, ES, AC, T.

36. AAAG-TFB to John M. Davis, January 8, 1868; AAAG-TFB to W. H. Cundliff, December 21, 1868, LS, AC, T; E. A. Daniel to AAAG-FMD, May 19, 1868, LR, CA, FMD, RG 393, NA; W. H. Cundliff to AAAG-TFB, October 13, 1868, LR, AC, T.

37. For the search for freedmen, see Circ. Letter, September 21, October 26, 1866; Reynolds to AC-Kentucky, September 18, 1868; Reynolds to 1 Lt. F. W. Liedtke, September 21, 1868, LS, AC, T; Reynolds to AAAG-C, November 6, 1868, LR, C. For fraudulent importation of hands, see Reynolds to AC-Georgia, February 3, 1868, ES, AC, T.

38. Circ. Letter, December 4, 1867, LS, C; Report on Refugees, July 16, August 18, September 14, 1868, RR, AC, T.

39. Circ. 3, May 12, 1868, Ms. Orders, C; AAAG-TFB to Mrs. L. H. Cunningham, February 26, 1868, LS, AC, T.

40. AAAG-TFB to Sinclair, October 7, 1867, ES, AC, T.

41. Garretson to AAAG-TFB, October 11, 1867, LR, AC, T.

42. Garretson to AAAG-TFB, October 14, 31, 1867, ibid.; GO 16, October 28, 1867, Ms. Orders, TFB. Wheelock reported for duty two weeks later; AAAG-TFB to Wheelock, November 13, 1867, LS, AC, T.

43. Howard to Reynolds, December 20, 21, 1867, March 12, 1868, LR, AC, T; Reynolds to Howard, January 4, July 29, 1868, LS, AC, T; GO 3, March 21, 1868, Ms. Orders, TFB.

44. GO 19, November 23, 1867; Circ. Letter, February 15, 1868; Ms. Orders, TFB. For Reynolds reminding a teacher of the salary by tuition only, see AAAG-TFB to Miss E. M. Evans, June 19, 1868, ES, AC, T.

45. Reynolds to Rev. J. J. Whipple, November 26, 1867; Reynolds to Rev. J. R. Shipard, October 8, 1868, LS, AC, T. An example of a teacher, Fannie Campbell at Austin, following bureau guidelines is in Reynolds to Howard, February 14, 1868, LS, AC, T. Government-paid transportation was limited to actual employees. For example, Superintendent Welch could not get his wife a free trip to Texas. See AAAG-C to AAAG-TFB, November 11, 1868, ES, C. Private teachers who wanted bureau help were told to seek sponsorship by a benevolent association first; AAAG-TFB to SS, November 20, 1868, ES, AC, T.

46. AAAG-TFB to Howard, March 21, 1868, LS, AC, T. See also Smallwood, *Time of Hope, Time of Despair*, 71–72; Elliott, "Freedmen's Bureau in Texas," 9 n. 22, 15; Hornsby, "Freedmen's Bureau Schools in Texas," 406.

47. AAAG-C to all ACs and SSs, October 6, 1868, LS, C; Reynolds to Howard, October 22, 1868, LS, AC, T.

48. For the Goliad incident, see A. McBride to AAAG-TFB, February 7, 29 (quotation), 1868, LR, AC, T; Cpt. P. E. Holcomb to AAAG-TFB, April 10, 1867, LR, AC, T. The Paris occurrence is in DeWitt C. Brown to AAAG-TFB, April 30, 1868, ROC, AC, T; Brown to AAAG-TFB, May 16, 1868, LR, AC, T. The Bowie County material is from W. G. Kirkman to AAAG-TFB, November 30, 1867, ROC, AC, T. The reward for those who burned Circleville's school is in GO 7, July 8, 1868, Ms. Orders, TFB. For other instances of opposition to black schools, see Smallwood, *Time of Hope, Time of Despair*, 76–84.

49. SO 39, 23, 1868, as modified by SO 48, August 11, 1868, Ms. Orders, TFB.

50. Sinclair to AAAG-TFB, August 25, 1868, ibid.

51. Sinclair to AAAG-TFB, July 25, August 24, 1868, ibid.

52. Sinclair to AAAG-TFB, August 18, 1866, LR, AC, T; Reynolds to Howard, August 25, LR, C; Reynolds to AGO, October 22, November 4, 1868, LS, FMD, RG 393, NA; GO 15, October 12, 1868, Printed Orders, FMD, RG 94, NA. A full

listing of crimes during Reconstruction reported to the bureau is in "Record of Criminal Offenses Committed in the State of Texas," 3 Ms. vols., AC, T. For those the army tracked, see "Register of Crimes Committed in Texas, 1866–1868," 3 vols. (listed by county), and "Abstracts of Crimes Committed in Counties of Texas, 1869–1870," 3 vols. (listed by date), RG 393, NA.

11: CARE AND CIRCUMSPECTION

1. Reynolds to Howard, February 15, 1868, LS, AC, T; AAAG-C to AAAG-TFB, May 26, 1868, ES, C. Examples of job applications and refusals to make any more appointments fill the 1868 series, LS, AC, T. Three exceptions to the rule were the appointments as subassistant commissioners for the harvest and settlement season of William J. Neely, a former civilian aide to Bvt. Maj. Gen. Francis Herron, and David Beath and William Holt, mustered-out sergeants from the Sixth Cavalry. See "Rosters of Officers and Civilians on Duty . . . ," September, 1868, Ms. vol. 9, AC, T.

2. All figures compiled from "Rosters of Officers and Civilians on Duty . . . ," October, 1867–December, 1868, Ms. vol. 9, AC, T. See also Special Orders, series 1867 and 1868, Ms. Orders, TFB.

3. "Rosters of Officers and Civilians on Duty . . . ," October, 1867–December, 1868, Ms. vol. 9, AC, T.

4. SO 98, August 10, 1866; SO 61, January 1, 1867; Ms. Orders, TFB; Mayer to AAAG-TFB, August 9, 23, September 30, October 6, November 5, December 27, 1866, June 9, September 25, 1867, LR, AC, T.

5. Mayer to AAAG-TFB, December 23, 31, 1866, January 2, 14, May 28, September 1 (including endorsement), 1867, LR, AC, T; Sinclair to Mayer, December 16, 26 (two letters), 1866, January 15, 1867, LS, AC, T; AAAG-TFB to Mayer, September 25, November 24, 1866, March 8, July 16, 1867, ES, AC, T; reports of Mayer, December, 1866, April–June, 1867, September–October, 1867, December, 1867, December, 1867, ROC, AC, T.

6. On the hiring of a clerk, see Mayer to AAAG-TFB, January 16, February 1, 3, 23, 1867, LR, AC, T; Sinclair to Mayer, January 4, 1867, ES, AC, T. The quarrel with headquarters staff is in Mayer to AAAG-TFB, January 25, May 20, December 2, 1867; Mayer to R. F. Cordura, May 19, 1867, LR, AC, T. Mayer's sickness and leave are in Sam Sharpe to AAAG-TFB, June 17, August 10, November 13, 1867; Mayer to AAAG-TFB, July 20, September 1, 2, October 24, December 16, 1867, LR, AC, T. The spat with Hancock is in Mayer to AAAG-TFB, January 15, 24, February 11, 1868, LR, AC, T; Mayer to AAAG-TFB, January 21, 24, 1868, LR, C; Mayer to AAAG-FMD, January 25, 1868, LR, CA, FMD, RG 393, NA. His resignation is in Mayer to AAAG-TFB, February 8, 23, 1868, LR, AC, T; Reynolds to Howard, February 15, 1868; AAAG-TFB to Mayer, February 15, 1868, ES, AC, T.

7. Cpt. E. Miller to AAAG-TFB, February 21, May 31, June 23, 26 (quotations), July 12, 15, September 3, 17, 23, October 23, December 6, 26, 30, 1867, LR, AC, T; AAAG-TFB to Miller, March 7, 13, 16, April 3, 20, 23, 1867; Reynolds to Howard, January 20, 1868, LS, AC, T; AAAG to Miller, March 12, 16, 18, April 4,

15, May 8, November 25, December 17, 1866, ES, AC, T; Miller's reports, February–November, 1867, ROC, AC, T; SO 95, October 7, 1867; SO 105, December 24, 1867, Ms. Orders, TFB.

8. On Sherman, see reports of 1 Lt. Thomas Tolman, April, 1867; 1 Lt. H. E. Scott, November, 1867–March, 1868; 2 Lt. E. C. Hentig, May–December, 1868, ROC, AC, T. On Kaufman, see reports of 1 Lt. S. H. Lincoln, September, 1867–August, 1868, ROC, AC, T; Lincoln to AAAG-TFB, September 5, December 10, 1867, LR, AC, T; AAAG-TFB to Lincoln, November 30, 1867, LS, AC, T; AAAG-TFB to Lincoln, July 18, August 27, 1867, ES, AC, T.

9. SO 112, September 17, 1866; SO 15, February 7, 1867; SO 20, February 18, 1867; SO 28, March 3, 1867; SO 33, May 22, 1868; GO 9, December 31, 1868, Ms. Orders, TFB; Davis to AAAG-TFB, September 4, 1866, January 17, February 23, March 7, 1867, May 30, June 30, 1868; Loyal League of Houston to AAAG-TFB, June 26, 1868, LR, AC, T; Kiddoo to Davis, September 16, 1866; Sinclair to Davis, January 3, 1867; Reynolds to Howard, May 15, 1868; AAAG-TFB to Davis, January 29, February 14, March 1, 1867; May 23, June 16, September 21, 1868, LS, AC, T; AAAG-TFB to Davis, July 24, October 23, 1868; Reynolds to Howard, August 29, 1868, ES, AC, T; reports of M. E. Davis, June–November, 1868, ROC, AC, T. Davis's relationship to Smith is in *Report of the Joint Select Committee to Investigate Facts*, 45. His military appointment as marshal is in SO 44, February 23, 1869, Printed Orders, FMD, RG 94, NA.

10. For Trinity County, see Sinclair to AAAG-TFB, July 18, 23, 1868, LR, AC, T; SO 114, May 5, 1869; SO 306, December 30, 1868, Printed Orders, FMD, RG 94, NA.

11. SO 17, February 3, 1868, Printed Orders, War Department, RG 94, NA; SO 12, February 24, 1868; GO 2, February 2, 1869, Ms. Orders, TFB; Stevenson to AAAG-TFB, February 29, March 5, 20 (two letters), 23, 25, 26, April 8, 9, 10, 21, 22, 24, 30, May 2, 11, June 15, July 31, September 21, November 18, LR, AC, T; AAAG-TFB to Stevenson, March 16, 23, April 17, July 16, September 25, LS, AC, T; Reynolds to E. M. Pease, April 13, 1868; AAAG-TFB to Stevenson, April 6, 23, July 3, 28, 31, Ocotber 7, 1868, ES, AC, T; reports of L. W. Stevenson, April–December, 1868, ROC, AC, T. The political removals and appointments are in SO 130, June 12, 1868, Printed Orders, DT; SO 59, October 16, 1868; SO 102, April 30, 1869; SO 119, May 20, 1869; Printed Orders, FMD, RG 94, NA.

12. SO 3, January 11, 1868; SO 74, December 23, 1868, Ms. Orders, TFB; Homer to AAAG-TFB, December 31, 1867, January 18, 20, 26, 27, 31, February 24, March 2, 17, 20, April 1, 2, 20, May 18, 25, July 3, 18, 1868, LR, AC, T; AAAG-TFB to Homer, January 10, 13, 29, 31, February 4, 28, August 21, December 26, 31, 1868, LS, AC, T; reports of A. B. Homer, January–November, 1868, ROC, AC, T. His political appointments are in SO 89, April 15, 1869; SO 179, October 10, 1869, Printed Orders, FMD, RG 94, NA; USOR (1869).

13. SO 50, August 25, 1868; SO 73, December 22, 1868, Ms. Orders, TFB; Reynolds to Howard, August 25, 1868, LS, AC, T; AAAG-TFB to Holt, September 10, 1868, ES, AC, T; Holt to AAAG-TFB, September 15, 1868, LR, AC, T; reports of W. Holt, September–December, 1868 (kindliest feeling [September], saucy nigger, head shot off [November]), ROC, AC, T.

14. On Lacy, see SO 98, August 8, 1868, Ms. Orders, C; SO 50, August 25,

1868; GO 9, December 31, 1868, Ms. Orders, TFB; Lacy to AAAG-TFB, September 15, 1868, LR, AC, T; AAAG-TFB to Lacy, September 25, October 8, December 31, 1868, LS, AC, T; reports of H. C. Lacy, September–November, 1868, ROC, AC, T.

15. SO 44, July 31, 1868, Ms. Orders, TFB; Reynolds to Howard, July 31, 1868; AAAG-TFB to Neely, July 31 (quotation), August 25, 1868, LS, AC, T; Neely to AAAG-TFB, August 31, October 1, 1868, LR, AC, T; AAAG-TFB to Neely, October 3, 1868, ES, AC, T; reports of Neely, August–October, 1868, ROC, AC, T. The political appointments of Neely as assessor and collector, alderman, and clerk of the county court are in SO 10, August 20, 1868; SO 212, May 5, 1869; SO 27, February 4, 1870; Printed Orders, FMD, RG 94, NA. There was a significant change in the local government, as Neely requested, in late 1868. See SO 55, October 12, 1868, Printed Orders, FMD, RG 94, NA.

16. Neely to AAAG-TFB, August 20, September 3, 9, October 20, 1868, LR, AC, T; AAAG-TFB to Neely, August 27, October 17, 1868, LS, AC, T; Reynolds to Howard, October 28, 1868; AAAG-TFB to AAAG-C, November 16, 1868, ES, AC, T; Reynolds to Howard, October 28, LR, C; AAAG-C to AAAG-TFB, August 13, November 7, 1868, ES, C; Reynolds to Howard, August 5, 1868, LS, AC, T; Howard to Reynolds, August 19, 1868, LS, C; SO 51, August 26, 1868, Ms. Orders, TFB; Sinclair to AAAG-TFB, September 7, 8, 1868, LR, AC, T.

17. SO 35, March 25, 1868; SO 62, October 17, 1868; GO 9, December 31, 1868, Ms. Orders, TFB; Clark to AAAG-TFB, September 27, 1867, April 25, July 14, 1868, LR, AC, T; AAAG-TFB to Clark, March 26, 1867, April 21, July 19, 1868, LS, AC, T; AAAG-TFB to Clark, June 13, 1867 (two letters), January 27, 1868; reports of H. Clark, April–July, September, 1867–December, 1868, ROC, AC, T.

18. Burke to AAAG-TFB, May 29 (telegram and letter), June 1, 2 (telegram and letter), 3, 1868, LR, AC, T; AAAG-TFB to Burke, May 30 (two letters), June 2, June 5, 1868; AAAG-TFB to Howard, May 30, June 2, 1868; LS, AC, T; SO 34, May 30, 1868, Ms. Orders, TFB.

19. Reynolds to Howard, June 10, July 13, 1868; AAAG-TFB to Sinclair, July 6, 1868, LS, AC, T; R. M. Bankhead and 120 others to AAAG-TFB, June 20, 1868; Stewart to AAAG-TFB, July 5, 1868; Sinclair to AAAG-TFB, July 5, 7, 13, 15, 1868, LR, AC, T; report of W. H. Stewart, June, 1868, ROC, AC, T. His political jobs are in SO 49, March 1, 1869; SO 241, October 13, 1869, Printed Orders, FMD, RG 94, NA. For his bureau appointment and resignation, see SO 36, June 10, 1868; SO 42, July 13, 1868, Ms. Orders. TFB.

20. SO 42, July 13, 1868, Ms. Orders, TFB; Reynolds to Bvt. Maj. Gen. O. O. Howard, July 13, 1868; AAAG-TFB to W. H. Howard, July 31, August 29, September 24, 26, October 2, 1868, LS, AC, T; Sinclair to AAAG-TFB, July 5, 1868; W. H. Howard to AAAG-TFB, September 21, 1868, LR, AC, T; reports of W. H. Howard, July, November–December, 1868, ROC, AC, T.

21. Howard to AAAG-TFB, July 30, August 6, 12, October 6, 29, November 6, [December __], 1868, LR, AC, T; Reynolds to Howard, July 31, 1868, LS, AC, T; AAAG-TFB to Howard, July 18, November 3, 1868, ES, AC, T; report of W. H. Howard, December, 1868 (quotation), ROC, AC, T. For Howard's court appointment, see SO 142, June 16, 1869, Printed Orders, FMD, RG 94, NA. Howard's quarrels with the local army commandant extended past the closing of the bu-

reau field offices at the end of 1868; Reynolds to AAAG-FMD, January 8, 1869, LS, AC, T.

22. Howard to AAAG-TFB, October 6, November 25, 1868, February 3, 1869 (all quotations), LR, AC, T.

23. On Bledsoe, see SO 33, May 22, 1868, Ms. Orders, TFB; Reynolds to A. Bledsoe, April 20, 1868; AAAG-TFB to Sam Jones, May 22, 25, 1868; AAAG-TFB to W. A. Bledsoe, May 22, June 11, July 13, 1868; Reynolds to Howard, May 23, July 13, 1868, LS, AC, T; A. Bledsoe to AAAG-TFB, May 8, 1868; W. A. Bledsoe to AAAG-TFB, June 3, 1868, LR, AC, T; report of W. A. Bledsoe, June, 1868, ROC, AC, T; SO 42, July 13, 1868, Ms. Orders, TFB. On the soldiers at Dallas, see reports of 1 Lt. Henry Norton, July–August, 1868; of Bvt. Maj. L. H. Sanger, November, 1868, ROC, AC, T.

24. Reynolds to Howard, March 18, April 24, 1868, LS, AC, T; Wood to AAAG-TFB, March 18, 1868, LR, AC, T. Wood's political appointment is in SO 195, November 1, 1867, Printed Orders, DT, RG 94, NA.

25. Reports of F. P. Wood, April–December, 1868, ROC, AC, T.

26. Wood to AAAG-TFB, June 26, 28, 30, July 6 (letter and telegram) 1868, LR, AC, T; AAAG-TFB to Wood, June 26, July 6, 1868, LS, AC, T; Wood to AAAG-FMD, August 22, 1868, LR, FMD, RG 393, NA; AAAG-TFB to Wood, December 26, 1868, ES, AC, T; GO 9, December 31, 1868, Ms. Orders, TFB.

27. Sinclair to AAAG-TFB, July 6, 1868, LR, AC, T.

28. AAAG-TFB to Foster, September 21, 1865, April 23, 1866, May 12, 1868, LS, AC, T; Foster to AAAG-TFB, April 13, 1868; Sinclair to AAAG-TFB, May 11, 1868, LR, AC, T; SO 30, May 12, 1868, Ms. Orders, TFB. For his political positions, see "Election Register (2-1/7)," vol. 261, Ms. copy, TSL.

29. Foster to AAAG-TFB, June 1, October 23, 1868, LR, AC, T; AAAG-TFB to Foster, June 5, 1868, LS, AC, T; AAAG-TFB to Foster, June 19, July 28, 1868, ES, AC, T; report of F. P. Wood, April, 1868; A. K. Foster, May, July, November, 1868, ROC, AC, T; GO 9, December 31, 1868, Ms. Orders, TFB; GO 5, January 11, 1870, Printed Orders, FMD, RG 94, NA.

30. SO 30, May 12, 1868; GO 9, December 31, 1868, Ms. Orders, TFB; Baker to AAAG-TFB, May 9, 31, July 18, 1868; Sinclair to AAAG-TFB, September 7, 8, 1868, LR, AC, T; AAAG-TFB to Baker, May 5, 12, June 2, July 17, 18, 1868, January 23, 1869; Reynolds to Howard, May 11, 1868; LS, AC, T; AAAG-TFB to Baker, August 13, 1868, ES, AC, T; reports of T. H. Baker, May–December, 1868, ROC, AC, T. Baker's political jobs are in SO 195, November 11, 1867, Printed Orders, DT; SO 223, September 22, 1869; GO 5, January 11, 1870; Printed Orders, FMD, RG 94, NA.

31. SO 18, March 3, 1868; GO 9, December 31, 1868, Ms. Orders, TFB; E. M. Harris to AAAG-TFB, July 29, 1867 (quotation); Griffin to AAAG-TFB, March 4, May 23, July 31, August 18, 1868, LR, AC, T; AAAG-TFB to Griffin, February 21, June 11, August 14, 1868; Reynolds to Howard, March 10, 1868, LS, AC, T; AAAG-TFB to Griffin, April 13, 1868, ES, AC, T; reports of T. C. Griffin, March–December, 1868, ROC, AC, T. Griffin's political positions are in SO 195, November 11, 1867, Printed Orders, DT; SO 91, April 17, 1869; SO 148, June 23, 1869, Printed Orders, FMD, RG 94, NA.

32. SO 85, June 20, 1866; SO 95, July 26, 1866; SO 122, October 16, 1866; SO

127, October 26, 1866; SO 148, December 14, 1866; SO 149, December 17, 1866; SO 74, December 23, 1868, Ms. Orders, TFB; Rock to AAAG-TFB, September 29, December 20, 1866, April 30, July 26, August 30, September 18, November 11, 1867, January 10, February 1, 3, 5, March 26, August 8, December 17, 1868; Sinclair to AAAG-TFB, December 21, 1866; Reynolds to Rock, February 7, 1867, February 7, 1868; William Sheriff to AAAG-TFB, July 2, 1867; M. Evans to AAAG-TFB, July 26, 1867; George C. Booth to AAAG-TFB, June 10, 1868; Howard to Reynolds, September 9, 1868; [Ku Klux Klan] to Martin McEnery, December 2, 1868, LR, AC, T; AAAG-TFB to Rock, July 31, August 14, September 4, October 3, 1866, May 1, July 24, 26, 29, November 4, 1867, February 4, May 22, 26, July 3, August 17, 19, 22, September 14, December 31, 1868; Kiddoo to Wright, June 7, 1866; Sinclair to Rock, December 28, 1866, January 1, 1867; Griffin to Rock, February 9, 1867; Reynolds to Rock, February 7 (two letters), 1868, LS, AC, T; Sinclair to Cook and Andrews (attorneys), January 9, 1867; Sinclair to 1 Lt. J. Hutchison, January 9, 1867; AAAG-TFB to AAAG-DT, July 20, August 27, 1867; AAAG-TFB to Rock, March 1, 1867, January 19, February 17, April 23, 30 (two letters), August 9, 10, October 3, 1868, ES, AC, T; reports of W. H. Rock, December, 1866–March, 1867, May–September, 1867, December, 1867–July, 1868, September–December, 1868, ROC, AC, T. The first historian to note Rock's importance to the bureau and Texas Reconstruction was Shook, "Federal Occupation and Administration of Texas," 251.

33. Reinhard to AAAG-TFB, August 25, November 12, 19, 1866, LR, AC, T; SO 104, August 27, 1866, TFB.

34. Statement of Thomas Holliman (free man of color), February 23, 1867; Reinhard to AAAG-TFB, February 18, April 12, 1867; D. C. Brown to AAAG-TFB, March 14, May 1, 1867; Cpt. J. H. Bradford to AAAG-TFB, April 8, 1868; John K. Potts to Griffin, February 20, March 18, 1868, LR, AC, T; AAAG-TFB to Reinhard, March 27, ES, AC, T; AAAG-TFB to Reinhard, April 2, 1867; AAAG-TFB to Bradford, July 25, 28, September 10, 1867; Griffin to Throckmorton, March 1, 1867, LS, AC, T. For a similar incident, in which whites opposed the creation of independent black settlements, see Felix, "Decline and Fall of Freedmen's Village," 247–50.

35. Cpt. S. I. Wright to Sinclair, October 22, 1866; Reinhard to AAAG-TFB, November 16, 1866, LR, AC, T; AAAG-TFB to Reinhard, November 27, 1866, LS, AC, T; Leathers, *Through the Years,* 53.

36. F. W. Harnes to AAAG-TFB, March 5, 1867; J. D. Stepp to AAAG-TFB, November 4, 1867; Norman B. Tunstall to AAAG-TFB, February 18, 1868; Reinhard to AAAG-TFB, April 5, 1868, LR, AC, T; Sinclair to Reinhard, January 29, 1867; AAAG-TFB to Reinhard, February 20, March 14, May 22, 1868, LS, AC, T.

37. SO 10, February 21, 1868, Ms. Orders, TFB; Sinclair to AAAG-TFB, March 4, 6 (two letters, quotation), 1868, LR, AC, T.

38. Dr. T. N. Mimms to AAAG-TFB, October 14, 1867; Reinhard to AAAG-TFB, December 10, 1867; J.R.R. Lynch and seven others to 2 Lt. Edwin Turnock, February 28, 1868; W. H. Cunliff to AAAG-TFB, August 24, 1868; A. T. Monroe and others to AAAG-TFB, August 17, 1868; A. T. Monroe to AAAG-TFB, August 20, 1868, February 28, 1868, LR, AC, T; AAAG-TFB to Reinhard, February 12, May 28, 1868; AAAG-TFB to W. H. Cunliff, October 22, 1868, LS, AC,

T; AAAG-TFB to Reinhard, December 30, 1867, ES, AC, T; reports of F. W. Reinhard, October, 1867, January, 1868, ROC, AC, T. Reynolds's removal of the sheriff and justice of the peace are in SO 95, April 2, 1869, Printed Orders, FMD, RG 94, NA.

39. Reinhard to AAAG-TFB, September 14, 1866, April 16, 1868, LR, AC, T; AAAG-TFB to Reinhard, April 2, 1867, May 28, 1868, LS, AC, T; SO 67, June 22, 1867; SO 74, July 10, 1867; SO 90, September 28, 1867; SO 4, February 8, 1869, Ms. Orders, TFB. See also SO 139, June 12, 1869; SO 43, February 24, 1870, Printed Orders, FMD, RG 94, NA; Sinclair to AAAG-TFB, March 9, 19, 30, April 1, 17, 1867, LR, AC, T.

40. SO 65, April 18, 1866, Ms. Orders, TFB. For the day-to-day business, see Randlett to AAAG-TFB, April 24, 28, June 14, 1866 (roughs), LR, AC, T; Randlett to AAAG-TFB, June 30, 1866, RR, AC, T; AAAG-TFB to Randlett, April 20, May 31, June 20, July 23, August 18, December 24, 1866, LS, AC, T; AAAG-TFB to Randlett, December 15, 1866, ES, AC, T; Griffin to AAAG-C, May 20, 1867, LR, C. The political business is in Randlett to AAAG-TFB, July 2, August 17, 1867 (good men), LR, AC, T; AAAG-TFB to Randlett, July 15, 1867; Griffin to SCA-DT, August 12, 1867; AAAG-TFB to SCA-DT, August 20, 1867, ES, AC, T. For the sheriff's appointment, see SO 16, January 22, 1868, Printed Orders, FMD, RG 94, NA.

41. Randlett to AAAG-TFB, December 25, 1866, September 23, November 13, December 30, 1867, LR, AC, T; AAAG-TFB to Randlett, December 24, 1867, January 20, 1868, LS, AC, T; Citizens of Anderson to Randlett, October 3, 1867, copy in Governor's Papers (Pease), TSL; Randlett's reports, December, 1866, March–May, 1867, July–September, 1867, November, 1867–January, 1868, ROC, AC, T; SO 156, December 31, 1866; SO 6, January 29, 1867; SO 29, March 8, 1867; SO 105, December 31, 1867; Ms. Orders, TFB.

42. SO 57, September 23, 1868; SO 62, October 17, 1868, Ms. Orders, TFB; Reynolds to AAAG-C, August 1 (containing the report of Randlett, dated July 23, with corrections dated August 4), August 7 (containing the Report of Gentry dated July 24), 1868, LR, C. For Randlett's resignation, see Randlett to AAAG-TFB, October 14, 1868, LR, AC, T; Reynolds to AAAG-TFB, October 17, 1868, LR, C. For Gentry's position, see GO 30, September 3, 1868, Printed Orders, FMD, RG 94, NA. See also Randlett's reports, February–September, 1868, ROC, AC, T. The importance of eliminating all potential black leadership is a theme in Crouch, "Freedmen's Bureau Records," 86–87; and Crouch, "Self Determination and Local Black Leaders in Texas," 344–55. Also of interest are: Felix, "Decline and Fall of Freedmen's Village," 247–50; O'Brien, "Reconstruction in Richmond," 259–81; Magdol, "Local Black Leaders in the South," 81–110; Magdol, *A Right to the Land*; Pitre, "Evolution of Black Political Participation," 36–45; Barr, "Black Legislators of Reconstruction Texas," 340–52; Smallwood, *Time of Hope, Time of Despair*, 128–58; Rankin, "Role of the Negro Office Holders"; Fennell, "Negro in Texas Politics"; Hale, "Political Leadership in Texas."

43. SO 39, April 3, 1867; SO 74, December 23, 1868, Ms. Orders, TFB; Randall to AAAG-TFB, March 23, April 10, May 11, June 7, July 13, 15, 19, August 9, September 20, 27, October 5, 19, November 4, December 24, 1867, January 18, 1868; E. H. Mitchell to AAAG-TFB, May 28, 1867; W. H. Libby to AAAG-TFB,

July 19, 1867; George W. Dyrant to AAAG-TFB, December 7, 1867; AAAG-TFB to AAAG-FMD, n.d., LR, AC, T; Randall to AAAG-TFB, August 31, 1867, RR, AC, T; AAAG-TFB to AAAG-DT, June 21, July 20, 23, 1867; AAAG-TFB to Randall, May 18, June 1, July 20, 23, August 8, October 12, 22, December 25, 1867, January 10, 27, February 4, June 11, November 4, December 31, 1868, LS, AC, T; AAAG-TFB to Randall, July 18 (two letters), October 11, 1867; AAAG-TFB to William Fair and others, December 6, 1867, ES, AC, T; reports of J. L. Randall, April–June (revolver and pony [May], no southern, if a nigger [June]), August 1867–December, 1868 (deplorably ignorant [August 1867], great care [October 1867]), ROC, AC, T. The few political appointments are in SO 195, November 1, 1867, Printed Orders, DT; SO 61, October 19, 1868, Printed Orders, FMD, RG 94, NA.

44. 2 Lt. John H. Archer to AAAG-TFB, June 25 (I would), September 19 (I propose), 1866; J. H. Archer to AAAG-TFB, August 26, October 18, 1868, LR, AC, T; AAAG-C to AAAG-TFB, September 17, 1868, ES, C; AAAG-TFB to Archer, September 28, 1868, LS, AC, T; SO 125, October 22, 1866, Ms. Orders, TFB.

45. Archer to AAAG-TFB, November 4 (two letters), 28, December 26, 31, 1866, January 11, 21, 29, 1867, LR, AC, T; Archer to AAAG-TFB, November 30, 1866, RR, AC, T; AAAG-TFB to Archer, November 7, December 1, 1866; Lathrop to Archer, December 16, 1866; Sinclair to Archer, December 28 (two letters), 1866, January 4, 14 (two letters), 18, 28, 1867, LS, AC, T; AAAG-TFB to Archer, November 12, 30, 1866, ES, AC, T; reports of J. H. Archer, December, 1866 (all quotations)–January, 1867, ROC, AC, T; SO 15, February 7, 1867, Ms. Orders, TFB.

46. Reports of J. H. Archer, March, 1867–December, 1868, ROC, AC, T; Archer to AAAG-TFB, September 10, 1867, September 18, 1868, LR, AC, T; AAAG-TFB to Archer, August 8, 1867, LS, AC, T; SO 86, August 8, 1867; SO 75, December 24, 1868; Ms. Orders, TFB. His appointment as judge is in SO 119, May 20, 1869, Printed Orders, FMD, RG 94, NA.

47. Raymond to AAAG-TFB, April 20, 1868, LR, AC, T; Sinclair to Raymond, June 29, 1868, LS, AC, T.

48. These paragraphs are a compilation of Collins's ideas as presented throughout his baker's dozen of reports while stationed at Brenham. See reports of Cpt. Edward Collins, March, 1867–March, 1868, ROC, AC, T.

49. Hancock to Howard, February 24, 1868, copy in LR, AC, T.

50. Reports at Bryan of Bvt. Maj. James Gillette, October–November, 1868, ROC, AC, T.

12: THE GRAND CYCLOPS HAS COME

1. Sinclair to AAAG-TFB, July 13 (bad habits, given to, disgraceful conduct), 15, August 18 (Grand Cyclops, I know how), 1868, LR, AC, T.

2. On Butler, see SO 45, August 1, 1868; SO 75, December 24, 1868, Ms. Orders, TFB; Butler to AAAG-TFB, April 20, June 9, July 31, August 20, 25, October 16, November 19, 1868; Sinclair to AAAG-TFB, July 13, 1868, LR, AC, T; Reynolds to Howard, August 3, 1868; AAAG-TFB to Butler, July 25, August 3, 8, 1868; LS, AC, T; Reynolds to Howard, August 27, 1868, ES, AC, T; AAAG-C

to AAAG-TFB, September 8, 1868, ES, C; reports of M. Butler, August–December, 1868, ROC, AC, T.

3. Sinclair to AAAG-TFB, August 18, 1868, LR, AC, T. On Metzner's term, see William C. Philips and ten others to AAAG-TFB, October 16, 1867; William King and others to AAAG-TFB, November 20, 1867; S. W. Blount to AAAG-TFB, November 23, 1867; Metzner to AAAG-TFB, November 25, 1866; Jacob Omerod to AAAG-TFB, December 6, 1867; Metzner to AAAG-TFB, April 17, June 23, 27, 1868, LR, AC, T; AAAG-TFB to Metzner, April 22, June 23, 1868, LS, AC, T; AAAG-TFB to Metzner, November 7, 1867, ES, AC, T. The relief is in Sinclair to AAAG-TFB, December 9, 1867, July 13, 1868, LR, AC, T; Reynolds to Howard, July 31, 1868, LS, AC, T; SO 44, July 31, 1868, Ms. Orders, TFB. See also Metzner's reports, January–May, 1868, ROC, AC, T.

4. SO 98, November 13, 1867, Ms. Orders, TFB; SO 153, October 3, 1867, Printed Orders, AGO, RG 94, NA; Taylor to Griffin, August 29, 1867; Taylor to Howard, August 29, 1867; Rolfe to AAAG-TFB, November 13, 25, December 9, 12, 20, 1867, LR, AC, T.

5. Sinclair to AAAG-TFB, January 2, 9, 1868, LR, AC, T.

6. SO 2, January 10, 1868, Ms. Orders, TFB; Sinclair to Rolfe, December 31, 1867; Sinclair to AAAG-TFB, January 2, 1868; Rolfe to Reynolds, January 20, 1868 (money), LR, AC, T; Sinclair's unnumbered order, December 31, 1867; Reynolds to Howard, January 9 (intemperance), 11, 1868; AAAG-TFB to Rolfe, January 9, 1868, LS, AC, T.

7. AAAG-TFB to Rolfe, January 9, 1868, LS, AC, T; Taylor to AAAG-TFB, February 15, 28, 1868, LR, AC, T.

8. SO 59, September 28, 1868; SO 65, November 2, 1868, Ms. Orders, TFB; AAAG-TFB to Sinclair, October 2, 1868; AAAG-TFB to Steinberg, October 24, 1868; Reynolds to Howard, October 1, November 6, 1868, LS, AC, T; Reynolds to Howard, October 1, 1868; AAAG-TFB, October 12, 1868, ES, AC, T; AAAG-C to Reynolds, October 14, 1868, LS, C; AAAG-C to AAAG-TFB, October 12, 1868, ES, C; Steinberg to AAAG-TFB, October 30, 1868, LR, AC, T. Steinberg's Alabama career, during which time he was part of a ring that stole over 10,000 freedmen's rations destined for the Garland Home Farm and resold them to groceries and planters around Greenville, can be followed in Steinberg to AAAG-AlaFB, May 17, June 3 (two letters), August 6, 16, 30, 1866, Judge B. F. Porter to Bvt. Maj. Wager Swayne (AC-Alabama), May 16, June 7, 22, 1866, Cpt. W. C. Arthur (AAIG-AlaFB) to AAAG-AlaFB, n.d. [July __, 1866], July 11, 1866, LR, AC-Alabama, RG 105, NARA; SO 47, March 14, SO 60, April 10, SO 63, April 16, SO 6, June 16, 1866, Ms. Orders, ibid.

9. SO 24, April 15, 1868, Ms. Orders, TFB; Horton to AAAG-TFB, April 30, May 2, 4, 18, June 3, 12, July 3, 21, 28, August 4, 5, September 6, 1868, LR, AC, T; AAAG-TFB to John B. Jones, June 4, 1868, LS, AC, T; reports of Horton, April–July, 1868, ROC, AC, T. See also SO 35, June 4, 1868, Ms. Orders, TFB; AAAG-TFB to Sinclair, June 6, 1868, LS, AC, T; Sinclair to AAAG-TFB, June 6, 8, 1868; Sinclair to Sheriff John B. Jones, June 27, 1868, ES, AC, T.

10. Horton to AAAG-TFB, September 8, 1868, LR, AC, T; AAAG-TFB to Horton, September 19, 1868, LS, AC, T.

11. SO 55, September 19, 1868, Ms. Orders, TFB; quotations from Horton to

AAAG-TFB, September 20, 1868, LR, AC, T. The accusations came from both Unionists and Horton's rebel enemies. See Reynolds to Howard, September 19, 1868, and enclosures, LR, C; T. G. Kendall to AAAG-TFB, April 10, 1868; John J. Good to AAAG-TFB, August 8, 28, 1868; S. S. Jones to AAAG-TFB August 12, 1868; Horton to AAAG-TFB, April 20, May 6, August 19, August 21, September 16, 1868, LR, AC, T. For the lawsuit, see Horton to AAAG-TFB, October 28, 30, LR, AC, T; AAAG-TFB to Horton, October 29, November 4, 1868, LS, AC, T.

12. SO 101, August 18, 1866, Ms. Orders, TFB; reports of Harris, April–May, July 1867, ROC, AC, T; most of the reports were either not filed or are missing, but the letter file is copious. See, for example, Harris to AAAG-TFB, November 30, December 12, 1866, January 18 (two letters), 31, March 7, April 10, 17, May 10, 22, June 17, July 1, 22, August 29, October 6, 1867; Sinclair to AAAG-TFB, December 8, 1867 (three letters); LR, AC, T; AAAG-C to AAAG-TFB, October 15, December 16, 1867, ES, C.

13. Harris to AAAG-TFB, October 8, 1867 (quotation), December 17, 1867; various legal documents in unassigned letters, 1867; R. V. Cook and J. H. Crisp to AAAG-TFB, October 2, 16, November 16, 1867; John H. Crisp to AAAG-TFB, December 30, 1867, LR, AC, T; AAAG-TFB to Harris, December 3, 1867; Reynolds to Bvt. Col. W. T. Gentry, December 3, 1867, LS, AC, T.

14. J. H. Crisp and R. V. Cook to AAAG-FMD, October 10, 11, 1867; John H. Crisp to Maj. Gen. W. S. Hancock, January 17, 1868, LR, FMD, RG 393, NA; Harris to AAAG-TFB, January 31, February 7 1868; AAAG-FMD to Harris, February 19, 1868; E. M. Pease to Reynolds, February 27, 1868, LR, AC, T; AAAG-TFB to Harris, February 19, 1868, LS, AC, T; AAAG-TFB to Wheelock, October 24, 1867; AAAG-TFB to Harris, February 3, 1868, ES, AC, T; Sinclair to AAAG-TFB, April 1, 1868 (quotation), LR, C; SO 8, February 7, 1868, Ms. Orders, TFB.

15. SO 102, November 22, 1867, Ms. Orders, TFB; Sinclair to AAAG-TFB, December 8 (two letters and quotations on teachers), 1867, January 30 (knock higher than a kite), 1868, LR, AC, T. Harris's removal is SO 8, February 7, 1868, Ms. Orders, TFB, effective on February 29, 1868.

16. F. W. Grassmeyer to AAAG-TFB, April 16, 1868, LR, AC, T; Bvt. Brig. Gen. F. D. Sewall to Howard, April 22, 1868; Reynolds to 1 Lt. William H. Hick, April 30, 1868; Reynolds to Sinclair, April 30, 1868; Sinclair to AAAG-TFB, May 6, 1868, LR, C. See also Sinclair to AAAG-TFB, May 4, 6, 11, 13, 20, 1868, LR, AC, T; AAAG-TFB to Sinclair, April 25, 1868, LS, AC, T. Sinclair did not fully settle the Harris audit until May, 1869. See Sinclair to AAAG-TFB, May 30, 1869, LR, AC, T.

17. Reynolds to Howard, April 17, 1868 [including copies of the Galveston *Republican*, April 6, 1868; Pease to Sinclair, April 14, 1866; and Sinclair to Reynolds, April 15, 1868], LR, C. A somewhat similar complaint against Sinclair, for allegedly favoring the appointment of his brother-in-law over another to a clerkship, is in Samuel Dodge to AAAG-C, April 20, 1866, LR, C. Dodge's complaint was disposed of in the same manner as the newspaper's; see Sinclair to AAAG-TFB, May 19, 1866, ES, AC, T. Harris and the now-retired black bureau agent, George T. Ruby, had been involved in an attempt to purge Sinclair's influence at headquarters in late 1867, with the aid of Reynolds's AAAG, 2 Lt. J. P. Richardson (Ruby to Harris, November 1, 1867, LS, AC, T). The fact that the letter is in headquar-

ters correspondence probably indicates that Sinclair and Reynolds found it during the audit, and were more than happy to get rid of Harris. Reynolds soon replaced Richardson with 2 Lt. Charles Vernou; GO 6, May 16, 1868, Ms. Orders, TFB.

18. SO 5, January 23, 1868; SO 77, December 30, 1868, Ms. Orders, TFB; Jenkins to AAAG-TFB, February 1, 13, March 4, April 1, May 2, July 13, September 23, October 7 (curses, I believe), 1868, LR, AC, T; Reynolds to Howard, January 20, 1868; AAAG-TFB to Jenkins, February 19, May 11, August 3, 20, December 31, 1868, LS, AC, T; reports of N. B. Jenkins, February–December, 1868 ("indespensible" [December]), ROC, AC, T.

19. On Cotton Gin, see 1 Lt. J. F. Hill to AAAG-TFB, December 21, 1867, LR, AC, T; reports of Bvt. Maj. R. P. Wilson, January–February, 1868, ROC, AC, T; SO 15, March 2, 1868, Ms. Orders, TFB.

20. SO 46, August 8, 1868, Ms. Orders, TFB; Beath to AAAG-TFB, July 9, August 14, 17, 19, 26, September 26, 29, 1868, LR, AC, T; AAAG-TFB to Beath, July 16, August 29, September 4, 1868; AAAG-TFB to John Morrison, September 4, 1868; Reynolds to Howard, August 1, 1868, LS, AC, T; Reynolds to Howard, August 27, 1868; AAAG-TFB to Beath, September 5, 1868, ES, AC, T; AAAG-C to AAAG-TFB, September 8, 1868, ES, C; reports of D. S. Beath, August–September, 1868, ROC, AC, T.

21. SO 55, September 19, 1868; SO 75, December 21, 1868, Ms. Orders, TFB; Beath to AAAG-TFB, October 29, November 6, 8, 30, December 1, 13 (two letters), 14, 16 (two letters), 18, 19, 21, 23, 24, 1868; W. T. Allen and others to AAAG-TFB, December 11, 1868; Allen to AAAG-TFB, December 26, 31, 1868; B. Trigg to AAAG-TFB, January 4, 1869, LR, AC, T; AAAG-TFB to Allen, October 9, 1868; AAAG-TFB to Beath, November 11, December 15, 1868, LS, AC, T; AAAG-TFB to Beath, November 21, December 26 (two letters), 1868, ES, AC, T; reports of D. S. Beath, October–December, 1868, ROC, AC, T. His postmastership is in "Postmaster's Appointment Record, 1867–1877," Texas Registers of Appointments, RG 28, NA.

22. 1 Lt. D. F. Stiles's reports, December 1867–February, 1868 ("anything but friendly" [February]), ROC, AC, T; Stiles to AAAG-TFB, February 12, 1868, LR, AC, T; AAAG-TFB to Stiles, February 17, 1868, LS, AC, T; Herring & Anderson (attorneys) to Maj. Gen. W. S. Hancock, February 5, 28, 1868, LR, AC, T. See also Sinclair to AAAG-TFB, January 10, 20, 1868, LR, AC, T.

23. SO 13, February 26, 1868; SO 66, November 16, 1868; SO 73, December 22, 1868; GO 4, February 8, 1869, Ms. Orders, TFB; Haughn to AAAG-TFB, February 20, March 20, April 17, May 15, 18, 28, June 11, 22, 24, 27, July 25, September 5, 10, 16, 18, 21, 26 (two letters), 29 (This Bureau), October 3, (two letters), November 14, 17, December 31, 1868, LR, AC, T; AAAG-TFB to Haughn, April 8, May 22, 29, July 29, August 25, September 3, 21, 22 (two letters), 25, 26, October 5, 6 (two letters), 10 (two letters), November 12, 1868, January 7, February 2, 4, 1869; Reynolds to Howard, February 26, 1868; Sinclair to Haughn, June 27, 1868; Bvt. Maj. Gen. E.R.S. Canby to Haughn, February 9 (two letters), March 16 (two letters), 1869, LS, AC, T; AAAG-TFB to Haughn, 20, 23, June 11, August 29, 1868, ES, AC, T; AAAG-C to AAAG-TFB, March 3, 25, 1869, ES, C; reports of C. Haughn, March–December, 1868 (You went and voted [April], Disloyal Rabble

[June]), ROC, AC, T. For his political positions, see SO 179, October 8, 1969; GO 18, February 1, 1870, Printed Orders, FMD, RG 94, NA.

24. See George F. Eber to AAAG-TFB, March 7, 31, 1868; Thomas C. Griffin to AAAG-TFB, April 11, 1868; Charles Haughn to AAAG-TFB, April 14, 1868 (quotation); A. Bledsoe to AAAG-TFB, May 8, 1868, LR, AC, T; AAAG-TFB to Howard, March 24, April 18, 1868; AAAG-TFB to Eber, March 24, 1868; AAAG-TFB to Sam Jones, May 5, 1868, LS, AC, T; SO 21, March 24, 1868, Ms. Orders, TFB.

25. Reports of 2 Lt. E. O. Gibson, June, August, 1867; of Cpt. T. M. K. Smith, September–December, 1867; of Bvt. Lt. Col. J. F. Grimes, January–February, 1868, ROC, AC, T; AAAG-TFB to Smith, August 17, 1867, LS, AC, T; AAAG-TFB to Smith, October 26, 1867; AAAG-TFB to Grimes, February 22, 1868, ES, AC, T.

26. SO 60, June 3, 1867; SO 1, January 3, 1868; SO 10, February 21, 1868; SO 77, December 31, 1868, Ms. Orders, TFB; Bvt. Lt. Col. James Fleming to AAAG-TFB, March 4, 1868; Ferguson to AAAG-TFB, May 20, September 28, 1867, March 4, April 15 (cowardly), 21, May 1, December 1, 5 (suicide, Ku Klux), 7, 20, 1868, January 29, 1869, LR, AC, T; AAAG-TFB to Ferguson, April 25, 1868, January 7, February 15 (two letters), 1869, LS, AC, T; reports of A. Ferguson, March–July, September–December, 1868, ROC, AC, T.

27. SO 124, October 19, 1866; SO 35, March 25, 1867, Ms. Orders, TFB; Lowrie to AAAG-TFB, July 29, August 12, September 13, October 22, 1867; Bvt. Lt. Col. J. C. Bates to AAAG-District of Louisiana, August 3, 1867; H. C. Pedigo to AAAG-TFB, September 17, 1867, LR, AC, T. Lowrie, a friend of Enon M. Harris, came highly recommended. See Kiddoo to Howard, August 25, 1866, LR, C; AAAG-TFB to Lowrie, September 10, 1866, ES, AC, T. See also reports of Bvt. Maj. L. H. Sanger, August, 1867–March, 1868, ROC, AC, T.

28. Lowrie to AAAG-TFB, January 4, May 6, July 26, December 5, 1867, September 9, 1868, LR, AC, T; AAAG-TFB to Lowrie, October 11, December 21, 1867, July 31, August 1, 1868, LS, AC, T; AAAG-TFB to Lowrie, May 15, September 4, 1867, ES, AC, T; reports of Lowrie, January, 1867, April, 1867–June, 1868, ROC, AC, T; SO 44, July 3, 1868, Ms. Orders, TFB.

29. Sinclair to AAAG-TFB, July 23, August 18 (all quotations), 1868, LR, AC, T.

30. See reports of Bvt. Lt. Col. D. L. Montgomery, April–June, 1867, August, 1867–March, 1868; of Bvt. Col. Levi Bootes, July, 1867, ROC, AC, T. See also AAAG-TFB to Montgomery and 1 Lt. Charles Garretson, November 2, 1867, LS, AC, T. For a detailed account of the work of the bureau among the freedmen at Tyler, see Crouch, "Freedmen's Bureau and the 30th Sub-district in Texas."

31. For the order to leave Barrett and his men behind, AAAG to Montgomery, March 27, 1868, LS, AC, T. The original order, which Montgomery did not heed, is in SO 15, March 2, 1868, Ms. Orders, TFB. See also reports of 1 Lt. Gregory Barrett, Jr., March–September, 1868, ROC, AC, T (quotations from March).

32. The Kennedy incident is in Barrett to AAAG-TFB, July 21, August 14, 1868, LR, AC, T; Reynolds to AAAG-FMD, July 23, 28, TR, FMD, RG 393, NA; Reynolds to Howard, August 3, 1868, LR, C.

33. Barrett to AAAG-TFB, July 25, August 31, September 2, 8, 30, 1868, LR, AC, T; for the sheriff's replacement, SO 16, August 27, 1868, Printed Orders, FMD, RG 94, NA. See also AAAG-TFB to Barrett, August 1, 28, 1868, LS, AC, T; for the

townspeople's complaints against Barrett, S. P. Donly to L. D. Evans, August 10, 1868, copy in LR, AC, T. Donly had been a judge on the state supreme court under A. J. Hamilton, and Evans was the area's current representative to the state constitutional convention.

34. Sinclair to AAAG-TFB, August 10, 1868, LR, AC, T.

35. Reports of 1 Lt. W. T. Hartz, October, 1868 (quotation); of Bvt. Maj. Horace Jewett, November–December, 1868, ROC, AC, T; Thomas Meador and 122 others to Reynolds, September 26, 1868, LR, AC, T; AAAG-TFB to Jewett, October 13, 1868, LS, AC, T.

36. SO 2, January 1, 1867; SO 3, January 8, 1867; SO 14, February 7, 1867; SO 20, February 18, 1867; SO 29, April 8, 1867, Ms. Orders, TFB; Brown to AAAG-TFB, January 4, March 14, April 28, May 1, 1867, LR, AC, T; AAAG-TFB to Brown, February 14, March 1, 14, 1867; LS, AC, T; reports of D. C. Brown, January–February, 1867, ROC, AC, T.

37. SO 66, June 21, 1867; SO 68, June 26, 1867, Ms. Orders, TFB; Brown to AAAG-TFB, May 8, 15, August 7, 15, 23, 26, 1867; Dr. J. F. Reed to AAAG-TFB, August 13, 1867, LR, AC, T; AAAG-TFB to Brown, May 15, June 10, 14, 21, 1867, LS, AC, T; report of D. C. Brown, May, 1867, ROC, AC, T.

38. SO 90, September 28, 1867; SO 64, October 30, 1868; SO 69, November 30, 1868, Ms. Orders, TFB; Brown to AAAG-TFB, October 10, 29, 1867, January 1, February 21, April 27, May 16, 18, 20, June 8, 12, August 14, 27, September 2, 5, 30, October 28, November 13, 17, 1868, LR, AC, T; AAAG-TFB to Brown, February 21, July 31, September 14, 26, 1868; AAAG-TFB to Hancock and West (attorneys), March 3, 1868, LS, AC, T; AAAG-TFB to Brown, December 10, 1867; AAAG-TFB to AAAG-DT, May 29, 1868, ES, AC, T; reports of D. C. Brown, November, 1867–October, 1868, ROC, AC, T. Brown's career is covered in depth in William L. Richter, "'The Revolver Rules the Day!': Colonel DeWitt C. Brown and the Freedmen's Bureau in Paris, Texas, 1867–1868," *Southwestern Historical Quarterly* 93 (1989–90), 303–32.

39. AAAG to Rand, February 15, 1869, LS, AC, T. Rand was also asked to file atrocity reports for his Matagorda station, but said he kept no records of them while there; Rand to AAAG, March 1, 1868, LR, AC, T.

40. Rand's daily business routines are from his monthly reports; Rand to AAAG, December 31, 1867, February 29, April 1, 30 (property seizure policy), May 31, July 1, 31, 1868, ROC, AC, T.

41. SO 15, March 2, 1868, TFB. The lack of cases is evident in the monthly reports, which specifically called for their delineation. See previous note. Rand's inactivity caused the neighboring agent, W. G. Kirkman, in Subdistrict Fifty-eight, to file an official complaint against him. See Kirkman to AAAG, March 31, 1868, ROC, AC, T.

42. Rand to AAAG, December 31, 1867 (bad men), February 1 (three or four cavalrymen), April 30 (cannot travel three miles), July 1 (freedmen reluctant to complain), 31, 1868 (cooperation of whites), ROC, AC, T.

43. Rand to AAAG, February 4, 1868, LR, AC, T.

44. Rand to AAAG, February 1, 29, April 1, 30, 1868, ROC, AC, T.

45. Rand to AAAG, July 21, 1868, LR, AC, T; Rand to AAAG, July 31, 1868, ROC, AC, T.

46. The account of the aftermath of Griffith's murder is from Rand to AAAG, July 21, August 2, 1868 (quoted), and Rand to U.S. senator [of New York] E. D. Morgan, September 11, 1868, all in LR, AC, T; Rand to AAAG, July 31, 1868, ROC, AC, T. The various Clarksville agents (Latimer, Roberts, Rand, Shorkley) will be treated fully in William L. Richter, "'This Bloodthirsty Hole': Opposition to the Freedmen's Bureau in Clarksville and Northeastern Texas, 1867–1868" (work in progress).

47. Kirkman has arguably the most complete set of detailed reports of any Texas bureau agent for the era. See reports of Kirkman, July, 1867–September, 1868, ROC, AC, T. The report for August, 1868, is missing, while that of August, 1867, is Kirkman to AAAG-TFB, August 31, 1867, LR, AC, T. See also Smallwood, "The Freedmen's Bureau Reconsidered," 309–20; William L. Richter, "'Shoot or Get Out!': The Murder of Freedmen's Bureau Agent William G. Kirkman" (work in progress).

48. Reports of Bvt. Col. S. H. Starr, September, 1867–January, 1869, ROC, AC, T; the enticement case is in W. E. Hart and D. P. Boyd to Hancock, January 28, 1868; Starr to AAAG-TFB, February 25, 1868, LR, AC, T; AAAG-TFB to Starr, November 5, 1867, March 6, 1868; AAAG-TFB to Messrs. Penn and Burke, February 27, 1868, LS, AC, T. The shutdown order is SO 15, March 2, 1868, Ms. Orders, TFB.

49. Reports of Bvt. Lt. Col. W. B. Pease, October–December, 1868 (quotation from November); of Bvt. Maj. George Shorkley, October–December, 1868 (quotations from October), ROC, AC, T.

50. Reports of Cpt. T. M. K. Smith, April–August, 1868, ROC, AC, T; Smith to AAAG-TFB, June 24, 28, 1868, LR, AC, T.

51. Reports of 1 Lt. Henry Sweeney, September–October, 1868, ROC, AC, T.

52. Reports of 1 Lt. E. C. Henshaw, November–December, 1868, ibid.

53. The best published account of events in Jefferson is Trelease, *White Terror,* 137–48. A good summary of events of the era is in Conner, "Rise and Decline of Jefferson, Texas," 60–80 (for the Smith murder, see 60–68). See also Bvt. Maj. James Curtis to AAAG-TFB, September 19 (fraud and outrage, mad dog, scour the country), 1868; GO 29, October 13, 1868, Post of Marshall, Sweeney to AAAG-TFB, October 12, 26, November 2 (prowling about), 1869, LR, AC, T. The anti-masking ordinance is GO 15, October 12, 1868. The results of the military commission (which allegedly indicted three black members of the Knights of the Rising Sun) are in GO 175, October 1869; GO 202, November 12, 1869, Printed Orders, FMD, RG 94, NA. The state constitutional convention adjourned for one day in memory of Smith's contribution to Reconstruction; *Journal of the Reconstruction Convention [of] 1868,* vol. 2, 7.

54. The campaign is in Richter, *Army in Texas,* 146–47. One suspects that 1 Lt. Cyrus S. Roberts, a headquarters aide, had much to do with planning this campaign, as it was exactly what he had called for thirteen months previously, when he served as subassistant commissioner at Clarksville. For Roberts's suggestion to make it more dangerous for citizens to shield the brigands than to aid the army; see Roberts to AAAG, November 12, 1867, LS, AC, T. Kirkman made a similar proposal in his monthly report, January 1, 1868, as did Shorkley, his successor, later in his report of October 31, 1868; both in ROC, AC, T.

55. Barthlomew, *Cullen Baker*, 84.

56. Canby's law-and-order policy through the use of mixed infantry and cavalry forces is put forth in his GO 4, January 16, 1869, Printed Orders, FMD, RG 94, NA. See also Richter, *Army in Texas*, 162–64, especially map on 163.

CONCLUSION

1. SO 72, December 9, 1868; SO 73, December 22, 1868; SO 74, December 22, 1868; SO 75, December 24, 1868; SO 76, December 29, 1868; SO 77, December 30, 1868; SO 78, December 31, 1868; GO 9, December 12, 1868; Ms. Orders, TFB; AAAG-TFB to AAQM&DO-TFB, January 4, 1869, LS, AC, T. For the paucity of many local agency records, see Everly and Pacheli, *Preliminary Inventory of the Field Offices of the Bureau of Refugees, Freedmen, and Abandoned Lands*, vol. 3, 452–72.

2. GO 91, November 4, 1868, AGO, RG 94, NA.

3. GO 1, January 18, 1869; GO 2, February 1, 1869; SO 4, February 8, 1869; Ms. Orders, TFB.

4. These questions are posted by Forrest McDonald in a presidential context, but they might be appropriate to help analyze any departmental executive, governmental or private. See McDonald and McDonald, *Requiem*, 165–66.

5. Sinclair, "Freedmen's Bureau in Texas," 2–6. Written more than twenty years ago, Sinclair's brief, yet singular, paper for the Johns Hopkins University Institute of Southern History analyzes the racial attitudes of the Texas assistant commissioners. Despite his narrow focus, his conclusions are remarkably valid as regards the Gregory administration, but more limited in scope in reference to the other Texas bureau heads. Gregory is comparable in time and policy to Thomas Conway in Louisiana; White, *Freedmen's Bureau in Louisiana*, 17–40, passim. The ouster of both men indicates the success of those who wished to compromise the bureau's announced objectives. See McFeely, *Yankee Stepfather*, 68–69, 166–75.

6. Sinclair, "Freedmen's Bureau in Texas," 6–11, deals with Kiddoo, but the complexities of the general's regime do not readily admit to a brief analysis. As with his friend and colleague, Brevet Major General Wager Swayne, the assistant commissioner in Alabama, Kiddoo saw Reconstruction from his Northern legal and military background. He opposed slavery, but through his conventional thinking and moderate actions he set up in its place a new system, based on the sharecrop and the lien, that resulted in minimal social adjustment and the pseudo-slavery of involuntary servitude. See White, "Wager Swayne," 92–109, esp. 106–109; Alderson, "Influence of Military Rule and the Freedmen's Bureau on Reconstruction in Virginia," 296–309; and McFeely, *Yankee Stepfather*, 77–78, 259–60. Kiddoo's counterpart in Louisiana would be Brevet Brigadier General Absalom Baird. See McFeely, *Yankee Stepfather*, 285–87; White, *Freedmen's Bureau in Louisiana*, 17–40, passim. Both military commanders and the assistant commissioners tended to underestimate, misinterpret, and dismiss Governor Throckmorton's potential during the era, as do present-day historians. See Richter, "General Phil Sheridan," 131–54. The lack of cooperation between Texas army and bureau commands con-

trasts with the smooth operations of the two entities in Virginia. See Alderson, "Influence of Military Rule and the Freedmen's Bureau on Reconstruction in Virginia," 29–64; 71–114, 279–95.

7. Sinclair, "Freedmen's Bureau in Texas," 11–15, treats Griffin's tenure in office but, like other historians of the era, he falls to appreciate the general's key importance to Texas Reconstruction. For a fuller treatment of the man who more than any other Federal official in the state appreciated the need for an imaginative Reconstruction effort that broke with the norms of the past, see Richter, *Army in Texas*, 79–115; Richter, "Tyrant and Reformer," 225–42. Griffin's attitude might be compared to that of Bvt. Maj. Gen. Joseph A. Mower. See Dawson, *Army Generals and Reconstruction Louisiana*, 63–69; White, *Freedmen's Bureau in Louisiana*, 17–40, passim. Griffin's effect in Texas seems to indicate that the army's influence on bureau operations was dependent upon the personality and benevolence of the commander, as postulated in McFeely, *Yankee Stepfather*, 291, 295–96, and in Alderson, "Influence of Military Rule and the Freedmen's Bureau on Reconstruction in Virginia," 296–309.

8. Sinclair, "Freedmen's Bureau in Texas," 15–19 (quotation from 16), recognizes Reynolds's political interests, and his analysis of the general is his next best after his treatment of Gregory. Reynolds had much of Kiddoo's intellectual outlook on slavery, emancipation, and Reconstruction, but lacked Kiddoo's interest in and commitment to blacks as free persons. The general's changing attitude concerning whom the state Republican party should rely on in its attempt to control the polls nicely parallels the confusion of the Republican party nationally as presented in Abbott, *Republican Party and the South*, x, xii, 109, 234, 237, 239–41, 243. Unfortunately, the result of Reynolds's political solution to Reconstruction falls to the same condemnation pronounced by one historian on similar efforts by Brevet Major General John Pope in Florida: excluding too many participants from the white majority, relying too heavily on a small black vote (which could not produce a majority under the best conditions in Texas), and practicing just enough apparent fraud to guarantee a counterrevolution the moment the Federal government withdrew its protection from the interior. See Peek, "Military Reconstruction," 380–400, esp. 398. Reynolds's effect in Texas confirms once again McFeely's notion of the importance of the personality and benevolence of the commander (*Yankee Stepfather*, 291, 295–96) and also shows it can be as unfortunate as that suggested in Alderson, "Influence of Military Rule and the Freedmen's Bureau on Reconstruction in Virginia," 296–309.

9. Richter, *Army in Texas*, 134, 138.

10. Goddin to AAAG-TFB, April 19, 1867, LR, AC, T. For others disillusioned by white intransigence and desiring a tougher Reconstruction, see Kidder Walker to Hamilton, June 5, July 15, 1865; A. A. Deavalon to Hamilton, July 10, 1865; J. M. McAlpine to Hamilton, August –, September 4, 1865; Thomas Ford et al. to Hamilton, September 6, 1865; S. J. Richardson to Hamilton, September __, 1865; N. U. Gunn et al. to Hamilton, October 8, 1865; John E. Thompson to Hamilton, October 8, 1865; W. Longworth to Hamilton, October 10, 1865; Louis Constant to Hamilton, October 18, 1865; D. J. Baldwin to Hamilton, November 7, 1865; Citizens of Lockhart to Bvt. Maj. Gen. George A. Custer, January 24, 1866,

all in Governor's Papers (Hamilton), TSL. Compare Trefousse, *Andrew Johnson*, 214–33. See also Woodward, "Irony of Southern History," 3–19.

11. Longworth to AAAG-TFB, March 28, 1866, LR, AC, T. The intensity of Southern resistance is generally an argument adopted in Rabel, *But There Was No Peace*, esp. 15, 191. A good statement on the lack of Northern commitment of time and resources is in Abbott, *Freedmen's Bureau in South Carolina*, 130–35.

12. This delay in placing agencies hints that Griffin was probably correct in his contempt for the inability of his predecessors to administer the Texas command aggressively. See Griffin to Howard, July 1, 1867, RR, AC, T. Griffin's total of seventy subassistant commissioners in 1867 compares to fifty-one in South Carolina (plus eighteen contract bureau surgeons), and twenty in Alabama at that time. See Abbott, *Freedmen's Bureau in South Carolina*, 20; Bethel, "Freedmen's Bureau in Alabama," 84. Alderson shows ("Influence of Military Rule and the Freedmen's Bureau on Reconstruction in Virginia," 29–31, 35) that Griffin's organization of Texas into subdistricts in April, 1867, only began to approach the thorough departmentalization and numbers of agents already achieved by Virginia's assistant commissioner, Colonel Orlando Brown, as early as July, 1865.

13. For Texas, see Smallwood, "Freedmen's Bureau Reconsidered," 309–20; Smallwood, "Charles E. Culver, a Reconstruction Agent in Texas," 350–61. Other profiles include May, "Freedmen's Bureau at the Local Level"; Price, "John C. Barrett," 51–74; Mugleston, "Freedmen's Bureau and Reconstruction in Virginia," 45–102; Campbell, "Freedmen's Bureau Diary by George Wagner," 196–214, 333–60; Hume, "Freedmen's Bureau and the Freedmen's Vote," 217–24; Stealey, "Reports of Freedmen's Bureau Operations in West Virginia," 94–129; Stealey, "Reports of Freedmen's Bureau District Officers on Tours and Surveys in West Virginia," 145–55.

14. White, "Black Lives, Red Tape," 241–58.

15. A good example is AAAG-TFB to Doubleday, P. Johnson, Lowrie, Collins, Plummer, Bradford, Latimer, Horton, Dix, Starr, and Harris, July 26, 1867, LS, AC, T. It may be unfair to blame the army for a quagmire that seemed to characterize not only its operations, but also the functioning of governmental bureaucracy in general. See, for example, White, *Republican Era*, 1–19; Bennis, "Beyond Bureaucracy," 3–16; Stillman, *American Bureaucracy*, chap. 6; Weber, *Theory of Social and Economic Organization*, 39, 54–55, 58–59, 73–74, 324–41. See also related material in Prucha, "New Approaches," 15–19; Unrau, "Civilian as Indian Agent," 405–20; and Sievers, "Malfeasance or Indirection?" 273–94. The bureaucratic notions, however, lend credibility to and inflate in scope McFeely's assertion that a lot of the work done by General Howard "served to preclude rather than promote Negro freedom," *Yankee Stepfather*, 5. Tragically, many bureau agents in Texas promoted little but paperwork.

16. Kirkman to AAAG-TFB, October 26, November 7, 30, 1867, April 3, 15, May 1 (two letters), 20, 24, 1868, LR, AC, T; AAAG-TFB to Kirkman, June 10, 23, July 26, 1867, LS, AC, T; AAAG-TFB to Kirkman, May 18, 1868, ES, AC, T. Examples of his summonses for one month are: Kirkman to James Garrett, October 29; to John Rochelle, November 2; to M. L. Ingrahm, November 5; to Charles Rochelle, November 5; to Edward Runnels, November 5; to Artis Copeland, November 7; to Richard McAdam, November 15; to Mrs. S. Hall, Novem-

ber 20; to Anderson R. Moore, November 22; to Wiley Murphy, November 25; to Henry Allison, November 26, 1867, all in LR, AC, T.

17. Mayer to AAAG-TFB, January 25, February 3, 27, May 19, 20, 1867, LR, AC, T; Mayer to AAAG-TFB, June 2, 1867, RR, AC, T; AAAG-TFB to Mayer, September 22, 1866; Sinclair to Mayer, January 4, 1867, ES, AC, T.

18. The best example of the process is Bvt. Lt. Col. D. L. Montgomery to AAAG-TFB (and endorsements), May 10, 1867. See also A. F. Manning to AAAG-TFB, May 1, 1867; 1 Lt. A. G. Mallory to AAAG-TFB, June 6, 1867, all in LR, AC, T.

19. On revenue stamps, see J. F. Brown to AAAG-TFB, February 28, 1866. For forms, books, and orders, see James Lowrie to AAAG-TFB, May 10, 1867; 2 Lt. E. O. Gibson to AAAG-TFB, May 15, 1867; Cpt. Horace Jewett to AAAG-TFB, October 14, 1868; Lt. Col. Charles H. Morse to AAAG-TFB, April 23, 1867; Bvt. Brig. Gen. Lewis R. Brown to AAAG-TFB, June 6, 1867; A. F. Manning to AAAG-TFB, May 1, 25, 1867, all in LR, AC, T.

20. For the hurry-up letters, see AAAG-TFB to William H. Howard, August 24, October 22, 1868; AAAG-TFB to John Morrison, September 26, 1868, LS, AC, T. Morrison had already complained about headquarters' unsympathetic attitude; Morrison to AAAG-TFB, March 18, 1868, LR, AC, T.

21. AAAG-TFB to William H. Rock, October 3, 1868; AAAG-TFB to William H. Howard, December 11, 1868, ES, AC, T; AAAG-TFB to William H. Howard, September 26, 1868 (quotation), LS, AC, T.

22. For oaths, see AAAG-TFB to James Lowrie, DeWitt C. Brown, William H. Rock, E. M. Harris, Hiram S. Johnson, Louis Jacobs, J. L. Randall, A. H. Latimer, Albert Evans, A. M. Bryant, John Dix, William Garretson, James Devine, Thomas Bayley, May 20, 1867; and AAAG-TFB to Michael Butler, August 3, 1868, LS, AC, T. Most of these men had oaths on file already but, for some unspecified reason, had to resubmit them. The other issues are in AAAG-TFB to Cpt. W. B. Pease, March 5, 1867; AAAG-TFB to L. J. Warner, November 5, 1866; AAAG-TFB to William H. Rock, January 19, 1868, ES, AC, T.

23. AAAG-TFB to William H. Rock, January 9, 1867, ES, AC, T; AAAG-TFB to Bvt. Maj. Horace W. Jewett, October 26, 1868, LS, AC, T; William H. Horton to AAAG-TFB, April 18, 1867; 1 Lt. Henry Norton to AAAG-TFB, October 3, 1868; G. T. Ruby to AAAG-TFB, October 24, 1867, LR, AC, T.

24. See any of Archer's reports for late 1867 or 1868 in ROC, AC, T. See also AAAG-TFB to Maj. J. W. Eckles, October 7, 1868, ES, AC, T.

25. See, for example, 1 Lt. I. M. Beebe to AAAG, May 26, June 6, 1866, LR, AC, T, for the ease with which headquarters forgot northeastern Texas in its administrative decisions.

26. An excellent analysis of the psychological rationale of the system of involuntary servitude that replaced slavery is in Friedman, "Search for Docility," 313–23. From a Texan point of view, consult Ledbetter, "White over Black in Texas," 406–18, which also has relevance to the Reconstruction period. Oakes, "Failure of Vision," 70, questions whether the native legal, social, political, and institutional forces that existed in the South after the war could have been overcome by any outside concept of freedom and equality. Another closely allied approach to understanding Texans' political and social attitudes is Buenger, "Stilling the

Voice of Reason," which adds recent historical research and depth to an earlier classic work by Jordan, "Imprint of the Upper and Lower South," 667–90. Buenger sees antebellum Texan society as much more complex than Jordan did, somewhat in the mold of the Owsley school. See Owsley, *Plain Folk of the Old South*. A good discussion of Owsley, his advocates, and his critics is in Link and Patrick, *Writing Southern History*, 153–56.

27. Mss. Monthly Troop Rosters, Fifth Military District and the District of Texas, Records of the Adjutant General, RG 94, NA. The disappointments of the postwar army are revealed in McConnell, *Five Years a Cavalryman*, 13, 17; Wilson, "Soldier of the Texas Frontier," 82–96, esp. 86. McConnell served as an enlisted man in the Sixth Cavalry; Wilson, an officer in the Twenty-sixth Infantry, was a bureau agent at Cotton Gin in Freestone County.

28. Sefton, *Army and Reconstruction*, 207–208.

29. Richter, *Army in Texas*, 119–86, passim, details the army's interest in Texas politics.

30. On the attitudes of loyalists, see ibid., 27, 62–63, 72, 95–97. The best statement of the loyalists' stand on race is in Carrier, "The Ball That Never Was," in his "Political History of Texas during the Reconstruction," 167–97. A similar view from another perspective is in Pitre. "A Thorn in the Side," *Through Many Dangers, Toils, and Snares*, 84–98. See also North, *Five Years in Texas*, 102–104. This compares closely with President Johnson's own attitudes as portrayed in Trefousse, *Andrew Johnson*, 214–33, 378–79.

31. On the code of the West and its Texas roots, see C. L. Sonnichsen, *I'll Die Before I'll Run*; Sonnichsen, *Tularosa*; Utley, *High Noon at Lincoln*, 20–21, 63, 116, 176–77; Utley, *Billy the Kid*, 4, 14–15, 198, 205, 211. For the Southern background to the code, consult Franklin, *Militant South*, and an intriguing masterpiece by Gorn, "'Gouge and Bite, Pull Hair, and Scratch'," 18–43. The use of violence to maintain white political, social, and economic domination is a theme in Hennessey, "To Live and Die in Dixie," 356, 403–406; and Woodman, "Sequel to Slavery," 523–54. See also White, "Outlaw Gangs of the Middle Border," 387–408; Elliott, "Crime and the Frontier Mores," 185–92; Holden, "Law and Lawlessness on the Texas Frontier," 188–203; and Adams, "Our Lawless Heritage," 732–40.

32. Roberts to AAAG, August 12 (quotation), November 12, 1867, LR, AC, T. The conditions in the Red, Sulphur, Neches, and Sabine valleys closely parallels the guerrilla-style butchery found in the Kansas-Missouri Border Wars as described in Fellman, *Inside War*, 23–80, 132–230. In most instances all one needs to do is change dates and placenames.

33. Roberts to AAAG, August 7, 12, 14, 17, October 3, November 12, 1867, LR, AC, T. The plans to centralize bureau operations are in Roberts to AAAG, November 12, 1867, LS, AC, T; Kirkman to AAAG, January 1, 1868; Shorkley to AAAG, October 31, 1868; ROC, AC, T; P. B. Johnson to AAAG-TFB, July 6, 1867, LR, AC, T. Their suggestions probably were the basis of General Canby's GO 4, January 16, 1869, RG 94, NA. Such a plan had been instituted in Virginia as early as July, 1865, and provided a basis for early Federal anti-guerrilla activity in Missouri. See Alderson, "Influence of Military Rule and the Freedmen's Bureau on Reconstruction in Virginia," 29–31, 35; Fellman, *Inside War*, 93.

34. On Baker's political campaign, see Bartholomew, *Cullen Baker*, 50, 54, 63,

127–28, 129. See also Johnson, "Cullen Montgomery Baker," 229–39, esp. 235. Otto H. Olsen, "Ku Klux Klan," 340–62, argues that the Ku Klux Klan and related organizations, such as Baker's gang in Texas, were backed heavily by conservative politicians and local community leaders who used the brigands to enforce their concept of what society should be like. Reconstruction whites called this establishing "law and order," but Olsen, as blacks and loyal whites of the era argued, sees this as a negation of Negro equality and participation in the democratic process. Although it is hard to find concrete evidence, a strong suspicion exists that this thesis is appropriate in parts of Texas, too, especially when local law enforcement officials seem to "disappear" or stand by whenever bureau agents are threatened (see, for example, Rand to AAAG-TFB, February 24, 1868, LR, AC, T; Rand to AAAG-TFB, February 1, 1868, ROC, AC, T), or when they refuse to cooperate with army patrols sent to pacify an area (Cpt. T. W. Tolman to AAAG-TFB, August 31, 1868; Bvt. Maj. A. R. Chaffee to AAAG-FMD, September 21, 27, October 5, 30, 1868, LR, FMD, RG 393, NA). The best example of cooperation between local authorities and Baker was the public meeting held in the town square at Paris, witnessed at a safe distance by bureau agent DeWitt C. Brown (Brown to AAAG, September 2, 5, 1868, LR, AC, T). The concept of social banditry—in which outlaws like Baker, Bickerstaff, English, Guest, and Bob Lee are perceived rightly or wrongly as "Robin Hood" types of heroes by the average citizen—is developed for the Missouri area in White, "Outlaw Gangs of the Middle Border," 387–408, which owes much to Hobsbawm, *Social Bandits and Primitive Rebels*. See also Wyatt-Brown, *Southern Honor*, which looks at the influence of klan and kinship in the role of violence, important to the South with its Scots-Irish heritage. Some of these studies are used by Robert Utley in his volumes on New Mexico violence, and less directly in C. L. Sonnichsen's examinations of Texas feuds and outlawry. For these and other citations see note 31. One could also place in this category the activities of Jean Lafitte, and possibly of John Murrell (and scores of others). See, for example, DeGrummond, *Baratarians and the Battle of New Orleans*; Harrison, *Outlaw of the Natchez Trace*.

35. Unlike other commanders, Griffin accompanied bureau appointments with automatic troop assignments. See, for example, AAAG-TFB to AAAG-DT, June 10, 23, 1867, LS, AC, T; AAAG-TFB to AAAG-DT, July 12, 1867; AAAG-DT to CO-Mt. Pleasant, July 12, 1867, LR, AC, T. For more on the question of violence in Texas, see Crouch, "Spirit of Lawlessness," 217–32, who characterizes Texas as possibly the most violent of all Southern states in the era to 1868, an assessment repeated as regards racial violence around the turn of the century in Shapiro, *White Violence and Black Response*, 28–29, 104–107. For Texas specifically, see also Keener, "Racial Turmoil in Texas"; Gregg Contrell, "Racial Violence and Politics in Reconstruction Texas, 1867–1868," 333–55; Shook, "Federal Occupation and Administration of Texas," 354–63, 419–67 passim; Richter, *Army in Texas*, 143–52, 162–65; Ramsdell, *Reconstruction in Texas*, 33–36, 67–68, 187–92, 217–25, 230–33, 245–47. The topic is covered nationally and very broadly in Shapiro, *White Violence and Black Response*; and more specifically as to the Reconstruction era in Rabel, *But There Was No Peace*; Trelease, *White Terror*; Carpenter, "Atrocities during the Reconstruction Period," 234–47. See also other state studies such as those of Phillips, "White Reaction to the Freedmen's Bureau in Tennessee," 50–62; "Law-

lessness in Florida," 164–85; Abbott, *Freedmen's Bureau in South Carolina*, 134–65; Shapiro, "Ku Klux Klan during Reconstruction," 34–55; White, *Freedmen's Bureau in Louisiana*, 114–29. Otto H. Olsen indicts loyal Southern state governments for not effectively using their political and military power to counter the violence brought against them by their opponents; Olsen, "Reconsidering the Scalawags," 316–20. He also points out ("Southern Reconstruction and the Question of Self-Determination," 113–41) the willingness of the Southern establishment to continue its war aims and to use methods of force to achieve them beyond the Appomattox cease-fire, which much of the North mistakenly saw as the end of the war, an error more recently repeated in Beringer et al., *Why the South Lost the Civil War*, 436–38.

36. On Missouri, see Mink, "General Orders No. 11," 132–36; Niepman, "General Orders No. 11 and Border Warfare," 185–210. The quotation is in Castel, "Order No. 11 and the Civil War," 357. An excellent overall account is Fellman, *Inside War*, passim, with the official government (Union and Confederate) policies discussed on 132–90. See also Smith, "Experiment in Counterinsurgency," 361–80.

37. Quotation from Sefton, *Army and Reconstruction*, 224. Perhaps the best statement on the limits of Federal action during Reconstruction is the essay by C. Vann Woodward, "Reconstruction," 183–200, first advanced in his review article, "Unfinished Business," *New York Review of Books* 35 (May 12, 1988), 22–24, 26–27. Woodward points out that more decisive Federal action on behalf of the blacks does not look viable in the light of the years that followed. To have confiscated plantation land to give to the blacks would merely have caused it to wind up shortly in the hands of railroads and Northern speculators, as did much of the land blacks obtained under the Southern Homestead Act. To have placed the blacks under a lengthy national benevolent guardianship would have been counterproductive, also, if Federal Indian policy is any indication. If Woodward is correct, then Reconstruction's shortcomings remain speculative and pretty near unsolvable, given America's nineteenth-century commitment to white supremacy. It might also bode little success for the whole concept of government-engineered revolution today, not only reinforcing "The Central Theme of Southern History" of historian Ulrich Bonnell Phillips (*American Historical Review* 34 [1928–1929], 30–43), but suggesting that it may be nationwide in its subtle influences. See McDonald, "Woodward's Strange Career," 46–47, and Woodman, "Sequel to Slavery: The New History Views the Postbellum South," 523–54. One of the more prolific critics of governmental action in the socio-economic field as superficial in its applications and counterproductive in its results is Thomas Sowell, who expands the critique from the narrow base of a particular period of American history to an international viewpoint. See Sowell, *Preferential Policies: An International Perspective*, 15–16, 19–22, 35–36, 106–107, 111–14, 119–65, 167, 179, 182–83. See also Sowell, *Ethnic America: A History*, 183–84, 195, 202, 211, 276–77, 296; Sowell, *The Economics and Politics of Race: An International Perspective*, 121, 123, 127, 183–206; Sowell, *Pink and Brown People and Other Controversial Essays*, 7–8, 74–75; Sowell, *Affirmative Action Reconsidered: Was It Really Necessary in Academia?* 45; and Sowell, *Civil Rights: Rhetoric or Reality?* 7–8.

38. Report of Bvt. Lt. Col. D. L. Montgomery, April 1867, ROC, AC, T.

39. DuBois, "Freedmen's Bureau," 354–65; White, "Wager Swayne," 92–109; Ira C.

Colby, "Freedmen's Bureau," 219–30; and Farnum, *Chapters in the History of Social Legislation*, 231–52. Given the course of American history both before and after the Reconstruction era, whatever their shortcomings in administration the bureau's programs seem much more radical or innovative than characterized by Nieman, *To Set the Law in Motion*, xvii, 190, 196, 222. See Foner, "Reconstruction Revisited," 82–100, esp. 95. The problem was not so much the concept as its lukewarm implementation in the South by various army and bureau employees; McFeely, *Yankee Stepfather*, 3, 5, 9, 322, 328. For a good analysis of the bureau as a twentieth-century concept lost in the nineteenth century, see Olds, "Freedmen's Bureau as a Social Agency," 14–28, 227–47. For an analysis of the agricultural system that followed slavery, see Daniel, *Shadow of Slavery*.

40. See, for example, Stampp, *Era of Reconstruction*, 215; Foner, *Reconstruction*, 602–603; Carpenter, *Sword and Olive Branch*, 135–56, 184; Bentley, *History of the Freedmen's Bureau*, 214; Abbott, "Free Land, Free Labor, and the Freedmen's Bureau," 156; Olds, "Freedmen's Bureau as a Social Agency," 239–43, 251–52; Crouch, "Freedmen's Bureau and the 30th Sub-district in Texas," 15–30.

41. No one has expressed the nagging doubts about Reconstruction's achievements more movingly than W. E. B. DuBois in his *Black Reconstruction*. His essay, "The Freedmen's Bureau," was first published in the *Atlantic Monthly* in 1901, and appeared as chap. 2 ("Of the Dawn of Freedom") in *The Souls of Black Folk*. Similar reservations are found in Foner, *Reconstruction*, 603. The reasons can be attributed to a moral lapse as in Gillette, *Retreat from Reconstruction*, and Logan, *Negro in American Life and Thought*, or more to a perceived demand of political calculation as described by Hirshon, *Farewell to the Bloody Shirt*. Also of interest is Hoogenboom, *Presidency of Rutherford B. Hayes*, 51–79, esp. 68–69. The Northern reluctance to reconstruct the nation vigorously lends credence to the ultimate conclusion in Woodward, "Emancipations and Reconstructions," 145–66. Compare his earlier essays, "Equality," 459–72, and "Seeds of Failure in Radical Race Policy," 214–47. Also of relevance is the prewar study by William W. Freehling, *The Road to Disunion: Secessionists at Bay*, 418–21. This failure threw the blacks back on their own ingenuity for survival, which had been their strength all along. See Genovese, *Roll Jordan Roll*; Litwack, *Been in the Storm So Long*; Guttman, *Black Family in Slavery and Freedom*; and for Texas specifically, Smallwood, *Time of Hope, Time of Despair*, and Pitre, *Through Many Dangers, Toils, and Snares*. The continued dedication of a small group of Northern whites to the cause of equality is portrayed in McPherson, *Abolitionist Legacy*.

42. Crowther, *Grammar and Vocabulary of the Yoruba Language*, 229.

43. Griffin to Howard, June 17, 1867, LS, AC, T.

44. Whether or not the Wormley Conference was a critical aspect of the end of Reconstruction, it remains a convenient symbol. See Woodward, *Reunion and Reaction*; Polakoff, *Politics of Inertia*; Peskin, "Was There a Compromise of 1877?" 63–75; Rabel, "Southern Interests and the Election of 1876," 347–61; Benedict, "Southern Democrats in the Crisis of 1876–1877," 489–524.

45. AAAG-DT to Col. John Kelly, June 28, 1865, OR, vol. 48, pt. 2, 1017–18.

Bibliography

NOTE: Because of the relevance of my earlier volume, *The Army in Texas during Reconstruction* to the current work, this bibliography includes all sources used in that volume as well as this.

A. Manuscript Collections

1. Federal Documents

Briefs of Dispatches Between Generals Grant and Sheridan, Movement of Troops to Texas, Violation of Surrender Terms by Kirby Smith, Mexican Affairs. Record Group 108, National Archives and Records Administration, Washington, D.C.

Letters Received by the Office of the Adjutant General (Main Series), 1861–1870. File 57M1868, Microcopy 619, Roll 634. Record Group 94, National Archives and Records Administration, Washington, D.C.

Postmaster's Appointment Record, 1858–1867, Texas Register of Appointments. Record Group 28, National Archives and Records Administration, Washington, D.C.

Records of the Bureau of Refugees, Freedmen, and Abandoned Lands, District of Texas. Record Group 105. National Archives and Records Administration, Washington, D.C.

Records of the Department of Justice. Record Group 60. National Archives and Records Administration, Washington, D.C.

Records of the Department of the Treasury (Internal Revenue Department). Record Group 56. National Archives and Records Administration, Washington, D.C.

Records of the Fifth Military District and the District of Texas. Record Group 393. National Archives and Records Administration, Washington, D.C.

Records of the U.S. District Court (Texas). Record Group 21. Regional Federal Records Center. Region No. 7. Fort Worth, Texas.

2. Texas State Papers

Election Register, 1865–70. Archives, Texas State Library, Austin.

Executive Correspondence, 1865–70. Archives, Texas State Library, Austin.

Secretary of State's Papers. Letterbooks and Proclamations of the Governors. Archives, Texas State Library, Austin.

Texas Adjutant General's Office. Transcript of Records, 1838–69. Archives, Barker History Center, University of Texas, Austin.

Bibliography

3. Personal Papers

Thomas Affleck Papers. Department of Archives and Manuscripts, Louisiana State University, Baton Rouge.

Amelia Barr Letters. Archives, Barker History Center, University of Texas, Austin.

James H. Bell Papers. Archives, Barker History Center, University of Texas, Austin.

R. W. Black Papers. Archives, Barker History Center, University of Texas, Austin.

Frank Brown Papers. Archives, Barker History Center, University of Texas, Austin.

J. R. Cressinger Civil War Letters. Archives, Barker History Center, University of Texas, Austin.

B. H. Epperson Papers. Archives, Barker History Center, University of Texas, Austin.

U. S. Grant Papers. Manuscripts Division, Library of Congress, Washington, D.C.

John L. Haynes Papers. Archives, Barker History Center, University of Texas, Austin.

Andrew Jackson Hamilton Papers. Archives, Barker History Center, University of Texas, Austin.

Samuel Peter Heintzelman Papers. Manuscripts Division, Library of Congress, Washington, D.C.

Charles Adelbert Herff Reminiscences. Archives, Barker History Center, University of Texas, Austin.

Andrew Johnson Papers. Manuscripts Division, Library of Congress, Washington, D.C.

James Larson Papers. Archives, Barker History Center, University of Texas, Austin.

W. W. Mills Papers. Archives, Barker History Center, University of Texas, Austin.

Charles H. Moore Reminiscences. Archives, Barker History Center, University of Texas, Austin.

James Pierson Newcomb, Sr., Papers. Archives, Barker History Center, University of Texas, Austin.

Pease-Niles-Graham Collection. Archives, Austin Public Library, Texas.

John Reid Papers. Department of Archives and Manuscripts, Louisiana State University, Baton Rouge.

Philip H. Sheridan Papers. Manuscripts Division, Library of Congress, Washington, D.C.

James Webb Throckmorton Papers. Archives, Barker History Center, University of Texas, Austin.

R. H. Watlington Reminiscences. Archives, Barker History Center, University of Texas, Austin.

Edward Clifton Wharton Papers. Department of Archives and Manuscripts, Louisiana State University, Baton Rouge.

B. Printed Official Materials

1. Congressional Documents

39th Cong., 1st Sess.
  House Executive Documents, No. 1 (Report of the Secretary of War, 1865).
  House Executive Documents, No. 70 (Freedmen's Bureau).

House Reports, No. 30 (Report of the Joint Committee on Reconstruction).
Senate Executive Documents, No. 2 (Condition of the South).
Senate Executive Documents, No. 26 (Provisional Governments of the Southern States).
Senate Executive Documents, No. 27 (Reports of the Assistant Commissioners of the Freedmen's Bureau).
Senate Executive Documents, No. 30 (Kidnapping of Colored Persons in the Southern States).
Senate Executive Documents, No. 43 (Report of Benjamin C. Truman).

39th Cong., 2nd Sess.
House Executive Documents, No. 1 (Report of the Secretary of War, 1866).
House Reports, No. 61 (Condition of Affairs in Texas).
Senate Executive Documents, No. 6 (Freedmen's Affairs).

40th Cong., 1st Sess.
House Executive Documents, No. 20 (Letter from the Secretary of War).
House Executive Documents, No. 30 (Correspondence with Ministers to Mexico).
House Executive Documents, No. 34 (Interpretation of the Reconstruction Acts).

40th Cong., 2nd Sess.
House Executive Documents, No. 1 (Report of the Secretary of War *ad interim* and the General, U.S.A., [1867]).
House Executive Documents, No. 25 (Mexican Affairs–Maximilian).
House Executive Documents, No. 57 (Removal of Hon. E. M. Stanton and others).
House Executive Documents, No. 342 (General Orders–Reconstruction).

40th Cong., 3rd Sess.
House Executive Documents, No. 1 (Report of the Secretary of War, 1868).
House Executive Documents, No. 97 (Constitutional Convention of Texas).

41st Cong., 2nd Sess.
House Executive Documents, No. 1 (Report of the Secretary of War, 1869).
House Executive Documents, No. 59 (Expenses of the Texas Election).
House Executive Documents, No. 60 (Oath in Texas).
House Executive Documents, No. 211 (Officers on Duty in the Southern States).
House Executive Documents, No. 228 (Sites of Military Posts in Texas).
House Executive Documents, No. 265 (Elections in the Second District of Texas).

41st Cong., 3rd Sess.
House Executive Documents, No. 1 (Report of the Secretary of War, 1870).
House Executive Documents, No. 145 (Burning of Brenham, Texas).

42nd Cong., 2nd Sess.
House Executive Documents, No. 22 (Affairs in the Late Insurrectionary States).
House Executive Documents, No. 216 (Political Complexion of Affairs on the Texas Frontier).

42nd Cong., 3rd Sess.
House Executive Documents, No. 39 (Depredations on the Frontier of Texas).

43rd Cong., 1st Sess.
   House Executive Documents, No. 222 (Protection of the Texas Frontier).

2. Other Printed Documents

Alford, John W. *Fifth Semi-Annual Report on Schools for Freedmen, January 1, 1868.*
   Washington, D.C.: Government Printing Office, 1868.
Andrews, Bvt. Maj. Gen. Christopher Columbus. *Early Steps in Reconstruction:
   Speeches by General C. C. Andrews of Minnesota in Texas and Arkansas.* Wash-
   ington, D.C.: Union Republican Congressional Committee, 1865.
Cullum, George W. *Biographical Register of the Officers and Graduates of the U. S.
   Military Academy at West Point, New York, from Its Establishment March 16, 1802
   to the Army Reorganization of 1866-1867.* 2 vols. New York: D. Van Nostrand, 1868.
Everly, Elaine, and Willna Pacheli, comps. *Preliminary Inventory of the Field Offices
   of the Bureau of Refugees, Freedmen, and Abandoned Lands.* 3 parts. Washington,
   D.C.: National Archives and Records Administration, 1974.
Gammel, Hans Peter Nielson, comp. *The Laws of Texas.* 10 vols. Austin: Gammel
   Book Company, 1898.
Heitman, Francis B. *Historical Register and Dictionary of the United States Army,
   from Its Organization, September 19, 1789 to March 2, 1903.* 2 vols. Washington,
   D.C.: Government Printing Office, 1903.
*Journal of the Reconstruction Convention Which Met at Austin, Texas, June 1, A.D.,
   1868.* 2 vols. Austin: Tracy, Siemering & Co., 1870.
Journal of the State Convention Assembled at Austin February 7, 1866. Austin: South-
   ern Intelligencer Office, 1866.
Kennedy, Joseph C. G., comp. *The Population of the United States in 1860; Compiled
   from the Original Returns of the Eighth Census. . . .* Washington, D.C.: Government Printing Office, 1864.
Matthews, James M., ed. *Statutes at Large of the Confederate States of America, Com-
   mencing with the First Session of the First Congress.* Richmond, Va.: R. M. Smith,
   1862-64.
Official Records of the Union and Confederate Navies in the War of the Rebellion. 26
   vols. Washington, D.C.: Government Printing Office, 1894-1926.
Richardson, James D., comp. *A Compilation of the Messages and Papers of the Presi-
   dents, 1789-1897.* 10 vols. Washington, D.C.: Government Printing Office, 1897.
*Report of the Joint Select Committee to Investigate Facts in Regard to the Burning of
   Brenham.* Austin: Jo. Walker at the *State Gazette* office, 1866.
Robards, Charles L. *Synopses of the Decisions of the Supreme Court of the State of
   Texas . . . for Writs of Habeas Corpus.* Austin: Brown & Foster, 1865.
*Roll of Honor: Names of Soldiers Who Died in Defense of the American Union Interred
   in the Eastern District of Texas; Central District of Texas; Rio Grande District, De-
   partment of Texas; Camp Ford, Tyler, Texas; and Corpus Christi, Texas.* Washing-
   ton, D.C.: Government Printing Office, 1866.
U.S., Department of War, Adjutant General's Office. *Official Army Register of the
   Volunteer Force of the United States Army, 1861-1865.* 8 vols. Washington, D.C.:
   Government Printing Office, 1865-67.
U.S., Federal Register Office. *Statutes at Large.* 104 vols. to date. Washington, D.C.:
   Government Printing Office, 1789-   .

U.S., Judge Advocate General. *Digest of Opinions . . . 1862–1868.* Washington, D.C., Government Printing Office, 1868.
Walker, Francis, A., comp. *The Statistics of the Population of the United States. . . .* Washington, D.C.: Government Printing Office, 1872.
War of the Rebellion: A Compilation of the Official Records of the Union and Confederate Armies. 70 vols. in 128 parts. Washington, D.C.: Government Printing Office, 1880–1901.

C. Periodicals, 1865–70

Appleton's Annual Cyclopaedia.
Army and Navy Journal.
Austin *Record.*
Austin *Republican.*
Bellville *Countryman.*
Brownsville *Daily Ranchero.*
Dallas *Herald.*
Denton *Monitor.*
Flake's Daily Bulletin (Galveston).
Galveston *Daily News.*
Georgetown *Watchman.*
Houston *Telegraph.*
Houston *Union.*
San Antonio *Herald.*
San Antonio *Ledger.*
San Antonio *News.*
Southern Intelligencer (Austin).
The Standard (Clarksville).
Texas Almanac.
Texas News (Bonham).
Texas State Gazette (Austin).

D. Secondary Materials

1. Books

Abbott, Martin. *The Freedmen's Bureau in South Carolina, 1865–1872.* Chapel Hill: University of North Carolina Press, 1967.
Abbott, Richard H. *The Republican Party and the South, 1855–1877.* Chapel Hill: University of North Carolina Press, 1986.
Ambrose, Stephen E. *Halleck: Lincoln's Chief of Staff.* Baton Rouge: Louisiana State University Press, 1962.
Bailyn, Bernard. *Ideological Origins of the American Revolution.* Cambridge: Harvard University Press, 1967.
Bancroft, Hubert Howe. *History of the North Mexican States and Texas.* 2 vols. San Francisco: A. L. Bancroft Co., 1889.

Bibliography

Barkley, Mary Starr. *History of Travis County and Austin, 1839–1899.* Waco: Texian Press, 1964.
Barr, Alwyn. *Reconstruction to Reform: Texas Politics, 1876–1906.* Austin: University of Texas Press, 1971.
Bartholomew, Ed Ellsworth. *Cullen Baker: Premier Texas Gunfighter.* Houston: Frontier Press, 1954.
Belz, Herman. *Emancipation and Equal Rights: Politics and Constitutionalism in the Civil War Era.* New York: W. W. Norton, 1978.
Benét, Stephen Vincent. *Treatise on Military Law and the Practice of Courts Martial.* 2nd ed. New York: D. Van Nostrand, 1868.
Bentley, George R. *A History of the Freedmen's Bureau.* Philadelphia: University of Pennsylvania Press, 1955.
Beringer, Richard E., Herman Hattaway, Archer Jones, and William N. Still, Jr. *Why the South Lost the Civil War.* Athens: University of Georgia Press, 1986.
Berlin, Ira. *Slaves without Masters.* New York: Pantheon, 1974.
Birkhimer, William E. *Military Government and Martial Law.* 2nd ed. Kansas City: F. Hudson Pub. Co., 1904.
Bluntschli, Johann Kaspar. *Das Moderne Kriegsrecht der Civilisierten Staaten als Rechtsbuch Dargestellt.* Nördlingen: C. H. Beck, 1866.
Boatner, Mark M., III. *The Civil War Dictionary.* New York: D. McKay & Co., 1959.
Bowers, Claude. *The Tragic Era: The Revolution after Lincoln.* Boston: Houghton Mifflin, 1929.
Branda, Eldon Stephen, ed. *The Handbook of Texas: A Supplement.* Vol. 3. Austin: Texas State Historical Association, 1976.
Brewer, J. Mason. *Negro Legislators of Texas and Their Descendants: A History of the Negro in Texas Politics from Reconstruction to Disfranchisement.* Dallas: Mathis Pub. Co., 1935.
Brown, John Henry. *History of Texas from 1685 to 1892.* 2 vols. St. Louis: L. E. Daniell, 1893.
Buenger, Walter L. *Secession and the Union in Texas.* Austin: University of Texas Press, 1984.
Bullock, Henry Allen. *A History of Negro Education in the South from 1619 to the Present.* Cambridge: Harvard University Press, 1967.
Burke, Ulick Ralph. *A Life of Benito Juarez, Constitutional President of Mexico.* London: Remington & Co., 1894.
Butchart, Ronald E. *Northern Schools, Southern Blacks, and Reconstruction: Freedmen's Education, 1862–1875.* Westport, Conn.: Greenwood Press, 1980.
Califf, Joseph Mark. *Record of the Services of the Seventh Regiment U.S.C.T. from September 1863 to November 1866. . . .* Providence, R.I.: E. L. Freeman, 1878.
Callcott, Wilfred Hardy. *Liberalism in Mexico, 1857–1929.* Palo Alto, Calif.: Stanford University Press, 1931.
Campbell, Randolph. *A Southern Community in Crisis: Marshall, Texas, 1850–1880.* Austin: Texas State Historical Association, 1983.
Carpenter, John A. *Sword and Olive Branch: Oliver Otis Howard.* Pittsburgh: University of Pittsburgh Press, 1964.

Bibliography

Carter, Dan T. *When the War Was Over: The Failure of Self-Reconstruction in the South, 1865–1867.* Baton Rouge: Louisiana State University Press, 1985.

Carter, Hodding. *The Angry Scar: The Story of Reconstruction.* Garden City, N.Y.: Doubleday, 1959.

Carter, W. H. *From Yorktown to Santiago with the Sixth U.S. Cavalry.* Baltimore: Friedenwald Co., 1900.

Casdorph, Paul D. *A History of the Republican Party in Texas, 1865–1965.* Austin: Pemberton Press, 1965.

Case, Lynn M., ed. *French Opinion on the United States and Mexico, 1860–1867: Extracts from the Reports of the Procureurs Généraux.* New York: D. Appleton-Century Co., 1900.

Catton, Bruce. *A Stillness at Appomattox.* New York: Doubleday, 1954.

Cimprich, John. *Slavery's End in Tennessee, 1861–1865.* University, Ala.: University of Alabama Press, 1985.

The Civil Record of Major General Winfield Scott Hancock, during His Administration in Louisiana and Texas. New Orleans: n.p., 1871.

Clark, Charles T. *Opdyke Tigers, 125th Ohio Volunteer Infantry: A History of the Regiment and of the Campaigns and Battles of the Army of the Cumberland.* Columbus, Ohio: Spahr & Glenn, 1895.

Clark, Mary Whatley. *David G. Burnet.* Austin: Pemberton, 1969.

Clendenen, Clarence C. *Blood on the Border: The United States Army and the Mexican Irregulars.* New York: Macmillan, 1969.

Cogley, Thomas Sydenham. *History of the Seventh Indiana Cavalry. . . .* Laporte, Ind.: Herald Co., 1876.

Connor, Seymour V., and Odie B. Faulk. *North America Divided: The Mexican War, 1846–1848.* New York: Oxford University Press, 1971.

Cornish, Dudley. *The Sable Arm: Black Troops in the Union Army, 1861–1865.* New York: Longmans, Green, 1956.

Corti, Egon Caesar. *Maximilian and Charlotte of Mexico.* Trans. Catherine Alison Phillips. 2 vols. New York: Knopf, 1928.

Coulter, E. Merton. *The South during Reconstruction.* Baton Rouge: Louisiana State University Press, 1947.

Craven, Avery O. *Reconstruction: The Ending of the Civil War.* New York: Holt, Rinehart, Winston, 1969.

Crocket, George Louis. *Two Centuries in East Texas: A History of San Augustine County and the Surrounding Territory, from 1685 to the Present Time.* Dallas: Southwest Press, 1932.

Crowther, Samuel Adjai, comp. *A Grammar and Vocabulary of the Yoruba Language.* London: Seeley, 1852.

Current, Richard N. *Those Terrible Carpetbaggers: A Reinterpretation.* New York: Oxford University Press, 1988.

―――. *Three Carpetbag Governors.* Baton Rouge: Louisiana State University Press, 1967.

Custer, Elizabeth B. *Tenting on the Plains, or General Custer in Kansas and Texas.* New York: C. L. Webster & Co., 1887.

Dabbs, Jack Autrey. *The French Army in Mexico, 1861–1867: A Case Study in Military Government.* The Hague: Moulton, 1963.

Daniel, Pete. *The Shadow of Slavery: Peonage in the South.* New York: Oxford University Press, 1973.

Davis, Burke. *To Appomattox.* New York: Rinehart, 1959.

Davis, Edwin Adams. *Fallen Guidon: The Forgotten Saga of General Jo Shelby's Confederate Command. . . .* Santa Fe, N. Mex.: Stagecoach Press, 1962.

Davis, George B. *A Treatise on the Military Law of the United States.* New York: John Wiley & Sons, 1912.

Davis, Susan Lawrence. *Authentic History: Ku Klux Klan, 1865–1877.* New York: Susan Lawrence Davis, 1924.

Davis, William R. *The Development and Present Status of Negro Education in East Texas.* New York: Columbia Teachers College, 1934.

Dawson, Daniel. *The Mexican Adventure.* London: G. Bell & Sons, 1935.

Dawson, Joseph G., III. *Army Generals and Reconstruction Louisiana, 1862–1877.* Baton Rouge: Louisiana State University Press, 1982.

DeGrummond, Jane. *The Baratarians and the Battle of New Orleans.* Baton Rouge: Louisiana State University Press, 1960.

Denison, C. W. *Illustrated Life, Campaigns, and Public Services of Philip H. Sheridan.* Philadelphia: T. B. Peterson & Bros., 1865.

Donald, David, ed. *Why the North Lost the Civil War.* New York: Collier, 1962.

Dowdey, Clifford. *Lee's Last Campaign.* Boston: Little, Brown, & Co., 1960.

Dowell, Cassius M. *Military Aid to the Civil Power.* Fort Leavenworth: General Service School, 1925.

DuBois, W.E.B. *Black Reconstruction: An Essay toward a History of the Part Which Black Folk Played in the Attempt to Reconstruct Democracy, 1860–1888.* New York: Harcourt, Brace & Co., 1935.

———. *The Souls of Black Folk.* Chicago: A. C. McClurg, 1903.

Dunning, William A. *Essays on Civil War and Reconstruction.* New York: Macmillan, 1904.

———. *Reconstruction, Political and Economic, 1865–1877.* New York: Harper Bros., 1907.

Dyer, Frederick H., comp. *A Compendium of the War of the Rebellion.* 3 vols. New York: Thomas Yoseloff, 1959.

Elliott, Claude. *Leathercoat: The Life History of a Texas Patriot [James Webb Throckmorton].* San Antonio: Standard Printing Company, 1938.

Erby, Frederick. *The Development of Education in Texas.* New York: Macmillan, 1925.

Evans, Thomas W. *The Second French Empire.* New York: D. Appleton & Co., 1905.

Fairman, Charles. *Reconstruction and Reunion, 1864–1888.* 2 vols. New York: Macmillan, 1971– .

Farnum, Henry W. *Chapters in the History of Social Legislation in the United States to 1860.* New York: AMS Press, 1970.

Fellman, Michael. *Inside War: The Guerrilla Conflict in Missouri during the American Civil War.* New York: Oxford University Press, 1989.

Field Record of Officers of the Veteran Reserve Corps, from the Commencement to the Close of the Rebellion. Washington, D.C.: Scriver & Swing, n.d.

Bibliography

Fields, Barbara Jane. *Slavery and Freedom on the Middle Ground: Maryland during the Nineteenth Century.* New Haven, Conn.: Yale University Press, 1985.

Fleming, Walter L. *Civil War and Reconstruction in Alabama.* New York: Columbia University Press, 1905.

Fletcher, Samuel H., and D. H. Fletcher. *A History of Company "A," 2nd [Illinois] Cavalry.* Chicago: n.p., 1912.

Foner, Eric. *Reconstruction: America's Unfinished Revolution, 1863–1877.* New York: Harper & Row, 1988.

Forbes, Archibald. *The Life of Napoleon III.* New York: Dodd, Mead & Co., 1897.

Forney, John W. *The Life and Career of Winfield Scott Hancock.* . . . Rochester, N.Y.: Lillingston & Co., 1880.

Fränkel, Ernst. *Military Occupation and the Rule of Law.* New York: Oxford University Press, 1961.

Franklin, John Hope. *The Militant South.* Cambridge: Harvard University Press, 1956.

———. *Reconstruction: After the Civil War.* Chicago: University of Chicago Press, 1961.

Freed, August T. *Hancock: The Life and Public Services of Winfield Scott Hancock.* Chicago: A. H. Sumner & Co., 1880.

Freehling, William W. *The Road to Disunion: Secessionists at Bay.* New York: Oxford University Press, 1990.

Fritz, Henry E. *The Movement for Indian Assimilation, 1860–1890.* Philadelphia: University of Pennsylvania Press, 1963.

Fulfer, Richard J. *A History of the Trials and Hardships of the Twenty-fourth Indiana Volunteer Infantry.* Indianapolis: Indianapolis Printing Co., 1913.

Garner, James W. *Reconstruction in Mississippi.* New York: Macmillan, 1901.

Geer, Walter. *Napoleon the Third: The Romance of an Emperor.* New York: Brentano's, 1920.

Genovese, Eugene D. *Roll Jordan Roll: The World the Slaves Made.* New York: Pantheon, 1974.

Gerteis, Louis S. *From Contraband to Freedman: Federal Policy toward Southern Blacks, 1861–1865.* Westport, Conn.: Greenwood Press, 1973.

Gillette, William. *Retreat from Reconstruction.* Baton Rouge: Louisiana State University Press, 1979.

Glatthaar, Joseph T. *Forged in Battle: The Civil War Alliance of Black Soldiers and White Officers.* New York: Free Press, 1989.

Gooch, G. P. *The Second Empire.* London: Longman's 1960.

Goodrich, Frederick E. *The Life and Public Services of Winfield Scott Hancock, Major General, U.S.A.* Boston: Lee & Shepard, 1880.

Graber, H. W. *The Life Record of H. W. Graber, A Terry Texas Ranger, 1861–1865.* [Dallas]: H. W. Graber, 1916.

Guedalla, Philip. *The Second Empire.* 2nd rev. ed. New York: G. Putnam's Sons, 1925.

Guerard, Albert. *Napoleon III: A Great Life in Brief.* New York: Knopf, 1955.

Guttman, Herbert G. *The Black Family in Slavery and Freedom, 1750–1925.* New York: Pantheon, 1976.

Hamilton, Holman. *Prologue to Conflict: The Crisis and Compromise of 1850.* New York: W. W. Norton, 1966.

Hamilton, J. G. de Roulhac. *Reconstruction in North Carolina.* New York: Columbia University Press, 1914.

Hancock, A[lmira] R[ussell]. *Reminiscences of Winfield Scott Hancock by His Wife.* New York: C. L. Webster & Co., 1887.

Hanna, Alfred Jackson, and Kathryn Abbey Hanna. *Napoleon III and Mexico: American Triumph over Monarchy.* Chapel Hill: University of North Carolina Press, 1971.

Harris, William C. *Presidential Reconstruction in Mississippi.* Baton Rouge: Louisiana State University Press, 1967.

Harrison, C. William. *Outlaw of the Natchez Trace.* New York: Ballantine, 1960.

Haskin, William Lawrence. *The History of the First Regiment of Artillery from Its Organization in 1821 to January 1, 1876. . . .* Portland, Maine: B. Thurston & Co., 1879.

Hawkins, Walace. *The Case of John C. Watrous, U.S. Judge of Texas: A Political Study of High Crimes and Misdemeanors.* Dallas: University Press of Dallas, 1950.

Heintzen, Michael R. *Private Black Colleges in Texas, 1865–1954.* College Station: Texas A&M University Press, 1985.

Henry, Robert Self. *The Story of Reconstruction.* Indianapolis: Bobbs-Merrill, 1938.

Hesseltine, William B. *Lincoln's Plan of Reconstruction.* Tuscaloosa: Confederate Pub. Co., 1960.

———. *U. S. Grant: Politician.* New York: Dodd, Mead & Co., 1935.

Heyman, Max L., Jr. *Prudent Soldier: A Biography of Major General E. R. S. Canby, 1817–1873.* Glendale, Calif.: A. H. Clark, 1959.

Higham, Robin D. S., ed. *Bayonets in the Streets: Use of Troops in Civil Disturbances.* Manhattan: Kansas State University Press, 1969.

Hirshon, Stanley P. *Farewell to the Bloody Shirt: Northern Republicans and the Southern Negro.* Bloomington: Indiana University Press, 1962.

A History of Texas, Together with a Biographical History of Milam, Williamson, Bastrop, Travis, Lee and Burleson Counties. Chicago: Lewis Pub. Co., 1893.

Hobsbawm, Eric J. *Social Bandits and Primitive Rebels.* Glencoe, Ill.: Free Press, 1959.

Holbrook, William C. *A Narrative of the Officers and Enlisted Men of the Seventh Regiment of Vermont Volunteers from 1862–1866.* New York: American Bank Note Co., 1882.

Hoogenboom, Ari. *The Presidency of Rutherford B. Hayes.* Lawrence: University Press of Kansas, 1988.

Horn, Stanley. *Invisible Empire: The Story of the Ku Klux Klan, 1866–1871.* Boston: Houghton Mifflin, 1939.

Howard, Oliver Otis. *Autobiography of Oliver Otis Howard.* 2 vols. New York: Baker & Taylor Co., 1908.

Howard, Victor B. *Black Liberation in Kentucky: Emancipation and Freedom, 1862–1884.* Lexington: University of Kentucky Press, 1983.

Hughes, W. J. *Rebellious Ranger: Rip Ford and the Old Southwest.* Norman: University of Oklahoma Press, 1964.

Huson, Hobart. *Refugio: A Comprehensive History of Refugio County from Aboriginal Times to 1953.* Woodsboro, Texas: Rooke Foundation, 1953.

Bibliography

Hutton, Paul Andrew. *Phil Sheridan and His Army*. Lincoln: University of Nebraska Press, 1985.

Hyman, Harold. *A More Perfect Union: The Impact of the Civil War and Reconstruction on the Constitution*. New York: Knopf, 1973.

Ives, Rollin A. *A Treatise on Military Law. . . .* New York: D. Van Nostrand, 1886.

Jensen, Merrill. *The New Nation: A History of the United States during the Confederation, 1781–1789*. New York: Knopf, 1950.

Johnson, Robert U., and Clarence C. Buel, eds. *Battles and Leaders of the Civil War*. 4 vols. New York: Century, 1888.

Jones, Jacqueline. *Soldiers of Light and Love: Northern Teachers and Georgia Blacks, 1865–1873*. Chapel Hill: University of North Carolina Press, 1980.

Jordan, Terry G. *German Seed in Texas Soil: Immigrant Farmers in Nineteenth Century Texas*. Austin: University of Texas Press, 1966.

Kendrick, B. B. *The Journal of the Joint Committee of Fifteen on Reconstruction*. New York: Columbia University Press, 1914.

Kerby, Robert L. *Kirby Smith's Confederacy: The Trans-Mississippi South, 1863–1865*. New York: Columbia University Press, 1972.

Kerwood, Asbury L. *Annals of the Fifty-seventh Regiment Indiana Volunteers. . . .* Dayton, Ohio: W. J. Shelby, 1868.

Kidd, J. H. *Personal Recollections of a Cavalryman with Custer's Michigan Brigade in the Civil War*. Ionia, Mich.: Sentinel Pub. Co., 1908.

Kimberly, Robert L., and Ephraim S. Holloway. *The Forty-first Ohio Veteran Volunteer Infantry in the War of the Rebellion, 1861–1865*. Cleveland: W. R. Smilie, 1897.

King, Alvy L. *Louis Wigfall: Southern Fire-Eater*. Baton Rouge: Louisiana State University Press, 1970.

Leathers, Francis Jane. *Through the Years, A Historical Sketch of Leon County, and the Town of Oakwood*. Oakwood, Texas: n.p., 1964.

Link, Arthur S., and Rembert W. Patrick, eds. *Writing Southern History: Essays in Historiography in Honor of Fletcher M. Green*. Baton Rouge: Louisiana State University Press, 1965.

Linn, John J. *Reminiscences of Fifty Years in Texas*. New York: D. & J. Sadlier Co., 1883.

Litwack, Leon. *Been in the Storm So Long: The Aftermath of Slavery*. New York: Knopf, 1979.

Logan, Rayford W. *The Negro in American Life and Thought: The Nadir, 1877–1901*. New York: Dial Press, 1954.

Lonn, Ella. *Desertion during the Civil War*. New York: Century Co., 1928.

Lothrop, Charles Henry. *A History of the First Regiment Iowa Cavalry. . . .* Lyons, Iowa: Beers & Eaton, Printers, 1890.

McConnell, H. H. *Five Years a Cavalryman; or, Sketches of Regular Army Life on the Texas Frontier, Twenty-odd Years Ago*. Jacksboro, Texas: J. N. Rogers & Co., 1889.

McDonald, Forrest, and Ellen Shapiro McDonald. *Requiem: Variations on Eighteenth Century Themes*. Lawrence: University of Kansas Press, 1988.

McFeeley, William S. *Yankee Stepfather: General O. O. Howard and the Freedmen*. New Haven, Conn.: Yale University Press, 1968.

McKee, Irving. *"Ben Hur" Wallace: The Life of General Lew Wallace*. Berkeley: University of California Press, 1947.

Bibliography

McPherson, James M. *The Abolitionist Legacy: From Reconstruction to the NAACP.* Princeton, N.J.: Princeton University Press, 1975.

Magdol, Edward. *A Right to the Land: Essays on the Freedmen's Community.* Westport, Conn.: Greenwood Press, 1977.

Main, Jackson Turner. *The Anti-Federalists: Critics of the Constitution, 1781–1788.* Chicago: Quadrangle Books, 1964.

Mantell, Martin E. *Johnson, Grant, and the Politics of Reconstruction.* New York: Columbia University Press, 1973.

Marcy, R. B. *Thirty Years of Army Life on the Border.* New York: Harper Bros., 1866.

Marshall-Cornwall, James. *Grant as Military Commander.* New York: Van Nostrand, Rinehart, 1970.

Matloff, Maurice, ed. *American Military History.* Washington, D.C.: Government Printing Office, 1969.

Meinig, D. W. *Imperial Texas: An Interpretive Essay in Cultural Geography.* Austin: University of Texas Press, 1969.

Memorial and Biographical History of Navarro, Henderson, Anderson, Limestone, Freestone, and Leon Counties. Chicago: Lewis Pub. Co., 1893.

Merington, Marguerite. *The Custer Story: The Life and Intimate Letters of General George A. Custer and His Wife Elizabeth.* New York: Devon-Adair, 1950.

Messner, William F. *Freedmen and the Ideology of Free Labor: Louisiana, 1862–1865.* Lafayette: Center for Louisiana Studies, 1978.

Miller, Edmund Thornton. *A Financial History of Texas.* Austin: University of Texas Press, 1916.

Mills, William Samuel. *History of Van Zandt County.* Canton, Texas: n.p., 1950.

Mohr, Clarence L. *On the Threshold of Freedom: Masters and Slaves in Civil War Georgia.* Athens: University of Georgia Press, 1986.

Monaghan, Jay. *Custer: The Life of General George Armstrong Custer.* Boston: Little, Brown, 1959.

Moneyhon, Carl. *Republicanism in Reconstruction Texas.* Austin: University of Texas Press, 1980.

Nance, Joseph M. *Early History of Bryan and the Surrounding Area.* College Station: Texas A&M University, 1962.

Neville, Alexander White. *A History of Lamar County, Texas.* Paris: North Texas Pub. Co., 1937.

Newton, Alexander Heritage. *Out of the Briars, An Autobiography and Sketch of the Twenty-ninth Regiment Connecticut Volunteers.* Philadelphia: A. M. E. Book Concern, 1910.

Nichols, James L. *The Confederate Quartermaster in the Trans-Mississippi.* Austin: University of Texas Press, 1964.

Nieman, Donald G. *To Set the Law in Motion: The Freedmen's Bureau and the Legal Rights of Blacks, 1865–1868.* Millwood, N.Y.: Kraus International, 1979.

Nolan, Claude H. *The Negro's Image in the South: The Anatomy of White Supremacy.* Lexington: University of Kentucky Press, 1967.

North, Thomas. *Five Years in Texas; or, What You Did Not Hear during the War from January 1861 to January 1866.* Cincinnati: Elm Street Pub. Co., 1871.

Norton, Oliver. *Army Letters, 1861–1865. . . .* Chicago: O. L. Deming, 1903.

Novak, Daniel A. *The Wheel of Servitude: Black Forced Labor after Slavery*. Lexington: University of Kentucky Press, 1978.

Nunn, W. C. *Escape from Reconstruction*. Fort Worth: Texas Christian University Press, 1962.

————. *Texas under the Carpetbaggers*. Austin: University of Texas Press, 1962.

O'Connor, Richard. *Sheridan the Invincible*. Indianapolis: Bobbs-Merrill, 1953.

Osthaus, Carl L. *Freedmen, Philanthropy, and Fraud: A History of the Freedmen's Savings Bank*. Urbana: University of Illinois Press, 1976.

Otis, George A., ed. *Medical and Surgical History of the War of the Rebellion*. 3 vols. in 6 parts. Washington, D.C.: Government Printing Office, 1876.

Oubre, Claude F. *Forty Acres and a Mule*. Baton Rouge: Louisiana State University Press, 1978.

Owsley, Frank L. *Plain Folk of the Old South*. Baton Rouge: Louisiana State University Press, 1950.

————. *State Rights in the Confederacy*. Chicago: University of Chicago Press, 1925.

Patrick, Rembert. *The Reconstruction of the Nation*. New York: Oxford University Press, 1967.

Penniger, Robert. *Fest-ausgabe zum 50 – järigen Jubiläum der Gründig der Stadt Friedrichsburg.* . . . Fredericksburg, Texas: n.p., 1896.

Perkins, Dexter. *The Monroe Doctrine, 1826–1867*. Baltimore: Johns Hopkins University Press, 1933.

Perman, Michael. *Reunion without Compromise: The South and Reconstruction*. New York: Cambridge University Press, 1973.

Phisterer, Frederick. *New York in the War of the Rebellion*, 5 vols. Albany: J. B. Lyon Co., 1912.

Pierce, Paul Skeels. *The Freedmen's Bureau: A Chapter in the History of Reconstruction*. Iowa City: State University of Iowa Press, 1904.

Pitre, Merline. *Through Many Dangers, Toils, and Snares: The Black Leadership of Texas, 1868–1900*. Austin: Eakin Press, 1985.

Polakoff, Keith Ian. *The Politics of Inertia: The Election of 1876 and the End of Reconstruction*. Baton Rouge: Louisiana State University Press, 1973.

Powell, Lawrence N. *New Masters: Northern Planters in the Civil War and Reconstruction*. New Haven, Conn.: Yale University Press, 1980.

Priest, Loring Benson. *Uncle Sam's Stepchildren: The Reformation of United States Indian Policy, 1865–1887*. New Brunswick: Rutgers University Press, 1942.

Proceedings of the State Assembly of the State of New York on the Life and Services of General Philip H. Sheridan, Held at the Capitol, April 9, 1889. Albany: J. B. Lyon, 1890.

Prucha, Francis Paul. *A Guide to the Military Posts of the United States, 1789–1895*. Madison: State Historical Society of Wisconsin, 1964.

Rabel, George C. *But There Was No Peace: The Role of Violence in the Politics of Reconstruction*. Athens: University of Georgia Press, 1984.

Ramsdell, Charles W. *Reconstruction in Texas*. New York: Columbia University Press, 1910.

Randall, James G. *Constitutional Problems under Lincoln*. Rev. ed. Urbana: University of Illinois Press, 1964.

Ransom, Roger L., and Richard Sutch. *One Kind of Freedom: The Economic Consequences of Emancipation.* Cambridge: Harvard University Press, 1977.

Ray, Gladys B. *Murder at the Corners.* San Antonio: Naylor, 1957.

Reagan, John H. *Memoirs, with Special Reference to Secession and the Civil War.* New York: Neal Pub. Co., 1906.

Reid, John Philip. *In Defiance of the Law.* Chapel Hill: University of North Carolina Press, 1981.

Richardson, Rupert N. *The Frontier of Northwest Texas, 1846–1876: The Advance and Defense by Pioneer Settlers of the Cross Timbers and Prairies.* Glendale, Calif.: A. H. Clark, 1963.

Richter, William L. *The Army in Texas During Reconstruction, 1865–1870.* College Station: Texas A&M University Press, 1987.

Ripley, C. Peter. *Slaves and Freedmen in Civil War Louisiana.* Baton Rouge: Louisiana State University Press, 1978.

Rippy, J. Fred. *The United States and Mexico.* New York: F. S. Crofts & Co., 1931.

Rister, Carl Coke. *Border Command: General Phil Sheridan and the West.* Norman: University of Oklahoma Press, 1944.

———. *Fort Griffin on the Texas Frontier.* Norman: University of Oklahoma Press, 1956.

———. *The Southwestern Frontier, 1865–1881: A History of the Coming of the Settler . . . and the Disappearance of the Frontier.* Cleveland: A. H. Clark, 1928.

Roark, James L. *Masters without Slaves: Southern Planters in the Civil War and Reconstruction.* New York: W. W. Norton, 1977.

Rodenbough, Theodore F., and William L. Haskin, eds. *The Army of the United States.* New York: Maynard, Merrill & Co., 1896.

Rogers, John William. *The Lusty Texans of Dallas.* New York: E. P. Dutton, 1951.

Rose, Willie Lee. *Rehearsal for Reconstruction: the Port Royal Experiment.* Indianapolis: Bobbs-Merrill, 1964.

Rushmore, Elsie Mitchell. *The Indian Policy during Grant's Administration.* Jamaica, N.Y.: Marion Press, 1914.

Schofield, John M. *Forty-six Years in the Army.* New York: Century Co., 1897.

Sefton, James E. *The United States Army and Reconstruction, 1865–1877.* Baton Rouge: Louisiana State University Press, 1967.

Shapiro, Herbert. *White Violence and Black Response: From Reconstruction to Montgomery.* Amherst: University of Massachusetts Press, 1988.

Sheridan, Philip H. *Personal Memoirs of Philip H. Sheridan.* 2 vols. New York: C. L. Webster & Co., 1888.

Shy, John. *Toward Lexington: The Role of the British Army in the Coming of the Revolution.* Princeton, N.J.: Princeton University Press, 1965.

Sierra, Justo. *The Political Evolution of the Mexican People.* Austin: University of Texas Press, 1969.

Simkins, Francis B., and Robert W. Woody. *South Carolina during Reconstruction.* Chapel Hill: University of North Carolina Press, 1932.

Simon, John Y., ed. *The Papers of Ulysses S. Grant.* 16 vols. to date. Carbondale: Southern Illinois University Press, 1963– .

Smallwood, James. *Time of Hope, Time of Despair: Black Texans during Reconstruction.* Port Washington, N.Y.: National University Publications, 1981.

Smith, Justin. *The War with Mexico*. 2 vols. New York: Macmillan, 1919.

Sonnichsen, C. L. *I'll Die Before I'll Run: The Story of the Great Feuds of Texas*. New York: Harper, 1950.

———. *Tularosa: Last of the Frontier West*. 2nd ed. Albuquerque: University of New Mexico Press, 1980.

Sowell, Thomas. *Affirmative Action Reconsidered: Was It Really Necessary in Academia?* Washington, D.C.: American Enterprise Institute, 1975.

———. *Civil Rights: Rhetoric or Reality?* New York: William Morrow, 1984.

———. *The Economics and Politics of Race: An International Perspective*. New York: William Morrow, 1983.

———. *Ethnic America: A History*. New York: Basic Books, 1981.

———. *Pink and Brown People and Other Controversial Essays*. Stanford, Calif.: Hoover Institute, 1981.

———. *Preferential Policies: An International Perspective*. New York: William Morrow, 1990.

Speer, John W. *A History of Blanco County*. Ed. Henry W. Armbruster. Austin: Pemberton Press, 1965.

Stackpole, Edward J. *Sheridan in the Shenandoah: Jubal Early's Nemesis*. Harrisburg, Penn.: Stackpole Co., 1961.

Stampp, Kenneth. *The Era of Reconstruction, 1865–1877*. New York: Knopf, 1965.

Steward, T. G. *The Colored Regulars in the U. S. Army . . . from the Period of the Revolutionary War to 1899*. Philadelphia: A. M. E. Book Concern, 1904.

Stillman, Richard J., II. *The American Bureaucracy*. Chicago: Nelson-Hall, 1987.

Summers, Mark W. *The Plundering Generation: Corruption and the Crisis of the Union*. New York: Oxford University Press, 1987.

———. *Railroads, Reconstruction, and the Gospel of Prosperity*. Princeton, N.J.: Princeton University Press, 1984.

Swint, Henry Lee. *The Northern Teacher in the South, 1862–1870*. Nashville, Tenn.: Vanderbilt University Press, 1941.

Taylor, Richard. *Destruction and Reconstruction: Personal Experiences of the Late War*. New York: D. Appleton & Co., 1879.

Thomas, Benjamin, and Harold Hyman. *Stanton: The Life and Times of Lincoln's Secretary of War*. New York: Knopf, 1962.

Thomas, David Y. *A History of Military Government in Newly Acquired Territories of the United States*. New York: Columbia University Press, 1904.

Thompson, Elizabeth. *Reconstruction in Georgia, 1865–1872*. New York: Columbia University Press, 1915.

Thompson, Jerry Don. *Vaqueros in Blue and Gray*. Austin: Presidial Press, 1976.

Thompson, J. M. *Louis Napoleon and the Second Empire*. New York: Noonday Press, 1955.

Thrall, Homer S. *A Pictorial History of Texas from the Earliest Visits of European Adventurers to A.D. 1879*. St. Louis: N. D. Thompson & Co., 1879.

Trefousse, Hans L. *Andrew Johnson: A Biography*. New York: W. W. Norton, 1989.

Trelease, Allan W. *White Terror: The Ku Klux Klan Conspiracy and Southern Reconstruction*. New York: Harper & Row, 1971.

Tucker, Glenn. *Hancock, the Superb*. Indianapolis: Bobbs-Merrill, 1960.

The Union Army: A History of the Military Affairs in the Loyal States, Records of the Regiments of the Union Army. . . . 8 vols. Madison, Wis.: Federal Pub. Co., 1908.

United States Army and Navy Manual of Military Government and Civil Affairs. Washington, D.C.: Government Printing Office, 1943.

Utley, Robert M. *Billy the Kid: A Short and Violent Life.* Lincoln: University of Nebraska Press, 1989.

———. *Frontiersmen in Blue: The United States Army and the Indian, 1848-1865.* New York: Macmillan, 1967.

———. *High Noon at Lincoln: Violence on the Western Frontier.* Albuquerque: University of New Mexico Press, 1987.

Van De Water, Frederic F. *Glory Hunter: The Life of General Custer.* Indianapolis: Bobbs-Merrill, 1934.

Vandiver, *Jubal's Raid.* New York: McGraw-Hill, 1960.

Vaughn, J. W. *The Reynolds Campaign on Powder River.* Norman: University of Oklahoma Press, 1961.

Wagandt, Charles L. *The Mighty Revolution: Negro Emancipation in Maryland, 1862-1864.* Baltimore: Johns Hopkins University Press, 1964.

Walker, Francis A. *General Hancock.* New York: D. Appleton & Co., 1894.

Wallace, Ernest. *The Howling of the Coyotes: Reconstruction Efforts to Divide Texas.* College Station: Texas A&M University Press, 1979.

———. *Texas in Turmoil.* Austin: Steck-Vaughn Co., 1965.

Waller, John L. *Colossal Hamilton of Texas: A Biography of Andrew Jackson Hamilton.* El Paso: Texas Western Press, 1968.

Warner, Ezra J. *Generals in Blue: Lives of the Union Commanders.* Baton Rouge: Louisiana State University Press, 1964.

Webb, Walter Prescott. *The Texas Rangers: A Century of Frontier Defense.* Austin: University of Texas Press, 1965.

Webb, Walter P., and H. B. Carroll, eds. *The Handbook of Texas.* 2 vols. Austin: Texas State Historical Association, 1952.

Weber, Max. *The Theory of Social and Economic Organization.* Trans. A. M. Henderson. Ed. with introd. Talcott Parsons. Glencoe, Ill.: Free Press, 1957.

Welles, Gideon, *Diary of Gideon Welles.* Ed. Howard K. Beale, 3 vols. New York: Houghton-Mifflin & Co., 1911.

Weigley, Russell F. *The American Way of War: A History of the United States Military and Strategic Policy.* New York: Macmillan, 1973.

———. *History of the United States Army.* New York: Macmillan, 1967.

Wheeler, Kenneth W. *To Wear a City's Crown: The Beginnings of Urban Growth in Texas, 1836-1865.* Cambridge: Harvard University Press, 1968.

White, Howard A. *The Freedmen's Bureau in Louisiana.* Baton Rouge: Louisiana State University Press, 1970.

White, Leonard D. *The Republican Era, 1869-1901: A Study in Administrative History.* New York: Macmillan, 1958.

Whiting, William. *War Powers under the Constitution.* New York: Lee, Shepard, & Dillingham, 1871.

Wilbarger, J. W. *Indian Depredations in Texas.* Austin: Hutchings Printing House, 1889.

Bibliography

Wilson, Theodore B. *The Black Codes of the South.* University, Ala.: University of Alabama Press, 1965.

Winfrey, Dorman H., and James M. Day, eds. *The Indian Papers of Texas and the Southwest, 1825–1916.* 4 vols. Austin: Pemberton Press, 1966.

Winthrop, William. *Military Law and Precedents.* Washington, D.C.: Government Printing Office, 1920.

Wood, William D. *Reminiscences of Reconstruction in Texas and Reminiscences of Texas and Texans Fifty Years Ago.* San Marcos, Texas: n.p., 1902.

Woodward, C. Vann. *Reunion and Reaction: The Compromise of 1877 and the End of Reconstruction.* Boston: Little, Brown & Co., 1951.

Wooster, Ralph A. *The People in Power: Courthouse and Statehouse in the Lower South.* Knoxville: University of Tennessee Press, 1969.

Works Progress Administration. *Houston: A History and a Guide.* Houston: Anson Jones Press, 1942.

Wortham, Louis J. *A History of Texas from Wilderness to Commonwealth.* 5 vols. Fort Worth: Wortham-Molyneaux Co., 1924.

Wyatt-Brown, Bertram. *Southern Honor: Ethics and Behavior in the Old South.* New York: Oxford University Press, 1982. Abridged version, *Honor and Violence in the Old South.* New York: Oxford University Press, 1986.

Young, Otis E. *The West of Philip St. George Cooke, 1807–1895.* Glendale, Calif.: 1955.

Young, S. O. *True Stories of Old Houston and Houstonians.* Galveston: O. Springer, 1913.

2. Articles and Essays

Abbott, Martin. "The Freedmen's Bureau and Negro Schooling in South Carolina." *South Carolina Historical Magazine* 57 (1956): 65–81.

———. "Free Land, Free Labor, and the Freedmen's Bureau." *Agricultural History* 30 (1956): 150–56.

Adams, James Truslow. "Our Lawless Heritage." *Atlantic Monthly* 142 (1928): 732–40.

Alderson, William T. "The Freedmen's Bureau and Negro Education in Virginia." *North Carolina Historical Review* 29 (1952): 64–90.

Alexander, Roberta Sue. "Hostility and Hope: Black Education in North Carolina during Presidential Reconstruction, 1865–1867." *North Carolina Historical Review* 53 (1976): 113–32.

Alexander, Thomas B. "Persistent Whiggery in the Confederate South, 1860–1877." *Journal of Southern History* 27 (1961): 305–29.

Ashcraft, Alan C. "Role of the Confederate Provost Marshals in Texas." *Texana* 6 (1968): 390–92.

———. "Texas in Defeat: The Early Phase of A. J. Hamilton's Provisional Governorship, June 17, 1865 to February 7, 1866." *Texas Military History* 8 (1970): 199–219.

Aston, B. W. "Federal Military Occupation of the Southwest." *Texas Military History* 8 (1970): 123–34.

Avillo, Philip A., Jr. "John H. Reagan: Unionist or Secessionist?" *East Texas Historical Journal* 11 (1973): 3–11.

———. "Phantom Radicals: Texas Republicans in Congress, 1870–1873." *Southwestern Historical Quarterly* 77 (1973–74): 431–44.

Baenziger, Ann Patton, "The Texas State Police during Reconstruction: A Reexamination." *Southwestern Historical Quarterly* 72 (1968-69): 470-91.

Baggett, James Alex. "Birth of the Texas Republican Party." *Southwestern Historical Quarterly* 78 (1974-75): 1-20.

———. "Origins of Early Texas Republican Party Leadership." *Journal of Southern History* 40 (1974): 441-50.

Ballantine, Henry W. "Martial Law." *Columbia Law Review* 12 (1912): 529-38.

———. "Unconstitutional Claims of Military Authority." *Yale Law Journal* 24 (1914-15): 201-202.

Barr, Alwyn. "Black Legislators of Reconstruction Texas." *Civil War History* 32 (1986): 340-52.

———. "The Making of a Secessionist: The Ante-Bellum Career of Roger Q. Mills." *Southwestern Historical Quarterly* 79 (1975-76): 129-44.

———, ed. "Records of the Confederate Military Commission in San Antonio, July 2-October 10, 1862." *Southwestern Historical Quarterly* 70 (1966-67): 93-109, 289-313, 623-44; 71 (1967-68): 247-78.

———. "Texas Coastal Defense, 1861-1865." *Southwestern Historical Quarterly* 65 (1961-62): 1-31.

Barton, Henry W. "The United States Cavalry and the Texas Rangers." *Southwestern Historical Quarterly* 63 (1959-60): 495-510.

Bauer, Raymond A., and Alice H. Bauer. "Day to Day Resistance to Slavery." *Journal of Negro History* 27 (1942): 388-419.

Beale, Howard K. "On Rewriting Reconstruction History." *American Historical Review* 45 (1940): 807-27.

Belz, Herman. "The Freedmen's Bureau Act of 1865 and the Principle of No Discrimination According to Color." *Civil War History* 21 (1975): 197-217.

Benedict, Michael Les. "Preserving the Constitution: The Conservative Basis of Radical Reconstruction." Journal of American History 41 (1974): 65-90.

———. "Southern Democrats in the Crisis of 1876: A Reconsideration of Reunion and Reaction," *Journal of Southern History* 46 (1980), 489-524.

Bennis, Warren G. "Beyond Bureaucracy." In Warren G. Bennis, ed., *American Bureaucracy* (Chicago: Aldine Pub. Co., 1970): 3-16.

Bestor, Arthur. "State Sovereignty and Slavery: A Reinterpretation of the Proslavery Constitutional Doctrine, 1846-1860." *Illinois State Historical Society Journal* 54 (1960): 117-80.

Bethel, Elizabeth. "The Freedmen's Bureau in Alabama." *Journal of Southern History* 14 (1948): 49-92.

Biesele, R. L. "The Relations between the German Settlers and the Indians in Texas, 1844-1860." *Southwestern Historical Quarterly* 31 (1927-28): 116-29.

———. "The Texas State Convention of Germans in 1854." *Southwestern Historical Quarterly* 33 (1929-30): 247-61.

Bigelow, Martha M. "Vicksburg: Experiment in Freedom." *Journal of Mississippi History* 26 (1964): 28-44.

Blackburn, J. K. P. "Reminiscences of the Terry Rangers." *Southwestern Historical Quarterly* 22 (1918-19): 143-79.

Bowen, Nancy Head. "A Political Labyrinth: Texas in the Civil War." *East Texas Historical Journal* 11 (1973): 3-11.

Bibliography

Brown, Ira V. "Lyman Abbott and Freedmen's Aid, 1865–1869." *Journal of Southern History* 15 (1948): 49–92.

Byrne, Frank L. "'A Terrible Machine': General Neal Dow's Military Government on the Gulf Coast." *Civil War History* 12 (1966): 5–22.

Campbell, Clarice T. "Exploring the Roots of Tougaloo College." *Journal of Mississippi History* 35 (1973): 15–27.

Campbell, Randolph. "Political Conflict within the Southern Consensus: Harrison County, Texas, 1850–1880." *Civil War History* 26 (1980): 218–39.

Campbell, William A., ed. "A Freedmen's Bureau Diary by George Wagner." *Georgia Historical Quarterly* 48 (1964–65): 196–214, 333–60.

Cantrell, Gregg. "Racial Violence and Politics in Reconstruction Texas, 1867–1868." *Southwestern Historical Quarterly* 93 (1989–90): 333–55.

Carpenter, A. H. "Military Government of Southern Territory, 1861–1865." *American Historical Association Annual Report* (1900): vol. 1, 465–98.

Carpenter, John A. "Atrocities during the Reconstruction Period." *Journal of Negro History* 47 (1962): 234–47.

Carper, N. Gordon. "Slavery Revisited: Peonage in the South." *Phylon* 37 (1976): 85–99.

Carter, Dan T. "Anatomy of Fear: The Christmas Day Insurrection Scare of 1865." *Journal of Southern History* 42 (1976): 345–64.

Castel, Albert. "Order No. 11 and the Civil War on the Border." *Missouri Historical Review* 57 (1963): 357–68.

Christensen, Lawrence O. "Schools for Blacks: J. Milton Turner." *Missouri Historical Review* 76 (1982): 212–35.

Cimbala, Paul A. "The 'Talisman Power': Davis Tillson, the Freedmen's Bureau, and Free Labor in Reconstruction Georgia." *Civil War History* 28 (1982): 153–71.

"The Civil Administration of Major General Winfield Scott Hancock, during His Administration in Louisiana and Texas." *Southern Review* 9 (1871): 906–23.

Cohen, Barry M. "The Texas-Mexico Border, 1858–1867. . . ," *Texana* 6 (1968): 153–65.

Cohen, William. "Negro Involuntary Servitude in the South, 1865–1940: A Preliminary Analysis." *Journal of Southern History* 42 (1976): 31–60.

Colby, Ira C. "The Freedmen's Bureau: From Social Welfare to Segregation." *Phylon* 46 (1985): 219–30.

Cox, John, and La Wanda Cox. "General Howard and the 'Misrepresented Bureau'." *Journal of Southern History* 19 (1953): 427–56.

Cox, La Wanda. "The Promise of Land for the Freedmen." *Mississippi Valley Historical Review* 45 (1958): 413–40.

Cox, Merlin G. "Military Reconstruction of Florida." *Florida Historical Quarterly* 46 (1967–68): 219–33.

Crook, Carland Elaine. "Benjamin Theron and French Designs in Texas during the Civil War." *Southwestern Historical Quarterly* 68 (1964–65): 432–54.

Crouch, Barry A. "Black Dreams and White Justice." *Prologue* 6 (1974): 255–65.

———. "The Freedmen's Bureau and the 30th Sub-district in Texas." *Chronicles of Smith County, Texas* 11 (1972): 15–30.

———. "Freedmen's Bureau Records: Texas, A Case Study." In Robert L. Clarke, ed., *Afro-American History: Sources for Research* (Washington: Howard University Press, 1981): 74–94.

————. "Hidden Sources of Black History: The Texas Freedmen's Bureau Records as a Case Study." *Southwestern Historical Quarterly* 83 (1980): 211–26.

————. "Self Determination and Local Black Leaders in Texas." *Phylon* 39 (1978): 344–55.

————. "A Spirit of Lawlessness: White Violence, Texas Blacks, 1865–1868." *Journal of Social History* 18 (1984): 217–32.

————. "'Unmanacling' Texas Reconstruction: A Twenty Year Perspective." *Southwestern Historical Quarterly* 93 (1989–90): 275–302.

Crouch, Barry A., and Larry Madaras. "Reconstructing Black Families: Perspectives from the Texas Freedmen's Bureau Records." *Prologue* 18 (1986): 109–22.

Crouch, Barry A., and L. J. Schultz. "Crisis in Color: Racial Separation in Texas Reconstruction." *Civil War History* 16 (1969): 37–49.

Cumberland, Charles C. "The Confederate Loss and Recapture of Galveston, 1861–62." *Southwestern Historical Quarterly* 51 (1947–48): 109–30.

Current, Richard. "Carpetbaggers Reconsidered." In David H. Pinckney and Theodore Ropp, eds., *A Festschrift for Frederick B. Artz* (Durham, N.C.: Duke University Press, 1964): 139–57.

Davis, Ronald L. F. "The U. S. Army and the Origins of Sharecropping in the Natchez District: A Case Study." *Journal of Negro History* 62 (1977): 60–80.

Dawson, Joseph Green, III. "Army Generals and Reconstruction: Mower and Hancock as Case Studies." *Southern Studies: An Interdisciplinary Journal of the South* 17 (1978): 255–72.

————. "General Phil Sheridan and Military Reconstruction in Louisiana." *Civil War History* 24 (1978): 133–51.

Degler, Carl N. "Rethinking Post–Civil War History." *Virginia Quarterly Review* 57 (1981): 255–56.

Delany, Robert W. "Matamoros, Port for Texas during the Civil War." *Southwestern Historical Quarterly* 58 (1954–55): 473–87.

Dennison, George W. "Martial Law: The Development of a Theory of Emergency Power, 1776–1861." *American Journal of Legal History* 18 (1974): 52–95.

Dill, Robert G. "The Soldiers' Homeward Voyage, a Thrilling Experience at the Close of the Late Civil War." *Magazine of American History* 11 (1884): 445–53.

Dimick, Howard T. "The [Davis B.] Bonfoey Murder Case." *Southwestern Historical Quarterly* 48 (1944–45): 469–83.

Donald, David H. "The Scalawag in Mississippi Reconsidered." *Journal of Southern History* 10 (1944): 447–60.

Dorris, J. T. "Pardon Seekers and Brokers: A Sequel to Appomattox." *Journal of Southern History* 1 (1935): 276–92.

DuBois, W. E. B. "The Freedmen's Bureau." *Atlantic Monthly* 87 (1901): 254–65.

Dugan, Frank H. "The 1850: Affair of the Brownsville Separatists." *Southwestern Historical Quarterly* 56 (1957–58): 270–87.

Duniway, C. A. "Reasons for the Withdrawal of the French from Mexico." *American Historical Association Annual Report* (1901): vol. 1, 313–28.

Duty, Tony E. "The Home Front—McLennan County in the Civil War." *Texana* 12 (1974): 197–238.

Dykes, J. C. "Dime Novel Texas; or, the Sub-Literature of the Lone Star State." *Southwestern Historical Quarterly* 49 (1945–46): 327–40.

Eason, Al. "Cullen Baker—Purveyor of Death." *Frontier Times* 40 (August–September, 1966): 6-12, 44-47, 67.

Ellem, Warren A. "Who Were the Mississippi Scalawags?" *Journal of Southern History* 48 (1982): 349-72.

Elliott, Claude. "The Freedmen's Bureau in Texas." *Southwestern Historical Quarterly* (1952-53): 1-24.

———. "Union Sentiment in Texas, 1861-1865." *Southwestern Historical Quarterly* 50 (1946-47): 449-77.

Elliott, Mabel A. "Crime and the Frontier Mores." *American Sociological Review* 9 (1944-45): 185-92.

Ellis, L. Tuffly. "Maritime Commerce on the Far Western Gulf, 1861-1865." *Southwestern Historical Quarterly* 77 (1973-74): 167-226.

Engdahl, David E. "Soldiers, Riots, and Revolutions: The Law of Military Troops in Civil Disorders." *Iowa Law Review* 57 (1971): 1-70.

Englesman, John C. "The Freedmen's Bureau in Louisiana." *Louisiana Historical Quarterly* 32 (1949): 145-224.

Estill, Harry F. "The Old Town of Huntsville." *The Quarterly of the Texas State Historical Association* 3 (1899-1900): 265-78.

Everly, Elaine C. "Marriage Registers of Freedmen." *Prologue* 5 (1973): 150-54.

Ewing, Floyd F., Jr. "Origins of Unionist Sentiment on the West Texas Frontier." *West Texas Historical Association Year Book* 32 (1956): 3-29.

Felix, James. "Decline and Fall of Freedmen's Village in Arlington, Virginia." *Negro History Bulletin* 37 (1974): 247-50.

Field, William T., Jr. "The Texas State Police, 1870-1873," *Texas Military History* 5 (1965): 131-41.

Fitzhugh, Lester N. "Saluria, Fort Esperanza, and Military Operations on the Texas Coast, 1861-1864." *Southwestern Historical Quarterly* 56 (1957-58): 66-100.

Fletcher, John. "Fort Phantom Hill." *Texas Military History* 3 (1963): 161.

Foner, Eric. "Reconstruction Revisited." *Reviews in American History* 10 (1982): 82-100.

Foster, Gaines M. "The Limitations of Federal Health Care for Freedmen, 1862-1868." *Journal of Southern History* 48 (1982): 349-72.

Franklin, John Hope. "Whither Reconstruction Historiography?" *Journal of Negro Education* 17 (1948): 446-65.

Freidel, Frank. "General Orders No. 100 and Military Government." *Mississippi Valley Historical Review* 32 (1945-46): 541-56.

Friedman, Lawrence J. "The Search for Docility: Racial Thought in the White South, 1861-1917." *Phylon* 31 (1970): 313-23.

Friend, Llerna B. "The Texan of 1860." *Southwestern Historical Quarterly* 62 (1958-59): 1-17.

Fuke, Richard Paul. "A Reform Mentality: Federal Policy toward Black Marylanders, 1864-1868." *Civil War History* 22 (1976): 214-35.

Furman, H. W. C. "Restrictions upon the Use of the Army Imposed by the Posse Comitatus Act." *Military Law Review* 79 (1959): 85-129.

Futrell, Robert F. "Federal Military Government in the South, 1861-1865." *Military Affairs* 15 (1951): 181-91.

Gabriel, Ralph. "The American Experience with Military Government." *American Historical Review* 49 (1944): 632-37.

Garner, James W. "General Orders 100 Revisited." *Military Law Review* 27 (1965): 1–48.

Gordon, Leonard. "Lincoln and Juarez – A Brief Reassessment." *Hispanic-American Historical Review* 48 (1968): 75–80.

Gorn, Elliott J. "'Gouge and Bite, Pull Hair, and Scratch': The Social Significance of Fighting in the Southern Backcountry." *American Historical Review* 90 (1985): 18–43.

Green, Fletcher M. "Democracy in the Old South." *Journal of Southern History* 12 (1946): 3–23.

Groff, Patrick. "The Freedmen's Bureau in High School History Texts." *Journal of Negro Education* 51 (1982): 425–33.

Gutman, Herbert G. "The Slave Family and Its Legacies." *Historical Reflections* 6 (1979): 183–211.

Hall, Martin H. "The Campbell-Sherman Diplomatic Mission to Mexico." *Historical and Philosophical Society of Ohio Bulletin* 13 (1955): 254–70.

Halstead, Jacqueline J. "The Delaware Association for the Moral Improvement and Education of the Colored People: 'Practical Christianity'." *Delaware History* 15 (1972): 19–40.

Hanna, Kathryn Abbey. "The Role of the South in the French Intervention in Mexico." *Journal of Southern History* 20 (1954): 3–21.

Harrison, Lowell H. "Supplying Texas Military Posts in 1876." *Texas Military History* 4 (1964): 23–24.

Hasson, Gail S. "Health and Welfare of Freedmen in Reconstruction Alabama." *Alabama Review* 35 (1982): 94–110.

Hermann, Janet S. "Reconstruction in Microcosm: Three Men and a Gin." *Journal of Negro History* 65 (1980): 312–35.

Highland, John. "Texas Collection." *Southwestern Historical Quarterly* 45 (1941–42): 197–98.

Hill, Lawrence F. "The Confederate Exodus to Latin America." *Southwestern Historical Quarterly* 39 (1935–36): 100–134, 161–99, 309–26.

Hoffnagel, Warren. "The Southern Homestead Act: Its Origins and Operation." *Historian* 32 (1970): 612–29.

Holden, W. C. "Frontier Defense, 1865–1889." *Panhandle-Plains Historical Review* 2 (1929): 43–64.

———. "Frontier Defense in Texas during the Civil War." *West Texas Historical Association Year Book* 4 (1928): 16–31.

———. "Law and Lawlessness on the Texas Frontier, 1875–1890." *Southwestern Historical Quarterly* (1940–41): 188–203.

Holdsworth, W. S. "Martial Law Historically Considered." *Law Quarterly Review* 18 (1902): 117–32.

Holsinger, Frank A. "How Does One Feel under Fire?" In *War Talks in Kansas: A Series of Papers Read before the Kansas Commandery of the Military Order of the Loyal Legion of the United States* (Kansas City, Mo.: Franklin Hudson Printing Co., 1906), 290–304.

Hornsby, Alton, Jr. "The Freedmen's Bureau Schools in Texas 1865–1870." *Southwestern Historical Quarterly* 76 (1972–73): 397–417.

Howard, Victor B. "The Kentucky Press and the Negro Testimony Controversy, 1866–1872." *Register of the Kentucky Historical Society* 71 (1973): 29–50.

Hume, Richard L., ed. "The Freedmen's Bureau and the Freedmen's Vote in the Reconstruction of Southern Alabama: An Account by Agent Samuel Gardner." *Alabama Historical Quarterly* 37 (1975): 217–24.

Humphrey, George D. "The Failure of the Mississippi Freedmen's Bureau in Black Labor Relations, 1865–1867." *Journal of Mississippi History* 45 (1983): 23–37.

Hyman, Harold. "Deceit in Dixie." *Civil War History* 3 (1957): 65–82.

———. "Johnson, Stanton, and Grant: A Reinterpretation of the Army's Role in Events Leading to Impeachment." *American Historical Review* 66 (1960): 85–100.

Jackson, Luther P. "The Educational Efforts of the Freedmen's Bureau and Freedmen's Aid Societies in South Carolina, 1862–1872." *Journal of Negro History* 8 (1923): 1–40.

Johnson, Boyd W. "Cullen Montgomery Baker: The Arkansas-Texas Desperado." *Arkansas Historical Quarterly* 25 (1966): 229–39.

Jones, Allen W. "Military Events in Texas during the Civil War, 1861–1865." *Southwestern Historical Quarterly* 64 (1960–61): 64–70.

Jordan, Terry G. "The Imprint of the Upper and Lower South on Mid-Nineteenth Century Texas." *Association of American Geographers Annals* 57 (1967): 667–90.

Kaczorowski, Robert J. "To Begin the Nation Anew: Congress, Citizenship, and Civil Rights after the Civil War." *American Historical Review* 90 (1987): 45–68.

Kassel, Charles. "Educating the Slave – A Forgotten Chapter of Civil War History." *Open Court* 40 (1927): 239–56.

———. "Edwin Miller Wheelock." *Open Court* 33 (1920): 564–69.

———. "Edwin Miller Wheelock and the Abolition Movement." *Open Court* 36 (1923): 166–75.

———. "Edwin Miller Wheelock: A Prophet of the Civil War Times." *Open Court* 35 (1923): 116–27.

———. "The Herald of Emancipation: A Memory of Edwin Miller Wheelock." *Open Court* 38 (1925): 230–42.

———. "An Interpreter of Destiny: Edwin Miller Wheelock and the War between the States." *Open Court* 37 (1924): 406–18.

———. "A Knight Errant in the Department of the Gulf: Episode in the Life of Edwin Miller Wheelock." *Open Court* 38 (1925): 563–76.

———. "The Labor System of General Banks – A Lost Episode in Civil War History." *Open Court* 42 (1929): 35–50.

Kimball, Philip Clyde. "Freedom's Harvest: Freedmen's Schools in Kentucky after the Civil War." *Filson Club Historical Quarterly* 54 (1980): 272–88.

Lale, Max S. "Military Occupation of Marshall, Texas, by the Eighth Illinois Volunteer Infantry, U.S.A., 1865." *Military History of Texas and the Southwest* 13 (1976): 39–47.

———. "Robert W. Loughery: Rebel Editor." *East Texas Historical Journal* 21 (1983): 3–15.

Lathrop, Barnes F. "Migration into East Texas, 1835–1860." *Southwestern Historical Quarterly* 52 (1948–49): 1–31, 184–208, 325–48.

Ledbetter, Billy D. "White over Black in Texas: Racial Attitudes in the Antebellum Period." *Phylon* 34 (1973): 406–18.

Legan, Marshall S. "Disease and the Freedmen in Mississippi during Reconstruction." *Journal of the History of Medicine and Allied Sciences* 28 (1973): 257–67.

Little, Robert D. "Southern Historians and the Downfall of the Confederacy." *Alabama Review* 3 (1950): 243–62; 4 (1951): 38–54.

Low, W. A. "The Freedmen's Bureau in the Border States." In Richard O. Curry, ed., *Radicalism, Racism, and Party Alignment: The Border States during Reconstruction* (Baltimore: Johns Hopkins University Press, 1969): 245–64.

Lynd, Staughton. "Rethinking Slavery and Reconstruction." *Journal of Negro History* 50 (1965): 198–209.

McClellan, Waymon L. "The Know Nothing Challenge in East Texas." *East Texas Historical Journal* 12 (1974): 33–44.

———. "The Know Nothing Party and the Growth of Sectionalism in East Texas." *East Texas Historical Journal* 14 (1976): 26–36.

McDonald, Forrest. "Woodward's Strange Career." *National Review* 41 (October 27, 1989): 46–47.

McDonald, Forrest, and Grady McWhiney. "The South from Self-sufficiency to Peonage: An Interpretation." *American Historical Review* 85 (1980): 1095–1118.

McDonough, James L. "John Schofield as Military Director of Reconstruction in Virginia." *Civil War History* 15 (1969): 237–56.

McKay, S. S. "Social Conditions in Texas in the Eighteen Seventies." *West Texas Historical Association Year Book* 14 (1938): 32–51.

Macy, William Madison. "The Civil War Diary of William Madison Macy." *Indiana Magazine of History* 30 (1934): 181–97.

Magdol, Edward. "Local Black Leaders in the South, 1867–1875: An Essay toward the Reconstruction of Reconstruction History." *Societas* 4 (1974): 81–110.

Maher, Edward R. "Sam Houston and Secession." *Southwestern Historical Quarterly* 55 (1951–52): 448–58.

Majeske, Penelope K. "Virginia after Appomattox: The Unites States Army and the Formation of Presidential Reconstruction Policy." *West Virginia History* 43 (1982): 95–117.

Maresh, Henry R. "The Czechs in Texas." *Southwestern Historical Quarterly* 50 (1946–47): 236–40.

Marten, James. "The Lamentations of a Whig: James Throckmorton Writes a Letter." *Civil War History* 31 (1985): 163–70.

May, J. Thomas. "Continuity and Change in the Labor Program of the Union Army and the Freedmen's Bureau." *Civil War History* 17 (1971): 245–54.

———. "The Freedmen's Bureau at the Local Level: A Study of a Local Agent." *Louisiana History* 9 (1968): 5–19.

———. "The Louisiana Negro in Transition: An Appraisal of the Medical Activities of the Freedmen's Bureau." *Bulletin of the Tulane University Medical Faculty* 26 (1967): 29–36.

———. "A 19th Century Medical Care Program for Blacks: The Case of the Freedmen's Bureau." *Anthropological Quarterly* 46 (1973): 160–71.

Mecklin, John W. "The Black Codes." *South Atlantic Quarterly* 16 (1917): 248–59.

Meek, Clarence I., III. "Illegal Law Enforcement: Aiding Civil Authorities in Violation of the Posse Comitatus Act." *Military Law Review* 70 (1975): 83–126.

Mehring, John V. "Persistent Whiggery in the Confederate South: A Reconsideration." *South Atlantic Quarterly* 69 (1970): 124–43.

Miller, Robert Ryal. "Lew Wallace and the French Intervention in Mexico." *Indiana Magazine of History* 54 (1963): 31–50.

———. "Matias Romero: Mexican Minister to the United States during the Juarez-Maximilian Era." *Hispanic-American Historical Review* 45 (1965): 228–45.

Mink, Charles R. "General Orders No. 11: The Forced Evacuation of Civilians during the Civil War." *Military Affairs* 34 (1970): 132–36.

Mitchell, Leon, Jr. "Camp Groce: Confederate Military Prison." *Southwestern Historical Quarterly* 67 (1963–64): 15–21.

Moneyhon, Carl. "George T. Ruby and the Politics of Expedience in Texas." In Howard N. Rabinowitz, ed., *Southern Black Leaders of the Reconstruction Era* (Urbana: University of Illinois Press, 1982): 364–78.

Moore, Richard. "Radical Reconstruction: The Texas Choice." *East Texas Historical Journal* 16 (1978): 15–23.

Moore, Wilton P. "The Provost Marshal Goes to War." *Civil War History* 5 (1959): 62–71.

———. "Union Provost Marshals in the Eastern Theater." *Military Affairs* 26 (1962): 120–21.

Moran, Robert E. "The Negro Dependent Child in Louisiana, 1800–1935." *Social Service Review* 45 (1971): 53–61.

Morris, Thomas D. "Equality, 'Extraordinary Law,' and Criminal Justice: The South Carolina Experience, 1865–1866." *South Carolina Historical Magazine* 83 (1982): 15–33.

Mugleston, William F., ed. "The Freedmen's Bureau and Reconstruction in Virginia: The Diary of Sterling Hopkins, a Union Officer." *Virginia Magazine of History and Biography* 86 (1978): 45–102.

Nackman, Mark E. "The Making of the Texas Citizen Soldier, 1835–60." *Southwestern Historical Quarterly* 78 (1974–75): 231–53.

Neal, Diane, and Thomas W. Kremm. "'What Shall We Do with the Negro?': The Freedmen's Bureau in Texas." *East Texas Historical Journal* 27 (2) (1989): 23–33.

Nieman, Donald G. "Andrew Johnson, the Freedmen's Bureau, and the Problem of Equal Rights, 1865–1866." *Journal of Southern History* 44 (1978): 399–420.

———. "The Freedmen's Bureau and the Mississippi Black Code." *Journal of Mississippi History* 40 (1978), 91–118.

Niepman, Ann Davis. "General Orders No. 11 and Border Warfare during the Civil War." *Missouri Historical Review* 66 (1972): 185–210.

Oakes, James. "A Failure of Vision: The Collapse of Freedmen's Bureau Courts." *Civil War History* 25 (1979): 66–76.

Oates, Stephen B. "John S. 'Rip' Ford: Prudent Cavalryman, C.S.A." *Southwestern Historical Quarterly* 64 (1960–61): 289–314.

———. "Recruiting Confederate Cavalry in Texas." *Southwestern Historical Quarterly* 64 (1960–61): 463–77.

———. "Texas under the Secessionists." *Southwestern Historical Quarterly* 67 (1963–64): 167–212.

Bibliography

O'Brien, John T. "Reconstruction in Richmond: White Restoration and Black Protest, April–June 1865." *Virginia Magazine of History and Biography* 89 (1981): 259–81.

Olsen, Otto H. "The Ku Klux Klan: A Study in Reconstruction Politics and Propaganda." *North Carolina Historical Quarterly* 39 (1962): 340–62.

———. "Reconsidering the Scalawags." *Civil War History* 12 (1966): 304–20.

———. "Southern Reconstruction and the Question of Self-Determination." In George M. Frederickson, ed., *A Nation Divided: Problems and Issues of the Civil War and Reconstruction* (Minneapolis: Burgess Pub. Co., 1975): 113–41.

Page, Thomas Nelson. "The Southern People during Reconstruction." *Atlantic Monthly* 87 (1901): 289–304.

Parmet, Robert D. "Schools for the Freedmen." *Negro History Bulletin* 34 (1971): 128–32.

Pate, J'Nell. "United States–Mexican Border Conflicts, 1870–1880." *West Texas Historical Association Year Book* 38 (1962): 175–94.

Pearce, Larry W. "The American Missionary Association and the Freedmen's Bureau in Arkansas, 1868–1878." *Arkansas Historical Quarterly* 30 (1971): 123–44, 246–61; 31 (1972): 246–61.

———. "Enoch K. Miller and the Freedmen's Schools." *Arkansas Historical Quarterly* 31 (1972): 305–27.

Peek, Ralph L. "Lawlessness in Florida, 1868–1871." *Florida Historical Quarterly* 40 (1961–62): 164–85.

———. "Military Reconstruction and the Growth of Anti-Negro Sentiment in Florida, 1867." *Florida Historical Quarterly* 47 (1968–69): 380–400.

Peskin, Allan. "Was There a Compromise of 1877?" *Journal of American History* 60 (1973): 63–75.

Pfanz, Harry W. "The Surrender Negotiations between General Johnston and General Sherman, April 1865." *Military Affairs* 16 (1952): 61–70.

Phillips, Paul D. "White Reaction to the Freedmen's Bureau in Tennessee." *Tennessee Historical Quarterly* 25 (1966): 50–62.

Pierson, William Wately. "Texas *versus* White," *Southwestern Historical Quarterly* 18 (1914–15): 341–67; 19 (1915–16): 1–36, 142–58.

Pitre, Merline. "The Evolution of Black Political Participation in Reconstruction Texas." *East Texas Historical Journal* 26 (1) (1988): 36–45.

———. "A Note on the Historiography of Blacks in the Reconstruction of Texas." *Journal of Negro History* 66 (1981): 340–48.

Powell, Lawrence N. "The Politics of Livelihood: Carpetbaggers in the Deep South." In J. Morgan Lousser and James M. McPherson, eds., *Region, Race, and Reconstruction: Essays in Honor of C. Vann Woodward* (New York: Oxford University Press, 1982): 315–47.

Price, Charles L. "John C. Barrett, Freedmen's Bureau Agent in North Carolina." *Papers in North Carolina History* 5 (1981): 51–74.

Proctor, Samuel, "Yankee 'Schoolmarms' in Post-war Florida." *Journal of Negro History* 44 (1959): 275–77.

Prucha, Francis Paul. "New Approaches to the Study of the Administration of Indian Policy," *Prologue* 3 (1971): 15–19.

Putney, Martha S. "The Baltimore Normal School for the Education of Colored Teachers: Its Founders and Its Founding." *Maryland Historical Magazine* 72 (1977): 238–52.

Rabel, George. "Southern Interests and the Election of 1876: A Reappraisal." *Civil War History* 26 (1980): 347–61.

Ramsdell, Charles W. "The Frontier and Secession," In James W. Gardner, ed., *Studies in Southern History and Politics Dedicated to William A. Dunning* (New York: Columbia University Press, 1914): 63–65.

————. "The Last Hope of the Confederacy—John Tyler to the Governor and Authorities of Texas." *The Quarterly of the Texas State Historical Association* 15 (1910–11): 129–45.

Raphael, Alan. "Health and Social Welfare of Kentucky Black People, 1865–1870." *Societas* 2 (1972): 143–57.

Rice, Paul Jackson. "New Laws and Insights Encircle the Posse Comitatus Act." *Military Law Review* 104 (1984): 109–38.

Richardson, Joe M. "An Evaluation of the Freedmen's Bureau in Florida." *Florida Historical Quarterly* 41 (1963): 223–38.

————. "The Florida Black Codes." *Florida Historical Quarterly* 47 (1968–69): 365–79.

————. "The Freedmen's Bureau and Negro Labor in Florida." *Florida Historical Quarterly* 39 (1960): 176–84.

Richter, William L. "The Army and the Negro during Texas Reconstruction." *East Texas Historical Journal* 10 (Spring, 1972): 7–19.

————. "'A Better Time Is in Store for Us': An Analysis of the Reconstruction Attitudes of George Armstrong Custer." *Military History of Texas and the Southwest* 11 (1973): 31–50.

————. "The Brenham Fire of 1866: A Texas Reconstruction Atrocity." *Louisiana Studies: An Interdisciplinary Journal of the South* 14 (1975): 287–314.

————. "'Devil Take Them All': Military Rule in Texas, 1862–1870." *Southern Studies: An Interdisciplinary Journal of the South* 25 (1986): 5–30.

————. "General Phil Sheridan, the Historians, and Reconstruction." *Civil War History* 33 (1987): 131–54.

————. "'It Is Best to Go in Strong-Handed': Army Occupation of Texas, 1865–1866." *Arizona and the West* 27 (1985): 113–42.

————. "'Outside My Profession': The Army and Civil Affairs in Texas Reconstruction." *Military History of Texas and the Southwest* 9 (1971): 5–21.

————. "'The Revolver Rules the Day!': Colonel DeWitt C. Brown and the Freedmen's Bureau in Paris, Texas, 1867–1868." *Southwestern Historical Quarterly* 93 (1989–1990): 303–32.

————. "'Shoot or Get Out': The Murder of Texas Freedmen's Bureau Agent William G. Kirkman." Work in progress.

————. "'Spread-Eagle Eccentricities': Military-Civilian Relations in Reconstruction Texas." *Texana* 8 (1970): 311–27.

————. "Texas Politics and the United States Army, 1866–1867." *Military History of Texas and the Southwest* 11 (1972): 159–86.

————. "'This Bloody Hole': Opposition to the Freedmen's Bureau in Clarksville and Northeastern Texas." Work in progress.

————. "Tyrant and Reformer: General Charles Griffin Reconstructs Texas, 1866–1867." *Prologue: The Journal of the National Archives* 10 (1978): 255–41.

————. "'We Must Rubb Out and Begin Anew': The Army and the Republican

Party in Texas Reconstruction, 1867–1870." *Civil War History* 19 (December, 1973): 334–52.

———. "Who Was the Real Head of the Texas Freedmen's Bureau?: The Role of Brevet Colonel William H. Sinclair as Acting Assistant Inspector General." *Military History of the Southwest* 20 (1990): 121–56.

Rister, Carl Coke, ed. "Early Accounts of Indian Depredations." *West Texas Historical Association Year Book* 2 (1926): 18–44.

———. "The Significance of the Jacksboro Indian Affair of 1871." *Southwestern Historical Quarterly* 29 (1925–26): 181–200.

Rosen, F. Bruce. "The Influence of the Peabody Fund on Education in Reconstruction Florida." *Florida Historical Quarterly* 55 (1977): 310–20.

Russ, William A., Jr. "Radical Disfranchisement in Texas 1867–1870." *Southwestern Historical Quarterly* 38 (1934–35): 40–52.

Ryan, James Gilbert. "The Memphis Riot of 1866: Terror in a Black Community During Reconstruction." *Journal of Negro History* 62 (1977): 243–57.

St. Clair, Kenneth E. "Judicial Machinery in North Carolina in 1865." *North Carolina Historical Review* 30 (1953): 415–39.

———. "Military Justice in North Carolina, 1865: A Microcosm of Reconstruction." *Civil War History* 11 (1965): 341–50.

Savitt, Todd L. "Politics in Medicine: The Georgia Freedmen's Bureau and the Organization of Health Care, 1865–1866," *Civil War History* 28 (1982), 45–64.

———. "The Use of Blacks for Medical Experimentation and Demonstration in the Old South." *Journal of Southern History* 48 (1982): 331–48.

Schlomowitz, Ralph. "The Origins of Southern Sharecropping." *Agricultural History* 53 (1979): 557–75.

Schoonover, Thomas. "Confederate Diplomacy and the Texas-Mexican Border." *East Texas Historical Journal* 11 (1973): 33–39.

———. "Documents Concerning Lemuel Dale Evans' Plan to Keep Texas in the Union in 1961." *East Texas Historical Journal* 12 (1974): 35–38.

Scott, Rebecca. "The Battle over the Child: Child Apprenticeship and the Freedmen's Bureau in North Carolina." *Prologue* 10 (1978): 101–13.

Sefton, James E. "Aristotle in Blue and Braid: General John Schofield's Essays on Reconstruction." *Civil War History* 17 (1971): 45–57.

Self, Zenobia. "The Court Martial of J. J. Reynolds." *Military Affairs* 37 (1973): 52–56.

Shapiro, Herbert. "The Ku Klux Klan during Reconstruction: The South Carolina Episode." *Journal of Negro History* 19 (1964): 34–55.

Shook, Robert W. "The Battle of the Nueces, August 10, 1862." *Southwestern Historical Quarterly* 66 (1962–63): 31–42.

———. "Custer's Texas Command." *Military History of Texas and the Southwest* 9 (1971): 49–54.

———. "The Federal Military in Texas, 1865–1871." *Texas Military History* 6 (1965): 3–53.

———. "Military Activities in Victoria, 1865–1866." *Texana* 3 (1965): 347–52.

———. "Toward a List of Reconstruction Loyalists." *Southwestern Historical Quarterly* 76 (1972–73): 315–20.

Sibley, Marilyn McAdams. "Charles Stillman: A Case of Entrepreneurship on the Rio Grande." *Southwestern Historical Quarterly* 27 (1973-74): 227-40.

Sievers, Michael A. "Malfeasance or Indirection?: Administration of the California Indian Superintendency's Business Affairs." *Southern California Quarterly* 56 (1974): 273-94.

Simkins, Francis B. "New Viewpoints of Southern Reconstruction." *Journal of Southern History* 5 (1939): 46-61.

Singletary, Otis A. "The Texas Militia during Reconstruction." *Southwestern Historical Quarterly* 60 (1956-57): 23-35.

Small, Sandra E. "The Yankee Schoolmarm in Freedmen's Schools: An Analysis of Attitudes." *Journal of Southern History* 45 (1979): 381-402.

Smallwood, James. "Black Texans during Reconstruction: First Freedom." *East Texas Historical Journal* 14 (1) (1976): 9-23.

———. "Charles E. Culver, a Reconstruction Agent in Texas: The Work of Local Freedmen's Bureau Agents and the Black Community." *Civil War History* 27 (1981): 350-61.

———. "Early 'Freedom Schools': Black Self-Help and Education in Reconstruction—Texas: A Case Study." *Negro History Bulletin* 41 (1978): 790-93.

———. "Emancipation and the Black Family: A Case Study in Texas." *Social Science Quarterly* 57 (1977): 849-57.

———. "The Freedmen's Bureau Reconsidered: Local Agents and the Black Community" (also subtitled, "The Case of William S. [*sic*] Kirkman," in other of Smallwood's publications). *Texana* 11 (1973): 309-20.

———. "G. T. Ruby: Galveston's Black Carpetbagger in Reconstruction." *Houston Review* 6 (1983): 24-33.

———. "Perpetuation of Caste: Black Agricultural Workers in Reconstruction Texas." *Mid-America* 61 (1979): 5-23.

Smith, Thomas H. "Ohio Quakers and the Mississippi Freedmen: 'A Field to Labor'." *Ohio History* 78 (1969): 159-71.

Smith, W. Wayne. "An Experiment in Counterinsurgency: The Assessment of Confederate Sympathizers in Missouri." *Journal of Southern History* 35 (1969): 361-80.

Smyrl, Frank H. "Texans in the Union Army." *Southwestern Historical Quarterly* 65 (1961-62): 234-50.

Sneed, Edgar P. "A Historiography of Reconstruction in Texas: Some Myths and Problems." *Southwestern Historical Quarterly* 72 (1968-69): 435-48.

Somers, Dale A. "James P. Newcomb: The Making of a Radical." *Southwestern Historical Quarterly* 72 (1968-69): 449-69.

Spindler, Frank MacD. "Concerning Hempstead and Waller County." *Southwestern Historical Quarterly* 59 (1955-56): 455-72.

———. "The History of Hempstead and the Formation of Waller County." *Southwestern Historical Quarterly* 63 (1959-60): 404-27.

Stealey, John Edmond, III, "The Freedmen's Bureau in West Virginia." *West Virginia History* 39 (1978): 99-142.

———. "Reports of Freedmen's Bureau District Officers on Tours and Surveys in West Virginia." *West Virginia History* 43 (1982): 145-55.

————. "Reports of Freedmen's Bureau Operations in West Virginia: Agents in the Eastern Panhandle," *West Virginia History* 42 (1980–81): 94–129.

Tarbell, Ida M. "How the Union Army Was Disbanded." *Civil War Times Illustrated* 6 (1967–68): 1–9, 44–47.

Temple, Henry W. "William H. Seward." In Samuel Flagg Bemis, ed., *The American Secretaries of State and their Diplomacy*, 10 vols. (New York: Knopf): 1927–29.

Terrell, Alexander W. "The City of Austin from 1839–1865." *The Quarterly of the Texas State Historical Association* 14 (1868–69): 113–28.

Thompson, C. Mildred. "The Freedmen's Bureau in Georgia in 1865–1866: An Instrument of Reconstruction." *Georgia Historical Quarterly* 5 (1921): 40–49.

Thornberry, Jerry. "Northerns and the Atlanta Freedmen, 1865–1869." *Prologue* 6 (1974): 236–51.

Trelease, Allen W. "Who Were the Scalawags?" *Journal of Southern History* 29 (1963): 445–68.

Unrau, William E. "The Civilian as Indian Agent: Villain or Victim?" *Western Historical Quarterly* 3 (1972): 405–20.

Vandiver, Frank E. "Some Problems in Writing Confederate History." *Journal of Southern History* 36 (1970): 400–10.

Wagstaff, Thomas. "'Call Your Old Master—"Master"': Southern Political Leaders and Negro Labor during Presidential Reconstruction." *Labor History* 10 (1969): 323–45.

Weigley, Russell F. "Philip H. Sheridan: A Personality Profile." *Civil War Times Illustrated* 7 (1968–69): 5–9, 46–47.

Weisberger, Bernard A. "The Dark and Bloody Ground of Reconstruction Historiography." *Journal of Southern History* 25 (1959): 427–44.

Wesley, Edgar B. "Forty Acres and a Mule and a Speller." *History of Education Journal* 8 (1957): 113–27.

West, Earle H. "The Peabody Fund and Negro Education, 1867–1880." *History of Education Quarterly* 6 (1966): 3–21.

Wharton, Vernon L. "Reconstruction." In Arthur Link and Rembert W. Patrick, eds., *Writings in Southern History: Essays in Honor of Fletcher M. Green* (Baton Rouge: Louisiana State University Press, 1965): 295–315.

Wheeler, T. B. "Reminiscences of Reconstruction in Texas." *The Quarterly of the Texas State Historical Association* 11 (1907–1908): 56–65.

White, Kenneth B. "The Alabama Freedmen's Bureau and Black Education: The Myth of Opportunity." *Alabama Review* 34 (1981): 107–24.

————. "Black Lives, Red Tape: The Alabama Freedmen's Bureau." *Alabama Historical Quarterly* 43 (1981): 241–58.

————. "Wager Swayne: Racist or Realist?" *Alabama Review* 31 (1978): 92–109.

White, Richard. "Outlaw Gangs of the Middle Border: American Social Bandits." *Western Historical Quarterly* 12 (1981): 387–408.

White, William W. "The Texas Slave Insurrection of 1860." *Southwestern Historical Quarterly* 52 (1948–49): 259–85.

Williams, T. Harry. "An Analysis of Some Reconstruction Attitudes." *Journal of Southern History* 12 (1946): 169–86.

Wilson, Aubrey A. "A Soldier of the Texas Frontier: Brevet Major Robert Patterson Wilson, United States Army." *West Texas Historical Association Year Book* 34 (1958): 82–96.

Winkler, E. W., ed. "The Bryan Hayes Correspondence." *Southwestern Historical Quarterly* 25 (1921–22): 274–99; 26 (1922–23): 58–70.

Wood, George A. "The Black Codes of Alabama." *South Atlantic Quarterly* 13 (1914): 350–60.

Wood, W. D. "The Ku Klux Klan." *The Quarterly of the Texas State Historical Association* 9 (1905–1906): 262–68.

Woodman, Harold D. "Sequel to Slavery: The New History Views the Postbellum South." *Journal of Southern History* 43 (1977): 523–54.

Woods, Randall B. "George T. Ruby: A Black Militant in the White Business Community." *Red River Valley Historical Review* 1 (1974): 269–80.

Woodward, C. Vann. "Emancipations and Reconstructions: A Comparative Study." In C. Vann Woodward, *The Future of the Past* (New York: Oxford University Press, 1989): 145–66.

———. "Equality: The Deferred Commitment." *The American Scholar* 27 (1958): 459–72.

———. "The Irony of Southern History." *Journal of Southern History* 19 (1953): 3–19.

———. "Reconstruction: A Counterfactual Playback." In C. Vann Woodward, *The Future of the Past* (New York: Oxford University Press, 1989): 183–200.

———. "Seeds of Failure in Radical Race Policy." In Harold Hyman, ed., *New Frontiers of the American Reconstruction* (Urbana: University of Illinois Press, 1966): 124–47.

Wooster, Ralph A. "An Analysis of the Membership of the Texas Secession Convention." *Southwestern Historical Quarterly* 62 (1958–59): 322–35.

———. "An Analysis of the Texas Know Nothings." *Southwestern Historical Quarterly* 52 (1966–67): 414–23.

———. "Texas." In W. Buck Yearns, ed., *The Confederate Governors* (Athens: University of Georgia Press, 1985): 195–215.

Wynne, Lewis N. "The Role of Freedmen in the Post Bellum Cotton Economy of Georgia." *Phylon* 42 (1981): 309–21.

Young, Jo. "The Battle of Sabine Pass." *Southwestern Historical Quarterly* 52 (1948–49): 398–409.

3. Unpublished Theses, Dissertations, and Papers

Adkins, John Robert. "The Public Career of A. J. Hamilton," M.A. thesis, University of Texas, 1947.

Albrecht, Winnell. "The Black Codes of Texas." M.A. thesis, Southwest Texas State University, 1969.

Alderson, William T. "The Influence of Military Rule and the Freedmen's Bureau on Reconstruction in Virginia, 1865–1870." Ph.D. dissertation, Vanderbilt University, 1952.

Anderson, Thomas Franklin. "A History of Indianola." M.A. thesis, University of Houston, 1951.

Arnold, Marcus Llewellyn. "The Later Phases of the Secessionist Movement in Texas." M.A. thesis, University of Texas, 1920.

Atkinson, Bertha. "The History of Bell County." M.A. thesis, University of Texas, 1929.

Baggett, James Alex. "The Rise and Fall of the Texas Radicals, 1867–1883." Ph.D. dissertation, North Texas State University, 1972.

Bain, Kenneth Ray. "The Changing Basis of the Republican Party, 1865–1877." M.A. thesis, North Texas State University, 1970.

Baker, George T. "Mexico City and the War with the United States: A Study of the Politics of Military Occupation." Ph.D. dissertation, Duke University, 1970.

Biesele, Rudolph Leopold. "The History of the German Settlements in Texas, 1831–1861." Ph.D. dissertation, University of Texas, 1928.

Boethel, Paul Carl. "The History of Lavaca County, 1685–1930." M.A. thesis, University of Texas, 1932.

Bohne, Edwin. "History of the Brenham *Banner Press*." M.A. thesis, Sam Houston State College, 1950.

Boon, Effie Mattox. "The History of Angelina County." M.A. thesis, University of Texas, 1937.

Boozer, Jesse Beryl. "The History of Indianola, Texas." M.A. thesis, University of Texas, 1942.

Bowen, Nancy Head. "A Political Labyrinth: Texas in the Civil War." Ph.D. dissertation, Rice University, 1974.

Bowles, Flora G. "The History of Trinity County." M.A. thesis, University of Texas, 1928.

Brown, Robert B. "Guns over the Border: American Aid to the Juarez Government during the French Intervention." Ph.D. dissertation, University of Michigan, 1951.

Budd, Harrell. "The Negro in Politics in Texas." M.A. thesis, University of Texas, 1925.

Buenger, Walter Louis. "Stilling the Voice of Reason: Texans and the Union, 1854–1868." Ph.D. dissertation, Rice University, 1979.

Carrier, John P. "A Political History of Texas during the Reconstruction, 1865–1874." Ph.D. dissertation, Vanderbilt University, 1971.

Cassles, Ann Ethel. "A History of Hunt County." M.A. thesis, University of Texas, 1935.

Chandler, Barbara Susan Overton. "A History of Bowie County." M.A. thesis, University of Texas, 1937.

Christopher, Nehemiah. "The History of Negro Public Education in Texas, 1865–1900." Ph.D. dissertation, University of Pittsburgh, 1948.

Chunn, Prentis W., Jr. "Education and Politics: A Study of the Negro in Reconstruction Texas." M.A. thesis, Southwest Texas State University, 1957.

Cole, Fred C. "The Texas Career of Thomas Affleck." Ph.D. dissertation, Louisiana State University, 1942.

Cooner, Ben C. "Rise and Decline of Jefferson, Texas." M.A. thesis, East Texas State University, 1965.

Cowling, Annie. "The Civil War Trade of the Lower Rio Grande Valley." M.A. thesis, University of Texas, 1926.

Bibliography

Cox, Alonzo Bettis. "The Economic History of Texas during the Period of Reconstruction," M.A. thesis, University of Texas, 1914.

Cravens, John Nathan. "The Life and Activities of James Harper Starr, 1809–1890." Ph.D. dissertation, University of Texas, 1948.

Curtis, Sara Kay. "A History of Gillespie County, Texas, 1846–1900." M.A. thesis, University of Texas, 1943.

Dawson, Joseph Green, III. "Five Generals in Louisiana Reconstruction." M.A. thesis, Louisiana State University, 1970.

Dobie, Dudley Richard. "History of Hays County, Texas." M.A. thesis, University of Texas, 1932.

Drago, Edmund L. "Black Georgia during Reconstruction." Ph.D. dissertation, University of California–Berkeley, 1975.

Drake, Richard B. "The American Missionary Association and the Southern Negro, 1861–1888." Ph.D. dissertation, Emory University, 1957.

Dugas, Vera Lee. "A Social and Economic History of Texas in the Civil War and Reconstruction Period." Ph.D. dissertation, University of Texas, 1963.

Ellsworth, Lois. "San Antonio during the Civil War." M.A. thesis, University of Texas, 1938.

Everly, Elaine C. "The Freedmen's Bureau in the National Capital." Ph.D. dissertation, George Washington University, 1972.

Felgar, Robert Pattison. "Texas in the War for Southern Independence." Ph.D. dissertation, University of Texas, 1935.

Fennell, Romey, Jr. "The Negro in Texas Politics, 1865–1874." M.A. thesis, North Texas State University, 1963.

Flannigan, Daniel. "The Criminal Law of Slavery and Freedom, 1800–1868." Ph.D. dissertation, Rice University, 1973.

Franzetti, Robert Joseph. "Elisha Marshall Pease and Reconstruction." M.A. thesis, Southwest Texas State University, 1970.

Ganus, Clifton L., Jr. "The Freedmen's Bureau in Mississippi." Ph.D. dissertation, Tulane University, 1953.

Goodlett, Margaret Amelia Nance. "The Enforcement of the Confederate Conscript Acts in the Trans-Mississippi Department." M.A. thesis, University of Texas, 1914.

Gray, Ronald N. "Edmund J. Davis: Radical Republican and Reconstruction Governor of Texas." Ph.D. dissertation, Texas Tech University, 1976.

Griffin, Roger A. "Connecticut Yankee in Texas: A Biography of Elisha Marshall Pease." Ph.D. dissertation, University of Texas, 1973.

Gunn, Jack Winston. "Life of Ben McCulloch." M.A. thesis, University of Texas, 1947.

Hale, Charles. "Political Leadership in Texas during Reconstruction." M.A. thesis, Lamar State University, 1965.

Hall, Ada Marie. "The Texas Germans in State and National Politics, 1850–1865." M.A. thesis, University of Texas, 1938.

Hasson, Gail Snowden. "The Medical Activities of the Freedmen's Bureau in Reconstruction Alabama, 1865–1868." Ph.D. dissertation, University of Alabama, 1982.

Heintzen, Frank W. "Fredericksburg, Texas, in Civil War and Reconstruction." M.A. thesis, St. Mary's University (San Antonio), 1944.

Hennessey, Melinda Meek. "To Live and Die in Dixie: Reconstruction Race Riots in the South." Ph.D. dissertation, Kent State University, 1978.

Hill, James Lyle. "The Life of Judge William Pitt Ballinger." M.A. thesis, University of Texas, 1937.

Holbert, Ruby Crawford. "The Public Career of James Webb Throckmorton, 1851–1867." M.A. thesis, University of Texas, 1932.

Holladay, Florence Elizabeth. "The Extraordinary Powers and Functions of the General Commanding the Trans-Mississippi Department of the Southern Confederacy." M.A. thesis, University of Texas, 1914.

Jordan, Edith Marian. "The History of Parker County." M.A. thesis, University of Texas, 1935.

Keener, Charles V. "Racial Turmoil in Texas, 1865–1874." M.A. thesis, North Texas State University, 1971.

King, Alma Dexta. "The Political Career of Williamson Simpson Oldham." M.A. thesis, University of Texas, 1929.

Lambert, Joseph I. "The Defense of the Indian Frontier of Texas by the United States Army." M.A. thesis, St. Mary's University (San Antonio), 1948.

Lambie, Agnes Louise. "Confederate Control of Cotton in the Trans-Mississippi Department." M.A. thesis, University of Texas, 1915.

Lancaster, James L. "The Scalawags of North Carolina, 1850–1868." Ph.D. dissertation, Princeton University, 1974.

Love, John Warren. "The Regulator-Moderator Movement in Shelby County." M.A. thesis, University of Texas, 1936.

Lowman, Berta. "Cotton Industry in Texas during the Reconstruction Period." M.A. thesis, University of Texas, 1927.

McGraw, John Conger. "The Texas Constitutional Convention of 1866." Ph.D. dissertation, Texas Tech University, 1959.

McKay, Seth Shepard. "Texas under the Regime of E. J. Davis." M.A. thesis, University of Texas, 1919.

Madole, Jewel Pickford. "A History of Salado, Texas." M.A. thesis, University of Texas, 1952.

Marr, John Columbus. "The History of Matagorda County, Texas." M.A. thesis, University of Texas, 1928.

Marshall, Elmer Grady. "The History of Brazos County, Texas." M.A. thesis, University of Texas, 1937.

Marten, James Allen. "Drawing the Line: Dissent and Loyalty in Texas, 1856 to 1874." Ph.D. dissertation, University of Texas, 1986.

Martin, James Lee. "History of Goliad, 1836–1880." M.A. thesis, University of Texas, 1937.

Maslowski, Peter. "'*Treason Must Be Made Odious*': Military Occupation and Reconstruction in Nashville, Tennessee, 1862–1865." Ph.D. dissertation, Ohio State University, 1972.

Matthews, Clifford. "Special Military Tribunals, 1775–1865." M.A. thesis, Emory University, 1951.

May, J. Thomas. "Medical Care of Blacks in Louisiana during Occupation and

Reconstruction, 1862–1868: Its Social and Political Background." Ph.D. dissertation, Tulane University, 1970.

Megee, Jonnie Mildred. "Confederate Impressment Acts in the Trans-Mississippi Department." M.A. thesis, University of Texas, 1915.

Meiners, Fredericka Ann. "The Texas Governorship, 1861–1865: Biography of an Office." Ph.D. dissertation, Rice University, 1975.

Meredith, Mary Owen. "The Life and Work of Thomas Jefferson Devine." M.A. thesis, University of Texas, 1930.

Merseberger, Marion. "A Political History of Houston, Texas, during the Reconstruction Period as Recorded by the Press, 1868–1873." M.A. thesis, Rice University, 1950.

Messner, William F. "The Federal Army and Blacks in the Gulf Department." Ph.D. dissertation, University of Wisconsin, 1972.

Miller, Benjamin Hillon. "Elisha Marshall Pease: A Biography." M.A. thesis, University of Texas, 1927.

Moore, Sue Estella. "Life of John Benjamin Long." M.A. thesis, University of Texas, 1924.

Morris, Robert C. "Reading, 'Riting, and Reconstruction: Freedmen's Education in the South, 1865–1870." Ph.D. dissertation, University of Chicago, 1976.

Myers, Ila Mae. "The Relations of Governor Pendleton Murrah of Texas with the Confederate Military Authorities." M.A. thesis, University of Texas, 1929.

Nackman, Mark E. "The Texas Experience, 1821–1861: The Emergence of Texas as a Separate Province and Texans as a Breed Apart." Ph.D. dissertation, Columbia University, 1973.

O'Bannion, Maurine Mattie. "The History of Caldwell County." M.A. thesis, University of Texas, 1931.

Olds, Victoria Marcus. "The Freedmen's Bureau as a Social Agency." Ph.D. dissertation, Columbia University, 1966.

Owen, James L. "The Negro in Georgia during Reconstruction, 1864–1872: A Social History." Ph.D. dissertation, University of Georgia, 1975.

Palm, Reba W. "Slavery in Microcosm: Matagorda, Texas." M.A. thesis, Texas A. & I. University, 1971.

Phillips, Paul D. "A History of the Freedmen's Bureau in Tennessee." Ph.D. dissertation, Vanderbilt University, 1964.

Pierson, Oris Emerald. "Norwegian Settlements in Bosque County, Texas." M.A. thesis, University of Texas, 1947.

Rankin, Dan F. "The Role of the Negro Office Holders in the Reconstruction Southwest [Arkansas, Louisiana, and Texas]." M.A. thesis, North Texas State University, 1954.

Raphael, Alan. "Health and Medical Care of Black People in the United States during Reconstruction." Ph.D. dissertation, University of Chicago, 1972.

Real, Matilda Marie. "A History of Kerr County, Texas." M.A. thesis, University of Texas, 1942.

Reese, James Verdo. "A History of Hill County, Texas, to 1873." M.A. thesis, University of Texas, 1961.

Roney, Johnson, III. "Marshall, Texas, 1860–1865." M.A. thesis, Baylor University, 1967.

Ruckman, Caroline Silsby. "The Frontier of Texas during the Civil War." M.A. thesis, University of Texas, 1926.

Ryan, Frances Dora. "The Election Laws of Texas, 1827–1895." M.A. thesis, University of Texas, 1922.

St. Clair, Gladys Annelle. "A History of Hopkins County, Texas." M.A. thesis, University of Texas, 1940.

St. Clair, Lawrence Ward. "History of Robertson County." M.A. thesis, University of Texas, 1931.

Sandlin, Betty Jeffus. "The Texas Reconstruction Constitutional Convention of 1868–1869." Ph.D. dissertation, Texas Tech University, 1970.

Scaief, James Seborn. "Texas in National Periodical Literature from 1865–1885." M.A. thesis, University of Texas, 1949.

Scarborough, Jane Lynn. "George W. Paschal: Texas Unionist and Scalawag Jurisprudent." Ph.D. dissertation. Rice University, 1972.

Schoonover, Thomas. "Mexican–United States Relations, 1861–1867." Ph.D. dissertation, University of Minnesota, 1970.

Sergeant, George W. "Early History of Tarrant County." M.A. thesis, University of Texas, 1953.

Shook, Robert W. "Federal Occupation and Administration of Texas, 1865–1870." Ph.D. dissertation, North Texas State University, 1970.

Sinclair, O. Lonnie. "The Freedmen's Bureau in Texas: The Assistant Commissioners and the Negro." Paper submitted to the Institute of Southern History, Johns Hopkins University, July 22, 1969.

Small, Sandra Eileen. "The Yankee Social Marm in Southern Freedmen's Schools, 1861–1871." Ph.D. dissertation, Washington State University, 1976.

Smyrl, Frank Herbert. "Unionism, Abolitionism, Vigilantism in Texas, 1856–1865." M.A. thesis, University of Texas, 1961.

Tausch, Egon Richard. "Southern Sentiment among the Texas Germans during the Civil War and Reconstruction." M.A. thesis, University of Texas, 1965.

Theisen, Lee S. "The Public Career of General Lew Wallace, 1845–1905." M.A. thesis, University of Arizona, 1973.

Thompson, Esther Lane. "The Influence of the Freedmen's Bureau on the Education of the Negro in Texas." M.A. thesis, Texas Southern University, 1956.

Ulrich, John William. "The Northern Military Mind in Regard to Reconstruction, 1865–1872: The Attitudes of Ten Leading Union Generals." Ph.D. dissertation, Ohio State University, 1959.

Volz, Harry A., III. "The Administration of Justice by the Freedmen's Bureau in Kentucky, South Carolina, and Virginia." Ph.D. dissertation, University of Virginia, 1975.

Vowell, Jack. "Politics at El Paso, 1850–1920." M.A. thesis, Texas Western University, 1950.

Wallis, Mary Ella. "The Life of Alexander Watkins Terrell, 1827–1912." M.A. thesis, University of Texas, 1937.

Wetta, Francis J. "The Louisiana Scalawags." 2 vols. Ph.D. dissertation, Louisiana State University, 1977.

White, Frank Edd. "A History of the Territory That Now Constitutes Waller County, Texas, from 1821 to 1884." M.A. thesis, University of Texas, 1936.

Bibliography

White, Michael Allen. "History of Education in Texas, 1860–1884." Ed.D. dissertation, Baylor University, 1969.

Winfrey, Dorman Hayward. "A History of Rusk County, Texas." M.A. thesis, University of Texas, 1951.

Yelderman, Pauline. "The Jaybird Democratic Association of Fort Bend County." M.A. thesis, University of Texas, 1938.

Index

431

Index

Index

Index